Understanding Constitutional Issues

Understanding Constitutional Issues

Selections from *The CQ Researcher*

WITHDRAWN
PRINT

CQ PRESS

A Division of Congressional Quarterly Inc.
Washington, D.C.

CQ Press
1255 22nd Street, N.W., Suite 400
Washington, D.C. 20037

(202) 729-1900; toll-free, 1-866-4CQ-PRESS (1-866-427-7737)

www.cqpress.com

☉ The paper used in this publication exceeds the requirements of the American National Standard for Information Sciences—Permanence of Paper for Printed Library Materials, ANSI Z39.48-1992.

Printed and bound in the United States of America

08 07 06 05 04   5 4 3 2 1

Cover photos from left to right: Peter Muhly, AFP Photo; Mark Wilson, Getty Images; Justin Sullivan, Getty Images

Library of Congress Cataloging-in-Publication Data
Understanding constitutional issues : selections from The CQ researcher.
     p. cm.
   Includes bibliographical references and index.
   ISBN 1-56802-885-7
  1. Constitutional law—United States. 2. Civil rights—United States. 3. United States—History—1969- 4. United States—Politics and government—2001- I. CQ Press. II. CQ researcher. III. Title.

   KF4550.Z9U537 2004
   342.73—dc22

                                      2004050304

Contents

Preface

Understanding Constitutional Issues: Selections from The CQ Researcher helps readers make important connections between contemporary issues and constitutional concepts and principles. Beginning with an overarching essay on the U.S. Constitution's history and its evolving impact, this volume organizes 17 *CQ Researcher* reports into four themes: Governmental Powers and Structure, Security, Liberty and Equality. Each thematic section sets its reports in context with an opening essay that ties them to relevant concepts in the Constitution and provides updated information such as recent court decisions.

The *CQ Researcher* itself is a periodical that focuses on a single topic in each report, bringing in-depth, objective and forward-looking analysis to often complicated and controversial issues on the public agenda.

Each *CQ Researcher* report follows a similar format. It begins with an overview of the topic that touches upon the areas explored in greater detail later. Following this introduction is a section that chronicles the important debates currently surrounding a topic, such as "Should colleges adopt other policies to try to increase minority enrollment?" or "Is enough being done to protect personal privacy on the Internet?" The answers to these key, or "issue," questions are never conclusive — the issues are too controversial for pat answers. Rather, they highlight the range of opinions among experts.

Next comes the "Background" section, which provides a history of the topic and insight into how current policy has evolved, detailing important government actions and court decisions. An examination of existing policy (under the heading "Current Situation") follows, providing an overview of important developments. The final "Outlook" section gives a sense of what might happen in the near future, anticipating new regulations, court rulings or possible legislative proposals.

Each *CQ Researcher* issue also contains additional features to augment the main text, including sidebars that examine related topics, an "At Issue" section in which two experts provide opposing answers to a relevant question, a chronology of key events and an annotated bibliography.

Acknowledgments

Several people deserve acknowledgment for their assistance with this book. We wish to thank the *CQ Researcher*'s talented staff of editors and writers. In particular, we thank those whose reports appear in this volume: Adriel Bettelheim, Sarah Glazer, Alan Greenblatt, Kenneth Jost and Patrick Marshall. Kenneth Jost also wrote the introduction and the thematic essays. We also wish to acknowledge the editorial assistance of Grace Hill and Lorna Notsch and the production work of Belinda Josey.

Introduction

"We the People"

John and Mary Beth Tinker never met James Madison. But in 1965 the two Iowa teenagers benefited from Madison's constitutional legacy after they were suspended from school for wearing black armbands to protest the Vietnam War. They had intended to participate in a protest to be held from December 16 until New Year's Day, and the armbands were to be worn on each of the days in between.

Des Moines school officials saw the planned protest as disruptive and decided to suspend any students who participated. Three of the five pupils suspended under the policy — John, Mary Beth, and a third teenager, Christopher Eckhardt — challenged their punishments in court. They claimed that the suspensions violated the First Amendment, which is the part of the U.S. Constitution that guarantees freedom of speech.

Nearly two centuries before any of this took place, James Madison, a Virginia lawyer in his mid-30s, had played a leading role in drafting a new constitution for the United States. The goal was to create a stronger national government. The Articles of Confederation, adopted in 1781 during the latter part of the Revolutionary War, had not proved to be the success the newly independent colonies had expected.

After the new U.S. Constitution was ratified in 1788, Madison also worked to quiet concerns about the new government by drafting a series of amendments to protect individual liberty. These amendments, the first ten to the Constitution, were approved in 1791 and became known as the Bill of Rights. Among them was one that said that Congress "shall make no law . . . abridging the freedom of speech, or of the press."

Another 135 years elapsed before the Supreme Court of the United States ruled that the First Amendment, of which the above phrase is a part, also prevented any state or local government from abridging freedom of speech. With that ruling, the court laid the groundwork for Americans from every walk of life — high school students included — to claim a constitutional right to speak free from undue interference by any arm of government.

Students "do not shed their constitutional right to freedom of speech or expression at the schoolhouse gate," the Supreme Court declared in 1969 when it overturned the Des Moines suspensions in *Tinker v. Des Moines Independent Community School District.* With only one of the nine justices dissenting, the court stressed that the protest had provoked "discussion" but no disorder. "In the circumstances," the court concluded, "our Constitution does not permit officials of the State to deny their [the students'] form of expression."

It may seem odd that a document written in the eighteenth century can determine how high school principals discipline students today in the twenty-first century. Yet in its 200-plus years of existence, the U.S. Constitution has come to occupy a special place not only in U.S. government but also in the nation's life and culture. The document itself is enshrined in the National Archives in Washington, D.C. But its spirit is everywhere, its provisions invoked for guidance or support in disputes of all sorts on a daily basis.

The 17 reports from the *CQ Researcher* included in this collection indicate the variety of constitutional issues in the United States today. Can the president order enemy combatants detained indefinitely with limited access to courts or even to a lawyer? Can someone who is mentally ill be executed for murder? Can state universities give preferences to minority applicants? Can the government give vouchers to students to attend parochial schools? In the United States, these are not merely political issues; they are constitutional questions on which courts — ultimately, the Supreme Court — often have the final say.

The Constitution deals with none of these issues in explicit terms. It begins with three articles that establish the powers and shape the relationships among the three branches of the national government: Congress, the president, and the judiciary. The Bill of Rights protects individual liberties, including freedom of speech and religion and the rights of suspects and criminal defendants. Three post–Civil War Amendments abolish slavery (Thirteenth), prohibit state and local governments from violating any person's right to "due process" and "equal protection of the law" (Fourteenth) and bar racial discrimination in voting (Fifteenth). Among the other Amendments — only twenty-seven altogether — the Eighteenth extends voting rights to women and the Twenty-Sixth guarantees eighteen-year-olds the right to vote.

Despite the later protections for individual rights, the Constitution was intended at its inception to strengthen the powers of the national government. The majestic preamble opens by declaring the goal "to form a more perfect Union," and the powers of Congress, the president and the judiciary are described in broad, open-ended terms. By keeping the branches separate, the Constitution also limits their powers — with each one operating as a check on the other two. The Framers envisioned that the inevitable conflicts would help prevent tyranny and safeguard liberty.

Article I sets out a long list of "enumerated" powers for the legislative branch of the government. Congress is authorized, among other powers, to raise and borrow money, to regulate interstate and foreign commerce and to raise and support an army and navy. The list ends with a catch-all authorization for Congress "to make all Laws which shall be necessary and proper for carrying into Execution the foregoing powers."

Article II vests "the executive power" in the president. The powers of the president are likewise broad but described in less detail. He — the masculine pronoun is used throughout — is to be commander in chief of the army and navy. He is authorized to make treaties with foreign countries and appoint executive branch officials and judges — but only with the "advice and consent" of the Senate. As in Article I, the list of presidential powers ends with a broadly phrased directive to "take care that the Laws be faithfully executed."

Article III places "the judicial power of the United States" in "one supreme Court" and "in such inferior Courts as Congress may from time to time ordain and establish." The article provides that the judicial power — never precisely defined — "shall extend" to cases arising under the Constitution and the laws of the United States and to a variety of other cases, including disputes between states and between citizens of different states. The article nowhere states that the courts can declare an act of Congress or a state law contrary to the Constitution. But the U.S. Supreme Court claimed that power as early as 1803, and the power, although controversial, is firmly secured today.

Opponents of the new Constitution argued during the ratification debate that the national government was too powerful and that its unchecked powers were a threat to individual liberty. Madison — sometimes called the Father of the Constitution — disagreed, but sought to allay the fears by proposing an omnibus collection of amendments in the historic First Congress that convened in 1789. Twelve amendments were submitted to the states; ten were ratified at the time. An eleventh — delaying any salary increase for senators or representatives until the start of a new Congress — finally gained approval from the necessary number of states 200 years later, in 1992. The other unsuccessful amendment dealt with the size of the House of Representatives.

The Bill of Rights made the Constitution a guardian of liberty as well as a source of power for the new government. The now familiar First Amendment protects freedom of speech, press and religion, along with the right to assemble peaceably and to petition the government for redress of grievances. The Fourth guarantees the right of the people to be "secure in their persons, houses, papers, and effects, against unreasonable searches and seizures." The Fifth and Sixth establish a privilege against self-incrimination, prohibit being tried twice for the same offense and guarantee the right to counsel and jury trial in criminal cases. The Eighth prohibits excessive bail or fines or "cruel and unusual punishments."

The Supreme Court limited the force of these provisions by ruling in 1833 that they did not apply to the states. The court adhered to that view until the 1920s, when it held for the first time that the states were bound by the free speech provisions of the First Amendment. Over the next forty years, the court relied on a so-called "incorporation doctrine" to apply most (though not all) of the Bill of Rights provisions to the states.

The federal system created under the Constitution left the states with many of their previous powers, and the Tenth Amendment specifically reserved to the states the powers "not delegated to the United States by the Constitution." But the sectional dispute over slavery that ended with the Union victory in the Civil War reshaped the constitutional landscape. The Reconstruction Congress proposed and won ratification of three constitutional amendments.

Of the three, the Fourteenth Amendment wrought the broadest and most lasting constitutional transformation. No state, the amendment declares, "shall deprive any person of life, liberty, or property, without due process of law; nor deny to any person within its jurisdiction the equal protection of the laws." Together, the Due Process and Equal Protection Clauses turned the Constitution into a guardian of individual liberty and equal justice against infringements not only from the federal government but also from state or local governments.

Congress, the president and the Supreme Court were all slow to realize the full implications of these broadly phrased constitutional guarantees. In the mid-twentieth century, however, the Supreme Court under Chief Justice Earl Warren invoked the provisions to force sweeping changes on the country. In the name of equal protection, the court ruled that legally mandated racial segregation — starting with "separate but equal" public education — was unconstitutional. In the name of due process, the court required states to afford suspects and criminal defendants the protections listed in the Bill of Rights. And the court struck a blow for political equality with the so-called "one person, one vote" rulings that forced states to shift representation in Congress and state legislatures from rural areas to rapidly growing cities and suburbs.

The expansion of constitutional rights slowed but did not stop under Warren's successors. Under Chief Justice Warren Burger, the court relied on due process to establish a woman's right to an abortion during most of a pregnancy. The court also ruled that equal protection limited the ability of the federal government or state governments to treat men and women differently under the law. In the First Amendment, the court found limits on how closely the federal or state governments could regulate campaign contributions and expenditures.

Since 1986 Chief Justice William H. Rehnquist has presided over a court less receptive to expanding individual rights. Instead, Rehnquist has led the court in a series of decisions that invoke state sovereignty to limit the power of Congress to enact or enforce laws that affect traditional functions of state governments. The court has also loosened the restrictions on government aid to religious institutions. Neverthe-less, the court has expanded individual rights in some areas. It found new constitutional limits on the power of government to regulate landowners' use of their property. In 2003 the court ruled state laws banning gay sex to be unconstitutional; Rehnquist was one of three dissenters.

As this history demonstrates, constitutional law has not followed a simple or consistent course. The country is constantly changing and as it does new issues arise and new claims of rights advance. The president pushes one way, Congress pulls another, and the courts stand to the side — sometimes ready to step in, other times not. The Constitution does not purport to give all the answers, but it provides a framework for the American people to find the answers. History books say the Constitution was written in 1787, but that is only part of the story. In truth, we the people are still writing the Constitution today.

"To Form a More Perfect Union"
— preamble to the Constitution of the United States

The Constitution created a national government with three separate branches — Congress, the executive, and the judiciary — that share power. Congress has the power to declare war, but the president is commander in chief. Congress passes laws, but the president must sign them. The president can veto a bill passed by Congress, but Congress can override that veto. The president nominates federal judges, but the Senate must confirm them. The Supreme Court can nullify laws passed by Congress or actions taken by the president as unconstitutional. The disputes between the separate branches throughout history have defined the extent — and the limits — of their constitutional powers. The disputes over President Bush's warmaking powers and his nominations to federal courts are the most recent of these constitutional clashes. Meanwhile, the political fortunes of members of Congress are being shaped by constitutional disputes in two areas: campaign finance regulation and redistricting.

"Presidential Power" examines the historic debate over warmaking powers in the context of President Bush's actions in the war against terrorism and the confrontation with Iraq. Bush asked Congress in advance for authority to use military force against Saddam Hussein; Congress approved the resolution with the condition that Bush first consult with lawmakers and show that diplomacy had failed. Some lawmakers were also tangling with the administration on how it was exercising new anti-terrorism powers granted by the USA Patriot Act, passed within six weeks of the 9/11 attacks.

The war in Iraq came after our report: the military victory did not prevent continuing debates over the U.S. occupation. Most notably, it did not silence questions regarding the failure to discover weapons of mass destruction. Legal challenges also emerged over a range of administration policies, with major cases argued before the Supreme Court in April 2004 and due to be decided by the end of June. (See "Civil Liberties Debates.")

"Campaign Finance Showdown" analyzes the broad constitutional challenge to a major new statute tightening regulation of campaign spending on House and Senate elections. The Bipartisan Campaign Reform Act — also known as the McCain-Feingold law — bans "soft money," the unregulated funds given to political parties by corporations, unions and wealthy donors. It also regulates funds raised for election-time radio and television advertising by corporations, unions or advocacy groups. A diverse array of plaintiffs — political parties, business groups, organized labor and free speech advocates — contended the law ran afoul of the First Amendment. After our report, the Supreme Court upheld all but two relatively minor sections of the law, by a 5–4 vote on most issues (*McConnell v. Federal Election Commission,* Dec. 10, 2003).

"Judges and Politics" covers the sharp conflicts between President Bush and Senate Democrats over federal judicial nominees. With his first appointments, Bush signaled his intention to find strong-minded conservatives for the federal bench. Senate Democrats promptly signaled their intention to try to block confirmation of nominees whom they regarded as outside the legal mainstream. Since our report, President Bush has won Senate confirmation of the vast majority of his judicial nominees. Democrats used filibusters to block votes on six nominees, but Bush circumvented the tactic twice in January 2004 by naming two of his choices as "recess appointees" who can hold their positions until the end of the next session of Congress.

"Redistricting Disputes" examines the difficult and contentious issues surrounding the redrawing of congressional district lines every ten years. Partisan conflicts have flared over drawing House districts throughout U.S. history, but the issues became more complex with the Supreme Court's "one-person, one-vote" decisions and its more recent rulings limiting racially motivated redistricting. In a new case, Pennsylvania Democrats asked the Supreme Court to throw out a Republican-written congressional map as an unconstitutionally partisan redistricting, or gerrymander. The court was to rule on *Vieth v. Jubilerer* by the end of June, 2004. Meanwhile, Texas Republicans pushed through an unusual, mid-decade redistricting aimed at helping the GOP pick up as many as six new House seats. Democrats unsuccessfully challenged the plan by arguing that redistricting was allowed only at the start of the decade.

1 Presidential Power

ADRIEL BETTELHEIM

S en. Robert C. Byrd, the self-appointed guardian of congressional prerogatives, was shaking with rage.

Standing on the floor of the Senate on Oct. 3, the 85-year-old West Virginia Democrat bitterly denounced the Bush administration for pressuring Congress to quickly approve a resolution authorizing the use of unilateral force against Iraq on the grounds that it poses a threat to U.S. interests.

"This is an unprecedented and unfounded interpretation of the president's authority under the Constitution, not to mention the fact that it stands the charter of the United Nations on its head," Byrd declared. "The president is using the Oval Office as a bully pulpit to sound the call to arms, but it is from Capitol Hill that such orders must flow."

Byrd saw the resolution as the latest example of the White House's attempt to steamroll the legislative branch on a key national security matter — this time by forcing the House and Senate to vote just weeks before the midterm elections on whether to launch a pre-emptive strike on a sovereign nation that intelligence reports indicated was amassing weapons of mass destruction. Lawmakers for the first time in history were put in the difficult position of having to give the commander-in-chief open-ended authority to begin firing when he pleases — or attaching conditions and appearing to tie his hands.

After more than a week of debate in the House and Senate, the administration got what it wanted. Congress

After meeting with President Bush, Senate Minority Leader Trent Lott announces that President Bush will resume briefing congressional leaders on anti-terrorism operations. Bush had restricted secret information after accusing lawmakers of leaking classified information. With Lott on Oct. 10, 2001, were, from left, House Speaker Dennis Hastert, Senate Majority Leader Tom Daschle and House Minority Leader Dick Gephardt. The November 2002 elections changed Congress' leadership.

passed compromise language empowering the president to wage war, though making it clear he should first gain support from the United Nations.
* While the House cleared the resolution by better than a 2-to-1 margin, and the Senate by better than 3-to-1, there was palpable concern on Capitol Hill about the precedents that were being set and the possible consequences. Some lawmakers like Byrd questioned the timing of the vote, while others wondered whether they were affirming an imperial presidency that would march to its own beat in international relations. [1]

"The Constitution clearly [creates a] separation of powers to stop the president from going off on foreign adventures without the express consent of the American people," says Rep. Sam

---

* The U.N. Security Council unanimously adopted a tough weapons-inspection mandate for Iraq on Nov. 6, 2002, calling on Saddam Hussein to scrap his weapons of mass destruction or face "serious consequences."

Farr, D-Calif., who voted against the resolution.

"We need to have a national dialogue," added Sen. Chuck Hagel, R-Neb., a decorated Vietnam veteran and Senate Foreign Relations Committee member, who initially questioned Bush's plan but supported a modified version of the resolution. "We didn't have that dialogue before we got into Vietnam. We have to be careful about what we're doing."

The Iraq debate reflected the tense state of relations between the Bush administration and Congress since the Sept. 11, 2001, terrorist attacks on New York and the Pentagon. The administration has used the threat of terrorism — and less specific challenges to U.S. interests — to try to wield a brand of clout similar to that seen during World War II and the Cold War. After trying to score narrow political victories in their first year in office, Bush Cabinet officials now are aggressively asserting authority over foreign and domestic affairs, aided by Bush's administrative fiat and Congress' general tendency to look to the executive branch for leadership.

Some scholars attribute the move to a strongly held belief within the administration that presidential power has slipped over the past two decades, evidenced most recently by former President Bill Clinton's unsuccessful invocation of executive privilege during the scandals that plagued his administration. The chief advocate of this view, according to many observers, is Vice President Dick Cheney, who in 1987 — as ranking Republican on the House select committee that investigated the Iran-Contra scandal — had scolded fellow lawmakers for stepping on then-President Ronald W. Reagan's toes. [2]

From *The CQ Researcher,* November 15, 2002.

AFP Photo/Tim Sloan

But the administration's tactics have angered Democrats and some Republicans in Congress, who increasingly believe they are being bypassed on key decisions and may be ceding too much power to the executive branch in the name of national security. Some, such as Byrd and House Judiciary Committee Chairman F. James Sensenbrenner Jr., R-Wis., are mulling ways to publicly express their displeasure, including holding hearings on administration policies, issuing subpoenas and possibly withholding funding for some presidential initiatives. [3]

"It's quite a tug-of-war, and Cheney and others in the administration think it is time Congress gives the executive branch its due," says Fred I. Greenstein, a presidential scholar at Princeton University. "Presidents have been constrained by other actors and constitutional complexities and have had to use all their wiles and political savvy to get their way. Congress goes back and forth on how much the president should be constrained. A lot of it boils down to whose ox is being gored."

The showdown over Iraq is only the latest friction point in the struggle between the two branches. For most of 2002, Bush and Congress have also fought over the merits of creating a domestic security agency. Then in June,

AFP Photo/Peter Muhly

Army MPs take a handcuffed detainee at Camp X-Ray in Guantanamo Bay, Cuba, for questioning at the Joint Interrogation Facility. Critics say that while many of the arrests of terrorism suspects appear legal under President Bush's authority as commander-in-chief, some unilateral decisions regarding prosecutions of terror suspects may conflict with existing laws.

facing declining approval ratings and questions about intelligence lapses prior to Sept. 11, the White House abruptly reversed its previous policy of rejecting congressional efforts to create a governmental counterterrorism agency. Bush proposed creating a homeland security department by combining 22 existing federal agencies with at least 170,000 employees and a budget of $37.5 billion. He then demanded that Congress give him more power over federal civil service employment practices — such as the authority to hire,

fire and transfer workers and to exclude some from civil service protections — all in the name of national security. Senate Democrats' resistance to those demands threatened to stall action on a homeland security bill in the 107th Congress.

The administration similarly pressed lawmakers for expanded authority soon after the Sept. 11 attacks, when it asked for, and received, new prosecutorial powers to track terror suspects and their sympathizers in an anti-terrorism law commonly known as the USA Patriot Act. But while lawmakers were debating and writing the legislation, the administration was separately instituting a series of rules without consulting Congress that allowed authorities to indefinitely detain suspects, listen in on conversations between some federal prisoners and their lawyers and more closely scrutinize visa applications from certain countries. The White House also authorized the use of military tribunals to try foreigners suspected of terrorism. The actions raised questions about whether Bush was deliberately shifting power away from Congress and into the domain of the executive branch and the courts. [4]

"The thread running through all of this is the feeling on the part of the administration that it can arrogate power to itself and dismiss review either by Congress or the courts, saying any questions will hurt the war on terrorism," said Neil Sonnett, former assistant U.S. attorney in Florida, who chaired an Amer-

Congress' Power of the Purse

Few congressional powers can tie a president's hands more than control of discretionary spending, known informally as "the power of the purse."

This constitutionally conferred prerogative is the most effective way to force a president to use military force — or make other policy changes — in ways he might otherwise not consider. But lawmakers run the risk of triggering a political backlash if their actions are viewed as jeopardizing the well-being of troops already committed in the field.

Since the Vietnam era, Congress frequently has used funding cutoffs or significant reductions to end or limit the use of military personnel abroad. Because the cutoffs usually are included in annual spending bills, they have to be renewed each year to have the effect of being permanent policy:

- Congress tried several times during the last years of the Vietnam War to restrict U.S. military activity in Indochina. A supplemental foreign-assistance appropriations act, cleared by Congress in December 1970, prohibited the use of funds to introduce ground combat troops in Cambodia or to provide U.S. military advisers to Cambodian military forces.
- A supplemental fiscal 1973 appropriations bill cut off funds for combat activities in Indochina after August of that year. Similar language was included in a stopgap funding measure passed in June 1973. Then Congress passed the Foreign Assistance Act of 1974, which set a personnel ceiling of 4,000 Americans in Vietnam within six months of

enactment, and 3,000 Americans within one year.
- More recently, the fiscal 1994 defense spending bill approved the use of U.S. combat forces in strife-torn Somalia for certain purposes — such as security roles and protecting United Nations units — but it cut off funding for other purposes after March 31, 1994. The fiscal 1995 defense-spending bill went further, stipulating no funds appropriated by the act could be used for a continued presence in the African nation.
- The fiscal 1995 defense-spending bill also cut off funding for military participation to address ethnic and other conflicts in the African nation of Rwanda, except for action to protect the lives of U.S. citizens.

Congress also has periodically used funding restrictions to limit military or paramilitary actions around the world. The fiscal 1976 defense-spending bill restricted military activity in Angola to intelligence gathering. Congress later made the ban permanent law through the International Security Assistance and Arms Export Control Act of 1976.

The 1984 dispute over funding anti-government guerrillas in Nicaragua known as "contras" also led to a funding ban on continuing CIA, Pentagon or other federal agency activities in the Central American nation in fiscal 1985. The legislation provided that, after Feb. 28, 1985, the president could spend $14 million on the contras, subject to congressional approval, if he specified why continued military assistance was necessary.

---

ican Bar Association task force that reviewed the administration's legal tactics.

The power tug-of-war goes beyond national security matters. Bush also has resisted congressional and public oversight on non-terrorism matters, such as denying requests for documents from an energy task force chaired by Cheney. Environmental and congressional critics said the panel, charged with crafting the administration's energy plan, was too closely aligned with the oil, coal and electricity industries. And Bush in November 2001 ordered that a sitting president could have unlimited time to decide whether to release presidential documents and new powers of censorship over those documents — a move that raised the hackles of archivists, historians and librarians. They said the order violated the spirit of the 1978 Presidential

Records Act, which gives the public access to old White House papers.

To some extent, Congress is at a natural disadvantage in power struggles with the executive branch, because its decentralized nature and highly charged partisan environment makes it difficult for the House or Senate to coordinate strategy or speak with one voice. In rare cases, courts have been left to decide whether a president overreached, such as when the Supreme Court in 1952 ruled that President Harry S Truman had no legitimate power to nationalize steel mills during the Korean War. [5]

Congress has had an especially difficult time reacting to the war on terrorists, because it has scrambled traditional concepts of deterrence and use of force. But scholars note that the legislative branch still has options. For in-

stance, Congress can influence public opinion by stretching out debate on administration initiatives so that the public dialogue takes into account opposing views. It also can shift its agenda to issues the administration wants to avoid, such as the sputtering economy. In extreme cases, it can even cut off funding for administration initiatives. However, lawmakers must propose solutions and not simply appear to be guarding their turf or trying to score political points, according to analysts.

"The president in the past benefited from a certain ambiguity in the way people perceive his role, because the bully pulpit allowed him to quickly stake a claim — such as declaring that the Cheney task force documents are confidential — and have it accepted," says George C. Edwards III, a professor of political science at Texas A&M

University. "Now, on the biggest issues, particularly the war, you're seeing Congress challenge him, and raise questions before it's too late."

In the aftermath of the midterm elections that delivered the Senate back into Republican hands, Congress is not expected to mount robust challenges immediately and create the perception that it is disloyal and unpatriotic. Indeed, Republicans are expected to eagerly work to advance the president's agenda — for example by trying to pass homeland defense legislation and enact tax cuts to spur the economy. Democrats, trying to regroup in time for the 2004 elections, may not have the appetite to quickly challenge the politically popular chief executive. But given the open-ended nature of the war on terrorism, many are contemplating how to regain institutional clout instead of being relegated to a long-term supporting role. [6]

As Congress mulls the executive branch actions and the constitutional system of checks and balances, here are some questions being debated:

Has the administration overstepped its authority in the war on terrorism?

House Judiciary Committee Chairman Sensenbrenner has a tempestuous relationship with the Bush administration. The veteran Republican congressman from the Milwaukee suburbs is a stickler for rules and insists on deference, frequently erupting in anger when he doesn't get it. Sensenbrenner was in a particularly cranky mood when he met with a group of *Milwaukee Journal-Sentinel* reporters and editors during Congress' August recess.

For two months, the Bush Justice Department had refused to answer questions from Sensenbrenner's committee about how the administration was using new powers conferred by the USA Patriot Act in its foreign intelligence investigations. The committee wanted to know, for example, how many times U.S. citizens or resident legal aliens had been electronically monitored, how many times authorities had been allowed to monitor suspects' conversations as they moved from phone to phone and how library, newspaper and bookstore records were being used. The committee said it needed the information to assess whether to reauthorize the law when it expires in 2004. But the administration was not rushing up to the Hill with answers, saying the information was secret and would only be shared later with the House Intelligence Committee, which does not have jurisdiction over the anti-terrorism law.

Quipping that the White House was playing "I've Got a Secret," Sensenbrenner told journalists: "I've never signed a subpoena in my five and a half years as chairman. I guess there's a first time for everything." [7]

Although the administration has since provided more details, such incidents and broader questions about its prosecutorial powers have fueled concerns that the White House is openly disregarding Congress and compromising civil liberties in the name of national security. The incidents also have raised questions about whether the administration is using a cloak of secrecy to dodge congressional and public oversight.

"They're not using the war to advance a hidden agenda, but their policies reflect what some would regard as a peculiar notion about executive branch power that emphasizes unilateral action and obstructs even the most routine requests for information," says Steven Aftergood, director of the project on government secrecy of the Federation of American Scientists.

Aftergood points to administration efforts such as a recent decision to define a new category of government information — tentatively called sensitive homeland security information, or SHSI — that could be withheld from the public on the grounds that making it public is tantamount to making it available to terrorists. While the White House has not said what the category would encompass, it could include everything from blueprints of government buildings to scientific research deemed useful for making biological or chemical weapons. [8]

Administration officials defend their actions, saying the stealthy and often lethal nature of terrorism requires a broad and swift response. They add some personal liberties may have to be sacrificed for national security.

"The mission of the Department of Justice has been transformed from a focus on prosecution of illegal acts to a focus on the prevention of terrorist acts," Attorney General John Ashcroft told the Eighth Circuit Judges Conference in Duluth, Minn., in August. "Like many Americans, I am concerned about the expansion of preventative law enforcement. That is why we . . . [are] mindful that we seek to secure liberty, not trade liberty for security."

One policy that has aroused concern and comment is the administration's secret detention of two U.S. citizens accused of terrorism and at least 147 others detained in the investigation of the Sept. 11 attacks. Lawmakers, including Sen. Arlen Specter, R-Pa., a former prosecutor, have questioned whether the detentions without access to a lawyer of U.S. citizens José Padilla and Yaser Hamdi as "enemy combatants" violates a 1971 law that bars citizens who haven't been charged with a crime from being imprisoned or detained indefinitely, except pursuant to an act of Congress. Padilla was detained for allegedly plotting to detonate a radioactive bomb. Hamdi was nabbed fighting for the Taliban in Afghanistan. The law was inspired by the controversial World War II internment of Japanese-Americans. [9]

Critics say the White House is trying to claim a right to detain citizens without charging them with a crime, creating a paradox in which a citizen charged with being an enemy combatant, such as so-called "American Taliban" John Walker Lindh, has more rights than the uncharged citizen detainees. The White House defends the prosecutorial strategy as legal, however, citing a 1942 Supreme Court ruling in a case dealing with Nazi saboteurs, which stated that the military may detain a U.S. citizen who joined the enemy or entered the country to carry out hostile attacks.

Similarly, critics complain about secret deportation proceedings against aliens detained in the Sept. 11 investigation that exclude the public, the press and even the families of the accused. Some were not initially told why they were being held. The 6th U.S. Circuit Court of Appeals ruled in August that the insistence on closed proceedings was unconstitutional because it denied the public's right to know whether the government is acting legally. The three-judge panel called the policy "profoundly undemocratic," warning that it could result in a "wholesale suspension of First Amendment rights." [10]

Congress separately is discussing whether to hold hearings into whether some detentions violate the USA Patriot Act, which gave law enforcement seven days to charge or release suspects or to begin deportation proceedings. The administration defends the secret proceedings, saying disclosure of charges could compromise ongoing investigations. Though lawmakers are not about to argue for quicker releases of suspects, it is pondering new legislation that would set stan-

dards for lengthy detentions.

"Instead of expending resources to prevent the release of information about detainees, the administration should show it has confidence in the Justice Department's investigation by opening the department's actions to public scrutiny," says Sen. Russell D. Feingold, D-Wis.

Even the ultrasecret federal court that oversees terrorism investigations is criticizing the administration. Last May, the Foreign Intelligence Surveillance Court refused to expand Justice De-

Flanked by Vice President Dick Cheney, left, and Defense Secretary Donald H. Rumsfeld, President Bush speaks in the White House Rose Garden on Oct. 23, 2002, before signing legislation increasing defense spending for 2003. Bush's insistence on blanket authority to pursue his anti-terrorism and war policies has antagonized some members of Congress, who believe they have been bypassed on key policy decisions.

partment powers to use intelligence information, saying the administration was trying to thwart the will of Congress and give criminal investigators free access to classified information.

The so-called FISA court meets in secret to approve warrants and almost never publishes opinions. But it said federal agents had misled the court in applications for secret eavesdropping warrants during both the Clinton and Bush administrations. It concluded the Bush administration's efforts to expand the use of classified information could

violate the Fourth Amendment, which prohibits unreasonable searches and seizures.

Ironically, the ruling could prompt Congress to give the administration more prosecutorial powers, albeit within specific guidelines. Specter, Sen. Charles E. Grassley, R-Iowa, and others on the Senate Judiciary Committee concerned about the effectiveness of ongoing probes are considering legislation to make it easier for the FBI and other investigative agencies to obtain warrants. The lawmakers were infuriated last summer on learning that the Minneapolis office of the FBI could not obtain a FISA warrant to inspect the laptop computer of terror suspect Zacarias Moussaoui in the weeks before the Sept. 11 attacks because there was no clear evidence linking the French Muslim to an international terror group.

"We need to give the government some expanded powers," says Sen. Charles E. Schumer, D-N.Y., a Judiciary Committee member. "The real trick is finding the right balance." [11]

While the administration's assertive strategy clearly has bruised egos and drawn admonitions, it remains unclear whether the president actually has overreached and skewered the system of checks and balances. Some scholars cite the strong congressional reaction as proof that the system is alive and well. In fact, they say, it has prevented the United States from following Europe's lead and enacting even tougher anti-terrorism measures. According to this line of thinking, Bush is no different from his predecessors who sought sweeping authority during wartime. But, the admin-

War Powers Act Pits Congress vs. President

Tensions between Congress and the Nixon administration already were reaching the boiling point in 1973 when lawmakers, on learning about the secret bombing of Cambodia, passed the War Powers Resolution, serving notice they were reasserting influence over the country's foreign affairs.

But in trying to limit the president's power to send U.S. forces abroad without congressional approval, they created a document that, nearly 30 years later, continues to stir controversy and confusion over presidential power.

When Congress approved the act, Richard M. Nixon's presidency was already weakened by the Watergate scandal, his firing of special prosecutor Archibald Cox and the scandal surrounding the Watergate tapes. [1]

Nevertheless, Nixon vetoed the resolution, arguing it would "seriously undermine the nation's ability to act decisively and convincingly in times of international crisis" and "give every future Congress the ability to handcuff every future president." [2]

But the House and Senate — intent on flexing their muscle — each overrode his veto and enacted the resolution into law, arguing that the president could only commit forces pursuant to either a declaration of war, specific statutory authorization or an emergency created by an attack on the United States. Without such approval, the resolution required terminating troop commitments within 60 days, with a 30-day extension, if necessary, to ensure safe withdrawals.

"If the president can deal with the Arabs, and if he can deal with the Soviets, then he ought to be able and willing to deal with the U.S. Congress," said then-House Majority Leader Thomas P. "Tip" O'Neill Jr., D-Mass. [3]

Every president since Nixon has viewed the War Powers Resolution as an unconstitutional infringement on the commander-in-chief's authority as head of the armed forces to defend vital national security interests. Congress has never used the resolution to compel the withdrawal of military forces against the president's will. But the mere existence of it has led the two sides to compromise over a series of foreign showdowns. [4]

One of the first deals was struck in September 1983, when President Ronald Reagan and Congress agreed to authorize the participation of U.S. Marines in a multinational peacekeeping force in Lebanon for 18 months. But the next month, a suicide truck bombing killed 220 Marines and 21 other U.S. service members at the Marines' compound in Beirut. Reagan announced he was pulling the Marines out, and in March 1984 he reported to Congress that U.S. participation in the multinational force had ended.

Six years later, at the outset of the Persian Gulf War with Iraq, Congress bristled at President George Bush's deployment of military personnel to Saudi Arabia to defend U.S. interests in the region without congressional approval.

Congress belatedly approved the use of military force against Iraq, but, citing the War Powers Resolution, lawmakers stipulated that the president must certify to Congress that such use of force was necessary and that diplomatic efforts had failed. While the sides ultimately agreed on the common

istration almost certainly would not have been able to enact a law like Britain's anti-terrorism act, which authorizes the government to record and store citizens' e-mails, Internet browsing habits and other electronic communications and to make the information available to authorities without a court order. The European Union in May authorized members to pass similar data-retention measures.

"So far, in the face of great stress, the system has worked relatively well," George Washington University law Professor Jeffrey Rosen wrote recently in *The Washington Post*. "The executive branch tried to increase its own authority across the board, but the courts and Congress are insisting on a more reasoned balance between liberty and security. Of all the lessons about

America's strength that have emerged since the attacks, this is one of the most reassuring." [12]

Did Congress give the president too much leeway by authorizing the use of force against Iraq?

As Congress returned from its August recess, President Bush aggressively worked to develop compromise language on the use-of-force resolution against Iraq that so upset Sen. Byrd. The administration dispatched high-level officials to Capitol Hill to offer private, classified briefings for undecided lawmakers about Iraqi weapons capabilities and to make the case for pre-emptive strikes. It also previewed proposed drafts of the resolution, which eventually would win a solid bipartisan majority in both houses.

But perhaps the president's most effective selling job took place 235 miles to the north. On Sept. 12 Bush addressed the United Nations and laid out his rationale for an attack, making his case in the context of international law and U.N. agreements, and finally warning that the United States was prepared to act with or without Security Council sanction. The appearance did not win over the world body, especially after Iraq agreed to a new round of U.N. weapons inspections.

However, his tough talk and bow to the international body unified congressional Republicans and even brought skeptical Democrats into the administration's corner. Senate Majority Leader Tom Daschle, D-S.D., dropped his plan to postpone a vote on a resolution until next year. And

objective, Bush made it clear that he never sought congressional authorization. Congress, however, characterized its action as the requisite authorization to proceed.

Another flareup over presidential authorization of combat activity occurred in March 1999, when President Bill Clinton notified Congress he had begun air strikes against Yugoslavia in response to its repression of ethnic Albanians in the province of Kosovo.

Congressional Republicans tried to use the War Powers Resolution to overturn the president's actions, and later attempted to withhold funding for the operation. In fact, 18 members of Congress, led by Rep. Tom Campbell, R-Calif., even sued Clinton in federal district court in Washington, alleging his actions violated the act. The suit was dismissed after the judge ruled the members lacked legal standing to bring the suit. The U.S. Court of Appeals for the District of Columbia Circuit upheld the ruling. The lawmakers appealed to the U.S. Supreme Court, but justices refused to hear the case, letting stand the appeals court decision.

Experts believe the resolution remains a useful and appropriate way to express congressional sentiment, even if presidents

War Powers Resolution
Sec. 4 — Consultation

"The President in every possible instance shall consult with Congress before introducing United States Armed Forces into hostilities or into situations where imminent involvement in hostilities is clearly indicated by the circumstances, and after every such introduction shall consult regularly with the Congress until United States Armed Forces are no longer engaged in hostilities or have been removed from such situations."

continue to argue it is not legally binding. Louis Fisher, a specialist in separation of powers at the Congressional Research Service, argues that if the legislative branch does not use the powers available to it and acquiesces to the executive branch, courts cannot be relied on to rule on abuses that may arise.

"Congress must be prepared, and willing, to exercise the ample powers within its arsenal," Fisher writes. "It needs also the institutional courage and constitutional understanding to share with the president the momentous decision to send U.S. forces into combat." [5]

---

[1] For background, see "Watergate Crisis, 1972-1976 Political Chronology," in *Congress and the Nation, 1973-76* (1977).

[2] See *1973 CQ Almanac*, pp. 905-917.

[3] *Ibid.*

[4] For background, see Congressional Research Service, "Congressional Use of Funding Cutoffs Since 1970 Involving U.S. Military Forces and Overseas Deployments," Report No. RS20775, Jan. 10, 2001.

[5] See James A. Thurber, ed., *Divided Democracy: Cooperation and Conflict Between the President and Congress* (1991), pp. 199-215.

House Democratic Leader Richard A. Gephardt of Missouri — like Daschle a possible 2004 presidential aspirant — unexpectedly one-upped his Senate counterpart, cutting a deal with the White House giving Bush authority to wage war but stipulating that he must first consult with Congress and provide evidence that diplomacy is no longer working. [13]

Bush's dual-track selling job came with polls indicating lukewarm public support for a U.S. attack on Iraq. Many lawmakers also were unconvinced that there is a real connection between Iraq and the war on terrorism. Analysts said the result was tribute to the president's effective use of the bully pulpit and his bare-knuckles political tactic of challenging Congress to defy him on a national se-

curity matter in an election year. Many also attributed the widespread Democratic acquiescence to a desire to dispense with the matter so they could concentrate on traditional party issues, like prescription drugs for the elderly and protecting Social Security.

"The president has run a successful campaign to win a vote," Thomas E. Mann, a senior fellow at the Brookings Institution, said after the vote on the resolution. "The president has not persuaded the public or the Congress that a full, careful, cost-benefit analysis has been done and that this is the wisest course to follow."

The Iraq vote could set a new precedent for a chief executive seeking war powers. Congress for the first time allowed the president to launch military strikes, without advance notice, under

conditions that preclude a lengthy debate. That conflicts with Article I, Section 8, of the Constitution, which gives Congress power "to declare war." Though Congress has only done so on five occasions — the War of 1812, the Mexican War, the Spanish-American War and the two world wars — institutionalists like Byrd fear future presidents will use a pre-emption doctrine to bypass the legislative branch when it suits them.

Since passage of the 1973 War Powers Resolution, Congress has used the act for leverage in debates over war. (*See sidebar, p. 8*) The law allows Congress to compel — against the president's will — the withdrawal of military forces from foreign deployments if Congress does not approve of the action. While Congress has never actually used it to pull back troops, the existence of the act has, from time to time, forced presidents to compromise even though they view it as an unconstitutional infringement on their authority. [14] Congress also has the politically risky option of not funding military actions — a move that can be viewed as not supporting U.S. troops in the field.

Congress was not sure how to react to the White House's insistence for war authority, especially given the speed with which the Iraq debate progressed and overshadowed other items on the House and Senate agendas. Some lawmakers chose to parse the dilemma from a legal perspective, questioning whether it is appropriate to react to a "continuing threat," as opposed to an "imminent threat." Skeptics like Senate Armed Services Committee Chairman Carl Levin, D-Mich., say lowering the threshold for a pre-emptive strike could lead unfriendly countries with weapons of mass destruction — such as Iran or North Korea — to strike unilaterally, possibly against U.S. interests. But during Senate and House debates, Levin and Rep. John M. Spratt Jr., D-S.C., each failed to persuade colleagues to add language requiring the White House to seek another congressional vote before launching unilateral strikes against Iraq, unless it were part of an international coalition.

Byrd questioned whether Bush's swagger will hinder future attempts to build international coalitions and accused him of timing the vote to coincide with the politically charged period before midterm elections. Byrd intended to use Senate rules to drag out debate beyond the elections, but Daschle thwarted him by using his own procedural tactics to change the order of the text of the resolution. The chamber adopted the resolution after two weeks of debate and within hours of the House. "We debated it at least as long as the debate we had in 1991 [over war with Iraq], and I think every-

one knows how they're going to vote," Daschle said. [15]

The final version attaches some conditions, though it generally is more broadly worded than similar resolutions in the past. It allows the president to wage war as long as he informs Congress within 48 hours after the start of military action. In contrast, the resolution authorizing President Bush's father to commence the 1991 Gulf War stipulated that the president had to tell Congress that diplomatic efforts had failed before he could launch an attack.

The new resolution requires the president to certify that non-military methods of eliminating the threat have failed and reaffirm that removing the threat posed by Iraq is consistent with, and an integral component of, the war on terrorism. The language also requires Bush to report to Congress every 60 days on relevant matters concerning the confrontation with Iraq, and reaffirms the 1998 Iraq Liberation Act, which said Iraqi President Saddam Hussein should be removed from power. [16]

Some observers suggest debates over how much power the president accumulates are pointless, because the Founding Fathers envisioned the president having to quickly authorize military action in self-defense, even when it was unilateral. They point out that Congress recognized this in 1798, when it authorized the first military action: to block France from interfering with U.S. maritime commerce. Since then, presidents have sent American troops into conflict at least 200 times without formal declarations of war, though most of the actions were authorized by congressional statute.

"We're living in a post-Cold War world where deterrence alone just doesn't do the job it used to," says Jack Spencer, security analyst at the conservative Heritage Foundation. "Our president has all the authority he

needs to address this new threat, and he should use it."

"The question isn't why now, but why not earlier," said Sen. Joseph I. Lieberman, D-Conn., as he supported the resolution during the Senate debate. "Over the last decade, Saddam has built up weapons of mass destruction, developed the means to deliver them on targets near and far and consistently ignored and violated U.N. resolutions. We've waited too long to address this threat."

Others contend, however, that Congress capitulated by giving the president extraordinary powers that cannot be challenged. They say Congress signed its authority away — and did so clearly understanding that the Bush administration is trying to overthrow the Iraqi regime. Some worry about similarities to the 1964 Gulf of Tonkin Resolution, in which Congress authorized President Lyndon B. Johnson to use force and effectively authorized the Vietnam War because of reports of an attack on U.S. vessels in Southeast Asian waters.

"To have the president draft the resolution, submit it to Congress and demand they pass it — it's incredible arrogance of power, but they did it," says Shirley Anne Warshaw, a political science professor at Gettysburg College. "The fear of terrorism has emasculated Congress."

BACKGROUND

'Imperial Presidency'

President Bush was sworn into office at a time when presidential clout was on the wane. Since the end of the Cold War, Congress has taken the initiative in areas once the exclusive domain of the chief executive,

Chronology

1780s–1820s

The office of the presidency is conceived and its powers spelled out.

1787
The Constitution spells out the president's executive powers, such as military command, involvement in the legislative process, pardon and the execution of laws. While the president is designated "commander-in-chief" of armed forces, Congress is given the power "to declare war."

1801-1803
Thomas Jefferson battles with the Supreme Court over the concept of judicial review. The question of whether ultimate authority rests with the president and elected representatives in Congress or in a fixed legal standard has come up repeatedly in U.S. history.

———•———

1830s–1860s

Presidents seek to expand executive powers, increasing their influence over legislation, military matters and responses to national emergencies.

1832
Andrew Jackson vetoes a congressional bill to re-charter the National Bank of the United States for four years, arguing for the first time that a veto is justified if the president had a policy disagreement with Congress. By demanding to be involved in the drafting of legislation, Jackson alters the relationship between the executive and legislative branches. Jackson later tries to kill off the bank, triggering a bitter power struggle over control of the executive administration.

1844-1848
James K. Polk further asserts presidential power, for the first time creating an executive branch budget and insisting on being the decisive authority in all military matters during the Mexican War.

1861-1865
Abraham Lincoln seizes extraordinary powers during Civil War, suspending habeas corpus and imposing martial law. Lincoln also pushes the anti-slavery 13th Amendment through Congress.

———•———

1900s–1960s

Economic and military crises help define a modern notion of presidential power.

1901-1908
Theodore Roosevelt expands executive power, claiming the president possesses a special mandate from the people. He wins authority to regulate railroad shipping rates, takes control of the Panama Canal Zone and intervenes in the Russo-Japanese War, for the first time recognizing one power's claim on the territory of another.

1918
Woodrow Wilson fails to win Senate approval to create the League of Nations, indicating the presidency still can be limited by Congress and public opinion.

1935-1937
Franklin D. Roosevelt triggers a constitutional crisis when he tries to "pack" the Supreme Court by replacing the oldest justices after the court strikes down a series of New Deal laws on the grounds they delegate too much authority to the executive. Roosevelt fails to get the plan through Congress. Roosevelt's actions spark a backlash, as conservative Democrats and Republicans block further presidential reform initiatives.

1952
Supreme Court, in *Youngstown Sheet and Tube Co. v. Sawyer*, rebuffs Harry S Truman's effort to assume emergency economic powers by trying to nationalize steel mills during the Korean War.

1964
Congress inadvertently authorizes the Vietnam War through the Gulf of Tonkin Resolution, which gave Lyndon B. Johnson the right to use force in response to what is claimed to be an attack on U.S. ships in Asian waters.

———•———

1970s–Present

Resurgent Congress seeks to make presidents more accountable to the legislative branch.

1973
Congress passes War Powers Act allowing Congress to compel the withdrawal of U.S. military forces from foreign deployment against the president's will.

Dec. 19, 1998
House impeaches President Bill Clinton on charges of lying under oath and obstructing justice over his affair with White House intern Monica Lewinsky. Senate acquits Clinton.

2001-2002
President Bush strengthens executive branch counterterrorism efforts after the Sept. 11 terrorist attacks, winning expanded prosecutorial powers from Congress and using administrative fiat to establish new rules for terrorism investigations.

Was Lincoln a Dictator?

Although President Bush's war on terrorism has raised questions about the boundaries of a president's legal authority in wartime, his actions fairly pale in comparison to those of Abraham Lincoln. The 16th president's forceful use of executive powers during the Civil War prompted charges that he had turned the presidency into a military dictatorship.

Lincoln unilaterally suspended the *writ of habeas corpus*, blockaded the nation's southern coast and added 40,000 enlisted men to the Army and Navy after Confederates bombarded Fort Sumter in April 1861. He believed that in times of crisis he had constitutional authority as commander-in-chief to prosecute the war without having to first seek congressional approval. Indeed, in calling for military enlistments beyond existing limits, Lincoln conceded he was overstepping statutory authority. [1]

Lincoln's actions were particularly notable because as a Whig member of Congress he had criticized President James K. Polk's aggressive leadership during the Mexican War, arguing that the Constitution gave "war-making power" to Congress.

Lincoln knew he was playing with a weak hand politically after only winning about 40 percent of the popular vote during the fragmented 1860 election. However, he believed that the extraordinary circumstances of the Civil War justified re-thinking the rules. By the time he was inaugurated in March 1861, six Southern states had seceded. Lincoln judged the action treasonous and vowed to enforce federal laws in all of the states, as the Constitution enjoined him to do.

He served early notice that he would use his executive powers forcefully. For instance, after issuing his first executive orders, he deliberately postponed a special session of Congress until July 4, even though the session had been called for in April. When Congress arrived, Lincoln submitted his early actions to the legislative branch for approval, and lawmakers rat-

The earliest known photo of Lincoln is believed to show him after he won his first seat in Congress, in 1846.

Library of Congress

ified them. In effect, Lincoln expected the legislative branch to rubber stamp his policies, but he respected the Constitution enough to submit his agenda to Congress for approval.

Some of Lincoln's most controversial moves involved prosecutorial powers. By suspending *habeas corpus*, he allowed citizens to be arrested without warrants and without authorities having to offer proof to a court. In September 1862, he began authorizing more power for military authorities — again without consulting the legislative branch — by declaring all draft resisters and suspected Confederate sympathizers subject to martial law and liable to be tried by military tribunals.

Congress put up some resistance, challenging the suspension of *habeas corpus* in an 1863 law that ordered the release of prisoners unless they were first indicted in civil courts. However, the legislature never succeeded in shifting the venue from military courts to civilian courts. The courts also refused to weaken the expanded prosecutorial powers while the war was on. It was not until after the war, in 1866, that the Supreme Court ruled, in *Ex Parte Milligan*, that Lincoln had violated constitutional guarantees of a fair trail, and that military courts could only be used if civil courts had been closed by the rebellion.

Scholars view Lincoln's tenure as extraordinary, because while he stretched the boundaries of the Constitution, he was, at times, scrupulous about maintaining some balance of power. He issued the "Emancipation Proclamation" in January 1863, then showed deference to the legislative branch by pushing it through Congress, arguing that freeing slaves in existing states was beyond the legislative branch's enumerated powers.

Lincoln based the proclamation on his war powers, arguing it was necessary in order to suppress rebellion. Congress ratified the 13th Amendment in 1865.

---

[1] For background, see Michael Newman, ed., *Congressional Quarterly's Guide to the Presidency* (1989), pp. 80-84.

forcing the president into political battles on an issue-by-issue basis and blocking him from assembling permanent working majorities in either the House or Senate. Myriad interest groups further complicated the president's task by weighing in on national debates and exerting strong pressure on various votes. [17]

Bush spent the first few months of his administration following a pattern set by his immediate predecessors — identifying fundamental problems and broaching solutions, while leaving the details of how they would be enacted to the legislative branch. But in contrast to Clinton, a perpetual campaigner who weighed in on a wide range of issues, Bush focused only on a small subset of priorities, such as education reform and tax cuts.

As leader of the first unified Republican government in half a century (with the GOP in control of the House and an evenly divided Senate that only later swung to Democratic control), Bush did not have to pander to each Republican constituency. Only occasionally did he seek to reassure core supporters by nominating reliable conservatives, such as Ashcroft.

"His style of governing and his claim to fame was to focus on a few big things and get them done," says Texas A&M political scientist Edwards. "It would be difficult to conclude they were taking an expansive view."

But after the terrorist attacks exposed a new and grave national security threat, Bush changed course, using an almost corporate "top-down" management style that envisioned minimal consultation with Congress. For example, he did not apprise members when he established a "shadow government" in secret locations along the East Coast to ensure that the executive branch could continue functioning in the event of a nuclear attack. Some saw his moves to establish broad institutional authority in national security and international affairs as an attempt to re-establish "the imperial presidency" that prevailed during World War II and the Cold War, according to historian Arthur Schlesinger Jr. [18]

Jackson's Model

Presidents always have had considerable elbowroom to define their jobs, in part because of the vagueness of the Constitution. While Congress' roles and responsibilities were clearly spelled out in Article I, opinions differed on whether the chief executive was a supreme leader or just an important part of a bigger plan built around the separation of powers. Adding to the ambiguity is the fact that the president is elected from much broader electoral coalitions than representatives and senators, who have narrow constituencies in districts and states and, thus, cannot represent the nation as a whole. [19]

The murky questions have left the balance of power between the branches in constant flux. Thomas Jefferson, elected president by the House of Representatives after a tie vote in 1801, regarded Congress, not the public, as his primary constituency, though he still held considerable sway as head of the new majority Democratic-Republican Party.

The concept of a strong chief executive was first affirmed two decades later by Andrew Jackson, who built the first modern political-party organization and installed a spoils system that inserted allies into key government jobs, triggering huge power struggles. The party system allowed Jackson to appeal directly to the public, thereby circumventing the elected representatives, when it suited him.

Abraham Lincoln built on Jackson's model by using political patronage to help pass a constitutional amendment abolishing slavery (he cut deals with a handful of House members to allow Nevada to enter the union and provide the deciding votes). As the Civil War split the nation, Lincoln asserted that the president was entitled to assume "war power" and did not need specific constitutional authority to act at home or on foreign soil. (*See sidebar, p. 12.*)

In the early 20th century, Theodore Roosevelt again adopted this model, after a change in public thinking following the Spanish-American War led the once-isolationist U.S. government to pursue more foreign policy objectives. Woodrow Wilson refined and modernized the approach, becoming the first president to propose and draft legislation, hold regular news conferences, lobby Congress and actively assess public opinion. Though Congress granted Wilson expanded war powers during World War I, he failed to convince lawmakers of the need to join the League of Nations after the conflict ended.

It was Franklin D. Roosevelt who most reshaped the concept of presidential power to fit modern times. Elected as a rattled nation tried to come to grips with the Great Depression, Roosevelt won huge victories as Congress ceded authority in fiscal policy, banking, housing and agriculture. He also gained unprecedented emergency authority to dispense economic relief and, later, to plan military actions in World War II.

Roosevelt's tenure created the expectation that the president should be a chief legislative leader. Dwight D. Eisenhower was able to centralize power in the White House after Congress created the Council of Economic Advisers and a National Security Council in the late 1940s. Congress continued to defer as the president grew more involved in global affairs. The Marshall Plan to rebuild Europe, the Bretton Woods agreement on an international gold standard and sending troops to Korea were all executive-branch initiatives.

In October 1962, John F. Kennedy similarly was ready to act on his own during the Cuban missile crisis, asserting that he had full authority as commander-in-chief to take military action against the island nation. Congress — worried that unilateral action would not reflect the collective judgment of the government and could threaten national prestige — passed a Cuba Resolution that did not authorize presidential action but did express sentiments in favor of keeping Cuba's regime in check. When Kennedy acted that month to block the delivery of weapons to Cuba, he based his action on his constitutional authorities "as endorsed by the resolution of the Congress."

Building Presidential Power

The Constitution clearly spells out Congress' roles and responsibilities but is less explicit about the role of the president. Consequently, chief executives always have had considerable elbowroom to define their jobs. Presidents who played key roles in shaping the power of the office include:

National Archives

Andrew Jackson (1829-37) — set the precedent for the concept of a strong chief executive. Jackson built the first modern political-party organization and installed a spoils system that inserted allies into key government jobs, triggering huge power struggles. The party system allowed Jackson to circumvent the elected representatives and appeal directly to the public.

Library of Congress

Abraham Lincoln (1861-65) — built on Jackson's model by using political patronage to help pass a constitutional amendment abolishing slavery (he cut deals with a handful of House members to allow Nevada to enter the union and provide the deciding votes). When the Civil War split the nation, Lincoln asserted that the president was entitled to assume "war power" and did not need specific constitutional authority to act.

Library of Congress

Woodrow Wilson (1913-21) — followed President Theodore Roosevelt's model and pursued more foreign-policy objectives. Wilson became the first president to propose and draft legislation, hold regular news conferences, lobby Congress and actively assess public opinion. Though Congress granted him expanded war powers during World War I, he failed to convince lawmakers to join the League of Nations.

FDR Library

Franklin D. Roosevelt (1933-45) — almost single-handedly reshaped the concept of presidential power to fit modern times. Amid the Great Depression, Congress ceded authority to FDR in fiscal policy, banking, housing and agriculture, plus unprecedented emergency power to dispense economic relief and later to plan military actions in World War II.

Library of Congress

Harry S Truman (1945-53) — pushed through executive-branch initiatives such as the Marshall Plan to rebuild Europe, the Bretton Woods agreement on an international gold standard and sending troops to Korea. In one of the rare instances where a court ruled against presidential power, the Supreme Court in 1952 held that Truman had no legitimate power to nationalize steel mills during the Korean War.

JFK Library

John F. Kennedy (1961-63) — prepared to act on his own during the 1962 Cuban missile crisis. Worried lawmakers passed a resolution that did not authorize presidential action but supported keeping Cuba's regime in check. When Kennedy blocked the delivery of weapons to Cuba, he based his action on his constitutional authorities "as endorsed by the resolution of the Congress."

Congress Pushes Back

But the run of unchallenged White House power ended during President Johnson's administration. Despite giving Johnson de facto power to fight a war in Vietnam through the 1964 Gulf of Tonkin Resolution, Congress — particularly Senate Foreign Relations Committee Chairman J. William Fulbright, D-Ark. — refused to accept the president's decision to send troops to the Dominican Republic to suppress a revolt. Fulbright later broke with precedent and held televised hearings into the legitimacy of military action in Vietnam.

Congress continued to assert itself during Richard M. Nixon's terms, first by reviewing U.S. overseas commitments and agreements. Nixon responded by refusing to release congressionally approved funds for programs he thought were wasteful or unnecessary. Congress struck back by passing legislation restricting presidential autonomy — most notably the 1973 War Powers Resolution — forcing the chief executive to obtain congressional blessing for extended military engagements. Congress also passed the 1974 Budget Act, which gave the legislative branch its own economic forecasts and deficit estimates, which sometimes challenge the conclusions of the White House Office of Management and Budget.

Congress finally exercised its most dramatic check on the president when it began impeachment proceedings against Nixon in connection with the burglary of the offices of the Democratic National Committee in the Watergate Hotel complex and the ensuing cover-up by the administration. The House Judiciary Committee recommended Nixon be impeached. But he resigned before a full session of the House could vote on the issue.

Similarly, dramatic institutional tensions existed during Reagan's terms, when congressional Democrats seized on a sputtering economy to fight the president's efforts to spend more on defense without raising taxes. Congress also used investigations and inquiries to assert its power and undercut the chief executive during the Iran-Contra scandal, which greatly diminished Reagan's public standing and effectively ended his conservative revolution.

Increased partisanship and an assertive Congress frustrated the administration of the first President George Bush and, in many instances, Clinton, who fought a Republican majority in Congress by using the appropriations process and the power of the veto. Scandals surrounding Clinton's personal behavior also led the House to impeach Clinton, though he was acquitted in the subsequent Senate trial. [20]

Some historians and commentators see the current President Bush as trying to rekindle the spirit of President Jackson by battling Congress over war powers, advocating aggressive use of U.S. power and trying to redefine the judicial notions of the rights of the accused. Bush, like Jackson, also advocates an America-first foreign policy, which rejects internationalist solutions to dilemmas like global warming and anti-ballistic-missile buildups. Bush believes global accords to address such problems do not necessarily serve U.S. interests, even though he may support their principal objectives. He has called for new approaches that better serve U.S. needs. [21]

But such an approach can pose perils. If Bush does not build a popular response for his policies and cannot stop terrorism and other threats at the U.S. borders, some fear a backlash that could give rise to nativist fears and discrimination.

"We are at the zenith of our power and influence," former Clinton administration national security adviser Samuel Berger told Cox Newspapers. However, he said most of the dire global threats — from terrorism to the AIDS pandemic — are very difficult to confront alone. "We live in a world in which we can often get a lot more done by cooperating than acting alone." [22]

"If Bush fails to contain terror and shape a popular response, you get something much tougher to deal with," said Walter Russell Mead, a historian at the Council on Foreign Relations. "I don't think the political alternative is moderation." [23]

CURRENT SITUATION

Homeland Security

As the 2002 midterm elections approached, Congress had yet to clear a major piece of unfinished Bush-agenda business: creation of a domestic security agency. The job of organizing nearly two-dozen federal agencies responsible for counterterrorism into a new Cabinet-level department at first seemed timely and non-controversial. In fact, many in Congress predicted they would complete the authorizing legislation by the symbolic first anniversary of the Sept. 11 attacks.

Yet the administration's insistence on having more authority over the department than it has over most other federal agencies turned the reorganization into an unexpectedly bitter partisan battle with Senate Democrats, for whom organized labor is a core constituency. Lawmakers abandoned the effort in mid-October, after a standoff over procedural rules, and agreed to resume debate in a less-partisan environment after the elections.

The controversy stemmed from the administration's insistence that Congress authorize it to develop a new personnel system for the department that, among other things, would allow managers to fire unionized employees or transfer some workers out of collective bargaining units on national security grounds. The administration explained it did not want individuals in important security positions walking off the job in labor disputes. The administration added that it needed more flexibility than the civil service system now provides in order to recruit the most qualified job candidates and to quickly shift department resources to meet changing terrorist threats.

But Democrats and their labor allies charged that the request amounted to a backdoor attempt to gut labor protections. Their suspicions were rooted partially in an administration decision in January 2002 to remove some 500 Justice Department workers engaged in terrorism investigations from collective bargaining units on similar national security grounds. [24]

"The unions have the votes and can influence the outcome," says Sen. George V. Voinovich, R-Ohio, the Senate's resident expert on civil service, who is friendly with organized labor. "There has to be some reconciliation."

The administration and unions have clashed in the past over workplace rules. After Sept. 11, the White House and Congress heatedly debated legislation that established the Transportation Security Administration. The White House wanted the freedom to hire federal employees to staff airport security checkpoints or to continue contracting for private personnel. Pro-labor forces prevailed, however, arguing that the checkpoints should be run only by federal workers. The transportation security agency was to become part of the new homeland security department, and policymakers on both sides of the debate seemed to anticipate that unions would try to organize approximately 3,000 federal screeners due to be at their posts by this November.

The administration is adamant that anything short of full authority to make work rules would diminish powers presidents have enjoyed since the height of the Cold War, when then-President Kennedy in 1962 ordered personnel flexibilities on national security grounds. Senate Democrats want language that would add conditions and force the president to justify shifting employees.

The dispute took up some of the most arcane aspects of the federal work force. Administration officials complained about restrictive union rules that, for example, would protect a hypothetical intoxicated Border Patrol agent who allows a potential terrorist to enter the country from being fired without a 30-day written notice, during which time he would continue being paid. The administration also argued that work rules could prevent the new department from quickly deploying teams of workers to respond to biological or chemical attacks. At the heart of the issue, however, was the perception that Congress was trying to micromanage the executive branch.

Election Politics

I t was unclear how quickly any compromise would emerge in the aftermath of the stunning 2002 midterm elections. Resounding GOP victories that will give the Republicans control

National Guard soldiers patrol San Francisco's Golden Gate Bridge on Sept. 11, 2002. The administration says the unusual nature of the terrorist threat justifies its aggressive stance, arguing it needs maximum flexibility to confront a dangerous enemy.

AFP Photo/John G. Mabanglo

of the Senate were largely due to Bush's active campaigning on national security matters. Nowhere was this more evident than in the Georgia Senate race, in which Republican Rep. Saxby Chambliss defeated incumbent Democrat Sen. Max Cleland, a Vietnam War hero who lost both legs and an arm in that conflict. Chambliss characterized Cleland's votes against Bush's reorganization plan and the work rules as evidence that Cleland was soft on national security matters.

The election results gave the White

House a chance to prevail on homeland security legislation during a "lame duck" post-election session of the 107th Congress. Former Republican Rep. James Talent's victory over incumbent Democratic Sen. Jean Carnahan of Missouri in a special election allowed Talent to be certified the victor and be seated immediately, before the start of the 108th Congress. The death of Democratic Sen. Paul Wellstone of Minnesota days before the election also prompted Independent Gov. Jesse Ventura to appoint fellow Independent Dean Barkley as an interim senator.

However, it was unclear whether Senate leaders would seek to do more than pass a long-term continuing resolution to ensure that the government keeps running until early 2003.

At a Nov. 7 press conference, President Bush strongly urged the Senate to pass a homeland security bill before the 107th Congress adjourns.

On Nov. 10, Senate Republican leader Trent Lott of Mississippi told NBC's "Meet the Press" that he hoped to get a homeland security bill passed within days after the Senate reconvened on Nov. 12, following its election hiatus. But Lott did not explain exactly how that could be achieved, since, technically, control of the Senate would not shift to the GOP for another two weeks, when Talent is to be sworn in. [25]

In the 108th Congress, Republicans will have at least a 51-seat Senate ma-

At Issue

Did the president act responsibly in seeking authority to pre-emptively strike Iraq?

SEN. PAT ROBERTS, R-KAN.
RANKING MEMBER, ARMED SERVICES SUBCOMMITTEE ON EMERGING THREATS AND CAPABILITIES

FROM A SPEECH TO THE SENATE, OCT. 9, 2002

*t*he United Nations has completely and unequivocally failed to disarm Iraq consistent with its own resolutions. . . . Saddam Hussein has demonstrated ad nauseam over the last 10 years that he will never permit the removal or destruction of his weapons of mass destruction, [which] are the very source of his authority. . . . He has [been] willing to use [such] weapons against his own countrymen and against other nations. And he rules by fear. So, . . . he [will never] disarm — ever.

Any notion that the United States itself is off-limits to a massive attack by groups cooperating with or supported by Baghdad should now be gone. It is [a] sanctuary for further terrorist attacks against our homeland. . . .

While "hard evidence" of an Iraqi role in the attacks of 9/11 may be hard to prove . . . I do not think we can afford to be naive. Particularly in the Middle East, terror groups and states work together when and where their interests are common. And their intent is the destruction of the United States, the murder of our citizens and the elimination of our influence, real and perceived. . . . If Iraq and other regimes are left unchallenged, it is only a matter of time before they transfer the capability for weapons of mass destruction to a terrorist cell that will use that capability against the United States.

The criminal-justice model of gathering evidence and presenting a case does not apply here. By the time you have evidence, it is too late. We will not lose buildings and thousands of people when that happens. We will lose whole cities and hundreds of thousands of people.

In light of the events of Sept. 11, 2001, this body has more reason to support action against Iraq than it had in the winter of 1991. . . . because preventing weapons of mass destruction from being acquired by terrorist cells should be the No. 1 policy priority of this government. This means neutralizing regimes that possess or seek such weapons and are predisposed to harboring, assisting [and] sympathizing with the bin Ladens of the world.

American survival must be assured. It is a first priority. It is our highest agenda. . . . We must be pre-emptive. . . . Yes, pre-emptive, that new doctrine that is causing a rethink of our foreign policy, our military strategy, our politics, our foreign relations. It is a brand new world. It is an asymmetrical world. This has nothing to do with partisan rivalry. This is about our future, both immediate and long term. This is the state of affairs we leave our children and our grandchildren.

SEN. ROBERT C. BYRD, D-W.VA.
MEMBER, ARMED SERVICES SUBCOMMITTEE ON EMERGING THREATS AND CAPABILITIES

FROM A SPEECH TO THE SENATE, OCT. 3, 2002

*w*e are rushing into war without fully discussing why, without thoroughly considering the consequences or without making any attempt to explore what steps we might take to avert conflict.

The newly bellicose mood that permeates this White House . . . is clearly motivated by campaign politics. Republicans are already running attack ads against Democrats on Iraq. . . . Before risking the lives of American troops, all members of Congress — Democrats and Republicans alike — must overcome the siren song of political polls and focus strictly on the merits, not the politics, of this most serious issue.

The resolution is . . . a product of presidential hubris. . . . [It] reinterprets the Constitution to suit the will of the executive branch. It would give the president blanket authority to launch a unilateral, pre-emptive attack on a sovereign nation that is perceived to be a threat. This is an unprecedented and unfounded interpretation of the president's authority under the Constitution, [which] stands the charter of the United Nations on its head.

Article I, Section 8, of the Constitution grants Congress the power to declare war and to call forth the militia "to . . . repel Invasions." Nowhere is it written that the president has the authority to call forth the militia to pre-empt a perceived threat. . . .

Think for a moment of the precedent this resolution will set, not just for this president, but for future presidents. . . . Other nations will be able to hold up the United States as the model to justify their military adventures. Do you not think that India and Pakistan, China and Taiwan, Russia and Georgia are closely watching the outcome of this debate?

A war against Iraq will affect thousands, if not tens of thousands of lives, and perhaps alter the course of history [and] affect the balance of power in the Middle East. It is not a decision to be taken in haste, under the glare of election-year politics and the pressure of artificial deadlines. And yet any observer can see that that is exactly what the Senate is proposing to do.

Let us be convinced that a reinvigorated inspection regime cannot work before we move to any next step, and let us, if we must employ force, employ the most precise and limited use of force necessary to get the job done. Let us guard against the perils of haste, lest the Senate fall prey to the dangers of taking action that is both blind and improvident.

jority, pending the outcome of a runoff in Louisiana. They also will continue to have control of the House, having added at least four additional seats to its majority there. But because legislation cannot carry over into a new Congress, a new homeland security reorganization bill — if it doesn't clear Congress this fall — will have to be reintroduced and make its way through both chambers, giving both parties a chance to reprise this year's debate.

Some believe the White House did not really want to compromise before the elections, preferring to charge that Democrats were endangering national security by pandering to political allies. Others contend the White House may have unwisely used the homeland security bill as a vehicle for broader civil service reforms.

"There's no doubt this is all about politics," says Ivo Daalder, senior fellow at the Brookings Institution. "If there is another terrorist attack, a lot of people are going to blame the Senate and the White House for dickering for months over how to reorganize instead of figuring out what a [counterterrorism] strategy should be."

Should the personnel issue be settled, Congress would likely resolve remaining differences over such matters as intelligence-sharing and contractor insurance and pass authorizing legislation creating the third-largest Cabinet department. The new homeland security department would contain 22 federal agencies, including the Federal Emergency Management Agency, Coast Guard, Secret Service, Immigration and Naturalization Service and Border Patrol. It would not include either the FBI or CIA, which the administration and Congress decided should remain independent. The new department would have a fiscal 2003 budget of $37.5 billion and a workforce of 170,000 employees, not including the new airport screeners.

But even if the department is created, Congress and the White House will have to agree on funding levels

for new counterterrorism initiatives. Increased spending on borders, infrastructure protection and "first responders" was to be dealt with in fiscal 2003 appropriations bills. But partisan friction in Congress prevented the House and Senate from completing action on most of those bills before the elections, freezing funding at 2002 levels. Observers estimate that further skirmishes will prevent the new department from being up and running before late 2003, at best.

"They're trying to balance everything these agencies already do with the new mission of homeland security, and they have to deal with all of the politics. It's an awesome task," says Donald Kettl, professor of public affairs and political science at the University of Wisconsin-Madison.

Other Bush Moves

While the homeland security debate simmers, the administration continues to assert executive branch prerogatives. In a series of recent statements issued when the president signs new legislation into law, Bush has advised Congress that he regards some mandated new requirements as "advisory," meaning they can be overridden by intrinsic executive branch authority.

The Federation of American Scientists' Aftergood says requirements that the administration disclose information to Congress or the public, in particular, are typically deflected by language stating the administration is construing the requirement "in a matter consistent with the constitutional authorities of the president to supervise the unitary executive branch." The boilerplate language also states the president can withhold information when disclosure may impair foreign relations, national security and the president's ability to do his job.

The administration has also been flexing its muscle outside of national

security matters — particularly in the environmental-regulation arena. Since taking office, President Bush has used his executive power to reverse an array of regulations and longstanding environmental-protection laws, usually by issuing "guidance" on regulatory matters, often without oversight and with little public notice. [26]

Conservationists say such actions jeopardize progress made in restoring environmental health since the 1970s, when bedrock environmental-protection laws were passed. They also contend that the president's policies favor oil producers, loggers, electric utilities and other industrial sectors that have long chafed at environmental regulations.

Administration officials say many of the old rules harm the environment and the economy. For instance, some rules delay removal of flammable deadwood from forests, triggering devastating forest fires in the West last summer. Others bar such activities as logging and oil and gas production and snowmobile use on certain public lands.

Critics say the administration is purposely using the "guidance" mechanism to avoid exposure to public scrutiny or debate. "Rulemaking requires a public process, while guidance can happen with almost no public process," says Gregory Wetstone, director of programs at the Natural Resources Defense Council (NRDC), an environmental advocacy group in New York City. "We've seen big changes in forest policy and policy on snowmobiles in national parks that weren't even [advertised as] rulemakings." Wetstone points to more than 100 separate actions by six federal agencies and the White House taken outside the regular rulemaking process.

This year, for example, the administration lifted a ban on new oil and gas drilling in the Rocky Mountains, changed tough air-conditioner efficiency standards and formally designated Nevada's Yucca Mountain as a nuclear-waste repository. In June, Bush announced a plan that critics say would weaken enforcement of Clean Air Act pollution limits. In August, the administration opposed a sweeping proposal by the World Summit on Sustainable Development to increase the use of renewable energy.

In addition to rewriting regulations, Bush has made other controversial environmental decisions. Within weeks of taking office, he reversed a campaign pledge to push for limits on industrial emissions of carbon dioxide and other "greenhouse gases," which most scientists believe are causing a potentially catastrophic warming of Earth's atmosphere. [27] Bush also renounced the Kyoto Protocol, an international treaty calling for mandatory carbon emission reductions designed to slow global warming.

Environmentalists say Bush's approach constitutes an unprecedented assault on the nation's commitment to protect the environment. "The Bush administration has the worst record of any presidential administration ever," Wetstone says. "I don't think we've ever seen a more sweeping or potent assault on our bedrock environmental laws."

Conservatives, on the other hand, extol Bush's policies as innovative alternatives to bureaucratic red tape. "The Bush administration wants to emphasize the next generation of environmental policy," says Steven F. Hayward, a resident scholar at the American Enterprise Institute (AEI), a conservative think tank. That policy will produce "less of the old-style, command-and-control regulation" from Washington, he explains, and more use of markets, incentives and regulatory flexibility to enable companies "to get around some of the rigidities in the way we've implemented environmental laws for the last 30 years."

OUTLOOK

Anti-terror 'Proxy'

Because the war on terrorism is open-ended and comprises so many aspects of domestic and foreign policy, many observers question whether the Bush administration will use it as a proxy for its entire agenda. The administration could cite national security to justify increasing police powers, changing labor laws, building highways and bridges, reforming immigration policies or advocating public-health initiatives like vaccinating the population against smallpox. For that reason, analysts believe Congress and the executive branch must develop a comprehensive strategy delineating options and priorities, committing the executive branch to a blueprint.

"Nowhere in the discussion about homeland security has there been anything indicating how the first additional dollar is to be spent," says Brookings' Daalder. "They have spent all this time talking about how to reorganize the government, but homeland security is about more than just being in the same department or wearing the same uniform."

Foreign policy experts believe the administration similarly may use the broad war on terrorism to justify continuing a policy of pre-emption that includes nation-building. While few object to overthrowing a despot like Hussein, they question whether the American public will tolerate a protracted military involvement that could cost hundreds or thousands of lives.

"I don't sense any appetite in the American body politic for this kind of large imperial role," says Harvard University political scientist Stephen Walt, who is skeptical about the United States' ability to reconstruct countries. "In Iraq, we're going to go in there and not be able to get out."

Realists like Walt believe there are limits to America's economic and military might, and that it may be more prudent to play traditional enemies against each other to serve America's interests. However, such sentiments conflict with so-called neoconservatives within the administration, who — encouraged by the rapid U.S. victory in Afghanistan — believe the president should flex his muscle in foreign affairs. [28]

Regardless of which paths the administration chooses, it must continue to deal with congressional oversight of its agenda and regularly consult with the legislative branch. With Republicans in control of both houses of Congress, Bush will lead a unified government and be able to push a more ambitious agenda. He likely will seek maximum flexibility in dealing with public labor unions and take other steps, such as indemnifying corporations that make anti-terrorism equipment — like bomb-detection systems — from lawsuits.

"The American people have indicated that they want the Congress, the House, the Senate and the president to work together to get things done," Lott said after the elections. "People do want security here at home. They didn't understand why we couldn't come to an agreement on creating a new homeland security department. They have confidence in this president's leadership in fighting the war on terror and taking on Al Qaeda. And they do want Congress to support and work with our president as the commander-in-chief."

However, Democrats caution the election results in no way constitute a mandate and already are putting the administration on notice that they will vigorously challenge its policies. For instance, they could use Senate rules to put "holds" on controversial nominees or filibuster legislation they deem questionable. And experts believe they may pick up Republican allies if the administration interprets its victory too broadly and is perceived as stepping on congressional toes.

"Right after Sept. 11 there was a kind of patriotic silence that stood for, 'Tell us what to do, sir,' " says Stephen Flynn, senior fellow for national security studies at the Council on Foreign Relations. "Now, there's a pendulum swing, and the Congress could be well-positioned to say, 'Yeah, but . . .' "

Notes

[1] See Gebe Martinez, "Concerns Linger for Lawmakers Following Difficult Vote for War," *CQ Weekly*, Oct. 12, 2002, pp. 2671-2678.

[2] For background, see Kenneth Jost, "Political Scandals," *The CQ Researcher*, May 27, 1994, pp. 457-480.

[3] See Adriel Bettelheim, "Congress Changing Tone of Homeland Security Debate," *CQ Weekly*, Aug. 31, 2002, pp. 2222-2225.

[4] For background, see David Masci and Patrick Marshall, "Civil Liberties in Wartime," *The CQ Researcher*, Dec. 14, 2001, pp. 1017-1040, and Patrick Marshall, "Policing the Borders," *The CQ Researcher*, Feb. 22, 2002, pp. 145-168.

[5] For background, see Linda Feldmann and Warren Richey, "Power Shift to President May Stick," *The Christian Science Monitor*, Oct. 3, 2002, p. 1.

[6] See Adam Nagourney, "Republicans Keep Hold on House," *The New York Times*, Nov. 6, 2002, p. A1.

[7] See Steve Schultze, "Sensenbrenner Wants Answers on Act," *Milwaukee Journal-Sentinel*, Aug. 19, 2002, serial online at www.jsonline.com.

[8] See Jeff Nesmith, "White House Proposes Security Information Rules," *Cox News Service*, Nov. 1, 2002.

[9] For background, see David Masci, "Reparations Movement," *The CQ Researcher*, June 22, 1001, pp. 529-552.

[10] See "Rights and the New Reality," *Los Angeles Times*, Sept. 10, 2002, p. B12.

[11] Quoted in David G. Savage, "A Year After Administration Defends Secret Searches in Terror War Security," *Los Angeles Times*, Sept. 11, 2002, p. A9.

[12] See Jeffrey Rosen, "Liberty Wins, So Far," *The Washington Post*, Sept. 15, 2002, p. B1.

[13] See Miles A. Pomper, "Senate Democrats in Disarray After Gephardt's Deal on Iraq," *CQ Weekly*, Oct. 5, 2002, pp. 2606-2610.

[14] See Jack Rakove, "Who Declares War?" *The New York Times*, Aug. 4, 2002, p. A13.

[15] See Mary Dalrymple, "Byrd's Beloved Chamber Deaf To His Pleas for Delayed Vote," *CQ Weekly*, Oct. 12, 2002, p. 2674.

[16] See Neil A. Lewis, "Congress Lets Slip The Dogs of War," *The New York Times*, Oct. 13, 2002, p. WK5.

[17] For background, see Adriel Bettelheim, "State of the Presidency: What Bush Inherits," *CQ Weekly*, Jan. 20, 2001, pp. 162-173.

[18] Arthur M. Schlesinger Jr., *Imperial Presidency* (1998).

[19] For background, see James A. Thurber, ed., *Divided Democracy: Cooperation and Conflict Between the President and Congress* (1991).

[20] For background, see Kenneth Jost, "Independent Counsels Re-examined," *The CQ Researcher*, May 7, 1999, pp. 377-400.

[21] For background, see Mary H. Cooper, "Transatlantic Tensions," *The CQ Researcher*, July 13, 2001, pp. 553-576.

[22] See Bob Deans, "Averse to Global Treaties, Is U.S. Embracing New Isolationism?" *Cox News Service*, July 29, 2001.

[23] See Dana Milbank, "Another Ol' Hickory in the White House?" *The Washington Post*, Sept. 17, 2002, p. A19.

[24] See Adriel Bettelheim, "Work Rules Throw Wrench in Homeland Security Bill," *CQ Weekly*, Aug. 3, 2002, pp. 2101-2103.

[25] Quoted in David Firestone, "Lott Says Senate Could Pass Security Bill Within Days," *The New York Times*, Nov. 11, 2002.

[26] For background, see Mary H. Cooper, "Bush and the Environment," *The CQ Researcher*, Oct. 25, 2002, pp. 865-896.

[27] For background, see Mary H. Cooper, "Global Warming Treaty," *The CQ Researcher*, Jan. 26, 2001, pp. 41-64.

[28] See Miles A. Pomper, "Philosophical Conflicts Complicate Iraq Debate," *CQ Weekly*, Aug. 3, 2002, pp. 2096-2100.

Bibliography

Selected Sources

Books

Greenstein, Fred I., *The Presidential Difference: Leadership Style from FDR to Clinton*, Princeton University Press, 2001.
A prominent presidential scholar analyzes 11 chief executives in areas such as communication, organization, political skill, vision and courage.

Jones, Charles O., *Separate But Equal Branches: Congress and the Presidency*, Chatham House, 2000.
An insightful look at how the system of checks and balances works, with particularly good chapters on the Carter and Reagan presidencies.

Jones, Gordon S., and John A. Marini (eds.), *The Imperial Congress: Crisis in the Separation of Powers*, World Almanac Books, 1990.
A series of lively and opinionated essays that assert Congress is taking over the powers of the presidency. Most seem more intent on bashing the legislative branch than explaining the nuances in the Constitution that gave rise to the system of checks and balances.

Neustadt, Richard E., *Presidential Power and Modern Presidents*, Free Press, 1991.
Another classic study of the presidency argues that presidents who lead by persuasion, as opposed to executive powers bestowed by the Constitution, are the most successful.

Schlesinger, Arthur M. Jr., *Imperial Presidency*, Replica Books, 1998.
This classic political-science text by the former Kennedy administration aide argues presidential power increases and decreases naturally, peaking during times of crisis.

Articles

"George Bush and Iraq: Your Moves," *The Economist*, Sept. 21, 2002, p. 27.
The president's speech to the United Nations about Iraq may transform domestic politics as well as international diplomacy.

"The Imperial Presidency," *The Economist*, Nov. 3, 2001.
Under the Bush administration, the United States is witnessing the most dramatic expansion in presidential power in a generation.

Brill, Steven, "On Guard, a Year Later," *Newsweek*, Sept. 16, 2002, pp. 38-41.
Balancing safety with civil liberties poses a difficult problem for the Office of Homeland Security.

Peterson, Peter G., "Public Diplomacy and the War on Terrorism," *Foreign Affairs*, Sept. 1, 2002, p. 74.
Faced with the multifront war that is terrorism, the president understands that changes are required in the executive power structure he inherited.

Pomper, Miles A., "Lawmakers Pushing Back From Quick Vote on Iraq," *CQ Weekly*, Sept. 14, 2002, pp. 2352-2357.
Congress confronts the war question and finds it has to make up its mind sooner rather than later.

Rogers, David, "Executive Privilege: Assertive President Engineers a Shift In Capital's Power," *The Wall Street Journal*, Oct. 22, 2002, p. A1.
George W. Bush, with the Sept. 11 terrorist attacks as a backdrop, is changing the balance of power between the White House and Congress.

Walsh, Kenneth T., "The Cheney Factor," *U.S. News & World Report*, March 25, 2002, pp. 16-20.
The vice president's hawkish approach puts him at odds with more moderate voices. But it appears his views are carrying the day.

Reports and Studies

"Assessing the Department of Homeland Security," *Brookings Institution*, July 2000.
A team of scholars from the left-of-center think tank concludes that, while the idea of creating a homeland security department is sound, Congress should modify key elements of the president's plan.

"Homeland Security: Human Resources Management," Congressional Research Service, RL31500, Sept. 26, 2002.
A lengthy analysis of proposed personnel provisions and work rules in House and Senate versions of homeland-security legislation.

"Homeland Security: Key Elements to Unify Efforts Are Underway but Uncertainty Remains," General Accounting Office, GAO-02-610, June 2002.
Congress' investigative arm assesses the governmentwide reorganization and notes it lacks a unified approach. Also discusses uncertainty about national priorities, roles, responsibilities and funding.

Bremmer, L. Paul III, and Edwin Meese III, "Defending the American Homeland," The Heritage Foundation, 2002.
A comprehensive study on homeland-security vulnerabilities and requirements considers recommendations of a task force convened by the conservative think tank.

Campaign Finance Showdown

KENNETH JOST

Art Linkletter was back on television this fall, but the legendary host of "Kids Say the Darndest Things" wasn't joshing with impish youngsters. In his customarily avuncular style, he was talking to senior citizens about their Medicare benefits.

"Your member of Congress has been fighting for real prescription drug coverage," the 90-year-old TV icon declared, urging viewers to tell their representatives to "keep standing up for America's seniors."

The 30-second spots ran in the weeks before the Nov. 5 elections in 19 districts where incumbent members of Congress faced opposition. The $12 million ad campaign — sponsored by the United Seniors Association, a self-described grass-roots organization largely funded by pharmaceutical companies — asked viewers to "call" their representative but said nothing about casting a vote.

The omission was no oversight. Without an express call to vote for or against a candidate, the ads circumvented longstanding federal laws that prohibit corporations or unions from using their general treasuries to contribute to candidates for federal office or spend money to influence federal elections. [1]

Such thinly disguised campaign ads have proliferated in recent years, but they may be gone — or significantly transformed — by the next congressional elections. The newly enacted Bipartisan Campaign Reform Act prohibits political parties, corporations, unions or nonprofit organizations from running broadcast ads that mention

From *The CQ Researcher,*
November 22, 2002.

Four lawmakers from both parties played key roles in passing the new Bipartisan Campaign Reform Act: From left: Sen. John McCain, R-Ariz., Reps. Martin Meehan, D-Mass., and Christopher Shays, R-Conn., and Sen. Russell Feingold, D-Wis. A legal challenge to the law — the first major overhaul of federal campaign laws in 30 years — is scheduled for a court showdown on Dec. 4.

specific federal candidates just before an election unless they pay for the spots with so-called "hard money" — funds raised and spent in accord with federal campaign finance laws.

The so-called McCain-Feingold law — principally sponsored by Sens. John McCain, R-Ariz., and Russell Feingold, D-Wis. — would prevent special interests from pouring millions of dollars into what the law's supporters call "sham issue advertising" during the run-up to presidential or congressional elections. It also bars national political parties from raising or spending "soft money" — unregulated donations from corporations, unions and wealthy individuals used for party-building activities ostensibly unrelated to federal campaigns. But opponents say the law violates the First Amendment and are challenging it in a federal lawsuit scheduled for a showdown before a three-judge court on Dec. 4. [2]

Supporters of the law say the soft-money and issue-advertising loopholes corrupt the political system by allowing special interests — corporations and unions — to gain sway over members of Congress despite laws banning them from contributing to federal candidates.

Opponents say that the effort to prevent corruption — which they say is exaggerated anyway — runs roughshod over paramount constitutional principles of free speech and federalism.

Opponents of the measure run the gamut from the U.S. Chamber of Commerce and National Rifle Association (NRA) to the AFL-CIO and the American Civil Liberties Union (ACLU). The lead plaintiff in the litigation is Sen. Mitch McConnell, R-Ky., who had blocked campaign finance bills for years until the onslaught of corporate scandals this year helped McCain-Feingold over the final congressional hurdles in March. (*For major provisions, see p. 26.*)

"The law violates First Amendment principles in numerous ways," says Washington lawyer Jan Baran, a longtime GOP election-law attorney on McConnell's legal team. "It unconstitutionally deprives political parties of legal funding. It unconstitutionally deprives officeholders of the ability to support and help grow their state political party organizations. And the law unconstitutionally restricts the ability of everyone, including political parties, to say certain things about politicians 60 days before an election."

Lawyers defending the measure, however, say the act is needed to close two major loopholes in federal campaign finance law. The soft-money system allows political parties to raise hundreds of millions of dollars from corporations, unions and wealthy donors, while circumventing contribution limits and prohibitions on corporate and union campaign spending. (*See graph, p. 24.*) Soft-money fundraising by the two major political parties rose from $86 million in the 1992 election to $495 million in the 1999-2000 cycle — and is expected to go even

Rise of 'Soft-Money' Fundraising

The two major political parties are expected to raise more than $500 million this year in soft money. That's a sixfold increase since 1992, the first election following adoption of the 1991 regulation requiring disclosure of soft money.

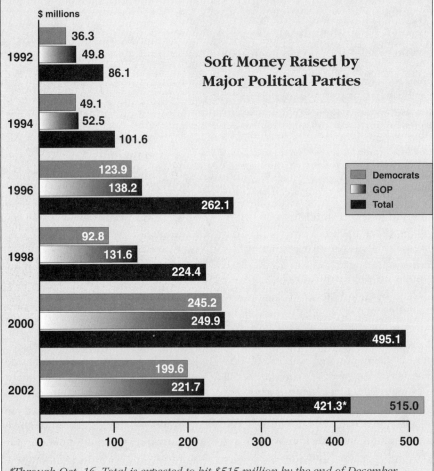

Soft Money Raised by Major Political Parties

$ millions

Year	Democrats	GOP	Total
1992	36.3	49.8	86.1
1994	49.1	52.5	101.6
1996	123.9	138.2	262.1
1998	92.8	131.6	224.4
2000	245.2	249.9	495.1
2002	199.6	221.7	421.3* / 515.0

*Through Oct. 16. Total is expected to hit $515 million by the end of December.

Source: Federal Election Commission

higher when final figures for 2002 are available.

Second, parties, corporations, unions and interest groups have spent millions of dollars on issue advertising that often has a transparent campaign purpose but avoids regulation by not specifically urging a vote for or against a federal candidate. Total spending on what critics call "sham advertising" was an estimated $509 million in the 1999-2000 election cycle (*p. 28*).

"We're seeing massive evasion of existing constitutionally upheld campaign finance laws," says longtime reform advocate Fred Wertheimer, president of the advocacy group Democracy 21 and former president of the citizens' group Common Cause. "This law is designed to end this evasion."

McCain-Feingold — also called Shays-Meehan after House sponsors Reps. Christopher Shays, R-Conn., and Martin Meehan, D-Mass. — is the first major overhaul of federal campaign laws since the Nixon-era Watergate scandal. [3] Con-

gress responded to evidence of illegal corporate contributions to President Richard M. Nixon's 1972 re-election campaign by passing a broad measure in 1974 that included spending and contribution limits, along with partial public financing for presidential candidates.

But the Supreme Court opened a big gap in the law two years later. In a controversial decision, *Buckley v. Valeo*, the court said the limits on candidate spending and on independent expenditures by individuals violated the First Amendment. [4]

Opponents of the new law mounted a broad constitutional attack this year on March 27, the same day President Bush signed it into law. The NRA, a longtime big spender on election-time issue advertising, was the first to file suit in federal district court in Washington. The law "places a burden on the NRA's ability to speak," says Charles Cooper, the attorney representing the group.

All told, some 84 plaintiffs — individuals and organizations — filed 11 separate complaints against the law. McConnell's wide-ranging suit — the second filed — was joined by the ACLU, plus an array of conservative organizations. (*See arguments, p. 32.*)

Suits contesting restrictions on political parties were filed by the Republican National Committee (RNC) backed up by state GOP organizations, as well as the California Democratic Party. The law "cripples the ability of state and local parties to carry out their functions," says Joseph Sandler, a former general counsel for the Democratic National Committee (DNC) representing the California parties in the litigation.

The Chamber of Commerce and the AFL-CIO have separate suits contesting the restrictions on issue advertising. The National Association of Broadcasters (NAB) says the limits on broadcast advertising within 30 days of a primary election or 60 days of a general election are unconstitutional. From an opposite perspective, liberal public interest groups are attacking provisions that raise the contribution limits for individuals and allow candidates facing wealthy, self-financed opponents to accept donations in even higher amounts.

The law — which went into effect on Nov. 6, the day after the midterm elections — provides a fast-track schedule for the legal challenge. It calls for a trial before a three-judge court, which is to expedite the case as much as possible. The court scheduled arguments in Washington on Dec. 4 and kept lawyers and witnesses to a grueling schedule for depositions and opposing briefs in advance of the hearing. Under the law, the court's decision will bypass the federal appeals court and go directly to the U.S. Supreme Court, which is widely expected to decide the case by the end of its current term in late June.

Lawyers defending the act say it conforms to Supreme Court precedent. "The provisions fit squarely within the court's previous decisions permitting campaign finance regulation because of the potential for corruption from large contributions and the appearance of corruption, which damages our citizens' faith in the democratic process," says Washington attorney Roger Witten, who represents six sponsors of the act joining the government and the Federal Election Commission (FEC) in defending the law. The lawmakers include McCain, Feingold, Shays and Meehan along with Sens. Jim Jeffords, I-Vt., and Olympia Snowe, R-Maine, who crafted an important part of the issue-advertising provisions.

On the opposite side, a legal team headed by Kenneth Starr — the former U.S. solicitor general and Whitewater independent legal counsel — says the law "shows utter contempt for governing Supreme Court precedent," including *Buckley v. Valeo*. "The law suppresses speech about political issues," the plaintiffs' lawyers write in their opening brief, "and fundamentally undermines the role of national and state political parties in our electoral system."

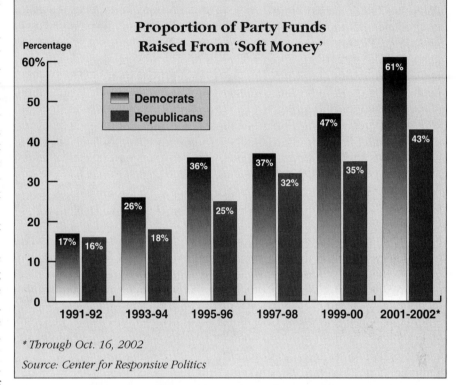

Parties' Growing Reliance on 'Soft Money'

Soft money has become an increasingly larger percentage of the funds raised by political parties, especially the Democrats. Soft money provided more than half the Democrats' funds this year, compared with only 17 percent in 1991-92; for Republicans, the percentage rose from 16 percent to more than 40 percent.

Proportion of Party Funds Raised From 'Soft Money'

Percentage

- Democrats
- Republicans

1991-92: 17% / 16%
1993-94: 26% / 18%
1995-96: 36% / 25%
1997-98: 37% / 32%
1999-00: 47% / 35%
2001-2002*: 61% / 43%

* Through Oct. 16, 2002

Source: Center for Responsive Politics

As the legal challenge moves toward its first courtroom showdown, here are the issues being debated both in and outside the courts:

Is the ban on political parties' use of unregulated "soft money" constitutional?

Federal Express — a big soft-money contributor to both parties for many years — successfully lobbied Congress at the end of the 1996 session for a small but important change in federal labor law. The Memphis-based delivery company wanted its truck drivers to be included under the federal Railway Labor Act, which covers airline and railroad employees, instead of under the more worker-friendly National Labor Relations Act.

Within the Senate Democratic caucus, then-Sen. Paul Simon of Illinois urged colleagues to oppose attaching the provision to a last-minute bill without hearings. As he recalls the meeting today, Simon says that a senior Democrat urged him to be more practical. "I'm tired of Paul always talking about special interests," Simon says, quoting the unnamed senator. "We've got to pay attention to who is buttering our bread."

McCain-Feingold's sponsors cite Simon's account, along with other comparable episodes from current or former members of Congress, to show what they consider the corrupting effects of soft-money contributions to political parties from corporations and unions. "We've documented that soft-money contributions result in corrup-

The Bipartisan Campaign Reform Act

The first major overhaul of federal campaign finance laws since 1974 — more than 90 pages long — is aimed principally at banning "soft money" and regulating election-time issue advertising on radio and television by corporations, unions and interest groups. Here are the major provisions of the law, also known as McCain-Feingold:

- **Soft money** — National party committees cannot accept or spend soft money — unregulated contributions from corporations, labor unions and wealthy individuals ostensibly intended for "party-building" activities, such as voter registration, but often used for campaign-related purposes.

- **State and local parties** — Non-national political parties cannot spend soft money on federal election activities. They may spend soft money on voter registration and mobilization under certain conditions.

- **Tax-exempt organizations** — National, state and local parties may neither solicit money from nor contribute to any nonprofit that spends money on federal elections. They also may not contribute to or solicit money from so-called 527 organizations that intervene in campaigns but do not expressly advocate any candidate's election or directly subsidize federal campaigns.

- **Hard-money contribution limits** — Effective Jan. 1, 2003, individual contribution limits for House and Senate candidates will be doubled to $2,000 per election, indexed to grow with inflation; aggregate contribution limits for individuals will be $95,000: $37,500 to candidates and $57,500 to parties and political action committees (PACs). Contribution limits for PACs are unchanged: $5,000 per candidate per election, plus $15,000 to a national party committee and $5,000 combined to state and local party committees.

- **Electioneering communications** — Broadcast, cable or satellite communications that name candidates for federal office or show their likeness and are targeted at candidates' states or districts — known as "electioneering communications" — may not be issued within 60 days of a general election or 30 days of a primary.

- **Unions and corporations** — Labor unions and corporations are prohibited from directly funding "electioneering communications" and can pay for such advertising only through political action committees (PACs) with regulated hard money.

- **Nonprofits and 527s** — One contingent provision bars "electioneering communications" by nonprofit organizations except through PACs. If that provision is ruled unconstitutional, an alternative provision would allow nonprofits to pay for such ads only with individual contributions, not from corporations or unions.

- **Independent and coordinated expenditures** — The Federal Election Commission (FEC) must issue new rules regulating coordination between candidates or parties and outside groups. The regulation cannot require formal evidence of coordination to treat spending by outside groups as a regulated "contribution" instead of an unregulated "independent expenditure."

- **Effective date/judicial review** — The law took effect Nov. 6, 2002, the day after the election, and provides for expedited judicial review, with a panel of three U.S. district court judges trying the case in Washington and the decision going directly to the Supreme Court, bypassing the U.S. Court of Appeals.

Source: "Campaign Finance Law Provisions," *CQ Weekly*, May 18, 2002, p. 1347 (www.cqoncongress.com). See also "Bipartisan Campaign Reform Act," Campaign Finance Institute (www.cfinst.org).

tion — the ability to exercise undue influence on the judgment of public officials — and certainly the appearance of corruption," Wertheimer says.

According to plaintiffs' lawyer Baran, however, "The evidence fails to identify any politician at any time who's been corrupted by a soft-money contribution to the party. As to the appearance of corruption, we'll have a debate about what that means and whether that justifies the enormous restrictions that are placed on political parties by this bill."

The law prohibits national parties from raising or spending soft money and allows state and local parties to use soft money for registration or get-out-the-vote activities only if the contributions do not exceed $10,000 and the expenditures are disclosed. Federal officeholders, including members of Congress, and candidates for federal office are barred from soliciting soft-money contributions, even for state party activities, though they are allowed to attend state party fundraisers.

The law's supporters say it simply enforces existing bans on corporate and union contributions. "The soft-money ban is designed to close loopholes on corporate contributions and union contributions — loopholes that have opened up in laws that have

commanded consensus support for nearly a century," Witten says.

But opponents contend the restrictions violate the First Amendment rights of national parties by limiting their freedom of speech relative to other organizations. "Political parties raise and spend soft money to help defray their administrative costs, to engage in party-building and to pay portions of their public advertising, including issue advertising," Baran says. "This law permits other non-party organizations and individuals to do exactly that, except during the 60 days before a general election."

Opponents also contend that the law infringes on states' rights under the 10th

Amendment. "This law essentially eliminates or trumps state law," Baran says. He notes that 29 states allow some corporate financing of campaigns, and 43 states permit union financing of state elections. But the law prohibits national parties from raising or spending corporate or union money in state elections and imposes a comparable ban on state parties in federal elections.

Supporters, however, say the restrictions on state activities are necessary and proper. "If you don't deal with the ability of state parties to influence federal elections, you're not going to close this loophole," Wertheimer says.

"These are federal elections," adds Trevor Potter, a former FEC commissioner and one of the lawyers representing the law's sponsors. "These are expenditures in connection with federal elections that have the purpose or effect of influencing federal elections."

In practical terms, opponents contend the new law will cripple parties by sharply reducing their financial base. "Out of the $1.2 billion raised in 1999-2000 by all the political parties, $500 million was soft money," Baran says. "So they will be diminished significantly in terms of the resources that they will have to finance their party activities and get-out-the-vote activities."

But supporters say the law will not hurt political parties. "National parties are raising hard money and will be able to raise more," Wertheimer says. "The party contribution limits have gone up. They will be able to raise adequate funds."

Are the restrictions on broadcast advertising at election time by corporations, labor unions and nonprofit groups constitutional?

The NRA blitzed key battleground states in the 2000 presidential election with 30-second spots and longer "infomercials" featuring the group's president, Charlton Heston, decrying the pro-gun control stance taken by the Democratic candidate, Vice President Al Gore. At the end of the infomercial,

Heston lifts aloft a musket and declares, "From my cold, dead hands, Mr. Gore."

All told, the NRA spent $20 million on issue advertising — much of it on radio and TV spots in the closing days before the Nov. 7 balloting. [5] Since the ads did not explicitly urge a vote against Gore, however, they did not count as campaign-related expenditures subject to federal campaign laws.

Supporters of the new law say that loophole allows political parties, corporations, labor unions and nonprofit groups to spend millions of dollars, while circumventing prohibitions against direct corporate or union spending to influence federal elections.

To close the gap, the new law brings under federal regulation what it calls "electioneering communications" — advertising on radio, television, cable or satellite within 30 days of a primary or 60 days of a general election that names or shows the likeness of a candidate for federal office. Political parties would have to count that advertising as a contribution to a federal candidate unless it was handled independently of the campaign. Labor unions and corporations could no longer pay for the ads, except through separate political action committees (PACs). And nonprofit organizations would also have to use PACs to pay for such ads or — if that provision is struck down — rely solely on contributions from individuals, not from unions or corporations.

Attorneys for the NRA and other advocacy groups say the new provision amounts to a ban on First Amendment-protected speech. "The law silences nonprofit corporations on issues of fundamental importance to their members," attorney Cooper says.

"We're dealing with independent speech here," says Baran, who is representing another big issue-advertising spender — the U.S. Chamber of Commerce — in the litigation. "The Supreme Court has repeatedly stated that the only type of independent political speech that can be regulated is speech that ex-

pressly advocates the election or defeat of a clearly identified candidate."

The legal issue turns on a footnote in the *Buckley v. Valeo* decision, which strictly defined expenditures "relating to" a candidate as including only advertising that explicitly called for electing or defeating a candidate by using what came to be known as "magic words," such as " 'vote for,' 'elect,' 'support,' 'cast your ballot for,' 'Smith for Congress,' 'vote against,' 'defeat,' 'reject.' "

Under this so-called "express advocacy" test, groups that pay for these ads say they fall in the First Amendment-protected area of independent speech. "They're independent issue advocacy by groups that believe in these ideas and want to communicate these ideas to the public and want to do it during election season, when the public is listening," says Joel Gora, a professor at Brooklyn Law School who is representing the ACLU in the litigation.

The law's supporters deride the election-time ads as "sham issue advertising." "Everybody knows what's going on, and everybody knows that these are ads being run to elect or defeat candidates," Wertheimer says. But they also stress that the law does not ban the advertising, as the opponents suggest. "We don't ban any speech," says reform advocate Wertheimer. "No one is being told they can't speak."

Individuals and groups can make unlimited expenditures during the 30- or 60-day window, he points out, but they will have to disclose what they are spending. "For corporations and labor unions, this is a battle over what kind of money they can use to run those ads — money from their general treasuries or from a PAC — not what ads they can run."

Such arguments amount to "sophistry," says Laurence Gold, the AFL-CIO's longtime general counsel. "Hard money is very hard to raise," he says, pointing to the source and contribution limits for federally regulated funds. "The AFL-CIO's PAC only raises $1 million per year. Our

Spending on Advocacy Ads Topped $500 Million

More than a half-billion dollars was spent on TV and radio issue-advocacy advertising in the 1999-2000 election cycle, about one-third of it by the two major political parties. Business-oriented groups concerned with health care were among the other big spenders.

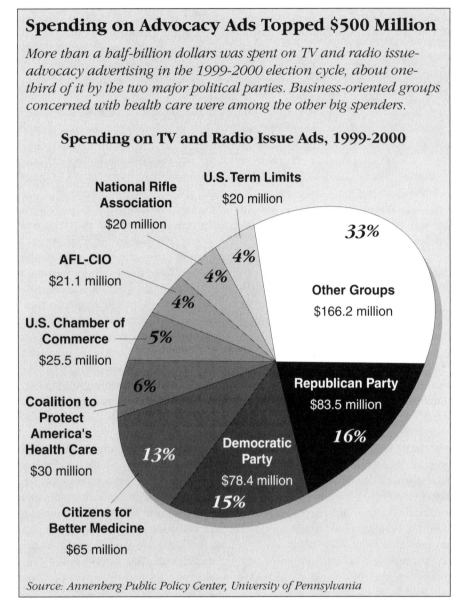

Spending on TV and Radio Issue Ads, 1999-2000

U.S. Term Limits $20 million — 4%

National Rifle Association $20 million — 4%

AFL-CIO $21.1 million — 4%

33% Other Groups $166.2 million

U.S. Chamber of Commerce $25.5 million — 5%

6%

Coalition to Protect America's Health Care $30 million

13% Citizens for Better Medicine $65 million

15% Democratic Party $78.4 million

16% Republican Party $83.5 million

Source: Annenberg Public Policy Center, University of Pennsylvania

broadcast costs have been many multiples of that year in and year out."

In its complaint, the NAB supports the general attack on the law but also says the law unconstitutionally discriminates against broadcast advertising. "It violates principles of equal protection to have a statute that says political ads on television and radio and satellite are in good part illegal within 60 days of an election and to limit that [restriction] to those forms of communication," says Floyd Abrams, the New York City attorney representing the NAB.

"That's the heart of the problem," counters Wertheimer. "This is campaign money being spent on broadcast ads at the central time of the campaign."

Are the increased contribution limits for candidates facing wealthy, self-financed candidates constitutional?

The $1,000 limit that Congress set in 1974 on individual contributions to federal candidates remained unchanged for a quarter-century, despite steadily growing support for raising the ceil-

ing. Politicians of both parties and campaign finance advocates and experts complained that the ceiling — never adjusted for inflation — forced candidates to spend an inordinate amount of time raising large numbers of individual contributions and made it especially difficult for third-party candidates to raise seed money needed to jump-start their campaigns.

The new law's provision doubling the contribution limit to $2,000 per candidate per election is winning general approval from both major political parties and from most parties to the litigation. But a coalition of individuals and liberal public interest groups — the so-called Adams plaintiffs (named after the lead plaintiff) — say the increased limit violates the constitutional guarantee of equal protection by discriminating against the non-wealthy.

"We're trying to get the idea of equality into the whole debate," says Bonnie Tenneriello, an attorney with the National Voting Rights Institute in Boston, who represents the Adams plaintiffs in the case. Under the new law, she says, "The stratification that exists in campaign finance today will be increased to such a drastic degree that people without money or without access to a network of wealthy donors simply won't be able to compete."

Lawyers representing both the sponsors and opponents of the act discount the argument against the increased contribution limit. "There is no case," Wertheimer says. "You may object to it on policy grounds, but I don't see any basis for the court saying that the $1,000 limit is constitutional, but the $2,000 limit is not."

"The Supreme Court has said they're not going to second-guess legislatures as to where they set limits, as long as the limits are not too low and do not interfere with the candidate's ability to communicate with voters," says GOP attorney Baran.

More controversially, however, the new law also includes a so-called "millionaires provision" that allows candidates facing wealthy, self-financed opponents to accept individual contributions up to $6,000 per election. Supporters say the special provision is needed to offset the advantages enjoyed by candidates able to bankroll their own campaigns.

Tenneriello says the special dispensation "exacerbates" the harm from raising contribution limits generally. The other critics of the law, however, say that from their perspective the millionaires provision suggests the $2,000 limit is illogically low.

"If the Congress has determined that [candidates] could receive up to $12,000 through the millionaires provision and not be corrupted, then I don't think there's any justification for the $2,000 limit," says James Bopp, one of the lawyers on the McConnell legal team. "It should be $12,000."

"It shows the hypocrisy and the mixed message of the sponsors of the bill," says Benjamin Ginsberg, a Washington lawyer representing the RNC in the case. He says the provision was inserted because sponsors "needed a few more votes" to win passage in the Senate.

Supporters of the law, however, say the millionaire's provision passes constitutional muster. "I don't see a constitutional problem with Congress determining to raise the limits and to decide in those particular instances the danger of corruption or the appearance of corruption is offset by the need to have robust speech on both sides," Witten says.

Tenneriello acknowledges her clients face an uphill road with their complaint. "This is the first time that this kind of challenge has been raised, saying that the state can't increase the advantage of the wealthy through campaign finance legislation," she says. But she says at least three Supreme Court justices — John Paul Stevens, Ruth Bader Ginsburg and Stephen G. Breyer — have written that campaign

finance laws can be justified on equality as well as anti-corruption grounds.

"Our suit goes far beyond the question of corruption," Tenneriello says. "We're saying that by multiplying the amount of hard money coming into the system, [the law increases] the disadvantage of non-wealthy candidates vs. their more wealthy and more connected opponents."

For his part, the ACLU's Gora credits the motivation behind the complaint but not its remedy. "There's a kernel of validity in the idea that you do want to make campaign resources more widely available to more candidates," he says. To deal with that concern, the ACLU favors public financing or other steps to increase candidates' ability to reach voters. "Build floors, not ceilings, for candidates," he explains.

BACKGROUND

Laws and 'Loopholes'

The rising cost of political campaigns and the Watergate scandals prompted Congress in the 1970s to replace a weak set of campaign finance laws with stronger limits on contributions and spending and public financing for presidential campaigns. Within a matter of years, however, two major gaps were created, first, by a Supreme Court decision barring most spending limits and then by actions by both the FEC and Congress to allow political parties to use unregulated funds — soft money — for activities ostensibly unrelated to federal election campaigns. [6]

Longstanding bans on campaign contributions to federal candidates by corporations and labor unions dated, respectively, from the progressive era of the early 1900s and the anti-union period immediately after World War

II. They did not prevent either corporate executives or labor unions from contributing to candidates. Unions and corporations also were able to form so-called political action committees to raise campaign funds voluntarily from union members or from company employees and shareholders. Federal laws dating from 1910 and 1911 also limited individual contributions to and overall spending by federal candidates. But candidates and contributors alike exploited loopholes in the laws to render them largely meaningless.

During the 1960s, the spiraling cost of campaigns — driven largely by spending on radio and television advertising — spurred widespread interest in strengthening federal campaign finance laws. The reformist push brought about passage of the Federal Election Campaign Act (FECA) in 1971, which required contributors to disclose identifying information, covered both political committees and candidates and set realistic spending limits on advertising. In the same year, Congress established public financing for presidential campaigns, funded by a voluntary income-tax checkoff; President Richard M. Nixon agreed to sign the law only after insisting that it take effect after the 1972 campaign.

Nixon's record-setting fundraising in the 1972 campaign included millions of dollars in illegal, laundered, corporate contributions that helped finance a secret fund used to pay for the break-in at DNC headquarters at the Watergate Hotel and other illicit activities. The scandal resulted in a fortified federal campaign finance law, the FECA Amendments of 1974, signed by President Gerald R. Ford two months after Nixon's forced resignation.

The new law set limits on individual, political committee and party donations to federal campaigns and set overall spending ceilings for advertising on House and Senate races. It also provided for partial public financing of presidential campaigns for candidates who agreed to abide by specified spending limits. And it established an independent agency, the Federal Election Commission (FEC), to enforce the law.

Barely 15 months later, the Supreme Court carved out part of the heart of the law in its *Buckley v. Valeo* ruling that the spending limits on candidates or on "independent" expenditures in support of candidates violated the First Amendment's protections for political speech. But the court upheld the law's limits on campaign contributions. The justices said contribution ceilings were justified by "the Act's primary purpose — to limit the actuality and appearance of corruption resulting from large individual financial contributions." The ruling also upheld public financing for presidential campaigns, along with the spending limits imposed on those accepting public funds.

The FEC created a second major loophole in 1978 with an advisory opinion that state parties need not comply with the federal laws in raising or spending money for get-out-the-vote and registration activities, even if federal candidates were on the ballot. The ruling — in response to a request from the Kansas Republican Party — reversed an advisory opinion issued two years earlier that required state parties to allocate a portion of such expenditures to the federal candidates. A dissenting commissioner called the new opinion "inexplicable," saying it allowed corporations and unions to "finance a major part of the costs associated with a partisan registration and get-out-the-vote drive out of general treasury funds." [7]

The next year, the FEC extended the ruling to national parties. Campaign finance operatives and experts coined the phrase "soft money" to refer to the unregulated funds because they were not subject to the "hard" limitations of general campaign finance laws. [8]

Growing Gaps

Within a few years of their enactment, the federal campaign finance laws were proving inadequate to achieve the goals supporters had sought. With spending limits thrown out, the costs of political campaigns rose unabated. And despite contribution limits, the influence of unions, corporations and interest groups rose with the proliferation of PACs.

Two other major gaps in the regulatory system have grown in importance over the past two decades. The use of soft money increased through the 1980s and then exploded in the '90s, despite calls to limit or ban the practice. And parties and interest groups circumvented spending limits and bans on corporate and union spending with election-time ads that avoided direct calls for electing or defeating particular candidates.

The two major national parties raised and spent around $20 million in soft money in 1980 and again in '84, with Republicans enjoying a substantial advantage in both years. [9] Common Cause responded by petitioning the FEC in 1984 to ban the practice. When the commission refused, the citizens' group took the issue to federal court, which eventually ordered the FEC to issue clearer rules for allocating expenditures between federal and non-federal races. An arduous regulatory proceeding ended with new rules that, for the first time, mandated full disclosure of soft-money contributions and expenditures and specified minimum hard-money allocation percentages for some party activities.

However, the regulations — which took effect Jan. 1, 1991 — did nothing to slow the accumulation of soft money. Soft-money funding by the two parties went from more than $86 million in the 1992 election cycle to $260 million in 1996 and $495 million in 2000. The FEC encouraged the explosion by ruling in 1995 — in response to a request from the RNC — that parties could use soft money to finance election-time broadcast advertising as long as the spots did not explicitly call for electing or defeating a particular candidate. [10]

Despite the GOP's efforts in obtaining the ruling, President Bill Clinton made the heaviest use of the widened role for soft money. He enticed wealthy soft-money donors with coffees and overnight stays at the White House, funneling millions of dollars to the DNC to pay for ads in key target states touting his administration's record. Republicans criticized Clinton for the contributions — some from foreign-born donors — and also criticized Vice President Al Gore for making fundraising calls from his office.

Despite the criticisms, Republicans also launched a soft money-funded advertising campaign, paid for by six-figure contributions from an array of corporate and wealthy individual donors. Meanwhile, both Clinton and GOP nominee Bob Dole ostensibly abided by voluntary spending limits tied to the public subsidies they accepted for their official re-election campaigns.

Common Cause took the lead in challenging the practices — again, without success. Attorney General Janet Reno turned down the group's call for appointment of an independent counsel to investigate both the Clinton and Dole campaigns and then declined to prosecute on her own. The FEC staff found that the ads by both campaigns were election-related and should have been paid for with hard money. But the full commission refused to require the two campaigns to repay the party committees for the ads and then closed the matter in 2000 by deadlocking 3-3 on the general counsel's recommendation to initiate enforcement actions against the two campaign committees.

The 1996 campaigns also marked a turning point in election-time advertising by outside groups. [11] In scattered rulings, federal courts had opened the

Chronology

Before 1970
Campaign disclosure and spending limits are virtually unenforced.

1907
Tillman Act bars corporations from contributing to candidates for federal office.

1910, 1911
First federal laws require campaign finance disclosure by House and Senate candidates and set spending limits; spending limits are raised in some Senate races in 1925.

1947
Taft-Hartley Act prohibits unions from contributing to candidates for federal office.

------●------

1950s-1970s
Concern about the rising cost of political campaigns spurs tougher campaign finance laws, but Supreme Court bars spending limits; FEC opens door to "soft money."

1971
Congress passes the Federal Election Campaign Act (FECA) to strengthen campaign disclosure and contribution limits; signed into law by President Richard M. Nixon in 1972.

1974
Congress amends FECA, limiting spending for congressional races and contributions by individuals and political action committees (PACs), creating public financing of presidential campaigns and creating Federal Election Commission (FEC) to enforce the law.

1976
Supreme Court (in *Buckley v. Valeo*)

says mandatory limits on campaign spending violate First Amendment, but upholds contribution limits.

1978
FEC advisory opinion allows state parties to use unregulated, non-federal funds — "soft money" — for get-out-the-vote and registration drives; the next year, commission sanctions same practice by national party committees.

------●------

1980s-1990s
Campaign finance proposals stall in Congress as soft-money fundraising grows and criticism of campaign finance laws grows.

1990
Supreme Court reaffirms validity of banning corporate spending in political campaigns (*Austin v. Michigan State Chamber of Commerce*). FEC, acting under court order, issues regulations to take effect Jan. 1, 1991, upholding soft money but requiring disclosure.

1995
FEC says parties can use soft money to pay for election-time "issue advertising."

1996
Both parties make major use of soft money in presidential campaigns . . . . AFL-CIO launches "issue advertising" in select House districts; business group follows. . . . President Bill Clinton heavily criticized for White House invitations to major soft-money donors.

1999
House passes Shays-Meehan bill on Sept. 14 to eliminate soft money and restrict issue-advocacy advertising. . . . Filibuster led by

Sen. Mitch McConnell, R-Ky., blocks Senate consideration of comparable McCain-Feingold bill.

------●------

2000-Present
Campaign finance overhaul enacted, challenged in court.

2000
Sen. John McCain, R-Ariz., uses campaign finance as central plank of bid for GOP presidential nomination, but withdraws in March after losing most primaries to Texas Gov. George W. Bush. . . . Supreme Court reaffirms constitutionality of campaign contribution limits to prevent corruption or appearance of corruption. (*Nixon v. Shrink Missouri Government PAC*). Two major political parties raise combined $495 million in soft money for campaigns.

2001
Supreme Court upholds limits on political parties' "coordinated" expenditures in congressional campaigns (*Colorado Republican II*). . . . Campaign finance reform bill brought to House floor falters when motion setting rules for debate fails to pass.

Feb. 14, 2002
House approves Bipartisan Campaign Reform Act (BCRA), 240-189; Senate approves it, 60-40, on March 20.

March 27, 2002
BCRA signed into law by President Bush; first of legal challenges filed in federal court in Washington on same day; 11 suits by more than 80 plaintiffs consolidated for argument before three-judge federal court on Dec. 4; case expected to reach U.S. Supreme Court in time for July 2003 decision.

Campaign Finance Suit Has Multiple Plaintiffs, Arguments

The legal challenge to the Bipartisan Campaign Reform Act — the "McCain-Feingold law" — comprises 11 separate complaints filed by more than 80 plaintiffs. Sen. Mitch McConnell, R-Ky., who led congressional opposition to the law, is the lead plaintiff. The case will be argued before a three-judge federal District Court in Washington on Dec. 4. The following excerpts are from the plaintiffs' complaints and the brief filed by the Justice Department and Federal Election Commission (FEC) in defense of the law.

Case and Plaintiffs	Plaintiffs' Arguments	Government's Argument
McConnell v. FEC Sen. Mitch McConnell, R-Ky., and 28 others, including, Libertarian National Committee, ACLU, Associated Builders and Contractors, Club for Growth, National Right to Life Committee, National Right to Work Committee, Southeastern Legal Foundation, U.S. d/b/a Pro-English	Act "impose[s] all manner of new federal rules that would radically alter . . . the ways citizens, corporations, labor unions, trade associations, officeholders, candidates, advocacy groups, tax-exempt organizations and national, state and local political party committees are permitted to participate in our Nation's democratic process."	"Congress has broad latitude to ensure that federal restrictions on the sources and amounts of campaign contributions are not evaded."
Republican National Committee v. FEC With GOP parties of Colorado, Ohio, New Mexico; Dallas County (Iowa) Republican County Central Committee	Act's "new rules . . . hamper the ability of national party committees . . . to support state parties and state and local candidates."	Ban on solicitation, receipt or use of soft money by national political parties is "closely drawn to prevent the appearance and reality of corruption in federal elections."
California Democratic Party v. FEC With Calif. Republican Party, Yolo County Democratic Central Committee; Santa Cruz County Republican Central Committee	Law is "attempt to impose a federal regulatory regime upon all political parties . . . down to the local subunits of each state political party."	Restrictions on state parties "are fully consistent with the 10th Amendment and principles of federalism."
Thompson v. FEC Rep. Bennie G. Thompson, D-Miss., with Rep. Earl F. Hilliard, D-Ala.	Act "unconstitutionally prevents *minority office holders* from effectively raising much needed outside funds in and outside their poorer districts."	Plaintiff's argument not specifically addressed; see *McConnell v. FEC*.

door to election-time ads financed outside the campaign finance regulation system by strictly applying the "express advocacy" rule from *Buckley*—for example, exempting "voter guides" from Christian and anti-abortion groups from contribution limits or disclosure. In 1995, the AFL-CIO stepped through the regulatory gap with a massive $35 million "issue" ad campaign targeted at congressional districts represented by vulnerable Republicans. Business groups countered in summer 1996 with ads praising the records of GOP incumbents.

The FEC had sought to close the gap with a 1995 regulation that strict-

ly defined express advocacy and imposed regulation if an ad's electoral purpose was "unmistakable" and "unambiguous" even though it did not expressly call for a particular vote. Federal courts threw out the second part, however, saying it went against Supreme Court precedent.

Pushing Reform

With growing criticism of campaign finance laws, lawmakers, outside groups and experts pushed a

variety of reform proposals throughout the 1980s and '90s, focused at first on PACs and then on soft money and issue advertising. A mixture of partisan interests and the inherent complexity of the subject caused those legislative efforts to be bottled up or defeated. In 2001 and '02, however, growing political pressure on the issue — aided by a web of corporate scandals highlighting the role of big-money campaign contributions — finally propelled the Bipartisan Campaign Reform Act through Congress and into law. [12]

Reform proponents came tantalizingly close to success several times in

Case and Plaintiffs	Plaintiffs' Arguments	Government's Argument
National Rifle Association v. FEC With NRA Political Victory Fund	"The law silences nonprofit corporations on issues of fundamental importance to their members."	"The explosion of sham 'issue' advocacy allowed evasion of . . . restrictions and disclosure requirements for independent expenditures."
U.S. Chamber of Commerce v. FEC With U.S. Chamber Political Action Committee, National Association of Manufacturers	Act "will seriously impair the plaintiffs' First Amendment right to speak out on public issues, to associate for public purposes, and to petition for redress of grievances."	"Corporations and labor unions have recently engaged in systematic evasion of . . . restrictions on campaign expenditures to influence the outcome of federal elections."
AFL-CIO v. FEC With AFL-CIO COPE Political Contribution Committee	Act "seeks to ban core political speech by labor organizations."	[See *U.S. Chamber of Commerce v. FEC*]
National Association of Broadcasters v. FEC	Act "criminalizes constitutionally protected speech broadcast on television and radio."	Act "does not violate either the First Amendment or principles of equal protection" by exempting non-broadcast communications.
Paul v. FEC Rep. Ron Paul, R-Texas, with Gun Owners of America, Citizens United	Act's provisions "deprive the plaintiffs of the freedom of the press in violation of the First Amendment."	Plaintiff's argument not specifically addressed; see *NRA v. FEC, National Assn. of Broadcasters v. FEC*
Adams v. FEC Victoria Jackson Gray Adams (founder of Mississippi Freedom Democratic Party), with 10 individuals, four state public-interest research groups, Fannie Lou Hamer Project, Association of Community Organizers for Reform	Increased contribution limits create "economic obstacles to equal participation" in political process; millionaire's provision "denies the right to equal participation to candidates with high levels of grass-roots support but without access to large contributors."	Millionaire provisions "increase the pool of potential candidates and promote robust competition in federal elections without limiting the spending of the self-funded candidate. . . ."
Echols v. FEC Emily Echols, with five other minors who are "active participants in politics."	"No government interest justifies" prohibiting minors from donating to candidates or campaigns.	" . . . [S]ome parents use their influence and their control over their children's assets to circumvent the limits on contributions. . . ."

the '90s. The House and Senate in 1990 approved similar bills with voluntary spending limits and restrictions on PACs but could not reach agreement on a final bill. In 1992, President George Bush vetoed a Democratic-backed bill to provide partial public financing and set congressional spending limits. In 1994, a Republican-led filibuster engineered by McConnell blocked consideration of a similar bill in the Senate.

A handshake agreement between President Clinton and Republican House Speaker Newt Gingrich in 1995 to create a special commission to take on the issues produced momentary optimism on breaking the partisan deadlock, but the idea fell by the wayside. The Clinton-Gore scandals of the 1996 campaign brought renewed attention to the issues and helped reformers twice — first in 1998 and then in 1999 — to win House passage of the Shays-Meehan bill focused on soft money and issue advertising. In both years, however, Republican-led filibusters blocked consideration of the comparable Mc-Cain-Feingold proposals in the Senate.

In January 2001, the current President Bush came to office claiming to support rewriting campaign finance laws. But the "reform principles" he announced on March 15, 2001, left issue advertising untouched and called for banning soft-money contributions only by unions and corporations, not by individuals. By then, however, McCain and Feingold had secured a promise from then-Senate Majority Leader Trent Lott, R-Miss., to allow a full-dress Senate debate on their bill early in the session. A two-week debate ended on April 2, 2001, with a 59-40 vote in favor of their bill limiting soft money and issue advertising, eased somewhat by the addition of higher hard-money contribution limits.

Supporters of the House version of the bill hit a major roadblock, however, when they tried to follow the Senate's action. In an effort to align their bill with the Senate's, Shays and Meehan prepared 14 amendments and asked for a single vote on the package on the House floor. The GOP-controlled House Rules Committee, however, proposed a parliamentary rule requiring separate votes — a move that Democrats said was designed to unravel the fragile coalition supporting the bill. Democrats combined with 19 Republicans and one independent on July 12 to defeat the Republican-backed rule. Without a rule, however, supporters had no immediate vehicle for bringing the bill to the floor.

Campaign finance receded as an issue in the wake of the Sept. 11 terrorist attacks, but it re-emerged after the Enron scandal broke in fall 2001. The energy giant's longtime chairman, Kenneth Lay, had been a major GOP soft-money contributor, and there was evidence that the donations had helped win access, or more, from the Bush administration on energy-related issues.

Shays-Meehan supporters exploited the scandal to reach the 218 signatures needed for a so-called discharge petition to force the House leadership to schedule the bill for floor debate. The bill came to the floor on Feb. 12; the next day, Bush himself weakened the opposition to the bill by signaling, through his spokesman Ari Fleischer, that he would sign any bill that would improve the system.

In the end, Shays and Meehan — their bill now almost aligned with the Senate's version — passed by a 240-189 vote on Feb. 14, after picking up 41 GOP votes. Most significantly, they also defeated all major amendments to the bill, thus eliminating the need for a House-Senate conference that opponents could use to try to thwart final passage.

With the Senate now in Democratic control, Majority Leader Tom Daschle of South Dakota promised to bring the

slightly amended version of the bill up for a final concurring vote before a scheduled recess in late March — threatening all-night sessions if necessary to break any filibuster mounted by opponents. McConnell made a last-ditch effort to slow the legislation with a package of ostensibly technical amendments, but then gave up the fight to turn to the anticipated court battle instead. The bill passed the Senate, thus clearing Congress, on a 60-40 vote on March 20.

In signing the bill into law six days later, Bush praised its provisions banning soft-money contributions by unions and corporations, raising contribution limits and speeding disclosure procedures. But he also said some provisions raised "serious constitutional concerns."

For his part, McConnell went to court the next day. "Today, I filed suit to defend the First Amendment right of all Americans to be able to fully participate in the political process," he said in a statement. "I look forward to being joined by a strong group of co-plaintiffs in the very near future." [13]

CURRENT SITUATION

Regulatory Skirmishes

P olitical parties and the Federal Election Commission (FEC) are under pressure to comply with the McCain-Feingold campaign finance law, even as it is being challenged in court. Supporters, however, say parties are circumventing its restrictions on soft-money fundraising and that the FEC is opening major loopholes in the law.

Congressional sponsors are already challenging soft-money regulations adopted by the FEC by a divided vote in June. The rules undermine the ban

on soft-money fundraising by federal candidates and give state parties too much leeway to use unregulated funds for election-time activities, they say. The lawmakers also criticize rules adopted in October governing issue advertising — so-called electioneering communications — but no court challenge has been filed yet. [14]

Meanwhile, political parties were setting up new organizations to raise unregulated soft money once McCain-Feingold went into effect on Nov. 6 — the day after the midterm congressional elections. Before the election, Republican and Democratic national committees raised soft money at a record-setting pace.

The latest available reports — covering the period through Oct. 16 — show that Republicans raised $221.7 million in soft money and Democrats $199.6 million. The total — $421.3 million — was nearly double the amount raised for the 1998 midterm elections. Additional fundraising before Nov. 5 was widely expected to push the total past the $495 million raised for 2000, a presidential election year. [15]

The FEC had to set an ambitious schedule to meet the act's Dec. 22 deadline for adopting regulations implementing the law. The six-member commission started with public hearings on the soft-money provisions in the spring and saved the other major issues — issue advertising, contribution limitations and coordinated expenditures — for the summer and fall.

The soft-money regulations provoked sharp disagreement between sponsors of the law and the four commissioners — three Republican appointees and the Democratic vice chairman, Karl Sandstrom — who provided the majority votes for the disputed portions. Some of the provisions were adopted against the recommendation of the agency's general counsel, Lawrence Norton; two Democratic commissioners dissented on the key issues. [16]

In one disputed provision, the panel

Vermont Tests Court's Ban on Spending Limits

Vermont lawmakers decided in 1997 to limit the amount of money candidates for state office could spend on their campaigns. They well knew, however, they were directly challenging a landmark 1976 Supreme Court decision barring campaign-spending limits on free-speech grounds.

Supporters of the Vermont statute won an unexpected victory in August when a federal appeals court upheld major parts of the law, including spending limits. But two months later, the court withdrew the opinion without explanation.

The spending limits ranged from $300,000 for gubernatorial candidates to $2,000 for state House races. Incumbents seeking re-election to statewide posts were limited to 85 percent of the maximum; incumbent state legislators could spend up to 90 percent of the ceiling. The law also set low contribution limits: $400 for donations to a gubernatorial candidate and $300 or $200 for state Senate or House candidates, respectively.

Vermont legislators had deliberately set out to challenge the prevailing interpretation of the Supreme Court's *Buckley v. Valeo* decision, which upheld contribution limits but struck down spending limits as an unconstitutional infringement of political speech. Despite criticism of the ruling from opposite sides of the campaign finance debate, the high court has stuck to the distinction — upholding contribution limits most recently in 2000, while barring efforts to set spending limits agreed to voluntarily in return for public campaign financing.

The Vermont law was challenged by an array of plaintiffs, including the state's Republican and Libertarian parties and the Vermont Right to Life Committee. The Boston-based National Voting Right Institute, representing the Vermont Public Interest Research Group and other liberal organizations, joined with the state attorney general's office to defend the law.

In a 10-day trial, current and former lawmakers offered what Brenda Wright, the institute's managing attorney, called "very candid and very courageous" testimony about campaign finance practices. One Democrat testified that she could not get cosponsors for a bill banning genetically modified food because party leaders felt they could not afford to alienate food manufacturers. "We proved that unlimited spending has had a very serious negative impact on the quality of democracy in Vermont and the access of ordinary citizens to their elected officials," Wright says.

Lawyers for the plaintiffs contended the spending limits were flatly unconstitutional under *Buckley* as well as unrealistically low. "Candidates cannot run an effective campaign under those limits," says James Bopp, an Indiana lawyer who has represented Republican and anti-abortion groups in many election law cases. "These limits are way below what people spend in competitive races."

U.S. District Judge William K. Sessions III found that the state had shown compelling justification for the law, but agreed with the plaintiffs that *Buckley* required him to invalidate the spending limits. He also struck down some other provisions, including limits on party contributions to candidates.

A divided panel of the 2nd U.S. Court of Appeals, however, upheld the spending limits.[1] Two judges appointed by President Bill Clinton — Chester Straub and Rosemary Pooler — said *Buckley* did not completely bar campaign spending limits and that the state had shown sufficient reason for capping expenditures. "The state's expenditure limits, in conjunction with the contribution limits, are necessary to ensure that access is not available only to those who pay for it," Straub wrote in the 66-page majority opinion.

In a 91-page dissent, Judge Ralph Winter argued that the law violated *Buckley* and other First Amendment cases. Spending limits, he wrote, "directly inhibit the most ordinary activities of democratic politics." Winter, who was appointed 1982 by President Ronald Reagan, dismissed testimony about the corrupting effects of campaign finance as "untested anecdotal evidence."

Plaintiffs filed a customary motion asking the full appeals court to rehear the case. Instead, the three-judge panel issued a brief and highly unusual order on Oct. 3, saying the decision had been "withdrawn" and that "further proceedings" would be held.

Wright believes the action may be an effort by the majority to strengthen the opinion. "It's possible the panel is making some modification to shore up support" for the opinion among other judges on the court, Wright says. "It's my belief that the majority will adhere to the original ruling."

Bopp laughs at Wright's speculation. "To withdraw an opinion is so unusual and so dramatic," he says. "It would be ridiculous to withdraw an opinion only to tinker."

Even if the original decision is preserved, most campaign finance reform advocates doubt the Supreme Court will change. "It's very hard to see how that case could survive at the Supreme Court," says Fred Wertheimer, former president of the Common Cause citizens' group and now president of a reform advocacy group, Democracy 21.

---

[1] The case is *Landell v. Sorrell*, decided Aug. 7, 2002. The withdrawn opinion can be found on the Stanford Law Library's campaign finance Web site (http://www.law.stanford.edu/library/campaignfinance/vermont.2002.landell.pdf) or on the National Voting Right Institute's site (http://www.nvri.org).

---

softened the ban on soft-money fundraising by applying it only to explicit requests for contributions. Norton had urged that the ban also apply to an action to "suggest" or "recommend" a contribution. The commission also exempted solicitations by federal candidates at state party fundraising events.

The rules also somewhat broaden the ability of state parties to use unregulated soft money for voter-mobilization activities when state elections are held simultaneously with congressional or presidential voting. Specifically, the rules require that regulated (hard) money be used only for activities that specifically "assist" voters immediately before an election — for example, for vans to transport voters to the polls. Soft money could continue to be used, however, for more general voter-mobilization efforts.

After the FEC's action, the four major sponsors of the law — McCain, Feingold, Shays and Meehan — angrily charged commissioners with undermining the law. "A majority of the FEC is willing to flout congressional intent and substitute its own policy preferences," the lawmakers said in a statement.

Majority commissioners, however, insisted they were trying to avoid overly broad readings of the law that would "federalize" state and local campaign activity. "I think I've strengthened our political process by giving a more reasonable reading to what would have been an extreme reading," Sandstrom told the *Los Angeles Times*.

Shays and Meehan filed suit challenging the soft-money regulations in federal district court in Washington on Oct. 8; McCain and Feingold were barred by Senate rules from filing suit, but are planning to file a friend-of-the-court brief. By coincidence, the case was assigned to U.S. District Judge Colleen Kollar-Kotelly, who is also presiding over the three-judge court hearing the main constitutional challenge to the McCain-Feingold law. The FEC has until Dec. 5 to file its answer on the soft-money regulations.

The issue-advertising rules — adopted Sept. 26 — also provoked criticism from McCain-Feingold sponsors and supporters. The commission exempted charitable and religious organizations from the soft-money ban on election-time advertising and exempted unpaid advertising from the hard-money requirement. However, the commission declined to write an exemption for election-time advertising with a genuine lobbying purpose. Groups supporting the law fear an overly broad reading of the issue-advertising restric-

tions could add to its constitutional difficulties.

Sponsors and supporters of the law are also taking issue with moves by both parties to set up new organizations to raise unregulated soft money after the election. [17] The FEC eased the way for the moves by ruling that groups formed by the national party committees would be deemed independent if created before McCain-Feingold went into effect. Under that ruling, the DNC spun off a new group, the Democratic State Party Organization, while the Democrats' principal Washington law firm was forming three new groups with the stated purpose of supporting Democratic candidates and issues.

On the Republican side, the former chief of staff to House Republican Whip Tom DeLay of Texas and a former GOP congressman are heading a newly formed group called the Leadership Forum, independent of other national Republican organizations. The Republican National Committee also moved before the elections to sever formal ties with the Republican Governors Association, thus enabling that group to raise soft money in the future.

Supporters question the ties between party committees and the supposedly independent groups. "There's going to be a very thin line between these so-called independent groups and the party committees," Larry Noble, executive director of the Center for Responsive Politics and a former FEC general counsel, told *The New York Times*. Lawyers for the parties, however, defend the moves. "It's not illegal for anyone to create a committee even under McCain-Feingold law," says GOP attorney Baran.

Legal Arguments

The three federal judges considering the constitutionality of the new campaign finance law have more than 800 pages of legal briefs and thou-

sands of pages of depositions and reports to help them decide the case. But the voluminous documents filed by the opposing sides under tight deadlines paint diametrically opposite pictures of the impact of the law and the governing legal principles.

Plaintiffs attacking the law say its multiple restrictions on political parties, corporations, unions and advocacy groups amount to "the most threatening frontal assault on core First Amendment values in a generation" — a reference to the 1974 campaign finance act. The government, however, says the new law is "closely drawn to combat the widespread circumvention of statutory limits on the sources and amount of spending on federal election campaigns."

Overseeing the pretrial work on the case, Judge Kollar-Kotelly gave lawyers and witnesses marching orders both precise and demanding. Depositions and cross-examination of the more than 100 witnesses from each side had to be completed by late October. Opposing sides filed opening briefs simultaneously on Nov. 6 — limited to around 350 pages for the consolidated plaintiffs' arguments and the separate presentations by the government and the six McCain-Feingold sponsors. Additional rounds of reply briefs were due on Nov. 20 and Nov. 27.

Kollar-Kotelly, appointed to the bench in 1997 by President Clinton, is joined in the case by two Republican-appointed jurists. Karen LeCraft Henderson was appointed to the federal appeals court in Washington by the first President Bush in 1990; Richard Leon was named to the district court by the current President Bush and confirmed by the Senate in February 2002.

In their briefs, the government and the law's sponsors take pains to lay out the rapid increase in soft money over the past decade to defend the new restrictions on political parties. Pointing to a host of examples — including Clinton's controversial 1996 fundraising practices — the lawmakers claim that soft

At Issue

Is the Bipartisan Campaign Reform Act constitutional?

SENS. JOHN MCCAIN R-ARIZ., AND RUSSELL FEINGOLD, D-WIS.

WRITTEN FOR THE CQ RESEARCHER, NOVEMBER 2002

*t*he Bipartisan Campaign Reform Act (BCRA) will have a dramatic impact on a campaign finance system awash in unregulated "soft money," but the new law is hardly revolutionary. BCRA seeks to restore constitutionally tested restrictions on campaign contributions by corporations, labor unions and wealthy individuals.

BCRA does two things: It limits the solicitation and use of soft money for federal election activity, and it calls the bluff on a narrow class of "sham issue ads" — broadcast advertisements that affect federal candidates, but which, by purporting to be about issues, brazenly skirt existing laws.

Federal law has banned the use of union and corporate treasury funds in connection with federal elections for most of the last century and capped contributions by individuals to candidates and parties since 1974. During the 2002 election cycle, however, the national parties are estimated to have spent more than $500 million in soft money. Much of this money was solicited by or on behalf of federal candidates, with checks for hundreds of thousands or millions of dollars coming from corporations, labor unions and wealthy individuals.

The Supreme Court has consistently recognized Congress' authority to regulate campaign finance and found such regulation consistent with the First Amendment. As the court stated recently in the *Shrink Missouri* case: "Leave the perception of impropriety unanswered, and the cynical assumption that large donors call the tune could jeopardize the willingness of voters to take part in democratic governance." The court has upheld laws restricting campaign contributions on two grounds: that unregulated contributions pose a serious threat to our democracy by creating the actuality or appearance of corruption, and that Congress can act to prevent circumvention of valid contribution limits.

Both of these grounds set a firm constitutional foundation for BCRA. Corruption, or the appearance of corruption, created by the massive unregulated soft money system has already led to the public cynicism the court warned about. Recent polls show a majority of the public believes that members of Congress vote based on what big-money contributors want, despite their constituents' interests and their own beliefs.

BCRA stops circumvention of existing law and closes loopholes through which hundreds of millions of dollars have flowed. It addresses the perception of impropriety that casts a shadow over everything the Congress does, and it does so in a way consistent with our cherished constitutional rights.

SEN. MITCH MCCONNELL, R-KY.

WRITTEN FOR THE CQ RESEARCHER, NOVEMBER 2002

i am proud to lead a group of approximately 80 co-plaintiffs in the case that will determine nothing less than the future of political speech in our nation. The BCRA, which took effect on Nov. 6, constitutes the most threatening frontal assault on core First Amendment values in a generation. The law suppresses speech about political issues, fundamentally undermines the role of national and state political parties in our electoral system and squarely attacks the Supreme Court's decision in *Buckley v. Valeo.*

The eclectic collection of plaintiffs challenging this law — unions and corporations, Democratic and Republican political parties, starkly divergent public interest groups, individual officeholders and citizens — share little except a concern that their voices will not be heard in the democratic process if BCRA is upheld.

The BCRA exhibits a total absence of proportionality and utter contempt for governing Supreme Court precedent. The "soft money" ban goes so far afield from core notions of federalism and the First Amendment as to bar the California Democratic Party from using funds lawfully raised under California law to pay for a radio advertisement urging California voters to reject a California initiative relating to affirmative action.

The issue-advocacy blackout provisions deviate so far from First Amendment principles as to criminalize advertisements by the National Right to Life Committee denouncing partial-birth abortion and encouraging viewers to call their senators to urge them to vote to ban that procedure.

The Constitution grants Congress some power to act in some circumstances, but we are never free simply to ignore competing constitutional interests, to disparage governing Supreme Court case law, and to disregard well-established and deeply rooted constitutional limitations. Nor is Congress free, in an effort to avoid criticism of itself and its members, to enact a statute plainly designed to protect incumbents who concluded we had "lost control of our campaigns."

Never before has the First Amendment been treated as some sort of impediment to progress, with speech about issues and candidates viewed as a threat to public health requiring quarantine lest too much of it be permitted. Never before has Congress wielded such a legislative sledgehammer when essential speech and federalism issues are at stake. No such law, dating from the Alien and Sedition Acts, has ever been deemed constitutional. It is my deepest hope that, for the sake of our Constitution and our democracy, this law will meet a similar fate.

money "has been used to evade the law and, in actuality and appearance, corrupts the political process."

Plaintiffs counter by emphasizing principles of federalism. Soft money, the RNC says, "is merely a byproduct of our federal system of government," with different structures and roles for political parties at the national and state levels. As to the Clinton scandals, McConnell's brief argues that two of McCain-Feingold's unchallenged provisions respond to those by tightening restrictions on campaign contributions by aliens and on fundraising on federal property.

Both sides claim the decision in *Buckley v. Valeo* supports their positions. The government looks to the anti-corruption rationale endorsed in Supreme Court cases from *Buckley* through the 2000 decision upholding state contribution limits against a First Amendment challenge. Plaintiffs, however, view *Buckley* as limiting Congress' power to regulate state campaign practices. And they point to two other recent decisions regarding political party spending as limiting Congress' power to impose special disadvantages on parties compared to other advocacy groups. [18]

Similarly, the government and McCain-Feingold's sponsors justify the restrictions on issue advertising by stressing what they call the "explosion" in election-time broadcast ads beginning in 1996 from unions, corporations and interest groups. The "sham" issue ads allow "evasion" of limits on corporate and union spending and of disclosure requirements, the lawmakers contend. And the government and the lawmakers both insist that the law establishes a "bright line" for groups to follow in separating lawful issue advocacy from restricted electioneering communications.

For their part, plaintiffs say the law restricts a vast amount of "core political speech" that — in the words of the NRA brief — is "absolutely protected by the First Amendment" and poses "no threat of corrupting the political process." As one example, the ACLU says the law

would have prevented it from running an ad earlier this year calling on House Speaker Dennis Hastert, R-Ill., to permit a vote on a federal gay-rights bill right before his primary election — even though he was unopposed.

For legal support, plaintiffs cite several well-established First Amendment cases along with the *Buckley* ruling striking down the limit on independent expenditures in federal campaigns. But the government and the lawmakers say the issue-advertising provisions do not ban speech, but only limit corporate or union funding as permitted most recently in a 1990 decision upholding a state ban on corporate spending in campaigns. [19]

The increased contribution limits and the "millionaire's provision" receive less attention in the briefs. The Adams plaintiffs contend the increased contribution limits are unnecessary and place "a substantial burden on the voting rights of the non-wealthy" — a burden "multiplied" by the millionaire's provision increasing the contribution limits for candidates facing wealthy, self-financed opponents.

Among the other plaintiffs, only the RNC attacks the millionaire's provision. It says the differential treatment is unjustified and calls for raising contribution limits for all candidates. The government counters that the provision will "promote robust competition in federal elections without limiting spending by the self-funded candidate."

OUTLOOK

Weighing the Stakes

Election Night 2002. Republicans and Democrats around the country watch nervously as returns come in that will determine which party controls the Senate for the next two years.

One by one, the key states report Republican victories: New Hampshire, Georgia, Colorado, and then — in the early morning hours of Nov. 6 — Missouri. Even with three states still undecided, the GOP victory in the "Show-Me" state ensures a Republican majority in the Senate. It also gives Republicans majorities in both chambers of Congress as well as control of the White House for the first time since 1954.

Not coincidentally, the states with closely contested Senate races were also the states where heavily spending advocacy groups — and both political parties — targeted their unregulated soft money in the closing days before the midterm elections. Along with ads on Social Security and prescription-drug benefits, United Seniors ran targeted ads touting President Bush's call for permanent tax cuts in Missouri and in two states where Democrats emerged victorious: Arkansas and South Dakota.

The conservative Club for Growth spent around $2.5 million in 17 states, most of it to mock Democratic candidates for the Senate as "bobble heads" alongside similar doll figures of then-Senate Majority Leader Tom Daschle of South Dakota and liberal Sen. Edward Kennedy, D-Mass.

David Keating, the group's executive director, hopes the ads influenced how people voted — and he believes they did. "The ads were clever enough that they had a lot of impact for the money spent," Keating says. "A lot of reporters told us that people were talking about them, that people considered them to be very funny."

The spending patterns for issue ads help belie the legal fiction that issue ads — paid for with funds raised outside the campaign finance system — are not intended to influence federal elections. Both Republican and Democratic national organizations transferred more than $4 million in soft funds each to state and local party committees in Missouri during the two-year election cycle. [20]

Supporters of the McCain-Feingold law say political realities explain the need to ban soft money-fundraising by the national parties and to control the soft money-funded issue ads by outside groups. "Let's be real about what's going on," says reform advocate Wertheimer. "This is not issue advocacy. This is about the clear and often articulated purpose of defeating or electing candidates."

Opponents, however, continue to maintain the law is unconstitutional. "We have rights to free speech," says Keating, whose group is one of the plaintiffs in the suit challenging the law. "If they want to repeal the First Amendment, they should do that rather than trying to do it through a backdoor way," he says.

As the Dec. 4 trial date approaches, both sides in the case are professing guarded optimism. "This law is an unconstitutional Rube Goldberg machine," says GOP lawyer Baran. "I don't expect the law to be struck down," counters attorney Witten, representing the six sponsors of the law who intervened in the case.

Whatever decision the three-judge court reaches is certain to be appealed — also on an expedited basis — to the Supreme Court.* The high court is divided on campaign finance issues roughly along a conservative-liberal fault line, with liberals supportive of and conservatives skeptical of campaign finance restrictions. In the two most recent decisions, however, centrist-conservative Justice Sandra Day O'Connor has joined with the four liberal-leaning justices to uphold challenged campaign finance laws.

With the law on the books for now,

---

* The Supreme Court agreed on Nov. 18 to hear a case testing whether advocacy groups formed as corporations can make direct contributions to federal candidates. Currently, such groups are subject to the general ban on corporate contributions. The case, *Federal Election Commission v. Beaumont*, is likely to be argued by March and decided by late June.

new soft-money organizations are sprouting up — ostensibly independent of national party committees, which are banned from raising or spending soft money under McCain-Feingold. "Everybody in the parties signaled from the beginning that this was going to happen," says Michael Malbin, executive director of the nonpartisan Campaign Finance Institute at George Washington University in Washington.

Malbin expects soft money will continue to flow even if McCain-Feingold is upheld. "A fair amount of the soft money will come back," he says. "How much it will be reduced depends on how restrictive the rules are." On that point, reform advocates continue to worry about the agency charged with enforcing the law — the FEC — which they have criticized as lax because of commissioners' ties to the two major political parties. [21]

Malbin also minimizes the law's likely impact on overall party fundraising. "I do not expect the parties to disappear," he says. "I do expect that parties will have to reinvigorate their fundraising bases."

Most outside groups also will be less affected than their lawyers are claiming, Malbin says. "The law permits them to continue to do exactly what they did before as long as they stop 61 days before the election," he says. "And they can do whatever they want through the mails, on the phone, or on the Internet. They will continue to try to get their case across."

The opposing lawyers, however, see much greater stakes. Baran says political parties "will be diminished significantly in terms of the resources that they will have to finance their party activities and get-out-the-vote activities." Cooper says the law burdens not only his client, the NRA, but all advocacy groups. "It's not just the NRA," he says. "It's Sarah Brady's pro-gun control group. It's the Sierra Club. It's all these voluntary, nonprofit membership organizations whose ability to

speak on issues has brought them into existence."

For his part, Witten also sees large stakes: the integrity of campaign finance laws and the political process itself. "The case tests whether campaign finance laws are real or whether they are going to be a mockery," he says. "The sham issue ads make a mockery of the law. The soft-money loophole makes a mockery of the law. And when you have a mockery of law, you have a public that is turned off. So what's at stake is the health of our democracy."

Notes

[1] Full text of ads can be found on United Seniors Association's Web site: www.united-seniors.org. For additional background, see Greg Hitt, "Drug Makers Pour Ad Money Into Final Days of Campaign," *The Wall Street Journal*, Nov. 4, 2002, p. A1.

[2] The case is *McConnell v. Federal Election Commission*, U.S. District Court for the District of Columbia, Civ. No. 02-0582. Case documents can be found on several Web sites, including http://www.law.stanford.edu/library/campaignfinance, www.camlc.org, and www.democracy21.org.

[3] For background, see Mary H. Cooper, "Campaign Finance Reform," *The CQ Researcher*, March 31, 2000, pp. 257-280; Kenneth Jost, "Campaign Finance Reform," *The CQ Researcher*, Feb. 9, 1996, pp. 121-144.

[4] *Buckley v. Valeo*, 424 U.S. 1 (1976).

[5] Kathleen Hall Jamieson, *et al.* (eds.), "Issue Advertising in the 1999-2000 Election Cycle," Annenberg Public Policy Center of the University of Pennsylvania, www.appcpenn.org/issueads.

[6] Some background drawn from Diana Dwyre and Victoria A. Farrar-Myers, *Legislative Labyrinth: Congress and Campaign Finance Reform* (1983), pp. 1-28. For an historical overview by a critic of campaign finance laws, see Bradley A. Smith, *Unfree Speech: The Folly of Campaign Finance Reform* (2001), pp. 17-38.

[7] Federal Election Commission Advisory Opinion 1978-10, "Allocation of Costs for Voter Registration," excerpted in Anthony Corrado *et al*, eds., *Campaign Finance Reform: A Sourcebook* (1997), pp. 190-193. The earlier

opinion — "Advisory Opinion 1976-72" — appears at pp. 187-189.

[8] For an early, critical account, see Elizabeth Drew, *Money and Politics: The New Road to Corruption* (1983), pp. 14-18.

[9] See Anthony Corrado, "Party Soft Money," in Corrado, *op. cit.*, p. 173. Since the funds were not subject to federal disclosure laws, Corrado cites what he calls the "best available estimates" for the two years: $15.1 million for Republicans and $4 million for Democrats in 1980, $15.6 million for Republicans and $6 million for Democrats in 1984.

[10] FEC Advisory Opinion 1995-25, "Costs of Advertising to Influence Congressional Legislation Allocated to Both Federal and Nonfederal Funds," excerpted in Corrado, *op. cit.*, pp. 214-216.

[11] For background, see Trevor Potter, "Issue Advocacy and Express Advocacy," in Corrado, *op. cit.*, pp. 227-239.

[12] For background, see Kenneth Jost, "Corporate Crime," *The CQ Researcher*, Oct. 11, 2002, pp. 817-840.

[13] The Bush and McConnell statements can both be found at http://www.law.stanford.edu/library/campaignfinance.

[14] See Thomas B. Edsall, "FCC to Allow 'Soft Money' Exceptions," *The Washington Post*, June 21, 2002, p. A1. For text of the soft-money rules, see "Prohibited and Excessive Contributions: Non-Federal Funds or Soft Money," *Federal Register*, Vol. 67, No. 145 (July 29, 2002), pp. 49064-49132 (www.fec.gov/register.htm). For text of the issue-advertising rules, see FEC, "Electioneering Communications," Vol. 67, No. 205 (Oct. 23, 2002), pp. 65190-65212 (www.fec.gov/register.htm).

[15] See Richard A. Oppel Jr., "Soft Money Rolls Into Coffers While It Can," *The New York Times*, Oct. 17, 2002; Thomas B. Edsall, "Republicans: Big Cash Edge; Advantage Likely to Grow," *The Washington Post*, Nov. 7, 2002, p. A27.

[16] For coverage, see Thomas B. Edsall, "FEC to Allow 'Soft Money' Exceptions," *The Washington Post*, June 21, 2002, p. A1; Mark Fineman, "New FEC Rules Add Loopholes in Soft-Money Ban," *Los Angeles Times*, June 21, 2002, p. A34.

[17] See Don Van Natta Jr. and Richard A. Oppel Jr., "Parties Create Ways to Avoid Soft Money Ban," *The New York Times*, Nov. 2, 2002, p. A1; Thomas B. Edsall, "Campaign Money Finds New Conduits as Law Takes Effect," *The Washington Post*, Nov. 5, 2002, p. A2.

[18] The state contribution-limit case is *Nixon v. Shrink Missouri Government PAC*, 528 U.S. 377 (2000). The political party cases are *Colorado Republican Federal Campaign Committee v. FEC (Colorado Republican I)*, 518 U.S. 604 (1996); and *FEC v. Colorado Republican Federal Campaign Committee (Colorado Republican II)*, 533 U.S. 431 (2001). See Kenneth Jost, *Supreme Court Yearbook, 1999-2000* (2000), pp. 70-75; *Supreme Court Yearbook, 2000-2001* (2001), pp. 86-91.

[19] The case is *Austin v. Michigan State Chamber of Commerce*, 494 U.S. 652 (1990).

[20] "National Party Transfers to State/Local Party Committees: January 1, 2001-October 16, 2002," www.fec.gov.

[21] See Jim Drinkard, "Agency That Referees Elections Protects Parties First," *USA Today*, Nov. 12, 2002, p. A1.

FOR MORE INFORMATION

American Civil Liberties Union, 125 Broadway, 18th Floor, New York, NY 10004; (212) 549-2500; www.aclu.org. Lobbies and litigates against limits on campaign contributions and spending; supports disclosure and public financing.

Campaign and Media Law Center, 1101 Connecticut Ave., N.W., Suite 330, Washington, DC 20036; (202) 736-2200; www.camlc.org. The University of Utah center acts as "the people's voice" in hearings on campaign finance laws.

Campaign Finance Institute, George Washington University, 1990 M St., N.W., Suite 380, Washington, DC 20036; (202) 969-8890; www.cfinst.org. The center aims to "identify campaign finance policies that can achieve meaningful results."

Center for Responsive Politics, 1101 14th St., N.W., Suite 1030, Washington, DC 20005-5635; (202) 857-0044; www.opensecrets.org. Nonpartisan center tracks money in politics and its effect on elections and public policy.

Common Cause, 1250 Connecticut Ave., N.W., Suite 600, Washington DC 20036; (202) 833-1200; www.commoncause.org. Citizens' group that has been a major advocate of campaign finance regulation since its founding in 1970.

Democracy 21, 1825 I St., N.W., Suite 400; Washington, DC 20006; (202) 429-2008; http://democracy21.org. Nonpartisan advocacy group, founded in 1997 by former Common Cause President Fred Wertheimer, supports campaign finance.

National Rifle Association, 11250 Waples Mill Road, Fairfax, VA 22030; (703) 267-1000; www.nra.org. Lead plaintiff in one of the consolidated suits challenging the Bipartisan Campaign Reform Act.

National Voting Right Institute, 27 School St., Suite 500, Boston, MA 02108; (617) 624-3900; www.nvri.org. Represents plaintiffs challenging the increased contribution limits established by the Bipartisan Campaign Reform Act.

U.S. Chamber of Commerce, 1615 H St., N.W., Washington, DC 20062-2000; (202) 659-6000; www.uschamber.org. Lead plaintiff in one of the consolidated suits challenging the Bipartisan Campaign Reform Act.

Bibliography

Selected Sources

Books

Birnbaum, Jeffrey, *The Money Men: The Real Story of Fund-Raising's Influence on Political Power in America*, Crown, 2000.

The Washington bureau chief of *Fortune* magazine presents a journalistic account of how campaign fundraisers actually do their work.

Corrado, Anthony, Thomas E. Mann, Daniel R. Ortiz, Trevor Potter and Frank J. Sorauf (eds.), *Campaign Finance Reform: A Sourcebook*, Brookings Institution Press, 1997.

Provides overviews and source documents from court cases, congressional materials, Federal Election Commission (FEC) rulings and other sources on major campaign finance issues, including "soft money" and issue advertising. Corrado, Ortiz and Sorauf are professors, respectively, at Colby College, University of Virginia Law School and the University of Minnesota; Mann is at the Brookings Institution; Potter is a Washington lawyer and director of the Campaign and Media Law Center. An updated edition is in preparation.

Drew, Elizabeth, *The Corruption of American Politics: What Went Wrong and Why*, Carol Publishing Group, 1999.

A veteran Washington journalist decries "the debasement of American politics over the past 25 years," which she blames in part on "the expanding corruption of money in all its pervasive ways." For Drew's earlier treatment of the issues, see *Politics and Money: The New Road to Corruption* (Macmillan, 1983).

Dwyre, Diana, and Victoria A. Farrar-Myers, *Legislative Labyrinth: Congress and Campaign Finance Reform*, CQ Press, 2001.

Provides a detailed accounting of efforts through 1999 to enact reform proposals to ban soft money and limit issue advertising. Dwyre is an associate professor of political science at California State University-Chico, Myers an assistant professor at the University of Texas-Arlington.

Magleby, David B. (ed.), *Financing the 2000 Election*, Brookings Institution Press, 2002.

The most recent quadrennial report on campaign finance in a series begun in 1960 includes chapters on "soft money" and interest-group advertising in the 2000 election. Magleby is dean of the College of Family, Home and Social Sciences and director of the Center for the Study of Elections and Democracy at Brigham Young University. He served as editor of *Outside Money: Soft Money and Issue Advocacy in the 1998 Congressional Elections* (Rowman & Littlefield Publishers, 2000).

Smith, Bradley A., *Unfree Speech: The Folly of Campaign Finance Reform*, Princeton University Press, 2001.

Smith was a professor at Ohio State University's Capital Law School when he authored this strongly critical examination of campaign finance laws and regulations as infringements on political speech; he is now a member of the Federal Election Commission. Includes chapter notes and a 20-page bibliography.

Articles

Drinkard, Jim, "Agency That Referees Elections Protects Parties First," *USA Today*, Nov. 12, 2002, p. A1.

Good backgrounder on the Federal Election Commission and its critics.

—, "Special-Interest Money Floods Races," *USA Today*, Nov. 3, 2002, p. A10.

Examines interest-group spending in midterm congressional elections.

Foerstel, Karen, "Campaign Finance Passage Ends a Political Odyssey," *CQ Weekly*, March 23, 2002, p. 799.

Details final passage of McCain-Feingold campaign finance law. Includes related articles, legislative chronology, citations to House and Senate bill numbers, major provisions and citations to previous coverage.

Van Natta, Don Jr., and Richard A. Oppel Jr., "Parties Create Ways to Avoid Soft Money Ban," *The New York Times*, Nov. 2, 2002, p. A1.

Recounts steps by the two major political parties to form new organizations to raise unregulated "soft money" after the Bipartisan Campaign Reform Act takes effect.

3 Judges and Politics

KENNETH JOST

If lawyers who argue before the U.S. Supreme Court had an all-star team, Jeffrey Sutton would be on it. This year he won all four of his cases.

President Bush has nominated the Ohio lawyer for a federal appeals court judgeship in Cincinnati. But Sutton may not be leaving private practice anytime soon. Several liberal organizations want the Senate to look closely at Sutton's record before voting on his confirmation for a lifetime appointment to the federal bench.

The critics are particularly exercised over Sutton's role in a number of high-profile cases urging the Supreme Court to limit Congress' ability to enforce civil rights laws against state governments.

"Jeffrey Sutton has a very problematic record because of what appears to be his [effort] to give more power to the states at the expense of Congress and its ability to pass protections for the people," says Marcia Kuntz, director of the Judicial Selection Project at the Alliance for Justice, a liberal group that monitors candidates for vacancies in the federal judiciary.

Sutton's admirers defend both his support for what they call "state sovereignty" and his qualifications for the federal bench. "Jeffrey Sutton is 40 years old, but he has a résumé that lawyers twice his age would envy," says Clint Bolick, vice president and litigation director for the libertarian Institute for Justice.

Sutton was one of 11 people Bush nominated for federal appeals court vacancies on May 9. In presenting the nominees at a White House ceremo-

From *The CQ Researcher,*
July 27, 2001.

Judge Roger Gregory, left, receives a warm reception July 11 from Senate Judiciary Committee Chairman Patrick Leahy, D-Vt., right, on his nomination for the federal appeals court. But President Bush's other nominees are expected to face tough questioning. Looking on is Rep. Robert C. Scott, D-Va.

ny, Bush said all had "sterling credentials," had met "high standards of legal training, temperament and judgment" and came from "diverse backgrounds." The nominees included three women, two African-Americans and one Hispanic. (*See sidebar, p. 46.*)

Bush also voiced hopes for a smooth confirmation process in the Senate — at the time under Republican control. After noting the "political battles" over judicial nominations in the recent past, Bush called for "the return of civility and dignity to the confirmation process." He urged "senators of both parties" to "provide a prompt vote to every nominee."

The president's hopes for smooth and quick confirmation suffered a major setback less than a month later, however, when the Democrats gained control of the Senate with the defection of Vermont Sen. James Jeffords from the GOP to independent status. Democrats had already vowed to closely scrutinize Bush's judicial nominees.

Now, with a Democratic chairman — Vermont's Patrick Leahy — the Senate Judiciary Committee is expected to be a more difficult hurdle for Bush's nominees.

Senators in both parties and conservative and liberal interest groups alike have waged war over the selection of federal judges for the past 20 years. The most prominent fights have been over U.S. Supreme Court nominations, but bitter battles also have been fought over nominees for the trial-level district courts and for the regional federal courts of appeals.

"Over the last 20 years, the degree of politicization has been ratcheted up and up until we're almost at a stalemate or a crisis," says Sheldon Goldman, a professor of political science at the University of Massachusetts at Amherst, who has written extensively on federal judicial nominations.

Federal courts handle only a small fraction of the country's legal business. The vast majority of cases — criminal prosecutions as well as civil lawsuits — are heard in state courts. But federal judges decide some of the most important cases — from civil rights and free-speech cases to major economic disputes like the Microsoft antitrust litigation. In addition, federal judges have the power to set aside state criminal convictions even after a defendant has exhausted all appeals through the state courts. [1]

The political battles are taking a toll on the federal judiciary. Currently, there are 110 vacancies — more than one-eighth of the 853 authorized district and appellate court judgeships. Democrats complained that the Republican-controlled Senate stalled dozens of Dem-

Appeals Courts Tilt Republican

Judges appointed by Republican presidents outnumber Democratic-appointed judges on seven of the 13 federal circuit courts of appeals, Democratic appointees outnumber Republican appointees on four, and the remaining two courts are evenly divided. Each of the numbered circuits plus the District of Columbia Circuit hears appeals from federal district courts within its region. The Federal Circuit hears appeals in patent and trade cases. Each appeals court is the final authority on issues of federal law within its circuit unless reversed by the U.S. Supreme Court.

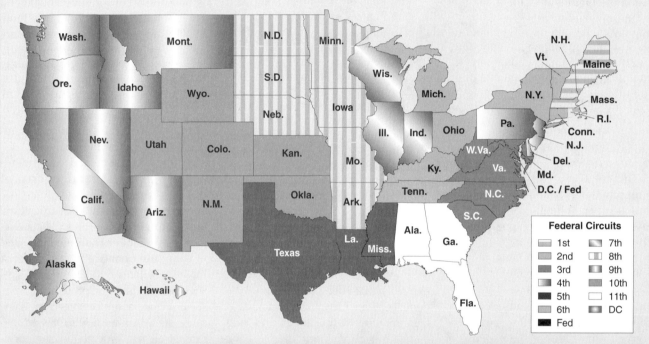

Federal Circuits	Lineup of Judges Based on Appointing President's Party	Vacancies	Authorized Judgeships
1st Circuit	3R-2D	1	6
2nd Circuit	2R-10D	1 (1 Bush nominee pending)	13
3rd Circuit	6R-6D	2	14
4th Circuit	5R-5D	5 (3 Bush nominees pending)	15
5th Circuit	9R-5D	3 (3 Bush nominees pending)	17
6th Circuit	5R-6D	6 (2 Bush nominees pending)	16
7th Circuit	8R-3D	—	11
8th Circuit	5R-3D	3 (3 Bush nominees pending)	11
9th Circuit	8R-17D	3 (2 Bush nominees pending)	28
10th Circuit	3R-5D	4 (3 Bush nominees pending)	12
11th Circuit	6R-5D	1	12
D.C. Circuit	5R-4D	3 (2 Bush nominees pending)	12
Federal Circuit	7R-4D	1 (1 Bush nominee pending)	12

Source: Administrative Office of the U.S. Courts

ocratic President Bill Clinton's nominees during his final years in the White House. Now, Republicans are complaining that Democratic senators are slowing action on Bush's nominees and preparing to use a political "litmus test" in voting on confirmations.

Politics also has taken a toll on state courts, especially in states where judges are subject to election rather than appointment. In recent years, business groups, plaintiffs' lawyers and anti-crime groups have become more active in supporting judicial candidates or opposing the re-election of incumbent judges. "A lot of people in those states are becoming very cynical about judges," says Stephen Burbank, a law professor at the University of Pennsylvania in Philadelphia and co-chair of a task force on judicial independence for the American Judicature Society, a court advocacy group. (*See sidebar, p. 48.*)

Bush made a calculated effort to soothe partisan feelings in Washington by including in his first batch of nominees two people whom Clinton had named to the federal bench. Bush proposed to elevate Judge Barrington Parker Jr. from the district court in New York City to the Second U.S. Circuit Court of Appeals. He also renominated Judge Roger Gregory to a seat on the Fourth U.S. Circuit Court of Appeals in Richmond, Va. Clinton named Gregory to a recess appointment after the Republican-controlled Senate failed to give him a hearing, but the temporary appointment expires at the end of this congressional session.

Both Parker and Gregory are African-American, and both are regarded as moderate to liberal. Bush's other choices, however, are widely viewed as conservative to varying degrees. "They seem to be moderately conservative types, but not screened for their ideological purity," says Robert Carp, a professor of political science at the University of Houston who studies the federal judiciary. [2]

Bush has been adding to his list of judicial nominees since May 9. Through July 15, he had made 20 appeals court nominations and nine for U.S. district courts.

Liberal groups have been poring over the nominees' records for evidence of what they regard as ideological bias. Meanwhile, conservative advocacy groups have been defending Bush's choices. Two organizations — the Family Research Council and the newly formed People for Common Sense Courts — have run television ads defending the president's choices.

On Capitol Hill, in the meantime, Senate Democrats are staging a rehearsal of sorts: a series of hearings about the nomination and confirmation process by the Judiciary Subcommittee on Administrative Oversight and the Courts. In an initial hearing, the subcommittee's chairman, Democrat Charles Schumer of New York, argued on June 26 that the Senate should consider a judicial nominee's ideology in the confirmation process. Schumer's statement prompted a sharp rebuttal from Sen. Orrin Hatch of Utah, the committee's ranking Republican, who served as chairman when the GOP was in control. (*See "At Issue," p. 57.*)

For his part, Michael Gerhardt, a law professor at the College of William and Mary in Williamsburg, Va., and author of a new book on the federal appointments process, says presidents and U.S. senators alike always consider ideology in picking federal judges. "It is an appropriate factor to take into account," Gerhardt continues. "The president and senators both are charged with monitoring the ideology and direction of the federal courts."

The stakes are high. All sides are anticipating a possible battle over a Supreme Court nominee if one or more of the justices retire during Bush's presidency. Any new appointment

could have a significant effect on a court that delivered the White House to Bush in December and remains closely divided between a conservative majority and a moderate-to-liberal minority.

As the White House, the Senate and opposing interest groups gird for the coming battles over federal judgeships, here are some of the questions being debated:

Is President Bush politicizing the selection of federal judges?

As the Bush administration got its judicial-selection process under way early this year, White House Counsel Alberto Gonzales insisted there were "no litmus-test questions" for prospective nominees.

"The truth of the matter is that a judge's personal views of an issue are irrelevant or should be irrelevant if a judge does her job right," Gonzales told *The New York Times*. "We ask them questions about their philosophy. We ask how they construe statutes, how do they resolve disputes and what do they believe is the appropriate role of judges." [3]

Liberal interest groups saw a different picture. "These people are fairly right-wing and out of step with the values of mainstream America," Kuntz of the Alliance of Justice declared following the president's initial nominations on May 9.

Two months later, liberal advocacy groups continue to depict Bush's nominees as ideologically motivated. "This first group of judges in the main are extremely conservative and very consistent with what we said in the beginning — that the Bush administration is trying to pack the federal judiciary with right-wing ideologues," says Ralph Neas, president of People for the American Way.

Conservative interest groups, however, say Bush's nominees are well qualified and share the president's philosophy of judicial restraint. "They're people

Many Bush Nominees Lean Right

President Bush's initial nominees for federal judgeships have a conservative cast that is likely to lead to close scrutiny when the Democratic-controlled Senate Judiciary Committee begins confirmation hearings this fall.

Four of the prospective judges are drawing special attention from liberals:

- **Jeffrey Sutton**, 40, came to prominence arguing states' rights cases before the U.S. Supreme Court as Ohio's state solicitor. His most recent victory in that area — argued as a private attorney — came this year with a 5-4 decision holding that states cannot be sued for damages for violating the federal Americans with Disabilities Act. He also represented cigarette companies in a case that struck down Massachusetts' restrictions on tobacco advertising. He was nominated for the Cincinnati-based Sixth U.S. Circuit Court of Appeals.

- **Michael McConnell**, 46, a University of Utah law professor, also has won significant Supreme Court decisions on a major conservative issue: lowering barriers to government support for religious activities. He won a 6-3 decision in 2000 giving the government greater leeway to support church-affiliated schools. He was nominated for the 10th Circuit in Denver.

- **John Roberts Jr.**, 46, an appellate specialist in Washington and former deputy U.S. solicitor general under the first President Bush, has represented a variety of clients — mostly business interests — in more than 30 arguments before the U.S. Supreme Court. This is his second chance to serve on the D.C. Circuit: former President Bush nominated him in 1992, but the Senate never acted on the nomination.

- **Miguel Estrada**, 39, now in private practice in Washington, was an assistant solicitor general in the first Bush administration and continued to serve through President Bill Clinton's first term. He has argued 15 cases before the U.S. Supreme Court. He also would serve on the D.C. Circuit.

The other initial Bush nominees included two state supreme court justices viewed as conservative: **Priscilla Owen**, 46, of Texas, nominated for the New Orleans-based Fifth Circuit, and **Deborah Cook**, 49, of Ohio, chosen for the Sixth Circuit in Cincinnati. The group included one other woman: **Edith Brown Clement**, 53, a federal judge in New Orleans, named to the Fifth Circuit.

Bush also picked two federal judges who formerly worked for Republican senators to serve on the Fourth Circuit: **Dennis Shedd**, 48, a former aide to Sen. Strom Thurmond of South Carolina; and **Terence Boyle**, 55, a former aide to Sen. Jesse Helms, R-N.C.

The president gave an air of bipartisanship to the initial group of nominees by picking two Democratic-appointed federal judges to appellate posts: **Barrington Parker Jr.**, 56, a federal district court judge named by Clinton in 1994, tapped for the New York-based Second Circuit; and **Roger Gregory**, 48, named to the Richmond, Va.-based Fourth Circuit by Clinton in a recess appointment in December after the Senate failed to act on his nomination. His appointment expires at the end of the current congressional session unless his renomination is confirmed.

Bush has nominated nine more candidates for appellate courts since the first appointments. Some also have well-known conservative records, most prominently **Carolyn Kuhl**, 48, a Los Angeles Superior Court judge and former assistant U.S. solicitor general under President Ronald Reagan, nominated for the liberal-dominated Ninth Circuit. She once signed a brief urging the Supreme Court to overturn the abortion-rights decision *Roe v. Wade*. For another vacancy on the Ninth Circuit, Bush turned to **Richard Clifton**, 50, a private lawyer in Hawaii who has served as attorney for the state's Republican Party.

Other nominees include **Charles Pickering**, 64, a federal judge in Mississippi and father of Rep. Skip Pickering, R-Miss. (Fifth Circuit); **Lavenski Smith**, 42, a black conservative and member of the Arkansas Public Service Commission; **William Riley**, 54, private attorney in Nebraska, and **Michael Melloy**, 53, federal judge in Iowa (all for the Eighth Circuit in St. Louis); **Timothy Tymkovich**, 44, a private lawyer and former Colorado state solicitor, and **Harris Hartz**, 54, a private lawyer and former New Mexico state appeals court judge (both for the 10th Circuit); and **Sharon Prost**, 50, an aide to Sen. Orrin Hatch, R-Utah. (Federal Circuit).

Bush's nine nominees for federal district courts are getting less attention so far. But one could draw fire: **Paul Cassell**, a University of Utah law professor and former prosecutor and Justice Department lawyer. Cassell waged a long campaign to uphold a federal law aimed at overturning the famous *Miranda* decision on police interrogation. The Supreme Court in 1999 rejected Cassell's argument, 7-2.

who understand the proper role of a judge," says Andrew Stephens, president of People for Common Sense Courts, which formed after Bush's election was assured in December. "The key question is: Are you willing to accept the limited role of the judge and resist the temptation to legislate from the bench?"

Bush raised concerns that he was politicizing the judicial selection process in March when he abandoned a practice dating to the 1950s of submitting possible candidates in advance to a special American Bar Association (ABA) committee. In a letter to ABA leaders, Gonzales said the White House

did not want to give the bar "a unique, quasi-official role" in evaluating judicial candidates. The move pleased conservatives, who have been critical of the ABA's role ever since the committee gave a divided recommendation on the controversial nomination of Robert Bork to the Supreme Court in 1987.

Liberal groups are now sifting through the records of Bush's nominees for evidence of ideological bias. At the same time, they are warning about what they regard as a partisan imbalance in the federal judiciary. They note that out of the 13 federal circuit courts of appeals, seven have a majority of judges appointed by Republican presidents, while only four have a majority of Democratic appointees. The remaining two are evenly split. (*See chart, p. 44.*)

"The circuit courts are not ideologically balanced," Kuntz says, "and it will only get worse. President Bush has made it very clear that at the top of his agenda is the intention to shift the judiciary further rightward."

Conservatives, however, say Bush is simply exercising the power that the Constitution gives to the president. "George W. Bush is president," says Andrea Lafferty, executive director of the Traditional Values Coalition. "As president, he has the right to appoint judges consistent with his philosophy."

The University of Pennsylvania's Burbank agrees that the president should consider a prospective judge's views in making his decisions. "There's nothing wrong with the president taking account of the political inclinations and affiliations of the people [he] is considering appointing to the federal court," he says. "It's the one opportunity for the president to influence the federal judiciary, and we'd be naive to think that federal judges aren't influenced by their life experiences and backgrounds."

But Burbank also says the Senate has a role in making sure that the president does not appoint "ideologues" to the bench. "When the president does that, the Senate has the right and indeed the responsibility to make sure that these people have their minds open so that they don't qualify as ideologues," he says.

Are Senate Democrats politicizing the confirmation process for federal judges?

As Democrats prepared to take over control of the Senate in early June, party leaders promised there would be "no payback" for what they regarded as the Republicans' mistreatment of President Clinton's judicial nominees while the GOP controlled the chamber. But incoming Judiciary Committee Chairman Leahy also warned that Democrats would use their power to block candidates they viewed as too ideological.

"Bill Clinton wouldn't have sent over a left-wing ideologue," Leahy declared. "And Bush can't send over a right-wing ideologue." [4]

Some Senate Republicans saw those kinds of remarks as signaling an intention by Democrats to approve judicial nominees only if they committed themselves to particular political views. "I am concerned that there will be a litmus test for judicial nominees," Sen. Kay Bailey Hutchison of Texas said in a June 6 appearance on NPR's "Talk of the Nation."

Today, conservative groups continue to accuse Democratic senators of seeking to impose their views on the federal judiciary. "This process is designed to prevent conservatives who believe in judicial restraint from becoming federal judges," Lafferty says. "Liberals only want activist judges who believe the Constitution is whatever they want it to be, whereas conservatives believe that the Constitution is to be interpreted according to the original intent of the writers."

Liberals, on the other hand, say the Senate has an obligation to give what Kuntz calls "the highest scrutiny" to Bush's judicial nominees. The Senate, she says, "should place the burden on the nominee to establish that he or she meets high standards, including a respect for Congress' ability to legislate and particularly to legislate [civil rights] protections."

The current debate is an echo of recriminations played out during the last six years of Clinton's presidency between the Democratic White House and the GOP-controlled Senate. The Senate formally rejected only one of Clinton's nominees — Ronnie White, a black state Supreme Court justice from Missouri — but it failed to act on many others. A total of 42 federal court nominees had not been acted upon at the end of 2000.

Conservatives, however, claim that the Democratic-controlled Senate treated the first President Bush even worse in his final year in office. Thomas Jipping, director of the Judicial Selection Monitoring Project of the conservative Free Congress Research and Education Foundation, cites statistics that 55 Bush judicial nominees were unacted on when he left the White House in January 1993.

This year, Senate Republicans themselves were responsible for a one-month delay in starting action on Bush's nominees. In their new minority status, they demanded changes in the confirmation process rules. They wanted assurances that the Judiciary Committee would allow a floor vote on any Bush nominee for the Supreme Court — even if a majority of the panel rejected the nomination. They also wanted to revise or abolish the so-called "blue slip" procedure, which allowed an individual senator to secretly put a hold on any nomination.

Republicans refused to approve a new organization measure for the Senate after Jeffords' departure until the issues were resolved. The impasse was resolved on June 29 by a joint letter from Leahy and Hatch saying that the committee would likely send any Supreme Court nominee to the floor regardless of the vote in the panel. The agreement also called for any senator's hold on a nomination to be publicly disclosed.

Selection of State Judges . . .

As cash weighed down the scales of justice, the narrator on a TV ad in last year's contentious Ohio Supreme Court races suggested that Alice Robie Resnick — a sitting justice — had sold her vote.

Resnick was re-elected, despite a $4 million, four-week advertising blitz by the U.S. Chamber of Commerce and an arm of its Ohio affiliate. The business groups were unhappy that Resnick, part of a four-vote majority, had often ruled in favor of consumers and organized labor.

Overall, candidates and interest groups spent $9 million on races for the two seats. In Michigan, bitter races for three Supreme Court seats cost at least $16 million.

In Tennessee and Nebraska, two Supreme Court justices lost their seats in 1996 retention elections when interest groups targeted them for their supposedly soft-on-crime votes in death-penalty cases.

The increasingly political nature of judicial elections is spurring efforts in at least a dozen states by lawmakers, courts, judicial organizations and citizens' groups to reform or eliminate the role of aggressive campaign politics in selecting state judges. Efforts are also afoot to replace elections with so-called merit selection, usually by governor-appointed panels. Currently, judges face elections in 39 states, according to the American Bar Association (ABA). [1]

The rising cost of state judicial elections led an ABA commission just this week to ask those 39 states to finance judges' campaigns from public funds. "There has been an alarming increase in attempts by special interests to influence judicial elections through financial contributions and attack campaigning," said ABA President Martha Barnett, as she released the report of the ABA Commission on Public Financing of Judicial Campaigns. [2]

Reform proposals run the gamut, including:

- Replacing elective systems for top state judges with appointive ones in Pennsylvania, Michigan and other big states.
- Providing public campaign financing for appeals court candidates in Wisconsin and North Carolina.
- Supplying more information to voters about races and monitoring the accuracy of interest-group advertising against candidates.

In Michigan, Republican Gov. John Engler wants to replace elections for the state Supreme Court with appointments. "The campaigns have a less than helpful effect in terms of the image of the judiciary," he said. [3] In Pennsylvania, Republican Gov. Tom Ridge convened a meeting of state groups in April to draft a constitutional amendment to appoint appellate judges rather than elect them, using a merit-selection system to screen candidates' judicial qualifications.

Alan Ashman, director of the Hunter Center for Judicial Selection at the American Judicature Society, says 34 states and the District of Columbia currently have merit-selection plans of various types. In 15 states and the District, judges are selected through nominating commissions.

Ashman says he supports merit selection in part because of "all the hoopla, money and politics" that surround elections. The reform effort has grown in states like Pennsylvania, Michigan and Ohio because "elections have become so nasty, so partisan," he says.

However, James Wootton, president of the U.S. Chamber's Institute for Legal Reform, defends the election process, including the money spent on campaigns, as part of the democratic process.

"The amount of money being spent is the wrong focus," he says. "The question is: Should people who have a point of view be able to communicate with the public about candidates? Judicial candidates are not in a special category and should not be protected from certain communications with the public. And those communications cost money."

The Ohio election prompted the state's League of Women Voters and other organizations to draft legislation requiring groups that advertise against judicial candidates to disclose where their money came from. Meanwhile, the national League of Women Voters is working with chapters in Oklahoma, Minnesota, Nebraska and other states to assess the amount of political pressure being exerted to influence judges. [4]

Although the Ohio justices retained their seats in the 2000 election, anti-crime groups in 1996 had successfully ousted sitting Supreme Court justices in Nebraska and Tennessee.

The case of former Justice Penny White of Tennessee reflects what happens when a judge is targeted in a retention election, Ashman says. Judges in Tennessee and many other states come to the bench through merit selection but are re-elected in retention elections, in which they run unopposed and voters vote "yes" or "no" to retain them.

Leahy moved immediately after the Fourth of July recess to hold the first hearing on a Bush nominee: Judge Gregory, the Clinton holdover for the Fourth Circuit. But Leahy says more controversial confirmation hearings will not begin until fall.

Supporters of Bush's nominations are less than pleased. "We would like the Senate to pick up the pace," Stephens says. But Neas says the Senate should allow time for "a serious advise-and-consent process that will take a serious look at all the nominees."

For his part, William and Mary's Gerhardt says Senate Democrats have done nothing improper — at least so far. "I think they're being open about their concerns," he says. "The openness of their concerns is to their credit. Lines are crossed when people use other factors as pretexts to go after nominees."

. . . Called Too Costly, Political

The elections of White and Supreme Court Justice David Lanphier of Nebraska were highly politicized contests in which special-interest groups pushed for their removal. "The electioneering that occurred in these two elections was the very type that legislatures in Nebraska and Tennessee sought to eliminate by installing merit selection and judicial retention elections," wrote Traciel V. Reid, a professor of political science at North Carolina State University. [5]

Reid noted "the success of special-interest groups in politicizing the elections raises serious questions about the public's role in selecting state court judges. Both defeats reflect the ability of political actors to unseat judges by galvanizing public frustration over a hot-button issue, such as the death penalty, or by manipulating the electorate through expensive, negative campaigning. Judicial retention elections thus become another access point by which special-interest groups can influence policy making." [6]

In the wake of the Lanphier and White defeats, several reform proposals were made in Tennessee and Nebraska to help inoculate judges against political attacks for unpopular decisions, including efforts to provide the public with objective information about judges' competence.

Roger Warren, president of the National Center for State Courts, says much could be done to improve judicial elections, short of abolishing them. "As currently conducted in many states, the judicial election campaigns undermine trust in the system, because of the conduct of the candidates and interest groups and by reason of the campaign and interest group expenditures."

A summit convened by the center made 20 recommendations for improving judicial selection, including improving voter awareness of candidates' qualifications and regulating conduct and expenditures. "If you want a system where the public decides," Warren says, "you must have an informed electorate, create sources of reliable information and get it into the hands of the voters."

Steven Collier, president of the Ohio Academy of Trial Lawyers, opposes efforts to replace judicial elections with merit selection, in which a panel typically selected by the governor selects judges. But Collier says expenditures must be publicly disclosed.

In Ohio, Collier says, the identity of the group that raised millions of dollars last fall to defeat Supreme Court candidates was kept secret. "We want disclosure of who is contributing," he says. "That is the only way for the public to find out the truth."

Collier opposes a merit system in Ohio because he says there are no checks and balances because the governor and legislative majority are from the same party. "The legislature passes what it wants, and the court rubber stamps it," he says. "We would rather let the people decide, like a jury. But the information they need is who is paying for these types of ads. In something as important as election to the Supreme Court, we need to do better."

In Florida, voters overwhelmingly rejected a ballot measure in November that would have replaced elections for trial court judges with an appointive system.

Proposals for public financing of judicial races are under consideration in North Carolina and Wisconsin, which has long provided some public funding to state candidates. Wisconsin's "impartial justice bill" would provide up to $900,000 for a Supreme Court candidate.

But opposition groups say such proposals are undemocratic. "We don't want our state tax dollars going to candidates who don't agree with our position," said Susan M. Armacost, legislative director of Wisconsin Right to Life. [7]

Wootton of the Institute for Legal Reform also opposes public funding because he says it takes away First Amendment rights of Americans to engage in the political process. Moreover, he says, it's not the money that politicizes the process but the elections themselves.

"The American people made a choice that they want to elect judges," he says. "The minute you have elections, then our tradition of free speech says the public and interest groups have a right to communicate with the public about those candidates."

---

[1] William Glaberson, "States Taking Steps to Rein In Excesses of Judicial Politicking," *The New York Times*," June 15, 2001, p. A1.

[2] From the ABA Web site: www.abanet.org/media/jul01/judicial.html.

[3] *Ibid.*

[4] *Ibid.*

[5] Traciel V. Reid, "The Politicization of Retention Elections," *Judicature*," September/October 1999.

[6] *Ibid.*

[7] *Ibid.*

Should bipartisan procedures be adopted to select federal judges?

After Illinois voters elected Republican Peter Fitzgerald to the U.S. Senate in 1998, the state's Democratic senator, Richard Durbin, proposed that the two lawmakers share responsibility for recommending federal judgeship nominees in the state.

They agreed to a power-sharing arrangement that allowed Fitzgerald to make one recommendation to President Clinton for district court appointments for every three recommendations that Durbin made. In addition, each senator could veto any recommendation that the other made.

"We went through four choices in a hurry," Durbin recalls. "He picked one that I thought was excellent. We ended up with a full complement of federal judges" in contrast to other states, where political differences often stalled action on nominees.

With a Republican in the White House now, the agreement is still in place, though Fitzgerald will get three recommendations to Durbin's one. The procedure will be tested soon, when one of Illinois' federal judges takes "senior status" — a form of semi-retirement — creating a vacancy for Bush to fill. For his part, Fitzgerald is satisfied with the agreement and expects to continue it, according to a press spokesman.

The Illinois senators' arrangement represents one of several ways used over the years to try to select better candidates for the federal bench and reduce partisan confrontations. In a different system, California's two Democratic senators — Dianne Feinstein and Barbara Boxer — agreed with the White House to form bipartisan screening committees for judicial vacancies in each of the state's four federal judicial districts. The six-member panels include three people named by the two senators and three chosen by the White House; any candidate must receive four votes in order to be recommended for a post.

Walter Dellinger, who served as acting solicitor general in the Clinton administration and now specializes in appellate litigation with a Washington law firm, goes so far as to suggest that Bush and the Democrats ought to agree on a power-sharing arrangement for appeals court appointments.

Dellinger says, for example, that Bush could balance his nomination of Republicans Miguel Estrada and John Roberts Jr. to the D.C. Circuit by picking a Democrat for a remaining vacancy. His suggestion: Seth Waxman, his successor as solicitor general, who now teaches at Georgetown University law school.

Interest groups on both sides, however, show no interest in bipartisan procedures to try to depoliticize the selection of federal judges.

"I'm not sure that it should be depoliticized, if you're equating ideology with politics," says Kuntz of the Alliance for Justice. "I think ideology is a very important factor and one that the Senate should look at very closely."

"I don't think [nominees] should be blocked for political reasons," Kuntz continues. "But they should be voted down if they're out of the ideological mainstream."

Conservatives reject the idea even more firmly. "I wouldn't like to see any formal mechanism put into place to require a particular procedure," says Stephens of People for Common Sense Courts. "The Constitution gives the president the power to appoint federal judges, and there's no reason for him to give that away."

"That is an unconstitutional approach," says Jipping of the Free Congress Research and Education Foundation. "It is not bipartisan to hijack a process and turn on its head what the Constitution requires."

Academic experts express more interest in bipartisan procedures but acknowledge any moves in that direction are unlikely for now. "You're not going to eliminate politics," says Goldman of the University of Massachusetts. "But you can provide for processes that make it more likely that qualified people are considered for the bench and that a diverse group of nominees will go forward."

Gerhardt says bipartisan procedures are "a good idea in the abstract." But, he adds, "The real problem now is that we're dealing with unprecedented circumstances," referring to the closely divided Senate and Bush's narrow election as president. "It's a recipe for chaos."

BACKGROUND

Advise and Consent

Partisan politics has been a major factor in judicial selection for the federal bench and in state courts through much of U.S. history — from the bitter fights between the Federalists and Anti-Federalists at the turn of the 18th century to the protracted disputes between conservatives and liberals from the Reagan presidency through today.

The Constitution gives the president the power to appoint — "by and with the advice and consent of the Senate" — judges of the Supreme Court and the lower federal courts later created by Congress. The compromise emerged after the Framers rejected as unwieldy a proposal to allow the Senate itself to make appointments. The evidence suggests — though not conclusively — that the Framers expected presidents to consult closely with the Senate in making appointments.

The federal judiciary became a battleground as political parties emerged after George Washington's presidency. Federalist judges appointed by President John Adams enforced the notorious Alien and Sedition Acts against the party's political opponents. Adams moved to entrench Federalist control of the judiciary by appointing a number of "midnight judges" as he left the White House in 1801. With President Thomas Jefferson in office, the Anti-Federalists sought to take revenge by trying — unsuccessfully — to cancel the appointments and later — again unsuccessfully — attempting to impeach Federalist Supreme Court Justice Samuel Chase in 1804.

Over time, partisan conflicts over the federal judiciary became more orderly if not less contentious. [5] As the federal judiciary was expanded after the Civil War, presidents routinely filled the bench with members of their own parties, which led to a long period of Republican domination of federal courts. Political practice also transformed the constitutional allocation of power as senators took on the major role in recommending candidates, especially for federal district courts. The result, as famously described by one political ob-

Chronology

Before 1960
Federal courts take shape, gradually gain independence and assume larger role with growth of federal government.

1789
Constitution gives president power to appoint judges "with advice and consent" of Senate.

1798-1804
Federalists and Anti-Federalists battle over federal courts; failed effort to remove Supreme Court Justice Samuel Chase helps ensure judicial independence.

Mid-1800s
By the century's midpoint, political affiliation becomes major criterion for presidential appointment of federal judges; senators take on major role in recommending nominees for district courts.

1861-1933
Republican-appointed judges dominate federal bench during the GOP's long period of White House control.

1913
American Judicature Society formed to promote "merit selection" of judges.

1933-1953
Democrats Franklin D. Roosevelt and Harry S Truman reorient federal judiciary; Democratic-appointed judges hold 80 percent of seats at end of Truman presidency.

1960s-1970s
Role of federal courts expands during civil rights era.

1969-1974
President Richard M. Nixon pledges to rein in liberal activism by Supreme Court; shifts high court to right, but two nominees are rejected by Democratic-controlled Senate.

1977-1981
Democrat Jimmy Carter pledges merit selection of federal judges; creates nominating commissions to screen candidates; expands number of women and minorities appointed to bench.

1980s *Reagan era shifts federal judiciary to the right.*

1981-1989
President Ronald Reagan forges conservative majority on Supreme Court despite rejection of Robert Bork in 1987; appoints prominent conservative academics to federal appeals courts, names other conservatives to lower courts; leaves office with Republican appointees dominating federal bench again.

1989-1993
President George Bush continues shifting federal courts to the right, but appoints greater percentage of women and minorities than Reagan; Democratic-controlled Senate leaves more than 50 Bush nominees unacted on at end of session.

1990s *President Bill Clinton picks moderates and liberals for federal bench.*

1993, 1994
Clinton names moderate-liberals Ruth Bader Ginsburg and Stephen G. Breyer to Supreme Court; Senate confirms both by wide margins.

1995-2001
Republicans gain control of Senate, initiating six years of delay and acrimony over Clinton's nominees for bench; many nominees withdrawn in face of GOP opposition; record number of women and minorities named, but Senate in 1999 rejects African-American nominee, Missouri Supreme Court Justice Ronnie White, on party-line vote.

2000-Present
Federal courts continue as partisan battleground after narrow presidential and congressional elections.

2000
George W. Bush promises to appoint "strict constructionists" to federal bench if elected; Senate leaves 42 Clinton judicial nominees unacted on; Democratic appointees slightly outnumber Republican appointees on federal bench as Clinton leaves office.

2001
White House ends pre-screening of judicial nominees by American Bar Association committee in March; Bush unveils first 11 nominees for federal appeals courts on May 9; liberal interest groups criticize group as too conservative; Democrats regain control of Senate on June 3, promise close scrutiny of Bush nominees; hearings on controversial nominees expected to begin in fall.

Inside the Federalist Society . . .

S ome call it a "vast right-wing conspiracy" determined to get conservative judges appointed to federal and state courts.

To others it is just a lawyers' debating club, dedicated to disseminating a limited-government view of constitutional issues.

Clearly, defining the Federalist Society depends on who is doing the defining.

The Washington, D.C.-based group was thrust into the media limelight recently when critics complained that an inordinate number of key Bush administration officials are either society members or supporters — including three Cabinet members and several lawyers who are screening potential federal judges. Several judges nominated by President Bush to the federal bench are also members or supporters, as are many sitting federal judges and three U.S. Supreme Court justices.

With such powerful supporters, critics say the group is strategically positioned to put its stamp on the nation's legal system, with effects that will ripple throughout society for decades to come. And that stamp, according to some critics, could threaten basic rights that most Americans take for granted, as well as environmental protections.

"The right-wing Federalist Society is calling the shots in the Bush White House," said Ralph G. Neas, president of People for the American Way, after the White House announced in March that it would no longer ask the American Bar Association (ABA) to evaluate potential federal judges. [1] Many observers think the Federalist Society convinced Bush to dump the ABA and instead consult with the society over judgeships.

The Federalists consider the ABA too liberal on civil liberties issues. Also, the society has never forgiven the group for its role in blocking former President Ronald Reagan's 1987 Supreme Court nomination of Robert H. Bork. He and Sen. Orrin Hatch, R-Utah, are co-chairmen of the society's Board of Visitors.

Allowing the Federalist Society to become a potential driving force behind President Bush's judicial nominees has deeply alarmed some liberals. "To have the Federalist Society replace the ABA in judicial selections is like having the creationist society screen high school science teachers," says Alfred Ross, president of the liberal New York-based Institute for Democracy Studies (IDS).

In April *The New York Times* quoted an administration official as saying that a quarter of the 70 potential judicial candidates being seriously considered by Bush had been recommended by the society's Washington headquarters, a claim denied by Executive Director Eugene B. Meyer.

"As an organization, we don't take positions on specific issues or lobby for specific candidates," Meyer says. However, he points out, many members with very strong views about the society's principles end up in public service. "If consulted on the merits of a particular judicial candidate, they would certainly give their opinion."

Influential leaders of the group — officially called the Federalist Society for Law and Public Policy Studies — include former Attorney General Edwin Meese III, former Christian Coalition President Donald P. Hodel, and C. Boyden Gray, White House counsel under former President George Bush and an adviser to President George W. Bush.

Much of the group's funding comes from conservative philanthropists, like Richard Mellon Scaife, who funded the Arkansas Project that investigated the activities of Bill and Hillary Clinton for the *American Spectator* magazine.

Bush Cabinet officials who are either founders or strong supporters of the Federalist Society include Attorney General John Ashcroft, Interior Secretary Gale Norton and Energy Secretary Spencer Abraham and his counsel, Lee Lieberman Otis, who helped select federal judges in the former Bush administration.

Newly appointed Solicitor General Theodore B. Olson — who won Bush's case before the Supreme Court in the contested 2000 presidential election — is a former president of the Washington, D.C., chapter. As solicitor general, he will represent the U.S. position in cases before the high court, where Justice Antonin Scalia is a society founder and Chief Justice William Rehnquist and Justice Clarence Thomas are supporters.

But the IDS and the Judicial Selection Project of the liberal Alliance for Justice are most concerned about the lesser-known society members in key positions in the White House general counsel's office and the Justice Department, which vet candidates for lifetime federal judgeships.

In an in-depth report on the society's activities, the IDS found that at least five lawyers at the White House and Justice de-

server, was a system in which senators appointed federal judges subject to the advice and consent of the president.

In the 20th century, the partisan make-up of the federal bench changed with successive presidencies of opposing parties. Democrat Woodrow Wilson (1913-1921) first created a Democratic majority among federal judges, which was reversed by 12 years of Republican presidents. When Democrat Franklin D. Roosevelt came to the White House in 1933, more than four-fifths of the federal judges were Republican appointees. At his death in 1945, the federal bench was both larger and more Democratic: More than two-thirds of federal judges were Democratic appointees.

Politics continued to play a major role in judicial appointments in the decades since the end of World War II. But several presidents also made attempts to raise the standards of the federal judiciary with mechanisms designed to place greater emphasis on

. . . Right-Wing Conspiracy or Debating Club?

partments are affiliated with the society. And IDS says White House Deputy Counsel Timothy Flanigan, who is not a member, received $256,958 from the society in 1998 for a biography he is writing about former Chief Justice Warren E. Burger.

According to the alliance, seven of President Bush's 20 appellate court nominees say they were members of the Federalist Society, including Jeffrey Sutton, a former Scalia clerk and leading advocate of states' rights; Michael McConnell, a University of Utah law professor who favors using public funds for religious schools, and Carolyn Kuhl, who once argued to overturn *Roe v. Wade*.

Groups like the IDS worry that if enough Federalist Society members are appointed to the federal bench, they would enact what Ross calls a "breathtaking" conservative judicial activist agenda to gut the federal government's administrative infrastructure that has been in place since the days of President Franklin D. Roosevelt. They cite a March 28 Federalist Society panel in Chicago entitled "Rolling Back the New Deal" and a recent society newsletter that outlined a case for abolishing the Securities and Exchange Commission.

"The right wing is making a dangerous power grab to remake the courts, and through them, the country . . . and only the Senate can stop it," said Neas. [2]

But Meyer says liberals are paranoid about the society's influence, and that the group's only agenda is "to encourage balanced, serious, open debate about fundamental principles of individual freedom, limited government and the notion that the courts should say what the law is and not what they want it to be."

Jim Grace, a board member of the Houston Federalist Society, believes assertions about the alleged synergy between the administration and the society have been exaggerated. He says it is only a coincidence that many Bush advisers are society members. "The Federalist Society has become a home for conservatives who are disenchanted with the ABA, but not all conservatives are," Grace said. [3]

The society was founded 20 years ago as a campus debating forum by conservative law students who felt their limited-government approach to constitutional issues was not being discussed or taught at the nation's elite law schools. Today it has a $3 million budget — funded largely by conservative founda-

tions — and 25,000 members in major cities and 140 law schools. Its chapters host hundreds of debates on legal topics, which are open to the public and generally include presentations by liberals, including Supreme Court Justices Stephen Breyer and Ruth Bader Ginsburg, former Democratic presidential candidate Michael Dukakis, Rep. Barney Frank, D-Mass., and former National Organization for Women President Patricia Ireland.

Flanigan likens the suspicions held by some about the society to left-wing McCarthyism. "This is not a society that sits around and plots the overthrow of the Constitution. It is a group of lawyers with a diversity of viewpoints who tolerate other views and who encourage debate," he said. "I find it offensive someone should suggest something nefarious about this group." [4]

Sen. Richard Durbin, D-Ill., said about the Federalist Society during a confirmation hearing in May, "I don't think they are a debating society. I think they have an agenda." UCLA law professor and society member Eugene Volokh responded in *The Washington Post*, "The Federalist Society is a group of conservatives, libertarians and moderates who share two things: an interest in law and a sense that the liberal legal establishment often (not always) gets things wrong." He continued: "Some of us are pro-choice, others pro-life. Some Federalists . . . think the Constitution should be interpreted primarily based on its original meaning. Others focus more on precedent or on evolving tradition." [5]

Volokh said it is "no surprise" that Bush has nominated some Federalists. "Democrats are likely to appoint lawyers associated with the ACLU and other liberal groups," he noted. "The same goes for Federalists during Republican presidencies." [6]

— Kathy Koch

[1] Quoted in Neil A. Lewis, "A Conservative Legal Group Thrives in Bush's Washington," *The New York Times*, April 18, 2001.

[2] Quoted in Robert Cohen, "Bush Slate of Judicial Nominees in Doubt: With the Jeffords Switch, Democrats Vow Scrutiny," *The Star-Ledger*, Newark, N.J., May 29, 2001.

[3] Quoted in Julie Mason, "Society of Conservative Lawyers Flexes Muscles at White House," *Houston Chronicle*, May 10, 2001.

[4] Ibid.

[5] Eugene Volokh, "Our Flaw? We're Just Not Liberals," *The Washington Post*, June 3, 2001.

[6] *Ibid.*

professional skills than political affiliation. President Harry S Truman began consulting the American Bar Association on candidates for federal judges — a practice institutionalized by his successor, Republican Dwight D. Eisenhower, and continued by presidents of both parties until Bush ended it in March.

In his 1976 campaign, Democrat Jimmy Carter pledged to appoint federal judges "strictly on the basis of merit." He sought to make good on the promise by creating nominating commissions for each of the federal courts of appeals and urging Democratic senators to use similar commissions for recommending candidates for

district court seats. At the end of his four-year presidency, merit-selection advocates said the commissions appeared to have produced judges who were by and large professionally competent and also aligned with Carter's political views. [6]

Divided Government

Ronald Reagan's election as president in 1980 culminated a conservative campaign aimed in part at reining in what he and other Republicans called judicial activism by the Supreme Court and lower federal courts. As president, Reagan sought to remake the federal judiciary — and succeeded to a substantial degree despite resistance from Democrats that peaked when they gained control of the Senate in his last two years in office. In the 1990s, Clinton faced a period of divided government for his last six years in office but still managed to shift the political leanings of the federal judiciary even with increased delays and acrimony over judicial appointments.

Reagan abolished Carter's appellate court nominating commission and brought control of judicial appointments — especially for the appeals courts — back tightly into the White House. He replaced Carter's emphasis on merit and diversity with a single-minded focus on judicial philosophy.

"The Reagan administration elevated ideology and legal policy to the highest concern," the University of Massachusetts' Goldman wrote. [7] Indeed, Reagan scattered academics well known for their conservative views onto federal appeals courts around the country. One prominent example: Antonin Scalia, named to the federal appeals court in Washington, D.C., in 1982 and elevated to the Supreme Court in 1986.

The full Senate never rejected any of Reagan's nominees for the lower courts, but one nominee was rejected in committee, and in Reagan's last two years in office more than a dozen languished without Senate action. [8] Despite that generally favorable record for Reagan nominees, conservatives defined judicial politics of the 1980s by the singular rejection of Supreme Court nominee Bork in 1987. Liberals sharply attacked Bork, then a federal appeals court judge, for his conservative views on a wide range of legal issues. Conservatives regarded the attacks — and his eventual defeat — as the illegitimate result of Democrats' politicization of the confirmation process.

President George Bush continued Reagan's effort to staff the federal judiciary with conservatives, but he turned more often to private lawyers than to academics. He also appointed more women (29 in four years, compared with Reagan's 24 in eight years) and more African-Americans (10 compared with Reagan's six). The Senate formally rejected none of Bush's nominees. But he left office with more than 50 nominations unacted on by the Democratic-controlled Senate. Some 66 Bush nominees, however, were approved that year — a record number for a presidential election year, when judicial confirmations normally slow down. [9]

Clinton halted the conservative transformation of the federal courts, but opposing advocacy groups disagree on the extent to which he shifted the judiciary to the left. Numerically, Clinton in eight years named 305 district court judges and 61 appellate judges — numbers comparable to Reagan's 290 district and 78 appellate judges. With Clinton's judges, Democratic appointees again constituted a majority in both the district and appellate courts. He also named a record number of women (96) and African-Americans (57) to the federal bench.

Nonetheless, Clinton gave lower priority to judicial selection than either Reagan, Bush or Carter — to the disappointment of liberal advocacy groups. He also encountered what Goldman calls "unprecedented delay . . . and acrimony" over his appointees." [10] Clinton responded by looking for somewhat moderate nominees — typified by his two Supreme Court appointees, Ruth Bader Ginsburg and Stephen G. Breyer. He also backed away from some nominees in the face of criticism from Republican senators — most notably, Peter Edelman, a Georgetown law professor who served as assistant secretary for Health and Human Services and who had been expected to be named to the D.C. Circuit.

"Clinton aimed for moderates, for mainstream lawyers and judges," Goldman says. "There are a few exceptions, one or two are on the right of the political spectrum, and a couple may be a bit on the left. But by no stretch of the imagination did he name liberal activists."

Bush's Judges

As a presidential candidate, George W. Bush repeatedly promised to appoint "strict constructionist" federal judges. Once in office, Bush staffed his judicial-selection machinery in the White House and the Justice Department with well-known conservatives. And his initial choices immediately drew sharp criticism from liberal advocacy groups — criticisms that became more potent when Senate Democrats gained majority status and with it the power to give critics ample time to develop campaigns against Bush's choices.

Bush's judicial appointments as governor of Texas (1995-2000) were widely described as moderate. His four appointees to the Texas Supreme Court included one woman and one Hispanic — Alberto Gonzales, now the White House counsel. All four are described as pro-business pragmatists, but three of the four — including Gonzales — supported the right to abortion at some point in divisive cases before the court. [11]

Campaigning for president, Bush adopted standard Republican rhetoric opposing "liberal, activist judges." In the first presidential debate on Oct. 3,

Bush declared, "I believe in strict constructionists, and those are the kinds of judges I will appoint." Bush listed Justices Scalia and Clarence Thomas as models for possible Supreme Court appointments.

Once he became White House counsel, typically the office most intimately involved in judicial selection, Gonzales staffed the office with eight lawyers with established conservative records, including two with direct roles in the investigations of President Clinton by the Senate Whitewater Committee or Independent Counsel Kenneth Starr. Six of them clerked for conservative Supreme Court justices. And two came directly from a Washington law firm active in conservative legal causes. Meanwhile, Bush named Viet Dinh, a conservative Georgetown law professor, as assistant attorney general for the Office of Legal Counsel — the Justice Department unit that oversees judicial nominations. [12]

Gonzales' role in judicial selection first gained attention in March, when he discontinued the practice of submitting candidates for judgeships in advance to the ABA's Standing Committee on the Federal Judiciary. The bar group and its supporters depicted the committee's role as screening potential nominees for professional qualifications. But the 15-member committee drew fire in 1987 when it gave a divided rating to Supreme Court nominee Bork: Four of the members gave him an unqualified rating for the high court.

After meeting with ABA leaders, Gonzales informed them of his decision on March 22 in a phone call and confirming letter. He said it would be "inappropriate" to give "a preferential, quasi-official role" to the ABA because it "takes public positions on divisive, political, legal and social issues that come before the courts." In response, ABA President Martha Barnett, a Tallahassee, Fla., lawyer, told a news conference, "This means that the role of

politics may be taking the place of professionalism in choosing judges." [13]

Senate Democrats, meanwhile, were mapping strategy for anticipated fights over judicial appointments — including one or more potential high-stakes appointments to the Supreme Court. "We're simply not going to roll over," Schumer of New York said following a private retreat of Democratic senators in late April. [14] With the president's first appointments expected soon, the Senate's Democratic leader, South Dakota's Tom Daschle, reportedly urged the 42 senators who attended the closed-door session to avoid any quick endorsement of Bush's nominees.

Bush raised the profile of his initial judicial appointments by assembling all 11 of the nominees for a White House ceremony on May 9. "Every judge I appoint will be a person who clearly understands the role of a judge is to interpret the law, not to legislate from the bench," Bush said. After praising the group's qualifications, Bush deplored the recent judicial fights that he said had "little to do" with individual nominees' fitness for the bench. "This is not good for the Senate, for our courts or for the country," Bush concluded.

CURRENT SITUATION

Political Maneuvers

The Senate Judiciary Committee gave an effusive reception on July 11 to the first of President Bush's judicial nominees to get a hearing before the panel: Roger Gregory, the black Virginia lawyer already serving on the Fourth Circuit bench under a recess appointment by President Clin-

ton in late December. But liberal interest groups are hard at work mining the records of Bush's other nominees for evidence to use in potential confirmation battles.

Gregory was introduced by the state's two Republican senators, John Warner and George Allen. "We stand united behind this distinguished nominee," Warner said. Committee Chairman Leahy was unrestrained in praise. "His life and career have been exemplary, and his qualifications for this position are stellar," Leahy said. Gregory is the first black judge to serve on the Fourth Circuit — whose five states (Maryland, North and South Carolina, Virginia and West Virginia) have the highest proportion of African-Americans (22 percent) of any of the federal circuits.

Gregory won unanimous approval from the committee on July 19 and confirmation from the full Senate the next day by a 93-1 vote, with GOP leader Trent Lott of Mississippi casting the only no vote. The Senate also approved confirmation of two district court judges for Montana, where vacancies had left the state with only one active federal judge.

Many of Bush's other nominees, however, appeared headed for more difficulties. "Democrats are on a campaign to obstruct as many of President Bush's nominees as possible," says Jipping of the Free Congress Research and Education Foundation.

Sutton drew opposition within days of his nomination from a national disability-rights organization: Americans with Disabilities Act Watch. Sutton "has been representing parties who are basically fighting to weaken and eliminate the protections" of the ADA, spokesman Jim Ward, said before a scheduled rally in Washington on May 19.

Sutton argued for the state of Alabama in the Supreme Court's Feb. 21 decision that Congress overstepped its power in subjecting states to damage suits for violating the ADA. Jipping de-

AP Photo/Columbus Dispatch

AP Photo/Richmond Times-Dispatch, Clement Britt

AP Photo/University of Utah, Kathleen Morgan

AP Photo/Pablo Martinez Monsivais

Nominees Under Fire

Four Bush judicial nominees seen as the most controversial and conservative are Jeffrey Sutton, top left, a leading states' rights advocate, for the 6th U.S. Circuit of Appeals in Ohio; John Roberts Jr., top right, a conservative Washington lawyer who has represented mostly business interests in more than 30 arguments before the U.S. Supreme Court, for the appeals court for the District of Columbia; Michael McConnell, lower left, a University of Utah law professor and a conservative Christian who has argued successfully in cases favoring lowering church-state barriers, for the 10th Circuit Court of Appeals in Denver; and Miguel Estrada, lower right, a staunch conservative, for the Court of Appeals in Washington, D.C.

fends Sutton's role in the case. "Jeff Sutton simply wants Congress to abide by the Constitution's limitations on congressional power," he says.

McConnell similarly drew fire quickly over his Supreme Court ad-

vocacy from a liberal interest group: Americans United for Separation of Church and State. "He's a conservative Christian who's willing to use the force of government to impose his viewpoint," the Rev. Barry W. Lynn,

the group's executive director, said in a statement.

But Jipping says McConnell wants to return to an earlier, less restrictive view of the barriers between church and state. "The Constitution has been made to mean something very different in recent years than it did when it was enacted," he says.

Criticism of Roberts centers on his work as deputy solicitor general under Kenneth Starr at the end of the first Bush administration. Abortion-rights supporters cite, in particular, his work on a brief in a 1991 case, *Rust v. Sullivan*, which attacked the Supreme Court's recognition of a right to abortion.

Jipping says Roberts was "doing his job — advocating a position for his client, the government." But Kate Michelman, president of the National Abortion and Reproductive Rights Action League (NARAL), says Roberts "was there in the first Bush administration in part because his views were in sync with that administration's hostility to reproductive rights for women." [15]

Estrada is drawing scrutiny, but so far no overt opposition. Michelman says NARAL has concerns about his views, as do two organizations representing Hispanics: the Mexican American Legal Defense and Educational Fund (MALDEF) and the Puerto Rican Legal Defense and Education Fund. In a letter to senators, Juan Figueroa, president of the Puerto Rican group, said Estrada's reported conservative views suggest that he is "totally insensitive to the interests, views and concerns of Hispanics and other minorities in our nation." But Brigida Benitez, who chairs the endorsement committee of the Hispanic Bar Association of Washington, says her group met with Estrada and was "impressed with his professional experiences and achievement." [16]

In fact, Bush's initial nominees are faring well in evaluations of their qualifications from the very group that the

At Issue:

Should the Senate consider ideology in acting on judicial nominees?

SEN. CHARLES E. SCHUMER, D-N.Y.

FROM A STATEMENT BEFORE THE SENATE JUDICIARY SUBCOMMITTEE ON ADMINISTRATIVE OVERSIGHT AND THE COURTS, JUNE 26, 2001.

*t*he ideology of particular nominees often plays a significant role in the confirmation process. Unfortunately, knowing when and to what degree ideology should be a factor for the Senate is far more obscure.

For whatever reason, possibly senatorial fears of being labeled partisan, legitimate considerations of ideological beliefs seem to have been driven underground. It's not that we don't consider ideology; we just don't talk about it openly.

And, unfortunately, this unwillingness to openly examine ideology has sometimes led senators who oppose a nominee to seek out non-ideological disqualifying factors, like small financial improprieties from long ago, to justify their opposition. This, in turn, has led to an escalating war of gotcha politics that has warped the Senate's confirmation process and harmed the Senate's reputation.

This was not always the Senate's practice. During the first 100 years of the Republic, one out of every four nominees to the Supreme Court was rejected by the Senate, many for clear ideological reasons. George Washington's appointment of John Rutledge to be chief justice and President Polk's nomination of George Woodward are two early examples of the Senate rejecting nominees on purely ideological grounds.

The power of the Senate in the nominations process, has, however, been accordian-like, and from 1895 to 1967 only one Supreme Court nominee was defeated. Since 1968, ideological considerations have occasionally surfaced, notably in Republican opposition to the [Abe] Fortas nomination to be chief justice and in Democratic opposition to the nomination of Robert Bork.

But since the Bork fight in 1987, ideology, while still an important factor for the Senate, has primarily been considered sub-rosa, fostering a search for a nominee's disqualifiers that are more personal and less substantive.

It is high time we returned to a more open and rational consideration of ideology when we review nominees. Let's make our confirmation process more honest, more clear and hopefully more legitimate in the eyes of the American people. And let's be fair to the nominees the president picks.

This era, perhaps more than any other before, calls out for collaboration between the president and the Senate in judicial appointments. It certainly justifies Senate opposition to judicial nominees whose views fall outside the mainstream and who have been selected in an attempt to further tilt the courts in an ideological direction.

SEN. ORRIN G. HATCH, R-UTAH

FROM A STATEMENT BEFORE THE SENATE JUDICIARY SUBCOMMITTEE ON ADMINISTRATIVE OVERSIGHT AND THE COURTS, JUNE 26, 2001.

*t*he shift of power in the Senate has focused a great deal of attention on the Judiciary Committee and how it will handle the confirmation of President Bush's judicial nominees. I hope that this heightened focus proves to be unwarranted, and that the new Democratic majority will fairly treat President Bush's nominees to our federal courts. In particular, fair treatment includes maintaining the committee's longstanding policy against injecting political ideology into the judicial confirmation process, and thus into the federal judiciary.

There are myriad reasons why political ideology has not been, and is not, an appropriate measure of judicial qualifications. Fundamentally, the Senate's responsibility to provide advice and consent does not include an ideological litmus test because a nominee's personal opinions are largely irrelevant so long as the nominee can set those opinions aside and follow the law fairly and impartially as a judge.

In our constitutional scheme, it is the members of the legislative branch elected by the people and accountable to the people, who make our laws. When the voters do not like these laws, they can, and, as we know all too well, do, vote their elected representatives out of office. This is what makes our system a representative democracy, founded on our faith in self-government.

Federal judges, by contrast, are unelected, have life tenure and by design are not accountable to the people. Their power is nonetheless justified — indeed, indispensable — to the extent it is only exercised by interpreting the written, duly enacted law. The role of federal judges is, quite simply, to apply the written law, be it the Constitution or enacted legislation, to the case before them.

But when federal judges deviate from the written law, and decide cases based on their own policy preferences or views of what is just or right, they in effect make up laws of their own despite the lack of legitimate authority for doing so. When judges twist the language of legislation to enact the policies they prefer, they usurp the role of the legislature and destabilize the balance of power. Even worse, when they read their own preferences and political agenda into the Constitution, judges directly thwart the will of the people. And voters have no recourse.

As a result, entire spheres of policy-making are, in effect, ruled off-limits from the people's elected officials, and instead are usurped by imperial judges — all-knowing guardians of justice. This is judicial activism, and it represents a direct attack on the democratic principles that are central to our constitutional system.

Judges' Rulings Reflect President's Party

Judges appointed to U.S. courts of appeal by Democratic presidents are more likely to hand down rulings in non-routine cases that support liberal positions than judges appointed by Republicans.

Percentage of Rulings That Were Liberal

Appointing President	Civil Rights	Criminal Rights	Labor/ Economic
Bill Clinton (D)	61%	71%	59%
Jimmy Carter (D)	60	69	62
Other Democratic presidents	68	64	74
George Bush Sr. (R)	50	54	46
Ronald Reagan (R)	49	64	48
Other Republican presidents	49	64	48

Source: American Judicature Society, Judicature*, March/April 2001, p. 278.*

White House decided to cut out of pre-nomination screening: the ABA's Standing Committee on the Federal Judiciary. Asked for evaluations by the Senate Judiciary Committee, the ABA group gave unanimous "well-qualified" ratings — the highest evaluation — to several of the 11 nominees, including Estrada, McConnell, Owen, Parker and Roberts. Two others — Edith Brown Clement and Dennis Shedd — were rated well qualified by a majority of the committee. The others were rated "qualified"; a minority of the committee gave Sutton the "well-qualified" rating.

Legal Stakes

Federal law prohibits employment discrimination based on race and ethnicity, gender, religion or disability. But workers who win verdicts against employers have a tough time when their cases reach federal appeals courts, according to a new study of federal court statistics.

Federal appeals courts reversed 44 percent of trial victories by plaintiffs in employment-discrimination cases in a 10-year period covered by the study, 1988-1997. By contrast, only 6 percent of employer victories were reversed on appeal during the same period

"Employment-discrimination plaintiffs fare miserably on appeal," Cornell University law Professors Theodore Eisenberg and Stewart Schwab wrote in the study, paid for by two plaintiffs' law firms. The scholars said the figures — taken from caseload data from the Administrative Office of U.S. Courts — indicate a "double standard on appeal" against workers and in favor of employers in job-bias suits. [17]

Business lawyers discounted the findings. "A reversal of a plaintiff's verdict generally means that the trial court sent something to the jury that shouldn't have gone there in the first place," says Ann Reesman, a lawyer with the Equal Employment Advisory Council, an employers' legal-defense group. "That's not surprising at all."

Whatever the explanation, the pat-tern indicates the impact that the largely obscure corps of federal appellate judges can have on the lives of people who find themselves in the court system. "The courts of appeals have a lot of power," Kuntz of the Alliance for Justice explains. "The Supreme Court hears less than 1 percent of the cases that come before it. So the courts of appeals are in a sense mini-Supreme Courts for the states."

Plaintiffs' lawyers attending the June 16 news conference to release the study said they see no partisan pattern in rulings on employment-discrimination cases. "I would say there's no difference between judges appointed by Republican presidents and judges appointed by Democratic presidents," said Lynn Bernabei, a Washington attorney.

Other studies, however, do find measurable differences between Republican and Democratic appointees on the federal bench. Two studies published this spring in the American Judicature Society's magazine *Judicature* both found somewhat more liberal voting by judges named by Clinton than by Reagan or Bush appointees — although Clinton's judges were less liberal than those named by other Democratic presidents.

Both studies used common journalistic definitions of "liberal" to mean greater support for criminal defendants, for civil rights litigants and for workers or other economic "underdogs." On that basis, the study of decisions by district court judges from 1993 through 1998 found that Clinton appointees issued liberal rulings in 44 percent of cases compared with 39 percent for Bush judges, 36 percent for Reagan judges and 52 percent for Carter judges. The gap was somewhat comparable in each of three categories of cases: criminal, civil rights and labor/economic. [18]

An analysis of voting by appellate judges in decisions from 1993 through 1999 found a somewhat similar pattern. After excluding so-called "easy" cases in which appellate courts unanimously upheld lower court rulings, the authors found that Clinton judges had records more liberal than Reagan or Bush judges, comparable to Carter judges and less liberal than those of two other Democratic presidents, Lyndon Johnson or John F. Kennedy. [19] (*See chart, p. 58.*)

The University of Houston's Carp describes Bush's current nominees as "moderately conservative business types" more comparable to judges appointed by his father than those appointed by Reagan. Goldman agrees. "They're not the outspoken right-wing ideologues that the Democrats have been worried about," he says.

Jipping of the Free Congress Research and Education Foundation says the fight over the nominees comes down to an issue of judicial activism. "President Bush's judges, whether they're liberal or conservative, are committed to applying the law as it's written." The question, he adds, "is whether the people or judges run the country."

"I agree that the issue is whether we're going to have activist judges," Kuntz replies. "Bush has nominated a group of people many of whom have records that suggest conservative activism that is antithetical to the interests of ordinary Americans."

OUTLOOK

Retirement Watch

Television reporters and camera operators were out in force in front of the Supreme Court building early on June 29, the day after the justices had issued their final decisions for the term. The reason: Rumors were running rampant that one of the justices — perhaps Chief Justice William

H. Rehnquist — was set to announce his retirement.

No retirement came that day — or as of yet. But the Supreme Court retirement watch forms an important part of the backdrop for the current skirmishing over President Bush's judicial nominees.

The court's membership has been unchanged since 1994 — the second-longest period without a vacancy in U.S. history. The court issued a record percentage of 5-4 decisions in the past term: 26 one-vote rulings out of 79. A new appointment could substantially affect the balance of power on the court — and opposing interest groups and lawmakers recognize that many of the issues in that fight will be similar to those being aired today concerning Bush's nominees for lower federal courts.

Bush's appeals court nominations take on added significance from speculation that some of them may be in line for a Supreme Court vacancy — if not now, then sometime in the future. Seven of the current justices — all but Rehnquist and Sandra Day O'Connor — served on federal appeals courts immediately before their appointments to the high court. Attention has focused in particular on Estrada — who, the speculation goes, could become the first Hispanic Supreme Court justice.

Before any high court vacancy materializes, however, Bush has to contend with getting his nominees through the Democrat-controlled Senate. He also faces determined opposition from several interest groups and some skepticism from the public, according to recent polls.

A *Washington Post*-ABC News poll in early June found that a majority of those surveyed — 52 percent — thought federal judges nominated by President Bush would be "about right," but 30 percent thought they would be "too conservative." (Twelve percent said his judges would be "too liberal.") In a *New York Times*-CBS News poll later last month, a majority — 51

percent — said they would trust Senate Democrats more than Bush "to make the right decisions about who should sit on the U.S. Supreme Court." Thirty-seven percent said they would trust Bush more; 12 percent voiced no opinion. [20]

When asked whether any of Bush's nominees will be defeated, Neas of People for the American Way says yes. "And I would hope," he adds, "that such a defeat will send a signal that George W. Bush has to consult with the Democrats and moderate Republicans and has to do this right and that the American people are not going to let the right wing take over the entire federal judiciary."

Supporters of Bush's nominees appear resigned to a difficult confirmation process, with delays and perhaps some defeats likely. "It would probably be unrealistic to say that every one of Bush's nominees is going to be confirmed," says Stephens of People for Common Sense Courts. Jipping, of the Free Congress Research and Education Foundation, says he expects Democrats to "delay or deny hearings to as many of President Bush's nominees as possible."

Lafferty of the Traditional Values Coalition predicts "an incredible backlash if [Democrats] continue to play these kinds of games." But Neas thinks rejection of one or more Bush nominees could reduce frictions in the long run by forcing the White House to work more closely with senators of both parties.

"To have real bipartisanship, you have to have mutual respect," Neas says. "Right now, the Bush administration has shown nothing but contempt for the Democrats and moderate Republicans."

For his part, William and Mary's Gerhardt expects most of Bush's nominees to win confirmation — but only with difficulty. He nonetheless defends the trend toward more rigorous examination of judicial nominees' views.

"Most of these nominees will make it through, but they're going to make it through a crucible," Gerhardt says. "The process has become a very tough one. But a more honest process isn't necessarily a bad one."

Notes

[1] For background, see Kenneth Jost, "The Federal Judiciary," *The CQ Researcher*, March 13, 1998, pp. 217-240.

[2] For profiles, see *Legal Times*, May 14, 2001, pp. 17-21. See also *CQ Weekly*, May 12, 2001, pp. 1071-1074.

[3] *The New York Times*, March 11, 2001.

[4] Quoted in *The New York Times*, June 4, 2001, p. A13.

[5] For background, see Deborah J. Barrow, Gary Zuk and Gerard S. Gryski, *The Federal Judiciary and Institutional Change*, 1996.

[6] See Larry C. Berkson and Susan B. Carbon, *The United States Circuit Judge Nominating Commission: Its Members, Procedures and Candidates*, 1979; Alan Neff, *The United States District Judge Nominating Commissions: Their Members, Procedures and Candidates*, 1980. Both books were published by the American Judicature Society, which began advocating merit selection for judges with its founding in 1913.

[7] Sheldon Goldman, "Federal Judicial Recruitment," in John B. Gates and Charles A. Johnson (eds.), *The American Courts: A Critical Perspective*, 1991, p. 194.

[8] See Sheldon Goldman, *Picking Federal Judges: Lower Court Selection From Roosevelt Through Reagan*, 1997, pp. 307-319.

[9] See Sheldon Goldman, "Bush's Judicial Legacy: The Final Imprint," *Judicature*, April-May 1993, pp. 282-297. Goldman counted 53 confirmations in this article, but revised the figure in a later article to 66. See Sheldon Goldman, "Clinton's Judges: Summing Up the Legacy," *Judicature*, March-April 2001, p. 233.

[10] *Ibid.*, p. 227.

[11] See *The Wall Street Journal*, March 20, 2001, p. A24.

[12] See *The Washington Post*, Jan. 30, 2001, p. A8.

[13] For coverage, see *The New York Times*, March 23, 2001, p. A13; *The Washington Post*, March 23, 2001, p. A1.

[14] Quoted in *The New York Times*, May 1, 2001, p. A17.

[15] Quoted in *Legal Times*, June 4, 2001, p. 14.

[16] Quoted in *Legal Times*, June 25, 2001, p. 12.

[17] Theodore Eisenberg and Stewart J. Schwab, "Double Standard on Appeal: An Empirical Analysis of Employment Discrimination Cases in the U.S. Courts of Appeals," July 16, 2001 (available at www.findjustice.com).

[18] Robert A. Carp, Kenneth L. Manning and Ronald Stidham, "President Clinton's District Judges: 'Extreme Liberals' or Just Plain Moderates?" *Judicature*, March-April 2001, pp. 282-290.

[19] Susan B. Haire, Martha Anne Humphries and Donald R. Songer, "The Voting Behavior of Clinton's Courts of Appeals Appointees," *Judicature*, March-April 2001, pp. 274-281.

[20] See www.washingtonpost.com/onpolitics; *The New York Times*, June 21, 2001, p. A16. Both polls were based on nationwide telephone surveys of approximately 1,000 persons.

FOR MORE INFORMATION

Alliance for Justice, 11 Dupont Circle, N.W., 2nd floor, Washington, D.C. 20036; (202) 822-6070; www.afj.org. The alliance, formed in 1979, is a coalition of predominantly liberal organization interested in legal affairs.

American Judicature Society, The Opperman Center at Drake University, 2700 University Ave., Des Moines, IA 50311; (515) 271-2281; www.ajs.org. The society, formed in 1913, promotes the independence and impartiality of the judiciary and public education about court systems.

Judicial Selection Monitoring Project, Free Congress Research and Education Fund, 717 2nd St., N.E., Washington, D.C. 20002; (202) 546-3000; www.judicialselection.org. The conservative foundation's judicial selection project monitors the nomination and confirmation of federal judges.

National Center for State Courts, 300 Newport Ave., Williamsburg, Va. 23185-4147; (888) 450-0391; www.ncsconline.org. The independent center was formed in 1971 to provide leadership and service to state courts.

People for the American Way, 2000 M St., N.W., #400, Washington, D.C. 20036; (202) 467-4999; www.pfaw.org/pfaw/general. The liberal organization, formed in 1981, advocates on a range of civil rights and civil issues.

Bibliography

Selected Sources

Books

Barrow, Deborah J., Gary Zuk and Gerard S. Gryski, *The Federal Judiciary and Institutional Change*, University of Michigan Press, 1996.

The book traces the growth of the federal bench and its partisan makeup from the 19th century through the early 1990s. The book includes detailed source notes. Barrow is a lawyer in Marietta, Ga.; Zuk and Gryski are professors of political science at Auburn University.

Gates, John B., and Charles A. Johnson (eds.), *The American Courts: A Critical Assessment*, CQ Press, 1991.

The book's 18 essays include overviews of judicial policy-making by the Supreme Court, federal appeals courts, federal district courts, state supreme courts and state trial courts, and separate examinations of state and federal judicial recruitment. Each essay includes detailed lists of references.

Gerhardt, Michael, *The Federal Appointments Process: A Constitutional and Historical Analysis*, Duke University Press, 2000.

Gerhardt, a professor at William and Mary law school, closes this thorough overview of presidential appointments with a chapter discussing various proposals to revise procedures for nominating and confirming federal judges. The book includes detailed source notes.

Goldman, Sheldon, *Picking Federal Judges: Lower Court Selection From Roosevelt Through Reagan*, Yale University Press, 1997.

Goldman, a professor of political science at the University of Massachusetts at Amherst and long-time student of federal judicial selection, provides a detailed history of judicial nominations and confirmation politics from FDR through Reagan. The book includes detailed source notes.

Songer, Donald R.; Reginald S. Sheehan, and Susan B. Haire, *Continuity and Change on the United States Courts of Appeals*, University of Michigan Press, 2000.

The book provides an overview of the federal appeals courts' increasingly important policy-making role in the late 20th century. Songer is a professor of political science at the University of South Carolina, Sheehan an associate professor at Michigan State University, and Haire an assistant professor at the University of Georgia.

Surrency, Erwin C., *History of the Federal Courts*, Oceana, 1987.

The director emeritus of the law library at the University of Georgia School of Law outlines the history of the federal courts from the writing of the Judiciary Act of 1791 through the 1980s, including a short chapter on judicial nominations.

Articles

"Clinton's Judicial Legacy," *Judicature*, March-April 2001.

The symposium includes a series of five articles comprehensively examining President Clinton's judicial legacy following an introductory essay by Professors Sheldon Goldman and Elliot Slotnick. The separate articles include: "Clinton's Judges: Summing Up the Legacy," "Clinton and the Diversification of the Federal Judiciary," "The Clinton Clones: Ginsburg, Breyer and the Clinton Legacy," "The Voting Behavior of Clinton's Courts of Appeals Appointees," and "President Clinton's District Judges: 'Extreme Liberals' or Just Plain Moderates?"

Jost, Kenneth, "The Federal Judiciary," *The CQ Researcher*, March 13, 1998, pp. 217-240.

The report describes the growth of the federal courts through U.S. history and the then-current debate between President Clinton and the Republican-controlled Senate over judicial appointments.

Oliphant, Jim, "Tipping the Scales: Circuit by Circuit," *Legal Times*, May 14, 2001, p. 1.

The article closely examines the effect of President Bush's initial judicial nominations on the makeup of the respective federal appeals courts. The issue also includes informative profiles of each of the 11 nominees. The Washington-based weekly has provided thorough, ongoing coverage of the judicial nominations and confirmation proceedings.

Palmer, Elizabeth A., "For Bush's Judicial Nominees, a Tough Tribunal Awaits," *CQ Weekly*, April 28, 2001, pp. 898-902.

The article describes the political debates and maneuvering surrounding federal court appointments shortly before President Bush was expected to begin making nominations.

Reports and Studies

Martin, Joanne, "Merit Selection Commissions: What Do They Do? How Effective Are They?" American Bar Foundation, 1993.

The 69-page monograph describes the history of the use of nonpartisan judicial nominating commissions, which were in use in 33 states and the District of Columbia at the time of the report.

4 Redistricting Disputes

KENNETH JOST

Martin Frost knows redistricting. The long-time Democratic congressman from Dallas-Fort Worth helped state lawmakers draw a congressional districting map in the early 1990s that gave Democrats control of Texas' delegation in the U.S. House of Representatives for a decade. Critics called the artfully drawn map a blatant "gerrymander."

During the 2001-2002 redistricting cycle, Frost had a chance to really help Democrats — as leader of the party's efforts to reshape congressional districts across the country.

But last year, Texas Republicans decided it was time to teach Frost a lesson about redistricting he would never forget. Aided by two other redistricting pros from Texas — House Majority Leader Rep. Tom DeLay and President Bush's top political adviser, Karl Rove — they redrew congressional districts so artfully that GOP congressional candidates could win 22 of the state's 32 House seats this November. [1]

As for Frost, his once-safe 24th District was decimated, its loyal Democratic voters in Fort Worth's Hispanic and African-American neighborhoods dispersed. Frost decided his best bet to win a 14th term this year would be to move to another district. He set his sights on the new, east-of-Dallas 32nd District and Rep. Pete Sessions — a four-term, conservative incumbent. The campaign is likely to be one of the most expensive, closely watched House contests this fall.

Frost avoids accusing the Republi-

From *The CQ Researcher,*
March 12, 2004.

Democratic lawmakers from Texas, led by Sen. Leticia Van de Putte, display voter mail last summer opposing redistricting plans that could give Republicans 22 of the state's 32 House seats this November. Democratic lawmakers staged an exodus from the state last summer in an unsuccessful effort to block voting on the new boundaries. Redistricting normally occurs every 10 years, but Texas and Colorado Republicans regained control of their legislatures and decided to redistrict mid-decade.

cans of singling him out. "I think they were trying to eliminate as many Democrats as possible," he says. "I happened to be one of the many Democrats that they were targeting."

For his part, Sessions says he is "surprised" that Frost decided to run against him, but adds, "I welcome him, red carpet rolled out. It won't be easy." [2]

Frost is among more than a half-dozen House Democrats who were thrown into new districts against each other or against Republican incumbents or stripped of large segments of their old constituencies. Meanwhile, Republicans in several safe districts shed some of their voters to aid the party's chances in others.

What happened in Texas could determine whether the Democrats regain control of the House next year. The new Texas map (*see p. 78*) could shift the state's House delegation from its

current 16-16 partisan balance to a GOP margin as wide as 22-10. A six- or seven-vote pickup for the Republicans would all but dash Democrats' already slim hope of regaining control of the House in November.

Republicans make no secret of their partisan motivations, but insist they were merely trying to bring the state's congressional delegation into line with Republican dominance throughout the state.

"We increased the number of Republican-opportunity districts to reflect the voting trend in the state of Texas," says Andy Taylor, a Houston attorney who represents the state in defending the redistricting plan in federal court. "We undid a Democratic gerrymander instead of creating a Republican gerrymander. We brought balance back to the districts because of the partisan shift in the way Texas voters vote."

But Democrats insist the GOP plan is indeed a partisan gerrymander and should be struck down. "The sole motivation of the Texas plan was to maximize partisan advantage, to discriminate against nearly half of the voters on the basis of their political affiliation," says Sam Hirsch, a Washington attorney representing Democrats challenging the plan. "This map is designed to lock down 22 out of 32 seats for the Republicans for the rest of the decade."

The bitter redistricting fight came after most observers thought the rough-and-tumble game of redrawing congressional district maps — which normally occurs every 10 years after a new census is released — was over until 2011. [3] But after gaining control of their state legislatures in 2002, Republicans in Texas and Colorado de-

GOP-Drawn Map Threatens Texas Democrats

Texas' new congressional redistricting plan, adopted by a Republican-controlled legislature, put 10 incumbent House Democrats in new, politically less favorable districts. One Democrat decided not to seek re-election, and another switched parties; the others are all running for new terms.

Democratic U.S. House member	Term	New political situation
Martin Frost	13th	Old Dallas-Fort Worth district carved up; seeking re-election in new 32nd District against four-term Republican.
Charles W. Stenholm	13th	Senior Agriculture Committee member lost two-thirds of his old Central/West Texas district; running against freshman Republican in 69 percent GOP district.
Ralph M. Hall	12th	Longtime conservative switched to GOP after more Republicans added to East Texas district.
Chet Edwards	7th	Lost major parts of his Central Texas district; new district is 64 percent GOP.
Gene Green	6th	Anglo representing Hispanic-majority Houston district; new district more Hispanic; ran unopposed for renomination in March 9 primary.
Lloyd Doggett	5th	Liberal representative from Austin; new district, heavily Hispanic, stretches to Mexican border; easily won renomination over Hispanic opponent in March 9 primary.
Max Sandlin	4th	East Texas district is 63 percent Republican, with 40 percent of previous constituency.
Jim Turner	4th	Old district virtually eliminated; Turner decided not to run.
Nick Lampson	4th	Lost major parts of his Houston suburban district.
Chris Bell	1st	White freshman elected from mixed Houston district redrawn into majority-black district; Bell lost bid for renomination against black opponent in March 9 primary.

Source: Politics in America 2004 *(CQ Press)*

Legislators Redraw Most Congressional Districts

In 40 states, the legislature or governor redraws new district lines, but the legislators have the final say. In three states, redistricting panels draw the maps and submit them to the legislatures for approval.* In seven states, special commissions control both drawing and approving the maps. Seven low-population states have only one congressional district, so they do not regularly go through the process. ** A significantly larger number of states use independent commissions to redraw state legislative district lines.

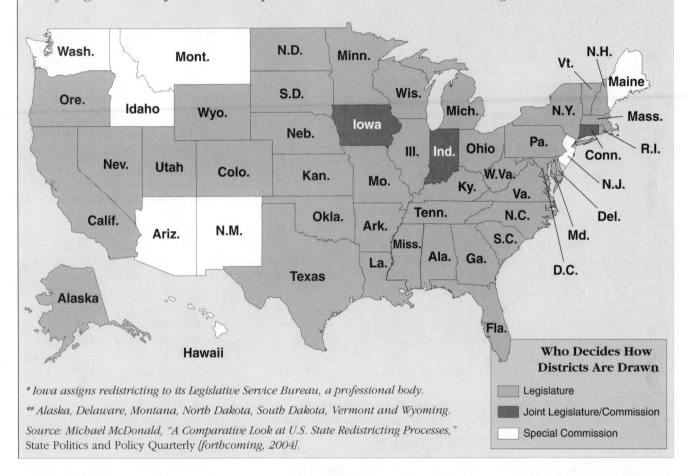

Who Decides How Districts Are Drawn

- Legislature
- Joint Legislature/Commission
- Special Commission

* Iowa assigns redistricting to its Legislative Service Bureau, a professional body.

** Alaska, Delaware, Montana, North Dakota, South Dakota, Vermont and Wyoming.

Source: Michael McDonald, *"A Comparative Look at U.S. State Redistricting Processes,"* State Politics and Policy Quarterly *[forthcoming, 2004].*

---

cided to revisit the task anew. GOP leaders in both states insisted they acted because their legislatures had deadlocked on redistricting in 2001, forcing courts to draw the districting plans used in the 2002 elections.

The unusual maneuver prompted Democrats — and many political observers — to say that redistricting is, or should be, allowed only once every 10 years. But Republicans and some academic experts say the Constitution's command to reapportion House seats among the states every 10 years based on census revisions does not limit redistricting to once per decade. Moreover, they say, mid-cycle remappings are more frequent than critics acknowledge.

One thing is certain: Redistricting can mean political life or death.

"It's no secret why everybody fights so hard," says Mark Braden, a Washington attorney for the Republican National Committee. "How you draw the lines has a huge impact on who sits in legislative chambers."

"You can devise districts in such a way that you can not only predict the outcome of the next election but also how they're going to perform in a series of elections over a decade," says Gerald Hebert, a Washington-area lawyer for Democrats. "You can actually rig elections in such a way that you can produce an electoral outcome almost regardless of what happens on Election Day."

Fights over redistricting date back to the nation's earliest days, but they have become more complex since the Supreme Court launched the reapportionment revolution in the 1960s, requiring the states to draw congressional and legislative districts with roughly equal populations. The high court introduced a new measure of complexity in the 1990s by limiting the use of race to create districts with majority-black or Hispanic populations. (*See box, p. 68.*)

Now the court is considering a constitutional challenge that could fundamentally alter redistricting. Pennsylvania Democrats argue the Republican-written congressional redistricting plan is unconstitutional because it gerrymanders on political — rather than population or racial — grounds. Republicans gained a 12-7 majority in Pennsylvania's congressional delegation under the new map. The court heard arguments in the case on Dec. 10, 2003. The case is *Vieth v. Jubelirer*, 02-1580.

Meanwhile, courts in Colorado and Texas were asked to announce a "once-per-decade" rule to strike down the new GOP redistricting plans. Democrats won in Colorado but failed with a similar argument in Texas. Democrats are appealing to the Supreme Court, but the justices refused to issue a stay — meaning the new map will be used for the Nov. 2 elections.

Political map-drawing is all the more intense today because of computers. "Partisan gerrymandering is becoming easier because of the sophistication of the technology," says Nathaniel Persily, a law professor and redistricting expert at the University of Pennsylvania. Using detailed census maps with racial and ethnic breakdowns and past election results, redistricters can customize a district neighborhood by neighborhood — even block by block.

Moreover, Persily says, "partisan preferences are more stable" today. Predictable voting patterns allow redistricters to use two common techniques for partisan advantage. "Packing" a rival party's voters into overly safe districts gives one's own party a better shot in others, while "cracking" a rival party's voters — dispersing them into several districts — can make the targeted district politically competitive for the party drawing the lines.

Some citizens' groups — such as Common Cause and the League of Women Voters — say that if independent bodies redrew the maps, partisan wrangling would be reduced and political competition enhanced. The Center for Voting and Democracy, in Takoma Park, Md., advocates replacing the single-member, winner-take-all system of congressional and legislative districts with some form of proportional or cumulative voting in multimember districts. Although voters would probably show little interest, politicians would probably adamantly resist either change. (*See sidebar, p. 67.*)

Meanwhile, some academics say redistricting is not really a big problem. "The political system does recover," says Mark Rush, a professor of political science at Washington and Lee University in Lexington, Va. Over time, voting behavior changes, incumbents retire and new candidates emerge, he says. "Elections go back and forth. The system works."

As redistricting cases work their way through the courts, and redistricting issues continue to divide political parties, here are some of the major questions being debated:

Should states redraw congressional district lines in the middle of a decade?

When Colorado's legislature deadlocked on a congressional redistricting plan in 2002, a federal court redrew the maps that were used for the seven House races that November. The result was a GOP-controlled legislature, and in May 2003 it adopted a new plan that favored Republicans in two politically competitive districts.

Democrats sued, complaining that both federal and state constitutions — as well as established political custom — limit redistricting to once a decade following the federal census. In December 2003, the Colorado Supreme Court agreed and threw out the new plan.

But Colorado appears to be one of only about a dozen states with such prohibitions. The Texas constitution limits legislative — but not congressional — redistricting to the session following a census. Constitutional or statutory redistricting provisions in other states are either silent or ambiguous on mid-decade enactments.

The U.S. Constitution requires that House seats be reapportioned among the states after the census. But neither the Constitution nor federal law explicitly says when congressional maps can be — or must be — redrawn.

Republicans in both Colorado and Texas insist they were merely fulfilling their constitutional responsibilities in order to replace court-crafted plans following the earlier legislative deadlock. "The legislature hadn't done its job this decade," says Texas attorney Taylor. "It fell to a federal court, and that court created a plan that we believe was a simple interim solution, not one designed for the remainder of the decade."

Hirsch, the Democrats' lawyer, counters that a redistricting plan approved at the start of a decade should be retained, whether adopted by the legislature or by a court. "If you redistrict more often, you're taking away [voters'] chance to vote for incumbents who've served them well — or against incumbents who've served them poorly," he says.

Many academic experts say successive redistrictings serve no purpose other than the partisan interests of the majority party. "No one in his right mind believes there's a good reason to do mid-decade redistricting except for political gain," says Bernard Grofman, a professor of political science at the University of California, Irvine.

"Redistricting occupies a lot of resources, it engenders litigation — all at taxpayer expense," Rush says. "The taxpayers' coffers are being drained to allow incumbents of one party to put incumbents of the other party out of business."

Reformers Target 'Winner-Take-All' System

About 40 percent of the population in Amarillo, Texas, is African-American or Latino, but during the 1990s no black or Hispanic sat on the school board.

To help minority groups elect a candidate of their choice, the League of United Latin American Citizens (LULAC) and the NAACP jointly filed a federal court suit asking to replace the system of at-large elections with single-member districts.

In a settlement with the Amarillo Independent School District, however, the two groups agreed instead to a different system known as cumulative voting, which allows voters in a multi-office election to cast multiple votes in any combination. For example, in an election for four school board seats, a voter could spread four votes among four candidates or cast all four for the same candidate.

The new system produced the hoped-for results. An African-American and a Hispanic won two of the four seats being filled in the first cumulative-voting election for the seven-member board, held in May 2000. Many voters had cast multiple votes for their respective minority candidates to enable them to win.

"The fact that we got two minorities on the board is awesome," said Nancy Bosquez, a local LULAC leader. "History was made in Amarillo." [1]

Amarillo's experience is often cited by the small number of academic experts and political reformers who want to replace the predominant use of single-member districts and winner-take-all elections for multimember bodies with some form of so-called limit voting designed to enhance representation for political, racial or ethnic minorities.

"Winner-take-all is horse-and-buggy technology," says Steven Hill, Western regional director of the Center for Voting and Democracy. "One side wins all the representation; the other side wins nothing."

Cumulative voting is one of three election systems suggested by reformers as alternatives to winner-take-all, according to Richard Engstrom, a professor of political science at the University of New Orleans. [2] Often imprecisely labeled "proportional representation," the proposed systems differ from those used in Israel and Europe, which allot parliamentary seats to party candidates in mathematical proportion to the party's overall vote. Rather, the U.S. reformers' methods would still focus on individual candidates, but change the methods of casting and counting votes.

Cumulative voting would give cohesive minority groups a chance to aggregate their votes for a select number of candidates. A second, less common method — known as limited voting — would allow voters to vote for fewer candidates than the total number of positions at stake, thus preventing a majority from taking every seat in a multimember election by eliminating the "sweep effect." A voter might get three votes, for example, if four seats are being filled.

A third, more complicated system, known as preference vot-

ing, would allow voters to write in a specified number of candidates in order of preference. After an initial tally of the first-preference votes, one or more candidates are eliminated, and the ballots for those candidates are redistributed according to the voters' second preferences. The counting continues until the number of candidates remaining equals the number of seats being filled.

Besides beefing up minority representation, Hill and Engstrom say, the alternatives avoid some of the redistricting problems experienced today. "Alternative election systems take the emphasis off the lines," Engstrom explains.

Some critics say the proposals are too complex, but Engstrom says, "There's nothing all that complicated. That's largely a red herring."

In Amarillo at least, voters appear satisfied. "It's a new system, and it takes some explaining, but we haven't had any resistance to it," Amarillo Assistant School Superintendent Les Hoyt remarked recently. [3]

Cumulative or limited voting has been instituted in 100 communities, according to Engstrom — typically in response to minority groups' suits brought under the federal Voting Rights Act. But Hill says the benefits go beyond minority representation: The alternatives would improve campaign discourse and increase political participation.

Winner-take-all encourages "negative campaigning," Hill says, because candidates are as interested in driving voters away from a rival as attracting voters to themselves. The alternative systems require candidates to "define themselves more precisely," he says.

Alternative systems would also increase turnout, he says, because they would increase competition. "All voters are swing voters, instead of a small select number of voters," he says.

But so far the proposals are only blips on the nation's political radar screen. A bill sponsored by Rep. Melvin Watt, D-N.C., in 1999 would have allowed states to choose House members from multimember districts with alternative voting arrangements. Watt, the African-American candidate elected from the majority-black district that was the focus of the Supreme Court's first ruling on racial redistricting in 1993, got a hearing on the bill, but it advanced no further. [4]

---

[1] Sonny Bohanan, "Voting System Lauded," *The* (Amarillo) *Globe-News*, May 8, 2000. The seven-member board now includes two Hispanics and one African-American.

[2] See Richard L. Engstrom, "The Political Thicket, Electoral Reform, and Minority Voting Rights," pp. 36-44, in Mark E. Rush and Richard L. Engstrom, *Fair and Effective Representation? Debating Electoral Reform and Minority Rights* (2001).

[3] Quoted in Zeke MacCormack, "Like a Candidate? Vote for Him Twice," *San Antonio Express-News*, May 1, 2003, p. 1B.

[4] See Engstrom, *op. cit.*, pp. 51-52.

"Reapportionment and redistricting are done every 10 years," says Paul Herrnson, director of the Center for American Politics and Citizenship at the University of Maryland, College Park. "That is the written law and a norm, practiced for a very long time."

Herrnson acknowledges that legislatures occasionally redraw maps mid-

Court Redistricting Decisions Affecting Race

The Supreme Court issued a series of decisions beginning in 1993 limiting states' ability to consider race in drawing majority-minority congressional and legislative districts.

Case	Date of Vote	Vote

***Shaw v. Reno*, 509 U.S. 630 (1993); 5-4** — White voters were allowed to challenge a highly irregular-shaped congressional district under the Constitution's Equal Protection Clause as an effort to separate voters by race; the challenge to North Carolina's majority-black 12th District was sent back to the lower court for trial.

***Miller v. Johnson*, 515 U.S. 900 (1995); 5-4** — Use of race as predominant factor in drawing voting-district lines can be upheld only if it serves a compelling government interest and is narrowly tailored to serve that interest; the ruling struck down a Georgia plan with three majority-black districts.

***Bush v. Vera*, 517 U.S. 952 (1996); 5-4** — Three majority-minority congressional districts in Texas were ordered redrawn because they were primarily motivated by race and not justified by legitimate state interests; in a fractured decision, majority of justices nevertheless said states can deliberately create majority-minority districts in some circumstances.

***Shaw v. Hunt*, 517 U.S. 899 (1996); 5-4** — North Carolina's 12th District was ruled unconstitutional because it was racially motivated and not justified by state interests; state responded by redrawing a more compact district with 47 percent black population; in new challenge, a three-judge court ruled the redrawn district was unconstitutional without full trial.

***Hunt v. Cromartie*, 526 U.S. 541 (1999); 9-0** — Federal court must hold a trial in racial gerrymandering case if the state's motivation for creating a challenged districting plan is in dispute; ruling sent challenge to North Carolina's redrawn 12th District back to lower court for full trial.

***Easley v. Cromartie*, 532 U.S. 234 (2001); 5-4** — Redistricting plan challenged on racial grounds must be upheld unless plaintiffs show state had ways to achieve legitimate political objectives with significantly greater racial balance; decision upheld North Carolina's redrawn 12th District.

***Georgia v. Ashcroft*, 539 U.S.___ (2003); 5-4** — States can reduce the number of blacks in majority-minority districts if they offset the reduced voting strength with gains in minority groups' political influence elsewhere; ruling sent challenge to redistricting plan for Georgia Senate back for trial on other issues; three-judge court in February 2004 ruled plan invalid because of excessive population deviations between districts.

Source: Supreme Court Collection, *CQ Press*

decade after a court strikes down lawmakers' first attempt. "What's taken place in Colorado and Texas goes beyond that," he says. "Basically, it's a power grab."

GOP lawmakers in Texas, however, insist they were merely bringing district lines into conformity with the state's predominantly Republican voting pattern. "We tried to make it consistent with general voting patterns," says state Rep. Phil King, R-Weatherford. "We took it from 15 seats to maybe 19, 20, or 21 or 22. That's a long way from a coup."

Grofman scoffs. "The Republican plan will exaggerate the extent to which Texas is a Republican state rather than mirror the politics of the state," he says.

Hebert, the Democrats' lawyer, says the Constitution envisions congressional lines being redrawn only in conjunction with reapportionment of House seats after the decennial census. "The Census Clause makes it pretty clear that the Framers intended for the House to be electorally stable," he says.

"There's no rule against it," counters GOP lawyer Braden. "Maybe there should be, but there isn't."

Academic opinion — even among critics of mid-decade redistricting — appears to side with the Republicans. "It makes sense to have it once a decade, but it's clear that there's no legal rule against it in most states," says Michael McDonald, a professor of government and politics at George Mason University, in Fairfax, Va.

And there's nothing in the Constitution about redistricting at all, Persily notes. "The Constitution does not mandate how the states draw district lines at all."

Democrats plan to press their argument by appealing the Texas decision to the U.S. Supreme Court. Declaring that redistricting should occur only once a decade is "one thing the court could do if it is looking for some clear way to put some brakes on the redistricting process — which has gone completely haywire," Hebert says. Braden notes that Congress also could limit congressional redistricting to once a decade.

But Taylor insists public disapproval is enough to deter legislators from successive redistrictings. "Public sentiment is a sufficient check and balance on the legislative redistricting front," the GOP lawyer says. "If voters don't think state legislatures should be changing districts, they'll let them know, either before or after."

Should courts limit partisan gerrymandering?

After Republicans gained control of both houses of the Pennsylvania legislature in 2000, they began drawing new congressional districts, cutting two districts to reflect declining statewide population. The GOP-crafted plan maximized the party's advantages. It paired Democratic incumbents in three redrawn districts — forcing them to fight against each other. It also put another Democratic incumbent in a district drawn to favor a senior Republican House member, and created two new open seats favorably situated for up-and-coming GOP state senators.

The strategy paid off. The state's congressional delegation shifted from a narrow 11-10 Republican majority in 2000 to a lopsided 12-7 edge for the GOP in 2002.

The Pennsylvania shift, combined with Republican gains from another GOP-drawn redistricting plan in Michigan, helped the Republicans pick up six additional House seats — an unusual midterm gain for a party controlling the White House.

Democrats complained in federal court that by "packing" Democratic voters into Democratic districts, the Republicans locked in a GOP advantage in most districts, regardless of any partisan shift in the statewide population.

"Republican votes count twice as much as a Democrat's vote," says Hirsch, one of the attorneys for Pennsylvania Democrats in the case now before the U.S. Supreme Court. In House races, he contends, "We Democrats could capture a majority of the

votes, [but] Republicans would get two-thirds of the seats."

Republicans counter that the new map simply reflects a statewide trend toward the GOP. The state has two Republican senators although it has voted Democratic in the past three presidential elections. [4]

"The state itself was becoming more Republican," says John Krill, a Harrisburg attorney for the Republicans. The predominantly Democratic cities of Philadelphia and Pittsburgh have lost population, and people have moved into Republican areas, such as

The term gerrymander was coined after Massachusetts Gov. Elbridge Gerry approved an irregularly shaped legislative district in 1812 that a critic said resembled "a salamander;" another critic promptly dubbed it "a gerrymander." This cartoon-map first appeared in the Boston Gazette on March 26, 1812.

central Pennsylvania, he says. "The legislature [had to accommodate] very significant demographic shifts."

Democrats have asked the high court to breathe life into a 1986 decision, *Davis v. Bandemer*, which allowed federal challenges to political gerrymandering. [5] A redistricting scheme could be unconstitutional if it caused "continued frustration of the will of a majority of the voters or effective denial to a minority of

voters of a fair chance to influence the political process," Justice Byron R. White wrote in the main opinion.

"The standard is very hard to meet," says Washington and Lee's Rush. In fact, the Supreme Court upheld, 7-2, the Indiana congressional redistricting plan at issue in the case. Since then, no federal court has used the *Davis v. Bandemer* case to strike down a legislative or congressional redistricting plan. [6]

Critics of gerrymandering hope the Supreme Court will use the Pennsylvania case to establish a new standard that challengers could more readily meet. The Pennsylvania Democrats say a plan drawn by one party should be held unconstitutional if "the rival party's candidates could be consigned to fewer than half the seats even if its candidates consistently won a majority of votes statewide."

Grofman endorses the Democrats' test. "It's a gerrymander when an even split always means one party wins," he says.

Somewhat oddly, Republicans at the national level are not averse to the court limiting partisan gerrymandering. Attorney Braden says he is "sympathetic" to the goal of getting "useful" standards from *Bandemer* and suggests a plan be struck down if the lines are "totally lacking in legitimate state interests."

Some experts, however, caution against judicial intervention in gerrymandering disputes. "There is a real risk that it will seriously affect the integrity of the judiciary," Persily says. Courts "are going to be in this incredible position of having to decide . . . which representatives live and die," he continues. "It would make confirmation fights more difficult, and it would reduce somewhat the impression of an impartial judiciary."

Rush says courts should avoid partisan gerrymandering disputes because — in contrast to racial lines in redistricting cases — voting patterns and voting behavior are inherently change-able. "History indicates that the damage done by a partisan gerrymander simply is not as clear as critics suggest," Rush says. For example, within a few years after Indiana Democrats failed to overturn the GOP-crafted redistricting plan challenged in *Bandemer*, the Democrats had regained a majority of the state's congressional delegation, he notes.

Critics of partisan gerrymandering are doubtful about the outcome of the Pennsylvania case. "It's clear from the questions of the justices that they were searching for a standard, and they can't find one," Grofman says.

Krill urged the justices to flatly over-rule *Bandemer*. "Any extreme attempts at partisan redistricting are self-cor-recting," he says, "sometimes in a very short time."

If the court chooses not to limit partisan gerrymandering, Congress could establish new redistricting standards. Congress passed a law in 1901 requiring "contiguous and compact" House districts but it lapsed after 1929.

Should states use nonpartisan or bipartisan bodies to oversee redistricting?

Arizona voters in 2000 approved creation of an independent, five-member, bipartisan commission to draw congressional and state legislative district lines that would encourage competitive political contests.

In January, however, Maricopa County Superior Court Judge Kenneth Fields agreed with Hispanic plaintiffs that the commission had hampered political competition by packing Hispanic voters into Democratic districts, thus giving Republicans too much of an edge elsewhere. [7]

The episode illustrates the difficulty of objective redistricting. Good-government groups — such as Common Cause and the League of Women Voters, which promoted the Arizona initiative — earnestly call for nonpartisan or bipartisan bodies to take the politics out of the process.

Many academic experts agree. Nonpartisan bodies "remove the prima facie basis for challenging a redistricting plan as being predatory," Washington and Lee's Rush says.

"Incumbents are looking to benefit themselves, and their parties are looking for partisan advantage," says the University of Maryland's Herrnson, who calls himself "a big fan" of using commissions.

But others insist that neutrality is simply unattainable in such an inherently partisan undertaking. "You can't just give off to technicians the responsibility for a plan," says the University of California's Grofman. "Any plan involves trade-offs. These are political questions, not purely technical matters."

Currently, 21 states use bipartisan or nonpartisan bodies for either congressional or legislative redistricting. Iowa assigns the task to its professional Legislative Service Bureau. The others use special bipartisan commissions. Typically, commission members include the attorney general, secretary of state or other government officials, or members appointed by the governor or legislative leaders.

The Arizona measure aimed to minimize partisan influence by using a judicial-appointments body to select a pool of potential commission members. Republican and Democratic legislative leaders appoint two members each from the pool. The fifth member is then chosen by the other four.

In some states, commissions propose districting maps for the legislature to consider; in others, the commission itself is the decision-making body. In Florida and Kansas, lawmakers submit a plan to the state supreme court, which can approve it or draw its own.

Iowa is often cited as proof that politics can be removed from the redistricting process. Four out of Iowa's five congressional districts are potentially competitive — a much higher percentage than in other states. "If you believe in representation and ac-countability, and that political competition leads to that, that's hard not to notice," Herrnson says.

Other experts, however, note that the Iowa legislature has thrice rejected redistricting maps drawn by the professional staff. They also say the Iowa system's relative success stems mostly from the state's somewhat less partisan political culture. "Nothing about the institutional form insulates it from partisan pressures," says Persily, at the University of Pennsylvania. "If you transfer that to New York, it wouldn't be nonpartisan."

Iowa does not have the same kind of racial and ethnic diversity that creates problems in other states, says McDonald, who supports the commission approach. "Iowa is like white bread," he says. "It doesn't matter how you slice it; you get back Iowa."

Elsewhere, commissions either split along party lines and produce a plan that favors the dominant party or reach a "compromise" favorable to both parties. "They tend to behave just like legislatures," Persily says.

GOP attorney Braden is dubious about reform proposals. "Bipartisan commissions are possible," he says, "but they've not been notoriously successful. It's a tricky matter to make it work. Some good intentions have been disasters."

Democratic lawyer Hebert, however, says independent bodies "ultimately are the solution," if they are truly nonpartisan. "It's an idea that needs to be studied."

BACKGROUND

Political Conflicts

In structuring the new national legislature, the Framers of the Constitution crafted a compromise to bal-

Chronology

Before 1960

Reapportionment and redistricting engender political conflicts; Congress and Supreme Court leave issues mostly to states.

1787

Constitution requires House of Representatives to reapportion seats following decennial censuses.

1842, 1872, 1901

Congress requires single-member, contiguous districts for House seats; subsequent versions require districts to be nearly equal in population (1872) and "compact" (1901). House declines to void elections for violations; law lapses after 1929.

1946

Supreme Court declines to nullify Illinois' malapportioned congressional districts; main opinion says court should stay out of "political thicket" of redistricting.

1950s

Cities, suburbs gain population, but most states fail to redraw districts to reflect shift.

1960s *Supreme Court launches reapportionment revolution; states forced to redraw legislative, congressional districts, shifting power to cities and suburbs.*

1962

Supreme Court rules that redistricting challenges are "justiciable" in federal courts (*Baker v. Carr*).

1963, 1964

Supreme Court establishes equal-population requirement — "one person, one vote" — for congressional districts and state legislatures.

1970s-1980s

Redistricting becomes routine, along with court challenges; partisan maneuvering, incumbent protection are dominant considerations.

1983

Supreme Court limits population deviations for congressional districts unless required for legitimate state interests.

1986

High court opens door slightly to federal court challenges to partisan gerrymandering (*Davis v. Bandemer*); separately, court sets standards for "minority vote dilution" cases under federal Voting Rights Act.

1990s *Supreme Court limits use of race in redistricting.*

1993

In *Shaw v. Reno*, Supreme Court rules that white voters can challenge the use of race to create "majority-minority" districts.

1995, 1996

Supreme Court tightens strictures on racial redistricting in cases from Georgia, Texas.

2000-Present

With Republican gains, partisan conflicts over redistricting intensify.

2001-2002

Democrats redraw congressional districts in Georgia to their advantage; Republicans do the same in Michigan, Pennsylvania; lesser partisan shifts approved in other states; Democrats challenge Pennsylvania plan as unconstitutional partisan gerrymander.

November 2002

Redistricting helps Republicans pick up seats in U.S. House; GOP also gains in gubernatorial and state legislative contests.

May 2003

GOP-controlled Colorado state legislature adopts new congressional map to replace court-drawn plan; Democrats file state, federal challenges.

October 2003

Texas legislature, controlled by Republicans, ends months of partisan rancor by approving new congressional map aimed to give Republicans 20-22 out of 32 House seats; Democrats challenge plan in federal court.

December 2003

Colorado Supreme Court bars second-in-decade redistricting on state constitutional grounds (Dec. 1) . . . U.S. Supreme Court hears arguments in Pennsylvania case on constitutional limits to partisan gerrymandering (*Vieth v. Jubelirer*, Dec. 10); decision expected by June 2004.

2004

Three-judge federal court rejects challenge to Texas' second-in-decade congressional redistricting (*Sessions v. Perry*, Jan. 6); Supreme Court refuses to stay ruling, allowing the plan to be used in the Nov. 2 elections.

Racial, Ethnic Politics Complicate Redistricting

Reps. Howard L. Berman and Brad Sherman represent adjoining congressional districts in Los Angeles County's San Fernando Valley, an area with a rapidly growing Hispanic population. The two Anglo Democrats back Latino positions on such issues as immigration and regularly receive Hispanic support in elections.

When it came time to redraw California's congressional map after the 2000 census, however, neither Berman nor Sherman wanted to have too many Latinos in his district — for fear of a successful challenge from a Latino opponent. Fortunately for Berman, the state's Democratic lawmakers had entrusted the task of redrawing congressional districts to his brother Michael, a behind-the-scenes force in the powerful local Democratic machine.

The new map, approved by the state legislature in September 2001 with support from most Latino lawmakers, shifted enough Hispanics out of Berman's district to protect him from a potential Latino rival. But Sherman, who now had double the number of Latino registered voters in his district, opposed the plan, although it still left Latinos far short of the numbers required to threaten him. [1]

The Mexican American Legal Defense and Educational Fund (MALDEF) challenged the configuration in court, arguing that the legislature deliberately fragmented Latino voters, creating "vote dilution" prohibited by the federal Voting Rights Act. MALDEF charged that the legislature had violated the act by removing thousands of Latino voters from Berman's district and placing them in Sherman's.

A three-judge federal court rejected the suit on the ground that Anglo prejudice against Latino candidates has diminished in recent years. "Whites and other non-Latinos are currently far more willing to support Latino candidates for office than in the past," the court ruled. [2]

The episode illustrates some of the complexities of racial and ethnic politics in the redistricting process, especially as it affects the nation's two largest minorities: Hispanics and African-Americans. Race-conscious redistricting in the 1990s contributed to a marked increase in blacks and Hispanics elected to the House. But a series of Supreme Court decisions now limits state legislatures' discretion to create so-called majority-minority districts. [3]

Meanwhile, the partisan implications of racial redistricting have become more evident. For Republicans, creating majority-minority districts can help GOP prospects in other districts with reduced minority voting strength. For Democrats, while the strategy helps elect African-Americans and Hispanics, it can put Anglo incumbents at risk — either from minority challengers in districts with concentrated minority populations or from Republican opponents in districts with fewer minority voters.

In Texas, partisan maneuvering meant that neither of the major parties supported Latino groups' call for an additional Latino majority district in South and West Texas. A Republican-drawn map reduced the Latino voting-age population in one district — the 23rd — below 50 percent to safeguard incumbent Republican Henry Bonilla. The five-term Hispanic Republican depended on Anglo votes to narrowly beat a Hispanic Democrat in 2002.

Democrats opposed the GOP-drawn map as a partisan gerrymander, but did not support the call for a new Latino district. Instead, they focused on line drawing elsewhere that put Anglo Democrats' political fortunes in jeopardy.

"In this round of redistricting, there was less willingness to create Latino-majority districts and little support from either political party to do it," says Nina Perales, a MALDEF regional counsel in San Antonio. "In terms of the redistricting struggle, there are Re-

ance the interests of large and small states. Congress was to consist of a Senate, with two members from each state, and a House of Representatives, with each state allotted a number of representatives tied to its population. Although the plan eased the way for ratification of the Constitution, it also set the stage for recurrent political conflicts over reapportionment and redistricting. [8]

Article I, Section 2, initially allocated 65 representatives among the 13 original states and required population-based reapportionment "within every subsequent term of ten years" — now done after each decennial census. However, the Constitution con-

tained no instructions about how states were to draw congressional districts — or even whether districts were required at all.

Nevertheless, the Framers apparently envisioned the division of states into congressional districts with equal population. In *The Federalist Papers No. 57*, for example, James Madison said each representative "will be elected by five or six thousand citizens." In the absence of a specific requirement, however, the states adopted varying practices. Six states elected representatives by districts, while five used at-large elections. Delaware and Rhode Island each were allotted only a single House member. [9]

More than a century of trial-and-error produced the current system of apportioning representatives among the states. Debates swirled around the size of the House and the method of allocating seats among states, given the inevitability of "fractional remainders" — the leftover fraction when a state's population is divided by the population of an ideal-size district. [10]

At first, leftover fractions were disregarded (1790–1830). A method used only in 1840 allotted an additional seat to any state with a surplus fraction greater than one-half the size of the ideal district. From 1850–1900, a new plan specified the size of the House

publicans, there are Democrats and there are Latinos. And our interests don't line up with either of the other two groups."

The push to create majority-minority districts began during the administration of the first President George Bush. The Justice Department interpreted the Voting Rights Act to require states to draw districts with majority-black populations wherever feasible. To comply, some Southern states — with Democratic-controlled legislatures — created bizarre-shaped districts to cover widely separated African-American neighborhoods.

Beginning in 1993, the Supreme Court set limits on the practice, ruling that race could not be the predominant factor in drawing district lines. In 2001, however, the high court gave states somewhat greater leeway by ruling that North Carolina had legitimate political reasons for creating a congressional district challenged on racial grounds. [4]

The court eased the state rules again in 2003 in a ruling on Georgia's Democratic-drawn plan for state Senate districts. Supported by 10 of 11 black senators — all Democrats — the plan reduced the African-American population in some senatorial districts to help spread the predominantly Democratic voters into others. But the Justice Department had said the plan improperly reduced minority voting strength.

Minorities Gained in Redistricting

Race-conscious redistricting in the 1990s contributed to a marked increase in the number of blacks and Hispanics elected to the U.S. House of Representatives. But recent Supreme Court decisions now limit legislatures' discretion to create so-called "majority-minority" districts.

African-American and Hispanic Members of U.S. House of Representatives

Year	Blacks	Hispanics
1991	26	11
2001	37	19
2003	37	22

Sources: CQ.com, CQ Weekly, American Political Leaders: 1789-2000, CQ Press.

In a 5-4 decision, the high court ruled that states could indeed move black voters out of "majority-minority" districts in order to increase the black population in "minority-influence" districts.

"The State may choose," Justice Sandra Day O'Connor wrote for the majority, "that it is better to risk having fewer minority representatives in order to achieve greater overall representation of a minority group by increasing the number of representatives sympathetic to the interests of minority voters." [5]

[1] For background, see David Rosenzweig and Michael Finnegan, "Latino Voter Lawsuit Rejected," *Los Angeles Times,* June 13, 2002, p. A1., and Kenneth Reich, "Latino Groups Sue Over Redistricting," *Los Angeles Times,* Oct. 2, 2001, Part 2, p. A1.

[2] The case is *Cano v. Davis,* 211 F.Supp.2d 1208 (C.D. Cal. 2002).

[3] For background, see Nadine Cohodas, "Electing Minorities," *The CQ Researcher,* Aug. 12, 1994, pp. 697-720.

[4] The decision is *Hunt v. Cromartie,* 526 U.S. 541 (2001). The most important of the earlier decisions are *Shaw v. Reno,* 509 U.S. 630 (1993); *Miller v. Johnson,* 515 U.S. 900 (1995) and *Bush v. Vera,* 517 U.S. 952 (1996).

[5] The decision is *Georgia v. Ashcroft,* 539 U.S. ___ (2003). The ruling sent the case back to a three-judge federal court for further consideration. The court struck the plan down because of population deviations. See Rhonda Cook, "Redistricting Shot Down," *The Atlanta Journal-Constitution,* Feb. 13, 2004.

---

with each new decade, allocated whole-number seats and assigned any left-over seats to states with the largest leftover fractions.

In 1910, Congress voted that the House would permanently consist of 435 members, and that seats would be apportioned using a system called "major fractions." A decade later, a Congress dominated by members from rural states stalemated when it appeared reapportionment would combine with the fixed-size provision to shift power to more urban states. For the only time in U.S. history, Congress went an entire decade without reapportioning House seats. [11]

Meanwhile, a debate between leading mathematicians produced a new apportionment method, which was eventually adopted in 1950 and remains in use today. The so-called Huntington method — named after its inventor, Edward Huntington of Harvard University — was deemed fairer than the earlier method. It assigns seats to the states based on a division of each state's population by $n(n-1)$, with n being the number of seats given so far to the state. The Supreme Court upheld this method in 1992 in a suit brought by Montana, which lost its second seat under the formula but would have been entitled to two seats under a different method. [12]

Congress followed a similarly meandering path on districting issues. In the early 1800s, the Senate three times approved a constitutional amendment requiring single-member congressional districts, but it failed to reach a vote in the House. Nevertheless, by 1840 most states were using single-member districts. In 1842, Congress required contiguous, single-member districts. The law lapsed after 1850 but was approved again in 1862. A decade later, Congress enacted a seemingly stricter law that required contiguous, single-member districts "as nearly as practicable" equal in population. That requirement was re-enacted in 1881 and 1891 and again in 1901 with an added requirement that districts be "compact."

But none of the laws were enforced. The House in 1844 voted — on partisan lines — to seat representatives from four states that had used at-large elections despite the law requiring single-member districts. In 1901, a House committee rejected a challenge to the election of a Kentucky congressman on the grounds that the state's redistricting law did not conform to federal statutes. Seven years later, a House committee approved a somewhat similar challenge involving a Virginia congressman, but the full House never acted on the recommendation.

The 1901 single-member districting requirement was not re-enacted when it expired in 1929, but a new version was adopted in 1967, which also barred at-large elections. By then, however, the Supreme Court had transformed the legal landscape by requiring that legislative and congressional districts be roughly equal in population — the "one person, one vote" standard.

Court Battles

Initially, the Supreme Court decided to stay out of what Justice Felix Frankfurter famously called the

James Madison recommended in The Federalist Papers No. 57 *that each representative to Congress "will be elected by five or six thousand citizens."* The Federalist Papers, *written with Alexander Hamilton and John Jay in 1787-88 and published in several New York newspapers, argued for ratification of the proposed Constitution.*

"political thicket" of legislative and congressional redistricting. In a series of momentous decisions in the 1960s, however, it ruled that federal courts had jurisdiction over equal-protection claims attacking malapportioned districting schemes and required states to devise districts essentially equal in population.

In its first brush with the issue, the Supreme Court in 1932 left standing a Mississippi redistricting law that was challenged as a violation of the 1911 federal statute. The majority ruled that the 1911 law had expired, but four other justices said they would have dismissed the suit "for want of equity" — in effect, a discretionary decision not to exercise jurisdiction. [13]

In 1946, the court shelved a broader attack claiming that an Illinois leg-

islative districting scheme favoring rural areas violated the voting rights of urban and suburban voters under the Equal Protection Clause. Three justices said the court had no jurisdiction. "Courts ought not enter this political thicket," Frankfurter wrote, although three other justices said they would have heard the case. Casting the deciding vote, Justice Wiley Rutledge concluded that courts could hear such claims, but that in this instance the court should refrain because of the potential "collision" with other branches of government. [14]

In the absence of judicial pressure, state lawmakers often did not bother to redistrict, leaving the nation's growing urban and suburban areas underrepresented. The disparity was greatest in state legislative districts: By 1960, all the nation's legislatures featured at least a 2-to-1 disparity between the most and the least heavily populated districts. Congressional districts were less imbalanced, but several states had lopsided plans. The most heavily populated congressional district in Texas, for instance, had four times as many inhabitants as its least populated, while Arizona, Maryland and Ohio had 3-to-1 disparities between districts.

Once again, city-dwellers took the equal-protection issue to the courts, this time in Tennessee, which had not reapportioned its legislature since 1901. The state courts declined to act, as did a lower federal court — citing the Supreme Court's 1946 decision. But the high court reversed itself in

1962, in its landmark *Baker v. Carr* decision. The urban residents' claim that the failure to reapportion violated their equal-protection rights presented "a justiciable constitutional cause of action upon which [they] were entitled to a trial and a decision," Justice William J. Brennan Jr. wrote in the 6-2 ruling. [15]

The decision set no standard and sent the case back to Tennessee. A year later, however, the high court was more explicit. In a legislative-reapportionment suit from Georgia, Justice William O. Douglas wrote for the majority that political equality "can mean only one thing — one person, one vote." The next year, the high court applied the same standard to congressional districting in another case from Georgia. "[A]s nearly as practicable, one man's vote in a congressional election is to be worth as much as another's," Justice Hugo Black wrote. [16] The dual rulings forced state lawmakers subsequently to redraw legislative and congressional district maps — significantly shifting power from rural to urban and suburban areas.

In applying the one-person, one-vote standard, the Supreme Court moved gradually toward strict mathematical equality for congressional districts, while allowing a bit more leeway for legislatures. The series of decisions on congressional maps culminated with a 1983 ruling in a New Jersey case, *Karcher v. Daggett*, which struck down a districting scheme where the disparity between the most and the least populous district was a tiny 0.69 percent — or 4,400 people. The court said that even small deviations were prohibited unless they were necessary to achieve some legitimate state interest. [17]

In separate opinions, Justice John Paul Stevens, who joined the majority, and Justice Lewis F. Powell Jr., who dissented, said they were more concerned about the partisan gerryman-

dering in New Jersey's plan. The court took up that issue more directly in Indiana's *Bandemer* case three years later, but the split decision fell short of a constitutional command against politically driven districting.

The 6-3 vote established that federal courts could entertain and rule on constitutional claims against political gerrymandering, but the fact that Indiana's politically driven congressional districting plan was upheld — plus the strict legal test set out in the main opinion — gave federal courts scant encouragement to review partisan gerrymandering cases. [18]

Building Blocs

Racial politics, partisan gamesmanship and computerized demographics combined in the 1990s to transform both congressional redistricting and judicial oversight of the process. Under pressure from a Republican Justice Department in the early 1990s, states used newly available, block-by-block census maps to draw intricate schemes concentrating minority voters in select districts to help elect African-American or Hispanic candidates.

White voters challenged the bizarrely shaped districts as "racial gerrymanders" that violated their equal-protection rights. The Supreme Court recognized the claims and told states that race could not be "the predominant factor" in drawing district lines.

Computer-aided redistricting was first proposed in the 1960s as an antidote to overly partisan line-drawing, according to Mark Monmonier, a geography professor at Syracuse University's Maxwell School of Citizenship and Public Affairs and author of a book on the subject. [19] Beginning with the 1970 population count, the Census Bureau started producing computerized street maps that could be used

in an interactive computerized process to draw increasingly precise district lines. With the 1990 census, the bureau produced what Monmonier calls "a more powerful and precise database." These electronic files, he explains, enabled redistricters to follow streets, streams, railways or other boundaries to produce districts with specified population counts — and predictable demographic makeups.

Meanwhile, slow, expensive "mainframe" computers were replaced by fast, cheap personal computers, spawning a growing niche industry that gave legislators, political parties, interest groups and others the data needed to fine-tune redistricting schemes to maximize their respective interests.

The new demographic information became available just as the Justice Department — under the first President George Bush — was advancing a new interpretation of the federal Voting Rights Act, which required states to maximize the number of majority-minority congressional and legislative districts. Legally, the department said it was acting to prevent "minority vote dilution," as defined by a pivotal 1986 decision by the Supreme Court. [20] But the legal position also served Republican interests by packing minority voters — overwhelmingly Democratic — into a few districts. Minority groups supported the government's position. Democrats had little choice but to go along, given their dependence on African-American votes.

States subject to the Voting Rights Act's "preclearance" requirement for redistricting plans met the Justice Department directive after the 1990 census by stitching minority neighborhoods together in sprawling, comically intricate districts. North Carolina's 12th wound snakelike through the center of the state to pick up African-American neighborhoods in three cities. Georgia's 11th stretched from Atlanta eastward to pick up black neighborhoods in Augusta and Savannah on the coast.

Louisiana's 4th gained the nickname "the mark of Zorro" for its Z-shaped path along the state's northern and eastern borders. Texas produced a congressional map with districts resembling Rorschach inkblots — some designed to elect African-American or Hispanic candidates, others aimed at protecting incumbents.

The Supreme Court had countenanced some use of racial criteria in legislative districting in a 1974 decision. But the racial redistricting of the 1990s — often discarding the traditional principle of compactness — did not sit well with the court's conservative majority. A series of 5-4 decisions challenging the North Carolina, Georgia and Texas maps established constitutional bounds on the practice.

First, the court ruled in the North Carolina case — *Shaw v. Reno* — that white voters could challenge racially drawn districts that were "highly irregular in shape." Two years later, in the Georgia case, the court said a redistricting plan had to meet the high constitutional standard of "strict scrutiny" if race was "the predominant factor" in placing "a significant number of voters" in or outside a district. A year later, the court made clear that the constitutional test was stringent by rejecting Texas' argument that its racially drawn districts were justifiable efforts to preserve minority voting strength or to protect incumbents in other districts. [21]

The court also helped resolve a second reapportionment-related issue over the use of statistical "sampling" in the population counts used to allocate congressional seats. The Census Bureau and most demographers argued that enumerators could not possibly find everybody in a nationwide count and that sampling techniques were reliable methods to adjust for the inevitable "undercount." [22] Democrats agreed, but Republicans said sampling was unreliable, unnecessary and illegal. In 1999, the court sided with the GOP, ruling 5-4 that the Census Act

did not allow sampling in congressional apportionment. [23]

By decade's end, the court's decisions in the racial redistricting cases had forced Georgia, North Carolina and Texas to redraw the challenged congressional districts and prompted other states to re-examine the use of race in map drawing. Meanwhile, political winds were blowing in a Republican direction. The GOP gained control of the House in 1994 and held on for the rest of the decade. In 2000, Republicans gained control of the White House and both chambers of Congress and improved their positions in statehouses and state legislatures. The GOP began the new century in a favorable posture and saw an opportunity for further gains in the coming redistricting cycle.

Escalating Warfare

Political pundits expected the post-2000 redistricting season to be the most contentious ever. Three years later, the predictions had proven well-founded. As both parties sought to maximize whatever political control they had over the process, the courts were again called in to referee, but the judiciary appeared reluctant to rein in partisan gerrymandering or limit redistricting to once a decade.

In Texas, a divided state legislature — with a Democratic-controlled House and GOP-controlled Senate — adjourned its regular session in May 2001 without seriously trying to redraw the congressional map to incorporate the two new seats Texas was apportioned following the 2000 census. GOP Gov. Rick Perry decided not to reconvene the legislature for a special session — leaving the matter up to the courts. In approving a new map on Nov. 14, a three-judge federal court relied heavily on the existing, Democratic-drawn map

in order to protect incumbents. [24]

Colorado followed a similar course after the Republican-controlled House and Democratic-controlled Senate deadlocked. A state judge adopted a Democratic-backed plan in January 2002 that largely protected the state's six incumbent House members — four Republicans and two Democrats — while favoring a Democratic candidate in a newly created district around Denver. [25]

Democrats already had won a victory in Georgia, where a Democratic-controlled legislature had adopted a redistricting plan. By "packing" GOP districts and pairing incumbent Republicans in two of them, Democrats hoped to shift the state's congressional delegation from an 8-3 GOP majority to a 7-6 Democratic edge. [26]

Some Pennsylvania Republicans cited the Democrats' Georgia remap as grounds for retaliation in their own state later that year. Facing the loss of two of Pennsylvania's 21 House seats, the GOP-controlled legislature threw two pairs of Democratic incumbents together and put another Democrat into a district with an incumbent Republican. The map, approved in early January 2002, appeared likely to enlarge the GOP's narrow 11-10 edge to a more comfortable 12-7 margin. [27]

Michigan, another GOP-controlled state that lost seats after the 2000 census, followed Pennsylvania's example by pairing six Democratic incumbents in three redrawn districts. Likewise, Democratic-controlled legislatures in North Carolina and Tennessee approved maps likely to net their party one seat in each, while a Democratic plan in Maryland added a hefty chunk of Democrats to the district of longtime moderate Republican Rep. Constance A. Morella. In other states, incumbent protection appeared the dominant goal. As the redistricting cycle ended, Republicans and Democrats alike pronounced themselves largely satisfied.

In November, however, redistricting

appeared to be a significant factor — along with President Bush's popularity and the population shift toward predominantly Republican Sun Belt states — in producing a net pickup of six House seats for the GOP. [28] It was only the third time since the Civil War that the president's party gained House seats in a midterm election.

Democrats lost six seats in Michigan and Pennsylvania, while Republicans gained new seats in Florida and Texas (two each) and Arizona and Nevada (one each). In Maryland, Morella fell to a Democratic opponent, but Democrats did not match their expectations in other states. Notably, Republicans held onto an 8-5 majority in the expanded Georgia delegation. In Colorado, a Republican eked out a surprise 122-vote victory for the new seat.

Republicans also made gains in state legislative contests and, significantly, won majority control of both chambers of the Colorado and Texas legislatures. Meanwhile, House Majority Leader DeLay hatched a plan for a second round of redistricting in Texas. Ironically, the idea bore fruit first in Colorado, where a Republican-crafted redistricting plan was introduced, approved and signed into law within five days in early May. Colorado's Democratic attorney general, Ken Salazar, promptly vowed to challenge the mid-cycle redistricting in court.

The path to the second-in-a-decade redistricting in Texas was more protracted. Republicans pushed the measure to the top of the House calendar as the regular legislative session was ending in May. But Democrats thwarted passage by decamping en masse to a motel in Oklahoma for the final four days — putting them beyond the reach of Texas authorities and leaving the chamber without a quorum. When Gov. Perry convened a special legislative session, the Senate's 12 Democrats staged a similar exodus to New Mexico. But the month-long boycott ended on Sept. 2 when one of the

Democrats decided to come back home after concluding that Perry could outlast them by calling a succession of special sessions. [29]

The legislature finally adopted the plan on Oct. 13. Democrats immediately sued, claiming the mid-decade redistricting violated the U.S. and state constitutions. Along with the Mexican American Legal Defense and Educational Fund (MALDEF), Democrats also contended that the map improperly diluted minority voter strength in violation of the Voting Rights Act. Republicans countered that the measure actually created a new, third "minority-opportunity" district for African-Americans in Houston and maintained the number of Hispanic opportunity districts at six.

Meanwhile, Pennsylvania Democrats were challenging the redistricting plan the GOP had pushed through in the regular post-census cycle. The measure was an unconstitutional gerrymander, they claimed, even under the Supreme Court's stringent *Davis v. Bandemer* standard. A three-judge federal court rejected the claim in January 2003, but the high court agreed in June to take up the case and scheduled oral arguments for Dec. 10.

As the December arguments approached, the stage was set for some of the most significant legal battles over redistricting since the start of the reapportionment revolution four decades earlier.

CURRENT SITUATION

Designing Districts

P ennsylvania Democrats want the Supreme Court to give courts more

power to strike down political gerrymandering, but they ran into strong resistance from several justices during arguments on Dec. 10, 2003. Even justices sympathetic to the Democrats' claim of unfairness appeared uncertain about what standard courts could use to police the practice. Meanwhile, lawyers for GOP legislators and the state urged the justices to bar partisan gerrymandering cases from federal courts altogether or give legislatures free rein in drawing district lines for partisan advantage. [30]

For the Democrats, Washington attorney Paul Smith opened the hour-long session by saying that lower courts had "effectively overruled" the high court's 1986 decision allowing challenges to partisan gerrymandering by setting an "impossible" burden of proof for plaintiffs. He urged that redistricting maps be ruled unconstitutional if plaintiffs showed it was "very clear" one party could win a majority of votes but have "no chance" of securing a majority of the seats.

Three justices openly disagreed with Smith — starting with the pivotal moderate conservative Sandra Day O'Connor, a dissenter in the original *Bandemer* decision. "Maybe the way to go is to just say hands off these things," O'Connor declared.

Justice Antonin Scalia reached the same conclusion after noting that the Constitution lets the states or Congress itself prescribe the "time, place, and manner" of House elections. "That suggests to me it is none of our business."

Chief Justice William H. Rehnquist, another of the dissenters in *Bandemer*, also sharply rejected Smith's proposed standard. "You're just pulling this thing out of a hat," he said.

For his part, Justice Anthony M. Kennedy conceded that the GOP-drawn congressional map might be "unfair . . . in common parlance," but still wondered what test courts could use. "It seems to me that we're at sea," he said.

"The government has no business

discriminating against people based on their partisan affiliation or their political viewpoint," Smith answered later. "There has to be an outer boundary."

Harrisburg attorney Krill, representing the GOP legislative leaders, urged the justices to bar federal courts from policing politically driven redistricting. Any test "requires inherent political choices" that are "inappropriate for the judiciary to make," Krill said.

Justice John Paul Stevens — who had voted in 1986 not only to allow legal challenges to gerrymandering but also to strike down the Indiana map at issue in the case — asked Krill whether a redistricting plan should be subject to challenge if "maximum partisan advantage" were the only justification for a line-drawing.

Yes, Krill answered, "It's a permissible legislative choice." When Stevens again asked whether the legislature had "any duty" to try to draw districts "impartially," Krill said the Constitution does not require fairness, but that "political forces" might pull lawmakers "in a multitude of directions."

In any event, Krill added, "The system is self-correcting," noting that Indiana Democrats gained control of the state's congressional delegation within a few years of losing their redistricting challenge. In Pennsylvania, he added, Democrats had won the House race in a district seemingly drawn to favor the GOP incumbent. "Voters are not disenfranchised," he concluded.

Representing Pennsylvania, Senior Deputy Attorney General J. Bart

DeLone said "the simplest and cleanest way" for the justices to "get out of the political thicket" was to overrule the *Bandemer* decision.

By the close of the argument, court-watchers counted four votes seemingly against the Democrats: Rehnquist, O'Connor, Scalia and the conservative Clarence Thomas, who followed his customary practice of asking no questions. Kennedy, a moderate conservative, seemed a likely fifth vote to reject the Democrats' claim.

Meanwhile, among the four liberal justices, only Stevens strongly favored an aggressive role for the courts on gerrymandering, and he did not embrace the standard proposed by Smith. Justices David H. Souter and Ruth Bader Ginsburg seemed possible votes for the Democrats' position, but Justice Stephen G. Breyer, an active questioner, had asked skeptical questions of both Smith and Krill.

"I expect the Supreme Court will reject the plaintiffs' cause of action," the University of Pennsylvania's Persily commented after attending the arguments. The justices, he said, "are afraid that they will get even more deeply into the political thicket."

A decision is due by July.

Taking Seconds

Democrats are one for two in challenging the mid-cycle congressional redistricting plans approved by GOP legislatures and governors in Colorado and Texas. But the Colorado Supreme Court's decision barring a second-in-a-decade redistricting set no broad precedent, because it depended on a provision in the state's constitution. So Democrats will have only a limited victory unless they can persuade the U.S. Supreme Court to overturn the Texas federal court ruling that the Constitution does not limit congressional redistricting to once every 10 years.

The Colorado court's decision, announced Dec. 1, came on a 5-2 vote, with the court's two Republican-appointed justices dissenting. [31] The ruling relied on a provision in Colorado's constitution requiring the general assembly to redistrict congressional seats whenever "a new apportionment shall be made by Congress." Writing for the majority, Chief Justice Mary Mullarkey said the provision mandated redistricting immediately after the census and barred a second remap — even if the

Getty Images/Jana Birchum

Texas' new congressional map threw several House Democrats into new districts against each other or against Republican incumbents or stripped them of large segments of their old districts. Voting in November in Texas could eliminate the Democrats' hopes of regaining control of the House next year.

At Issue

Should federal courts limit partisan gerrymandering?

SAM HIRSCH
COUNSEL FOR APPELLANTS IN VIETH V. JUBELIRER,
JENNER & BLOCK LLP

WRITTEN FOR *THE CQ RESEARCHER*, FEBRUARY 2004

i nviting federal courts to wade deeper into the "political thicket" always raises difficult issues of federalism and separation of powers. But sometimes the risks are worth taking. That was the case in the 1960s, when malapportionment had effectively doubled the voting strength of rural voters, at the expense of city-dwellers and suburbanites. It is the case again today, when partisan gerrymandering has effectively doubled the power of a class of voters defined solely by their political viewpoint. Like malapportionment 40 years ago, severe gerrymandering today threatens to make a mockery of our democratic system.

In the first general elections after the 2001-2002 redistricting, only four congressional challengers ousted incumbents — a record low. In California, none of the 50 general-election challengers garnered even 40 percent of the vote. Indeed, in 80 of the 435 districts nationwide, one of the two major parties did not even field a candidate. This lack of competition was peculiar to House elections, where redistricting has an impact: On the same day when barely one out of 12 House elections were decided by 10 percentage points or less, roughly half of all gubernatorial and Senate elections were that close. Most of the House is now locked in cement.

While historic levels of uncompetitiveness infected redistricting nationally, severe partisan bias was confined to a handful of states where one political party had unilateral control over the legislature and the governorship. For example, although Florida, Pennsylvania, Ohio and Michigan are all highly competitive "toss-up" states, redistricting handed the Republican Party 51 of their 77 House seats — an artificial 2-to-1 advantage.

Partisan gerrymandering is also transforming Congress. With little reason to fear voters, representatives increasingly cater to party insiders and donors, rather than to the political center where most Americans reside. Bipartisan compromise around moderate policies takes a backseat to party loyalty, resulting in historic levels of polarization. And further polarization only fuels the bitterness that promotes more gerrymandering.

The partisan-gerrymandering wars have spilled out of the legislatures and into the courtrooms. But with little prospect of prevailing on a forthright claim of partisan gerrymandering, aggrieved partisans instead often allege racial gerrymandering or minority-vote dilution under the Voting Rights Act. The incentive to couch partisan disputes in racial terms corrodes our politics. By putting teeth into the constitutional limits on partisan gerrymandering, federal courts can halt the racializing of redistricting, while restoring to the American people a House of Representatives worthy of its name.

JOHN P. KRILL, JR.
COUNSEL FOR APPELLEES IN VIETH V. JUBELIRER,
KIRKPATRICK & LOCKHART LLP

WRITTEN FOR *THE CQ RESEARCHER*, FEBRUARY, 2004

c ourt-imposed limits on partisanship in redistricting would create, not solve, problems. Redistricting is inherently political. Any line drawn anywhere has partisan repercussions, and no criteria are "neutral." For example, trying to follow county and municipal lines would give preference to 19th-century political boundary decisions, while disfavoring emerging communities of interest in our sprawling, non-compact suburbs.

Turning judicial preferences into constitutional principles would create a drag on democratic change. Although legislators are free to envision the future, the judicial role is essentially to apply precedent and past legislative policy choices to restrict future conduct. If the courts had intervened in an earlier age, and had applied principles of so-called partisan fairness based on past electoral strength, they might well have kept the Whig Party from collapsing. But a party whose base is shrinking should not be propped up by judges giving weight to the past preferences of voters who have died, moved or switched.

If judges start second-guessing elected legislatures about fundamental choices for future representation, the judiciary will inevitably be criticized for partisanship. Although the courts often redraw maps in one-person, one-vote cases, they must use past legislative districting decisions as guidance, so as to avoid making political choices. But if the courts start making such policy choices themselves, the unavoidable partisan impact will put judicial legitimacy at risk. We can't afford to have respect for the courts turn into cynicism about political bosses in black robes.

In any event, redistricting, even with the aid of modern computers, cannot control the choices of voters. Good candidates vector toward the politics of their districts, regardless of their party affiliation. That is why Congress has conservative Democrats and liberal Republicans and vice versa. Some districts will elect a conservative regardless of party and vice versa. Recognizing this point leads to the realization that partisan affiliation is not the be-all, end-all of elections, except to the parties themselves. The parties care about partisan control of legislative bodies more than about the politics of the members of their caucuses. Voters care more about the responsiveness and personalities of their representatives.

The states have used districting for partisan effect since the ratification of the Constitution. For example, Pennsylvania enacted different plans for congressional elections in 1788, 1790, 1792 and 1794, as Federalists struggled with Anti-Federalists for control of the delegation. Partisan conflict is no fiercer now. Judicial restraint is just as important now.

new plan was drawn by a court following a legislative deadlock.

"The state constitution limits redistricting to once per census, and nothing in state or federal law negates this limitation," Mullarkey wrote in her 63-page opinion. "Having failed to redistrict when it should have, the General Assembly has lost its chance to redistrict until after the 2010 federal census."

Mullarkey also cited previous state practice and policy considerations as weighing against a second-in-a-decade redistricting. "The Framers knew that to achieve accountability there must be stability in representation," she wrote. "Limiting redistricting to once per decade maximizes stability."

Justice Rebecca Kourlis, one of the two dissenters, argued that the state constitution's provision specifying redistricting "when" Congress reapportions did not prohibit a subsequent remap, nor did the state court's adoption of new congressional maps prevent the legislature from "reclaiming its authority to redistrict."

In the Texas case, all three federal judges said mid-decade redistricting is not prohibited by the Constitution, federal statute, Texas law or tradition — at least when a new map substitutes for a court-drawn plan. But two of the judges recommended Congress ban the practice, citing "compelling arguments" why states should "abstain from drawing district lines mid-decade." [32]

The judges divided sharply, however, on whether the redistricting violated the Voting Rights Act by improperly weakening Hispanics' political clout. Two Republican-appointed judges upheld the decision to disperse Hispanic voters from a South Texas district held by a Republican incumbent — a Hispanic — because the move was offset by creation of a new Hispanic-majority district. The Democratic-appointed judge on the panel disagreed.

In the main opinion, Judge Patrick Higginbotham — a federal appeals court judge appointed in 1982 by President Ronald Reagan — rejected the Democratic plaintiffs' arguments that the Census Clause limits redistricting to once per decade. The clause, Higginbotham wrote, "does not mention the states or their power to redistrict, and we fail to see how it can limit a power it never references." The Democratic-appointed judge on the panel, John Ward, also said mid-decade redistricting was prohibited, but added, "There may be legitimate state interests advanced by the effort."

In the main opinion, Higginbotham rejected claims by Democrats and minority-advocacy groups that the Voting Rights Act was violated by dispersing blacks and Hispanics — changes affecting 11 of the state's previous districts, including Frost's old 24th. Higginbotham wrote that because the two groups together constituted only 46 percent of the voting-age population in the old district — less than a majority — the argument against the reconfiguration was political, not racial or ethnic.

Higginbotham also upheld the redrawing of GOP Rep. Henry Bonilla's 23rd district to reduce its Hispanic voting-age citizen population to 46 percent from 57 percent — chiefly by splitting the border city of Laredo. The move was aimed at boosting Bonilla, who won only 8 percent of the Hispanic vote when he narrowly defeated a Hispanic Democrat in 2002. But Higginbotham said the offsetting creation of a new Hispanic-majority district — the 25th, stretching 300 miles from the Austin suburbs south to the border — satisfied the Voting Rights Act. Ward — a federal district judge appointed by President Bill Clinton — said the redrawn 23rd district violated Supreme Court rulings against "minority vote retrogression."

Democrats asked the Supreme Court to stay the effect of the ruling and leave the existing districting map in place for the 2004 election, but the justices declined without comment. Democrats now plan a full appeal to the Supreme Court, but Republicans are confident about the outcome.

"We are in very good shape," says GOP lawyer Taylor. If the court does hear the case, oral arguments would not be held until fall 2004.

OUTLOOK

Winners Take All?

The House of Representatives undergoes some turnover at the start of each decade when seats are reapportioned among states and districts redrawn within the states. But House elections in 2002 saw considerably less turnover and less political competitiveness than in comparable years in any of the previous three decades — and, in fact, less turnover and less competitiveness than in a typical election year.

Only 16 incumbent House members were defeated in 2002 — compared to an average of 35 following redistricting in 1972, 1982 and 1992. In addition, fewer members retired: 35 in 2002 compared to an average of 48 for the first post-redistricting elections in the previous three decades. And — in a telling statistic compiled by Democratic attorney Hirsch — 338 of the House's 435 members were elected in 2002 with at least 60 percent of the vote in their districts. [33]

Hirsch views the lack of political competitiveness as a consequence of partisan gerrymandering and the courts' refusal to rein in the practice. He wants courts — federal or state — to consider the political effects of redistricting plans and require what he calls "a reasonable degree" of partisan fairness, competitiveness and stability.

Surprisingly, perhaps, Republican attorney Braden agrees on the diagnosis, but not on the cure. "Turnover in 2002 was way too low," Braden says. He blames "partisan" gerrymanders, where both parties used control of the process to protect incumbents, as well as "bipartisan" gerrymanders, where Republicans and Democrats combined to spare incumbents from competitive races.

But Braden says he is "adamantly opposed to the courts getting more politicized." States may want to add competitiveness to the factors to be considered in redrawing districts, he says, but federal courts should keep hands off. "My concern doesn't make it a constitutional issue," he says.

Supporters of redistricting reforms — such as independent commissions or the more far-reaching step of devising some form of proportional representation — also cite lawmakers' self-preservation instinct as a drawback of current practices. Academic experts who worry about the problem see no easy solution.

"No politician likes competitive seats," says the University of California's Grofman. "It's hard to imagine a situation where you will have a lot of seats that will shift back and forth.'

"Incumbents are quite powerful," says Washington and Lee's Rush. "How to repair that, I can't say."

For now, most Supreme Court-watchers do not expect the justices to use the Pennsylvania case to increase the judicial review of partisan gerrymandering. "I'm not very optimistic that *Bandemer* is going to be resuscitated," Grofman adds. "It's more likely that the final nail will be laid."

Without any judicial controls, partisan gerrymandering is likely to continue and perhaps increase, the University of Maryland's Herrnson predicts. "Once the precedent allows for extremely selfish behavior on the part of politicians, it will be followed until things become so out of hand that reform is ultimately enacted," he says.

Predictions about the future of mid-decade redistricting are more tentative. Some experts say if the courts give the practice a green light, both parties will draw new maps for partisan advantage whenever and wherever they can. Others question whether legislators of either party have much stomach for reopening the partisan warfare unless forced to.

For his part, state Sen. Todd Staples, a Republican architect of Texas' mid-decade redistricting, says he has no desire to redraw congressional maps anytime soon. "I want to take up redistricting again in the year 3011," Staples quips.

But Democratic attorney Hirsch notes that GOP lawmakers have not promised to stick with the map approved in 2003, which was designed to elect 22 Republicans. "If they get only 20 or 21 seats, it will be interesting to see if they try again in 2005 or 2007," he says.

Hirsch's Democratic colleague Hebert agrees judicial intervention is necessary to check partisan-driven redistricting. "It won't get better as long as the fox guards the district and just makes more foxes," he says. "It's time for the Supreme Court to step in; it's not going to happen in any other fashion."

But GOP attorney Krill in Pennsylvania says a Supreme Court decision allowing greater review of redistricting cases would damage the political process and the judicial system itself.

"If they adopt a more relaxed standard, then there's litigation all over the country," says Krill — not only over Congress but also over state legislatures, city councils, school districts and so forth. "It will be wasteful litigation that will immerse judges in every level — federal, state and local. It will be bad for the public perception of the judicial system."

Notes

[1] For detailed information, including maps, see the Web site of the Texas Legislative Council: www.tlc.state.tx.us.

[2] Quoted in Dave Leventhal, "Sessions, Frost Ready to Rumble," *The Dallas Morning News*, Jan. 18, 2004, p. 1B.

[3] For background, see Jennifer Gavin, "Redistricting," *The CQ Researcher*, Feb. 16, 2001, pp. 113-128.

[4] "Candidate and Office Histories," CQ Voting and Elections Collection, CQ Electronic Library, accessed Feb. 26, 2004; http://library2.cq-press.com/elections/histories.php.

[5] *Davis v. Bandemer*, 478 U.S. 109 (1986).

[6] In the only decision to cite *Davis v. Bandemer* to mandate an electoral change, a federal court in North Carolina required the state to elect state supreme court justices by district rather than statewide; the court said at-large elections disenfranchised Republicans. See *Republican Party v. Martin*, 980 F.2d 943 (4th Cir. 1992).

[7] Chip Scutari and Robbie Sherwood, "Legislative Districts Map Thrown Out; Judge Orders New Boundaries Drawn," *The Arizona Republic*, Jan. 17, 2004, p. 1B. The ruling upheld the commission's congressional district map. For background on the initiative, see Chip Scutari, "Citizens Panel to Redraw Districts," *The Arizona Republic*, Nov. 8, 2000, p. 11E.

[8] Background drawn from "Reapportionment and Redistricting," in *Congressional Quarterly's Guide to Congress* (5th ed., 2000), pp. 891-911. See also David Butler and Bruce Cain, *Congressional Redistricting: Comparative and Theoretical Perspectives* (1992), pp. 17-41.

[9] "Reapportionment and Redistricting," *op. cit.*, p. 900. States with districts were Maryland, Massachusetts, New York, North Carolina, South Carolina and Virginia; at-large states included Connecticut, Georgia, New Hampshire, New Jersey, and Pennsylvania.

[10] A chart summarizing the various formulas can be found in Butler and Cain, *op. cit.*, p. 19.

[11] For a history, see Charles W. Eagles, *Democracy Delayed: Congressional Reappor-*

tionment and Urban-Rural Conflict in the 1920s (1990).

[12] The case is Department of Commerce v. Montana, 503 U.S. 442 (1992).

[13] Wood v. Broom, 287 U.S. 1 (1932).

[14] Colegrove v. Green, 328 U.S. 549 (1946).

[15] The citation is 369 U.S. 186 (1962). For a history of the case, see Gene Graham, One Man, One Vote: Baker v. Carr and the American Levelers (1972).

[16] The cases are Gray v. Sanders, 372 U.S. 368 (1963), and Wesberry v. Sanders, 376 U.S. 1 (1964).

[17] The citation is 462 U.S. 725 (1983). The leading case on population deviations in legislative redistricting is Mahan v. Howell, 410 U.S. 315 (1973), which approved a Virginia plan with a 16 percent variation between the largest and smallest population districts.

[18] The citation is 478 U.S. 109 (1986). Stevens and Powell dissented from the decision to uphold Indiana's districting plan.

[19] Mark S. Monmonier, Bushmanders and Bullwinkles: How Politicians Manipulate Electronic Maps and Census Data to Win Elections (2001). Background drawn from "What a Friend We Have in GIS [Geographic Information Systems]," pp. 104-120.

[20] The case is Thornburg v. Gingles, 478 U.S. 30 (1986). The decision held that minority plaintiffs could establish a claim of improper "vote dilution" under the Voting Rights Act by proving racially polarized voting, a legacy of official discrimination in voting or other areas, and campaign appeals to racial prejudice.

[21] The citation for Shaw v. Hunt is 509 U.S. 630 (1993). The other cases are Miller v. Johnson, 515 U.S. 900 (1995) (Georgia) and Bush v. Vera, 517 U.S. 952 (1996) (Texas).

[22] For background, see Kenneth Jost, "Census 2000," The CQ Researcher, May 1, 1998, pp. 385-408.

[23] The case is Department of Commerce v.

FOR MORE INFORMATION

Center for Voting and Democracy, 6930 Carroll Ave., Suite 610, Takoma Park, MD 20912; (301) 270-4616; www.fairvote.org.

Common Cause, 1250 Connecticut Ave., N.W., Suite 600, Washington DC 20036; (202) 833-1200; www.commoncause.org.

Democratic National Committee, 430 South Capitol St., S.E., Washington, DC 20003; (202) 863-8000; www.dnc.org.

National Conference of State Legislatures, 7700 East First Place, Denver, CO 80230; (303) 364-7700; www.ncsl.org.

Republican National Committee, 310 1st St., S.E., Washington, DC 20003; (202) 863-8500; www.rnc.org.

United States House of Representatives, 503 U.S. 442 (1999).

[24] See Mary Clare Jalonick, "Court-Ordered Remap Aids Texas Incumbents," CQ Weekly, Nov. 17, 2001, p. 2758.

[25] Gregory L. Giroux, "Judge's Ruling Puts New House District Up for Grabs," CQ Monitor News, Jan. 25, 2002.

[26] Gregory L. Giroux, "Georgia Remap Merges 2 GOP-Held Districts," CQ Weekly, Oct. 6, 2001, p. 2001.

[27] Jonathan Allen, "GOP Scores Major Win in Pennsylvania Redistricting," CQ Monitor News, Jan. 4. 2002.

[28] See Gregory L. Giroux, "Redistricting Helped GOP," CQ Weekly, Nov. 9, 2002, p. 2934. See also Gregory L. Giroux, "Redistricting Increases Polarization," in Politics in America 2004: The 108th Congress (2003), p. xxiii.

[29] See Gregory L. Giroux, "Texas GOP Outlasts Renegades, Prepares for New Congressional Map; Democrats Put Their Hope in Court," CQ Weekly, Sept. 6, 2003, p. 2145; Gebe Martinez, "In Texas Redistricting

Game, DeLay Holds the High Cards," CQ Weekly, July 12, 2003, p. 1728.

[30] For coverage, see Stephen Henderson, "Spirited Debate at High Court on Pa. Redistricting," Philadelphia Inquirer, Dec. 11, 2003, p. A19; Michael McGough, "Justices Treading Warily in Pa. Case," Pittsburgh Post-Gazette, Dec. 11, 2003, p. A12.

[31] The decision is Salazar v. Davidson, 03SA133. For the most extensive coverage in Colorado newspapers, see John J. Sanko, "Dems Are Big Winners on Congressional Map," Rocky Mountain News, Dec. 2, 2004, p. 6A.

[32] The decision is Sessions v. Perry, 2:03-CV-354. For the most extensive coverage in Texas newspapers, see David Paztor and Chuck Lindell, "Map Survives Court Challenge," The Austin American-Statesman, Jan. 7, 2004, p. A1.

[33] Sam Hirsch, "The United States House of Unrepresentatives: What Went Wrong in the Latest Round of Congressional Redistricting," Election Law Journal, Vol. 2, No. 2 (November 2003), Table 1, p. 3.

Bibliography

Selected Sources

Books

Butler, David, and Bruce Cain, *Congressional Redistricting: Comparative and Theoretical Perspectives*, Macmillan, 1992.

Surveys the history and contemporary practices of U.S. congressional redistricting; compares practices in other democracies. Butler is a professor at Nuffield College, Oxford, England; Cain is director of the Institute of Governmental Studies, University of California, Berkeley.

Clayton, Dewey M., *African Americans and the Politics of Congressional Redistricting*, Garland, 2001.

An assistant professor of political science at the University of Louisville argues that the case for deliberately drawing majority-black congressional districts "remains compelling."

Grofman, Bernard (ed.), *Political Gerrymandering and the Courts*, Agathon Press, 1990.

Essays by 15 political scientists examine the Supreme Court's decision to allow federal challenges to gerrymandering. Includes 12-page list of references. Grofman is a professor of political science at the University of California, Irvine.

— (ed.), *Race and Redistricting in the 1990s*, Agathon Press, 1998.

Essays by 16 political scientists examine Supreme Court decisions in the 1990s limiting the use of race in redistricting.

Hill, Steven, *Fixing Elections: The Failure of America's Winner Take All Politics*, Routledge, 2002.

The Western regional director of the Center for Voting and Democracy strongly criticizes redistricting and the single-member, winner-take-all system, advocating proportional representation to increase political competition.

Kousser, J. Morgan, *Colorblind Injustice: Minority Voting Rights and the Undoing of the Second Reconstruction*, University of North Carolina Press, 1999.

A professor of social sciences at California Institute of Technology and frequent witness for minority groups in voting-rights cases analyzes the history of minority voting rights during post-Civil War Reconstruction and following passage of the Voting Rights Act in 1965. Includes 36-page bibliography.

Monmonier, Mark S., *Bushmanders and Bullwinkles: How Politicians Manipulate Electronic Maps and Census Data to Win Elections*, University of Chicago Press, 2001.

A professor of geography at Syracuse University's Maxwell School of Citizenship and Public Affairs examines the implications of high-tech, super-precise redistricting.

Rush, Mark E., *Does Redistricting Make a Difference? Partisan Representation and Electoral Behavior*, Johns Hopkins University Press, 1993.

A professor of politics at Washington and Lee University argues that concern about partisan gerrymandering is based on an inaccurate understanding of voting behavior and contributes to political divisiveness.

Rush, Mark E., and Richard L. Engstrom, *Fair and Effective Representation? Debating Electoral Reform and Minority Rights*, Rowman & Littlefield, 2001.

Two political science professors offer conflicting views on using proportional representation instead of winner-take-all, single-member districts. Includes excerpts from nine major Supreme Court decisions. Rush is at Washington and Lee University, Engstrom at the University of New Orleans.

Thernstrom, Abigail M., *Whose Votes Count? Affirmative Action and Minority Voting Rights*, Harvard University Press, 1987.

A senior fellow at the conservative Manhattan Institute argues that maximizing minority office-holding may inhibit political integration.

Articles

Hirsch, Sam, "The United States House of Unrepresentatives: What Went Wrong in the Latest Round of Congressional Redistricting," *Election Law Journal*, Vol. 2, No. 2 (November 2003), pp. 179-216.

A Washington lawyer for Democrats in redistricting cases strongly criticizes courts' reluctance to carefully scrutinize "severely partisan incumbent-protecting gerrymanders."

McDonald, Michael, "A Comparative Look at U.S. State Redistricting Processes," *State Politics and Policy Quarterly* [forthcoming, 2004].

An assistant professor of government and politics at George Mason University analyzes redistricting processes and lawmakers' use of them to influence electoral outcomes.

Persily, Nathaniel, "In Defense of Foxes Guarding Henhouses: The Case for Judicial Acquiescence to Incumbent-Protecting Gerrymanders," *Harvard Law Review*, Vol. 116 (2002), pp. 649-683.

A University of Pennsylvania law professor defends courts' deference to partisan-motivated redistricting.

"Reapportionment and Redistricting," in *Congressional Quarterly's Guide to Congress* (5th ed.), CQ Press, 2000, pp. 891-911.

Overview of relevant issues from the Constitutional Convention to present day. Includes selected bibliography.

"Insure Domestic Tranquility"
— preamble to the Constitution of the United States

The framers of the Constitution wrote it with fresh memories of a six-month-long armed rebellion by debt-laden farmers in western Massachusetts. Shays' Rebellion, finally suppressed in February 1787, convinced the leaders of the young republic that there was a need for a stronger national government. Two centuries later, the threats to domestic tranquility are much different: violent and drug-related crime, particularly in metropolitan areas; and the threat of terrorism, domestic or foreign. The legal context has also changed. The law enforcement powers of the federal government and state governments are stymied by protections in the Bill of Rights for suspects and criminal defendants. The effort to balance security and liberty has produced a range of vexing issues — none more difficult perhaps than the current debates over Bush administration policies in the war against terrorism.

"Civil Liberties Debates" examines the aggressive stance President Bush has taken on security issues in the wake of the 9/11 terrorist attacks. At Bush's urging, Congress passed the USA Patriot Act to give the government increased search-and-surveillance powers in terrorism investigations. Meanwhile, the administration held hundreds of people captured during the war in Afghanistan as "enemy combatants" at Guantanamo Naval Base in Cuba. Two U.S. citizens were also held as enemy combatants in a naval brig in the United States. Civil liberties advocates filed court challenges to all of these policies and actions. After our report, the Supreme Court agreed to hear arguments in April 2004 on two of the disputes. The citizen-enemy combatant cases are *Padilla v. Rumsfeld* and *Rumsfeld v. Hamdi;* the consolidated Guantanamo detainee cases are

Rasul v. Bush and *Al Odah v. United States.* Decisions in all the cases are due by the end of June.

"Rethinking the Death Penalty" updates the continuing debate over capital punishment. The Supreme Court overturned all existing death sentences in 1972 on the grounds that, as administered, the death penalty violated the Eighth Amendment's ban on "cruel and unusual punishments." Just four years later, however, the court allowed states to re-enact death penalty laws under new guidelines. New issues have emerged year after year — among them, the constitutionality of executing juvenile or mentally retarded offenders. After our report, the Supreme Court ruled by a 6–3 vote that the Eighth Amendment bars execution of a mentally retarded offender (*Atkins v. Virginia,* June 20, 2002). More recently, the court agreed to re-examine the constitutionality of execution of juveniles in a Missouri murder case, *Roper v. Simmons,* to be argued in fall 2004.

"Three-Strikes Laws" covers the tough anti-crime statutes passed in twenty-five states that impose long prison terms for repeat offenders. California's law is the most severe. It imposes mandatory terms of twenty-five years to life on a defendant convicted a third time of any one of a long list of offenses, including some nonviolent crimes. Proponents say the laws are needed to get repeat offenders off the streets and help reduce crime. Civil liberties and criminal defense groups contend that the laws are unconstitutional and that the drop in crime is due to other causes. The Supreme Court agreed to hear a constitutional challenge to the California law in companion cases. After our report, the court upheld the California law by a 5–4 vote (*Ewing v. California, Lockyer v. Andrade,* March 5, 2003).

5 Civil Liberties Debates

KENNETH JOST

Top government officials trumpeted the arrest of José Padilla in May 2002 as a major coup in the war on terrorism. The one-time Chicago gang member and convert to Islam allegedly conspired with a leader of the al Qaeda terrorist network to build and detonate a radioactive bomb in the United States, possibly Washington, D.C.

"We have significantly disrupted a potential plot," Attorney General John Ashcroft told a news briefing on June 10. Padilla, a U.S. citizen, had been arrested on May 8 as he arrived in Chicago — carrying $10,000 in cash — after a flight from Pakistan via Egypt and Switzerland.

More than a year later, however, Padilla, also known as Abdullah al-Muhajir, embodies what many critics of the Bush administration view as the dark side of the war on terrorism: a disregard for civil and constitutional rights.

Padilla has been held incommunicado in a Navy brig in Charleston, S.C., under an order signed by President Bush as commander-in-chief designating him as an "enemy combatant" — in effect, as a captured enemy soldier. Padilla has not been charged with a crime, but for the past 16 months he has had no access to lawyers or family members: no visits, no telephone calls, no letters.

"It's not justice. It's the absence of justice," said Donna Newman, one of two New York City lawyers representing Padilla. "It's a void of rights. It's a black hole." [1]

Newman and co-counsel Andrew Patel have been fighting since June

From *The CQ Researcher,*
October 24, 2003.

Terrorism suspect José Padilla, a U.S. citizen, has been held incommunicado for 16 months in a Navy brig in Charleston, S.C., as an "enemy combatant." He has not been charged with a crime but has had no access to lawyers or family members. Critics of the Bush administration's war on terrorism say such detentions violate civil and constitutional rights.

AFP Photo/Broward County Florida Sheriff's Office

2002 to win Padilla's release from military custody through a habeas corpus action. They won a partial victory in December 2002 when U.S. District Judge Michael Mukasey ordered the government to allow Padilla to meet with one or both of the lawyers.

Padilla's right to contest his detention "will be destroyed utterly if he is not allowed to consult with counsel," Mukasey, chief federal judge for the Southern District of New York, wrote in a 102-page opinion.

However, the government balked at even that limited step. In an appeal, the Justice Department contends that allowing enemy combatants access to lawyers would risk "critically compromising the military's efforts to obtain vital intelligence." The case — *Padilla v. Rumsfeld* — is now set for argument before the 2nd U.S. Court

of Appeals in New York on Nov. 17.

Padilla's detention is only one of a long list of government moves since the Sept. 11, 2001, terrorist attacks that critics say are compromising the individual rights — of both citizens and foreigners — protected by the U.S. Constitution:

- The government rounded up more than 750 Arab residents, the so-called 9/11 detainees, and refused to release their names. It held many of them for weeks or months and deported hundreds after secret immigration hearings — all without charging any in connection with the attacks.

- Congress passed and Bush signed a sweeping law — the USA Patriot Act — enlarging the government's powers to conduct electronic surveillance or obtain personal records not only in terrorism cases but also in other criminal investigations. [2]

- The Justice Department broadened the FBI's discretion to conduct surveillance on domestic organizations, even as the Patriot Act made it easier for the CIA to share information with the FBI or other domestic law enforcement agencies.

- Some 660 foreigners captured in Afghanistan as "enemy combatants" are being held at Guantánamo Naval Base in Cuba without charges, access to lawyers or any form of judicial review, while the government plans military trials critics say will provide few procedural rights. Two cases challenging the detentions are pending before the U.S. Supreme Court.

- Besides Padilla, two other men are being held incommunicado at

Most Americans Concerned About Civil Liberties

A majority of Americans worry about how the war on terrorism is affecting civil liberties, according to a recent Associated Press poll.

How concerned are you that new measures to fight terrorism in this country could end up restricting our individual freedom?

Very or somewhat concerned — **65.9%**

Not too concerned or not at all — **32.2%**

Do you think that in its efforts against terrorism, the United States has or has not violated the legal rights and individual freedom of people living in the United States?

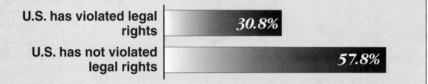

U.S. has violated legal rights — **30.8%**

U.S. has not violated legal rights — **57.8%**

Do you think the Bush administration has gone too far, not gone far enough or has been about right in using new laws that give the government more power to fight terrorism?

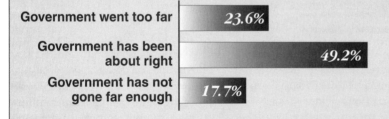

Government went too far — **23.6%**

Government has been about right — **49.2%**

Government has not gone far enough — **17.7%**

Source: Random telephone poll of 1,008 adults over age 18 conducted Sept. 4-8, 2003, for The Associated Press by ICR/International Communications Research

the Charleston brig as "enemy combatants"; one of them is a U.S. citizen: Yasser Hamdi, captured in Afghanistan while fighting for the Taliban regime. His case is now pending before the Supreme Court. *

U.S. officials insist the moves are both effective and constitutional. "We are winning the war on terror," Ashcroft said in a series of speeches in August and September aimed at rebutting criticism of the administration's tactics.

"We are safer" today than before Sept. 11, Assistant Attorney General Daniel Bryant remarked, "without having sacrificed any of our constitutional liberties and traditions." [3]

Civil liberties advocates disagree on both counts. "Since Sept. 11, there has been a steady assault on many fundamental liberties in the name of fighting terrorism but in ways that have nothing at all to do with catching terrorists," says Kate Martin, executive director of the Center for National Security Studies in Washington.

"I worry that in the name of fighting terrorism we haven't done some of the things that could be effective and, instead, are doing some things that will do much more harm than good," says Elliot Mincberg, vice president and legal director of People for the American Way. [4]

Independent legal experts have mixed views about the impact the administration's anti-terrorism tactics have had on civil liberties. Some, like Stuart Taylor, a veteran legal-affairs writer and columnist for *National Journal*, says the civil libertarians' warnings are "at best shrill and overblown and at worst flat-out false."

Other experts, however, lambaste the administration's broad claims that it can act unilaterally in secret and without normal judicial review. "They cut out the courts, they cut out defense counsel, they cut out the press, they cut out the public generally," says Stuart Schulhofer, a professor at New York University Law School and author of a report on the issues for the Century Foundation. "This is not a good prescription for effective government." [5]

So far, legal challenges to the administration's actions have proved fruitless. Suits by civil liberties advocates failed to open the secret immigration hearings for the 9/11 detainees or even to force the administration to identify those being held. (*See sidebar, p. 90.*)

---

* The third person being held as an enemy combatant in the brig in Charleston is Ali Saleh Kahlah al-Marri, a Qatari who lived in Peoria, Ill. Prosecutors said he had more than 1,000 credit-cards in files on his laptop computer along with oaths to protect al Qaeda leader Osama bin Laden, photos of the 9/11 attacks and files detailing weaponry and dangerous chemicals.

A federal appeals court upheld the government's incommunicado detention of Hamdi earlier this year. In his ruling in the Padilla case, Mukasey also upheld the government's power to hold enemy combatants but reserved a limited role for courts to review the basis for the detentions.

Somewhat surprisingly, Congress has proven to be a bit more responsive to civil liberties concerns. With a measure of bipartisan support, Congress derailed proposals for a national identification card, killed a plan to ask the general public to report suspicious activities and stymied another plan for scanning computer databases to try to identify suspected terrorists.

"When we think about the greatest civil liberties victories since 9/11, most have come from Congress," says Jeffrey Rosen, an associate professor at George Washington University Law School in Washington and legal-affairs editor for *The New Republic.*

Many previous episodes have tested Americans' support for civil liberties in the face of security threats, both domestic and international. Political dissidents were subjected to surveillance, investigation and, in some cases, prosecution during and after both of the 20th century's world wars, much of the Cold War and the domestic upheavals of the 1960s and '70s. Ethnic Germans were harassed during World War I, while 110,000 persons of Japanese ancestry — most of them U.S. citizens — were forced into internment camps during World War II.

The government's roundup of Muslims and Arabs strikes many critics as a repetition of episodes now widely acknowledged as shameful. "We've targeted the liberties of foreign nationals, and especially Arabs and Muslims," says David Cole, a professor at Georgetown University Law Center in Washington. [6]

Most observers, however, say any infringements on civil liberties in the current war on terrorism are less severe than those of the past. "We [may] come to regret some of the laws and

technologies established after Sept. 11," Rosen says. "But I don't think any of them compare to the excesses committed after the previous wars."

The administration and its supporters counter all of the criticisms with one overarching fact: the absence of any repeat of a 9/11-type terrorist incident. "Another major victory is that we've gone two-plus years, and it hasn't happened again," says Paul Rosenzweig, senior legal research fellow at the Heritage Foundation and an adjunct professor at George Mason University Law School in Fairfax, Va. "We can be pretty darn happy that the Golden Gate Bridge is still standing, Mount Rushmore is still there, the Arch in St. Louis hasn't been bombed."

Critics, however, are less inclined to credit the administration with having prevented any new terrorist attacks. "It is as if I say I have an elephant gun in my office and there are no elephants in my office, therefore the gun has been successful," said Laura Murphy, Washington office director for the American Civil Liberties Union (ACLU). "We cannot protect the American people by military might and increased law enforcement powers alone." [7]

As the country struggles with liberty and security issues, here are some of the major questions being debated:

Are parts of the Patriot Act unconstitutional?

Congress wasted little time after the 9/11 attacks in overwhelmingly approving new law enforcement powers in the fight against terrorism when it passed the Patriot Act in October 2001. Less than two years later, however, a solid bipartisan majority in the House of Representatives voted to bar funding for one of the act's provisions broadening the government's power to conduct so-called "sneak and peek" searches with delayed notification to the subjects of the investigations.

"This is the first of a whole group of assaults we are going to launch on

the Patriot Act," said Rep. C. L. "Butch" Otter, R-Idaho, before the House voted 309-118 to approve the prohibition as part of the Justice Department appropriations bill. "It was built in a day," Otter continued. "We're going to have to tear it down piece by piece." [8]

Bush administration officials appeared likely to win support in the Senate for stripping out the provision and hinted at a presidential veto if it stayed in the bill. But the legislative maneuver highlights the growing controversy around many of the Patriot Act's provisions for expanded law enforcement powers.

Critics contend a number of the act's provisions — including the sneak-and-peek provision, Section 213 — broaden the government's powers so much as to violate the Fourth Amendment's restrictions on law enforcement searches and surveillance. (*See box, p. 97.*) "The Patriot Act went too far, too fast in taking away basic checks and balances on government surveillance and other law enforcement powers," says Timothy Edgar, legislative counsel in the ACLU's Washington office. [9]

The administration insists that the provisions enlarge law enforcement powers only marginally and fully satisfy constitutional standards. "We must be better equipped to strike hard blows against terrorism," Bryant says. "At the same time, however, the Justice Department is committed to honoring and strengthening constitutional liberty so that we will not strike foul blows." [10]

Besides the sneak-and-peek provision, one other section of the law has been the principal target of opponents: Section 215, which makes it easier for the government to obtain personal records held by so-called "third parties" without notice to the subject of the search. The section has been dubbed the "angry librarian" provision because it could be used to obtain records of a person's library borrowings. But it also applies to a person's financial or medical records — or, in the act's terms, "any tangible thing." The provision al-

Inspector General Criticizes 9/11 Detentions

After the Sept. 11, 2001, terrorist attacks, federal agents searching for terrorists in the United States arrested hundreds of foreign nationals — mostly Arab and Muslim men.

In New York City, an Egyptian cabdriver with an expired visa was arrested carrying pictures of the World Trade Center. He was held for five months and then released.

In Louisville, 40 Mauritanians were detained because one of them was rumored to be taking flying lessons. Four were charged with overstaying their visas and held in jail for more than a month. [1]

Most of the detainees were jailed for months in federal detention centers on immigration violations but were never charged with crimes. Immigration violators are not automatically granted legal counsel, so many detainees had trouble retaining lawyers. Secret hearings determined their fate, and because the government refused to disclose their whereabouts, frantic relatives struggled to find them.

The government also detained terrorism suspects on minor criminal violations. Two Somali men were stopped in Texas for carrying a fake ID and a pocketknife one-quarter inch longer than legal. They were released the next day. [2]

The Department of Justice (DoJ) claimed the detentions were vital to national security. "Taking suspected terrorists in violation of the law off the streets and keeping them locked up is our clear strategy to prevent terrorism within our borders," Attorney General John Ashcroft said six weeks after 9/11. [3]

But a report on the detention of 762 illegal aliens by the DoJ's inspector general in the 11 months following Sept. 11 sharply criticized Justice Department tactics.

The report found "significant problems in the way the detainees were handled." Some were beaten while incarcerated. In other instances, the government violated immigration policy by failing to promptly tell the detainees why they were being held. [4]

"People were denied access to lawyers; they were beaten up in jail and held in abusively harsh conditions when they weren't ever even charged with a crime," says Kate Martin, director of the Center for National Security Studies.

In fact, none of the detainees were ever charged with crimes related to Sept. 11, writes Georgetown University law Professor David Cole in a new book about civil liberties and terrorism, and only two or three proved to have any terrorism ties, such as donating money to organizations with links to terrorists. [5]

According to the inspector general, the government cast too wide a net. "The FBI should have taken more care to distinguish between aliens whom it actually suspected of having a connection to terrorism from those aliens who, while possibly guilty of violating federal immigration law, had no connection to terrorism but simply were encountered in connection with an investigative lead," the report said.

The report also criticized the government's "hold until clear" policy, which kept immigrants behind bars longer than necessary because overworked FBI agents often took months to clear detainees of any terrorism ties.

lows the government to obtain the records by certifying to a special, secret federal court that the investigation is terrorism-related. And it provides for no notice to the person whose records are being sought and prohibits anyone holding the records from divulging the government's request for them.

The provision "violates the Fourth Amendment because it allows the government to obtain a vast array of personal records about any person in the United States without first establishing probable cause that the target has done anything wrong," says Ann Beeson, an ACLU lawyer. She is representing six Arab-American and Islamic organizations in a federal court suit in Detroit challenging the constitutionality of the provision. [11]

"These charges are nonsense," writes Heather Mac Donald, a senior fellow with the Manhattan Institute, a New York City-based conservative think tank. "Critics of Section 215 deliberately ignore the fact that any request for items under the section requires judicial approval." [12]

Beeson says the provision also violates the First and Fourth Amendments by "gagging" anyone from talking about the search and barring notice to the target. But Mac Donald says those restrictions are "crucial for the Justice Department's war-making function."

Justice Department officials say the provision changes existing law only slightly because the government already had the power to obtain personal records through a grand jury subpoena. Some independent experts agree at least in part. "Critics have certainly distorted [Section 215] in suggesting that it completely changes the legal landscape," Rosen says.

Beeson points out, however, that the new law allows the federal secret court to use a lower standard of evidence to approve a records search than is generally required by grand juries. Moreover, she notes, the secrecy surrounding the records searches — notably the gag rule — is new legal landscape.

Rosen acknowledges that the act makes "troubling" changes in previous practices — most significantly by imposing the gag rule. "That degree of opacity is something the government hasn't sought before," he says. "It seems hard to justify."

Ashcroft announced in September that the government, in fact, has never used the new section. "We're relieved that it hasn't been used," Beeson says, "but we don't have any reason to believe the attorney general won't start using it tomorrow."

"The government's use of immigration laws as a pretext for holding people indefinitely turned out to be a terrible policy for civil liberties," says Timothy Edgar, legislative counsel for the American Civil Liberties Union (ACLU). "Immigration law is not the detention of aliens statute; it's the statute that allows the government to remove people from the country." Normally, immigration detainees are held for a day or two, not months, Edgar adds.

The inspector general's report outlined 21 recommendations for improving immigration detentions, including streamlining the FBI clearance process, clarifying the rights of detainees and improving jail conditions.

The Justice Department said it was implementing some of the recommendations. [6] But Barbara Comstock, a DoJ spokeswoman, said, "We make no apologies for finding every legal way possible to protect the American public from further terrorist attacks." [7]

Last month, the inspector general said the Justice Department was addressing many of its concerns but that "significant work remains before the recommendations are fully implemented."

Some legal experts say the government has a right to detain immigrants suspected of being terrorists. "The inspector general did not find any actual rights violations, nor did he question the legal authority of the government to detain people. He just questioned the way the detentions were carried out," says Heather Mac Donald, a fellow at the conservative Manhattan Institute, a think tank.

Mac Donald also says that national-security issues trump concerns over civil rights: "The government was doing what was perfectly appropriate to protect the security of the country, which is its paramount duty, and without which, nothing else matters."

A leading architect of the administration's anti-terrorism policies, however, now acknowledges the government overstepped its bounds. "The [inspector general's] report was a very dramatic wake-up call," says Viet Dinh, the author of the USA Patriot Act who served as assistant attorney general under Ashcroft for two years until returning to Georgetown University Law Center in Washington as a professor in summer 2003. "The Department of Justice rightly said, 'We regret the mistakes, and we are taking steps to rectify them.' "

— Benton Ives-Halperin

[1] Human Rights Watch, *Presumption of Guilt*, August 2002, pp. 13-14.

[2] *Ibid.*

[3] National Public Radio, "Weekend All Things Considered," Oct. 27, 2001.

[4] U.S. Department of Justice, Office of Inspector General, "The September 11 Detainees: A Review of the Treatment of Aliens Held on Immigration Charges in Connection With the Investigation of the September 11 Attacks," April 29, 2003. www.usdoj.gov/oig

[5] David Cole, *Enemy Aliens* (2003), p. 22.

[6] Richard B. Schmitt and Richard A. Serrano, "U.S. Finds Abuses of 9/11 Detainees," *Los Angeles Times*, June 3, 2003, p. A1.

[7] Eric Lichtblau, "Ashcroft Defends Detentions as Immigrants Recount Toll," *The New York Times*, June 4, 2003, p. A23.

Should Congress give the government additional powers in anti-terrorism cases?

On the eve of the second anniversary of the 9/11 attacks President Bush called for new legislation to strengthen the government's hand against terrorists. In Sept. 10 remarks to the FBI Training Academy in Quantico, Va., Bush asked for legislation to deny bail to suspected terrorists and broaden the death penalty for terrorism-related offenses.

Most controversially, the president said the government should be able to obtain records in terrorism investigations with "administrative subpoenas" issued by federal law enforcement agencies rather than judicial subpoenas issued by courts.

Bush pointed out that administrative subpoenas are used in "a wide range of criminal and civil matters," including health-care fraud. "If we can use these subpoenas to catch crooked doctors," Bush said, "the Congress should allow law enforcement officials to use them in catching terrorists." [13]

Bush's proposal was more limited than a draft bill circulated by the Justice Department in early January 2003 but later disavowed. That 120-page proposal included provisions to bar the release of information about persons detained in terrorism investigations, create a DNA database on suspected terrorists and allow the government to strip someone of U.S. citizenship for supporting a terrorist organization. [14]

Despite the limited agenda, Bush's proposal drew fire from civil libertarians and skepticism even from leading Republicans on Capitol Hill. Anthony Romero, the ACLU's executive director, said in a press release that it was "unfortunate" that Bush had used the 9/11 anniversary to "continue to endorse the increasingly anti-civil liberties policies" of the Justice Department. Meanwhile, Senate Judiciary Committee Chairman Orrin Hatch, R-Utah, said it was unlikely that any proposals would be enacted this year. [15]

Administrative subpoenas are already used in some federal law enforcement contexts, but typically in regulatory-type cases where government attorneys consider civil penalties as well as criminal prosecutions. Assistant Attorney General Bryant says allowing their use in terrorism investigations would save government the time and trouble of finding a judge to authorize the subpoena.

"It comes down to a question of speed," Bryant says. "If we're going to prevent a terrorist episode, speed is of the essence."

Advocates on the left and the right say the administration has not made the case for the change. "Where is the need to not have a little bit of independent check by the judicial branch?" says Mincberg of People for the American Way. "That independent check is very important."

The Heritage Foundation's Rosenzweig is also unenthusiastic. "Administrative subpoenas are rare in situations where the tools available to the government are exclusively criminal in nature," he says. "Before accepting this proposed change, I would want more data and more information as to their actual practical necessity."

But columnist Taylor goes even further than the administration proposals, calling for a "systematic re-assessment" of civil liberties rules that limit the government's powers to investigate terrorism and hold suspected terrorists. Writing in *The Brookings Review* in January 2003, Taylor specifically proposed easing the rules on search warrants in terrorism cases and permitting "coercive" interrogation or "preventive detention" of suspected terrorists if necessary to prevent a terrorist attack. [16]

Of the three proposals, preventive detention appears to be the one most likely to draw serious consideration. Taylor argued that the administration already is effectively exercising a preventive-detention power by holding suspected terrorists as "enemy combatants" or as "material witnesses" under existing federal law. He noted that civil liberties groups had accused the administration of misusing the material-witness statute and argued that a carefully drawn preventive-detention law could provide greater protection for individual liberties than existing practices.

Mincberg agrees — up to a point.

"I support the idea . . . so that the president and Congress can debate it and make a conscious decision as to whether it's appropriate," he says. "We may well decide that it's not appropriate, but the advantage is that it brings the issue out in the open."

Rosenzweig is openly supportive. "Instead of using existing laws on an ad hoc and inappropriate basis, we would have a law more suitably targeted to those very few situations where it would be appropriate," he says. "Great Britain has such a law, and it hasn't diminished the level of civil liberties there."

Taylor's proposal would allow what he called a "preventive search or wire-

U.S. Army MPs take a terrorist suspect detained at the U.S. Naval Base in Guantánamo Bay, Cuba, to an interrogation facility.

tap" of anyone whom the government has reasonable grounds to suspect of preparing or helping others prepare for a terrorist attack. On interrogation, he says law enforcement agents should be allowed to use "psychological coercion short of torture or brutality" if neces-

sary to prevent a terrorist attack — even if the statements might be inadmissible in a criminal prosecution.

Rosenzweig endorses both suggestions. "If we have more significant needs than criminal punishment, we can forgo the criminal punishment for purposes of saving a million lives," he says.

Mincberg disagrees, particularly about coercive interrogation. "Once you allow what is explicitly considered coercive, the line between that and physical and mental torture is an awfully thin line," he says.

Is the administration misusing the power to detain "enemy combatants"?

The Bush administration has strongly defended its treatment of the 660 foreigners captured in Afghanistan and held since early 2002 as "enemy combatants" at the U.S. naval base at Guantánamo Bay, Cuba. But, departing from its usual practice of confidentiality, inspectors from the International Committee of the Red Cross (ICRC) have strongly criticized the legal basis for and the mental-health effects of the protracted detentions.

"U.S. authorities have placed the internees in Guantánamo beyond the law," the ICRC said in a report dated Aug. 25 but first publicized in October. "This means that, after more than 18 months of captivity, the internees still have no idea about their fate, and no means of recourse through any legal mechanism." [17]

White House spokesman Scott McClellan rejected the ICRC criticism. "I remind you these are enemy combatants that are being detained at Guantánamo Bay," he said in a regular news briefing. "They are treated humanely." At the same time, Maj. Gen. Geoffrey Miller, the commander of the

Army task force that runs the detention center, defended the prolonged captivity.

"We don't want the enemy combatants here to stay one day longer than is necessary," Miller told *The New York Times*. He added, however, that questioning of the detainees was "producing intelligence of enormous value" but necessarily took time.

Despite the White House brush-off, the Red Cross' unusual public statement adds to the growing chorus of complaints about the administration's use of its power to hold "enemy combatants," both at Guantánamo Bay and within the United States. Even some of the administration's supporters have criticized the decision to hold two U.S. citizens as enemy combatants within the United States and to deny them access to families or lawyers or direct review by the courts. And several major human rights groups have criticized the uncertain legal status of the detainees held at Guantánamo.

"The situation increasingly looks like a case of indefinite detention, which is something the United States condemns when it takes place in other countries," says Tom Malinowski, Washington advocacy director for Human Rights Watch.

The Guantánamo detainees include alleged Taliban and al Qaeda fighters. Miller has said all of the detainees are terrorists or terrorism supporters and may be held until the war on terrorism is over. The administration refuses to classify the detainees as prisoners of war, but nevertheless claims they are being treated in accord with the Geneva Conventions. [18]

Malinowski acknowledges the United States acted legally in the original captures, but claims the Taliban fighters were entitled to prisoner-of-war status and thus should have been repatriated to Afghanistan unless they are to be tried for war crimes. The Heritage Foundation's Rosenzweig disagrees.

He says most, if not all, of the detainees, including the Taliban captives,

were "clearly unlawful combatants" under the rules of war that require, for example, soldiers to be in uniform. "They were fighting illegally, and are therefore not entitled to the protections of the Geneva Convention."

Even so, Rosenzweig says the administration should process the detainees faster. "As a matter of American policy we should be working toward sorting them appropriately so that those who are potentially innocent or pose no dangers can be released," he says.

The administration has even less support for its decision to hold U.S. citizens Hamdi and Padilla as enemy combatants. Civil liberties advocates and independent legal experts have criticized the moves in the strongest of terms, and vocal support for the administration is minimal.

People for the American Way, for example, says the moves are evidence of "the administration's unilateral form of justice." NYU Law Professor Schulhofer calls the administration's actions "utterly unjustified." Columnist Taylor calls the incommunicado detentions "outrageous." And even Rosenzweig voices doubts. "I'm troubled by the idea that an American citizen in prison on American soil doesn't have access to a lawyer," he says.

Defending the administration, Mac Donald of the Manhattan Institute describes Padilla's as a "hard case." She says the Constitution gives Padilla the right to a lawyer only if he is being criminally prosecuted, but notes that Judge Mukasey appointed two attorneys to represent him in a habeas corpus action.

More broadly, Mac Donald argues that allowing attorneys to meet with Padilla would interfere with the government's ability to interrogate him about al Qaeda operations. "What if Padilla were about to crack and give up his superiors just before a lawyer began consulting with him?" Mac Donald writes. "The opportunity to pierce al Qaeda's structure could be lost forever."

But Schulhofer strongly disagrees. "There is nothing more central to civil liberties than the power of the executive branch to detain citizens," he says. "The whole history of habeas corpus going back to the 13th century has been a fight over this exact point: whether the executive can arrest people and throw them into jail without ever having to answer to the courts."

BACKGROUND

Wartime Fears

Civil liberties have been compromised repeatedly in the past when the country was at war or in fear of attack from without or from subversion within. In historical hindsight, the government's actions during many of those episodes have come to be widely, though not universally, regarded as mistakes. [19]

Less than a decade after ratification of the Bill of Rights, Congress in 1798 approved a package of laws — the Alien and Sedition Acts — ostensibly aimed at preventing attack or subversion from Napoleonic France. The Alien Act, which was never enforced, authorized the president to deport any non-citizen he deemed dangerous without any judicial review. The Sedition Act — which outlawed criticism of the government, Congress or the president — became notorious because it was largely used against President John Adams' political opponents.

Both laws expired after two years, and President Thomas Jefferson pardoned all those convicted under the Sedition Act. As Georgetown's Cole notes, however, Congress also passed a law still on the books — the Enemy Alien Act — authorizing the president to detain or expel any citizen of a country with which the United States is at war. The Supreme Court upheld the law as recently as 1948. [20]

During the Civil War, President Abraham Lincoln on eight separate occasions suspended the writ of habeas corpus — the centuries-old judicial procedure by which prisoners may challenge the legality of their detention. Lincoln acted so the government could deal with rebel sympathizers and anti-draft rioters. The broadest order, issued in September 1862, suspended habeas corpus nationwide. The military used this authority to imprison as many as 38,000 civilians. In one case, Chief Justice Roger Taney ruled that Lincoln had exceeded his authority, but the president ignored the ruling. A year after war's end — and Lincoln's assassination — the Supreme Court held that the president has no power to unilaterally suspend habeas corpus, even in time of war, if ordinary civil courts are functioning. [21]

After the United States entered World War I in 1917, Congress passed a law, the Espionage Act, which made it a crime to cause insubordination or disloyalty within the military or to advocate resistance to the draft. The Sedition Act, passed in 1918, was aimed more broadly at anarchist or communist dissent. It prohibited "any disloyal, profane, scurrilous, or abusive language" regarding the form of the U.S. government, the Constitution or the flag. More than 2,000 persons were prosecuted under one or the other of the laws. The Supreme Court reviewed only a handful of the convictions, upholding all of them typically by unanimous votes. [22]

The crackdown on dissent continued after the war. A series of terrorist mail-bombs that began in April 1919 prompted Attorney General A. Mitchell Palmer to launch a series of raids that resulted over the next two years in the arrest of an estimated 4,000 to 10,000 aliens for suspected communist views. Hundreds were deported as a result of the so-called "Palmer Raids." More would have been arrested but for the oppo-

sition to the mass arrests by Labor Secretary Louis Post, then in charge of immigration matters. [23]

In the most notorious wartime infringement of civil liberties, more than 110,000 people — mostly Americans of Japanese descent — were removed from their homes and interned in concentration camps during World War II. The forced removals resulted from an executive order that President Franklin D. Roosevelt issued on Feb. 19, 1942 — two-and-a-half months after the Japanese bombing of Pearl Harbor. Citing fears of Japanese attacks along the West Coast, Executive Order 9066 authorized the Army to designate "strategic areas" from which all persons of Japanese ancestry would be excluded. The Army also issued a curfew for anyone of Japanese descent.

In successive decisions, the Supreme Court upheld both the curfew and the relocations in 1943 and 1944. [24] In 1988 — more than 40 years later — Congress passed a law formally apologizing to and providing reparations for Japanese-Americans interned during the war. [25]

In his book detailing the events of the Civil War and the two world wars, Chief Justice William H. Rehnquist concludes that it is "neither desirable nor . . . remotely likely that civil liberty will occupy as favored a position in wartime as it does in peacetime." [26]

But Geoffrey Stone, a professor and former dean at the University of Chicago Law School, viewed the history less favorably in a speech to the Supreme Court Historical Society. "In time of war or national emergency," Stone said, "we respond too harshly in our restriction of civil liberties, and then, later, when it is too late, we regret our behavior." [27]

Cold War Scares

C ivil liberties were again tested — this time for a protracted period

— during the decades-long Cold War against global communism and the domestic upheavals occasioned by the civil rights and anti-war movements of the 1960s and '70s. Congress and the states passed an array of laws aimed at limiting the rights of communists or other "subversives." Some were eventually struck down as infringing on political and free-speech rights. The FBI and the CIA conducted surreptitious surveillance and infiltrated civil-rights and anti-war groups, and when the activities were exposed, Congress and presidents of both parties acted to prevent similar abuses in the future. [28]

The anti-subversive laws included the so-called Smith Act — Title I of the Alien Registration Act of 1940 — which made it a crime to advocate the overthrow of the government by force or violence or to belong to a group dedicated to that purpose. A decade later, the McCarran Act — formally, the Internal Security Act of 1950 — required communist or so-called communist-front organizations to register with the government and disclose their membership lists. Members of registered groups were barred from holding federal jobs. Many states also passed laws barring communists or suspected subversives from holding various jobs — notably, as teachers.

Meanwhile, congressional investigations by the House Un-American Activities Committee (HUAC) and a Senate subcommittee headed by Sen. Joseph R. McCarthy, R-Wis., pressured federal agencies to ferret out and fire suspected subversives. Congressional probes also drove movie studios and television networks to "blacklist" current and former Communist Party members and others with leftist political views from jobs in the entertainment industry.

The anti-communist investigations — viewed as "witch-hunts" by critics — eventually petered out, but only after grievous harm to the lives and

Chronology

Before 1945

Civil liberties restricted during times of war and threats of war.

1798
Fearing war with France, Federalist-controlled Congress passes Alien and Sedition Acts targeting foreigners, political opponents.

Civil War
President Lincoln suspends right of habeas corpus, allowing military trials of rebel sympathizers, draft resisters; Supreme Court rules Lincoln went beyond constitutional powers.

World War I
Espionage Act bars draft resistance; Sedition Act prohibits "disloyal" language; more than 2,000 prosecutions under one or the other law; Supreme Court upholds laws.

World War II
Japanese-Americans interned in concentration camps; Supreme Court upholds government actions.

1946-1990
Civil liberties tested during Cold War and civil rights and anti-war movements.

1950s
Federal and state laws and congressional investigations target communists, "subversives"; Supreme Court upholds laws at first.

1960s
FBI and CIA infiltrate and disrupt civil rights, anti-war groups.

1970s
CIA barred from domestic intelligence-gathering; FBI curbed in investigations of domestic political groups; Foreign Intelligence Surveillance Act of 1978 permits but limits wiretaps within U.S.

1990s
Terrorism tied to Islamic fundamentalist group al Qaeda strikes U.S. soil.

1993
Bomb at World Trade Center kills six.

1996
Antiterrorism and Effective Death Penalty Act, signed in April. . . . Truck bomb at U.S. barracks in Saudi Arabia claims 19.

1998
Twelve Americans among 224 killed in bombings at U.S. embassies in Kenya, Tanzania.

2000
Suicide bombers kill 17 seamen aboard USS *Cole* in Yemen.

2001-Present
Terrorist attacks lead to new anti-terrorism powers for government.

Sept. 11, 2001
Al Qaeda operatives crash hijacked airliners into World Trade Center, Pentagon and Pennsylvania field. . . . Hundreds of Musliims are detained on immigration charges.

October 2001
U.S. leads invasion of Afghanistan to topple Taliban regime for harboring al Qaeda network. . . . USA Patriot Act provides new anti-terrorism tools.

November-December 2001
Taliban regime falls in Afghanistan; hundreds of Taliban, al Qaeda fighters later brought to Guantánamo Naval Base in Cuba.

April-May 2002
Yaser Esam Hamdi, U.S. citizen captured as Taliban soldier, challenges his detention as "enemy combatant."

May-June 2002
José Padilla, accused May 8 of plotting to detonate radioactive bomb; designated as "enemy combatant" in early June and transferred to military brig.

December 2002
Federal judge in New York City rules government must allow Padilla access to lawyers; government's appeal to be argued on Nov. 17 before federal court.

Spring-Summer 2003
Federal appeals court in Washington in March rejects challenge by families of Guantánamo detainees. . . . Justice Department watchdog group blasts treatment of 9/11 detainees in June, but appeals court blocks release of names. . . . Federal appeals court in Richmond, Va., says Hamdi not entitled to lawyer.

July 2003
House bars "sneak and peek" search warrants under Patriot Act; Senate unlikely to follow suit.

August 2003
Attorney General Ashcroft launches public relations offensive to defend Patriot Act after criticism grows.

October 2003
Supreme Court opens new term, facing petitions on 9/11 detainees, Guantánamo internees, Hamdi.

reputations of the people caught up in the probes. In 1954 the Senate censured McCarthy for his tactics; in the 1960s HUAC shifted its focus to civil rights and anti-war groups before being renamed and then abolished in 1975.

The Supreme Court's response was "mixed and evolved over time," according to Professor Stone. The court during the early 1950s upheld both the Smith and the McCarran acts as well as laws barring communists from the bar, the ballot or public employment. In the late 1950s and the '60s, however, the court issued rulings that restricted the scope of the Smith Act, limited legislative investigations of individuals based on political views and narrowed governmental discretion to bar public employment on the basis of political beliefs or association. [29]

The FBI's targeting of civil rights and anti-war groups in the 1960s utilized the same kinds of surveillance, infiltration and disruption that the agency, under its longtime director J. Edgar Hoover, had first used against subversive organizations in the 1950s. Under the bureaucratic acronym COINTELPRO, FBI agents monitored and sometimes infiltrated dissident groups, compiled political-intelligence files on more than 500,000 Americans and worked to discredit and disrupt organizations the agency deemed to be subversive. Among the most notorious episodes was the FBI's wiretapping of the Rev. Dr. Martin Luther King Jr. over a period of several years.

Meanwhile, the CIA — limited by its 1947 charter to foreign intelligence activities — also joined in clandestine surveillance of domestic groups. Operation CHAOS, launched in 1967, eventually compiled files on 13,000 people, including 7,000 U.S. citizens, and 1,000 domestic organizations. Investigations encompassed an array of questionable tactics, some of them arguably illegal, including wiretaps, burglaries, opening of mail and inspection of income tax records.

The FBI and CIA abuses were exposed first in news stories and then thoroughly documented in the mid-1970s by two congressional committees and a blue-ribbon commission appointed by President Gerald Ford and headed by Vice President Nelson Rockefeller. Reforms followed. Ford issued an executive order in 1976 reiterating the bar on CIA involvement in domestic intelligence-gathering and barring information-sharing with law enforcement agencies, including the FBI. Ford's attorney general, Edward Levi, issued guidelines aimed at narrowing the FBI's discretion in surveillance and intelligence-gathering of political groups — guidelines reinforced under President Jimmy Carter's attorney general, Griffin Bell. And Congress in 1978 approved the Foreign Intelligence Surveillance Act which required a warrant for all but one category of foreign intelligence surveillances conducted within the U.S.

The reforms quieted the controversy, but the new focus on terrorism has caused a re-examination. Kate Martin of the Center for National Security Studies says the changes have served the country well. "There's certainly much more awareness of Fourth Amendment privacy and First Amendment speech and religion being protected," she says.

But Richard Morgan, a professor of political science at Bowdoin College in Brunswick, Maine, and author of a book on the issues, says the changes went too far. "We really did overcorrect in the late 1970s," Morgan says. "We built firewalls between domestic and foreign intelligence which cost us grievously."

Terror Attacks

New threats to U.S. security at home and abroad emerged in the 1980s and '90s in the form of terrorism —

both international and domestic. Nothing prepared the country, however, for the horrific attacks of Sept. 11, 2001, that left nearly 3,000 people dead and the entire country in grief and shock. President Bush declared war on global terrorism, and Congress passed the Patriot Act to strengthen the government's hand against terrorist organizations. Civil libertarians' warnings about the moves found little support at first, but drew more attention as the government tested the reach of the new powers. [30]

The earliest of the terrorist incidents directed against the United States occurred overseas. An elderly American, Leon Klinghoffer, was thrown overboard during the hijacking of an Italian cruise liner by Palestinian terrorists in October 1985. More than 270 persons were killed when a bomb planted by Libyan intelligence agents caused Pan American Flight 103 to crash in Scotland in December 1988.

International terrorism arrived on domestic soil in February 1993 when a bomb exploded beneath New York City's World Trade Center, killing six and injuring more than 1,000. The perpetrators were Islamic fundamentalists later linked to al Qaeda. International terrorists were initially blamed when a powerful truck bomb destroyed a federal office building in Oklahoma City in April 1995, killing 168 people. The deed was, instead, masterminded by a domestic terrorist: Timothy McVeigh, an Army veteran turned anti-government zealot.

Congress responded to the growing threat of terrorism in 1996 by passing the Antiterrorism and Effective Death Penalty Act, a complex statute that combined several modest anti-terrorism provisions with major restrictions on the use of federal habeas corpus in state death penalty cases. Among other provisions, the law allowed the government to block fund-raising by terrorist organizations and to deny visas to foreigners who belonged to such groups. [31]

Calls for stronger action later in the

Key Provisions of the Patriot Act

The sweeping 2001 law known as the USA Patriot Act expands the search-and-surveillance powers of federal law enforcement agents in anti-terrorism and other investigations. Several provisions amend the Foreign Intelligence Surveillance Act (FISA) — the 1978 law that created a special, secret court for authorizing searches and surveillance in foreign-intelligence investigations. [1] Here are major provisions of the act:

Roving wiretaps (Section 206) — Allows the FISA court to authorize wiretaps or intercepts on any phone or computer that may be used by the target of an investigation if the target's actions "may have the effect of thwarting . . . identification"; previously, only a specific computer or phone could be tapped.

"Sneak and peek" searches (Section 213) — Permits delayed notice of execution of search warrant in any criminal investigation if immediate notification "may have an adverse result"; the warrant must provide for notice to the target "within a reasonable time," but the period may be extended by court "for good cause shown."

Pen registers; "trap and trace" (Section 214) — Sets a minimal standard allowing government to obtain an order from the FISA court to trace outgoing telephone calls (pen registers) or incoming calls ("trap and trace") if "relevant to protect an ongoing investigation of international terrorism or clandestine intelligence activities." Previously, the minimal standard — less than the general "probable cause" requirement — applied only in foreign intelligence investigations.

"Angry librarians" provision (Section 215) — Allows FBI to apply to the FISA court for order requiring libraries, booksellers and other businesses to produce "any tangible things (including books, records, papers, documents, and other items)"

for an "authorized investigation . . . to protect against international terrorism or clandestine intelligence activities"; "no person" may disclose that the FBI has sought or obtained items under this section. Previously, FISA authorized such orders only "for purposes of conducting foreign intelligence" and required target to be "linked to foreign espionage."

Internet surveillance (Section 216) — Permits government to monitor "the processing and transmitting of wire or electronic communications" — specifically, by obtaining information about "dialing, routing, addressing or signaling," but not "the contents" of any communication; allows any court to issue such order if information likely to be obtained "is relevant to an ongoing criminal investigation" — that is, not solely for anti-terrorism investigations. Previous law had no explicit provision for Internet surveillance.

Business records (Section 218) — Allows physical searches, wiretaps and subpoenas of business records as authorized in proceeding before FISA court if foreign intelligence-gathering is a "significant purpose" (rather than "the purpose" under original law).

Nationwide wiretaps (Section 220) — Allows single federal court to issue nationwide search warrant for electronic evidence. Previously, a court could authorize searches only within its geographic district.

Sources: Congressional Research Service; Dahlia Litwick and Julia Turner, "A Guide to the Patriot Act," Slate, Sept. 8-11, 2003 (www.msn.com).

[1] The title of the law is an acronym for Uniting and Strengthening America by Providing Appropriate Tools Required to Intercept and Obstruct Terrorism (USA PATRIOT) Act of 2001, Pub. L. No. 107-56, 115 Stat. 272 (Oct. 26, 2001).

---

decade went largely unheeded, even after two attacks on U.S. facilities abroad. A truck bomb exploded outside a U.S. military barracks in Saudi Arabia in June 1996, killing 19 Americans. Two years later, bombs damaged U.S. embassies in Kenya and Tanzania on the same day — Aug. 7, 1998 — killing 224 persons, including 12 Americans. In a third incident, 17 U.S. seamen were killed when the USS *Cole* was severely damaged in an explosion in October 2000 while refueling in Aden, Yemen. All three bombings are now linked to al Qaeda.

The previously unimaginable quantum of death and destruction wrought by the carefully coordinated airline hijackings of Sept. 11, 2001,

destroyed any trace of complacency about terrorism within the United States. President Bush rallied the nation and the world to a war against global terrorism in general and specifically against Osama bin Laden's al Qaeda network and the Taliban government in Afghanistan that provided him safe haven. Domestically, Bush proposed and Congress passed within six weeks an omnibus bill — 342 pages long — aimed at strengthening law enforcement powers to prevent terrorist incidents and prosecute and punish suspected terrorists. The Patriot Act raised penalties for terrorism-related offenses, created new anti-money laundering procedures aimed at drying up funding for for-

eign terrorist groups and gave immigration officials new powers to detain or deport suspected foreign terrorists. [32]

Along with the immigration provisions, the search-and-surveillance powers were the focus of most of the debate in Congress. The final bill included some Justice Department requests — such as roving wiretaps — that Congress had previously turned aside. In a compromise, the bill also included a "sunset" clause terminating some of the new search-and-surveillance powers in 2005 unless reauthorized by Congress. Two major provisions, however, are not subject to the sunset clause: the expanded authority for the government to use sneak-and-peek search warrants

Critics Denounce Military Tribunals

On Nov. 12, 2001 — two months and a day after the terrorist attacks on New York and the Pentagon — President Bush ordered the use of secret military tribunals to try suspected terrorists captured in Afghanistan and elsewhere during the war on terrorism. Legal experts and human-rights activists immediately denounced the tribunals as unfair and unconstitutional. [1]

Almost two years later, 660 prisoners from 42 countries have been detained by U.S. and allied forces and are being held — virtually incommunicado — at the military's high-security Camp Delta prison in Guantánamo Bay, Cuba. Though none have been formally charged, six detainees — including two Britons and an Australian — could be tried at Guantánamo soon.

"We want to take the time and make sure it's done right," says Maj. John Smith of the Defense Department's Office of Military Commissions, adding that the military is "working expeditiously" to bring the six to trial.

But Defense Secretary Donald Rumsfeld has suggested that most of the inmates could be held without trial for the duration of the war on terrorism. "Our interest is not in trying them and letting them out," he said in September. "Our interest is in . . . keeping them off the streets." [2]

To date, the military has released 68 detainees to their home countries. Most were sent to Afghanistan and freed, but four were transferred to Saudi Arabia for detention there. [3] Smith says the released prisoners were no longer a threat and possessed no untapped intelligence.

Meanwhile, lawyers for several of the remaining detainees are seeking an explanation for why they are being held. They maintain that the prisoners are entitled to a status hearing under international law and the Geneva Convention.

"Due process goes where we go. That's what democracy means," said Barbara Olshansky, assistant legal director for the Center for Constitutional Rights in New York, which is representing two Britons and two Australians who have filed writs of habeas corpus.

Two federal courts have dismissed their petitions, ruling with the administration that the detainees have no legal rights since they are being held in Cuban territory. The case has been appealed to the Supreme Court. In October, a group of former judges, diplomats and prisoners of war filed several friend-of-the-court briefs on behalf of the detainees. [4]

Military-tribunal procedures have been criticized by human-rights activists for concentrating too much power in the executive branch. Activists say they allow the Defense Department to serve as prosecutor, defense lawyer, judge, jury and final arbiter of appeals. [5]

The tribunals also allow the military, in the interest of homeland security, to suspend procedural rights, such as denying detainees and their civilian lawyers access to evidence being used in the trial; barring civilian lawyers from proceedings on "sensitive" matters; and banning civilian lawyers from discussing the case.

and to obtain business and other records held by third parties.

In the two years since enactment, sentiment about the law has shifted both on Capitol Hill and among the public at large. Discontent with the sneak-and-peek and records search provisions boiled up this summer as Congress considered the Justice Department appropriations measure. On July 22 the House attached a rider to the bill barring use of any funds for sneak-and-peek warrants; the 309 members voting for the amendment included almost all of the chamber's Democrats (195); nearly half of the Republicans (113) and the lone independent, Bernard Sanders of Vermont. Sanders had a similar amendment to bar funding for any records searches under the law, but a procedural dispute blocked consideration. [33]

Meanwhile, popular discontent with the law was increasing, fueled by civil libertarians' critiques of the search-and-surveillance powers. By early October 2003, the ACLU was claiming that 194 communities in 34 states had adopted resolutions that criticized parts of the act. The Justice Department discounted the resolutions, but the actions helped prompt Ashcroft to launch his recent unusual public relations offensive to defend the law.

In the first of his speeches defending the law — an Aug. 19 address to the conservative American Enterprise Institute think tank — Ashcroft said the act "gave law enforcement improved tools to prevent terrorism in the age of high technology" and "began to tear down the walls" between law enforcement and intelligence agencies. "We have used these tools to provide the security that ensures liberty," Ashcroft said.

CURRENT SITUATION

Legal Challenges

As the head of a resettlement services center for Middle Eastern refugees, Mary Lieberman did not pay much attention to the Patriot Act as Congress was approving the anti-terrorism law in October 2001. But she got a crash course on the law in November 2002, when the FBI delivered a subpoena under the act's controversial Section 215 demanding personal files on all of the center's current and past Iraqi-born clients.

Such rules are even more restrictive than those imposed on Japanese and Nazi leaders at the war-crimes trials after World War II, said Don Rehkoph, co-chair of the Military Law Committee of the National Association of Criminal Defense Lawyers (NACDL). The NACDL has said it would be "unethical" to represent a client under the current rules. [6]

The American Bar Association has called on the administration and Congress to revise the regulations to allow civilian lawyers to more actively participate in the trials. [7]

But administration officials insist that the courts can provide a "full and fair" hearing of the evidence and urge skeptics to wait and see. They say they're unlikely to overhaul the regulations, though they could fine-tune them. "It's very easy to be critical of the process when you haven't seen it in action," Maj. Smith says, noting that such legal tenets as presumption of innocence and the right to remain silent will apply in the tribunals. "It will look very much like a standard courtroom proceeding."

"There is clear authority under international law to set up and try people under the military tribunals," says John Norton Moore, a law professor at the University of Virginia and chairman of the national and international security section of the conservative Federalist Society. "There is very solid ground for the administration to be utilizing tribunals for combatants when they have violated a number of fundamental principles of international law. Indeed, I think it's the preferred method of proceeding. It protects na-

tional security. Moreover, domestic criminal litigation is not geared for war-fighting settings."

Meanwhile, human-rights activists and veterans' groups worry that U.S. policy will be used to justify other unlawful detentions abroad. Already, the de facto law minister of Malaysia has argued that its imprisonment of 70 alleged Islamic militants without trial is "just like the process in Guantánamo." [8]

And activists warn that it could "create a free license for tyranny in Africa" as well. [9] "We've exported a situation where the rule of law doesn't apply," Olshansky says.

— *Kelly Field*

[1] American Bar Association, "Task Force on Treatment of Enemy Combatants," Aug. 12, 2003, p. 1.

[2] Matt Kelley, "U.S. Defense Chief Says Trials are Likely But Most Will Remain in Detention for War's Duration," The Associated Press, Sept. 11, 2003.

[3] Neil A. Lewis, "Red Cross Criticizes Indefinite Detention in Guantánamo Bay", *The New York Times*, Oct. 10, 2003, p. A1.

[4] Jennifer C. Kerr, "Court Urged to Review Guantánamo Appeals," The Associated Press, Oct. 9, 2003.

[5] American Bar Association, *op. cit.*, p. 2.

[6] The Associated Press, "U.S. May Ease Tribunal Rules," *Newsday*, Aug. 14, 2003, p. A18.

[7] "Injustice in Guantánamo," *The New York Times*, Aug. 22, 2003, p. A22.

[8] Sean Yoong, "Malaysia Slams Criticism of Security Law Allowing Detention Without Trial," The Associated Press, Sept. 9, 2003.

[9] Shehu Sani, "U.S. Actions Send a Bad Signal to Africa," *International Herald Tribune*, Sept. 15, 2003, p. 6.

"I don't want a terrorist to destroy this country any more than anyone else," says Lieberman, who serves as executive director of Bridge Refugee and Sponsorship Services in Knoxville, Tenn. But the "broad-brush" subpoena struck her as an invasion of privacy for the 40 or so Iraqi refugees that the center had helped over the past decade. "The far greater red flag for me is the violation of their civil liberties," she explains.

The center eventually negotiated with the FBI to provide names and addresses of its clients but no further information. But Lieberman was still discontented enough to agree readily when the ACLU asked the center to join a federal lawsuit challenging the constitutionality of the act's provision broadening the government's power to obtain third-party records in foreign intelligence or anti-terrorism investigations.

The suit — filed on behalf of the center and five organizations representing Arab- or Muslim-Americans — is one of several legal challenges to the administration's anti-terrorism tactics, including three now pending before the Supreme Court. The Justice Department is vigorously defending the administration's actions in all of the cases and so far has prevailed in all but one. In the only exception, a federal judge in New York City ordered the government to allow accused "dirty bomb" suspect Padilla access to a lawyer to challenge his detention as an "enemy combatant."

The government's appeal — scheduled for argument before the U.S. Court of Appeals for the Second Circuit on Nov. 17 — is shaping up as a pivotal showdown between the administration and a broad array of legal and civil liberties groups from across the ideological spectrum. [34] Friend-of-the-court briefs

supporting Padilla's right to counsel have been filed by civil liberties groups ranging from the Cato Institute and Rutherford Institute on the political right to People for the American Way and the ACLU on the left. The American Bar Association also urged the appeals court to uphold the December 2002 order by Judge Mukasey in New York demanding that the government allow Padilla to meet with his lawyers.

In its appeal, the U.S. argues the Supreme Court upheld the president's power as commander-in-chief to detain enemy combatants captured on U.S. soil in a World War II decision — *Ex parte Qirin* (1942) — involving captured German saboteurs. The government contends the same principle applies in the war against terrorism even if the "enemy combatant" is a U.S. citizen and not a uniformed soldier for a recognized government.

The brief goes on to argue that Padilla has no right to counsel under either the U.S. Constitution or the Geneva Convention, which established internationally recognized rules for waging war. "The laws of war recognize no right of access to counsel for persons detained as enemy combatants," the brief states.

In their brief for Padilla, attorneys Newman and Patel argue that because he is a U.S. citizen and not a uniformed soldier for a foreign government he cannot be held as an enemy combatant. They contend that under the Constitution's Due Process Clause Padilla is entitled to "plenary review" of the basis for his detention. And they argue that denying him access to counsel "has effectively blocked Padilla's ability to present a defense" to the accusations against him.

The appeals court decision is likely to be several months away. Legal observers say the losing side is all but certain to appeal to the Supreme Court. The high court already has been asked to review a decision in a similar case that upheld the government's authority to deny a U.S. citizen held as an enemy combatant access to lawyers.

The detainee in that case, Hamdi, was captured in Afghanistan and later found to have been born in Louisiana. In a January 2003 ruling, a three-judge panel of the U.S. Court of Appeals for the Fourth Circuit overturned a lower court decision that would have allowed Hamdi to challenge his detention. The full appeals court voted 8-4 on July 9 to let the panel's decision stand. [35] Hamdi's lawyers have asked the high court to review the decision. The government's response is due on Nov. 3.

The Supreme Court has two other terrorism-related legal challenges before it. In companion cases, relatives of Guantánamo detainees are challenging the government's decision to hold them without judicial review on constitutional and international law grounds. The U.S. Court of Appeals for the District of Columbia Circuit ruled in March 2003 that the detainees had no access to

American courts because they were not being held on U.S. soil. [36]

In the other challenge, a coalition of groups led by the Center for National Security Studies is pressing a Freedom of Information Act (FOIA) request for the names of the immigrants rounded up in the U.S. immediately after 9/11. In a 2-1 decision, the D.C. Circuit ruled in June 2003 that the government did not have to disclose the information because of a "law enforcement" exemption in the FOIA law. [37]

The government won one other important ruling that, for procedural reasons, will not get to the Supreme Court. In its first-ever appellate case, the three-judge Foreign Intelligence Surveillance Court of Review in November 2002 upheld the Justice Department's position that the Patriot Act authorizes sharing of foreign intelligence surveillance information with domestic law enforcement agencies. The 48-page ruling reversed a May 2002 decision by the seven judges who serve as trial courts for foreign intelligence wiretaps. That ruling had imposed restrictions on the government's surveillance and information-sharing procedures. [38]

Political Debates

The Bush administration's anti-terrorism tactics are drawing increased criticism from members of Congress, seemingly dooming any likelihood of new legislation to expand law enforcement powers. But Republicans and even many Democratic lawmakers continue to express support for most of the provisions of the Patriot Act, suggesting that any wholesale rollback of the law is also unlikely.

The mixed views were apparent as the Senate Judiciary Committee opened the first of a planned series of oversight hearings on the administration's anti-terrorism prosecutions and investigations. Chairman Orrin Hatch, R-Utah, opened the Oct. 21 hearing by casting doubt

on what he called the "rhetoric, confusion, and distortion" surrounding the administration's domestic counterterrorism program. But Sen. Edward M. Kennedy, D-Mass., accused the administration of "extreme measures which may well threaten basic freedoms more than they prevent acts of terrorism."

Democrats aimed their strongest criticisms at the detentions of U.S. citizens as enemy combatants, the post-9/11 roundup of aliens and the detention of foreign enemy combatants at Guantánamo Naval Base in Cuba. On the Patriot Act itself, some Democrats said provisions of the law went too far, citing the expanded authority for "sneak and peek" search warrants and business-records searches. Other Democrats, however, discounted the criticisms. Sen. Joseph R. Biden Jr. of Delaware, a former Judiciary Committee chairman, called criticism of the law "incorrect and overblown."

Justice Department officials appearing as witnesses at the hearing also rejected criticisms of the law. "The various misperceptions that have been perpetuated about the Patriot Act are disturbing and simply wrong," said Christopher Wray, assistant attorney general for the criminal division. Echoing Attorney General Ashcroft's speeches in defense of the law, Wray pointed out that the law required judicial approval for records searches and delayed notification search warrants. He also noted that no library borrowing records have been sought under the law, but said that such information could be useful in some cases in identifying and thwarting suspected terrorists.

Civil liberties concerns were raised as Congress was working on the Patriot Act in September and October 2001 and had some effect. Some lawmakers, for example, voiced support for a national identification card to help shield against foreign terrorists, but the proposal fell by the wayside in the face of criticism from civil libertarians.

A year later, then-House Majority Leader Dick Armey, R-Texas, helped kill

At Issue

Is the government misusing the USA Patriot Act?

TIMOTHY EDGAR
LEGISLATIVE COUNSEL,
AMERICAN CIVIL LIBERTIES UNION

WRITTEN FOR THE CQ RESEARCHER, OCTOBER 2003

*i*nevitable abuse — by this administration or the next — is why the opposition to Patriot Act powers can't easily be pigeonholed with traditional labels. Groups like the American Conservative Union and the Free Congress Foundation fear a partisan Democrat could misuse its powers to investigate gun rights or anti-abortion activists.

Members of Congress feared the Patriot Act was really just a prosecutor's wish list, not limited to terrorism. They were right. In touting Patriot Act "successes," the government has often pointed to garden-variety cases such as drugs and fraud. Congress agreed to the Patriot Act, despite misgivings, because Attorney General John Ashcroft said it was vitally needed to prevent terrorism. But the ink was not yet dry on the act when the Department of Justice (DoJ) began training agents to use their new powers in ordinary criminal cases.

In June 2003, DoJ's own inspector general found serious flaws in the government's treatment of hundreds of people detained after 9/11. Many detainees languished incommunicado for months until they were finally cleared. The effect of the policy was to evade the safeguards incorporated in the never-used detention provision of the Patriot Act — a painstaking compromise hammered out after Congress rejected the administration's call for indefinite detention without judicial review.

Responding to librarians' concerns that the Patriot Act could be used to monitor the records of Americans' reading habits, Ashcroft declassified all the records orders issued under one part of the act — which turned out to be zero. He side-stepped whether other Patriot Act powers are being used to monitor Americans. The American Civil Liberties Union (ACLU) has obtained pages of blacked-out lists of these orders under the Freedom of Information Act. What types of records? Unfortunately, that remains classified.

The American public is skeptical of the Patriot Act. More than 180 local governments have urged a rollback of its expansive powers. And, in a recent poll, more than two-thirds of the respondents agreed that, whether or not civil liberties have been abused already, the government's overbroad powers will be abused at some point.

The Patriot Act contains many appropriate provisions, like those that provide more security along the Northern border and encourage hiring translators in national security positions. However, some of its expansive powers tempt federal agents to operate outside the bounds of our democratic traditions.

To keep America safe and free, some parts of the Patriot Act must be narrowed.

PAUL ROSENZWEIG
SENIOR FELLOW, HERITAGE FOUNDATION
ADJUNCT PROFESSOR OF LAW, GEORGE MASON UNIVERSITY

WRITTEN FOR THE CQ RESEARCHER, OCTOBER 2003

*h*ow ironic that the war on terrorism — meant to ensure our safety — itself inspires fear in some Americans. But those fears are born largely of confusion: Critics of the Patriot Act constantly confuse potential abuse with actual abuse.

For example, one "icon" of alleged abuse — Section 215 of the act — has turned out to be nothing of the sort. For months, librarians complained that Section 215 allows the government to get the library reading lists of political opponents. From the beginning, this criticism was overwrought, at best.

It ignored the fact that library records already could be (and often had been) subpoenaed — without prior judicial approval — by grand juries investigating offenses such as organized crime and white-collar crime. It also ignored the fact that Section 215 orders are subject to prior judicial approval under a probable-cause standard already ruled constitutional by the Supreme Court.

Most instructive, though, is the simple truth that the government has never exercised its Section 215 power — not once in two years. Critics have confused the theoretical possibility of abuse with actual wrongdoing — a confusion that doesn't help the discussion.

To be sure, the possibility of abuse calls for great vigilance. But oversight, not prohibition, is the answer to potential abuse. So long as we keep an eye on law-enforcement activity, so long as the federal courts remain open and so long as the debate about governmental conduct remains vibrant, the risk of excessive encroachment on fundamental liberties is remote.

Critics of the Patriot Act err in exalting the protection of liberty as an absolute value. That vision reflects an incomplete understanding of why Americans formed a civil society. As Thomas Powers, author of *Intelligence Wars: American Secret History From Hitler to Al-Qaeda*, recently wrote: "In a liberal republic, liberty presupposes security; the point of security is liberty."

Thus, government has a dual obligation: to protect civil safety and to preserve civil liberty. That goal can be achieved, but we must recognize that security need not be traded off for liberty in equal measure.

Maintaining "balance" between freedom and security is not a zero-sum game. Policy-makers must respect and defend our Constitutional liberties when they act, but they also cannot fail to act when we face a serious threat from a foreign enemy.

Showdown With a Terrorist

The federal government is in a high-stakes legal showdown with Zacarias Moussaoui, the only person so far to be criminally prosecuted in connection with the 9/11 terrorist attacks. [1]

The dispute threatens to block the government from seeking the death penalty against the burly, French-born Moroccan and member of the al Qaeda terrorist organization. But it could also lead the government to take the case from federal court to a military tribunal — where Moussaoui would have fewer procedural rights than in a normal criminal prosecution.

The impasse stems from the refusal by U.S. prosecutors to comply with a federal judge's orders that Moussaoui be allowed to interview three al Qaeda prisoners to try to support his defense that he did not play a part in planning the 9/11 hijackings.

Under the Sixth Amendment, a criminal defendant is generally entitled to present witnesses in his behalf and to interview potential witnesses before trial. But U.S. Attorney Paul McNulty Jr., the lead prosecutor, says Moussaoui is "an avowed terrorist" who should not be allowed to meet with "terrorist confederates."

U.S. District Judge Leonie Brinkema, who sits in Alexandria, Va., rejected the government's positions in an order first issued in January 2003 and reaffirmed in September. When the government defied the order, Brinkema scheduled a hearing on what penalty to impose.

Zacarias Moussaoui, a French national of Moroccan descent arrested in Minnesota, was supposed to be the 20th hijacker on Se[pt. 11, the government alleges.

AFP Photo

Moussaoui — who is representing himself — asked that the case be dismissed. In an unusual legal maneuver, the government also filed a motion to have the case dismissed — a move aimed at getting an immediate appeal. Brinkema responded with a ruling on Oct. 2 that barred the government from introducing evidence tying Moussaoui to the 9/11 attacks — the only charges that could warrant the death penalty.

"It would simply be unfair to require Moussaoui to defend against such prejudicial accusations while being denied the ability to present testimony from witnesses who could assist him in contradicting those accusations," Brinkema ruled.

The government has appealed the ruling to the Fourth U.S. Circuit Court of Appeals, in Richmond, Va. Appellate arguments are scheduled for Dec. 3.

The government alleges Moussaoui was supposed to be the 20th hijacker. He entered the U.S. in February 2001 and enrolled at a flight school in Norman, Okla. After washing out, he enrolled in a school in Eagan, Minn., where he used flight simulators designed to train commercial pilots. His instructors became suspicious and called the FBI, which arrested Moussaoui on Aug. 17 on immigration charges.

At the time of his arrest, FBI agents applied to the Department of Justice for permission to go to court for a special warrant to examine the contents of Moussaoui's computer but were turned down.

---

[1] Account drawn from Associated Press dispatches, September-October 2003.

---

a plan that Ashcroft pushed to create a nationwide program to collect reports of suspicious activity from people who work in a community, such as postal employees or utility repair personnel. The proposed Terrorist Information and Prevention Systems — dubbed Operation TIPS — would have set up a central hotline to call to file such reports. Civil libertarians on the left and the right said the government should not encourage mass snooping by non-law enforcement personnel. Armey insisted the plan be dropped as a condition of allowing legislation authorizing the new Department of Homeland Security to move through the House. [39]

Congress balked again in early 2003 at a controversial Defense Department proposal to scan computer databases to try to detect possible terrorist activities. The so-called "Total Information Awareness" program would have used state-of-the-art computer technology to spot patterns of suspicious behavior. Electronic privacy advocates and lawmakers from both parties criticized the proposal as government surveillance with Orwellian overtones. A provision barring use of any funds for the proposal for the time being was inserted into an omnibus appropriations bill approved in February 2003. [40]

OUTLOOK

Liberty and Security?

Judging by the names of their respective Web sites, the Justice Department and the American Civil Liberties Union apparently agree on one point in the debate over the administration's anti-terrorism tactics: Liberty and security are not mutually exclusive. The Justice Department named its special site on the war on terror www.lifeandliberty.gov; the ACLU calls its site www.safeandfree.org.

The American people, however, disagree. In a recent poll, two-thirds of those responding said they are concerned that anti-terrorism measures could result in restricting individual freedom. So far, however, most people — 58 percent — believe the government has not violated legal rights, and a near majority — 49 percent — believe the administration has been "about right" in using new laws to fight terrorism. [41]

Attorney General Ashcroft and other administration officials stoutly maintain that no rights have been infringed and none are in jeopardy. "These reforms have been rooted in constitutionally tried and true, court-tested regimes," says Assistant Attorney General Bryant.

Civil liberties groups counter that individual rights have already suffered and will suffer more if the administration does not change course. The Justice Department and other federal agencies "have impeded some of the most basic freedoms enjoyed in this country," People for the American Way says. [42]

The administration also claims that its tactics are paying off in terms of successful criminal prosecutions. In his Sept. 10 speech, Bush said that more than 260 "suspected terrorists" have been charged in U.S. courts and that more than 140 had already been convicted. Bush also said the government had "shut down phony charities that serve as terrorist fronts" and "thwarted" terrorists in half a dozen locations around the country, including Buffalo, N.Y., and Portland, Ore.

Bush's statistics are subject to doubt, however. The General Accounting Office, the congressional watchdog agency, reported in January that nearly half of the terrorism-related convictions claimed by federal prosecutors in 2002 were "misclassified." [43]

Some of the successful criminal prosecutions have also been questioned on civil liberties grounds. Attorneys for John Walker Lindh, the California man who pleaded guilty in July 2002 to aiding the Taliban, had earlier charged the FBI with interrogating him under inhumane conditions. [44] The government may have used the threat of military trials to help win guilty pleas in 2003 from six defendants charged with being members of an al Qaeda cell in Lackawanna, N.Y., outside Buffalo. [45] Civil liberties advocates also criticize the government's acknowledged decision to use Patriot Act powers in non-terrorism-related cases. [46]

On the other hand, federal prosecutors in the recent "Portland Seven" cases — which yielded guilty pleas by six defendants to plotting to aid the Taliban — cited evidence from monitored conversations that the Patriot Act was helping to dry up financial support for terrorist groups. The plea agreements "would have been more difficult to achieve, were it not for the legal tools provided by the USA Patriot Act," Ashcroft told a news conference as the last of the guilty pleas were being entered on Oct. 16. [47]

One major question mark among advocates and experts is the Supreme Court's likely attitude toward the terrorism-related case to come before the justices. Some civil liberties advocates hope the justices will be skeptical. "I do think the Supreme Court is very sensitive to its legacy and very reluctant to get itself in the position again of deferring blindly to the government during war and regretting it 20 years later," says Steven Shapiro, the ACLU's national legal director.

John Norton Moore, a University of Virginia law professor and chairman of the national and international security section of the conservative Federalist Society, predicts the court will uphold the government's actions in some of the pending cases. But he also says he expects the court to be "vigilant" in guarding against excesses. "It is precisely the role of the court to provide that kind of balancing and assessment," he says.

For their part, liberal expert Schulhofer and conservative Rosenzweig both agree that the presumed tradeoff between liberty and security is neither inevitable nor desirable. "I don't think it's a zero-sum game," Rosenzweig says. "I think we can do both."

"There's absolutely no reasons to think that you have to give up some liberty to buy some additional security," Schulhofer says. "And even if you can buy some security by giving up some liberty, it's by no means clear that giving up the liberty is the best way to buy that security." The debate, Schulhofer adds, "is distracting people from some of the issues that should be more salient."

Notes

[1] Quoted in Thomas Adcock, "Defense of 'Enemy Combatant' Turns Solo's Life Upside Down," *American Lawyer Media*, Aug. 29, 2003.

[2] The title of the law is an acronym for Uniting and Strengthening America by Providing Appropriate Tools Required to Intercept and Obstruct Terrorism (USA PATRIOT) Act of 2001.

[3] Ashcroft's speeches can be found at www.usdoj.gov; Bryant's remarks were before a panel discussion sponsored by the Washington Legal Foundation, Sept. 25, 2003.

[4] See Center for National Security Studies, "Aftermath of September 11," www.cnss.gwu.edu; People for the American Way, "Two Years After 9/11: Ashcroft's Assault on the Constitution," Sept. 9, 2003 (www.pfaw.org).

[5] See Stephen J. Schulhofer, "The Enemy Within: Intelligence Gathering, Law Enforcement, and Civil Liberties in the Wake of September 11," The Century Foundation, Sept. 5, 2002 (www.tcf.org).

[6] See David Cole, *Enemy Aliens: Double Standards and Constitutional Freedoms in the War on Terrorism* (2003).

[7] Appearance on PBS' "The NewsHour with Jim Lehrer," Aug. 19, 2003 (www.pbs.org/newshour).

[8] See Jennifer A. Dlouhy, "House Moves to Eliminate Search-and-Seizure Provision of Anti-Terrorism Law," *CQ Weekly*, July 26, 2003, p. 1905 (www.cq.com).

[9] The ACLU site includes the text of the act and various analyses and commentaries (www.safeandfree.org).

[10] For the text of the act, analysis and commentary, see this Justice Department Web site: www.lifeandliberty.gov.

[11] The case is *Muslim Community Association of Ann Arbor v. Ashcroft*, 03-72913 filed in U.S. District Court for the Eastern District of Michigan, July 2003. Other plaintiff organizations are American-Arab Anti-Discrimination Committee; Arab Community Center for Economic and Social Services; Bridge Refugee and Sponsorship Services; Council on American-Islamic Relations; and Islamic Center of Portland (Ore.).

[12] Heather Mac Donald, "Straight Talk on Homeland Security," *City Journal*, Vol. 13, No. 3 (July 2003), pp. 28-41 (www.manhattan-institute.org).

[13] See "Weekly Compilation of Presidential Documents," Sept. 15, 2003, pp. 1190-1195.

[14] The draft proposal is posted on at www.publicintegrity.org.

[15] See Keith Perine, "Legislators Hesitant to Expand Law Enforcement Authority as Comity Wanes on the Hill," *CQ Weekly*, Sept. 13, 2003, p. 2231.

[16] Stuart Taylor Jr., "Rights, Liberties, and Security: Recalibrating the Balance after September 11," *The Brookings Review*, winter 2003, pp. 25-31.

[17] International Committee of the Red Cross, "Guantanamo Bay: Overview of the ICRC's work for internees," Aug. 8, 2003 (www.icrc.org/eng).

[18] For background on the POW debate, see David Masci, "Ethics of War," *The CQ Researcher*, Dec. 13, 2002, pp. 1013-1032.

[19] Background drawn in part from David Cole, *op. cit.*; Peter Irons, *Justice at War* (1983); William H. Rehnquist, *All the Laws but One: Civil Liberties in Wartime* (1998). See also Geoffrey Stone, "Civil Liberties in Wartime," *Journal of Supreme Court History*, Vol. 28, No. 3 (forthcoming December 2003), pp. 215-251.

[20] Cole, *op. cit.*, pp. 91-92. The Supreme Court decision is *Ludecke v. Watkins* (1948).

[21] Taney's decision, issued as circuit justice for Maryland, is *Ex parte Merryman* (1861); the full court's postwar decision is *Ex parte Milligan* (1866).

[22] See, e.g., *Schenck v. United States* (1919). The court's only decision with a dissent was *Abrams v. United States* (1920).

[23] See Cole, *op. cit.*, pp. 119-129.

[24] The cases are *Hirabayashi v. United States* (1943) (curfew) and *Korematsu v. United States* (1944) (relocations).

[25] For background, see David Masci, "Reparations Movement," *The CQ Researcher*, June 22, 2001, pp. 529-552.

[26] Rehnquist, *op. cit.*, pp. 224-225.

[27] Stone, *op. cit.*

[28] Background on the intelligence agency controversies drawn from Morton H. Halperin et al., *The Lawless State: The Crimes of the U.S. Intelligence Agencies* (1976); and Richard Morgan, *Domestic Intelligence: Monitoring Dissent in America* (1980).

[29] See Stone, *op. cit.* Two of the major decisions are *Dennis v. United States* (1951) and *Yates v. United States* (1957).

[30] Background drawn in part from the following *CQ Researcher* reports: Mary H. Cooper, "Combating Terrorism," July 21, 1995, pp. 633-656; David Masci and Kenneth Jost, "War on Terrorism," Oct. 12, 2001, pp. 817-840; David Masci and Patrick Marshall, "Civil Liberties in Wartime," Dec. 14, 2001, pp. 1017-1040.

[31] See *1996 CQ Almanac*, "President Signs Anti-Terrorism Bill," pp. 5-18 to 5-25.

[32] *2001 CQ Almanac*, pp. 14-3 to 14-13.

[33] Dlouhy, *op. cit.*

[34] The case is *Padilla v. Rumsfeld*, 03-2235.

[35] The full court's decision is *Hamdi v. Rumsfeld*, 337 F.3d 335 (4th Cir. 2003). The petition for certiorari was filed with the Supreme Court on Oct. 1 (03-6696).

[36] The decision is *Rasul v. Bush*, 321 F.3d 1134 (D.C. Cir. 2003). The petitions for certiorari in the companion cases, *Rasul v. Bush* and *Al Odah v. United States*, were filed with the Supreme Court on Sept. 2 (03-334, 03-343).

[37] The decision is *Center for National Security Studies v. Department of Justice*, 331 F.3d 918 (D.C. Cir. 2003). The petition for certiorari was filed with the Supreme Court on Sept. 29 (03-472).

[38] The case is *In re Sealed Case No. 02-001* (D.C. Cir 2003), issued Nov. 18, 2002.

[39] See Jackie Koszczuk, "Ashcroft Drawing Criticism From Both Sides of the Aisle," *CQ Weekly*, Sept. 7, 2002, p. 2286.

[40] Jonathan Riehl, "Lawmakers Likely to Limit New High-Tech Eavesdropping," *CQ Weekly*, Feb. 15, 2003, p. 406.

[41] *Rasul v. Bush, op. cit.*

[42] People for the American Way, *op. cit.*

[43] U.S. General Accounting Office, "Justice Department: Better Management Oversight and Internal Controls Needed to Ensure Accuracy of Terrorism-Related Statistics," GAO-03-266, January 2003. See Mark Fazlollah and Peter Nicholas, "U.S. Overstates Arrests in Terrorism," *The Philadelphia Inquirer*, Dec. 16, 2001, p. A1.

[44] Lindh pleaded guilty on July 15, 2002, to two felony counts and was sentenced to 20 years in prison. For a detailed, somewhat critical examination of the case, see Jane Mayer, "Annals of Justice: Lost in the Jihad," *The New Yorker*, May 10, 2003.

[45] For a critical examination of the case, see Matthew Purdy and Lowell Bergman, "Unclear Danger: Inside the Lackawanna Terror Case," *The New York Times*, Oct. 12, 2003, p. A1.

[46] See Eric Lichtblau, "U.S. Uses Terror Law to Pursue Crimes From Drugs to Swindling," *The New York Times*, Sept. 28, 2003, p. A1.

[47] See Blaine Harden and Dan Eggen, "Duo Pleads Guilty to Conspiracy Against U.S.," *The Washington Post*, Oct. 17, 2003, p. A3.

FOR MORE INFORMATION

American Civil Liberties Union, 125 Broad St., 18th floor; New York, N.Y. 10004; (212) 549-2500; 122 Maryland Ave., N.E., Washington, DC 20002; (202) 544-1681; www.aclu.org.

Center for National Security Studies, 1120 19th St., N.W., 8th Floor, Washington, DC 20036; (202) 721-5650; cnss@gwu.edu.

Century Foundation, 41 East 70th St., New York, NY 10021; (212) 535-4441; www.tcf.org.

Federalist Society, 1015 18th St., N.W., Suite 425, Washington, DC 20036; (202) 822-8138; www.fed-soc.org.

Heritage Foundation, 214 Massachusetts Ave., N.E., Washington DC 20002-4999; (202) 546-4400; www.heritage.org.

People for the American Way, 2000 M St., N.W., Suite 400, Washington, DC 20036; (202) 467-4999; www.pfaw.org/pfaw/general.

Bibliography

Selected Sources

Books

Cole, David, *Enemy Aliens: Double Standards and Constitutional Freedoms in the War on Terrorism*, The New Press, 2003.

A Georgetown University law professor argues that anti-terrorism measures aimed at aliens are unconstitutional and counterproductive, and pave the way for infringement of citizens' rights. Includes detailed notes.

Hentoff, Nat, *The War on the Bill of Rights — and the Gathering Resistance*, Seven Stories Press, 2003.

The longtime *Village Voice* columnist strongly criticizes — on civil liberties grounds — various governmental activities in the war on terrorism. Hentoff's syndicated column is called "Sweet Land of Liberty."

Irons, Peter, *Justice at War*, University of California Press, 1983.

The director of the Earl Warren Bill of Rights Project at the University of California, San Diego, chronicles the wartime internment of Japanese-Americans and the court cases challenging the action. A 1993 edition discusses the government's subsequent decision to apologize for the internment and pay reparations.

Morgan, Richard E., *Domestic Intelligence: Monitoring Dissent in America*, University of Texas Press, 1980.

A professor of law and government at Bowdoin College succinctly reviews the domestic-intelligence abuses revealed in the 1970s and the reforms later adopted to prevent future abuses. Includes detailed notes. For a more argumentative account, see Morton H. Halperin, *et al*, *The Lawless State: The Crimes of the U.S. Intelligence Agencies* (Penguin, 1976).

Rehnquist, William H., *All the Laws but One: Civil Liberties in Wartime*, Knopf, 1998.

The chief justice of the United States details the history of President Lincoln's suspension of habeas corpus during the Civil War and recounts more briefly the civil liberties disputes during World War I and World War II. Includes reference notes and a five-page bibliography.

Rosen, Jeffrey, *The Naked Crowd: Reclaiming Security and Freedom in an Anxious Age*, Random House, forthcoming January 2004.

An associate law professor at George Washington University and legal-affairs editor of *The New Republic* examines the effect on security and liberty of new technologies for surveillance and "data-mining." Includes reference notes.

Articles

Lithwick, Dahlia, and Julia Turner, "A Guide to the Patriot Act," *Slate*, Sept. 8-11, 2003 (www.slate.msn.com).

The four-part series provides a detailed and balanced examination of the law's major provisions.

Mac Donald, Heather, "Straight Talk on Homeland Security," *City Journal*, Vol. 13, No. 3 (July 2003), pp. 28-41 (www.manhattan-institute.org).

A senior fellow at the conservative Manhattan Institute defends the government's actions in the war on terrorism, calling criticisms "false and dangerous."

Stone, Geoffrey, "Civil Liberties in Wartime," *Journal of Supreme Court History, Vol. 28, No. 3* (December 2003), pp. 215-251.

A former dean of the University of Chicago Law School surveys civil liberties conflicts in U.S. history from the Alien and Sedition Acts through the Cold War.

Taylor, Stuart, Jr., "Rights, Liberties, and Security: Recalibrating the Balance after September 11," *The Brookings Review*, Vol. 21, No. 1 (winter 2003), pp. 25-31 (www.brookings.org).

A *National Journal* columnist and *Newsweek* contributing editor calls for re-examining civil liberties rules limiting surveillance and detention because of "the threat of unprecedented carnage at the hands of modern terrorists."

Reports and Studies

Olshansky, Barbara, "Secret Trials: Military Tribunals and the Threat to Democracy," Seven Stories Press, 2002.

The 80-page report by the assistant legal director of the Center for Constitutional Rights sharply criticizes the Bush administration's creation of special military tribunals to try non-citizens suspected of terrorism.

People for the American Way, "Two Years After 9/11: Ashcroft's Assault on the Constitution," Sept. 9, 2003 (www.pfaw.org).

A detailed report by the liberal civil rights group says the government's actions in the war on terrorism have had a "devastating" impact on basic rights.

Schulhofer, Stephen J., "The Enemy Within: Intelligence Gathering, Law Enforcement, and Civil Liberties in the Wake of September 11," The Century Foundation, Sept. 5, 2002 (www.tcf.org).

A New York University law professor says individual freedoms have been "sacrificed" in the war on terrorism while concerns about effectiveness have been "neglected."

6 Rethinking the Death Penalty

KENNETH JOST

D aryl Atkins never did well in school. He never lived on his own or held a job. He scored 59 on a standard intelligence test — below the benchmark IQ level of 70 commonly used to define mental retardation.

Atkins' mental deficiencies did not, however, prevent a jury in southeastern Virginia from sentencing him to death for the 1996 robbery-abduction-killing of a U.S. airman.

The Virginia Supreme Court was also unmoved. "We are not willing to commute Atkins' sentence of death to life imprisonment merely because of his IQ score," the court wrote in a 5–2 decision in September 2000. [1]

One year later, however, the U.S. Supreme Court agreed to use Atkins' case to reconsider an issue it had decided 12 years earlier: whether it is constitutional to execute someone who is mentally retarded. In 1989 the court had held that sentencing a mentally retarded offender to death does not violate his Eighth Amendment right not to be subjected to "cruel and unusual punishments." [2]

Atkins' lawyers say things have changed since then. "The Eighth Amendment does not have a static meaning," the lawyers wrote in a petition asking the high court to hear the case. They noted that nearly half of the states with capital punishment now specifically bar execution of mentally retarded offenders.

Mental retardation advocacy groups agree. "The death penalty is supposed to be reserved for the most culpable

Members of the Georgetown Campaign to End the Death Penalty collect petition signatures from fellow students at Georgetown University in Washington, D.C., during Death Penalty Awareness Week in October. Students started the campaign five years ago, when public opposition to capital punishment began increasing.

of people," says Doreen Croser, executive director of the American Association on Mental Retardation. "By definition, a person with mental retardation doesn't meet that standard."

Some law enforcement advocates disagree. "The assessment of the retarded in criminal justice, as in all other aspects of life, ought to be on an individualized basis," says Barry Latzer, a professor at the John Jay College of Criminal Justice, City University of New York.

Atkins' case is one of the most recent manifestations of a broad re-examination of capital punishment in the United States over the last several years. While polls still show a solid majority of Americans favor use of the death penalty, critics have made headway with arguments about the fairness and reliability of the system for meting out death sentences. DNA profiling, or so-called genetic fingerprinting, has been used in scores of cases in the United States since 1987 to exonerate wrongfully convicted defendants — including many on death row or serving long sentences. [3]

"Over the last few years there has been a lot of movement on the death penalty issue around the country, spurred largely by revelations about innocent people freed from death row but also by some unfairness in the process — poor representation, disparities of economics and even geography," says Richard Dieter, executive director of the Washington-based Death Penalty Information Center.

"There's a healthy skepticism about the death penalty and its reliability," Dieter adds. "That's a different tone than existed five or 10 years ago, where the emphasis was to speed up the death penalty and even to expand it."

Death penalty supporters acknowledge the gains opponents have made, but they believe the erosion in support was ending before the Sept. 11 terrorist attacks and the issue has been relegated to a back burner since then.

"The opposition had gained some momentum, but I think a lot of the steam has gone out of that," says Kent Scheidegger, legal director of the Sacramento, Calif.-based Criminal Justice Legal Foundation, which supports capital punishment. "They got a lot of very good press with some very dubious studies. [But] some reality was beginning to set in even before Sept. 11. Since then, I haven't seen much interest."

Death penalty critics scored some of their gains by arguing that the legal system, as it now operates, risks allowing an innocent person to be executed. The issue moved onto a front burner in July 1997 when Dieter's group published a report claiming that 69 "innocent" persons had been freed from death rows since the reinstitution of capital punishment in the United States in 1976. "The risk that innocent people will be caught up in

From *The CQ Researcher,* November 16, 2001.

A Quarter-Century of Capital Punishment

More than 700 men and women have been executed in the United States in the 25 years since the Supreme Court allowed the reintroduction of capital punishment in 1976. Executions have been carried out in 32 of the 38 states with the death penalty, with more than 80 percent of them taking place in the South. Overall, executions are down this year. In fact, in the top three death penalty states — Texas, Virginia, and Florida — only 15 people have been executed so far in 2001, compared with 54 last year.

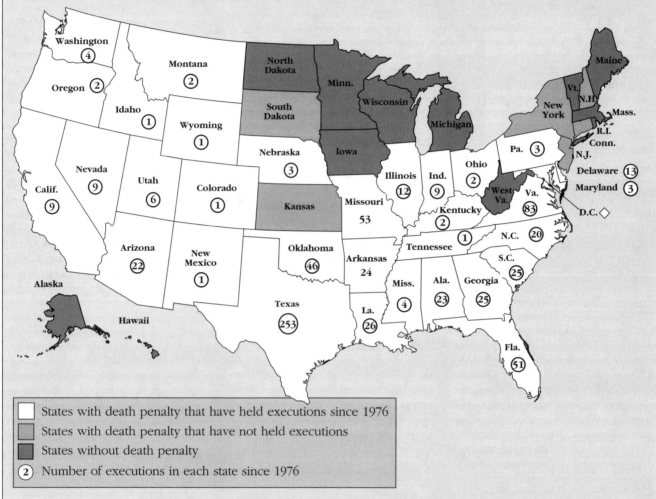

Note: A total of 741 executions were carried out in the U.S. since 1977 through Nov. 12, 2001, including two federal executions in 2001, both at the U.S. penitentiary in Terre Haute, Ind.: Timothy McVeigh for the 1995 bombing of the Murrah federal building in Oklahoma City that killed 168 people and Texas drug kingpin Juan Raul Garza for three murders. They were the first federal executions since 1963.

Source: Death Penalty Information Center

the web of the death penalty is rising," the report said. [4] Today, Dieter puts the number at 98.

But death penalty supporters note that the count includes cases in which a defendant won a reversal of his conviction or sentence because of legal error, not an actual finding of factual innocence. In addition, death penalty supporters say — and Dieter acknowledges — that critics have failed to document a single instance in which an incontrovertibly innocent person was put to death in the United States in the 20th century.

"A thorough review finds that the risk of executing the innocent has been significantly overstated by death penalty opponents," says Dudley Sharp, resource director of the Houston-based victim advocacy group Justice for All.

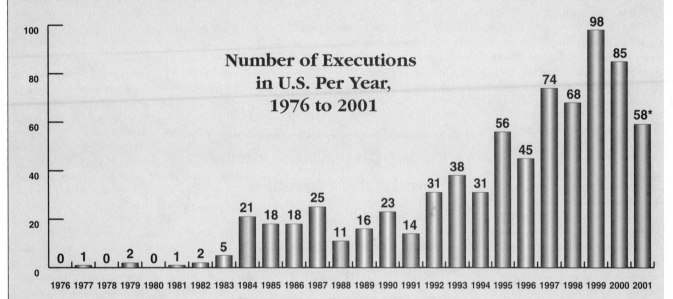

Number of Executions Declining

If this year's execution rate continues as expected, 2001 will mark the first time since the death penalty was reinstated in 1976 that executions have declined for two consecutive years. While a majority of Americans support capital punishment, questions about the fairness and reliability of the judicial system have contributed to the decline.

Number of Executions in U.S. Per Year, 1976 to 2001

Year	Executions
1976	0
1977	1
1978	0
1979	2
1980	0
1981	1
1982	2
1983	5
1984	21
1985	18
1986	18
1987	25
1988	11
1989	16
1990	23
1991	14
1992	31
1993	38
1994	31
1995	56
1996	45
1997	74
1998	68
1999	98
2000	85
2001	58*

* As of Nov. 12, the number of executions in 2001 was 58. An additional 11 executions were scheduled during the rest of the year, four of which were considered unlikely to occur.

Source: Death Penalty Information Center

"The risk is extraordinarily low."

Nonetheless, critics emphasize the seemingly frequent reversals of capital sentences or convictions as evidence of flaws in the trial and appellate procedures in death penalty cases. "The death penalty system is not functioning in a rational or effective measure [when] judged by the standards we would apply to any other process in the private or public sector," says James Liebman, a law professor at Columbia University in New York City and lead author of a major study of appellate court decisions in death penalty cases over the last 25 years. (*See sidebar, p. 110.*)

Death penalty supporters counter that the number of reversals demonstrates the careful scrutiny that death penalty cases receive not only before and during trials but also afterward. "The American death penalty has, by far, the greatest due-process protections of any criminal sanction in the world," Sharp says.

Concerned about potential errors in Illinois' death penalty system, Gov. George Ryan, a Republican, last January temporarily halted executions in his state. Similarly, Rep. Jesse L. Jackson Jr., D-Ill., introduced a bill in Congress last March imposing a moratorium on federal executions and calling on states to follow suit. No hearings have been held. (*See "At Issue," p. 121.*)

In recent years, many state legislatures have considered other proposals tinkering with the death penalty system. In 2001, five more states prohibited the execution of mentally retarded offenders, although Texas Gov. Rick Perry vetoed such a bill.

State courts are also re-examining a variety of death penalty issues. In the first such ruling in the nation, the Georgia Supreme Court in early October outlawed electrocution. [5] The decision left Alabama and Nebraska as the only states still using electrocution as the sole method of execution; Georgia had already passed a law shifting to lethal injection if a court prohibited use of the electric chair.

Meanwhile, the number of executions is declining somewhat after having reached a peak of 98 in 1999. As of Nov. 12, 58 persons have been executed in the U.S. in 2001 — including Timothy McVeigh, the Oklahoma City bomber, who became the first federal prisoner to be put to death since 1963. Currently there are some

Study Cites Flaws in Death Penalty System

Death penalty critics got new ammunition last year with a highly publicized academic study concluding that courts are twice as likely to reverse as to uphold death sentences on appeal. But death penalty supporters began attacking the study as soon as it was published and continue to describe it as methodologically flawed and ideologically biased.

The nine-year study by Columbia University Law School researchers bore a somewhat academic title: "A Broken System: Error Rates in Capital Cases, 1973-1995." [1] From the opening paragraphs, however, the authors bluntly described the death penalty system as marred by "serious error" in "epidemic proportions."

The study, based on an examination of some 4,700 death penalty cases reviewed by state or federal courts over a 23-year period, found that sentences were reversed in 68 percent of the cases. Only 18 percent of defendants were sentenced to death on retrial, the researchers found. The overwhelming majority — 75 percent — received a lesser sentence, and 7 percent were found not guilty.

The most frequent reasons for reversals, the study found, were "egregiously incompetent defense lawyers" who failed to look for evidence favorable to the defendant or "police or prosecutors who did discover that kind of evidence but suppressed it."

James Liebman, the Columbia professor who led the study, likens the courts' handling of capital cases to a "seriously flawed" manufacturing process. "Any given death sentence is much more likely — twice as likely — to get overturned, sent back and have to be redone or scrapped entirely than every one that is approved by the system's own inspectors," Liebman says.

"That's a system that appears to be costing a lot of money, producing a lot of faulty products, requiring a huge inspection system and in the end producing cases with not the results that are intended," he continues. "You not only waste a lot of time and money and frustrate the expectations of those who support the system, but you also run the huge risk that some of the errors that are being made will not be caught."

The study drew attention immediately, thanks in part to a front-page story in *The New York Times*. [2] It also promptly drew sharp attacks from death penalty supporters. In a three-page riposte, the Criminal Justice Legal Foundation termed the study "a political document, timed to impact congressional hearings" and depicted the large number of reversals in capital cases as evidence that the system had been "successfully obstructed by opponents of capital punishment." [3]

More than a year later, critics continue to discount the significance of the reversals. Barry Latzer, a professor at John Jay College of Criminal Justice, City University of New York, says the study merely demonstrates the "hypersensitivity of appellate courts"

in reviewing death penalty cases. "When you have an appellate reversal, it has nothing to do with innocence or guilt," Latzer says. "An appellate reversal is about procedural errors at trial."

In addition, Latzer and a colleague — Assistant Professor James Cauthen — argued strenuously in a leading journal on judicial affairs that Liebman's study was misleading because it failed to separate cases in which appellate courts reversed a death sentence and those in which convictions themselves were reversed. "Once the distinction between guilt and sentence is taken into account," Latzer and Cauthen wrote, "only about 27 percent of capital convictions — not two-thirds — are set aside." [4]

In fact, the debate over the study got off on the wrong foot in part because of an error in the lead paragraph of the *Times'* story, which described the study as showing reversals of "convictions" in two-thirds of death penalty cases studied. Liebman says he called the error to the *Times'* attention, which published a correction the next day.

The continuing debate between Liebman, who worked for the anti-death penalty NAACP Legal Defense and Educational Fund before joining the Columbia faculty, and Latzer, who was an assistant district attorney in Brooklyn for two years, is both ideological and statistical.

Liebman says Latzer's estimate for the rate of conviction reversals in death cases — 27 percent — is low because of a flawed methodology in analyzing a sample of state appellate decisions. While his initial study did not separate sentence and conviction reversals, Liebman says a study to be published soon will show that guilt reversals are more numerous than sentence reversals.

Whatever the exact number, Latzer and Cauthen say that counting sentence reversals along with conviction reversals overstates the charge of "systemic failure." "Judges and jurors disagree about the appropriateness of death sentences," they write.

Replying in the same publication, Liebman says that minimizing the importance of erroneous death sentences is "out of line with American criminal and constitutional law."

> "Capital trials produce so many mistakes that it takes three judicial inspections to catch them — leaving grave doubt whether we do catch them all."

[1] James S. Liebman, Jeffrey Fagan and Valerie West, "A Broken System: Error Rates in Capital Cases, 1973-1995," June 12, 2000. The study was published originally on the Internet; it is on several Web sites, including that of the anti-death penalty Justice Project (www.thejusticeproject.org).

[2] Fox Butterfield, "Death Sentences Being Overturned in 2 of 3 Appeals," *The New York Times*, June 12, 2000, p. A1.

[3] Criminal Justice Legal Foundation, "Death Penalty 'Error' Study Has Errors of Its Own," June 19, 2000.

[4] Barry Latzer and James N.G. Cauthen, "Capital Appeals Revisited," *Judicature*, Vol. 84, No. 2 (September/October 2000), pp. 64-69. Liebman, Fagan and West replied in the same issue; a second exchange appeared in *Judicature*, Vol. 84, No. 3 (November/December 2000). The entire exchange is posted on the John Jay College's Web site: www.lib.jjay.cuny.edu/docs/liebman.htm.

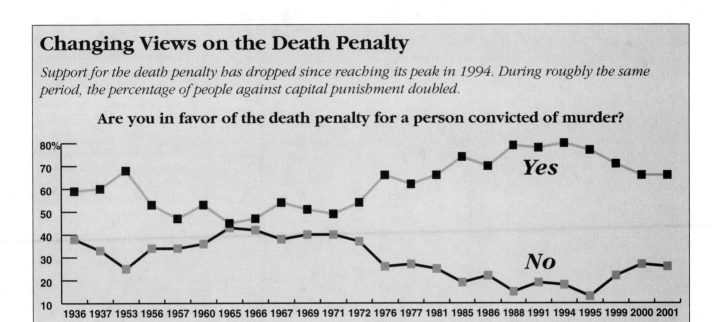

Changing Views on the Death Penalty

Support for the death penalty has dropped since reaching its peak in 1994. During roughly the same period, the percentage of people against capital punishment doubled.

Are you in favor of the death penalty for a person convicted of murder?

Yes

No

1936 1937 1953 1956 1957 1960 1965 1966 1967 1969 1971 1972 1976 1977 1981 1985 1986 1988 1991 1994 1995 1999 2000 2001

Source: The Gallup Poll

3,700 prisoners on death rows across the country.

Many of the issues surrounding the death penalty have been argued for decades, with opposing advocates and experts unable to persuade the other side. Here are some of the questions being debated in the current re-examination of capital punishment:

Is public support for the death penalty declining?

In her 20 years on the Supreme Court, Justice Sandra Day O'Connor has voted to reject most broad attacks on the death penalty and to make it harder for death row inmates to challenge their convictions or sentences in federal courts. But when O'Connor spoke to the Minnesota Women Lawyers group in Minneapolis last summer, she voiced some seemingly uncharacteristic doubts about the death penalty in the United States.

"Minnesota doesn't have it," O'Connor said, "and you must breathe a sigh of relief every day." She warned that the death penalty system "may well be allowing some innocent defendants to be executed" and called for establish-

ing "minimum standards" and "adequate compensation" for appointed counsel in death cases. [6]

Opponents seized on O'Connor's criticism to buttress their claims that public and official support for capital punishment has been declining in the past few years. "The climate seems to have taken a rather dramatic turn as of a few years ago," says Herbert Haines, a professor of anthropology and sociology at the State University of New York (SUNY) in Cortland and the sympathetic author of a history of the recent anti-death penalty movement. "It suddenly became politically and socially acceptable to have some degree of misgivings about the death penalty."

Supporters of capital punishment acknowledge that support has sagged recently. "There is no doubt that public support for executions has declined," says Sharp of Justice for All. But he and others stress that polls still register support for the death penalty from a substantial majority of the public: 67 percent in the most recent Gallup Poll on the issue. Support is "still quite high," says Latzer of John Jay College.

Supporters and opponents point to

several possible explanations for the slippage, including the drop in the nation's crime rate. [7] But death penalty supporters claim the shift is due to biased media coverage.

"The media has simply reported what the anti-death penalty movement says with little or no critical review," Sharp says. "This is an extraordinary obstacle for getting an objective presentation to the public."

Both sides agree that the so-called innocence issue has played a major part in changing public attitudes toward the death penalty. "[Now] it's a debate about the management and effectiveness of this system based upon what actually happens in the system, rather than being a debate about morality in an abstract way, which is the way the debate had been before," says Columbia's Liebman.

Opponents see evidence of weakening public support for capital punishment both in polls and in the slowed pace of executions over the past two years, as well as the flurry of congressional and state proposals to overhaul death penalty procedures. Among the reforms being sought are enforceable standards for defense counsel in death penalty trials and assured DNA testing for death row inmates who challenge their convictions. "The public strongly supports these reforms," says Peter Loge, director of the criminal justice reform campaign of the Washington-based Justice Project.

Death penalty supporters do not oppose those proposals in principle, but they disagree on details. "I know of no one opposing DNA testing," Sharp says. But, he adds, "Testing only makes sense in those cases where such testing is determinative of guilt or innocence." Similarly, Sharp says standards for defense counsel are "appropriate," depending on what those standards are.

Whatever the outcome of legislative debates, however, some prosecutors see little change in attitudes among jurors. "We haven't seen any change in support for the death penalty here, and I think most states fall in that category," says Robert McCulloch, St. Louis district attorney and chairman of the National District Attorneys' Association's committee on capital litigation.

"Nothing has changed in the 20 years I've been doing this," McCulloch adds. "We get some [jurors] who say that if they convict someone for murder, they will automatically vote for death, and others who say, 'No matter what, I won't vote for death.' But those numbers haven't changed much over the past 20 years."

Is capital punishment administered fairly?

The American Bar Association (ABA) has no official position on capital punishment. But for the past four years, the 600,000-member group has favored a moratorium on executions until states comply with a set of policies intended to ensure that death penalty cases are "administered fairly and impartially" and to "minimize the risk that innocent persons may be executed." [8]

In promoting the moratorium at the ABA's annual meeting in August, outgoing President Martha Barnett termed the existing death penalty system "absolutely unacceptable." In a letter to Congress, the Tallahassee, Fla., lawyer urged lawmakers to pass two bills — the Innocence Protection Act and the National Death Penalty Moratorium Act — as "immediate steps" to improve the fairness of the system.

Death penalty opponents say the fairness issues are helping shift public opinion in ways that the broad attacks on capital punishment failed to do. "It's not . . . that people are discovering that the death penalty is morally wrong," Dieter says, "but more a practical assessment that . . . innocent lives may be lost, that there is much that remains arbitrary and unfair about the death penalty."

Supporters of the death penalty sharply dispute the accusations of unfairness. "Capital trials are . . . among the fairest trials in the world," Latzer says. "The procedural protections are heightened. All of the parties — the lawyers, the prosecutors, the judges — are all aware of the stakes. The prosecutors are the most experienced, and the defense lawyers are increasingly being certified to handle those cases."

However, critics say a variety of factors demonstrate the unfairness of the system. Death penalty defenders dispute each of the points.

For one thing, Dieter notes that death sentences are "much more likely" to be imposed in murder cases with white victims than in those with African-American victims. Sharp acknowledges the statistic, but explains that whites are much more likely than blacks to be victims of the kinds of murders punishable by death — murders with aggravating factors such as robbery or carjacking or killings of police officers.

Death penalty opponents also emphasize the stark geographical disparities in the use of capital punishment.

They note that 80 percent of the executions since 1976 have taken place in one region of the country — the South — with more than half from just three states: Texas, Virginia and Florida. In addition, Dieter says that 40 percent of the federal cases in which U.S. attorneys have sought the death penalty have come from just five of the country's 94 federal districts. [9]

Supporters blame geographic disparities on delaying tactics of death penalty opponents themselves. "Opponents want no enforcement of capital punishments," Sharp of Justice for All says, "and it is their efforts that continue to encourage any disparity which exists between states."

Critics also say the death penalty is more likely to be imposed on indigent defendants with court-appointed lawyers. "If you can afford good quality representation, you're much less likely to get the death penalty," Dieter says. But Sharp says there is "no systemic evidence that wealthier capital murderers are less likely to be executed than poorer [ones]."

Some death penalty supporters do acknowledge a problem in uneven legal representation. Latzer, for one, calls for "more money for defense counsel" in capital cases. Death penalty critics note that court-appointed lawyers are paid well under $100 an hour in most jurisdictions. [10]

To critics, the various fairness issues point to the need for a nationwide moratorium on executions. "The evidence has accumulated to a degree that we should stop what we're doing," Dieter says. The number of people freed from death rows, he says, amount to "a national alert that we're taking too many risks. We should stop and find out whether this system is irredeemably broken or whether it can be fixed."

Death penalty supporters, however, note that under the current system there is already a long time — an average of 12 years — between conviction and execution. "On average, every

Should the Mentally Retarded Be Executed?

While psychologists disagree over whether convicted murderer Daryl Renard Atkins is mentally retarded or merely slow and unmotivated, lawyers disagree over whether putting him to death would be unconstitutional.

Sometime next year, the U.S. Supreme Court is expected to decide the second question. A constitutional ban on executing the mentally retarded — which the court refused to impose in 1989 — would significantly raise the stakes on an issue that already is difficult for lawyers, judges and jurors alike.

Death penalty supporters warn that a constitutional ban on executing mentally retarded offenders will encourage fabricated defenses on an issue with inevitably imprecise standards for judges or jurors to apply. Advocates for the mentally retarded insist that the condition has a clear and accepted definition, and that courts can easily weed out any false claims of mental impairment.

However the court rules on Atkins' constitutional plea, the case demonstrates how mental retardation claims can easily engender sharp evidentiary disputes between prosecutors and defense lawyers. Competing experts offered diametrically opposed opinions when Atkins was tried in York County in southeastern Virginia for the 1996 murder of U.S. airman Eric Michael Nesbitt. Atkins was 18 at the time, Nesbitt 21.

One other indicator of the scope of likely disagreements: Death penalty critics say at least 35 mentally retarded offenders have been put to death in the past 25 years. [1] Proponents of capital punishment call the count exaggerated and insist there are few, if any, retarded offenders awaiting execution today.

In Atkins' 1998 trial, evidence showed that he and a co-defendant, William Jones, abducted Nesbitt outside a store, forced him to withdraw $200 from an automated teller machine, and then shot him eight times. Jones claimed — and Atkins denied — that Atkins did the shooting. (Jones pleaded guilty in exchange for reduced charges.)

The jury convicted Atkins of capital murder and after a separate hearing sentenced him to death. The sentence was reversed because the jury form did not include the option of life imprisonment, but Atkins was again given the death penalty after a new sentencing hearing in 1999.

The jurors in the second proceeding heard testimony from two forensic psychologists: Evan Nelson for the defense and Stanton Samenow for the prosecution. Nelson, who administered a standard intelligence test to Atkins and examined his school records and other psychological data, concluded that Atkins was mentally retarded. Samenow, who interviewed Atkins twice but did not administer an IQ test, disagreed.

In his testimony, Nelson said that Atkins was "mildly" mentally retarded based on an IQ score of 59 and on what he called Atkins' "limited capacity for adaptive behavior." Nelson emphasized Atkins' record of "academic failure." Atkins consistently scored in the bottom fifth in standardized tests, failed the second and 10th grades and never graduated from high school.

By contrast, Samenow described Atkins as "of average intelligence." Samenow said that Atkins correctly identified the previous two U.S. presidents and the state's current governor and also appeared capable of carrying out such day-to-day activities as laundry and cooking. "There was no lack of ability to adapt and to take care of basic needs, certainly," Samenow concluded.

The two psychologists agreed, however, that Atkins knew that shooting Nesbitt was wrong and that Atkins fit the "general criteria" of an antisocial personality disorder. The prosecution introduced evidence that Atkins had prior convictions for robbing and maiming.

In upholding the death sentence, the Virginia Supreme Court said that the mental retardation issue was "a factual one" for the jury to decide. [2] But the majority in the 5-2 decision signaled agreement with Samenow's conclusion by saying that defense witness Nelson had failed to identify any "deficits" other than Atkins' low IQ score and academic failure. The dissenting justices said it was "clear" that Atkins was mentally retarded and called Samenow's testimony "incredulous."

Atkins' lawyers are now urging the Supreme Court to declare that executing a mentally retarded offender is unconstitutional under the Eighth Amendment. "It is time for this court to assess whether American society has changed significantly over the past decade to the point that the execution of the mentally retarded now violates American standards of decency," they wrote in a petition with the high court.

Lawyers for the Virginia attorney general's office disagree. "There simply is no national consensus against execution of the mentally retarded," the lawyers wrote in their brief before the state Supreme Court last year. Eighteen states prohibit execution of the retarded.

The court is likely to hear arguments in February, with a decision sometime before July. Even if the court adopts a constitutional rule against executing the mentally retarded, it most likely would send Atkins' case back to Virginia courts for further proceedings under the new standard.

Daryl R. Atkins

Virginia Dept. of Corrections

---

[1] See Death Penalty Information Center, "Mental Retardation and the Death Penalty," www.deathpenaltyinfo.org.

[2] *Atkins v. Commonwealth*, 534 S.E.2d 312 (Va. 2000).

death row inmate already has a nearly 12-year moratorium on their individual case during appeals," Sharp says.

Questioning the true motive behind the moratorium proposals, he says, "The nationwide effort for a moratorium on executions is a prelude to doing away with the death penalty altogether."

Is it "cruel and unusual" punishment to execute mentally retarded criminals?

When the Supreme Court considered the issue in 1989, only two jurisdictions in the United States — Georgia and the federal government — specifically exempted mentally retarded individuals from the death penalty. With no "national consensus" on the issue, the court concluded — by a 5-4 vote — that execution of a mentally retarded offender was not "cruel and unusual" punishment prohibited by the Eighth Amendment. [11]

Today, nearly half of the states that allow capital punishment — 18 out of 38 — prohibit execution of the mentally retarded. On that basis, an array of mental health, civil liberties and human rights groups are urging the court to adopt a constitutional rule in line with what they see as the national consensus against the practice.

"We as a society, through our laws, through our organizations, have expressed an abhorrence of the execution of those with a low IQ, those with mental retardation; and therefore it's unconstitutional," says Dieter of the Death Penalty Information Center.

"We said it was cruel and unusual punishment [in arguments in the 1989 Supreme Court case], and they said they would look to the states for some consensus on the issue," says Croser of the mental retardation advocacy group. "Since that time, we've been pretty successful" in getting states to ban capital punishment for mentally retarded offenders.

Supporters of capital punishment are ambivalent about the issue. Some

acknowledge the arguments against executing someone who is mentally retarded. "As a matter of policy, I would have no problem with a general rule that says we're not going to execute someone who is in fact retarded," says Scheidegger of the Criminal Justice Legal Foundation.

At the same time, most death penalty supporters appear to oppose a court-made constitutional rule against the practice. "Based on current law and legal opinion, execution of the mentally retarded is not cruel and unusual punishment," Sharp says. Prosecutor McCulloch in St. Louis agrees: "I don't think it would qualify today as cruel and unusual under the Eighth Amendment," he says, "but I think generally it's not going to be acceptable."

Mental retardation — commonly defined by an IQ below 70 — differs from two other conditions that sometimes become issues in criminal trials: competency and insanity. Competency refers to the ability to understand trial proceedings or consult with counsel; courts are not supposed to try a defendant who is not competent in that sense. Legal insanity denotes the inability to distinguish between right and wrong at the time of an offense; a defendant may be found "not guilty by reason of insanity" or "guilty but insane" and then committed to a mental institution for treatment rather than sentenced to prison. The Supreme Court in 1986 ruled that the Constitution prohibits the execution of someone who is insane. [12]

Mental health advocacy groups say no retarded person should be put to death because they lack the mental capacity to be treated as fully culpable of their crimes. "We're talking about people with intellectual capacity in the bottom 2 percent of the population," Croser says.

However, many death penalty supporters oppose a blanket exemption for the mentally retarded. Eliminating consideration of the death penalty without examining a defendant's "individ-

ual moral culpability," Latzer says, "is a miscarriage of justice. That is a guarantee of unequal treatment."

Sharp also favors case-by-case determinations. "The current system is the best," he says. "Determine competency before trial. Establish if the defendant knew right from wrong, if the defendant can constructively participate in his own defense. And establish if he understands the nature of his punishment. And review those issues, again, on appeal."

But Dieter says case-by-case decisions put an unfair burden on a mentally retarded defendant. "It's difficult for [a jury] to decide a separate question" about whether a mentally retarded defendant should be subject to the death penalty, he says. "Their sympathies are going to be with the victim. Their feelings are going to overwhelm any feeling that there should be mercy for the defendant."

With five more states this year banning the execution of mentally retarded offenders, supporters of a ban feel momentum is on their side. "Mental retardation is an issue that has legs," Haines of SUNY-Cortland says.

Death penalty supporters acknowledge the point. Asked whether there is now a national consensus against the death penalty for mentally retarded defendants, Scheidegger replies: "It's borderline." To the same question, Croser answers without hesitation, "Absolutely."

BACKGROUND

Death Penalty Debates

Death penalty laws have been on the books in America since Colonial times and have been enforced continuously except for the nine-year pe-

Chronology

Before 1960

Capital punishment taken for granted in U.S., but use gradually narrows over time; number of executions peaks in 1930s, declines sharply in '50s.

1960s-1970s

Executions continue to decline; Supreme Court bans death sentences in 1972, but four years later allows capital punishment to return.

1972
Supreme Court invalidates all existing death sentences in 5-4 ruling, citing uneven enforcement in states.

1976
Supreme Court restores capital punishment in 7-2 decision upholding "guided discretion" schemes with separate death penalty hearings, use of "aggravating" and "mitigating" factors to determine sentence; bars mandatory death penalty laws.

1977
Gary Gilmore, after dropping appeals, becomes first person executed in U.S. in 10 years; Supreme Court bars death penalty for rape.

1979
First involuntary execution in the U.S. since 1967.

1980s
Use of death penalty rises; Supreme Court narrows use of capital punishment in some cases, but rejects broad race-based challenge.

1987
Supreme Court rejects effort to invalidate death penalty on grounds it is most often imposed in murder cases where victim is white.

1988
Supreme Court bars executions for crimes committed at age 16 or under.

1989
Supreme Court refuses to bar execution of the mentally retarded, but says retardation is a factor to be considered in death cases.

1990s
Congress, Supreme Court limit death row challenges; death penalty opponents step up warnings that system could result in execution of innocent persons.

1994
President Clinton signs Violent Crime Control and Law Enforcement Act expanding federal death penalty; public support for death penalty peaks at 80 percent in Gallup Poll.

1995
New York becomes 38th state to provide death penalty for specified types of murder.

1996
Antiterrorism and Effective Death Penalty Act sets procedural hurdles for death row inmates in federal habeas corpus cases.

1997
Death Penalty Information Center names 69 "innocent" defendants released from death rows; American Bar Association calls for national moratorium on executions.

1999
Number of executions peaks at 99 — highest total since 1951.

2000s
Number of executions declines; calls for moratorium increase.

Jan. 31, 2000
Illinois Gov. George Ryan declares moratorium on executions in state, citing risk of executing innocent person.

June 2000
Report by Columbia University Law School researchers says two-thirds of death sentences reversed on appeal because of "serious errors"; death penalty supporters dispute study.

June 11, 2001
Timothy McVeigh is executed for Oklahoma City bombing; first federal execution since 1963.

July 3, 2001
Supreme Court Justice Sandra Day O'Connor voices doubts about death penalty; says system may allow the innocent to be executed.

Sept. 25, 2001
Supreme Court agrees to hear Virginia case testing constitutionality of execution of mentally retarded offenders; arguments due in February 2002.

Oct. 5, 2001
Georgia Supreme Court bars electric chair for executions.

Nov. 6, 2001
New Mexico becomes 32nd state to carry out death sentence since 1976, with its first execution since 1960.

"Death by electrocution, with its specter of excruciating pain and its certainty of cooked brains and blistered bodies, violates the prohibition against cruel and unusual punishment . . . of the Georgia Constitution."

— *From the majority opinion in* Dawson v. State

"Because today's decision reflects not the evolving standards of decency of the people of Georgia, but the evolving opinions of the majority members of this court, I dissent."

— *From the dissenting opinion in* Dawson v. State

AP Photo/The Paducah Sun-Seth Dixon

In the first such ruling in the nation, the Georgia Supreme Court on Oct. 5 outlawed electrocution. The decision in Dawson v. State *left Alabama and Nebraska as the only states that use electrocution as the sole method of execution.*

riod, 1968-76, marked by the Supreme Court's temporary abolition of capital punishment in 1972. Anti-death penalty campaigns in the 19th and 20th centuries succeeded in limiting executions, but failed to persuade Americans to follow the example of other industrialized democracies in banning capital punishment altogether. [13]

Early death penalty laws prescribed public execution by hanging as the mandatory punishment for various crimes against the state, persons or property. Over time, the use of capital punishment was narrowed; but some states allowed the death penalty for non-homicides, including robbery and rape, as late as the 1960s and '70s.

Beginning in the 19th century, in what was seen as a positive change, juries were given discretion in imposing the death penalty. Public executions were banned over time: the last states to perform public hangings stopped in the 1930s. The method of executions also changed with the introduction of the electric chair in the late 19th century, lethal gas a little later, and, most recently, lethal injection — now the most common method.

Anti-death penalty movements, which dated from Colonial times, were the most influential in amending death penalty practice. Abolitionist sentiment crested during the reform period of the 1830s and '40s, during the Progressive era at the end of the 19th and start of the 20th century, and again in the 1950s

and '60s. The movements drew some support from people with religious or moral scruples about capital punishment. But they achieved their limited successes only by focusing on more practical arguments. Progressive era reformers, for example, focused on the possibility of rehabilitating criminals, while evidence of racial discrimination in imposition of the death penalty strengthened opposition to capital punishment in the mid-20th century.

The number of executions peaked at about 190 a year in the late 1930s, began declining during World War II, and then dropped sharply in the 1950s and early '60s. By the middle of the decade, historian Hugo Adams Bedau — a confirmed opponent —

wrote approvingly that "nearly half the states now use the death penalty so sparingly that it plays almost no part in their program of law enforcement and criminal treatment." [14] Only one person was executed in 1966, two in 1967, and none for the next decade.

Death penalty opponents had shifted their focus by this time to courts rather than legislatures. [15] They mounted constitutional attacks claiming that the death penalty was "cruel and unusual" under the Eighth Amendment or that it was administered in an arbitrary and discriminatory fashion in violation of the Due Process or Equal Protection clauses of the 14th Amendment.

The Supreme Court turned aside a due process challenge in 1971, but in 1972 it invalidated all existing death penalty sentences by a 5-4 vote. [16] Although the five justices in the majority in *Furman v. Georgia* each wrote separately, the ruling effectively declared that the death penalty was so irrational — "wantonly and freakishly imposed," in the words of Justice Potter Stewart — that it amounted to cruel and unusual punishment under the Eighth Amendment.

Within a matter of months, state legislatures began passing new laws aimed at fixing the problems the court had cited. Ten states sought to comply with *Furman* by passing mandatory death penalty laws for certain types of murder. Many — 25 in all — chose instead to pass so-called guided discretion schemes that provided for separate death penalty hearings after conviction and listed specific aggravating and mitigating factors for jurors to consider in deciding whether to impose capital punishment.

The Supreme Court in 1976 by a 5-4 vote struck down the mandatory death laws (*Woodson v. North Carolina*), but upheld the discretionary schemes, 6-3 (*Gregg v. Georgia*). States had the green light to resume executions. [17]

Death Penalty Restored

Over the next quarter-century, the number of executions in the United States gradually increased, although they remained below pre-1950 levels. The number of death row inmates increased even faster — fueling complaints from death penalty advocates about court-imposed delays. Public support for capital punishment also increased to a record level as part of a general law-and-order trend during a period of rising crime rates. Opponents, outvoted in state legislatures and frustrated in courts, tried to develop new strategies to slow the pace of executions, but with limited success. [18]

Executions resumed slowly at first. Gary Gilmore, convicted of a 1976 robbery-murder of a motel clerk, was put to death in Utah on Jan. 17, 1977, after ordering his attorneys to drop all appeals. Two years later, Florida on May 25, 1979, executed John Spenkelink for the robbery-killing of a fellow drifter; unlike Gilmore, Spenkelink fought his sentence to the end. Through the 1980s, U.S. executions reached a peak of 25 in 1987 and another peak of 56 in 1995, before dipping slightly, and then rising again to 98 in 1999 — the highest level since 105 were executed in 1951.

Death row populations increased more rapidly, creating a backlog of hundreds and then thousands of inmates awaiting execution. The delays resulted in part from the three kinds of appeals allowed in all state criminal cases: ordinary appeals through state courts and to the U.S. Supreme Court, state post-conviction review, and federal *habeas corpus* petitions used to challenge state convictions or sentences. Anti-death penalty litigators used all those procedures more tenaciously than defense lawyers in other cases did. The result was a recurrent scene of last-minute court filings — up to and including the U.S. Supreme Court — seeking stays of execution to permit consideration of new legal claims.

The delays and apparent disorder frustrated death penalty proponents and resulted in significant changes over time. Beginning with a pivotal decision in 1983, the Supreme Court gradually made it harder for death row inmates to use *habeas corpus* to challenge their convictions or sentences. Some state courts once hospitable to death row appeals were also transformed. Pro-death penalty groups played a major role in 1986 in defeating three liberal justices on the California Supreme Court; their successors, appointed by the state's Republican governor, quickly proved to be more favorable to prosecutors and victims' rights groups.

Then in 1996, after McVeigh bombed the federal building in Oklahoma City, Congress passed a major rewrite of federal *habeas corpus* law. As part of the Antiterrorism and Effective Death Penalty Act, Congress set a new time limit: one year in most cases — but only six months in capital cases — for state inmates to file a federal *habeas corpus* petition after the end of all state appeals. Federal judges were directed to defer to rulings of state judges on constitutional and other issues unless the rulings were "unreasonable." In addition, the law required state prisoners seeking to file a second or subsequent habeas corpus petition to obtain permission from a federal appeals court, which could allow the new petition only if it was based on a new constitutional rule or on "clear and convincing" evidence of innocence.

Death penalty opponents responded to the unfavorable political and legal climates with new strategies that yielded only limited results. In the most important broad-based challenge, opponents claimed that capital punishment was racially discriminatory because the death penalty was most often imposed in murder cases with white victims. The Supreme Court rejected the argument in 1987 by a 5-4 vote. [19]

Major Capital Punishment Decisions

Here are the key U.S. Supreme Court decisions on capital punishment since the court reinstituted the death penalty in Gregg v. Georgia *in 1976.*

Case Name / Date of Decision	Vote	Holding
Gregg v. Georgia (1976)	7-2	Upholds death penalty under "guided discretion" statutes
Woodson v. North Carolina (1976)	5-4	Bars mandatory death penalty laws
Coker v. Georgia (1977)	6-2-1	Bars death penalty for rape
Enmund v. Florida (1982)	5-4	Bars death penalty for "minor" participation in felony-murder
Eddings v. Oklahoma (1982)	5-4	Strengthens requirement to consider "mitigating" factors in capital-sentencing hearings
Barefoot v. Estelle (1983)	6-3	Allows evidence of "dangerousness" in capital sentencing hearings; allows federal courts to expedite death-row challenges
Ford v. Wainwright (1986)	5-4	Bars execution of insane offenders
Booth v. Maryland (1987)	5-4	Bars victim impact statements in capital cases
McCleskey v. Kemp (1987)	5-4	Rejects race-based challenge to death penalty
Thompson v. Oklahoma (1988)	5-3	Bars execution of someone under age 16
Stanford v. Kentucky (1989)	5-4	Allows execution of 17- and 18-year-olds
Penry v. Lynaugh (1989)	5-4	Declines to bar execution of mentally retarded, but says retardation must be considered by jury
Payne v. Tennessee (1991)	6-3	Allows victim impact statements, overruling *Booth*
Herrera v. Collins (1993)	6-3	Rejects constitutional right to present claim of innocence in federal habeas corpus petition
Simmons v. South Carolina (1994)	7-2	Requires jurors to be told of life-without-parole option if dangerousness issue raised
Schlup v. Delo (1995)	5-4	Allows "actual innocence" claim if conviction "probably" resulted from constitutional violation
Felker v. Turpin (1996)	5-4	Upholds but softens limits on federal habeas corpus
Jones v. United States (1999)	5-4	Declines to require telling jurors in federal cases that judge is limited to death or life-without-parole
Penry v. Johnson (2001)	6-3	Sets aside death sentence in retrial because instruction on mental retardation again defective
Atkins v. Virginia (2002)	---	Ruling due on constitutionality of executing the mentally retarded

Sources: Joan Biskupic and Elder Witt, Congressional Quarterly's Guide to the U.S. Supreme Court *(3d ed.), 1996; Kenneth Jost,* The Supreme Court Yearbook *(annual series).*

Over the years, the high court also narrowed the use of the death penalty, at least in some instances. In 1977, for instance, it barred the death penalty for rape; in 1988 it outlawed executions for crimes committed by a defendant who was 16 or under at the time.[20] However, in 1989 the court refused, by a 5-4 vote, to bar the execution of mentally retarded offenders.

By the mid-1990s, the death penalty seemed once again to be a fact of life of American law and politics. A Gallup Poll in 1994 registered the highest support for capital punishment in the history of polling: 80 percent. A year later, New York became the 38th state to authorize capital punishment; only one of the 12 holdout states — Michigan — was among the top 10 in population.

The Innocence Issue

O ver the last five years death penalty critics have managed to put supporters on the defensive for the first time in three decades. Their major weapon has been a concentrated attack on the reliability of the death penalty system, including sharp warnings about what they say is the significant risk of executing innocent persons. Supporters have defended the system and strongly contended that critics have failed to document a single instance in which an innocent person has been put to death. But the arguments have failed to reverse a slippage in public support for the death penalty.

Anti-death penalty advocates and experts cited a 1987 study, which purported to show that 23 innocent people had been put to death in the United States in the 20th century; death penalty supporters discounted the findings. [21] A few years later, the House Judiciary Subcommittee on Civil and Constitutional Rights — chaired by Rep. Don Edwards, a liberal Democrat from California — asked the Death Penalty Information Center to study the issue. The report, published in 1993, added to the previous study by claiming that 48 persons had been released from death rows because of "subsequently discovered evidence of innocence." [22]

An updated study by the center in 1997 said a total of 69 death row inmates had been released after evidence of their innocence had emerged. "The danger that innocent people will be executed because of errors in the criminal justice system is getting worse," the study warned, citing restrictions on federal habeas corpus and reduced spending for capital defense lawyers in trials and post-conviction challenges. [23]

Death penalty supporters continued to criticize the conclusions. "The death penalty system is working and is working apparently at 100 percent accuracy," Paul Kamenar, an attorney with the conservative Washington Legal Foundation, said. He said the report listed "very few" cases where an innocent defendant was released and stressed that it cited "no case in the last 50 years where an innocent person was executed." [24]

A second academic study published in June 2000 buttressed the opponents' arguments. The study by Columbia law Professor Liebman and two colleagues purported to show that appellate courts reversed the death sentences in more than two-thirds of the cases reviewed over a 23-year period. Capital sentences in the United States are "persistently and systematically fraught with error that seriously undermines their reliability," the report concluded. [25] Again, critics disputed the methodology and the conclusions. They claimed that the study significantly overestimated the number of death-sentence reversals and that the number of reversals, in fact, demonstrated the adequacy of existing safeguards against legal mistakes in death penalty cases.

Critics fashioned legislative proposals to try to remedy what they saw as deficiencies in the death penalty system. In Congress, the major proposal became the Innocence Protection Act, a bill introduced in February 2000 with bipartisan sponsors in both the House and the Senate. The bill is designed to give federal and state inmates a right to DNA testing for post-conviction challenges if the testing would produce new evidence that the inmate did not commit the crime.

The measure also would create a commission to establish standards on qualifications and experience for defense counsel in death penalty cases and deny federal funding to states that fail to comply with the standards. In its current form, the bill has more than 200 cosponsors in the House, 24 cosponsors in the Senate.

More concretely, Illinois Gov. Ryan cited the risk of wrongful executions in his decision in January 2000 to impose a moratorium on executions in that state. "[U]ntil I can be sure with moral certainty that no innocent man or woman is facing a lethal injection, no one will meet that fate," Ryan told a Jan. 31 news conference. Ryan's action came after a multipart series in the *Chicago Tribune* questioning the operation of the death penalty system in the state and well-publicized investigations by Northwestern University journalism students that led to the exoneration of three Illinois death row inmates. [26]

In its annual report, the Death Penalty Information Center called 2000 "the most significant single year affecting death penalty opinion in United States history." [27] The report noted that several conservatives — including columnist George Will and television evangelist Pat Robertson — had joined death penalty critics in raising doubts about the system's fairness and reliability.

Death penalty supporters were surprised by the moratorium and the criticisms from prominent conservatives. But they attributed the slippage in public support to biased coverage in the news media. "That constant imbalance of coverage had taken its effect on the polling data," Sharp of Justice for All says today.

CURRENT SITUATION

Action in the States

J ust a week after the terrorist attacks on the World Trade Center, the New York state legislature made it a capital offense to kill someone in a terrorist act. The bill had bipartisan support, despite a few naysayers who questioned the bill's necessity, since terrorism cases typically are prosecuted by the federal government, not the state.

"If people want to create evil, then we're going to punish them very, very severely," said Senate Majority Leader Joseph Bruno, an upstate Republican. Assembly Speaker Sheldon Silver, a Democrat from Manhattan, said the bill was needed to show "unity of purpose."

The New York legislators' speed and near unanimity in approving the bill was reminiscent of the many times in the 1980s and '90s when state and federal lawmakers rushed to approve measures expanding or streamlining the use of capital punishment. But now the New York measure stands out as an exception to the rule: most of the bills introduced and most of the measures enacted into law this year either narrowed the use of the death penalty or added safeguards to protect defendants' rights.

This year five states enacted laws banning the execution of mentally retarded offenders: Arizona, Connecticut, Florida, Missouri and North Carolina. Three states adopted measures to allow prisoners to use DNA testing to challenge convictions: Maryland, Texas and Virginia. Texas and Virginia also passed laws aimed at establishing standards for capital defense counsel. And two states — Connecticut and Delaware — set up commissions to study death penalty policies. The Delaware study is due Jan. 8; the Connecticut study is to be submitted to the state's legislature a year later. [28]

Death penalty critics also succeeded in getting moratorium proposals introduced and debated in many states. In February, a North Carolina legislative committee recommended a moratorium on executions after a year's study, but the proposal was never brought up for a vote. In Maryland, supporters believed they had enough votes to win passage of a moratori-

Death Row USA	
No. of Inmates	**3,717**
White	1,695 (45.6%)
Black	1,602 (43.1%)
Hispanic	334 (9.0%)
Native American	45 (1.2%)
Asian/Other	41 (1.1%)
Male	3,663 (98.5%)
Female	54 (1.5%)
Juveniles*	84 (2.3%)

States with most inmates on death row	
California	600
Texas	454
Florida	383

*Under 18 at time of crime

Source: Death Penalty Information Center, NAACP Legal Defense Fund

um bill in the state Senate, but opponents blocked a vote in April with a filibuster as the legislature was about to adjourn. Moratorium proposals were also considered in California, Connecticut, Nevada, Tennessee, and Texas.

Opponents of the death penalty also came very close to abolishing capital punishment in two states — New Hampshire and New Mexico. On Feb. 10, a death penalty bill in New Mexico failed by a single vote in the state Senate, and on April 5 the New Hampshire House defeated a similar measure by a 188-180 vote. By contrast, the Massachusetts House on March 12 handily defeated a bill to bring back capital punishment, 94-60. Death penalty bills failed to advance in two of the other holdout states: Michigan and Minnesota.

In August, Illinois Gov. Ryan vetoed one of the few state bills to win legislative approval this year that would have expanded capital punishment. The measure would have provided the death penalty for anyone who com-

mits a murder "in furtherance" of a gang. Ryan said the bill was vague and duplicative and that it unfairly targeted minorities. In Connecticut, however, the bill banning executions for mentally retarded offenders extended the death penalty to murders committed while trying to avoid arrest or prevent the victim from carrying out his or her official duties.

In Texas, Gov. Rick Perry on June 17 vetoed the bill to ban executions of mentally retarded offenders after prosecutors and victim advocacy groups lobbied against it. Perry, a Republican, said the bill was unnecessary because existing law required juries to consider mental issues in imposing sentences in capital cases. The bill "is not about whether to execute mentally retarded capital murderers. We do not. It's about who makes the determination in the Texas judicial system," Perry said at a news conference.

Dieter, of the Death Penalty Information Center, calls the new state laws limiting the death penalty "a good first step in addressing a system that many feel is broken," but says it is uncertain whether they will be sufficient to make the system "fair and reliable."

Sharp, of Justice for All, emphasizes critics' failure to win enactment of moratorium proposals. "Death penalty opponents have marshaled huge resources in people, money and organizations to push the moratorium agenda," he says. "In that context, it is remarkable how unsuccessful they have been."

Signals From the Court?

Some Supreme Court justices are giving tantalizing hints of increasing skepticism toward the operation of the death penalty system in the United States. The court continues to reject most pleas from death row inmates, and none of the justices holds the view that capital punishment is flatly unconstitutional. Still,

At Issue

Should there be a national moratorium on executions?

REP. JESSE L. JACKSON JR., D-ILL.

WRITTEN FOR THE CQ RESEARCHER, NOVEMBER 2001

*j*ustice Harry Blackmun said, "The execution of a person who can show that he is innocent comes perilously close to simple murder."

Undoubtedly, taking a life is the supreme expression of a state's power over its citizens. It should not be used without offering the accused every possible opportunity to present evidence that may keep the state out of the unimaginable position of executing the innocent.

Today, science provides the criminal justice system with a means of definitively answering many questions of guilt or innocence without eyewitness testimony or circumstantial evidence. There have been great, new, scientific and technological advances in DNA and forensic evidence testing that can explore evidence previously unusable.

However, we should not overemphasize technology. Minorities and the poor often cannot pay for adequate or competent representation. They cannot afford "dream teams" who negotiate with prosecutors to eliminate the possibility of a death sentence before a trial begins — as with O.J. Simpson. Innocent people are often unable to adequately address their legal problems with definitive evidence of their innocence.

In the past, many complained that death row inmates were given too many chances to appeal a conviction, dragging out the process for years and tying up the courts. So, Congress passed the Anti-terrorism and Effective Death Penalty Act (AEDPA), limiting an inmate's right to appeal a capital conviction. However, in doing so, Congress also limited the ability of Americans wrongfully convicted to prove their innocence.

The Death Penalty Information Center reported that the average time between a capital conviction and execution is eight years. The average time that innocent people have spent on death row before proving their innocence is seven years. The provisions in AEDPA effectively cut the time between sentencing and execution in half, thus, virtually guaranteeing that innocent people will be executed.

My Accuracy in Judicial Administration Act of 2001 (AJA) calls for a minimum seven-year national moratorium on all executions until all inmates currently sitting on death row have an opportunity to explore potentially exculpatory DNA and similar evidence.

I'm opposed to the death penalty for moral, social, political and practical reasons. But even its proponents should support AJA (HR 321). It is a narrowly tailored piece of legislation that protects one of America's most fundamental constitutional rights — the right to substantive due process.

REP. LAMAR SMITH, R-TEXAS
CHAIRMAN, HOUSE JUDICIARY SUBCOMMITTEE ON IMMIGRATION AND CLAIMS

WRITTEN FOR THE CQ RESEARCHER, NOVEMBER 2001

*i*n this world of laws, our justice system will inevitably have some flaws. However, capital punishment is not one of them. If there is a defect, it is in the way we administer it.

From before the 1972 Supreme Court decision that outlawed it, to after the 1976 decision that reinstated it, the death penalty has been a topic of debate. It is described as racist, unreliable and ineffective. But no matter how detractors twist the issue, the vast majority of Americans continue to support this type of punishment.

It must be remembered that there is another party besides the murderer involved in every murder, and that is the victim. By the unjustified taking of another's life, the murderer has forfeited his own.

We are not obligated to support murderers for the rest of their natural life. If one murderer is granted life in prison while another is executed, it is only because of the extraordinary degree of leniency that we have in our American system of jurisprudence, and not because of any intrinsic unfairness.

Critics of capital punishment have sought to hobble it in every way possible. And the statistics they use to try and justify its abolition are misleading. As Mark Twain once said, "First get your facts; then you can distort them at your leisure." The fact is, however, the facts are just not there.

Some charge that capital punishment is racist. But the rates of execution reveal that white murderers are twice as likely to be executed as their black counterparts.

Others say that no deterrent effect is produced by capital punishment. The rub here is that it is impossible to prove the effect of something that didn't happen. Common sense tells us that some people refrain from murder because they fear death themselves, many others refrain from it because they consider it socially reprehensible; one of the reasons they consider it reprehensible is because people are put to death for it.

We don't need a moratorium on the death penalty. What we need is a death penalty applied in a more consistent and timely manner that will serve as a more effective deterrent to would-be murderers.

This is real justice. It is not only for society but also for the victims that we must uphold this ultimate sanction on the ultimate wrong.

some of the justices in their opinions and in comments off the bench are voicing greater doubts about the fairness and reliability of the system.

O'Connor has given the strongest — and most surprising — indication of new thinking toward the death penalty. Her remarks to the Minnesota lawyers group in July drew wide attention and surprised court observers. "Startling," says Alan Raphael, a professor at Loyola University of Chicago School of Law who watches the court's criminal law decisions. O'Connor repeated her views even more strongly in a little-noticed speech to the Nebraska State Bar Association last month. "More often than we want to recognize, some innocent defendants have been convicted and sentenced to death," she told the Nebraska lawyers. [29]

Two other justices — Ruth Bader Ginsburg and Stephen G. Breyer — have also made passing remarks critical of the handling of death penalty cases in recent months. [30] Ginsburg, in a speech in Washington on April 9, pointedly criticized legal representation for capital defendants. "I have yet to see a death case, among the dozens coming to the Supreme Court on the eve of execution petitions, in which the defendant was well represented at trial," Ginsburg said.

Breyer, in an interview with Radio France International, said, "There is much more discussion [about capital punishment] than there was five years ago." He added, "I also think that DNA will perhaps make a difference, because if we find that someone is really innocent, if we could prove this with DNA, maybe that would make a difference."

The court's decisions during the past term also displayed greater scrutiny of trial courts' handling of death cases. In two cases from Texas and South Carolina, the court set aside death sentences because of faulty jury instructions. [31] The Texas case involved the same defendant, Johnny Paul Penry, who had been involved in the 1989

case when the court refused to bar the execution of mentally retarded offenders. In the new decision, the court ruled, 6-3, that jurors at his retrial were not properly told they could consider his retardation as a mitigating factor. In contrast to this year's rulings, the court in 1999 and 2000 issued three decisions upholding death sentences despite somewhat similar challenges by defendants to jury instructions.

In the current term — which began Oct. 1 — the court already has three death penalty challenges on its docket, including the mental retardation case. The justices signaled a strong desire to decide the mental retardation question by issuing stays of execution in three cases raising the issue this spring. At the time, the court agreed to review one of the cases — an appeal by a North Carolina inmate, Ernest Paul McCarver. But after North Carolina in August banned the execution of mentally retarded offenders, the justices on Sept. 25 dropped McCarver's case and put the Atkins appeal on the court's calendar instead. Arguments are expected in February.

In one of the other cases, a Virginia death row inmate, Walter Mickens Jr., is seeking to overturn his conviction for the stabbing death of a teenager during an alleged homosexual rape-murder; Mickens claims his court-appointed lawyer had a conflict of interest because he had previously represented the murder victim. The court heard arguments in the case Nov. 5. In the second case, a South Carolina defendant, William Arthur Kelly, is challenging a judge's failure to instruct jurors that under state law a defendant convicted of capital murder but not sentenced to death is automatically given a life sentence without possibility of parole; arguments are set for Nov. 26. [32]

Dieter says the justices' comments indicate a desire for the states to improve death penalty procedures. "They would first like the states to monitor and control their processes, but . . . [the justices] are going to step in when it's called for," Dieter says. From the other side, Sharp criticizes the justices' remarks. "I have never heard the justices comment on how many innocent lives are protected by use of the death penalty," he says. "If they are going to be actively involved in the public debate, one wonders why they don't comment on both sides of this policy discussion."

For his part, Ron Wright, a criminal-law professor at Wake Forest University Law School in Winston-Salem, N.C., agrees that the justices are sending "signals" on death penalty issues, but notes that the court is also continuing to keep "a tight rein" on legal doctrines used to challenge convictions after the end of normal appeals. "They can say they're troubled, they can send a signal, but in the end they don't do anything about it," he says.

OUTLOOK

Mixed Feelings?

As New Mexico prepared for its first execution in nearly 42 years, the state's department of corrections had to go to neighboring Texas to hire two experts to oversee the procedure. The state also had to defend itself against a lawsuit contending that a state health department physician acted improperly by obtaining the drugs to be used in the lethal injection. [33]

Despite the difficulties, Terry Clark was executed as scheduled on Nov. 6 for the 1986 rape-murder of a 9-year-old girl. Clark had tried to prevent any last-minute appeals on his behalf, and Gov. Gary Johnson had declined to commute the sentence to life imprisonment.

With Clark's execution, New Mexico became the 32nd state to carry out a death sentence since the United States restored capital punishment in 1976, leaving only six death penalty states that have not done so. But in New Mexico — as in the rest of the country — ambivalence about capital punishment appears to be increasing.

Johnson, a Republican, supports the death penalty, but in the weeks before Clark's execution said he would listen to opposing views. A bill to repeal the death penalty failed by a single vote in the state Senate in February. A September 2000 poll had determined that popular support for the death penalty in New Mexico had slipped to 65 percent. And the same survey found that a plurality of New Mexicans — 47 percent to 41 percent — would oppose capital punishment if the state had the option of imposing a life sentence without possibility of parole. [34]

Nationwide, support for the death penalty also stands at 67 percent, according to the most recent Gallup survey, taken earlier this year. As in New Mexico, support drops when surveys include the life-without-parole option. The survey found that 52 percent favored the death penalty compared to 43 percent for life imprisonment; the margin had been closer — 49 percent to 47 percent — in September 2000.

Supporters and critics of the death penalty are waiting to see whether the Sept. 11 terrorist attacks will affect public opinion on the issue. "All bets are off since the 11th," says death penalty opponent and SUNY-Cortland Professor Haines. "It's very hard to know how that's going to affect the climate the issue plays out in."

"I think this would probably boost support for the death penalty," says John Jay College professor and death penalty supporter Latzer. "I can't imagine too many people would oppose the death penalty for someone who hijacked an airplane and somehow managed to live, certainly if he caused other deaths."

At the least, death penalty opponents acknowledge, the war against terrorism has deflected attention from capital punishment issues. "Obviously, Congress is distracted," says Loge of the Justice Project, conceding that lawmakers are unlikely to act soon on either the Innocence Protection Act or a nationwide moratorium on executions.

But Loge also says death penalty reform fits a post-Sept. 11 agenda. "The best way to fight these attacks is by strengthening our rights at home," he says.

Death penalty supporters are confident that the pro-reform moves of the past few years are coming to an end. "Politically, I don't think the opponents are going to make too much more headway," says Scheidegger of the Criminal Justice Legal Foundation. "Legally, doctrine is pretty well set. And I don't see a big push for statutory changes."

Critics still hope more states will follow Illinois' lead in temporarily halting executions. "Lots of states are toying with a moratorium," says Haines. But death penalty supporters predict those efforts will come to naught. "When reason and the facts prevail, moratorium bills have failed," says Sharp of Justice for All.

The opposing camps apparently agree on one issue: They both favor the use of DNA testing to verify death row inmates' claims of innocence, though supporters would adopt more restrictive standards for allowing such challenges. Some death penalty supporters also second critics' calls to strengthen defendants' legal representation in capital cases.

But supporters continue to discount critics' most effective issue of the past few years: the risk of executing the innocent. "There is a risk, and that risk is ineradicable," says Latzer. "But I think the risk is a minimal one, and there is no evidence that an innocent has been executed in the last 25 years."

In any event, Latzer says he believes the death penalty serves both of the major purposes of criminal law: retribution and deterrence. Society benefits, even if the evidence on deterrence is unclear or disputed, he adds, "because we can be confident that there are some deterrent impacts. What's to lose?"

But Haines believes public support for the death penalty will continue to decline. "A lot of people like the death penalty very much," he says. "But the death penalty they like is one that gets the guilty, not the innocent; that doesn't break the taxpayers' purse; that isn't racist; that doesn't make mistakes. They want a perfect death penalty, but I don't think that's possible."

"The complexities of making the death penalty work the way people want it to work in an ideal world are too great, and that will become apparent," Haines adds. "In the end, you can't have it all."

Notes

[1] *Atkins v. Commonwealth*, 534 S.E.2d 312 (Va. 2000).

[2] The case is *Perry v. Lynaugh*, 492 U.S. 302 (1989). For an in-depth backgrounder, see Raymond Bonner and Sara Rimer, "Executing the Mentally Retarded Even as Laws Begin to Shift," *The New York Times*, Aug. 7, 2000.

[3] For background, see Kenneth Jost, "DNA Databases," *The CQ Researcher*, May 28, 1999, pp. 449-472; Mary H. Cooper, "Death Penalty Update," *The CQ Researcher*, Jan. 8, 1999, pp. 1-24; Richard L. Worsnop, "Death Penalty Debate," *The CQ Researcher*, March 10, 1995, pp. 193-216.

[4] Richard C. Dieter, *Innocence and the Death Penalty: The Increasing Danger of Executing the Innocent*, Death Penalty Information Center, July 1997 (www.deathpenaltyinfo.org).

[5] The case is *Dawson v. State* (http://www2. state.ga.us/Courts/Supreme/s01a1041.pdf).

[6] Maria Elena Baca, "O'Connor Critical of Death Penalty," (Minneapolis) *Star-Tribune*, July 3, 2001 (www.startribune.com). See Charles Lane, "O'Connor Expresses Death Penalty Doubt," *The Washington Post*, July 4, 2001, p. A1. Lane, writing from Washington, noted that O'Connor did not provide a transcript of her remarks.

[7] For background, see Sarah Glazer, "Declining Crime Rates," *The CQ Researcher*, April 4, 1997, pp. 289-312.

[8] Quoting from resolution adopted by the American Bar Association House of Delegates, Feb. 3, 1997 (www.abanet.org). Other ABA materials also found on the site.

[9] See U.S. Dept. of Justice, "The Federal Death Penalty System: A Statistical Survey (1988-2000)," Sept. 12, 2000. The report and the Death Penalty Information Center's summary can be found at www.deathpenaltyinfo.org (click on "Information Topics," then on "Federal Death Penalty"). See also U.S. Dept. of Justice, "The Federal Death Penalty System: Supplementary Data, Analysis and Revised Protocols for Capital Case Review," June 6, 2000, also available on the center's site.

[10] The Spangenberg Group, "Rates of Compensation for Court-Appointed Counsel in Capital Cases at Trial: A State-By-State Overview," 1999. The report was prepared for the American Bar Association's Bar Information Program.

[11] See *Penry v. Lynaugh*, 492 U.S. 302 (1989). A Maryland law banning execution for the mentally retarded took effect in 1989, after the court's decision.

[12] See *Ford v. Wainwright*, 477 U.S. 399 (1986).

[13] Background drawn in part from Hugo Adams Bedau (ed.), *The Death Penalty in America: Current Controversies* (1997), pp. 3-25; Herbert H. Haines, *Against Capital Punishment: The Anti-Death Penalty Movement in America, 1972-1994* (1996), pp. 3-22.

[14] Hugo Adams Bedau (ed.), *The Death Penalty in America* (1964), p. 31.

[15] See Joan Biskupic and Elder Witt, Congressional Quarterly's *Guide to the Supreme Court* (3d ed.), 1996, pp. 608-615.

[16] The case is *Furman v. Georgia*, 408 U.S. 238 (1972).

[17] The citations are *Gregg*, 428 U.S. 153 (1976), and *Woodson*, 428 U.S. 280 (1976).

[18] Some background drawn from Bryan Vila and Cynthia Morris (eds.), *Capital Punishment in the United States: A Documentary History* (1997). See also Haines, *op. cit.*

[19] The case is *McCleskey v. Kemp*, 481 U.S. 279 (1987).

[20] The cases are *Coker v. Georgia*, 433 U.S. 583 (1977) (rape); *Thompson v. Oklahoma*, 487 U.S. 815 (1988) (juveniles).

[21] Hugo Adam Bedau and Michael L. Radelet, "Miscarriages of Justice in Potentially Capital Cases," *Stanford Law Review*, Vol. 41, No. 1 (Nov. 1987). For a critique of the study and a reply, see Stephen J. Markman and Paul G. Cassell, "Protecting the Innocent: A Response to the Bedau-Radelet Study," *Stanford Law Review*, Vol. 41, No. 1 (Nov. 1988), pp. 121-160; Hugo Adam Bedau and Michael L. Radelet, "The Myth of Infallibility: A Reply to Markman & Cassell," *Ibid.*, pp. 161-171.

[22] "Innocence and the Death Penalty: Assessing The Danger of Mistaken Executions," Staff Report, Subcommittee on Civil and Constitutional Rights, Committee on the Judiciary, 103 Cong., 1st Sess. (1993).

[23] Dieter, *op. cit.*

[24] ABC News, "Innocence and the Death Penalty," "Nightline," July 14, 1997.

[25] James S. Liebman, Jeffrey Fagan and Valerie West, "A Broken System: Error Rates in Capital Cases, 1973-1995," June 12, 2000. The report, published originally on the World Wide Web, can be found on several sites, including the site maintained by the anti-death penalty organization The Justice Project (www.thejusticeproject.org). An abridged version was published in *Texas Law Journal* in October 2000.

[26] Ken Armstrong and Steve Mills, "Illinois Is First State to Suspend Death Penalty," *Chicago Tribune*, Feb. 1, 2000, p. N1.

[27] "The Death Penalty in 2000: Year End Report," Death Penalty Information Center (December 2000) (www.deathpenaltyinfo.org).

[28] See "Changes in the Death Penalty Around the U.S., 2000-2001," Death Penalty Information Center (www.deathpenaltyinfo.org/Changes.html).

[29] John Fulwider, "O'Connor Lectures Lawyers, Recollects for Students in Lincoln," *Nebraska StatePaper*, Oct. 18, 2001 (www.nebraska.statepaper.com).

[30] See Lane, *op. cit.*

[31] The cases are *Penry v. Johnson* (June 4, 2001); *Shafer v. South Carolina* (March 20, 2001). See Kenneth Jost, *Supreme Court Yearbook, 2000-2001* (forthcoming).

[32] The cases are *Mickens v. Taylor*, 00-9285; *Kelly v. South Carolina*, 00-9280.

[33] Some medical groups oppose having doctors involved in the execution process, so most states that use lethal injection for executions obtain the drugs directly from the manufacturer. See Michael Janofsky, "Execution Set in New Mexico Draws Rarity of a Challenge," *The New York Times*, Nov. 1, 2001.

[34] The telephone poll of 422 registered voters by Mason-Dixon Polling & Research Inc. was conducted for the Santa Fe newspaper, *The New Mexican*.

FOR MORE INFORMATION

American Bar Association, 750 North Lake Shore Dr., Chicago, Ill. 60611; (312) 988-6000; www.abanet.org. The ABA supports a national moratorium on executions.

Criminal Justice Legal Foundation, P.O. Box 1199, Sacramento, Calif. 95816; (916) 446-0345; www.cjlf.org. The pro-law enforcement public interest law firm often files friend-of-the-court briefs with the U.S. Supreme Court in death penalty cases.

Death Penalty Information Center, 1320 18th Ave., N.W., 5th Floor, Washington, D.C. 20036; (202) 293-6970; www.deathpenaltyinfo.org. The anti-death penalty center's Web site provides extensive information on the death penalty system.

Justice for All, P.O. Box 55159, Houston, Texas 77255; (713) 935-9300; www.prodeathpenalty.com. The victims' advocacy group maintains a Web site with extensive information and pro-death penalty articles.

Justice Project, 730 12th St. N.E., Washington, D.C. 20002; (202) 638-5855; http://justice.policy.net. The organization, founded by U.S. veterans, lobbies to change "our deeply flawed capital justice system."

Bibliography

Selected Sources

Books

Bedau, Hugh Adam (ed.), *The Death Penalty in America: Current Controversies*, Oxford University Press, 1997.

A Tufts University professor and unabashed opponent of capital punishment presents an historical and contemporary overview plus some 20 essays on related issues, including public opinion toward executions. Almost all the contributors oppose the death penalty. Includes a 30-page bibliography.

Haines, Herbert H., *Against Capital Punishment: The Anti-Death Penalty Movement in America, 1972-1994*, Oxford University Press, 1996.

A sociology professor at the State University of New York-Cortland provides a recent history, with detailed notes and a 17-page bibliography. An updated paperback edition was published in 1999.

Jackson, The Rev. Jesse L., Rep. Jesse L. Jackson Jr. and Bruce Shapiro, *Legal Lynching: The Death Penalty in America*, New Press, 2001.

The authors critique the death penalty based on the frequency of legal errors, government misconduct and racial and economic discrimination. Includes a three-page list of readings and contact information for anti-death penalty groups. The senior Jackson is founder of the Rainbow/PUSH Coalition; his son is a Democratic representative from Illinois; Shapiro writes for *The Nation* and Salon.com.

Latzer, Barry, *Death Penalty Cases: Leading U.S. Supreme Court Cases on Capital Punishment*, Butterworth-Heinemann, 1998.

The John Jay College of Criminal Justice professor presents excerpts of 22 leading Supreme Court decisions in death penalty cases from 1972 through 1991. Includes a 17-page overview of capital punishment issues and a one-page list of references.

Lifton, Robert Jay, and Greg Mitchell, *Who Owns Death? Capital Punishment, the American Conscience and the End of Executions*, William Morrow, 2000.

The authors interview those directly involved in capital punishment, including wardens, prosecutors, jurors, ministers, judges and relatives of murder victims. Lifton directs the Center on Violence and Human Survival at John Jay College of Criminal Justice; Mitchell is a journalist. Includes 10 pages of chapter notes.

Sarat, Austin, *When the State Kills: Capital Punishment and the American Condition*, Princeton University Press, 2001.

A professor of law at Amherst College argues for what he calls a "new abolitionism" in the fight against capital punishment that would focus on "the impact of state killing on our politics, law and culture." Includes detailed source notes.

Vila, Bryan, and Cynthia Morris (eds.), *Capital Punishment in the United States: A Documentary History*, Greenwood Press, 1997.

The authors seek to present an objective collection of documentary materials on capital punishment from Colonial times through the mid-1990s, including lists of major Supreme Court decisions and organizations and an 11-page bibliography.

Westervelt, Saundra D., and John A. Humphrey, *Wrongly Convicted: Perspectives on Failed Justice*, Rutgers University Press, 2001.

The book includes 14 essays by experts from several disciplines focusing on the causes of wrongful convictions; social characteristics of the wrongly convicted; case studies and suggested reforms. Westervelt and Humphrey teach at the University of North Carolina at Greensboro.

***Note:** Most recent books on the death penalty system are written from a critical perspective. The pro-death penalty group Justice for All provides a list of books and tapes on capital punishment and individual murder cases, some of which reflect support for the death penalty (www.prodeathpenalty.com).*

Reports and Studies

Liebman, James S., Jeffrey Fagan and Valerie West, "A Broken System: Error Rates in Capital Cases, 1973-1995," June 12, 2000.

A Columbia University law professor and his colleagues purport to show that two-thirds of death sentences are reversed or set aside. The study can be found on several groups' Web sites, including The Justice Project (www.thejusticeproject.org). An abridged version appeared in the *Texas Law Journal* in October 2000.

Latzer, Barry, and James N.G. Cauthen, "Capital Appeals Revisited," *Judicature*, Vol. 84, No. 2 (September/October 2000), pp. 64-69.

Two professors at John Jay College of Criminal Justice offer the major academic critique of the Liebman study. Liebman et al replied in the same issue; a second exchange appeared in *Judicature*, Vol. 84, No. 3 (November/December 2000). The entire exchange is posted on the John Jay College's Web site: www.lib.jjay.cuny.edu/docs/liebman.htm.

7   Three-Strikes Laws

PATRICK MARSHALL

I s 25-years-to-life in prison too high a price for Gary Ewing to pay for trying to steal three golf clubs from a country club pro shop? What about 50-years-to-life for Leandro Andrade for shoplifting videotapes from Kmart?

Both men were sentenced under a popular but controversial California law designed to put habitual criminals behind bars for 25-years-to-life for even relatively minor crimes.* Twenty-five states and the federal government have three-strikes laws, but California's is by far the toughest. All the states have laws requiring prosecutors to seek tougher sentences for repeat offenders.

Now the Supreme Court will decide whether Andrade's and Ewing's sentences were so out of line as to violate the defendants' constitutional protection against "cruel and unusual punishment." The 9th U.S. Circuit Court of Appeals in San Francisco thought so. In throwing out Andrade's sentence, the court said it was "grossly disproportionate" to the crime of stealing $153 worth of videotapes.

Andrade and Ewing were given stiff sentences because on the third offense California's three-strikes law considers some misdemeanors, including shoplift-

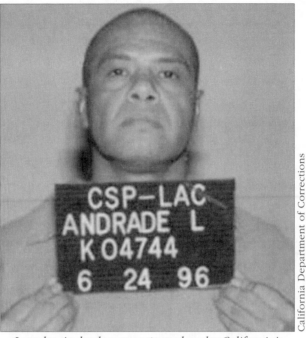

Leandro Andrade was sentenced under California's three-strikes law to 50-years-to-life in prison for trying to steal nine videotapes from two Kmart stores. The longtime heroin addict had previous convictions for marijuana sales and several arrests for burglary. The U.S. Supreme Court agreed in April to hear his appeal.

California Department of Corrections

ing, as felonies. (In the case of a criminal's second felony conviction, the sentence can be doubled.) California voters approved the law overwhelmingly in 1994, largely in response to the kidnap-murder of 12-year-old Polly Klaas by a repeat offender out on parole.

While a narrowly focused Supreme Court decision would affect only the California law, some experts say the court could, if it wanted, have a broad impact on mandatory-minimum sentencing laws in other states. Supporters of tough sentencing laws worry that the high court may overly intrude on the states' rights to manage their own sentencing practices — something the court has avoided in the past.

"The big question [in the *Andrade* and *Ewing* cases] is whether it will apply to mandatory-sentencing laws," says Michael Rushford, president of the Criminal Justice Legal Foundation, a California-based group that advocates tougher

sentencing. "There are mandatory-sentencing laws all over the country. If we're now going to decide that this is not OK, that's going to cause a lot of turmoil."

Kevin Meenan, president of the National District Attorneys' Association, agrees. "There is pretty strong sentiment that each state legislature should control its statutory scheme, as long as it's within the parameters of the Constitution," he says. "Every state has a different scheme. A crime that may get you 10 years in Wyoming might get you three years in New York . . . or it might not even be prosecuted in some other state."

"Is this necessarily fair?" he continues. "Well, we assume that each state has the ability within their boundaries to set those parameters."

The two cases have focused wider attention on the effectiveness and costs of incarceration, as well as the fairness of sentencing policies.

"We go through cycles," says Terry J. Hatter, a U.S. District Court judge in Los Angeles. "You get politicians who are just looking for some kind of political cover, and they start talking about soft-hearted judges and they go from 'indeterminate' sentencing to 'determinate' sentencing."

Determinate sentences require criminals to serve a specified term in prison and limit a judge's sentencing discretion. Indeterminate sentences give judges broad latitude in sentencing and allow the time a convict actually serves to be shortened by good behavior in prison or parole.

The three-strikes movement continues the trend toward determinate sentencing, which began in the 1980s and has lasted longer than previous cycles, Hatter says. But he can see pressure

---

* Andrade got 50 years because he stole the tapes from two different stores, doubling the 25-year minimum. Under a 25-years-to-life sentence, an offender must serve at least 80 percent of the minimum of 25 years and is then eligible to apply for parole. If parole were never granted, the offender would be required to remain in prison for life.

From *The CQ Researcher,*
May 10, 2002.

Most California Third-Strikers Are Over 29

Of the 4,368 defendants sentenced for a third strike in California from 1994 to 1998, more than three-quarters were 30 or older. Critics say the three-strikes law needlessly targets older defendants, who are already at the end of their careers as violent criminals.

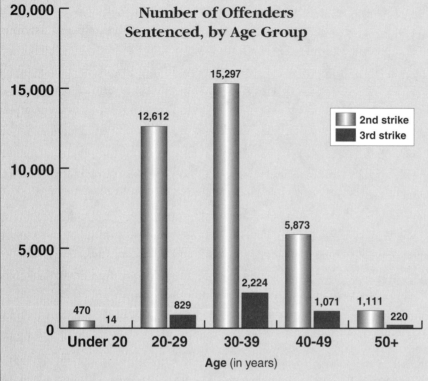

Number of Offenders Sentenced, by Age Group

Source: California Department of Corrections, "Second Strike Cases, Third Strike Cases," June 1998

fornia, he says, at least in part because of the influential California Correctional Peace Officers union, which was one of the primary financial backers of the three-strikes lobbying effort. "Now the prison guards are putting more into the governor's coffers than anyone else," Hatter says.

Critics say that mandatory-sentencing schemes simply waste money by giving long sentences to petty criminals who don't need lengthy confinement. "Three-strikes-and-you're-out is resulting in enormous costs and use of prison space for significant numbers of offenders who don't require such extremely punitive sentences," says Marc Mauer, assistant director of the Washington, D.C.-based Sentencing Project. "Inevitably, we sweep up the low-level offenders along with the kingpins. That doesn't contribute to justice, and it isn't a very efficient use of resources."

But California Attorney General Bill Lockyer defends both the cost and strictness of mandatory sentencing. "Nothing in the Constitution requires society to wait for another person to be victimized by another serious or violent crime before isolating [habitual offenders] for a substantial period of time," he said in appealing the 9th Circuit's decision in the Andrade case.

As politicians, prisoners and corrections officials await the Supreme Court's decision, here are some of the questions being debated:

Is California's three-strikes law working?

Supporters of California's three-strikes law credit it with an almost immediate and dramatic decline in serious crime.

"Of all the statistics, the one that means the most . . . is the fact that 5,694 of our fellow Californians are alive today that would not have been alive if crime hadn't been substantially reduced," California Secretary of State Bill Jones, who helped shape the law, told a crime victims' conference in

building for change. "A lot of people read about some of the worst kinds of offenses by the state, when someone who has stolen a loaf of bread all of a sudden faces 25 years to life," Hatter says. "Some of those things just don't make sense, and they make the system lose credibility with the public. That's something we don't want to see happen."

While debate continues to rage over whether tougher sentencing deters crime, both critics and advocates of tougher sentencing recognize that such policies carry a price. "The biggest problem that we as a society grapple with is the cost of incarceration," Meenan

says. "We do incarcerate a lot of people."

In fact, mandatory-sentencing laws adopted over the past two decades have helped push prison populations steadily upward. The number of inmates in state prisons rose from 684,544 in 1990 to 1,179,214 in June 2000, while the federal inmate population more than doubled, rising from 58,838 to 131,496. [1]

When prisons filled up in the past, politicians would return to indeterminate sentencing to enable judges and corrections officials to manage the flow of criminals in and out of the penal system, Hatter says.

But that hasn't happened in Cali-

1999. "I'm not saying three strikes is the sole reason for that. But in a state as diverse and complex as California, if you have a 51 percent reduction in the homicide rate in five years, I guarantee you, three strikes is a big part of the reason." [2]

Opponents point out, however, that the figures can be deceptive. Justice Department statistics indeed show California's homicide rate declining by 54.5 percent from 1994 to 1999. But Oregon — a state without three strikes — showed an even greater drop — 58.6 percent — over the same period. [3]

Statistics aside, advocates argue that anecdotal evidence shows the law is having a significant impact. "My wife teaches at the Placer County Jail," says J. Richard Couzens, a Superior Court judge in Northern California. "Whenever there is a class on the three-strikes law, it is well attended by the inmates, who are very concerned about it. And I hear of people who have actually left California for fear that they may get caught in the web. I think, on balance, that the law has had an effect on the crime rate, but I couldn't begin to guess how much."

"The three-strikes law is the biggest topic of conversation in most of the jails in this state," echoes Rushford, of the Criminal Justice Legal Foundation. "That's because they know what's going to happen to them the next time, and they don't like it."

However, those who doubt the effectiveness of the three-strikes law point to studies showing wide variations in enforcement of the law throughout California. For example, data from 22 California counties indicated "no statistically significant relationship exists between crime rates and third- and second-strike conviction rates, according to Samara Marion, a public defender in Santa Cruz and professor of law at Santa Clara University." [4] Another study outside California found "no differences in crime rates among large urban areas with and without three-strikes laws." [5]

Critics of the three-strikes law also argue that it tends to lock away older criminals, who were already at or near the end of their crime careers. (*See graph, p. 128.*) Despite research showing that the majority of chronic offenders stop committing crimes after age 28, the average age of those sentenced under the three-strikes law is in the mid-30s. [6] A study that examined convictions in San Diego found that nearly three-quarters of those sentenced under three strikes were over 30, and that most had committed nonviolent and petty offenses. [7]

"The implications of this aging of the prison population are very significant both for crime control and cost issues," writes Mauer of the Sentencing Project. "If one goal of incarceration is to reduce crime by incapacitating known offenders, there will be less of an impact, on average, derived from the imprisonment of a 50-year-old than a 20-year-old.

"This aging population will place an extraordinary burden upon the resources of the California penal system, particularly given the increased expense of housing older inmates." [8] Older prisoners cost more to incarcerate than younger inmates in large part because of their increasing need for expensive health care.

Even if it were proven that the three-strikes law actually did cut crime rates, critics say the unfairness and disparity in sentences outweigh those benefits.

"This is a law that is so overly punitive it's laughable," says Geri Silva, co-chair of Families Against California Three Strikes (FACTS). "You also have to cry about it. There are 3,500 people serving life sentences in the state for what amount to petty, minor offenses. It's unheard of in civilized society."

Although proponents argued initially that a three-strikes law would reduce sentencing disparities, studies indicate the reality may be quite different. According to Marion, who analyzed conviction data from San Diego, "The law's

attempt to remove all discretion from sentencing has created even more arbitrary and disparate sentencing patterns, which often bear little relationship to the seriousness of the offender or the crime." [9]

Marion found, for instance, that individuals who had committed two violent crimes received an average prison sentence of 9.6 years for the second conviction, while the average prison term for those committing a single violent crime was 11.7 years. But criminals who had not committed any violent offenses received an average prison sentence of 17 years. "The result," writes Marion, "is a selective application of law where — outside of those offenders who have committed numerous violent crimes — no consistent, identifiable factors distinguish those who received a life sentence from those who have not." [10]

Critics also note that, unlike laws in some other states, California's three-strikes law contains no time limit. Thus, someone who committed two serious crimes 20 years ago, thus earning two strikes, could, in principle, receive a 25-year sentence for committing a petty crime now.

Proponents of the law argue that district attorneys and judges have discretion in applying the law, and thus can ameliorate such inequities, particularly after a 1996 California Supreme Court decision gave judges discretion to remove old "strikes" from a criminal's record.

"If the priors are quite ancient and otherwise the fellow has led a pretty OK life, that should be taken into account," Judge Couzens says. "Many judges feel that a 25-to-life sentence for petty theft is just too much, and they just won't do it. I personally won't do it." At the same time, Couzens notes, "You get some of these jurisdictions where the district attorneys are very dogmatic, and the judges are very conservative."

Some third-strike advocates suggest that regional differences in how the law is applied may be a good thing. Rushford says that, to some extent, communities must be allowed to determine what kind of sentencing they want from their elected judges.

"Legislators in Sacramento should not be deciding charging policies for the whole state," he says. "If San Francisco doesn't want to enforce three strikes, as long as people keep electing their district attorney, then that's what they want."

Are mandatory-sentencing policies fair and effective?

Third-strike laws are one of many approaches to mandatory sentencing. All states and the federal government impose various types of mandatory-minimum sentences for specific crimes. The primary goals of such sentences are to ensure that sentences are actually imposed and to reduce or eliminate the wide discrepancies in sentences often received by those convicted of similar or identical crimes.

"When a man arrives in prison for first-degree burglary from San Francisco and he's doing a term of 12 months, and he meets a guy from Bakersfield who's doing three years for the same crime, it can create discontent," explains Alan Carlson, president of the Justice Management Institute in Kensington, Calif. "Mandatory sentencing has gotten rid of some of these discrepancies within the state."

Rushford of the Criminal Justice Legal Foundation agrees. "When we had indeterminate sentencing, the wiggle room for judges was so substantial that I could shoot you in San Diego and get a much better term than if I shot you

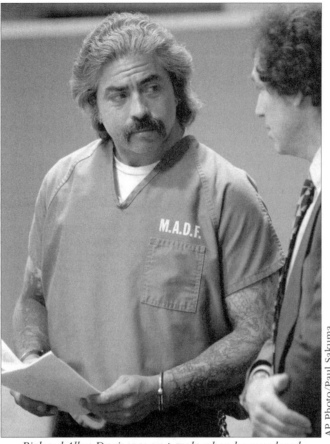

Richard Allen Davis was on parole when he murdered 12-year-old Polly Klaas in 1993 after abducting her from a slumber party in Petaluma, Calif. Davis was convicted of murder and is on death row at San Quentin Prison. Public outrage over Polly's death at the hands of a convicted felon sparked three-strikes laws around the country.

in Eureka," he says. The current system does not allow that discretion.

Critics argue, however, that mandatory-minimum sentences have not eliminated inequities in sentencing.

"The punishment often doesn't fit the crime," Judge Hatter says. "I've seen too many first-time, non-violent offenders filling up our prisons, and more and more prisons being built, rather than the money going to education and other kinds of things that would hopefully keep people from ever getting involved in the criminal-justice system to begin with."

Under mandatory-minimum sentencing laws, when prosecutors decide what crime to charge an offender with, they largely determine what kind of sentence will be imposed in a given case. Thus, instead of the rationale for a given sentence being delivered in court, by the judge, it is hidden in back rooms, Hatter says.

"We have far less truth now than ever before," Hatter says, noting that after state prosecutors leave public service, they often become defense attorneys. "Then they come back and go into the prosecutor's office to work out a deal" for their clients, he says. A defendant represented by an attorney without those connections is at a distinct disadvantage, Hatter contends.

"The only one who can make a departure below a mandatory minimum is this young fellow or young gal in the prosecutor's office," Hatter complains. "[They're] appointed individuals — not lifetime judges. This is really unfair. And it's not just unfair to the defendants, it's unfair to society."

Douglas Berman, a professor of law at Ohio State University, says mandatory-minimum sentencing might seem to be an effective tool at first, but it is too crude to work in the long run. "Yes, if we lock up any group of 10,000 people, crime will go down," Berman says. "But that doesn't mean it's a just approach."

The problem, he points out, is that judicial-system participants — judges, prosecutors, defense attorneys, police and even victims — quickly adjust to the system, creating new inequities. "People will underreport [crime] if there's a sense of unduly harsh sentencing at the back end," Berman says. "Or they may get the person out of the justice system at an earlier point."

U.S. Justice System Is Toughest

Most countries in Europe, as well as the United States, Canada and Australia, have similar legal and penal systems, which is not surprising given their several centuries of overlapping cultural traditions

Nonetheless, significant differences exist in the various systems, especially with respect to the use of mandatory-minimum sentencing schemes and sentencing guidelines.

Compared to other Western countries, the United States chooses incarceration more often than other alternatives, such as fines or community service. Out of every 100,000 people in the United States, 645 are in prison. The next highest ratio is 145 per 100,000 population in both New Zealand and Portugal. At the low end of the incarceration scale, Greece, Finland and Norway all have only 55 citizens in prison per 100,000 population. [1]

What's more, sentences are generally harsher in the United States than in most Western countries.

Most notably, the United States continues to use the death penalty and life sentences without the possibility of parole, while the rest of the Western world has abandoned the death penalty and rarely imposes sentences longer than 10 years.

"But there are many more differences than this," write Michael Tonry, director of the Institute of Criminology at Cambridge University, and Richard Frase, a professor of criminal law at the University of Minnesota. "In some countries, for example, Germany and Austria, prison sentences shorter than six months are regarded as destructive and serving no valid penal purpose and are therefore strongly discouraged. In others, including Sweden and Finland, certainty of punishment is seen as important, but not severity, and, as a result, many sentences of days or weeks of imprisonment are imposed.

And there is wide divergence in the use of community punishments. Community service is a commonly used prison alternative in England, Scotland and the Netherlands, but it is seldom used as a primary punishment in many other countries. Fines are often imposed in Germany and much of Scandinavia but are not used at all in both English-speaking and other countries (e.g., the Netherlands) and only sparingly in still others (e.g., France).

Most other Western countries also have refrained from adopting the "get-tough" policies introduced in the United States in the 1980s and '90s.

"There are few legislatively imposed mandatory-minimum prison sentences outside the United States, and many of those that exist are either short (by U.S. standards) or were not truly mandatory," Frase and Tonry write. "Second, all Western jurisdictions outside the United States retained parole-release discretion (although

a few have partially adopted the U.S. concept of 'truth in sentencing') by limiting or abolishing sentence reductions for 'good conduct' in prison. Third, no jurisdiction outside the United States has adopted legally binding sentencing guidelines of the type found in U.S. federal and some state courts." [2]

Instead, other countries use "more flexible means" to limit sentence disparities, including sentencing guidelines and procedures. Dutch courts, for example, must explain their rationale for imposing a sentence exceeding the prosecutor's recommendation or for refusing a defendant's offer to perform community service instead of going to prison.

Other Western countries also are generally more reticent about "enhancing" sentences in light of prior records or multiple offenses.

Although some U.S. states limit consecutive prison terms, most allow the judge broad discretion to impose cumulative punishments from related offenses up to the statutory maximum for each offense.

"But in Germany, consecutive sentences may not exceed a total of 15 years and must also total less than the sum of the maximum terms allowed for each charge," Frase and Tonry write. "In the Netherlands, a defendant found guilty of multiple offenses can only receive an enhancement of up to one-third of the maximum allowed for the most serious offense; a similar rule also applies in Sweden. In France, no enhancement is allowed above the maximum authorized for the most serious offense, whether sentenced in a single trial or serially."

There are signs, however, that some Western countries may be moving more in the direction of U.S. penal policies, a trend bemoaned by many scholars. "Unfortunately, 'bad' ideas have also spread across national boundaries — mandatory-minimum penalties, three-strikes laws and prison boot camps, although widely rejected by U.S. scholars and judges, have recently been adopted in England and Australia," according to the two criminologists. [3]

But Tonry and Frase view the trend toward U.S.-style justice as motivated by politics rather than by the desire to find appropriate responses to social and criminal issues. "The evidence is clear: National differences in imprisonment rates result not from differences in crime but from differences in policy," they write. [4]

---

[1] Michael Tonry and Richard S. Frase, eds., *Sentencing and Sanctions in Western Countries* (2001), p. 9.
[2] *Ibid.*, p. 272.
[3] *Ibid.*, p. 265.
[4] *Ibid.*, p. 7.

"It's unjust on every level," Berman continues. "Mandatory sentences result in much harsher sentences for a certain percentage of offenders, but then no sentence at all for others, because

they've been worked out of the system in a less legitimate way."

While politicians, prosecutors and law-enforcement officials continue to favor mandatory minimums, judges and aca-

demicians often argue that sentencing guidelines rather than mandatory sentencing would offer the best balance.

Under the federal system, mandatory-minimum sentences apply to roughly a third of the cases moving through the courts; the rest are handled under sentencing guidelines, which allow a range of sentences for each crime. The judge is empowered to vary from the guidelines, but must state on the record his or her reasons for doing so. Federal mandatory minimums apply primarily to firearms violations and drug crimes — particularly those involving crack cocaine.

"If these were just guidelines, I think most judges would welcome them," Hatter says. "I know I would. Sentencing is the toughest thing that the judge has to do, and any guidance you get is helpful. But to have your discretion removed is too much."

A National Institute of Justice study supports sentencing guidelines. "Measured in terms of their stated purposes, sentencing guidelines have been the more successful innovation," the report says. "Evidence . . . indicates that sentencing guidelines have reduced unwarranted disparities (in general and in relation to race and gender), have enabled policymakers to make statewide changes in sentencing policy and have permitted states to coordinate sentencing and prison-use policies." [11]

BACKGROUND

Colonial Severity

Mandatory-minimum sentences are not new. As far back as 1790, some states established mandatory penalties for capital offenses. Third-strike laws also have a long pedigree. Thieves and burglars caught for the third time were subject to the death penalty in Colonial Massachusetts. And throughout the 19th century, Congress on several occasions passed laws requiring specific prison terms for a variety of crimes.

Until recently, however, the enactment of mandatory-minimum laws was generally "an occasional phenomenon . . . not comprehensively aimed at whole classes of offenses," notes a 1991 report by the U.S. Sentencing Commission, which Congress created to help establish sentencing guidelines. [12]

In fact, throughout the 1800s most U.S. jurisdictions adopted flexible, indeterminate sentences. "Flat sentences were regarded as inconsistent with reformatory principles," wrote criminologist Tamasak Wicharaya. "Appropriate treatment required both reward for cooperation and penalty for disobedience as incentives for the process of reforming the offender. Thus, imprisonment was no longer necessary once the offender was reformed." [13]

According to Wicharaya, this philosophy led to the development of a "good-time" system — which allowed for the commutation of sentences for prisoners' good behavior — during the 1820s and eventually to a formal parole system in 1877.

Indeterminate sentencing with the possibility of parole was widely used throughout the United States during the first half of the 20th century. Legislatures would establish maximum penalties for specific offenses, and judges imposed a minimum and maximum term on those convicted. The actual time served was determined by a parole board, based on the prisoner's conduct while incarcerated.

Swinging Pendulum

The first real step away from the indeterminate model at the federal level took place in 1956, with the Narcotic Control Act. The law mandated minimum and, in many cases, lengthy prison terms for most drug-trafficking offenses and eliminated parole for those convicted of specified drug crimes.

Nearly 15 years later, Congress changed its mind. The Comprehensive Drug Abuse Prevention and Control Act of 1970 repealed all mandatory sentences for drug violations, with lawmakers noting in a report that such sentences "had not shown the expected overall reduction in drug-law violations." [14]

Despite the 1970 law undercutting mandatory sentencing for drug crimes, the main trend was toward mandatory sentencing. As the U.S. Sentencing Commission has noted, indeterminate sentencing was under fire at both the state and federal level. "Critics posited that rehabilitation was difficult to accomplish and measure, and that wide-open judicial discretion and parole actually exacerbated the problems of controlling crime," the report says. "They urged that a system of determinate sentencing would increase sentencing effectiveness by requiring sentences that are more certain, less disparate and more appropriately punitive." [15]

"[Indeterminate sentencing] was challenged from both the left and the right in the 1970s," writes Mauer of the Sentencing Project. "Liberals became concerned that broad discretion available to sentencing judges and parole boards left room for decisions based on race, gender, judicial district and other factors. Conservatives believed that the prison system represented 'revolving-door justice,' and that only a more restrictive sentencing structure could address the growing crime problem." [16]

To address these concerns, both sides came to favor a more determinate sentencing structure, giving judges and parole boards less discretion. "The main disagreement was over the length of sentences," Mauer notes, "with liberals generally favoring shorter, fixed terms and conservatives longer ones."

In 1973, New York state passed the so-called Rockefeller drug laws, named after then-Gov. Nelson Rockefeller. The laws were the harshest in the nation,

Chronology

calling for lengthy sentences for drug crimes and limits on plea-bargaining. "Within just a few years of their adoption, the Rockefeller laws were found wanting, both because of the distortions of the court system and their excessive punitiveness," Mauer writes. A 1978 evaluation, for example, concluded that the number of drug cases that went to trial had tripled; one consequence of the additional trials was a doubling of the time required to process each case. [17]

Sentencing Reform

Despite the concerns raised by the New York laws and others, 49 of the 50 states had passed mandatory-sentencing laws by 1983.

The Sentencing Reform Act of 1984 was the next major step in the development of mandatory federal sentencing. It established the U.S. Sentencing Commission, which developed federal sentencing guidelines and abolished parole for federal inmates. Companion legislation created the 1986 Firearm Owner's Protection Act and the Anti-Drug Abuse Act, which reintroduced mandatory-minimum sentences for a variety of drug and firearm-related crimes. The two new laws also required enhanced, or tougher, sentences for subsequent convictions for the same crimes.

Throughout the 1980s and '90s, Congress broadened the reach of mandatory minimum sentences. The 1990 Omnibus Crime Bill, for example, required a 10-year mandatory sentence for those convicted of organizing, managing or supervising a continuing financial-crimes enterprise.

Also in the 1990s, the concept of "truth in sentencing" became popular. The Federal Violent Crime Control and Law Enforcement Act of 1994 promised criminal-justice system funds to states that guaranteed that offenders actually served at least 85 percent of their sentence before being released. As a re-

1800-1950 *The United States gives judges broad discretion to set sentences.*

———— • ————

1950-Present *Congress and the states adopt "get-tough" sentencing policies.*

1956
Narcotic Control Act establishes minimum sentences for drug crimes.

1970
Congress repeals mandatory sentences for drug violations.

1972
The first clear call for sentencing guidelines comes from federal District Judge Marvin Frankel in his groundbreaking book, *Criminal Sentences: Law Without Order.*

1973
New York state's so-called Rockefeller laws require lengthy sentences for drug crimes.

1980
U.S. Supreme Court issues key ruling applying the Eighth Amendment's ban on cruel and unusual punishment. In *Rummel v. Estelle* it upholds a life sentence for a man convicted of obtaining $120 under false pretenses after two prior credit-card, forgery convictions. Defendant is eligible for parole after 12 years.

1983
In another key Eighth Amendment ruling, Supreme Court in *Solem v. Helm* overturns a mandatory life-without parole sentence for a defendant convicted of passing a $100 bad check.

1984
Sentencing Reform Act of 1984 creates the U.S. Sentencing Commission. The act also reintroduces mandatory-minimum sentences for drug and firearms offenses.

1986
The Firearm Owner's Protection Act and the Anti-Drug Abuse Act require enhanced sentences for subsequent convictions.

1991
In *Harmelin v. Michigan*, Supreme Court upholds mandatory life for a first-time offense of possessing about 1.5 pounds of cocaine. Justice Anthony M. Kennedy's plurality opinion notes the Eighth Amendment prohibits sentences "grossly disproportionate" to the offense but says this sentence is justified because of the "grave harm" posed by illegal drugs.

1993
Washington becomes first state to enact a three-strikes law. Within a few years, 24 other states pass similar laws.

1994
California voters approve the country's harshest three-strikes law: 25-years-to-life for a third conviction, even for petty crimes, if the two prior convictions were for serious felonies. The Violent Crime Control and Law Enforcement Act provides funds to states that require offenders to serve 85 percent of their sentences.

2002
Supreme Court agrees to hear the *Lockyer v. Andrade* and *Ewing v. California* cases, concerning individuals sentenced for petty crimes under California's three-strikes law.

sult, more than half the states have truth-in-sentencing requirements.

Voters in Washington state approved the nation's first three-strikes law in 1993 — the Persistent Felony Offender Act. It requires a sentence of life without the possibility of parole for criminals convicted of a third serious felony. The next year, 13 states, including California, followed Washington's lead and passed some form of a three-strikes law.

California prosecutors have imposed their three-strikes law in far more cases than any other state. By the end of 1999, 40,511 criminals had been convicted under California's law; the state with the next-highest total was Georgia, with 942 convictions.

CURRENT SITUATION

Supreme Court

There are indications that the United States may be retreating from the harsh, determinate sentencing that has been in vogue since the mid-1980s. The most obvious indication of the possible new trend is the U.S. Supreme Court's recent decision to hear the *Andrade* and *Ewing* cases challenging the legitimacy of California's three-strikes law.

While the California law widely differs from those in most other states, observers are uncertain whether the high court will rule narrowly on the California cases or hand down a broad decision that affects third-strike laws nationally.

"I am utterly amazed that this hasn't come up before now," says Judge Couzens. "This law has been around since 1994, and it's amazing to me that it has not reached the Supreme Court before. I'm not willing to pre-

dict how that's going to come out. It's going to be really close."

If the court decides the *Andrade* and *Ewing* cases narrowly, focusing on the constitutionality of California's law not requiring the third strike to be a serious felony, the laws in other states would not be affected. Couzens notes, however, that the court could also rule on much broader grounds, affecting every state.

In a decision — *Brown v. Mayle* — handed down a few months after the *Andrade* case, the 9th Circuit held that it was not proper to consider past violent conduct in judging a current non-violent offense.

"That goes to the heart of three-strikes law," Couzens says. "Since *Brown v. Mayle* is rooted firmly on *Andrade*, I would guess that the Supreme Court may pick it up." Noting that more than 60 percent of third-strike convictions in California are for non-violent offenses, Couzens adds, "there are serious concerns about how far the three-strikes law is going to go because of that decision."

Larry Brown, executive director of the California District Attorneys Association, is hopeful that the court will move in the other direction and overturn the 9th Circuit Court's ruling in *Andrade*. "We're accustomed in California to having rulings from the 9th Circuit go against our interests, which are then overturned by the high court," Brown says. "It has one of the highest reversal rates of all the federal circuit courts."

As the Supreme Court deliberates, there are moves in the state legislature to amend the law. A bill sponsored by Democratic Assemblywoman Jackie Goldberg of Los Angeles would require the third strike to be a serious or violent felony. Some backers of the bill, including Silva of FACTS, feel it does not go far enough.

"The bill includes burglary as a serious crime," Silva says. "In many cases, those are committed during the daytime in an unoccupied dwelling. They are basically crimes of an addict. I'm

sorry that those are included in Goldberg's bill, because a lot of them are just desperate addicts."

The California District Attorneys Association opposes Goldberg's bill. "We're strongly opposed to weakening the California three-strikes law," Brown says. "It has proven highly effective in removing hard-core, habitual felons from our streets."

Efforts in Other States

Outside California, there are also signs of a move away from harsh sentencing policies. "Sentencing reforms in a number of states in 2001 represent a significant shift in policy with regard to non-prison options for certain drug offenders and other non-violent offenders," according to a National Conference of State Legislatures report. [18]

The report notes that a new Indiana law allows offenders charged with distributing drugs to opt for treatment in place of prosecution. And a new law in Connecticut allows the court to deviate from mandatory-minimum sentences for specified drug crimes if there was no threat of violence. In addition, measures enacted in 2001 in Arkansas, Montana, North Dakota, Mississippi and Louisiana eased mandatory-sentencing laws.

While there are no specific measures in the works to change the federal system of sentencing guidelines and mandatory minimums, it has come under increasing fire in recent years.

Ohio State's Berman puts much of the blame on Congress and the Sentencing Commission, contending that in setting specific sentences for specific crimes, Congress went too far.

"Whenever Congress goes beyond providing general policy directives," he says, "that to me is Congress going beyond its proper lawmaking role." Berman also notes that "the Sentencing Commission itself has been criticized, and I think validly criticized, for

At Issue:

Should California's three-strikes law be weakened or eliminated?

GAIL BLACKWELL
DIRECTOR OF OPERATIONS, FAMILIES TO AMEND CALIFORNIA'S THREE STRIKES (FACT)

WRITTEN FOR THE CQ RESEARCHER, MAY 2002

Clifornia is in a crisis situation. More than 57,000 men and women are serving prison sentences under the three-strikes law. As of Dec. 31, 2001, California had convicted 7,072 defendants for third-strike offenses and 34,656 for second-strike offenses. More than 3,500 received 25 years to life for non-violent offenses, and more than 35,000 are serving 10 to 20 years in state prison for similar non-violent offenses on a second strike. Most offenses committed by second- and third-strikers are not violent crimes, but possession of a controlled substance.

No one deserves to have their life stolen from them for a non-violent offense. The three-strikes law is cruel and unusual punishment, and it should be amended to apply to violent crimes only. Let the time fit the crime!

Some politicians proclaim that the three-strikes law is a great deterrent. But current data do not suggest this to be the case. There is some logic to the argument that if you increase punishments for some crimes, some deterrence will probably occur. For instance, if you impose the death penalty on traffic violators, many people will probably slow down their driving (and probably decrease the number of deaths on our highways). The question, however, is whether such a penalty would be "just."

One of the foundations of American justice has been that people should not be punished for what they might do, but what they actually have done. Committing a couple of burglaries of unoccupied dwellings and then having a drug-possession charge is a far cry from committing extremely violent acts.

More than 65 percent of those convicted under the three-strikes law were arrested for drug-related offenses. A good deal of evidence shows that putting many three-strikers in rehabilitation programs would cost society much less overall than putting them in prison for 25 years or more.

In the quest for punishment, the state of California has expended very little effort to try to rehabilitate or educate offenders. Throwing them in prisons and dehumanizing every aspect of their existence leaves little or no opportunity for treating them as humans and trying to help them develop into better human beings.

The three-strikes law needs to be amended, and we can't do it fast enough.

KENT SCHEIDEGGER
LEGAL DIRECTOR, CRIMINAL JUSTICE LEGAL FOUNDATION

WRITTEN FOR THE CQ RESEARCHER, MAY 2002

Clifornia must be doing something right. Between 1993 and 2000, while the nation's crime rate dropped 25 percent, California's plunged 42 percent. In 1993, Californians were 18 percent more likely to be victimized than the national average, but in 2000 they were 9 percent less likely.

What America generally is doing right — but California is doing even better — is cracking down on crime with tough sentencing laws. The centerpiece of California's get-tough policy is the much-maligned 1994 measure mandating 25-years-to-life for a person convicted of a felony who has two prior convictions from a list of "serious or violent" felonies. These are people who simply have no intention of ever "going straight," and they will continue to prey upon innocent people unless and until we forcibly restrain them.

Opponents of tough sentencing bemoan the use of prison cells to house "non-violent" criminals. But the gentle burglar is a myth. Criminals typically do not specialize. The crook who crawls in your window when he thinks you are not home may very well kill you if you are. Effective sentencing means locking up those who have demonstrated a readiness to do evil and an unwillingness to change.

International comparisons further reinforce the conclusion that tough sentencing works. Absolute crime rates depend on other factors besides sentencing, of course. America's uninhibited, individualistic culture has long given us higher crime rates than Europe and Japan.

The changes in rates in recent years, though, are revealing, as we have cracked down and the Europeans have not. The British Home Office compared changes in violent crime rates in various countries between 1995 and 1999: The U.S. rate dropped 20 percent; the European Union average climbed 11 percent, and the French rate skyrocketed 31 percent. The risk of victimization by so-called contact crime is now higher in most of Europe than in the United States. The stunning support for far-right candidate Jean-Marie Le Pen in the recent French election indicates that the Europeans are finally waking up to what we have long known, and they are prepared to throw out officeholders who sacrifice innocent lives on the altar of political correctness.

Tough sentencing policies are saving innocent people from the trauma of robbery, rape, burglary and murder. To repeat the mistake of the 1960s and go soft on crime again would be a tragic folly.

micromanaging, making sentencing guidelines far more detailed, far more intricate and far more directive rather than persuasive. They were supposed to draw guidelines, and instead they drew up mandatory rules."

"It's striking that if you look at something like mandatory sentencing, outside of prosecutors, you have a hard time finding much support for this," says Mauer of the Sentencing Project. "The federal judges, in particular, have been extremely outspoken about this, but with no result. Here are your federal judges, nominated by the president, confirmed by the Senate — people at the peak of their careers — who are put on the bench and told to just follow whatever is in the guidebook. They are very angry about it."

OUTLOOK

Politics and Money

Both critics and advocates of mandatory-sentencing laws agree that the tide is turning away from longer, harsher sentences for many crimes.

"I do see a change coming, for two reasons," Ohio State's Berman says. First, crime rates are down, so crime is less on voters' radar screens and politicians are less compelled to constantly establish their tough-on-crime credentials. "The political force that has traditionally been driving the move toward mandatory sentences is weakening."

Secondly, states are strapped for cash right now, he points out. "We just can't afford to take this lock-'em-up-and-throw-away-the-key approach," he says.

Even so, Berman cautions that while political pressures may ease they will not disappear. "The change is going to be slow and nuanced by the reality that even as the politics get a little bit more sober, it's still going to be dangerous for folks in close races to appear soft on crime," he says.

Politics aside, some experts warn that society should not just rush into abandoning tough sentencing laws. "To just willy-nilly reject these laws would be a terrible step backwards," says Meenan of the National District Attorneys' Association. "Some adjustments can be made in the schemes [to] allow discretion and avoid the inequities. But the cost to society would be horrific if suddenly these people were just released."

Judge Hatter believes that the political sensitivity of the issue means that real change will require the assistance of those on the political right. "It's going to take some conservative standing up in Congress and saying, 'I'm tired of these rules having led us down the garden path,' " Hatter says. "It's a very sad situation all around, but I do think it is going to change."

According to some experts, in the aftermath of Sept. 11 states are struggling with increased security costs and the effects of a general economic slowdown. Thus, they say, the increasing cost of incarceration will bring the political right on board and trigger calls for moderating or eliminating three-strikes and other mandatory-sentencing policies.

"Budget shortfalls in nearly every state have driven many states to consider cutting corrections budgets," said a recent Sentencing Project report. While state officials have proposed substantial shifts in funding for criminal-justice programs, they say the shifts build on policy changes that could reduce incarceration costs while continuing to support crime reduction. [19]

Notes

[1] Allen J. Beck and Jennifer C. Karberg, "Prison and Jail Inmates at Midyear 2000," Bureau of Justice Statistics, March 2001.

[2] Andy Furillo, "3 Strikes Benefits Trumpeted: Author Says it Prevented Million Crimes," *Sacramento Bee*, Feb. 27, 1999, p. A3.

[3] Bureau of Justice Statistics, www.ojp.usdoj.gov/bjs.

[4] Samara Marion, "Justice by Geography? A Study of San Diego County's Three Strikes Sentencing Practices from July-December 1996," *Stanford Law and Policy Review*, V. 11:1, 1999, p. 32.

[5] Peter W. Greenwood, *et al.*, *Three Strikes Revisited: An Early Assessment of Implementation and Effects* (1998), pp. 8-21

[6] Mike Males and Dan MacAllair, "Striking Out: The Failure of California's Three Strikes and You're Out Law," *Stanford Law and Policy Review*, V. 11:1, 1999.

[7] Marion, *op. cit.*, p. 35.

[8] Ryan S. King and Marc Mauer, "Aging Behind Bars: Three Strikes Seven Years Later," Sentencing Project, August 2001.

[9] Marion, *op. cit.*, p. 32.

[10] *Ibid.*, p. 40.

[11] Michael Tonry, "Intermediate Sanctions in Sentence Guidelines," National Institute of Justice, May 1997.

[12] U.S. Sentencing Commission, "Mandatory Minimum Penalties in the Federal Criminal Justice System," August 1991, p. 6.

[13] Tamasak Wicharaya, *Simple Theory, Hard Reality: The Impact of Sentencing Reforms on Courts, Prisons and Crime* (1995), p. 27.

[14] House Report No. 1444 (1970).

[15] *Ibid.*, p. 8.

[16] Marc Mauer, "Why Are Tough on Crime Policies So Popular?" *Stanford Law and Policy Review*, Vol. 11:1, 1999, p. 14.

[17] *Ibid.*, p. 10.

[18] Donna Lyons, "State Crime Legislation in 2001," National Conference of State Legislatures, 2002.

[19] Ryan S. King and Marc Mauer, "State Sentencing and Corrections Policy in an Era of Fiscal Restraint," Sentencing Project, February 2002, p. 1.

Bibliography

Selected Sources

Books

Tonry, Michael, *Sentencing Matters,* **Oxford University Press, 1996.**

An international expert on sentencing offers a readable overview of sentencing issues, mainly focused on the U.S.

Tonry, Michael, and Richard S. Frase, *eds., Sentencing and Sanctions in Western Countries,* **Oxford University Press, 2001.**

A collection of essays comparing sentencing in the United States, England, Australia and Europe. Tonry is director of the Institute of Criminology at Cambridge University; Frase is a professor of criminal law at the University of Minnesota.

Wicharaya, Tamasak, *Simple Theory, Hard Reality: The Impact of Sentencing Reforms on Courts, Prisons and Crime,* **State University of New York Press, 1995.**

A criminologist explores the history and impact of sentencing reforms in the United States.

Articles

Berman, Douglas A., "A Common Law for This Age of Federal Sentencing: The Opportunity and the Need for Judicial Lawmaking," *Stanford Law and Policy Review,* **Vol. 11:1, 1999.**

An Ohio State University law professor criticizes the federal sentencing system and urges more discretion for federal judges.

Jones, Bill, "Why the Three Strikes Law is Working in California," *Stanford Law and Policy Review,* **Vol. 11:1, 1999.**

California's secretary of state argues that the law he helped create should not be watered down.

Marion, Samara, "Justice by Geography? A Study of San Diego County's Three Strikes Sentencing Practices from July-December 1996," *Stanford Law and Policy Review,* **Vol. 11:1, 1999.**

A law professor at Santa Clara University finds that most convictions in San Diego are for non-violent crimes and that most of those convicted are over 30.

Reports

King, Ryan S., and Marc Mauer, "Aging Behind Bars: Three Strikes Seven Years Later," Sentencing Project, August 2001.

An assessment of three-strikes legislation finds it tends to imprison criminals whose careers are winding down.

Lyons, Donna, "State Crime Legislation in 2001," National Conference of State Legislatures, 2002.

A useful compendium of the states' legislative action regarding sentencing and incarceration.

U.S. Sentencing Commission, "Special Report to the Congress: Mandatory Minimum Penalties in the Federal Criminal Justice System," August 1991, p. 6.

A useful history of sentencing reforms and policies in the United States.

FOR MORE INFORMATION

Criminal Justice Legal Foundation, P.O. Box 1199, Sacramento, CA 95812; (916) 446-0345; www.cjlf.org. A nonprofit, public-interest law organization dedicated to restoring a balance between the rights of crime victims and the criminally accused.

Families Against California Three Strikes, 3982 S. Figueroa St., Suite 207A Los Angeles, CA 90037; (213) 746-4844; www.facts1.com. An advocacy group comprised in part of relatives of offenders convicted under three-strikes legislation.

Justice Management Institute, 821 Coventry Road, Kensington, CA 94707; (415) 816-3341; www.jmijustice.org. A consulting and education organization that provides services to courts and other justice-related organizations.

National District Attorneys' Association, 99 Canal Center Plaza, Suite 510, Alexandria, VA 22314; (703) 549-9222; www.ndaa-apri.org. Provides information on criminal justice, the courts, child abuse and other issues.

Sentencing Project, 514 10th St., NW, Suite 1000, Washington, DC 20004; (202) 628-0871; www.sentencingproject.org. A nonprofit organization that promotes more effective and humane alternatives to incarceration.

U.S. Sentencing Commission, 1 Columbus Circle, N.E., Suite 20500, South Lobby, Washington, DC 20002-8002; (202) 502-4500; www.ussc.gov. Establishes sentencing guidelines and policy for all federal courts.

"Secure the Blessings of Liberty"
— preamble to the Constitution of the United States

The framers of the Constitution sought to safeguard individual liberties as they were understood at the time: notably, freedom of speech and the press, freedom of religion and legal protections in the home and in court. Today, the Bill of Rights and the Due Process Clause of the Fourteenth Amendment are construed as limiting the power of the federal or state governments in areas and settings beyond what the framers knew or could have imagined. Most significantly, the Supreme Court has recognized a constitutional right of privacy that protects sexual and reproductive freedom, including a woman's qualified right to choose to have an abortion. Courts have also had to consider how to apply freedom of speech to modern communications technology, including the Internet, and how to apply the First Amendment's provisions for religious freedom to proposals for government funding of religious activities and organizations.

"Abortion Debates" updates the intense controversy generated by the Supreme Court's 1973 decision *Roe v. Wade* that guarantees women a right to an abortion during most of a pregnancy. The court's 7–2 ruling was hailed by women's rights advocates, but fueled a strong backlash. The court has largely reaffirmed the original ruling, but it has also upheld some laws restricting abortion practices and allowed state and federal governments to refuse to fund abortions for low-income women. Most recently, antiabortion groups have called for banning a procedure that they call "partial-birth abortion." The Supreme Court ruled Nebraska's law on the issue unconstitutional, but since our report Congress has passed a federal statute to bar the procedure — a law promptly challenged by abortion rights advocates (Partial Birth Abortion Ban Act, PL 108–105, Nov. 5, 2003).

"Privacy Under Attack" covers efforts to protect a right nowhere named in the Constitution from practices and policies that the framers could not have envisioned. Police can use high-tech equipment to peer into homes. Businesses can monitor consumers' Internet activity. Government and business alike collect vast amounts of personal information from individuals and store the data on computers, some-

times with few effective limits on using the information or sharing it with others. Privacy advocates want courts and Congress to establish protections against unwarranted intrusions by government or industry. Businesses contend that self-regulation adequately protects consumers, while the Bush administration — after our report — won authority for increased surveillance of individuals and groups as part of its war against terrorism after the 9/11 attacks (USA Patriot Act, PL 107-56, signed Oct. 26, 2001).

"Libraries and the Internet" brings the First Amendment into the twenty-first century by examining the free-speech implications of efforts to limit children's access to sexually explicit materials on the Internet. Despite the many wonders of the worldwide interconnected computer network, the Internet also has a dark side that makes material unsuitable for youngsters too readily accessible. Congress tried to deal with the problem in part by requiring schools and libraries to install software filters on computers to block out indecent material. Libraries and other free speech advocates challenged the law, saying the government should deal with the problem without unnecessarily restricting adults' access to constitutionally protected materials. After our report, the high court upheld the law on a 6–3 vote (*United States v. American Library Association,* June 23, 2003).

"School Vouchers Showdown" details the most recent church-state confrontation over schools: proposals to give students government vouchers to pay for education at private — including religiously affiliated — schools. Voucher proponents and opponents sharply disagree on whether the plans help or hurt public schools. The constitutional issue is whether paying for tuition at religiously affiliated schools violates the Establishment Clause, as church-state separationists contend. The Supreme Court took up the issue in a challenge to a Cleveland voucher program that students used almost exclusively to attend parochial schools. After our report, the court upheld the program by a 5–4 vote (*Zelman v. Simmons-Harris,* June 27, 2002). In February 2004, however, the court dealt school choice proponents a setback by ruling that states could refuse to permit general scholarships to be used for students training for the ministry (*Locke v. Davey,* February 25, 2004).

"Faith-Based Initiatives" describes President Bush's proposals to permit federal funding to religiously affiliated social service organizations. Bush and other proponents contend that faith-based organizations have effective programs in such areas as drug treatment and prisoner rehabilitation and that they should be eligible for federal grants on the same basis as secular organizations. Critics maintain that such effectiveness by faith-based groups is unproven and that government funding in any event breaches the separation of church and state. Since our report, President Bush's legislation stalled in Congress, but he issued companion executive orders allowing five federal departments to increase funding to faith-based groups (Dec. 12, 2002). Court rulings have gone both ways, but in the most extensive decision a federal appeals court upheld a prison-based program that allowed drug offenders a choice between religious or secular treatment (*Freedom From Religion Foundation, Inc. v. McCallum,* Seventh U.S. Circuit Court of Appeals, April 2, 2003).

8   Abortion Debates

KENNETH JOST

A rmed with prayer book, rosary and anti-abortion literature, Christine Walsh takes up her post on a chilly Saturday morning recently outside a Planned Parenthood clinic within sight of the White House. As women approach, the teenage college student rushes to their side and tries with soft-spoken insistence to dissuade them from having an abortion.

Invariably, the women quickly turn away and are shepherded inside by volunteer "escorts" from the Washington Area Clinic Task Force. Wearing orange vests, they lock arms to block Walsh or her fellow "sidewalk counselors" from going farther once the patients reach the clinic's grounds.

Thirty years after the Supreme Court's landmark *Roe v. Wade* decision allowing abortions, the abortion wars continue — in Congress and state legislatures, in the courts and outside women's clinics across the country.

The sidewalk confrontations are usually orderly, but the potential for violence lurks in the background. The clinic has bullet-resistant windows and a 600-pound steel door; doctors often wear bulletproof vests. [1]

The number of protesters and clinic escorts grows on special occasions — notably, every Jan. 22, the anniversary of the *Roe* decision. Sometimes, the two sides get into shoving matches. "It's like a war zone," Walsh comments as two motorcycle police officers set up watch across the street in case of a disturbance.

From *The CQ Researcher*, March 21, 2003.

Anti-abortion militant James Kopp faces up to life in prison after being found guilty on March 18 of second-degree murder in the 1998 shooting of Barnett Slepian, a Buffalo, N.Y., doctor who carried out abortions. Violence directed against abortion providers and clinics has ebbed over the past few years, but legislative and judicial fights between anti-abortion and abortion-rights groups continue unabated 30 years after the Supreme Court's landmark Roe v. Wade *decision establishing a constitutional right to abortion.*

Getty Images

Walsh says she simply wants prospective patients to "take a step back" and think about their choices. "They're killing children here," she explains, "and we're here trying to offer alternatives."

Rebecca Fox, 24, the leader of a team of 10 escorts, says the "anti-choice harassers," as she calls them, never succeed. In four years, she says, she has never seen a sidewalk change-of-mind. "The women know what their choices are," Fox says, "and they've made their decision."

The arguments are no less fervent for being well worn. [2] Abortion-rights advocates praise *Roe v. Wade* as a landmark guarantee of what they call a woman's "right to choose." Anti-abortion groups bitterly assail the 1973 ruling and defend what they call the "right to life" of the "unborn child." Public opinion polls generally favor a woman's right to choose an abortion but also

favor certain restrictions on that right, many of which have been enacted at the state and federal levels in recent years. (*For state laws, see chart, p. 146; public opinion polls, p. 144.*)

Today, with Congress and the White House in Republican hands, anti-abortion groups see their best chance in more than a decade of winning federal passage of parts of their agenda. The GOP has been closely aligned with anti-abortion forces since 1980, when the party platform first supported a "right-to-life" constitutional amendment.

"We're in better shape as pro-lifers than we have been in a while," says Connie Mackey, vice president for government affairs at the Family Research Council, a Christian-oriented family-advocacy group. Republican control "should give us a leg up that we haven't had in a while."

"Abortion rights are in great peril," says Elizabeth Cavendish, legislative director for the newly named NARAL Pro-Choice America — formerly, the National Abortion Rights Action League. "We're likely to see a renewed assault on a woman's right to choose."

At the top of the right-to-life agenda is a bill to ban so-called partial-birth abortions — in which a fetus is brought partly outside a woman's body before being aborted, usually after 20 weeks gestation. "This is closer to infanticide than it is to abortion," Sen. Rick Santorum, R-Pa., told a March 10 news conference, three days before the Senate voted 64-33 to ban the procedure.

The bill is expected to win easy House approval and be signed into law by President Bush, but still faces legal hurdles. The Supreme Court in 2000 struck down a Nebraska ban on

Number of Abortions Has Been Dropping

CON

The number of abortions performed in the United States each year increased through the 1970s, leveled off in the 1980s and has been falling since 1990. The decline is attributed to a decline in sexual activity by adolescents and increased use of contraceptives, including the "morning-after" pill. Anti-abortion groups also note a public-opinion shift against abortion except under limited circumstances.

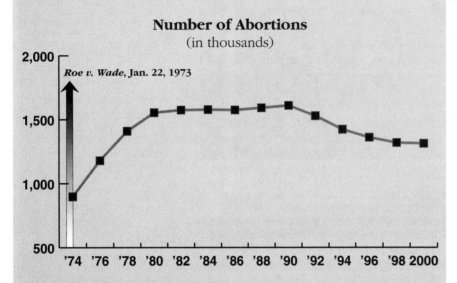

Number of Abortions
(in thousands)

Source: Lawrence B. Finer and Stanley K. Henshaw, "Abortion Incidence and Services in the United States in 2000," Perspectives on Sexual and Reproductive Health, January/February 2003, The Alan Guttmacher Institute.

the procedure, but supporters of the measure say it was rewritten to meet the court's objections. [3]

But abortion-rights groups say the new bill suffers from the same constitutional defects cited in the Supreme Court's Nebraska decision. "Make no mistake," says NARAL President Kate Michelman, "this bill goes directly to the heart of a woman's constitutional right to choose."

Anti-abortion groups are pushing three other bills to regulate abortion practices in the United States. The measures would:

• Make it a federal crime to help a minor cross state lines to get an abortion without parental notification or consent;

• Allow hospitals and doctors to refuse to perform, and health in-surers to refuse to cover, abortions without risking loss of federal funding; and

• Make it a federal crime to injure or kill a fetus during the commission of any one of a specified list of other violent offenses.

Anti-abortion groups will also continue to try to block any international aid for groups that promote abortion. And they have strongly backed legislation to ban any form of human cloning — a measure the House approved, 241-155, on Feb. 27.

Some of the bills were approved previously in the House, where anti-abortion groups have held narrow but secure majorities for several years. But they stalled in the Democratic-controlled Senate. Now — as evidenced by the Senate's March 13 ban on partial-birth

abortions — the Republican-controlled Senate is expected to be more hospitable to anti-abortion measures, even though it is still considered more abortion-rights-minded than the House.

Most important, anti-abortion groups believe they have a strong and reliable ally in President Bush. On his first workday in office, he reinstated a Reagan-era ban on U.S. funding of overseas groups that promote abortions. He has also appointed well-known abortion foes to key agency positions dealing with abortion policy, and his administration has instituted a laundry list of what abortion-rights advocates call "anti-choice" executive orders, regulatory policies and legal briefs championed by anti-abortion groups.

"On every pro-life legislative measure [the administration] has been effectively involved," says Douglas Johnson, director of federal legislation for the National Right to Life Committee (NRLC). "And on matters of administrative discretion, they have come down on the side of a culture of life."

In addition, Bush has nominated conservatives to federal judgeships — some of them openly critical of abortion rights — and endorsed anti-abortion measures in Congress, including the partial-birth abortion ban. Pro-choice groups are also bracing for a full-scale confrontation over a Bush Supreme Court appointee if one or more vacancies arise — as many political and legal observers expect to happen as early as this summer.

"It's very possible that President Bush will have the opportunity to reshape the court," Cavendish says. If one of the "pro-choice" justices is replaced, she says, the court could end up approving some "draconian" restrictions on abortion, including a revised partial-birth abortion ban. With two new appointments, she warns, the court might formally overrule *Roe*.

The political situation is mixed in the states, although anti-abortion groups appear to have the upper hand. NARAL estimates that 335 anti-choice measures have been enacted by state legislatures since 1995. Moreover, the NRLC claimed "critical gains" in state legislative races in the November 2002 elections. "We're in a better position than we were last year," said Mary Balch, NRLC's director of state legislation. [4]

In its annual state-by-state report, NARAL counts 23 states with anti-abortion majorities in both houses, but claims the number of "pro-choice" governors increased from 15 to 22 after the November elections. [5] Cavendish predicts that at least 12 and as many as 17 states might ban abortion altogether if the Supreme Court overturns *Roe* and gives states discretion to regulate abortions with minimal constitutional constraints.

As the abortion debates continue, here are some of the major questions at issue:

Should Roe v. Wade be overturned?

As he was completing his opinion for the Supreme Court in *Roe v. Wade*, Justice Harry A. Blackmun cautioned his colleagues that the decision "will probably result in the Court's being severely criticized." [6] Thirty years later, the ruling indeed remains controversial: praised by abortion-rights advocates, bitterly opposed by anti-abortion groups and held in some disrepute among legal scholars.

Anti-abortion groups want to overturn the decision, even though they have failed to nullify the ruling by constitutional amendment or to persuade the high court to overrule the decision itself. "It's been an enormous tragedy," says Johnson of the National Right to Life Committee.

For their part, abortion-rights groups say *Roe* has survived only in a weakened state — and could be overruled if President Bush gets the chance to name one or more new justices to the Supreme Court. "*Roe* is in jeopardy," says NARAL's Cavendish.

Criticisms of *Roe* stem not only from

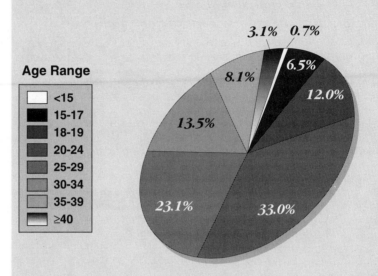

Women in Their 20s Get Most Abortions

Three-quarters of all abortions in 2000 were for women under 30. About one-fifth were obtained by teenagers.

Percentages of Women Having Abortions, 2000
(by age group)

Age Range
☐	<15
■	15-17
▨	18-19
▨	20-24
▨	25-29
▨	30-34
▨	35-39
▨	≥40

3.1% 0.7%
0.7%
6.5%
8.1%
12.0%
13.5%
23.1%
33.0%

Source: Rachel K. Jones, et al., "Patterns in the Socioeconomic Characteristics of Women Obtaining Abortions in 2000-2001," Perspectives on Sexual and Reproductive Health, September/October 2002, p. 228, The Alan Guttmacher Institute.

its outcome but also from the structure of the opinion. Legal critics have long said Blackmun based his opinion more on medical policy than constitutional law. They also contend that the decision's trimester approach — allowing unregulated abortion during the first three months of pregnancy, some regulations up to the point of fetal viability and a near-ban except to save the life of the mother during the final trimester — amounts to what Johnson calls "the apex of judicial legislation."

"There is consensus within the legal academy, whether one is pro-life or pro-abortion, whether one is liberal or conservative, that *Roe* had no grounding in the Constitution or in constitutional jurisprudence," says Douglas Kmiec, dean of the Columbus School of Law at the Catholic University of America in Washington, D.C.

"That's just not true," counters Louis Michael Seidman, a constitutional-law expert at the Georgetown University Law Center in Washington. "If you did a survey of constitutional-law professors, I'd be pretty confident that a majority think *Roe* was correctly decided."

Seidman acknowledges the criticism of the trimester approach, but says such line-drawing is common in constitutional decisions. "To give meaning to constitutional rights, it's sometimes necessary for justices to draw what may seem like arbitrary lines," he says. "You have to draw them someplace."

In a showdown case two decades after the 1973 decision, the Supreme Court reaffirmed what three of the justices — Sandra Day O'Connor, Anthony M. Kennedy and David H. Souter — called, in an unusual joint opinion, *Roe's* "essential holding." Their

Public Favors Abortion Rights

More Americans favor a woman's right to have an abortion than oppose it. But a majority of Americans also approve of placing some restrictions on abortions.

Would you describe yourself as being more pro-choice — supporting a woman's right to have an abortion — or more pro-life — protecting the rights of the unborn children?

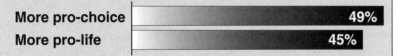

More pro-choice	49%
More pro-life	45%

Do you favor the Supreme Court ruling that women have the right to an abortion during the first three months of their pregnancy?

Favor	55%
Oppose	40%

Do you favor or oppose the following proposals?

	Favor	Oppose
Law requiring women seeking abortion to wait 24 hours	78%	19%
Law requiring doctors to inform patients about alternatives	88	11
Law requiring women under 18 to get a parent's consent	73	24
Law to make it illegal to perform an abortion procedure in the last six months of pregnancy, known as a partial-birth abortion, except to save the mother's life	70	25

Sources: Time/CNN poll conducted Jan. 15-16, 2003 (questions 1-2); Survey Research Center, University of California-Berkeley, fall 2002 (questions 3-6).

ruling in *Planned Parenthood v. Casey* rebuffed repeated calls from the Justice Department under Presidents Ronald Reagan and George Bush to overturn *Roe*. But the decision also appeared to discard the trimester approach and to allow states to regulate abortion unless the laws imposed an "undue burden" on women's rights. [7]

The three justices sought to strengthen the constitutional basis of the ruling by explicitly tying the abortion right to the "liberty interest" protected by the 14th Amendment's Due Process Clause. They also defended the decision not to overrule *Roe*, in part on the legal doctrine of *"stare decisis"* — Latin for let the decision stand.

Johnson calls that part of the decision especially unjustifiable. "They didn't try to defend the constitutional analysis," Johnson says. "They just said, 'That's what we did. If we changed it now, people would be upset.' "

Some critics also fault the *Roe* court for taking the issue out of the hands of state legislatures — several of which were moving in the early 1970s to liberalize abortion laws. Today, though, Johnson says most Americans support more restrictions on abortion than are allowed under the Supreme Court's decisions.

"There is a great gulf between the policy that is supported by the majority of Americans and the regime that has been imposed by judicial decree," Johnson says.

Abortion-rights advocates, however, note that polls show most Americans agree that the abortion decision should rest with women rather than the government. In any event, they say women's reproductive freedom should not be subject to the legislative process. "It would be a terrible thing for women to have to lobby for their liberty state by state, year by year, and legislature by legislature," Cavendish says.

Indeed, abortion-rights advocates say the court itself has already undermined *Roe*. "It's already been eroded by cases like *Casey*," Cavendish says.

Johnson disagrees. "The notion that *Casey* was a rollback of *Roe* is pure fiction," he says.

As for a direct overruling of *Roe*, anti-abortion groups are hopeful and abortion-rights groups fearful. But experts on both sides of the issue discount the likelihood.

"It's just not going to happen," says Ronald Rotunda, a conservative professor at George Mason University Law School in Fairfax, Va., outside Washington. "It's just like asking whether we should change the speed of light."

Seidman agrees: "In my lifetime, *Roe* will not be overruled."

Should Congress ban so-called "partial-birth" abortions?

Anti-abortion groups describe the procedure in stark terms: a late-stage fetus is brought through the woman's dilated cervix feet first; then — because the head is too big to pass through — the skull is pierced, the contents suctioned out and the skull

Anti-Abortion Tactics Test Free-Speech Limits

The Web site opened by a militant anti-abortion group in January 1997 sent a chilling message. The site listed the names of some 200 physicians identified as "abortionists." Some of the names were grayed out. "Wounded," the home page explained. Other names had a horizontal strikethrough — for "fatality."

Among the doctors named on the site were four Oregon physicians who also had been pictured two years earlier on a Wild West-style poster released by the American Coalition of Life Activists. The poster bore the headline "Guilty" and identified the 13 physicians shown as "baby butchers."

At a time when abortion clinic violence was at a peak, the Oregon doctors viewed the Web site and poster as threats on their lives. Along with taking security precautions, the physicians also filed a federal court suit hoping to take down the postings and collect damages from the groups and individuals responsible.

A jury in Oregon awarded $107 million to the four doctors and two women's clinics that joined as plaintiffs. A federal appeals court upheld the award in May 2002, but dissenting judges in the 6-5 decision strongly argued that the anti-abortion messages were constitutionally protected speech. [1]

Now, the anti-abortion groups' appeal is presenting the Supreme Court with another in a series of difficult cases testing the limits of free speech in the context of anti-abortion activities that entail violence or disruption, actual or threatened. The Bush administration also appears to be struggling with the case. The court asked the Justice Department's solicitor general's office to submit a brief on the case in mid-December, but as of mid-March nothing had been filed. The justices would normally wait for the government's brief before deciding whether to hear the appeal.

The closely watched case comes against the backdrop of a decade of abortion-related violence that included shootings, bombings, arson and clinic blockades. At least seven people have been killed: three physicians, two clinic employees, a clinic escort and an off-duty police officer who died in a Birmingham, Ala., clinic bombing in 1998. [2]

James Kopp, the defendant in the most recent of the shootings, went on trial in Buffalo, N.Y., on March 17. Kopp has admitted shooting Barnet Slepian at his home in Amherst, N.Y., in 1998, but claimed he meant only to wound the doctor. Kopp was convicted of second-degree murder on March 18; he faces a minimum prison term of 15 years and a maximum of 25 years to life.

Violence and disruption have been ebbing for the past three years. For 2002, the National Abortion Federation (NAF), which represents abortion clinics, counted 265 incidents of "violence," but almost all were in the least serious categories of trespassing, vandalism or stalking. The federation listed one arson and one "invasion" for the year. It also counted four clinic blockades, with no arrests.

NAF President Vicki Saporta attributes the decline in violence to federal law enforcement. She notes that former Attorney General Janet Reno put Kopp and another anti-abortion fugitive — Eric Rudolph — on the FBI's "Ten Most Wanted" list. Kopp was arrested in France and extradited to the U.S. Rudolph, charged in the Birmingham bombing, is still at large.

Operation Rescue, once the largest of the militant anti-abortion groups, is now bankrupt and defunct; none of the existing groups matches its size or visibility. Major anti-abortion organizations routinely condemn violence. The National Right to Life Committee says it prohibits any violence or illegal activity by its members. Still, Saporta says she fears trials such as Kopp's give militant organizations "the chance to recruit the next assassin."

The Supreme Court has bolstered clinics' legal efforts against violence with a series of divided rulings over the past decade. [3] Three rulings in 1994, 1997 and 2000 allow court injunctions or state laws to establish "buffer zones" requiring protesters to keep some minimum distance from clinic entrances or clinic personnel and patients as they enter or leave the premises. Dissenting justices in each of the decisions argued the rulings infringed on free speech.

A separate ruling in 1994 allowed women's clinics to sue demonstrators for damages under the federal anti-racketeering law commonly known as RICO. Under that ruling, women's clinics later won a $250,000 verdict in the case, but the Supreme Court on Feb. 26 threw out the award. The court ruled, 8-1, that the demonstrators' conduct did not amount to extortion for purposes of the racketeering law. [4]

---

[1] *Planned Parenthood v. American Coalition of Life Activists*, 290 F.3d 1058 (CA9 2002). Plaintiffs included Robert Crist, James Hern, Elizabeth Newhall and James Newhall; defendants included two organizations — American Coalition of Life Activists and Advocates for Life Ministries — and 15 individuals. For coverage, see Henry Weinstein, "Abortion Foes Are Ruled a Threat," *Los Angeles Times*, May 17, 2002, p. B1.

[2] Summary information on the cases can be found on the National Abortion Federation's Web site: www.naf.org.

[3] For a summary, see Claire Cushman (ed.), *Supreme Court Decisions and Women's Rights* (2001), pp. 204-206.

[4] The case is *Scheidler v. National Organization for Women, Inc.*

---

finally crushed or collapsed. "A partial-birth abortion brutally and painfully takes the life of a human baby who is inches away from being born alive," the NRLC's Johnson says.

Abortion-rights groups bristle at the terminology, which they call medically inaccurate and politically inflammatory. In fact, the medical term is "dilation and extraction" — short-

ened to "D&X" — or, alternatively, an "intact D&E" for "dilation and evacuation."

The opposing groups also disagree over the frequency of the procedure. Abortion-rights advocates generally depict the procedure as relatively rare and used only when medically necessary. Anti-abortion groups insist the procedure is more common than acknowledged and never medically justifiable.

Public opinion polls that use the term partial-birth abortion indicate substantial public support for banning the procedure: 70 percent in the most recent Gallup survey in January. [8] When a state law banning the procedure reached the Supreme Court, however, the justices voted 5-4 to strike it down on the ground that the statute interfered with women's abortion rights.

The court's 2000 decision in *Stenberg v. Carhart* said the Nebraska law was defective because it could be construed to apply to the more common D&E procedure, where the fetus is dismembered while still in utero. The court also held that the law failed to include a constitutionally required exemption to permit the procedure necessary to protect the woman's health. [9]

Now, anti-abortion groups are celebrating the March 13 Senate passage of a measure banning the procedure nationwide. Family Research Council President Ken Connor said the Senate's action would help "put an end to this unnecessary and grisly procedure which has taken the lives of thousands of partially born children and hurt so many women."

Abortion-rights groups assailed the bill as unnecessary, ill-advised and constitutionally flawed. "It's pretty much flagrantly unconstitutional," says NARAL's Cavendish. She contends that anti-abortion groups are pushing the proposal in the hope that by the time the issue reaches the Supreme Court again, there will be one or more new justices who will vote for a different outcome.

The Nebraska law defined a partial-birth abortion as a procedure performed after "delivering into the vagina a living unborn child, or a substantial

Most States Limit Abortion Rights

Forty-three states required parents to be notified before an abortion is performed on a minor child in 2002, and more than 30 states had informed-consent, TRAP laws or measures banning "partial-birth" abortion or other procedures.

Selected State Abortion Rates and Limits, 2002
(x = state has such a law)

States	Rate (per 1,000 women)	Informed Consent	Parental Notification	Waiting Period	Abortion Methods Banned*	TRAP Laws**
Alabama	14.3	x	x	x	x	x
Alaska	11.7	x	x		x	x
Arizona	16.5		x		x	x
Arkansas	9.8	x	x	x	x	x
California	31.2	x	x			x
Colorado	15.9	x				
Connecticut	21.1	x			x	
Delaware	31.3	x	x	x		
Dist. of Columbia	68.1					
Florida	31.9	x	x		x	x
Georgia	16.9		x		x	x
Hawaii	22.2					x
Idaho	7.0	x	x	x	x	x
Illinois	23.2		x		x	x
Indiana	9.4	x	x	x	x	x
Iowa	9.8		x		x	x
Kansas	21.4	x	x	x	x	
Kentucky	5.3	x	x	x	x	x

Continued ⟶

* *Includes partial-birth abortions and certain other procedures.*

** *So-called TRAP (targeted regulations of abortion providers) laws govern what an abortion doctor must do before performing an abortion, such as requiring a woman to first undergo an ultrasound procedure.*

Sources: "Who Decides: A State-by-State Review of Abortion and Reproductive Rights, 2003," NARAL, pp. iii-xxv; rates are from Lawrence B. Finer and Stanley K. Henshaw, "Abortion Incidence and Services In the United States in 2000," Perspectives on Sexual and Reproductive Health, *January/February 2003, The Alan Guttmacher Institute.*

portion thereof." To narrow the definition, the new bill pending in Congress prohibits an abortion in which "the entire fetal head" or "any part of the fetal trunk past the navel" is "outside the mother."

Johnson says the new phrasing meets the Supreme Court's objection that the Nebraska law covered com-

monly used techniques. "By no stretch of the imagination could it be subject to that construction," he says.

Abortion-rights advocates, including abortion providers, disagree. "The law is not what they say it is," says Vicki Saporta, president of the National Abortion Federation (NAF), an organization of abortion clinics and physicians. "It's

Selected State Abortion Limits, 2002
(x = state has such a law)

States	Rate (per 1,000 women)	Informed Consent	Parental Notification	Waiting Period	Abortion Methods Banned*	TRAP Laws**
Louisiana	13.0	x	x	x	x	x
Maine	9.9	x	x			
Maryland	29.0		x			
Massachusetts	21.4	x	x	x		x
Michigan	21.6	x	x	x	x	x
Minnesota	13.5	x	x			x
Mississippi	6.0	x	x	x	x	x
Missouri	6.6	x	x		x	x
Montana	13.5	x	x	x	x	
Nebraska	11.6	x	x	x	x	x
Nevada	32.2	x	x		x	x
New Hampshire	11.2					
New Jersey	36.3		x		x	x
New Mexico	14.7		x		x	
New York	39.1					x
North Carolina	21.0	x				x
North Dakota	9.9	x	x	x	x	x
Ohio	16.5	x	x	x	x	x
Oklahoma	10.1		x		x	x
Oregon	23.5					
Pennsylvania	14.3	x	x	x		x
Rhode Island	24.1	x	x		x	x
South Carolina	9.3	x	x	x	x	x
South Dakota	5.5	x	x	x	x	x
Tennessee	15.2	x	x	x	x	x
Texas	18.8		x			x
Utah	6.6	x	x	x	x	x
Vermont	12.7					
Virginia	18.1	x	x	x	x	x
Washington	20.2					
West Virginia	6.8		x		x	
Wisconsin	9.6	x	x	x	x	x
Wyoming	1.0		x			
		31	43	22	31	35

a pre-viability ban, with a definition so vague as to encompass more than one procedure," she says.

The new bill seeks to meet the Supreme Court's insistence on a health exception with a series of "congressional findings" that the procedure is "never medically indicated to preserve the health of the mother," is "unrec-ognized as a valid procedure by the mainstream medical community" and "poses additional health risks for the mother."

"The court has recognized in the past that Congress has a fact-finding role of its own that's entitled to deference," Johnson says.

But Saporta calls the findings "non-sense," with "no basis in scientific medical evidence."

Congress put the issue on hold immediately following the Supreme Court's 2000 decision, but the House again passed a ban in 2002. With the Democrats in control of the Senate, however, then-Majority Leader Tom Daschle of South Dakota blocked consideration of the measure.

The major legislative fight in the Senate turned on failed amendments sponsored by Democratic senators who wanted to add a health exception to the bill. A health exception "would ban no abortions at all," argued Sandy Rios, president of the Concerned Women for America, a conservative policy group.

NARAL's Cavendish countered that the proponents' refusal to agree to a health exception "just reveals that they really want to shackle doctors and have the government inserted squarely into medical decision-making."

Whatever happens in Congress, both sides expect the issue to be settled again in the courts — eventually, at the Supreme Court. Catholic University's Kmiec, a leading constitutional scholar on the anti-abortion side, doubts the bill will be upheld. "Not unless the Supreme Court changes its mind," he says.

The more explicit definition of the procedure "may convince five justices," he says, "especially if there's a new justice looking at it for the first time." But the law will be struck down, he predicts, if it does not allow the procedure when necessary to protect the woman's health. "I don't think you get around the health exception," Kmiec concludes.

Should Congress and the states enact additional restrictions on abortion?

State legislatures have adopted hundreds of laws regulating or limiting abortions in recent years. One type of anti-abortion law — requiring parental notification or consent before an abortion can be performed on a minor — has been adopted by at least 20 states, and 15 others are considering similar measures.

But anti-abortion groups say Planned Parenthood and other abortion-rights organizations help teenagers get around these laws by referring them to women's clinics in states without parental-involvement statutes.

To counteract the practice, anti-abortion groups are urging Congress to make it a federal crime punishable by up to a year in prison for anyone other than a parent to transport a minor from a parental-consent state to a non-parental-involvement state in order to obtain an abortion. Abortion-rights groups strongly oppose the bill, saying it would endanger girls in dysfunctional families and expose relatives, such as aunts or grandmothers, to prosecution.

Twice approved by the House, the proposal is one of several abortion-related measures sought by anti-abortion groups, girded with greater confidence now that Republicans also control the Senate.

Meanwhile, state legislatures are engaged in pitched battles over other abortion measures. NARAL Pro-Choice America counts 23 states as considering either informed-consent measures — which require that women be given certain information about fetal development and the procedure itself before an abortion can be performed — or bills requiring that a woman wait at least 24 hours before an abortion. Nine states are considering measures to ban most or all abortions.

Both sides in the debate agree the restrictions already on the books have reduced the number of abortions. "The states that have passed pro-life legislation have had a significant impact on their abortion rates, birth rates and the number of abortions generally," says the NRLC's Balch. "They've all gone down."

Abortion-rights groups point in particular to waiting-period laws, which in some states require a woman to make two trips to a clinic before undergoing

an abortion. One study suggested such laws reduced the number of abortions by 10 percent or more in two states: Mississippi and Utah. [10] "It definitely has an impact," says Erica Smock, legislative counsel for the Center for Reproductive Rights, a national litigation center based in New York City. "It increases burdens for women who already face obstacles."

Anti-abortion groups say the proposed federal Child Custody Protection Act will strengthen state parental-involvement laws by making it illegal to take a minor to another state for an abortion if state law requires parental-involvement in a minor's abortion. "Parental-notification laws are being systemically evaded by organized activity," Johnson says. "Elements of the abortion industry set up systems for shunting girls across state lines to get abortions without notifying their parents."

Abortion-rights groups say young women with abusive or unsupportive parents need to be able to turn to other relatives or other "trusted adults" in the event of an unwanted pregnancy. "This bill would endanger young women and isolate them when confronted with a crisis pregnancy," says NARAL's Cavendish. "The government cannot force healthy family communication where it doesn't already exist."

Among other bills pending in Congress, the Unborn Victims of Violence Act would make harming or killing a fetus a federal crime if the injury or death resulted from any one of 68 existing federal offenses, whether or not the assailant knew the woman was pregnant or intended to harm the fetus. Many states already have such laws.

Abortion-rights advocates say such laws are unnecessary. "The crime is on the pregnant woman who loses a wanted fetus or a wanted embryo," Cavendish says. She says the bill is "part of a strategy to undermine the foundations of *Roe* by weaving throughout the law a fabric of fetal personhood or embryonic personhood."

Anti-abortion groups say the bill

simply recognizes that crimes that result in injury or death to a fetus have "two victims, not one." And Johnson denies any intention of using the bill to undercut *Roe*. "Pro-abortion groups try to enforce a policy that the unborn child must be invisible," he says. "Most Americans, whatever their views on abortion, don't think of it that way."

A so-called right-to-refuse bill — passed by the House in September 2002 — is designed to prevent health-care providers with religious or moral objections to abortion from being forced to perform the procedure. Supporters say it merely clarifies a "conscience clause" inserted into federal public-health law after the 1973 *Roe* decision. But opponents say the bill expands existing law by allowing hospitals, as well as health insurers, to prevent physicians or others from performing abortions or providing referrals to abortion counseling.

The child custody, right-to-refuse and fetal-protection bills all passed the House during the past (107th) Congress but failed to come to a vote in the Democratic-controlled Senate. Today, even with Republican control, the Senate is still regarded as a difficult hurdle for anti-abortion groups. Johnson counts 53 senators — a majority — on the record in support of *Roe v. Wade*. Nonetheless, he says, "some of those senators will support specific pro-life legislation."

BACKGROUND

Road to *Roe*

Abortion laws — adopted by nearly all the states by the end of the 19th century — came under strong attack from a reform movement beginning in the 1950s. It was slowly gaining ground when the U.S. Supreme Court in 1973 dramatically

Chronology

Before 1970

Most states enact laws in 19th century generally prohibiting abortions; movement to reform or repeal statutes forms in 1950s, advances slowly through 1960s.

———•———

1970s
Abortion-reform movement gains in state legislatures, then wins constitutional ruling from U.S. Supreme Court; decision spawns "right-to-life" movement.

1970
New York and three other states pass abortion "repeal laws."

1973
Supreme Court's *Roe v. Wade* decision establishes a woman's qualified constitutional right to abortion during most of pregnancy; "right-to-life" groups seek to limit or overturn ruling.

1977
Supreme Court allows states to deny abortion funding under Medicaid; three years later, court similarly upholds Hyde amendment barring use of federal funds for abortion for poor women.

———•———

1980s
Presidents Reagan and Bush support anti-abortion initiatives; Supreme Court, in conservative shift, upholds some abortion regulations.

1983
Parental consent for abortion for minors upheld by Supreme Court

if law allows "judicial-bypass" procedure; court invalidates "informed consent" and waiting-period provisions.

1984
Reagan adopts "Mexico City" policy to bar U.S. funds to groups that promote abortion overseas.

1989
Missouri abortion law upheld by Supreme Court in 5-4 vote; four justices criticize *Roe*, one short of majority.

———•———

1990s
Supreme Court reaffirms Roe's "essential holding," with modification; President Clinton adopts abortion-rights stands on several issues.

1991
Supreme Court upholds rule barring abortion counseling at federally funded family-planning clinics.

1992
Three-justice plurality provides key votes for Supreme Court to reaffirm *Roe* while giving states leeway to regulate abortion unless laws impose "undue burden" on women's rights; ruling upholds most provisions of Pennsylvania law, including waiting period and informed consent.

1993
President Clinton reverses several Reagan-era anti-abortion policies on *Roe's* 20th anniversary. . . . First killing of doctor who performs abortions.

1994
Congress approves Freedom of Access to Clinic Entrances Act to establish criminal and civil penal-

ties for use of force to intimidate abortion-clinic staff, patients.

1996, 1997
Clinton vetoes bills passed by Congress to ban "partial-birth abortions."

———•———

2000-Present
President Bush supports anti-abortion initiatives in Congress, controlled by Republicans after midterm elections.

2000
Supreme Court on June 28 strikes down Nebraska statute banning "partial-birth" abortions. . . . Food and Drug Administration in September approves the "abortion pill" RU-486. . . . Texas Gov. George W. Bush soft-pedals anti-abortion views during presidential campaign, wins disputed election.

2001
President Bush re-establishes "global gag rule" on his first workday, barring federal funds for international organizations that promote abortions; draws fire from abortion-rights groups on judicial nominations.

2002
Bush signs Born-Alive Infants Protection Act on Aug. 5. . . . Health and Human Services regulation approved Sept. 27 allows states to define fetus as "unborn child" for purposes of prenatal care under federal health-insurance program.

2003
Roe's 30th anniversary marked by demonstrations by both sides. . . . Partial-birth abortion ban approved by Senate March 12, with House expected to follow and send to Bush to become law subject to certain court test.

invalidated all existing abortion laws with its landmark decision in *Roe v. Wade*. The ruling triggered a bitter fight between opposing forces now in its fourth decade.

The common law that the United States carried over from the Colonial period generally permitted abortion until "quickening," or the first movement of the fetus. [11] Connecticut became the first state to pass an abortion statute with an 1821 law prohibiting the inducement of abortion through dangerous poisons. By 1900, almost all the states had passed anti-abortion laws, largely in response to urgings from doctors. The laws typically permitted abortions when necessary in a doctor's opinion to preserve the life of the woman.

The laws remained on the books through the mid-20th century, but enforcement was uneven at most. Middle- and upper-class women often found ways to circumvent the laws by finding doctors willing to certify the procedure as medically necessary. Low-income women resorted to illegal abortions performed figuratively, if not literally, in the back alleys of metropolitan areas, often by people with little, if any, formal medical training. As of the late 1960s, the number of illegal abortions performed annually in the United States was variously estimated at between 200,000 and 1.2 million. In 1965, an estimated 200 women died from botched abortions, some of them crudely self-administered. [12]

The abortion-reform movement of the 1950s and '60s drew from the work of family-planning groups such as Planned Parenthood, anti-poverty organizations and the nascent women's-liberation movement. The movement gained ground despite strong opposition from the Roman Catholic Church and public ambivalence about what were then termed "elective" abortions.

Colorado in 1967 became the first state to liberalize its abortion law; by 1970, a dozen states had passed laws generally legalizing abortion in cases of rape, incest or to protect a woman's health or life. Then, in early 1970, New York dramatically became the first of four states to pass a "repeal law," virtually eliminating any barriers to abortion.

Reformers also had challenged abortion laws in courts, but with little success at first. In 1971, however, the justices agreed to hear challenges to laws in two states: Texas' 1857 ban on abortions except to save the woman's life and Georgia's 1968 "reform" statute allowing abortions if approved by a hospital committee after examination by two physicians other than the woman's personal doctor. The plaintiffs sued under the pseudonyms Jane Roe and Mary Doe, but years later identified themselves as Norma Jane McCorvey and Sandra Race Cano. Both women gave birth in 1970 after they were unable to obtain abortions in their states.

The Supreme Court struggled with the case, hearing arguments twice: once in December 1971 and then again in October 1972 after Justice Blackmun's initial draft of a decision failed to satisfy colleagues. Blackmun's second draft — strengthened by a summer's worth of research at the Mayo Clinic in Minnesota — eventually won concurrence from six other justices, including Chief Justice Warren Burger. Blackmun relied heavily on medical history, but based the decision on a "personal-liberty interest" protected under either the Ninth Amendment's "unenumerated rights" provision or the 14th Amendment's Due Process Clause. In a short dissent, then-Associate Justice William H. Rehnquist said the court's "conscious weighing of competing factors" was "far more appropriate to a legislative judgment than a judicial one."

From *Roe* to *Casey*

Anti-abortion forces responded to *Roe v. Wade* first with protests and then with well-organized campaigns that failed to overturn the decision but won enactment of a host of restrictive state and federal laws. Over the next two decades, the Supreme Court struck down some of the restrictions but upheld others. The court rejected pleas during the 1980s to reconsider the *Roe* decision, but significantly modified the ruling with its 1992 decision in *Casey* fortifying the states' discretion to regulate abortion procedures. [13]

The court fights played out against a political backdrop that became increasingly polarized over time. At the national level, President Ronald Reagan decisively aligned the Republican Party with the anti-abortion movement by such steps as prohibiting abortion counseling at federally funded family-planning clinics (the so-called "gag rule"), cutting off federal funds for international family-planning organizations promoting abortions (the "Mexico City policy") and barring the importation of the so-called abortion pill RU-486.

The first President George Bush continued the policies in his four years in the White House. Both Reagan and Bush also appeared to be choosing federal judges — including Supreme Court justices — likely to be skeptical at best of expanding abortion rights. As the GOP stance hardened, the Democratic Party equally committed itself to supporting abortion rights and opposing legislated restrictions or judicial efforts to overturn *Roe*.

Along with political organizing and lobbying, some elements of the anti-abortion movement turned to civil disobedience and violence. The National Abortion Federation counted some 161 incidents of arson or bombings against abortion clinics from 1977-1992. There were more than 100 clinic blockades each year in 1988 and 1989, resulting in more than 10,000 arrests per year. Most ominous were death threats and actual killings. Anti-abortion activists killed five people in 1993 and 1994: a physician at a Pensacola, Fla., clinic in March 1993; a second physician and a volunteer escort outside another Pensacola clinic in July 1994; and receptionists at separate Brookline, Mass., clinics on Dec. 30, 1994. [14]

The Supreme Court, meanwhile, gave anti-abortion forces major victories with decisions in 1977 and 1980 that permitted first the states and then the federal government to deny abortion funding under the Medicaid program for the indigent. Through the 1980s, the so-called Hyde amendment — named after Rep. Henry J. Hyde, R-Ill. — barred federal funding of abortions except to save the life of the woman. The court, on the other hand, struck down provisions requiring spousal consent, waiting periods or informed consent before an abortion could be performed.

After some wavering, the court in 1990 ruled that states could require parental notification for a minor to obtain an abortion, but only with a judicial procedure to bypass the requirement under certain circumstances. The court in 1991 also upheld the "gag rule" on family-planning clinics.

By the end of the 1980s, Reagan had appeared to shift the high court in a conservative direction with four appointments: Rehnquist's elevation to chief justice in 1986 and the selection of Justices O'Connor in 1981, Antonin Scalia in 1986 and Kennedy in 1987. The shift encouraged anti-abortion groups to view a challenge to a Missouri abortion law as a vehicle for overturning *Roe*. In fact, the court in 1989 upheld the law by a 5-4 vote, with four of the justices explicitly criticizing *Roe*: Rehnquist, Scalia, Kennedy and Byron R. White. But O'Connor declined to reconsider *Roe* and instead upheld the Missouri law because it did not create what she had described in previous opinions as an "undue burden" on a woman's right to an abortion.

The first President Bush appeared to shift the court further to the right with his appointments of Justice Souter in 1990 and Clarence Thomas in 1991. A new showdown came in a case challenging a Pennsylvania law that required a waiting period, informed consent and spousal consent — provisions seemingly barred by previous decisions. The Bush administration defended the law and expressly urged the court to overturn *Roe*. In an unusual move, however, three of the Republican-appointed justices — O'Connor, Kennedy and Souter — filed a pivotal joint opinion that reaffirmed what they called *Roe's* "essential holding" but nonetheless upheld all of the Pennsylvania law except the spousal consent portion, arguing that the measure met O'Connor's "undue burden" test.

Blackmun praised the three for "personal courage" while lamenting the apparent narrowing of *Roe*. From the opposite side, four justices — including Thomas — said abortion regulations should be permitted if "rationally related to a legitimate state interest."

Abortion-Rights Gains

The election of Democrat Clinton as president in 1992 brought an abortion-rights supporter to the White House for the first time in 12 years. Clinton reversed several Reagan-Bush abortion policies, supported abortion-rights measures in Congress and — perhaps most significantly — fortified the Supreme Court's abortion-rights bloc with his appointments of Justices Ruth Bader Ginsburg and Stephen G. Breyer. Those appointments helped produce a pivotal victory for abortion-rights forces with the court's 5–4 decision in 2000 striking down a state ban on "partial-birth abortions." [15]

Clinton cheered abortion-rights groups by changing three Reagan-Bush policies on his second day in office: Jan. 22, 1993 — the 20th anniversary of *Roe*. By executive order, Clinton ended enforcement of the "gag rule" on family-planning clinics and overturned the Mexico City policy on aid to international family-planning organizations. He also lifted a ban on abortions at overseas military facilities and directed the Department of Health and Human Services (HHS) to study whether to allow the importation of RU-486.

With Democratic majorities in the House and the Senate, Clinton also won enactment in 1994 of a law aimed at countering blockades of women's clinics. The Freedom of Access to Clinic Entrances Act — dubbed FACE — provided criminal and civil penalties for anyone using force or the threat of force against clinic workers or patients. In addition, Congress eased the Hyde amendment by allowing federal funding for abortions in cases of rape, incest or to protect the life of the mother. Abortion-rights supporters also won House and Senate committee approval of the "Freedom of Choice Act," aimed at writing the *Roe* decision into federal law. Neither bill was brought up for a floor vote, however, and anti-abortion forces gained the upper hand when Republicans won control of the House in the 1994 elections.

Ginsburg, a pioneer in women's-rights litigation before her appointment to the federal bench in 1980, and Breyer, a one-time aide to abortion-rights supporter Sen. Edward M. Kennedy, D-Mass., have both supported abortion rights after their appointments to the high court in 1993 and 1994, respectively. For several years, however, the court dealt with abortion issues only tangentially. In two decisions in 1994, the court ruled that judges could restrict anti-abortion demonstrations by setting up "buffer zones" around abortion-clinic entrances and that abortion clinics or patients could sue anti-abortion protesters for damages under the federal anti-racketeering law. Dissenting justices said the rulings limited anti-abortion groups' free-speech rights.

Beginning in 1995, anti-abortion groups were lobbying for laws to ban the procedure that they provocatively termed "partial-birth abortion." A fed-

Abortion Rates Higher for Low-Income Women

Abortion rates have been increasing dramatically among low-income women while declining among wealthier women.

Woman's Economic Status	Abortion Rate (No. of abortions per 1,000 women)	
	1994	2000
Income below poverty level	36	44
Income up to twice poverty level	31	38
Income two to three times poverty level	25	21
Income more than triple poverty level	16	10

Source: Rachel K. Jones, et al., "Patterns in the Socioeconomic Characteristics of Women Obtaining Abortions in 2000-2001," Perspectives on Sexual and Reproductive Health, *September/October 2002, pp. 226-235, The Alan Guttmacher Institute.*

eral ban won approval in the GOP-controlled House and the Democratic-controlled Senate in 1996, but Clinton vetoed the measure in a White House ceremony on April 10, attended by several women who insisted the procedure had saved their lives and their future ability to bear children. A second legislative push also ended with a veto in 1997. Anti-abortion groups were more successful with state legislatures; by the end of the decade, some 30 states had banned the procedure.

A challenge to one of those state laws — Nebraska's — reached the high court in 2000. In an opinion by Breyer, the court ruled that the measure created "an undue burden on a woman's right to make an abortion decision." First, he said, the law could be construed to prohibit the commonly done dilation and extraction (D&E) procedure. In addition, Breyer said, the law conflicted with *Roe* and subsequent cases because it did not include an exception for the procedure if necessary to protect the woman's health. In a pivotal concurring opinion, O'Connor suggested a more carefully drawn statute might pass constitutional muster. For the dissenters, Thomas likened the procedure to "infanticide." [16]

As the presidential campaign unfolded later that year, the Supreme Court's composition became a proxy for the opposing views of Republican George W. Bush and Democrat Al Gore. [17] Bush said he would appoint future justices in the mold of the court's strongest abortion opponents: Thomas and Scalia. Gore countered by pledging his support for abortion rights and warning of a likely reversal of *Roe v. Wade* if Bush made good on his pledge.

The two candidates staked out contrasting positions on other abortion issues, including partial-birth abortions and RU-486, but they also appeared to play down the issue to avoid alienating swing voters. For his part, Bush said he supported a constitutional amendment to ban abortions, but cautioned that it would not be adopted "until a lot of people change their minds."

Anti-Abortion Advances

During his first two years in office, President Bush has cheered anti-abortion groups with an array of policy moves and appointments. Anti-abortion bills won approval in the Republican-controlled House but stalled in the Senate after the Democrats gained control in May 2001. The GOP's recapture of the Senate in the 2002 midterm congressional elections improved the chances for the anti-abortion agenda, including the ban on partial-birth abortions. But abortion-rights advocates vowed to continue opposing the bills — and immediately to challenge the partial-birth abortion measure if it became law.

Bush touched off fierce fights before his inauguration by naming determined abortion opponents to two key Cabinet posts: John Ashcroft, a former Missouri governor who had been defeated for re-election to the Senate, as attorney general; and Wisconsin Gov. Tommy G. Thompson as HHS secretary. Then two days after his inauguration, Bush marked *Roe's* 28th anniversary by sending greetings to the annual "March for Life" and, more tangibly, by reinstating the Mexico City policy of barring U.S. funds to international family-planning organizations that promote abortion.

Abortion-rights supporters had no leverage to try to block the reinstated funding policy. They tried hard but failed to block Ashcroft's confirmation. In his confirmation hearings, however, Democratic senators secured Ashcroft's promise to enforce federal laws protecting abortion rights — including the access-to-clinic-entrances act. He also said he would not try to overturn *Roe v. Wade*. Despite the concessions, anti-abortion groups hailed the Senate's 58-42 vote to confirm him on Feb. 1. Thompson had won easier confirmation earlier, after initial opposition to the nomination failed to harden.

Abortion politics also shaped the reaction to Bush's judicial nominations, including his first batch of 11 nominees for federal appeals courts, announced on May 9, 2001. [18] Abortion-rights groups criticized several of the nominees for taking anti-abortion stands as academics, lawyers or judges. Under Democratic control, the Senate held up many of Bush's nominees in 2001 and 2002, including the most controversial. Priscilla R. Owen, a Texas Supreme Court justice chosen for the federal appeals court in New Orleans, failed to win approval by the Judiciary Committee last September after being criticized for arguing in a dissenting opinion for a restrictive interpretation of the state's parental-notification law. (Owen is expected to be approved by the committee, now under Republican control, in the next two weeks.)

As Bush began his second year in office, he renewed his anti-abortion credentials with a more detailed message to the annual "March for Life" on Jan. 22. In an eight-paragraph statement read by telephone, Bush promised his administration would oppose partial-birth abortion and public financing of abortions and support teen abstinence, crisis-pregnancy centers and parental consent and notification laws. He also vowed to support "a comprehensive and effective ban on all forms of human cloning." [19] Some abortion opponents believe cloning human embryos to extract the cells for biomedical research is the equivalent of murder.

The administration also won praise the same month from anti-abortion groups — and strong opposition from abortion-rights organizations — with a proposed rule to define a fetus as a child eligible for government-subsidized health care under the Children's Health Insurance Program. Congress created the program in 1997 to benefit children in near-poverty families ineligible for Medicaid. Thompson said the proposed rule would allow states to increase insurance coverage for prenatal care and delivery. But abortion-rights advocates said the proposal was really a backdoor attempt to establish a legal precedent for recognizing the fetus as a person; they called for simply adding pregnant women to the program's coverage.

The debate continued through the administrative rulemaking process. Nearly 7,800 comments were received on the proposed rule before Thompson gave final approval on Sept. 27 for the regulation to go into effect 30 days later. [20] The fight then shifted to the states. Abortion-rights advocates said they would urge states to reject the option and instead ask HHS for permission to include pregnant women in the program. Two states had already taken that approach: New Jersey and Rhode Island.

In the meantime, Bush had signed into law a bill sought by anti-abortion groups to guarantee legal protection to babies born alive at any state of development. The Born-Alive Infants Protection Act defined a child as born alive if he or she has been expelled from the mother; is breathing; and has a beating heart, a pulsating umbilical cord or muscle movement, even if the expulsion occurred during an abortion. The bill included a disclaimer that it was not intended to infringe on abortion rights. Abortion-rights supporters in Congress called the measure unnecessary but did not oppose it. Bush signed the measure on Aug. 5, saying that it would give legal rights to "every infant born alive — including an infant who survives an abortion procedure."

As midterm elections approached, the House on Sept. 25 passed by a comfortable 229-189 margin the right-to-refuse bill, exempting health-care providers with religious or moral objections from being forced to perform abortions. But the anti-abortion agenda remained blocked in the Democratic-controlled Senate. The GOP gains in the midterm elections immediately buoyed the anti-abortion forces, who counted eight of the 10 newly elected senators as "pro-life." Three of those took seats previously held by Democrats who had supported abortion rights. The election results helped clear one logjam when the Senate shifted to GOP control, with the early swearing in of two of the new

Republicans. The move allowed confirmation of one of Bush's judicial nominees: Michael McConnell, a conservative law professor named to the federal appeals court in Denver, who had been opposed by abortion-rights groups because of writings critical of *Roe*.

On the 30th anniversary of the decision, Bush again spoke to the anti-abortion march by telephone. [21] "You and I share a commitment to building a culture of life in America," the president said, "and we are making progress."

The crowd numbered in the tens of thousands, leading abortion-rights groups to sound urgent alarms. "Pro-choice America has to wake up," NARAL's Cavendish declared.

CURRENT SITUATION

'Abortion-Pill' Controversy

For more than a decade, American women waited to learn whether a new drug developed in Europe — the so-called abortion pill — would be approved for use in the United States. Finally, in August 2000, the Food and Drug Administration (FDA) gave the official green light for doctors who wanted to prescribe the drug, known most commonly as RU-486. [22]

Some observers speculated that use of the drug — now called mifepristone — could defuse the abortion controversy. But today RU-486 remains a source of contention between the opposing camps. Anti-abortion groups call it unsafe and are asking the FDA to rescind its approval, while abortion-rights groups are actively promoting what they prefer to call the "early-option pill."

The dispute underscores the chasm that continues to separate the opposing camps in the abortion debate on virtually every issue relating to women's reproductive health. Occasional efforts to find common ground appear to make little headway, as the rhetoric remains hot and accusatory. Anti-abortion groups call their opponents "the abortion industry" or more provocatively "baby killers," while abortion-rights organizations label their adversaries not just "anti-choice" but sometimes "antiwoman."

Whatever its political impact, RU-486 appeals to abortion-rights advocates as an additional and, at first blush, more convenient option for women to terminate unwanted pregnancies. Two years after FDA approval, the drug had been used to complete more than 100,000 abortions in the United States, according to Danco Laboratories, the New York-based company that markets the drug here. [23] The Alan Guttmacher Institute — a nonprofit research center affiliated with Planned Parenthood — estimates that pill-induced, or medical, abortions comprised about 6 percent of all abortions in the first half of 2001, the most recent period covered in its survey.

Abortion providers insist RU-486 is both safe and effective. "This has been a very acceptable method for women," says the National Abortion Federation's Saporta. Medical abortion can be completed earlier than surgical procedures — an important advantage, Saporta says. "Earlier abortion by any method is safer," she explains.

Anti-abortion groups, however, say RU-486 can cause hemorrhaging, or even death, and its approval was the result of political pressure in the last year of the Clinton administration. "The evidence would seem to show that it is not safe for the woman and obviously not safe for the baby," says Wendy Wright, senior policy director for Concerned Women for America (CWFA). The Christian-oriented organization petitioned the FDA in August 2002 to rescind its approval of RU-486

because of safety complaints and alleged procedural flaws in the approval process.

The National Abortion Federation is working on a response to correct what it calls the "medical misinformation" in CWFA's petition. "There isn't any question that mifepristone is safe and effective," says Saporta. "We don't believe the FDA will change its approval."

Anti-abortion groups emphasize — and an NAF fact sheet acknowledges — that use of RU-486 is not so simple as some news coverage might suggest. The drug works by blocking the body's production of progesterone, a hormone crucial to the early progress of pregnancy. The treatment requires at least two visits to a clinic or medical office, can take anywhere from three days to three to four weeks and fails about 5 percent of the time — necessitating a surgical procedure. Anti-abortion groups also say that a pill-induced abortion has a greater emotional impact on the woman because she is likely to see the aborted fetus when it is expelled.

For abortion-rights advocates, on the other hand, RU-486 helps to circumvent the persistent problem of limited availability of abortion providers. "Access is probably the biggest problem facing women who choose to have an abortion," Saporta says. The number of abortion providers has declined by more than one-third since 1982, according to the Guttmacher Institute. More than one-third of American women live in a county without an abortion provider. [24]

Doctors today often are not trained in how to perform an abortion. Fewer than half of the obstetrics-gynecology residency programs require or even offer abortion training, Saporta says. To remedy the problem, NAF and other abortion-rights groups are calling for laws — like an executive order issued by New York City Mayor Michael Bloomberg in April 2002 — to require abortion training in residency programs at pub-

lic hospitals. Anti-abortion groups say such requirements run afoul of existing federal law that prohibits discrimination against any health-care entity for refusing to provide abortion training.

In another fight, opposing camps have squared off on the question of whether women who have abortions have a heightened risk of developing breast cancer. Although most cancer experts doubt any link, the National Cancer Institute — part of the National Institutes of Health within the HHS Department — acceded to lobbying from anti-abortion lawmakers last summer and changed its Web site to describe the research on the subject as "inconsistent." [25]

Abortion-rights groups strongly criticized the revision. The institute responded by convening a closed-door conference on the issue in February that ended by reverting to the previous position. In a conference summary posted on its Web site, the institute now states flatly: "Induced abortion is not associated with increased breast cancer risk."

Legislative Battles

Anti-abortion groups are exulting in the Senate's quick approval of legislation to ban so-called partial-birth abortions and predicting easy passage in the House in April en route to being signed into law by President Bush. Meanwhile, other parts of the anti-abortion groups' agenda are progressing in Congress and in some state legislatures.

The Senate's March 13 ban on partial-birth abortions came after two days of debate and unsuccessful efforts by opponents to soften the measure. With some Democratic votes, the Republican majority rejected by margins of more than 20 votes each of two Democratic-sponsored amendments to add a health exception to the bill.

Abortion-rights advocates scored a symbolic victory with a 52–46 vote on

At Issue

Should Congress ban so-called partial-birth abortions?

REP. CHRISTOPHER H. SMITH, R-N.J.
CHAIRMAN, BIPARTISAN CONGRESSIONAL PRO-LIFE CAUCUS

WRITTEN FOR THE CQ RESEARCHER, MARCH 2003

a society is measured by how well — or poorly — it treats the most vulnerable in its midst, and partial-birth abortion, like all abortions, is horrific violence against women and children.

Justice Clarence Thomas accurately described the procedure in his *Stenberg v. Carhart* (2000) dissent: "After dilating the cervix, the physician will grab the fetus by its feet and pull the fetal body out of the uterus into the vaginal cavity. At this stage of development, the head is the largest part of the body. . . . the head will be held inside the uterus by the woman's cervix. While the fetus is stuck in this position, dangling partly out of the woman's body, and just a few inches from a completed birth, the physician uses an instrument such as a pair of scissors to tear or perforate the skull. The physician will then either crush the skull or will use a vacuum to remove the brain and other intracranial contents from the fetal skull, collapse the fetus' head, and pull the fetus from the uterus."

Most partial-birth abortions are committed between the 20th and 26th week of pregnancy. At this stage, a prematurely delivered infant is usually born alive. These are babies who are extremely sensitive to pain — whether inside the womb, fully born or anywhere in-between.

An overwhelming majority of Americans are outraged that this procedure is legal in our country. A January Gallup Poll found that 70 percent favored and 25 percent opposed "a law that would make it illegal to perform a specific abortion procedure conducted in the last six months of pregnancy known as 'partial birth abortion,' except in cases necessary to save the life of the mother."

In a January speech, President Bush agreed: "Partial-birth abortion is an abhorrent procedure that offends human dignity."

I have written two torture-victims relief laws and many other pieces of human-rights legislation including a law to stop exploitation of women by sex traffickers. Partial-birth abortion is torture of baby girls and boys, and I am ashamed of my colleagues who stand on the House floor to defend it.

Abortion methods are violence against children. There is absolutely nothing compassionate or benign about dousing a baby with superconcentrated salt solutions or lethal injections or hacking them to pieces with surgical knives, and there is absolutely nothing compassionate or caring about sucking a baby's brains out.

REP. LOUISE SLAUGHTER, D-N.Y.
CO-CHAIR, PRO-CHOICE CAUCUS

WRITTEN FOR THE CQ RESEARCHER, MARCH 2003

i do solemnly swear that I will support and defend the Constitution of the United States against all enemies, foreign and domestic. . . ." Before taking office, Members of Congress pledge these words to uphold the Constitution. Yet, again this year, anti-choice legislators introduce legislation that disregards the Constitution and the precious rights it guarantees.

The right to privacy as recognized in *Roe v. Wade* and reaffirmed in *Planned Parenthood v. Casey* is a fundamental American value. Opponents of a woman's right to choose have failed in their efforts to eliminate this constitutionally protected right, so they have changed tactics. Their strategy now is to whittle away at a woman's right to choose until all that remains are hollow guarantees in a faded court opinion.

The legislative centerpiece of this strategy is misleadingly titled Partial Birth Abortion Ban Act of 2003. Three years after the Supreme Court addressed this issue in the landmark *Stenberg v. Carhart* decision overturning Nebraska's prohibition of so-called "partial-birth" abortions, opponents of reproductive freedom want to force through Congress legislation that contains the same serious constitutional flaws as the Nebraska ban.

The court ruled that the Nebraska law was unconstitutional because it did not provide an exception to protect a woman's health. Further, it ruled that the law was an undue burden on women's rights to privacy, because the vague description of partial-birth abortions covered multiple procedures, including the most common form of second trimester abortion.

The legislation's authors could have drafted a bill that complies with constitutional standards, yet they have not done so. This bill does NOT include an exception for the health of the woman, and it does NOT prohibit a specific abortion procedure.

Congress should not invade the doctor-patient relationship. These intensely personal choices must be made by women, their doctors and their families — not by politicians. We should praise doctors who care for women faced with this difficult decision, not make them federal criminals. This legislation is an attack on the power of the Supreme Court, the Constitution and women's health and dignity.

Forcing members of Congress year after year to consider a bill that is clearly unconstitutional is a waste of taxpayers' money. Instead of continually reintroducing unconstitutional legislation, proponents of this measure should put their energies and resources into promoting women's health by improving access to contraception and supporting comprehensive family-planning programs.

Seeking Common Ground

Cristina Page and Amanda Peterman are both thirty-something college graduates and self-described feminists with a common interest in promoting women's health and family welfare. Since they first met a little over two years ago, they have become fast friends. They happen to disagree, however, on one major issue: abortion.

Page works as program director for the New York affiliate of NARAL Pro-Choice America, while Peterman serves as life media director for Right to Life of Michigan. Nonetheless, Page and Peterman marked the 30th anniversary of *Roe v. Wade* in January with a jointly bylined op-ed article in *The New York Times* calling for the opposing camps in the abortion debate to find common ground on such issues as pregnancy prevention, high-quality child care and "family friendly" workplace policies.

"If the pro-choice and pro-life movements work together to support legislation to expand the social safety net for low-income mothers, and to lobby for more family-friendly policies for working parents, their power would be formidable," Page and Peterman wrote. "But sadly, they are issues that often get lost in the larger debate." [1]

Since they met on the eve of the 2000 election, Page and Peterman have traveled together and talked at length. Page took Peterman to an abortion clinic in Pittsburgh to try to dispel the image of counselors rushing women to have the procedure. For her part, Page says she better appreciates that many people in the right-to-life movement are turned off by violence and harsh rhetoric.

Together, Page and Peterman are now working to raise money for a new organization to collaborate on what Page calls "the surprising number of important issues on which we agree."

The project is both ambitious and delicate. Page says her abortion-rights colleagues have been supportive for the most part, but Peterman bowed out of a scheduled interview in March because of what she called "stuff inside my ranks. It's a very slow process to educate both sides," Peterman said apologetically.

"There's a lot of distrust, there's been a lot of violence," Page says. "We can retrace the disagreements, but that's what we've been doing for 30 years."

---

[1] Cristina Page and Amanda Peterman, "The Right to Agree," *The New York Times*, Jan. 22, 2003, p. A21.

March 12 adding a "sense of the Senate" amendment in support of *Roe v. Wade*, but the language is certain to be rejected by the House and stripped out in conference. More substantively, abortion-rights advocates suffered a narrow loss on March 11 with a failed amendment to require health insurance plans to provide coverage for birth control pills. The measure was approved, 49-47, but under Senate rules needed 60 votes to overcome a point of order because it would have raised federal spending.

On final passage, 16 Democrats joined 48 of the chamber's 51 Republicans in voting for the ban. Democrats voting aye included Minority Leader Daschle. The three GOP "no" votes came from moderate New Englanders: Lincoln Chafee of Rhode Island and Maine's Olympia J. Snowe and Susan Collins. Sen. James M. Jeffords, I-Vt., also voted no. The three non-voting senators were all Democrats, including two declared presidential candidates — John Kerry of Massachusetts and John Edwards of North Carolina — and Delaware's Joseph Biden, Jr.

President Bush issued a statement commending the Senate for voting to outlaw what he called "an abhorrent procedure that offends human dignity."

Opponents continued to insist, however, that the bill will not survive a court test. "Anti-choice senators simply ignored Supreme Court precedent," said NARAL's Michelman, referring to the 2000 decision striking down Nebraska's partial-birth ban. But the NRLC's Johnson noted that four justices had voted to uphold the Nebraska law and voiced hope for a different outcome when a case testing the federal law reaches the high court.

Meanwhile, anti-abortion groups are also advancing a variety of restrictive bills in state legislatures around the country. But the only major bills to win final legislative approval by mid-March were a package of measures in Virginia that faced a possible veto from the state's Democratic governor, Mark Warner. Abortion-rights groups, however, are having some success with bills designed to reduce the need for abortions by easing women's access to emergency contraception — so-called morning-after bills.

The bills approved by the Virginia legislature include a new ban on so-called "partial-birth infanticide" to replace the state's previous law that was invalidated following the Supreme Court's decision in the Nebraska case. The bill prohibits "any deliberate act that is intended to kill a human infant (or that does kill an infant) who has been born alive but who has not been completely extracted or expelled from its mother." A second measure would require a minor to obtain the consent from one parent before an abortion; current state law only requires notice.

Warner says he may veto the measures, which he calls "a frontal assault on a woman's right to choose." But both bills originally passed with veto-proof majorities; the legislature is to return on April 1 to consider any gubernatorial vetoes. Opponents vow to challenge the partial-birth abortion bill in court if it does become law. [26]

Some of the other bills gaining in state legislatures are examples of what abortion-rights groups call "TRAP laws" — for "targeted regulation of abortion providers." A Kansas House committee has approved a bill setting safety standards for abortion clinics; opponents say the bill is unnecessary and designed to impose unaffordable costs. [27]

Some other bills are largely symbolic. A Georgia lawmaker is proposing to require a judge to issue a death warrant before an abortion can proceed. In South Carolina, a legislator has a bill to erect a six-foot statue of a fetus outside the statehouse as a memorial to "unborn children who have given their lives because of legal abortion."

For their part, abortion-rights advocates won legislative approval in two states — Hawaii and New Mexico — requiring hospitals to inform sexual-assault survivors about emergency contraception. Hawaii also passed a bill to allow women to obtain emergency contraception from pharmacists without an individual prescription from a physician; similar proposals were pending in other states, including New York, Oregon and Texas.

OUTLOOK

Unabated Conflict

The abortion wars show no signs of abating.

The dueling press releases issued after the Senate passed the partial-birth abortion bill carried forward the harsh debates from the Senate floor. The

NRLC accused opponents of "extremism in defense of abortion," while NARAL said the bill took "direct aim at a woman's right to choose."

The bill's ultimate fate rests with the courts — most likely, the Supreme Court itself. The justices have shied away from abortion disputes since their 2000 decision striking down the Nebraska ban. In February, for example, the court declined to hear a women's-clinic challenge to an Indiana waiting-period law upheld by the federal appeals court in Chicago. The justices are likely to feel obliged to take up a case testing a new federal law, but any legal challenge will take more than a year to reach them.

By then, the court may have one or more new justices, but its tilt on abortion issues depends on who retires. The court's three oldest members are Rehnquist, 78, who opposes abortion rights; and Justices John Paul Stevens, 82, a strong abortion-rights supporter, and O'Connor, nearly 73, who helped preserve *Roe v. Wade* in 1992 but has voted to uphold most state restrictions on abortion.

Rehnquist's retirement would not give President Bush the chance to shift the court's balance toward the anti-abortion side; Stevens' or O'Connor's departure might. Any vacancy, however, will result in a likely confirmation fight between liberals and conservatives in the narrowly divided Senate.

The opposing abortion-related groups are both using a fight over one of Bush's judicial nominees as a rehearsal of sorts for a potential Supreme Court fight. Anti-abortion groups are strongly supporting and abortion-rights organizations strenuously opposing confirmation for Miguel Estrada, a Washington lawyer and former assistant U.S. solicitor general, to the federal appeals court in Washington. Republicans say they have sufficient votes — 54 — to approve the nomination, but they have been unable to muster the 60 votes needed to overcome a Democratic filibuster.

Legislatively, anti-abortion lawmakers enjoy the upper hand on Capitol Hill, but they still face significant hurdles. As the new Congress convened, NARAL estimated that it had only prevailed in 25 out of 148 votes on reproductive rights issues since 1996. With the newly strengthened GOP hold in Congress, abortion-rights advocates already have been on the losing end of two major votes — the House's ban on human cloning in February and the Senate's partial-birth abortion ban in March. Abortion-rights advocates are likely to face more rough sledding over the next two years.

Meanwhile, the debates continue not only in legislative chambers but also on the sidewalks outside women's clinics, where abortion-rights advocates appear determined but beleaguered. "I don't think *Roe v. Wade* will be overturned," clinic escort Fox says. "But it's going to continue to be broken down until we only have a right to abortion under very limited parameters."

For her part, "sidewalk counselor" Walsh is equally determined and seemingly more hopeful of eventual victory in the fight against *Roe v. Wade*. "With the way our society is, our government is, it would take a miracle" to overturn *Roe*, Walsh says. "But God does do miracles. The most effective thing we can do is pray. So with God's grace, one day it will happen."

Notes

[1] For background, see Charles S. Clark, "Abortion Clinic Protests," *The CQ Researcher*, April 7, 1995, pp. 297-320.
[2] For background, see Sarah Glazer, "Roe v. Wade at 25," *The CQ Researcher*, Nov. 28, 1997, pp. 1033-1056.
[3] See *1996 CQ Almanac*, pp. 6-42 to 6-45; *1997 CQ Almanac*, pp. 6-12 to 6-18.
[4] Mary Balch, "Pro-Lifers Celebrate Gains in State Legislative Elections," *NRLC News*, December 2002 (www.nrlc.org/news/2002).

5 NARAL Pro-Choice America Foundation, "Who Decides? A State-by-State Review of Abortion and Reproductive Rights," January 2003 (www.naral.org/mediaresources/publications.html).

6 "Memorandum to the Conference," Nov. 21, 1972, cited in Barbara Hinkson Craig and David M. O'Brien, *Abortion and American Politics* (1993), p. 21.

7 *Planned Parenthood of Southeastern Pennsylvania v. Casey*, 505 U.S. 833 (1992). For accounts of the case, see David J. Garrow, *Liberty and Sexuality: The Right to Privacy and the Making of Roe v. Wade* (1998), pp. 681-701; N.E.H. Hull and Peter Charles Hoffer, *Roe v. Wade: The Abortion Rights Controversy in American History* (2001), pp. 249-258.

8 *Time*/CNN/Gallup Poll conducted Jan. 15-16, 2003, among 1,010 adult Americans age 18 or older.

9 *Stenberg v. Carhart*, 505 U.S. 833 (2000).

10 The studies are discussed in a recent federal appeals court decision upholding Indiana's waiting-period law. See *A Woman's Choice-East Side Women's Clinic v. Newman*, 7th U.S. Circuit Court of Appeals, 01-2107, Sept. 16, 2002.

11 For historical background, see Hull and Hoffer, *op. cit.*, pp. 11-88; James C. Mohr, *Abortion in America: The Origins and Evolution of National Policy, 1800-1900* (1978).

12 The Alan Guttmacher Institute, "Trends in Abortion in the United States, 1973-2000," January 2003.

13 For a compact summary of Supreme Court decisions from *Roe* through the partial-birth abortion decision in *Stenberg v. Carhart* (2000), see "Abortion" in Claire Cushman (ed.), *Supreme Court Decisions and Women's Rights* (2001), pp. 188-206.

14 See Dallas A. Blanchard, *The Anti-Abortion Movement and the Rise of the Religious Right: From Polite to Fiery Protest* (1994), pp. 53-60; Garrow, *op. cit.*, p. 705.

15 For summaries, see *Congress and the Nation, Vol. IX, 1993-1996* (1998), pp. 536-541, 563-565; *Congress and the Nation*, Vol. X, 1997-2000 (2002), pp. 455-459, 472-475.

FOR MORE INFORMATION

Alan Guttmacher Institute, 120 Wall St., New York, NY 10005; (212) 248-1111; www.agi-usa.org. Nonprofit research center on reproductive issues; "special affiliate" of Planned Parenthood Federation.

Center for Reproductive Rights, 120 Wall St., New York, NY 10005; (917) 637-3600; www.crlp.org.

Concerned Women for America, 1015 15th St., N.W., suite 1100, Washington, DC 20005; (202) 488-7000; www.cwfa.org. Opposes abortion.

Family Research Council, 801 G St., N.W., Washington, DC 20001; (202) 393-2100; www.frc.org. Opposes abortion.

NARAL Pro-Choice America, 1156 15th St., N.W., Suite 700, Washington, DC 20005; (202) 973-3000; www.naral.org.

National Abortion Federation. 1755 Massachusetts Ave., N.W., Suite 600, Washington, DC 20036; (202) 667-5881; www.prochoice.org. Represents abortion clinics.

National Right to Life Committee, 512 10th St., N.W., Washington, DC 20004-2293; (202) 626-8800; www.nrlc.org.

16 For an account, see Kenneth Jost, *Supreme Court Yearbook 1999-2000* (2000), pp. 34-41.

17 Account drawn from Mary Leonard, "Both Candidates Keep Quiet on Abortion," *The Boston Globe*, Nov. 1, 2000, p. A23.

18 For background, see Kenneth Jost, "Judges and Politics," *The CQ Researcher*, July 27, 2001, pp. 577-600.

19 The complete text can be found on *National Right to Life News*, February 2002 (www.nrlc.org/news).

20 See Robert Pear, "Bush Rule Makes Fetuses Eligible for Health Benefits," *The New York Times*, Sept. 28, 2002, p. A13; Laura Meckler, " 'Unborn Child' Coverage Rule Set," The Associated Press, Sept. 29, 2002.

21 See Robin Toner, "At a Distance, Bush Joins Abortion Protest," *The New York Times*, Jan. 23, 2003, p. A16.

22 Some background drawn from interest-group Web sites: National Abortion Federation (www.naf.org); National Right to Life Committee (www.nrlc.org). For a journalistic account, see Sharon Bernstein, "Persistence Brought Abortion Pill to U.S.," *Los Angeles Times*, Nov. 5, 2000, p. A1.

23 Marc Kaufman, "Abortion Pill Sales Rising, Firm Says," *The Washington Post*, Sept. 25, 2002, p. A3.

24 Stanley K. Henshaw and Lawrence B. Finer, "The Accessibility of Abortion Services in the United States, 2001," *Perspectives on Sexual and Reproductive Health*, Vol. 35, No. 1 (January/February 2003), pp. 15-24 (www.agi-usa.org/journals).

25 See Daniel Costello, "An Enduring Debate: Cancer and Abortion," *Los Angeles Times*, March 10, 2003.

26 Warner quoted in Warren Fiske, "Now, the Vetoes," *The* (Norfolk) *Virginian-Pilot*, Feb. 28, 2003, p. A1. See also Tammie Smith, "Lawmakers Focus on Abortion," *The* (Richmond) *Times-Dispatch*, Feb. 23, 2003, p. A11.

27 See David Crary, "Abortion Foes Step Up Efforts Nationally," The Associated Press, March 11, 2003.

Bibliography

Selected Sources

Books

Blanchard, Dallas A., *The Anti-Abortion Movement and the Rise of the Religious Right: From Polite to Fiery Protest*, **Twayne Publishers, 1994.**

Critically examines the movement from *Roe* through *Casey* (1992). Blanchard is professor emeritus at the University of West Florida. Lists major anti-abortion publications and organizations.

Cook, Elizabeth Adell, Ted G. Jelen and Clyde Wilcox, *Between Two Absolutes: Public Opinion and the Politics of Abortion*, **Westview Press, 1992.**

Detailed analyses of public opinion on abortion with extensive statistical information over 20-year period. Cook is now an editor at the *American Political Science Review*; Jelen teaches at the University of Nevada-Las Vegas, and Wilcox at Georgetown University. Jelen is also editor or co-editor of *Abortion Politics in the United States and Canada* (with Marthe A. Chandler), Praeger, 1994; *Perspectives on the Politics of Abortion*, Praeger, 1995.

Craig, Barbara Hinkson, and David M. O'Brien, *Abortion and American Politics*, **Chatham House, 1993.**

Analyzes the politics of the abortion issue from *Roe* through *Casey*. Craig is a professor emerita at Wesleyan University, O'Brien teaches at the University of Virginia. Includes major statutes and case index.

Garrow, David J., *Liberty and Sexuality: The Right to Privacy and the Making of Roe v. Wade*, **Macmillan, 1994 [updated edition, University of California Press, 1998].**

Definitive history of Supreme Court decisions on reproductive rights. Historian Garrow, an abortion-rights advocate, is a professor at Emory Law School. Includes voluminous notes, 30-page bibliography.

Gorney, Cynthia, *Articles of Faith: A Frontline History of the Abortion Wars*, **Simon & Schuster, 1998.**

Details the personalities and issues in the "abortion wars" by focusing on one of the most contentious battleground states: Missouri. Gorney is associate dean at the University of California's Graduate School of Journalism in Berkeley. Includes long source list.

Hull, N.E.H., and Peter Charles Hoffer, *Roe v. Wade: The Abortion Rights Controversy in American History*, **University Press of Kansas, 2001.**

Compactly traces history of abortion law from 19th-century state laws through *Casey*. Hull teaches at Rutgers University, Hoffer at the University of Georgia. Includes lengthy chronology and bibliographical essay.

Tribe, Laurence H., *Abortion: The Clash of Absolutes*, **W.W. Norton, 1990.**

The prominent Harvard Law School professor, an abortion-rights advocate, tries to look at the issue anew. In a 1992 edition, Tribe describes the *Casey* decision as watering down *Roe* by permitting states new powers to restrict abortion.

Articles

Savage, David, "As Roe vs. Wade Turns 30, Ruling's Future Is Unsure," *Los Angeles Times*, **Jan. 21, 2003, p. A1.**

Analyzes possible impact on abortion-rights ruling if President Bush gets to fill one or more Supreme Court vacancies.

Tumulty, Karen, and Viveca Novak, "Under the Radar," *Time*, **Jan. 27, 2003, pp. 38-41.**

Examines the White House strategy to undercut abortion rights legalized by *Roe v. Wade*.

Zernike, Kate, "Thirty Years After Abortion Ruling, New Trends but the Old Debate," *The New York Times*, **Jan. 20, 2003, p. A1.**

Discusses views on abortion among women, activists and others against backdrop of decline in abortion rate to lowest level since 1974. Package includes sidebar by same reporter: "An Abortion Doctor's View."

Reports and Studies

Finer, Lawrence B., and Stanley K. Henshaw, "Abortion Incidence and Services in the United States in 2000," *Perspectives on Sexual and Reproductive Health* **(January/February 2003) (www.agi-usa.org/journals).**

Documents a decline in U.S. abortions; a second article in the issue details information about abortion providers: Stanley K. Henshaw and Lawrence B. Finer, "The Accessibility of Abortion Services in the United States, 2001." The authors are researchers at the Alan Guttmacher Institute, a research center affiliated with Planned Parenthood but accepted as reliable by both sides in abortion debates.

NARAL Pro-Choice America, "Who Decides? A State-by-State Review of Abortion and Reproductive Rights," January 2003 (www.naral.org/mediaresources/publications/2003).

The advocacy group's 12th compendium of state abortion laws details what it calls the "further erosion" of *Roe v. Wade*.

National Right to Life Committee, "NRL News," monthly series (www.nrlc.org/news).

The anti-abortion group's monthly newsletter provides up-to-date information and perspective on legislative and legal developments.

9 Privacy Under Attack

PATRICK MARSHALL

I magine police officers cruising your neighborhood, using sophisticated surveillance devices to peer through the walls of your house to see if you're doing anything illegal. Or imagine being turned down by an insurance company because they've monitored your Web surfing and discovered that you've repeatedly visited a breast cancer site or bought mountain climbing gear.

Sound far-fetched? For Danny Lee Kyllo of Florence, Ore., the first scenario is a very real one. He was arrested after police used a thermal imager to detect the heat pattern generated by high-intensity lamps he was using in his attic to grow marijuana. On June 11, the Supreme Court ruled that using the device constituted an illegal search of Kyllo's house.

And while people haven't been turned down for insurance because of their Web surfing habits, some experts say it could happen. "The potential to abuse privacy is very likely," Larry Chiang, chief executive of the online advertising company MoneyForMail.com, told a congressional hearing late last year. "Certain data files could be used to discriminate against consumers."

For example, he said, mortgage companies could deny loans to people who perpetually visit online job-search sites. "The mere act of visiting a job-listing board could signify job instability," he said. "Or, an insurance company could determine that people who purchase adventure gear — ski equipment, sky diving supplies or mountain climbing ropes — are not a good risk." [1]

From *The CQ Researcher*, June 15, 2001.

Police arrested Danny Lee Kyllo in 1992 at his home in Florence, Ore., above, after using a thermal-imaging device to detect high-intensity lamps for growing marijuana.

The connection between emerging technologies and intrusions on personal privacy has been recognized for more than a century. In 1890, Louis D. Brandeis, soon to be a Supreme Court justice, wrote: "Recent inventions and business methods call attention to the next step which must be taken for the protection of the person and for securing to the individual . . . the right 'to be let alone.' Instantaneous photographs and newspaper enterprise have invaded the sacred precincts of private and domestic life; and numerous mechanical devices threaten to make good the predication that 'what is whispered in the closet shall be proclaimed from the house-tops.' " [2]

Recent rapid advances in technology — especially computer technology — have made personal privacy intrusions possible on a scale that Brandeis would never have imagined. And the advances are arriving faster than expected. For instance, in 1999 Reg Whitaker, a political science professor at Toronto's York University, predicted that face-recognition tech-

nology could be in widespread use by 2004.

With the right software, he warned, facial features could be reduced to a digital code, which could then be entered into a database of face patterns. The output of video surveillance cameras could then be compared to the database, allowing individuals to be picked out of a crowd. "The technology would exist to make it very hard to hide, or to be lost. Of course, just because something is possible does not mean that it will ever happen." [3]

But Whitaker's prediction became a reality in January — three years early — when the faces of fans pouring through the turnstiles for the Super Bowl were scanned by video cameras, and the images were compared to faces in a police database. Nineteen petty criminals in the crowd were identified. (*See story, p. 166.*)

Carnivore, the Federal Bureau of Investigation's (FBI) controversial new software, is another example of rapidly emerging technologies that some fear could infringe on individuals' privacy. The FBI uses the program to cull through Internet transmissions — including e-mails, chat room messages and other data — from drug dealers, child pornographers, terrorists and other wrongdoers.

But it's not just government agencies that may be using the Internet to snoop into your private life. In 1998, a New Hampshire woman was stalked and killed as she left her office after her stalker got her Social Security number and work address online.

Other threats are more prosaic but more serious today than in the past because of new technologies. Scam artists for years have found ways to "steal" the identities of individuals by acquiring their Social Security numbers and

States Offer Range of Protections

Areas Protected by State Law

	Off-Duty Behavior	Sexual Bias	Personnel Records	Polygraph Limits	Right to Privacy	Drug/Alc. Use	Arrest Record
Ala.				P			
Alaska				X	X	P	
Ariz.				P	X	P	P
Ark			X			X	
Calif.			X	X	X	X	X
Colo.	X	X	P				X
Conn.		X	X			X	X
Del.		X	X	X		P	
D.C.		X	X	X			
Fla.		X			X	X	
Ga.		X				P	X
Hawaii		X		X	X	X	X
Idaho		X		X			
Ill.	X	X	X		X	P	X
Ind.		X	P				
Iowa		X	X	X		X	
Kan.		X	P	X		X	X
Ky.		X	P		X		P
La.		X	X		X	X	X
Maine		X	X			X	
Md.		X		X		X	
Mass.		X	X				X
Mich.		X	X	X			X
Minn.		X	X	X		X	X
Miss.	X					X	X
Mo.	X	X				P	
Mont.	X	X		X	X		
Neb.		X	P	X		X	
Nev.	X	X	X	X		P	
N.H.		X	X				
N.J.		X		X			
N.M.		X		X			
N.Y.		X		X			X
N.C.		X	P				X
N.D.		X		P		X	X
Ohio		X					X
Okla.		X	X			X	X
Ore.		X	X	X		X	X
Pa.		X	X	X			X
R.I.		X	X	X	X	X	X
S.C.		X	P			P	
S.D.		X	P			P	
Tenn.		X	X			X	
Texas		X	X	X		X	
Utah		X	P			X	X
Vt.		X		X		X	
Va.		X		X			X
Wash.				X	X	X	
W.Va.		X		X			
Wis.	X	X	X	X	X		
Wy.		X					

P - Law applies to public sector only.
Source: American Management Assn.

using them to obtain fraudulent credit cards, bank accounts and other credit accounts. Now, there is a vibrant trade in stolen Social Security numbers on the Internet.

Most citizens, however, need look no further than their workplace to find threats to their privacy. More than three-quarters of major U.S. corporations collect information on employees in one way or another, whether through video-taping, monitoring Internet and e-mail use or hiring outside investigators. And nearly half of those companies do not tell employees the data are being collected. (*See graph, p. 164.*)

"Privacy, one of the fundamental rights underpinning our society, is under assault as perhaps never before," Michael O'Neill, a law professor at George Mason University in Fairfax, Va., told Congress last year. [4]

Although most Americans believe they have a right to privacy, there is no such constitutional guarantee. The Fourth Amendment protects citizens from unwarranted searches or seizures of their "persons, houses, papers, and effects" but only in the case of actions by government entities. It does not apply to intrusions by non-governmental organizations, retailers, employers or individuals.

Most federal laws apply only to activities of government agencies or to interstate commerce. Thus, personal privacy is largely protected by a patchwork of state laws.

But both federal and state privacy laws have historically been difficult to craft and enact. "Privacy almost by definition involves a lot of jurisdictions in Congress and in the executive branch, and that's one reason nobody has yet addressed it comprehensively," explains Evan Hendricks, editor of *Privacy Times* newsletter. "You really can't address, for example, the Social Security number issue without looking at the broader issue of privacy in general."

Privacy legislation is also difficult to

craft because it must envision threats that may appear in the future, as new technologies are constantly emerging. By the time a proposal wends its way through the laborious legislative process, it can be rendered obsolete by new technology.

Some privacy advocates contend that rapidly developing technologies, coupled with widespread public apathy, produce a powerful threat to individual privacy.

"It is surprising how recent changes in law and technology have been permitted to undermine sanctuaries of privacy that Americans took for granted throughout most of our history," writes Jeffrey Rosen, a professor at George Washington University (GWU) Law School. "But even more surprising has been our tepid response to the increasing surveillance of our personal and private life."

Rosen says if Americans want to, they could regain their privacy protections. "We have the ability to rebuild the private spaces we have lost," writes Rosen. "But do we have the will?" [5]

In recent years an increasing number of bills aimed at protecting privacy have been introduced in Congress, but very few have attracted enough votes for passage.

Pending legislation focuses more on protecting specific kinds of data than on providing a comprehensive privacy policy. Most of the attention focuses on privacy in three key areas: consumer data, medical data and the Internet. In debating such legislation,

policy-makers are asking the following questions:

Are tighter controls needed on companies that collect data from consumers?

While some citizens may be apathetic about the increase in privacy intrusions, others are very concerned.

Kevin O'Connor heads DoubleClick.com, which tracks consumers' Internet surfing habits.

Newsmakers Photo/Robin G. Londor

Indeed, polls sponsored by the Direct Marketing Association (DMA) in May 2000 found that more than half of consumers (56 percent) are concerned about providing personal information to businesses. Even more (68 percent) were concerned about providing personal information over the Internet.

"Data sharing among businesses is rampant," says Hendricks, of *Privacy Times.* "It means big money for marketers and major intrusions for consumers."

In 1999, for example, the state of Minnesota sued U.S. Bancorp for sharing credit-card names and numbers with a telemarketing firm, which then offered customers 30-day free trials for travel services, dental plans and other services. After the 30-day period, customers' credit cards were automatically charged for the services.

"Every piece of information has a price," wrote journalist Charles J. Sykes, in his 1999 book *The End of Privacy.* "Your salary and consumer credit report can be obtained from an information broker for $75; your stock, bond and mutual-fund records for $200. For $450, brokers can obtain your credit-card number; for $80 to $200 they can put their hands on your telephone records. Your personal medical history for the last 10 years is for sale for $400. Not all of this information can be obtained ethically, or even legally. But it can be obtained." [6]

While government agencies must first obtain a warrant before they can search a citizen's home, personal belongings or data, there are relatively few restrictions on what private companies can do.

Until recently, the only significant protection for consumers' personal credit data was the Fair Credit Reporting Act of 1971. The law regulates how credit agencies can collect and distribute consumer information and requires credit agencies to show consumers their

Most Firms Monitor Workers

Seventy-eight percent of major U.S. corporations use at least one technique to monitor employees' on-the-job phone calls, e-mail, Internet use and computer files, often without notice. The percentage of firms that monitor workers has doubled since 1997, according to the American Management Association.

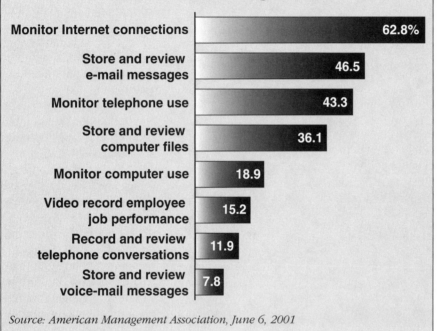

Percentage of firms conducting electronic monitoring in 2001

Monitor Internet connections	62.8%
Store and review e-mail messages	46.5
Monitor telephone use	43.3
Store and review computer files	36.1
Monitor computer use	18.9
Video record employee job performance	15.2
Record and review telephone conversations	11.9
Store and review voice-mail messages	7.8

Source: American Management Association, June 6, 2001

own credit reports so they can challenge false information.

In 1999 Congress passed the Gramm-Leach-Bliley Act. The measure's primary purpose was to tear down legal barriers that since the 1930s have prevented the mergers of banks, insurance companies, brokerage houses and other financial institutions. But because consumers were concerned that such mergers would result in massive shared databases of consumer information, Congress required the financial institutions to notify customers how their personal information would be used and offer them the chance to "opt-out" of having that information shared with third parties.

"This gives consumers the information they need to shop around," says Steve Bartlett, president of the Financial Services Roundtable, a financial-industry lobbying group. "If a consumer doesn't like her financial institution's stated privacy policy she can go someplace else."

However, privacy advocates like Hendricks argue that Gramm-Leach-Bliley was a "watered down, murky version" of the protections consumer advocates sought. As a result, the privacy notices that financial institutions are currently sending to consumers in order to abide by the law are unreadable and confusing, Hendricks says. "Rather than informing customers about privacy, they demonstrate how little financial institutions care about privacy," he says.

At least some in Congress agree. Already this year several bills have been introduced that would extend the protections offered by the act. For example, a bill introduced by Sen. Bill Nelson, D-Fla., would extend Gramm-Leach-Bliley so it would also protect individuals' medical information. And it would require individuals' prior approval before their data could be disclosed to a third party.

Another bill, introduced by Sen. Paul S. Sarbanes, D-Md., would beef up enforcement provisions and restrict the use of consumer information.

Finally, several proposals would limit the use of Social Security numbers for database matching, a measure that industry organizations claim will reduce efficiencies and add costs that will ultimately be passed on to consumers.

According to a Financial Services Roundtable study, current information-sharing practices save bank customers about $17 billion a year through reduced costs for data collection and management. But complying with the Gramm-Leach-Bliley Act will cost about $400 million, the study found. [7]

Moreover, industry groups argue, further measures are unnecessary now that consumers are protected by the Fair Credit Reporting Act, the new Gramm-Leach-Bliley law and a recent court decision prohibiting direct marketers from obtaining credit "header" information from credit reports, such as their name, address and Social Security numbers. "The concerns that people have had can be allayed," says Pat Faley, vice president for ethics and consumer affairs at the DMA.

Faley was referring to a recent federal court decision that credit bureaus and other companies could no longer sell names, addresses, Social Security numbers and other personal data from credit records without the consumers' consent. [8]

In addition, says Faley, the DMA has imposed strict self-regulation that will further protect consumers. "The

DMA has established a very strong self-regulatory program to address the privacy issues," Faley says. "If our members don't follow our 'privacy promise,' they are no longer members." [9]

In addition, the DMA now requires members to post their privacy policies on the Internet. "Many of the actions the Federal Trade Commission has taken recently have been about companies who have posted policies but haven't lived up to them," Faley notes.

Privacy advocates, however, caution against expecting industry self-regulation to do the job. "There has to be a remedy for individuals if something goes wrong," says Hendricks. "No self-regulatory program is going to offer people a remedy when things go wrong."

"Clearly the DMA is doing more on privacy, and that's better than not doing more," he adds. "But to claim that now people don't have to worry, that's insulting to the intelligence of the American people."

Is medical data kept private between patient and doctor?

While Americans are sensitive about their financial data being collected and shared, they are even more touchy when it comes to their medical information. According to a recent CNN-Time poll, for example, more than 90 percent of respondents believe insurance companies and employers should not have access to a person's genetic record. [10] (*See sidebar, p. 176.*)

Francis Collins, director of the National Human Genome Research Project, says legislation is needed to ensure that genetic information is kept private.

AFP Photos/Staff

Currently, most health-care providers routinely ask their patients to sign release forms before sharing medical information, but it is not mandatory that they ask. There is no single, comprehensive federal law protecting Americans' medical privacy, although some state laws provide some protection.

As a result, instances of intrusions are rife. In 1997, for example, it was revealed that a Maryland banker who sat on the state's Public Health Commission cross-checked his list of loans with the records of people who had cancer. He then canceled the loans of those he found on the list. [11] What's more, according to the American Civil Liberties Union (ACLU), 35 percent of *Fortune* 500 companies

check medical records before they hire. [12] Generally speaking, such employer practices are legal.

Although Congress has been unable to summon the votes to pass legislation protecting patients' medical information, in 1996 it passed the Health Insurance Portability and Accountability Act, which gave Congress until Aug. 21, 1999, to pass comprehensive health-privacy legislation. If no such measure was enacted by then, the law required the Department of Health and Human Services (HHS) to develop regulations providing such protections.

The regulations went into effect on April 14 despite pressure from the health-care industry to delay implementation. The industry now has two years to comply with the rules.

Under the regulations, patients must be able to see and receive copies of their medical records, and health-care providers, insurance companies and pharmacies must get patient permission before sharing patient histories.

Industry representatives fought the rules tooth and nail, claiming they will be too costly and will make it more difficult for health-care providers to do their jobs. "As drafted, the regulations are certain to compromise the quality of patient care by impeding the beneficial and necessary flow of information within the health care system and by adding unnecessarily to the cost of health coverage," Chip Kahn, president of the Health Insurance Association of America (HIAA), told reporters on April 2. [13]

According to Kahn, the regulation is so complicated that health plans will

No, You're Not Paranoid ...

You don't have to be a sports fan to remember this year's Super Bowl. The name of the winner may have faded from memory, but who can forget the furor over the surveillance system used to scan the faces of 100,000 fans as they entered Tampa stadium?

Although signs advised fans that they were being videotaped, most probably never realized the extent of the surveillance. The Facefinder biometric system picked out 19 petty criminals whose faces matched mugshots in a police database. Since it was just an experiment, no one was arrested, but the surveillance sparked a flood of media attention and a call for public hearings by the American Civil Liberties Union (ACLU).

The experiment — dubbed "Snooper Bowl" by the ACLU — renewed debate about how new technologies are shrinking the sphere of privacy that Americans once considered a birthright. Some also say the test was just another step toward broad and permanent surveillance of American society.

"We need a modern-day Paul Revere riding from city to city warning people: 'The cameras are coming! The cameras are coming!' " said Norman Siegel, former executive director of the New York chapter of the ACLU. After conducting a block-by-block inspection of Manhattan, the chapter discovered almost 2,500 cameras aimed at New Yorkers in public places. [1]

In Illinois, state officials have used face-recognition technology to transform all photos taken for drivers' licensing purposes into an electronic "mug" book of nearly every adult in the state.

Actually, the Super Bowl was not the first use of the technology. Casinos have been matching the faces of gamblers captured on video surveillance cameras to a database of known cheaters since 1997, when the first such system was installed at Trump Marina in Atlantic City, N.J.

And, of course, banks, hospitals, jewelry stores and other commercial establishments have been conducting video surveillance without the database matching capabilities since the early 1960s. But during the 1990s, as the price and size of video equipment decreased and the quality of the images improved, videotaping people in public — and sometimes in private — became a widespread practice.

Now video cameras record activity on freeways, subways and buses and in elevators, public

Tiny video cameras are hidden in these objects.

MATCO Inc.

parks, parking garages, schools, stores, restaurants and post offices. Moreover, the growing popularity of the Internet has given the practice worldwide coverage. In cities across the country, bars are installing Webcams — video cameras broadcasting live over the World Wide Web — enabling Web surfers to check out the action at their local pubs before they go out on the town.

Legal experts say surveillance cameras and face-recognition software are constitutional when used in public places where privacy expectations are low. [2] But in several recent cases, landlords and building supervisors have been caught watching tenants from hidden video cameras they've installed in their tenants' bathrooms or bedrooms. Video cameras have been discovered in public restrooms and tanning salons.

And the United States is not alone. In Britain — where terrorist bombings became commonplace in recent decades — authorities began installing video cameras in public places more than two decades ago. With more than 1.5 million closed-circuit television cameras monitoring streets, parks and public buildings, Britain is perhaps the most-watched country on Earth.

be uncertain about their responsibilities, patients will not understand their rights and costs will go up as insurers and health plans spend more to comply with the law.

Privacy advocates say industry complaints are unwarranted. "The industry has misread the regulation, and they've overreacted," says Janlori Goldman, director of the Health Privacy Project at Georgetown University. "Fortunately,

they didn't prevail in their attempts to get the administration to back down on letting the regulation go into effect. But I don't think they're going to give up. They don't want this law to cover them."

Goldman says industry estimates about the cost of implementing the rules are out of line. She cites government estimates that the industry will save $80 billion over 10 years by shar-

ing data. "The cost of putting privacy in place was estimated at only $17 billion, which means that ultimately you're still looking at a cost savings."

"I'm sure the health care industry would like the data sharing without the privacy protections, but it doesn't work that way," she says.

The law allows minor rule changes over the next two years, and the Bush administration would like the regula-

... Video Cameras ARE Watching

Privacy advocates in the United States argue that just because a technology exists and is legal does not mean it should be used. And they worry that the new technology could lead to unexpected invasions of privacy, just as some employers used pre-employment drug testing as a subterfuge for secretly conducting pregnancy tests on prospective employees.

Public outcry in Britain over the growing use of video surveillance led to passage in 1998 of the Data Protection Act, requiring that signs be posted in surveillance areas and limiting how long a videotape could be retained.

U.S. privacy advocates want similar legislation. The New York ACLU, for instance, has asked the state legislature to require that warning signs be posted at every surveillance zone, that access to surveillance tapes be limited and that tapes be archived for a limited time.

"Americans should be alarmed at the growth of surveillance in society without even minimal standards or regulation," Siegel says. [3]

Currently, police and other government agencies in the United States are not required to obtain search warrants to make soundless video or still pictures of individuals in public places. But if audio tracks are recorded, the surveillance falls under the Electronic Communications Privacy Act of 1986, which limits police wiretaps.

The Supreme Court has offered a two-step test to determine whether an act of surveillance might violate citizens' Fourth Amendment constitutional rights to protection against unreasonable search and seizure by government agencies. First, does the surveillance occur from and across public airspace? Secondly, is the surveillance physically non-intrusive? [4]

But the Constitution only protects citizens from unwarranted video surveillance by government entities. There is no constitutional protection from surveillance by businesses and other private parties.

And clearly such private surveillance is on the rise. The American Management Association, for example, estimates that video surveillance by employers rose from 33.7 percent of companies in 1997 to 37.7 percent in 2001. [5]

Law enforcement officials say technologies like face-recognition software can eventually give people more privacy, not less. For instance, police officers armed with face-recognition technology could identify suspects without having to resort to racial profiling or constitutionally questionable stop-and-frisk tactics. In addition, the identity of those using automated teller machines (ATMs) can be immediately verified with the technology, making it more difficult for someone to steal another person's money or personal identity.

And in some cases, video surveillance is conducted to protect the vulnerable — such as children in a day-care centers or elderly patients in nursing homes.

But while videotaped evidence has been critical in solving crimes and obtaining convictions in several high-profile cases, it's not clear just how effective video surveillance is in deterring crime. In a 1995 study, Washington state prisoners serving time for robbing convenience stores ranked video recording a distant 11th on a list of deterrents. [6] Yet a 1991 study found that convenience store robberies declined 53 percent during the first year after video cameras were installed. [7]

Privacy advocates are skeptical of the value of video surveillance. "The only value of videotaping is to preserve evidence after the fact," says Robert Ellis Smith, publisher of *Privacy Journal*. "I don't think it's very effective in decreasing response times or even in deterring criminal activity."

[1] Quoted in M.J. Zuckerman, "Chances are, somebody's watching you," *USA Today*, Nov. 30, 2000.

[2] Scott Sher, "Continuous Video Surveillance and Its Legal Consequences," Public Law Research Institute, University of California, Hastings College of the Law, November 1996.

[3] Zuckerman, *op cit*.

[4] *Florida v. Reilly*, 488 U.S. 445 (1989); *California v. Ciraolo*, 476 U.S. 207 (1986).

[5] American Management Association, "2001 AMA Survey: Workplace Monitoring & Surveillance," http://www.amanet.org/research/pdfs/ems_short2001.pdf.

[6] Lorraine La Femina, "For Electronic Security Firms, Crime Pays," *LI Business News*, March 25, 1996, p. 27.

[7] National Association of Convenience Stores, "Convenience Store Security: Report and Recommendations," November 1991.

tion amended to allow parents to view their minor children's medical records.

"We'll be vigilant to prevent that from happening," says Ronald Weich, an ACLU lawyer. "Teenagers have a constitutional right to obtain certain health services, particularly with respect to reproductive rights and other sensitive services such as substance abuse and mental health counseling. We think

minors should have the same privacy rights as others."

The health industry also wants to eliminate a provision requiring healthcare providers to give the minimum amount of medical information necessary when a third party legitimately requests personal health data. Richard Coorsh, spokesman for the Health Insurance Association of America, says the provision limiting information-

gathering would make it harder for health plans and health insurers to provide popular disease-management programs.

"That's just blatantly wrong," responds Goldman. Under the rules, she says "there's a free flow of information allowed for treating people, for paying for their care and for this broad area called 'health-care operations.' " Healthcare providers can insist on getting the consent of patients for such purposes, she says.

Rather than being too onerous, the HHS rules are "probably one of the most important privacy laws to go into effect in decades," Goldman argues, because they fill "an incredibly shameful gap in public policy."

But it's only a baseline, she says. "Now we can talk about how to build on it," she adds. "How to fill the remaining gaps."

Privacy advocates point to two major shortcomings in the HHS rules. First, they allow health-care providers to share medical information with marketers, such as pharmaceutical companies. "Patients should not be receiving mailings [from drug marketers] unless they specifically ask for them," the ACLU's Weich says. Currently, the first time a patient receives such a mailing he must indicate if he wants to opt out. "We think there shouldn't even be a first time."

Privacy advocates also complain that individuals can do nothing except complain to the Office of Civil Rights at HHS if their rights under the rules are violated. "People cannot go to court and say, 'My rights were violated,' " Goldman says. "It doesn't make sense to have a law that is not enforceable by individuals being able to sue, particularly a privacy law."

Is enough being done to protect personal privacy on the Internet?

The Internet is a broad expanse of uncharted seas for those seeking to en-

sure individual privacy. Concerns include credit card security when making online purchases, third parties posting others' personal information on Web sites, government and employer monitoring of e-mail and chat room messages and surreptitious collection of user data.

"The huge amounts of data speeding through the Internet — including phone numbers, addresses, credit card numbers and bank account information — have facilitated a booming online crime wave," Sen. Orrin Hatch, R-Utah, told a Senate Judiciary Committee hearing last September. "America's Internet users are legitimately concerned that surfing the Internet is like walking in a big city at night: The enjoyment is tempered by a fear of what's lurking unnoticed in the dark alleys." [14]

There is certainly no lack of examples of the risks awaiting Internet users. Last December the software company Egghead.com reported that 3.7 million customer credit card numbers

had been stolen from its Web site. Even more chilling was the experience of several Raytheon Co. employees who had conversed about the company in an online chat room. When the company learned of the discussions it sued Yahoo!, the provider of the chat room, to learn the identities of the participants. Yahoo! relented, handed over the names and Raytheon dropped its suit. [15]

Congress has not acted on Internet privacy issues in the past couple of years, even though threats to individual privacy have increased. For instance, two of the most dramatic new threats to privacy to emerge from cyberspace in recent years are the FBI's Carnivore system and online marketer DoubleClick Inc.'s tracking of consumers' Internet surfing habits. [16]

Carnivore is a suite of software used by the FBI to monitor millions of pieces of Internet traffic each day. Although the bureau claims Carnivore is subject to the same tight controls that govern the use of wiretaps — including the need to get a court order to initiate an interception — privacy advocates argue that Carnivore is different and more dangerous.

"Unlike a conventional wiretap, Carnivore gives the FBI access to all of the traffic over an Internet service-provider's network, and asks us to trust the government's filters to identify communications from a specified target," GWU's Rosen told a congressional hearing last October. According to Rosen, the idea of trusting the government has been rejected by businesses. [17]

A robbery suspect is caught on video surveillance while leaving a bank in Oshkosh, Wis., in February. Computer technology now enables police to match photos of suspects with mug shots of known criminals.

AP Photo/ Oshkosh Northwestern, Andy White

When Big Brother Is Watching You Work

The Fourth Amendment to the Constitution protects citizens from unreasonable searches and seizures by government officials, but it does not protect employees' privacy in the workplace.

"Most of the constitutional protections we enjoy as private citizens vanish when we go to work," writes William S. Hubbart, a human resources consultant. "While the government, as an employer, is subject to constitutional privacy limitations, laws impose few limitations on the private employer." [1]

The stakes are potentially high. An employee in San Diego, for example, was fired when it was discovered that he had tried to access a pornographic Web site, whitehouse.com. The man claimed that he had meant to go to the White House Web site, whitehouse.gov.

In many cases, employees do not even know they are being monitored. According to a recent University of Illinois survey, half of the corporations that collect information on employees monitor surreptitiously. Even more disconcerting, two-thirds of the organizations responding to the survey use investigative firms to collect information about employees. Of those companies, 25 percent do not review the policies and practices of the investigative firm. [2]

Whether the employee monitoring is done in-house or is farmed out to investigative firms, companies are doing a great deal of it, especially when it comes to computer and telephone use. According to the American Management Association, 63 percent of companies monitor employees' Internet connections and nearly half — 47 percent — store and review e-mail messages. [3] Many companies also mandate random drug testing of employees, even when there is no evidence of drug use by the employee. [4]

Few laws govern monitoring of employee performance and behavior. The only monitoring activity specifically covered by federal legislation is the use of polygraph tests. Under the Employee Polygraph Protection Act of 1988, employers may not require polygraphs for pre-employment screenings. Polygraphs may be used to investigate a company loss, but three conditions must be met. The employee must have had access to the lost or destroyed property. There must be reasonable suspicion that the employee was involved. And the employer must provide a written statement to the employee describing the incident being investigated.

A patchwork of state laws protect some workers from such practices as blacklisting, reference checking, drug and alcohol testing and other privacy invasions. Fourteen states limit what information employers can collect about employees.

If employees feel their privacy has been breached by their employer in ways that are not regulated by state or federal laws, they may seek redress through common law. But common-law protections are vague and can only be tested on a case-by-case basis.

Common law recognizes four basic grounds for actions against employers and other citizens with respect to privacy issues:

- ***Intrusion upon seclusion*** — When an employer's actions intrude in a manner that would be highly offensive to a "reasonable" person.

- ***Public disclosure of private facts*** — When an employer gives undue publicity to private facts about an employee.

- ***Publicly placing a person in a false light*** — When an employer misrepresents an employee's behavior or character to the public.

- ***Appropriation of an employee's name or likeness*** — When an employer uses an employee's name or likeness without his or her permission.

While Congress appears concerned about Internet privacy and about controlling the use of Social Security numbers, it seems to have little interest in employer monitoring.

"Workplace privacy is still an issue, but it doesn't seem to have a push behind it right now," says Evan Hendricks, editor of Privacy Times. "There's no congressional leader who has decided to take it on."

---

[1] William S. Hubbart, *The New Battle Over Workplace Privacy*, American Management Association, 1998, p. 2.

[2] Survey Research Laboratory, Univerity of Illinois, 1996, http://www.kent-law.edu/ilw/erepj/v1n1/linowes.html.

[3] "2001 AMA Survey: Workplace Monitoring & Surveillance," www.amanet.org/research/pdfs/ems_short2001.pdf.

[4] For background, see Kathy Koch, "Drug Testing," *The CQ Researcher*, Nov. 20, 1998, pp. 825-848.

But John Collingwood, assistant director of the FBI's office of public and congressional affairs, says the general public misunderstands how Carnivore is used. It does not "snoop" through e-mail by searching for key words or reading the "subject line" or any other content, he told Congress in a letter last Aug. 16. "That would be a crime," he wrote. The software only captures and records "e-mail between two criminals." [18]

Before intercepting a communication, he said, the bureau must first demonstrate — and a judge must conclude — that there is probable cause to believe that a serious crime is being or has been committed by the suspect, that the e-mails sought are related to that crime and that the interception is necessary to gather evidence, Collingwood said.

When all those legal standards have been met and a judge authorizes, for instance, the interception of e-mail from one drug dealer to another, he added, Carnivore "allows the interception of those particular e-mails to the exclusion of all others and all other types of computer traffic, regardless of what it is or who sends or receives it."

DoubleClick threw the Internet community into turmoil last year when it announced plans to combine consumer information it stored in off-line databases with "clickstream" data it collected from tracking users' Web surfing. Clickstream data is a record of mouse clicks a user performs while moving through the Internet.

The announcement caused an outcry among Web users, who saw it as a threat to their anonymity.

"A lot can be culled from clickstream data," warns Chris Hoofnagle, staff counsel for the Electronic Privacy Information Center, a privately funded public interest research center. "If you're interested in certain flavors of politics you'll visit certain sites, and if your dog has a certain kind of disease you'll visit other sites." If someone can record where you visit on the Web, they can learn a lot about you, Hoofnagle says. "There's very little regulation in this area."

The result, he says, is that people are getting very wary of using the Internet. "Some people simply won't shop online," he says, "while others won't go online at all. Still others will use false information to identify themselves."

After a public outcry and pressure from federal regulators, DoubleClick decided against its plan to combine clickstream data with consumer databases.

While conceding that consumers have some legitimate privacy concerns with respect to the Internet, industry representatives have urged caution in placing controls on the medium. They cite three primary reasons for going slowly: cost, uncertainty about the need for controls and the alternative of self-regulation.

As for cost, a recent study by Robert Hahn, director of the American Enterprise Institute-Brookings Joint Center for Regulatory Studies, claims that the costs of proposed privacy legislation "easily could be in the billions, if not tens of billions of dollars." [19] Hahn says "more information should be obtained on the benefits and costs of proposed online privacy laws prior to passing regulations."

Privacy advocates, however, argue that we can't afford not to implement regulations to ensure privacy. "Consumers left nearly $12 billion in online transactions uncompleted last year because they were worried about how their credit card data would be used," notes Rep. Anna Eshoo, D-Calif., sponsor of an Internet privacy bill. "E-commerce transactions are the business backbone of the Internet. If we put into place the protections that give people the confidence to transact online, then I think we will have accomplished something."

Regardless of the costs, industry representatives say it's too soon to determine just what types of privacy protections are needed. "All of us in the private and public sectors could use a very detailed dialogue before it's time to figure what the ideal approach is," says Brian Adkins, director of government relations for the Information Technology Industry Council (ITIC). Most important, he says, is the need to figure out what people mean when they say they're concerned about privacy.

Once privacy concerns are delineated, self-regulation and an effective enforcement program will be enough to assure users, industry representatives say. "While industry self-regulation is not the complete solution, we think the private sector has done a good job of responding to privacy concerns during the seminal growth of e-commerce," Scott Cooper, manager of technology policy at Hewlett-Packard Co., told a Senate hearing last October. "Self-regulation and credible third party enforcement . . . is the single, most important step businesses can take to ensure that consumers' privacy will be respected and protected online." [20]

Privacy advocates don't buy that argument. "Self-regulation? If self-regulation works, what would the landscape look like if it didn't work?" Hoofnagle asks sarcastically. "It's difficult to look at the landscape and conclude that self-regulation is working. There's an incredible traffic in personal data going on here that's largely unregulated."

Nor does the Federal Trade Commission (FTC) agree that industry self-regulation is up to the task. Reversing a position it had taken several years before, the FTC asked Congress in May 2000 to pass legislation ensuring a minimum level of privacy and establishing basic standards of practice for online information collection.

The FTC's recommendation was based on a recent survey showing that the quality of privacy protection that even the most responsible Web sites provide is "far from adequate," said FTC Commissioner Mozelle W. Thompson. In fact, the survey showed that 40 percent of the most popular — and presumably most sophisticated and responsible — Web sites "still do not provide consumers with adequate notice and choice, the most fundamental elements for any privacy policy," he continued.

Thompson called the survey results "especially disappointing" because they demonstrate "substantial deficiencies in providing what most industry leaders agree should serve as the bedrock of privacy self-regulatory efforts." [21]

BACKGROUND

A New Concept

P rivacy is a relatively modern concept. In Colonial America there was virtually no opportunity to be alone. People lived in towns and villages where everyone knew everything that took place with any member of the community. Most communities even had laws prohibiting people from living alone.

Chronology

1825-1934 Congress and the courts grapple with basic privacy issues.

1825
Congress makes it illegal for anyone to tamper with U.S. mail.

1877
Supreme Court rules that the Fourth Amendment protects mail.

1928
Supreme Court rules that police did not need a warrant to tap a bootlegger's telephone.

1934
Congress passes Federal Communications Act, which protects communications from interception without a court order.

1960s-1990
Early computer networks created by the military and universities eventually evolve into the Internet. The federal government and others begin considering privacy rights in the Information Age.

1969
Pentagon's Defense Advanced Research Projects Agency (DARPA) establishes ARPANET, a precursor to the Internet.

1973
A privacy task force created by the Department of Health, Education and Welfare (HEW) develops basic principles to safeguard personal health information stored on computers.

1980
The Organization of Economic Co-operation and Development establishes privacy standards based largely on the HEW principles.

1986
Electronic Communications Act broadens the protections of the 1968 Omnibus Crime Control and Safe Streets Act to include virtually any type of electronic communication.

1988
Computer Matching and Privacy Protection Act sets standards for federal computer-matching programs. Video Privacy Protection Act prohibits video rental stores from disclosing which films a customer has rented. Employee Polygraph Protection Act bars the use of polygraphs in hiring employees.

1991-Present
The increased use of personal computers and modems leads to the dramatic growth of Internet use. Privacy advocates begin calling for legal protections for Internet users.

1991
Telemarketing Protections Act of 1991 limits the use of dialing machines and recordings in making automated sales calls.

1995
The European Union adopts a Directive on Personal Data Protection.

1996
Health Insurance Portability and Accountability Act provides for data sharing among health-care providers and for the development of regulations to protect privacy of medical records.

1998
The number of Internet users is estimated at 60 million in the United States alone. The FCC releases a report to Congress on Internet Privacy. The FCC settles with the Web site GeoCities for alleged privacy violations. Congress passes legislation aimed at protecting children's privacy online. The European Union's Directive on Personal Data Protection takes effect.

1999
Congress misses its August deadline for passing a law protecting medical data; Department of Health and Human Services (HHS) steps in and begins writing regulations. Gramm-Leach-Bliley Act allows financial institutions to share consumer data but also requires protection of consumer privacy.

2001
The Bush administration implements HHS regulations protecting privacy of medical records. On Feb. 9, Sen. Tom Daschle, D-S.D., announces the formation of the Senate Democratic Privacy Task Force, to be headed by Sen. Patrick Leahy, D-Vt. "Whether it is bank records, or medical files or Internet activities, Americans have a right to expect that personal matters will be kept private," Daschle said. On Feb. 10, Sens. Richard C. Shelby, R-Ala., and Richard Bryan, D-Nev., and Reps. Edward Markey, D-Mass., and Joe Barton, R-Va., establish the Congressional Privacy Caucus.

"For the good of families and the community as a whole, the church regarded living together in a family unit as the best possible arrangement," writes Smith of *Privacy Journal*. "The rule applied to widows and young persons alike." In fact, he pointed out, records in Middlesex County, Mass., show that in 1668 the court systematically searched residences for single persons and placed them with families. [22]

And while the concept of a man's home being his castle was brought over from the old country to the new, there was precious little privacy within its walls. As Smith relates, in the late 1600s and early 1700s, even in houses in sophisticated Boston "there were no ceilings over the rooms, so sounds could easily be heard from room to room, and anybody willing to climb to the roof beams could peer into another room. Many homes, of course, had no room partitions at all." [23]

Nor could Colonial Americans rely upon their mail being confidential. It was not uncommon for the person delivering a letter to read it and even, on occasion, add to it. As a result, those needing to be sure of confidentiality generally wrote in code.

By the time the framers of the Constitution did their work — in strictest secrecy, by the way — there was a greater desire for privacy. George Washington, for example, made his interest in solitude well known after his two terms as president.

Unfortunately for those who valued solitude, there was no legal structure to protect their privacy, except the Fourth Amendment, which protected only against unreasonable searches and seizures by government, not from intrusions by other citizens or corporations.

From that point on, the story of privacy in America is a leapfrogging tale of new technologies emerging, legislation responding to those new inventions and then court decisions interpreting how the law applies to the new technologies.

In 1825, as literacy expanded and more Americans came to rely upon the mail system, Congress made it illegal for anyone to tamper with the mails. But not until 1877 did the Supreme Court rule that mail was protected by

Rep. Asa Hutchinson, R-Ark., has proposed legislation establishing a privacy commission to advise Congress.

CQ/Scott Ferrell

the Fourth Amendment. That ruling made it necessary for a government official to get a court order to open mail.

The new telegraph technology did not immediately receive the same protections as the mails. While Western Union had a practice of not disclosing the contents of telegrams to anyone but the recipient, there was no protection in the law. In fact, in January 1877 Congress subpoenaed, and Western Union delivered, 30,000 telegrams for examination by the House Committee on Privileges and Elections.

It also took quite some time for the law to catch up with the new technology of telephones. When they first came into use, there was no expectation of privacy. Virtually every line was a party line, and callers knew operators or neighbors could be listening at any moment. However, when automatic call routing came into use in the 1890s Americans began to expect privacy during telephone calls.

That expectation was apparently unwarranted. In 1928, the Supreme Court ruled that police did not need a warrant to tap a bootlegger's telephone. In an oft-quoted dissent to the majority opinion, Justice Brandeis argued that the Constitution "conferred, as against the government, the right to be let alone — the most comprehensive of rights and the right most valued by civilized men."

But the practices continued, and in 1935 and 1936 wiretaps were discovered on the telephones of two Supreme Court justices.

Several states prohibited interception of telephone calls, and in 1934, six years after Brandeis' objection in the bootlegging case, Congress enacted the Federal Communications Act, which prohibited anyone but those authorized by the sender from intercepting or divulging the contents of any communication.

Privacy Act

Privacy issues did not begin to receive significant and sustained attention in Congress until the 1970s. With enactment of the Privacy Act of 1974, Congress for the first time directly addressed the broad issue of citizen privacy. It prohibits data collected by the government for one purpose from being used for another purpose. It also gives citizens the right to see any government records kept on them and to have an opportunity to correct any errors.

However, privacy advocates argue that the Privacy Act has at least two major shortcomings: It applies only to activities conducted by federal agencies and departments, and information can be shared between agencies as long as the use of such information is for a purpose that is "compatible" with the purpose for which it was collected.

In some cases, the executive branch has interpreted that provision very broadly, privacy advocates say. In 1977, for example, federal welfare rolls were matched with federal payroll records in an effort to snag instances of welfare fraud.

The numbers of such computer cross-checks rose dramatically over the next decade until 1988, when Congress passed the Computer Matching and Privacy Act, which set guidelines for computer-matching programs by the government. Under the act, agencies are required to specify the exact purpose of any database matching and its expected results. What's more, agencies are prohibited from taking adverse action against an individual without independently verifying the information that results from the matching program.

Congress passed several other pieces of privacy legislation in 1988, including the Employee Polygraph Protection Act, which eliminated the use of polygraphs in employment screening, and the Video Privacy Protection Act, which prohibited video rental stores from disclosing customer information.

Partly as a result of legislation controlling government use of citizen data, many federal agencies have begun relying on private databases instead of maintaining their own. Generally speaking, databases maintained by private companies are not regulated by any federal law.

The FBI, the IRS and other federal agencies, for example, can access information on taxpayers' assets, driving records, addresses, phone numbers and other personal information by logging into databases owned and managed by ChoicePoint Inc., which is available to anyone who can afford their subscription services.

According to Hoofnagle, of the Electronic Privacy Information Center, this outsourcing trend is simply a way for federal agencies to get around the Privacy Act of 1974. "You find the suspect you're interested in and then buy the information [about him]," he says.

And the amount of detail about individuals available to anyone who can afford it is staggering, Hoofnagle says. "If you're willing to pay for it, you can order the names and addresses of all women within a one-mile radius of your store who wear a size 2 dress," he says.

CURRENT SITUATION

Action in Congress

Americans today may have more privacy than Colonial Americans, but they also have higher expectations of privacy. Meanwhile, threats to privacy — whether in the form of minia-ture surveillance cameras, programs that track your visits to Web sites or databases that collect information on all your purchases — are so subtle that a person may not even know his privacy has been violated.

Many citizens are also becoming increasingly concerned about information long available to the public in document form — such as court records — that is now easy to obtain online. The city of Kirkland, Wash., for example, recently sued several individuals who ran a Web site listing publicly accessible information about police officers — including telephone numbers, addresses, salaries, birth dates and Social Security numbers. The King County Superior Court ruled that the Web operators must remove the Social Security numbers from the site, but not the other publicly accessible information.

Privacy advocates are also concerned that some states are making court documents, including divorce records, available online. "Court files can contain intimate details of people's lives, such as Social Security numbers, birth dates and bank account numbers," writes Stephen Keating, executive director of the Privacy Foundation, a Denver-based advocacy group. "A reporter reviewing such files at the courthouse is unlikely to publish that data. But when the court file is online, anything goes." [24]

Finally, a bill proposed by Rep. Asa Hutchinson, R-Ark., would establish a privacy commission. "We haven't had a comprehensive look at privacy in more than 25 years," Hutchinson says. "Most of the proposals out there right now are very narrow. We need a broad look at privacy that is very comprehensive.

"There's a growing awareness and concern about privacy," according to Hutchinson, who says most consumers are shocked when they learn how much of their personal information is available either publicly or for a fee. "At the same time, there's a growing awareness of the benefits that consumers enjoy from the exchange of information" by companies and governmental agencies.

The proposed privacy commission "would try to figure out how to balance the need to protect consumers' privacy with the benefits consumers enjoy from having companies exchange data about them," Hutchinson says.

Even if the commission examines the big picture, agreeing on comprehensive legislation will be difficult, he says, because of the splintered nature of the groups lobbying on various privacy concerns. Except for consumer protection groups, most of those lobbying on the issue are only interested in how proposed legislation would affect their own narrow sliver of the privacy pie, he says. "One of the purposes of the commission would be to reach some kind of consensus for a more comprehensive approach to privacy protection," he says.

Hutchinson hopes to attach his bill to some other, more narrowly focused privacy bill, such as a proposal being developed by Rep. Billy Tauzin, R-La., chairman of the House Commerce Subcommittee on Telecommunications, Trade and Consumer Protection. Tauzin held hearings this spring on medical privacy and online consumer fraud.

A wide variety of privacy bills already have been introduced in the 107th Congress, with more expected soon. Among the legislation already introduced are two bills — one introduced by Rep. Eshoo, and another introduced by Rep. Gene Green, D-Texas — that would require Web sites collecting personal information to disclose to visitors how that information will be used and offer visitors the opportunity to "opt-out."

In addition, the Financial Institution Privacy Act, introduced by Sen. Nelson, would extend Gramm-Leach-Bliley to include medical information in protected data. It would also allow the U.S. attorney general to sue companies that

violate provisions of the bill and set civil penalties of $100,000 for each violation.

Another bill, the Financial Information Privacy Protection Act of 2001, sponsored by Sen. Paul S. Sarbanes, D-Md., covers much the same ground but also enables states to bring actions against violators.

Other bills would regulate so-called "Web bugs" and other tracking tools that follow users' movements on the Internet. And others would limit the use of individuals' Social Security numbers by marketers.

At least two bills would control the use of satellite-generated signals to show the location of a consumer using either a wireless phone or other device. Some companies want to use that information to forward "sales pitches" to wireless users who are near their stores, restaurants or business locations.

A wide variety of privacy bills already have been introduced in the 107th Congress, including proposals requiring Web sites that collect personally identifiable information to disclose to visitors how that information will be used.

Industry lobbyists, who successfully prevented passage of any significant privacy legislation in the last Congress, are expected to be at work in the current Congress. "The industry is very strong in lobbying," says Smith of the *Privacy Journal*. Unfortunately, he says, "there's no lobby that goes to Congress to express concern about the circulation of pho-

tographs without consent on the Internet. They hear only a corporate viewpoint because that's who funds Congress, for instance, right now."

Privacy Commission

Rep. Eshoo says legislation has been slow in coming — particularly with respect to the Internet — because legislators are working in unfamiliar territory. "It's one thing to have an interest," she says. "It's another thing to put pen to paper to draw something up that could have unintended consequences. And since the Congress has not adopted any kind of privacy legislation [regarding the Internet] there isn't any floor to build upon."

Industry organizations counter that it's still too soon for legislators to establish controls. "The debate has proceeded as if these bills are the answer to the whole broad spectrum of privacy issues," say the ITIC's Adkins. "They're not."

Adkins suggests that legislators step back before enacting new measures. "There's a need to stir the pot in this area," he says. "We need a more comprehensive dialog and then [we'll] see what needs to be done. It's so big it's hard to guess where it leads at this time."

Hendricks, of *Privacy Times*, agrees. "The current debate fractionalizes the privacy issues," he says of the current batch of legislation before Congress. "We may well end up with stronger protections for online activities than for off-line activities, or we could end up with better protections at the Web site for L.L. Bean than for our medical records. We need a comprehensive strategy."

Rep. Hutchinson's proposed Privacy Commission Act offers a more comprehensive approach. It would create a privacy commission made up of 17

At Issue

Should direct marketers be required to obtain consumers' approval before using their personal information?

EVAN HENDRICKS
EDITOR, PRIVACY TIMES

WRITTEN FOR THE CQ RESEARCHER, JUNE 2001

a central goal of privacy advocates is ensuring that uses of personal data are based upon the individual's informed consent. The problem with the so-called opt-out approach to getting permission to use data is that it puts the burden on the consumer to say "no." That leaves too much leeway for organizations to exploit personal data without the individual's informed consent while giving the appearance of offering "choice." The opt-in approach is clearly a more effective means for ensuring informed consent because it requires the individual to take an affirmative step and explicitly give approval for information to be used.

Another concern of privacy advocates, and one that obsesses marketers, is consumers' "right to be left alone" — to be free from unsolicited communications. The Telephone Consumer Protection Act uses the opt-out approach to regulate junk phone calls. Telemarketers are free to intrude upon the dinner hour until a legally knowledgeable consumer orders that firm to place him on its "Do-Not-Call List." If the telemarketer rings again, it is liable for small claims damages. At best, the law has led to modest improvements. But most Americans can easily testify that they are far from safe from unwanted and annoying sales calls.

The spam debate has followed a similar route. Spam — unsolicited or "junk" e-mail — continues to plague consumers, but most of the legislative proposals to deal with it rely on the opt-out approach. On the other hand, the wireless industry already is supporting a legally enforceable opt-in standard for everything from spam to cellular phone calls. They understand that e-commerce-styled spam would ruin cell phones as a medium for e-commerce.

In some contexts, it may prove difficult to establish requirements that individuals opt-in to receiving commercial messages. Companies assuredly have a First Amendment right to communicate their messages. Marketers have tried to claim that they also have a First Amendment right to traffic in people's personal data. The federal courts generally have not agreed, instead finding that privacy is a compelling societal interest that Congress is free to protect through statute. The problem is we don't have enough adequate privacy statutes.

That is why the larger issue is the legal standard for using personal data collected for one purpose but used for secondary purposes. That standard must be opt-in. There must also be access, so individuals can find out "where the spammers got my name."

FRED H. CATE AND MICHAEL E. STANTON
FROM "PROTECTING PRIVACY IN THE NEW MILLENNIUM: THE FALLACY OF 'OPT-IN' "

DIRECT MARKETING ASSOCIATION, JUNE 2001

i nformation is the lifeblood of the U.S. economy. Legislators, regulators and privacy advocates have been pushing vigorously for new limits on information flows in an effort to protect personal privacy. One of the most recent and severe of these restrictions has been the adoption of laws prohibiting the use of information unless the individual to which the information pertains "opts-in" to the use by giving explicit consent. These "opt-in" requirements replace the traditional standard of privacy protection — "opt-out." Under opt-out, personal information about an individual may be freely used within defined legal limits as long as the individual does not "opt-out" of its use.

Opt-in is frequently portrayed as giving consumers greater privacy protection than opt-out. In fact, opt-in provides no greater privacy protection than opt-out but imposes significantly higher costs with dramatically different legal and economic implications. Consider these critical distinctions:

- Opt-in and opt-out both give consumers the final say about whether their information is used.
- An opt-in system is always more expensive than an opt-out system. An opt-out system sets the default rule to free information flow and lets privacy-sensitive consumers remove their information from the pipeline. In contrast, an opt-in system sets the default rule to no information flow, thereby denying to the economy the very lifeblood on which it depends. Companies that seek to use personal information to enter new markets and improve customer service must rebuild the pipeline by contacting one customer at a time to gain their permission.
- Opt-in reduces competition and raises prices. Switching from an opt-out system to an opt-in system would make it more difficult for new and often more innovative firms and organizations to enter markets and compete. It would also make it more difficult for companies to authenticate customers and verify account balances, and thus would frustrate the ability to counteract fraud.
- Opt-in will increase the burden of unsolicited calls. By requiring an explicit statement of permission prior to use of personal information, an opt-in system necessarily requires businesses to make extra contacts with consumers.

The conclusion is clear: Opt-in is an exceptional tool that imposes high costs and harmful unintended consequences and should therefore be reserved for exceptional situations where the risk of those costs and consequences is justified.

Fighting Genetic Discrimination

Dave Escher is working on the railroad again, and now he doesn't have to worry about his genetic privacy being violated. And if Congress finally passes a landmark genetic-testing bill sponsored by Rep. Louise M. Slaughter, D-N.Y., no other American workers will be at risk either.

Escher, of McCook, Neb., has been a railroad man for 25 of his 47 years, working on the Burlington Northern Santa Fe Railroad outside Omaha. By all accounts, he has been a hard worker. Last year, after filing a workman's compensation claim with the railroad for carpal tunnel syndrome, he was given a medical examination, and several blood samples were taken.

Escher discovered the samples had been subjected to genetic testing without his consent, and on Feb. 7, 2001, along with another Burlington worker who had refused to give blood for testing, he complained to the Equal Employment Opportunity Commission (EEOC).

On April 8, the railroad promised not to test its employees for genetic defects as part of a landmark workplace-discrimination settlement between the railroad and the EEOC. Burlington Northern also promised not to retaliate against workers who refused to submit a blood sample for the tests. The settlement, the first of its kind about genetic discrimination, "sends a clear message about what not to do to the entire employer community," said EEOC Chairwoman Ida L. Castro.

The Burlington workers were not the first to complain about genetic testing. Last December, a federal court approved a settlement in a case involving the genetic privacy rights of workers at the Lawrence Livermore Laboratory in California, who for decades were tested without their knowledge for syphilis, pregnancy and the genetic test for sickle cell disease. [1]

Slaughter's proposal (HR 602) would ban discrimination in the workplace and in health insurance on the basis of genetic information. It has more than 240 co-sponsors in the House. Senate Majority Leader Tom Daschle, D-S.D., is the lead sponsor of companion legislation (S 318) in the Senate, along with co-sponsors Edward M. Kennedy, D-Mass., Tom Harkin, D-Iowa, and Christopher Dodd, D-Conn.

"This legislation could affect everyone," Slaughter said at a press conference on June 7. "It is estimated that each of us has between five and 50 faulty genes. Any one of us could be the target of genetic discrimination on the job or when we try to get health insurance."

Rep. Louise M. Slaughter, D-N.Y.

CQ/Scott Ferrell

Slaughter, who has degrees in microbiology and public health, calls genetics "one of the greatest advances since the development of germ theory. It would be a shame to allow this wonderful science to go by the wayside because people are afraid to be tested."

Slaughter was joined at the press conference by Escher, Daschle, Harkin and Francis Collins, director of the National Human Genome Research Institute, who strongly backs legislation banning genetic discrimination.

"We cannot wait until we have finished sequencing the human genome to pass important legislation that protects a person from being discriminated against by health insurance companies or employers," he said. "We do not need thousands of casualties before acting on this important issue."

Collins' support for legislation has been echoed by Edward R.B. McCabe, chairman of the Secretary's Advisory Committee on Genetic Testing. The committee "recognizes the tremendous potential benefits of genetic testing but also acknowledges that genetic testing can result in harm if information derived from the tests is used inappropriately," he says. "The public's concern reinforces [the committee's] belief that fear of genetic discrimination is a deterrent to advances in the field of genetic testing and that this may limit the realization of the benefits of genetic testing."

President Clinton last year banned genetic discrimination against federal employees, but Congress has not extended the rule to the private sector. The Health Insurance Portability and Accountability Act of 1996 became the first federal law to directly address genetic information. The law prohibits health-insurance discrimination based on any "health status-related factor," including genetic information, for government group-health plans.

Several states acted against employers' use of genetic information in the 1970s and '80s to prohibit employer discrimination against applicants with the sickle cell trait. Wisconsin prohibited genetic testing and discrimination by employers in 1991, and New Jersey enacted the first comprehensive workplace anti-discrimination law based on genetic information in 1996. Michigan joined the group this year, bringing to 21 the number of states that make employment discrimination based on genetic information illegal.

---

[1] Dana Hawkins, "The Dark Side of Genetic Testing," *U.S. News & World Report*, Feb. 19, 2001.

members appointed by Congress and the president, which would study the array of privacy issues and make recommendations to Congress. The bill died in the previous Congress, although it received a majority vote on the House floor.

The idea of a privacy commission, however, draws skepticism from both industry and privacy advocates in Congress. "We're not supporting a privacy commission at this point," says Faley of the Direct Marketing Association, pointing out that the FTC, the Department of Commerce, many states and Congress have been actively promoting privacy protection. "We would be happier with federal legislation if legislation were needed. But we're not convinced legislation is needed."

Rep. Eshoo argues that legislation — rather than an independent commission — is needed. "I think the Congress needs to delve into this," Eshoo says. "Step by step in the Congress, you can really learn a lot. I don't think we need a commission. Congress can handle it."

OUTLOOK

Signs of Hope?

Some privacy advocates are clearly discouraged by the way Congress has handled privacy issues.

"Washington's focus is on the most benign problems," says the *Privacy Journal*'s Smith, citing pending legislation to control consumer information collected by Web sites. "The circulation of photographs and of third-party information on the Internet, and the buying and selling of Social Security numbers are three much more serious problems, and they're not being addressed."

Smith cites a wide array of other issues not being addressed by either proposed legislation or existing regulations. "I don't know of anybody addressing video surveillance at all," he says, nor is anyone doing anything about workplace privacy or identity theft. "I place Internet issues about fifth on the priority list," he says, "even though they seem to place it much higher in Washington."

But other privacy advocates see signs of hope. The Health Privacy Project's Goldman cites the recent HHS medical privacy regulations as a major step forward. "I hope at some point the industry will put their resources and energy into putting these rules into place," she says.

President Bush surprised everyone when he gave a green light to the medical privacy rules, points out Hendricks of *Privacy Times*, who calls the move "pretty huge."

"Clearly, this is the first action by the president on privacy," he says, "and the message is that he cares. I certainly have to take him at his word at this point, but we'll be watching him very closely."

What's more, Hendricks sees signs that both government and business may be starting to see the light on the need to provide true assurances of privacy to citizens. "Enlightened self-interest may bring industry on board," he says.

Pointing to the potential cost savings for both government and business in integrating data into electronic databases, Hendricks says the lure is too great to resist. "It makes sense to aggregate our data in one place," he says. "But if you always have to worry about a dark side it won't fly. We have to come out with a 'privacy first' policy."

Hendricks adds that the very lack of laws in the United States may spur action. "The Europeans have a comprehensive law and an independent office of privacy, but they've had the law so long there is a sort of complacency among the public, who maybe assume their privacy is being protected," he notes. "Ironically, in the United States, since we don't have much law there are many more abuses and a much

higher consciousness level. So we have the potential to surpass the Europeans."

There is no organized opposition to a comprehensive federal privacy law. Instead, the opposition tends to be industry by industry. The health-care industry, for example, has lobbied against regulations controlling the use of patients' medical records but not against measures controlling the collection of personal information by Web sites.

The strongest opposition to a comprehensive federal privacy law appears to come from privacy advocates who fear that a poorly designed law may do more harm than good. "If you try to get socks on the octopus at this time," warns Rep. Eshoo, "the entire effort may fail and we will be left without any privacy protections."

Notes

1 Comments made on Oct. 11, 2000, during a hearing on consumer privacy protections before the House Commerce Subcommittee on Telecommunications, Trade and Consumer Protection.

2 Samuel D. Warren and Louis D. Brandeis, "The Right to Privacy," 4 *Harvard Law Review* 193 (1890).

3 Reg Whitaker, *The End of Privacy: How Total Surveillance is Becoming a Reality* (1999), p. 84.

4 Comments were made at a Sept. 6, 2000, Senate Judiciary Committee hearing on electronic surveillance and privacy.

5 *Ibid.*

6 Charles J. Sykes, *The End of Privacy* (1999), p. 29.

7 "Customer Benefits from Current Information Sharing by Financial Services Companies," Ernst & Young, December 2000. http://www.bankersround.org/PDFs/custbenefits.PDF.

8 Glenn R. Simpson, "Judge Upholds Tough New Restrictions on Sales of Certain Personal Credit Data," *The Wall Street Journal*, May 8, 2001.

9 The DMA's "privacy promise" requires member companies to notify customers of their ability to opt out of information exchanges; honor customer opt-out requests; accept and

maintain consumer requests to be on an in-house suppress file to stop receiving solicitations from a company; and, use the DMA Preference Service suppression files, which now exist for mail and telephone lists — and will soon exist for e-mail lists.

[10] CNN/*Time* Poll conducted by Yankelovich Partners, Dec. 17-18, 1998.

[11] Sykes, *op. cit.*, p. 100.

[12] American Civil Liberties Union, "Defend Your Data," http://www.aclu.org/privacy.

[13] HIAA press release, April 2, 2001.

[14] Senate Judiciary Committee hearing, Sept. 6, 2000, *op cit.*

[15] *Privacy Journal*, June 1999.

[16] See David Masci, *The CQ Researcher*, "Internet Privacy," Nov. 6, 1998, pp. 953-976.

[17] Comments made during an Oct. 3, 2000, hearing on consumer Internet privacy before the Senate Commerce, Science and Transportation Committee.

[18] See the letter and other documents related to Carnivore on the FBI's Web site, at www.fbi.gov.

[19] Robert W. Hahn, "An Assessment of the Costs of Proposed Online Privacy Legislation," conducted for the Association for Competitive Technology, May 7, 2001, p. 24.

[20] Comments made during the Oct. 3, 2000, Senate hearing (*See footnote 17*).

[21] Statement of FTC Commissioner Mozelle W. Thompson, May 22, 2000.

[22] Robert Ellis Smith, "Ben Franklin's Web Site: Privacy and Curiosity from Plymouth Rock to the Internet," *Privacy Journal*, 2000.

[23] *Ibid.*, p. 19.

[24] "Push to hide court records leaves public vulnerable," *USA Today*, June 5, 2001, p. A14.

FOR MORE INFORMATION

American Civil Liberties Union, 125 Broad St., New York, N.Y. 10004-2400; (212) 549-2500; www.aclu.org. A nonprofit, member-supported group that advocates the protection of civil liberties.

Direct Marketing Association, 1120 Avenue of the Americas, New York, N.Y. 10036-6700; (212) 768-7277; www.the-dma.org. The largest trade association for users and suppliers in the direct, database and interactive marketing field.

Electronic Frontier Foundation, 454 Shotwell St., San Francisco, Calif. 94110; (415) 436-9333; www.eff.org. A nonprofit, non-partisan organization working to protect civil liberties, including privacy and freedom of expression related to computer and Internet use.

Electronic Privacy Information Center, 1718 Connecticut Ave., N.W., Suite 200, Washington, D.C. 20009; (202) 483-1140; www.epic.org. A public interest research center established in 1994 to protect privacy, the First Amendment and constitutional values.

Financial Services Roundtable, 1001 Pennsylvania Ave., N.W., Suite 500 South, Washington, D.C. 20004; (202) 289-4322; www.fsround.org. An industry-supported lobbying and educational group that focuses on issues of concern to the finance industry.

Health Insurance Association of America, 601 Pennsylvania Ave., N.W., South Bldg., Suite 500, Washington, D.C. 20004, (202) 824-1600; www.hiaa.org. A trade association representing the private health-care system.

Health Privacy Project, 1120 19th St., N.W., 8th Floor, Washington DC 20036; (202) 721-5632; www.healthprivacy.org. A nonprofit organization that studies health-privacy issues.

Information Technology Industry Council, 1250 Eye St., N.W., Suite 200, Washington, D.C. 20005; (202) 737-8888; www.itic.org. Advocates free-market policies for the information-technology industry.

Online Privacy Alliance, 555 13th St., N.W., Washington, D.C. 20004; (202) 637-5600; www.privacyalliance.org. An industry-support organization that encourages self-regulatory initiatives to protect privacy online and in electronic commerce.

Privacy Foundation, 2255 E. Evans Ave., Suite 435, Denver, Colo. 80208; (303) 871-6295; www.privacyfoundation.org. A nonprofit research and education organization that informs the public about privacy issues.

Privacy Rights Clearinghouse, 3100 5th Ave., Suite B, San Diego, Calif. 92103; (619) 298-3396; www.privacyrights.org. A nonprofit organization that informs consumers about their privacy rights.

Bibliography
Selected Sources Used

Books

Alderman, Ellen, and Caroline Kennedy, *The Right to Privacy*, Vintage Books, 1997.

Despite the co-authorship of Caroline Kennedy, the daughter of President John F. Kennedy, the book doesn't go into depth on the politics of privacy but mainly offers a compilation of anecdotes and case studies.

Garfinkle, Simson, *Database Nation: The Death of Privacy in the 21st Century*, O'Reilly, 2000.

This chilling book does an excellent job of describing who is collecting what and how few laws control what they can do with the information.

Hubbart, William S., *The New Battle Over Workplace Privacy*, American Management Association, 1998.

Written by a human resources consultant, this book is a primer for businesses on how to deal with privacy issues in the workplace. It offers a good deal of historical background, legal context and practical advice.

Rosen, Jeffrey, *The Unwanted Gaze: The Destruction of Privacy in America*, Random House, 2000.

Rosen, a law professor, takes a broad journalistic approach to considering the threats to privacy, explaining the linkage between emerging technologies, social trends and the challenges to privacy.

Rothstein, Mark A., ed., *Genetic Secrets: Protecting Privacy and Confidentiality in the Genetic Era*, Yale University Press, 1997.

This collection of essays by leading experts explores the ethical, legal and social issues arising from the explosion of genetic research with respect to their implications for privacy.

Smith, Robert Ellis, *Ben Franklin's Web Site: Privacy and Curiosity from Plymouth Rock to the Internet*, Privacy Journal, 2000.

Smith, editor of Privacy Journal, presents a must read for anyone interested in privacy issues. The book is especially strong in providing a history of legal and legislative developments.

Sykes, Charles J., *The End of Privacy: The Attack on Personal Rights — at Home, at Work*, On-Line and in Court, St. Martin's Griffin, 1999.

This journalistic look at new technologies and the threats they pose to privacy is rich with well-documented case studies and historical accounts.

Whitaker, Reg, *The End of Privacy: How Total Surveillance is Becoming a Reality*, The New Press, 1999.

A professor of political science at York University in Toronto takes a social scientist's approach to examining the effects of new technologies on privacy and society.

Articles

Masci, David, "Internet Privacy," *The CQ Researcher*, Nov. 6, 1998.

Although somewhat dated by the rapid pace of events on the Internet, Masci's article nevertheless provides excellent background on the issues.

Rosen, Jeffrey, "Why Internet Privacy Matters," *The New York Times Magazine*, April 30, 2000.

The nature of the World Wide Web, law Professor Rosen writes, "has blurred the distinction between oral and written gossip by recording and publishing the kind of private information that used to be exchanged around the water cooler."

Rubin, Alissa J., "Lobbyists Go Full Tilt in Bid to Ease Patient Privacy Rules," *Los Angeles Times*, March 24, 2001, p. A1.

A broad coalition of hospitals, HMOs, insurers and pharmaceutical companies has launched an intensive campaign to persuade the Bush administration to scale back a landmark patient-privacy regulation approved by former President Bill Clinton.

Simpson, Glenn R., "Big Brother-in-Law: If the FBI Hopes to Get the Goods on You, It May Ask ChoicePoint," *The Wall Street Journal*," April 13, 2001, p. A1.

Simpson reports on how the FBI, the IRS and other government agencies are turning to private-sector databases of information on citizens.

Reports and Studies

Hahn, Robert W., "An Assessment of the Costs of Proposed Internet Legislation," Association for Competitive Technology, May 7, 2001, p. 24; http://www.actonline.org/pubs/Hahn-Study.pdf.

Hahn's study is based on some very broad and questionable assumptions about the costs of privacy measures, but it is still worth reading both because the industry frequently cites it and because it does at least broach most of the important privacy issues.

10 Libraries and the Internet

KENNETH JOST

Kathleen R.'s 12-year-old son Brandon was spending a lot of time at the Livermore, Calif., public library, ostensibly working on his homework. But when Kathleen looked inside his gym bag one day, she found something besides dirty clothes: a cache of dirty pictures from pornographic Web sites.

"He was spending the whole time at the library downloading pornography and taking it to my brother's house and printing it," Kathleen recalls today. "I had a fit."

Kathleen—who shields her last name to protect her son from publicity—complained to the librarian, who said there was nothing she could do. So Kathleen went to court to force the library to install software filters to block sites with sexually explicit material. "I can't have porno day in my house for the neighborhood kids," she explains. "So I want to know why the library can."

California courts rejected Kathleen's suit, but the state legislature is now considering a bill to require public libraries to install filters to block pornographic sites. "We lost the battle," Kathleen says, "but we're winning the war." [1]

In fact, Congress is on her side on the issue, which is roiling librarians and library boards throughout the country. A new law, approved by Congress in late December and signed by President Bill Clinton, requires all federally subsidized school and public libraries to install software on their computer terminals to block "visual depictions" of obscenity, child pornography and sexual matter deemed "harmful to minors."

From *The CQ Researcher,*
June 1, 2001.

Numerous computer workstations are available at the New York Public Library's Science, Industry and Business Library, one of four NYPL research libraries. Many of the system's 85 branches provide computer training.

New York Public Library

Some patrons, however, say they want no limits on Internet access from library computers. Carol Williams, an administrative assistant to a civil liberties organization in Philadelphia, says her teenaged niece, Marnique Tynesha Overby, needs an unfiltered gateway to the Internet in her local public library. "With the filtering system, you put in breast cancer or sexually transmitted diseases, and you couldn't possibly get to some of the sites out there," says Williams. She points out that young people may use Web sites to find information about sexual subjects that they do not feel comfortable discussing with their parents or caregivers.

Williams cannot afford a personal computer in her home, so the library's terminals are essential to her niece, who lives with her. Williams says filtering is just wrong. "It's censorship," she concludes.

The library establishment agrees with Williams. The American Library Association (ALA) strenuously opposed the filtering legislation as it worked its way through Congress and filed suit in federal court as it was about to take effect. The group contends the measure violates the free-speech rights of libraries and library patrons.

"Filters are anathema to what we as librarians want to accomplish," says Judith Krug, director of the ALA's Office of Intellectual Freedom. "The best filter is the individual. Every bit of information is not appropriate for every individual, but the best person to make that decision is the individual or, for children, in concert with their parents or guardians."

Supporters of the law, however, contend that the measure is needed to make libraries safe for young people. "This simply says the federal government is not going to subsidize getting hard-core pornography in the libraries," says Bruce Taylor, president of the National Law Center for Children and Families, an anti-pornography group. Without filters, Taylor says, "the library becomes the peep show section of adult bookstores."

The law—the Children's Internet Protection Act or CIPA (known as CIPA, or sometimes, CHIPA)—represents Congress' third attempt in four years to limit young people's access to sexually explicit material on the Internet. The Supreme Court struck down the first of the laws: the 1996 Communications Decency Act (CDA). Congress responded by enacting a modified Child Online Protection Act (COPA) in 1998, but federal courts have blocked that law from going into effect, too.

For libraries, the filtering issue merges a new technology that is revolutionizing access to information with a 60-year tradition of battling for intellectual freedom. [2] Computer terminals are now nearly universal in school and public libraries. Students who once went to the library to use books and encyclopedias to do their homework now find the information they need on the Web.

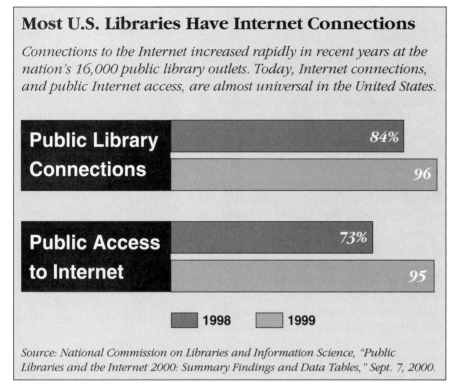

Most U.S. Libraries Have Internet Connections

Connections to the Internet increased rapidly in recent years at the nation's 16,000 public library outlets. Today, Internet connections, and public Internet access, are almost universal in the United States.

Public Library Connections
84%
96

Public Access to Internet
73%
95

1998   1999

Source: National Commission on Libraries and Information Science, "Public Libraries and the Internet 2000: Summary Findings and Data Tables," Sept. 7, 2000.

"It's a big part of the way we provide the public access to information," says Ginny Cooper, library director for Multnomah County, Ore., serving Portland. Her library system is the lead plaintiff in a second lawsuit challenging the new law, filed by lawyers for the American Civil Liberties Union (ACLU).

Before the new law went into effect, only a small number of the nation's estimated 16,000 public library outlets * were using filters, according to a survey by the U.S. National Commission on Library and Information Science. The survey, completed last year, showed that about 10 percent of public libraries used blocking software on all computer terminals and another 15 percent provided blocking at some workstations. (*See graph, p. 186*) By contrast, about three-fourths of school libraries use filtering or blocking software,

according to the National Center for Education Statistics.

Librarians opposed to filters say they clash with their understanding of providing free and open access to information. "The major loss is the loss of First Amendment rights and the concern about people's ability to find information freely and openly," says Leigh Estabrook, dean of the University of Illinois Graduate School of Library and Information Science at Champaign. "It's an enormously high price to pay concerning the fundamental freedoms that we have."

Librarians who support filters, however, argue that most parents do not want their children using library terminals to view sexually explicit material or being exposed to pornographic images on screens being viewed by other patrons. "Many people would feel uncomfortable enough to stop coming to the libraries," says David Biek, manager of the main library in Tacoma, Wash.

David Burt, a former librarian in the Portland, Ore., suburb of Lake Oswego,

says sentiment in support of filtering among librarians is increasing. "The problems have gotten so much worse as the Internet has gotten more pervasive in libraries and pornography is much more pervasive in libraries," he says.

As for the threat to intellectual freedom, some librarians say the ALA's arguments are overblown. "The dogma that the ALA establishment frequently espouses is put forward as an absolute: If you touch this, everything else will fall," says Donald Davis, a professor at the University of Texas Graduate School of Library and Information Science in Austin. "There is a danger of that, but it is exaggerated."

In addition to the legal and philosophical arguments, there is a practical technological question: Do the filters work? Theoretically, filtering software looks through a Web site for objectionable material and blocks the site when the program finds the words or images specified by the programmer.

Critics, however, say filtering programs are notoriously inaccurate in practice: They block sites that should not be blocked ("overblocking") while sometimes failing to block sites that should be ("underblocking"). In a test of six well-known filters, *Consumer Reports* found that several failed to test certain "inappropriate" sites and that some blocked "harmless" sites—in some cases based on what the magazine called "moral or political value judgments." [3]

But Burt, who now works for N2H2, a filtering-software company in Washington state, says the critics are off base. Other filtering companies also defend their products. "Filters do work; they work very well," says Susan Getgood, a vice president of the California-based company SurfControl. "Our customers buy them and renew them year after year because they do work well."

For the moment, the government has decided that libraries have until July 2002 to decide whether to install filters without fear of losing federal aid or fed-

---

* The figure for library outlets includes all branches of the nation's 8,967 library systems.

erally mandated discounts for Internet services.

As librarians and library patrons continue to make greater and greater use of the Internet, here are some of the major questions being debated:

Can filtering protect children from objectionable materials on the Internet?

A commission created by Congress spent nearly two years studying ways to reduce youngsters' access to sexually explicit materials on the Internet. The report by the 18-member group called on schools and libraries to voluntarily adopt Internet-use policies, but stopped short of recommending mandatory use of filtering software.

"No single technology or method will completely protect children from harmful material online," Donald Telage, chairman of the commission, said in announcing the commission's 95-page report. Filters are "hopelessly outgunned."[4]

Filtering opponents hailed the commission's report. "We hope Congress sees this as a wake-up call" to reject mandatory filtering, an ACLU spokeswoman said. But some commission members repeated their support for the legislation. "If you use federal money for the Internet, we want you to take appropriate steps to make sure that kids are safe when they're online using our money," said Donna Rice Hughes, vice president of the anti-pornography group Enough Is Enough.

The simplest filters block Web sites that contain designated words or phrases anywhere on the site. Critics say this type of filter carries an inevitable risk of "overblocking"—preventing access to a site about "breast" cancer, for example, or even a site about the "Mars explorer" because of the embedded three-letter sequence "s-e-x." At the same time, opponents say, some filters fail to block Web sites with patently objectionable material ("underblocking").

Filtering supporters, however, say newer software is finer-tuned—looking

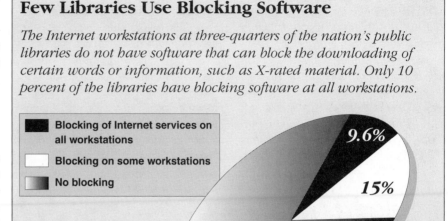

Few Libraries Use Blocking Software

The Internet workstations at three-quarters of the nation's public libraries do not have software that can block the downloading of certain words or information, such as X-rated material. Only 10 percent of the libraries have blocking software at all workstations.

■ Blocking of Internet services on all workstations
□ Blocking on some workstations
▨ No blocking

9.6%

15%

75.5%

Note: Total does not add to 100% due to rounding.

Source: National Commission on Libraries and Information Science, "Public Libraries and the Internet 2000: Summary Findings and Data Tables," Sept. 7, 2000.

at entire sites, not just an isolated word or phrase—and are therefore less susceptible to inaccurate blocking. "The modern generation of filters do a very good job," says Taylor of the National Law Center for Children and Families. And filters will get better, he says, because the new law "uses federal incentives to foster advances in filtering technology."

"There is a small amount of error," says Burt of N2H2. "But when we talked with schools or with libraries, we found that's something that they don't encounter much. And when they do encounter it, the librarian can override it."

Opponents of filtering are unconvinced. "Filtering software does not work," says Margaret Dempsey, head of Chicago's public library system. "It arbitrarily blocks words over which we have no control, and it inhibits access to legitimate research sites."

"Experts continue to uncover thou-

sands and thousands of [blocked] sites that people could not conceivably think are unsuitable for minors," says ACLU attorney Ann Beeson. "I'm not talking about controversial sites."

Defending the law, Taylor stresses that it requires libraries to block access only to visual depictions—not text—that fall into three categories that are already illegal.

"Libraries have responsibilities to block illegal materials: obscenity, child pornography and material that is harmful to minors within state law," he says.

But Teresa Chmara, a Washington lawyer representing the ALA in challenging the law, says all three categories require judgments that cannot be made by a computer program. "Filters cannot make the legal determination whether material is obscene or harmful to minors," she says.

Burt counters, however, that librarians are already charged with making those kinds of judgments. "People who work for filtering companies can apply a standard just as readily as a librarian can," he says.

The law includes a fail-safe provision that allows a librarian to "disable" a filtering program in order to give a patron access to blocked material "for bona fide research or other lawful purposes." "Even if a filter inadvertently blocks something," says Taylor, librarians "have the ability to unblock it."

But librarians and civil liberties advocates say that procedure is an unfair burden on library patrons' privacy. "Most adults will be too stigmatized to go ask a librarian for access to a site that has already been blocked," Beeson says. In addition, librarians say it is unclear how they are to decide what constitutes "bona fide research" for purposes of the law.

Even if filters did work as advertised, many librarians believe that the law gives them a responsibility for monitoring children's Internet usage that instead ought to lie with parents. "I am not going to become the parent in absentia," the ALA's Krug says. "It's not our role. It's not our responsibility, either legally or by virtue of being a librarian."

But Burt says libraries have always had the responsibility to select the informational materials in their collections. "This is a very reasonable approach to a serious problem," Burt says, "and it's within the traditional mission of public libraries."

Can other policies protect children from objectionable Internet materials?

The Tacoma library uses a filtering software designed by its systems manager to block visual depictions of sex-

ual acts or full nudity on computer terminals. By analyzing the logs of Internet sessions, librarians compiled some interesting information about the extent of the use of library computers for access to sexually explicit materials.

The findings, detailed in a paper prepared for a branch of the National Academy of Sciences, show that Tacoma library patrons made nearly 28,000 attempts to access sexually explicit materials on the Internet during the cal-

Marnique Tynesha Overby, 15, tells a press conference why she joined the ACLU in challenging a new federal law requiring federally subsidized libraries to install "blocking" software on their computers. She said she relies on public libraries for Internet access to help with homework projects on health and cultural issues.

American Civil Liberties Union

endar year 2000. Most of those efforts—about 53 percent—were by youngsters under age 18. And three-quarters of the logged entries occurred in the late afternoon, after kids leave school but before they go home for dinner.

Librarian Biek found the numbers disturbing. "Certainly, staff at the Tacoma Public Library would not have guessed that Internet users made nearly 28,000 attempts to access sexually explicit materials last year," Biek wrote in the 17-page report. "Many young people are not making 'good choices'

in their use of the Internet, and it is debatable whether classes and tips offered by the library will affect this." [5]

Biek's support for filtering in libraries puts him at odds with the position of the ALA and most librarians who have joined in the public debate. They argue that a combination of formal Internet policies, patron education and librarian oversight will adequately control misuse of library computers by minors or adult users.

"There are all kinds of ways libraries have developed in working with their communities," says the ALA's Krug. "Some libraries have contacts with kids, some have contacts with the kids and their parents. If libraries have policies, they will say you are not following the rules."

Librarians opposed to filtering emphasize their efforts to educate young patrons on using the Internet. "The Internet is not a very fine tool," says Portland library director Cooper. "It's still pretty difficult to get information there. And with kids, we feel we have a special responsibility to help them get information that's appropriate for them."

The Chicago Public Library employs tech-savvy college and high school students as "cyber-navigators" to assist young patrons in using the Internet. The program, funded by AT&T, "has been really wonderful," says Chicago library chief Dempsey.

Tacoma's Biek agrees that young patrons need instruction on using the Internet, but he says training is unlikely to reduce the misuse of library terminals to view pornography. "Most of these were very obviously intentional acts," Biek says, referring to the Tacoma library study. "No amount of edu-

Protecting Kids From Web Porn

The Commission on Online Child Protection recommended the following measures to help reduce access by minors to sexually explicit material on the Internet:

Public Education

- Major education campaign by government and private sector to promote awareness of technologies and methods to protect children online.
- Promotion of acceptable use policies by government and industry.

Consumer Empowerment

- Independent evaluation of child protection technologies.
- Steps by industry to improve child-protection mechanisms and make them more accessible online.
- "Broad, national, private-sector conversation" on development of next-generation systems for labeling, rating and identifying content.

Law Enforcement

- Government funding of "aggressive programs" to investigate, prosecute and report violations of federal and state obscenity laws.
- Listing by state and federal law enforcement of Internet sources found to contain child pornography or obscenity.
- Federal rulemaking to discourage deceptive or unfair practices that entice children to view obscene materials.

Industry Action

- Voluntary adoption by Internet service provider industry of "best practices" to protect minors.
- Voluntary steps by online commercial adult industry to restrict minors' access to adult content.

---

cation is going to change a person who wants to look for sexually explicit materials on the Internet if that's their intent."

Filtering opponents suggest several other steps. Some libraries use privacy screens to block other patrons' view of a user's screen. Time limits on computer use—necessitated by the demand for terminals—also help control viewing of objectionable materials, librarians say. And most libraries, it appears, set terminals in children's areas to log onto customized home pages designed for kids with links to other age-appropriate sites.

But supporters of filtering say these steps are inadequate. "We had privacy screens," Burt says of his experience in the Lake Oswego Library. "That seemed to encourage people. We had one man in particular who took delight in taking the privacy screen off and having women see what he was looking at."

Supporters of filtering believe that librarians simply disagree with the goal of regulating young people's use of the Internet in libraries. "They won't because they don't want to," says Taylor of the National Law Center for Children and Families. "They have said that they think it's their job as libraries to provide unfiltered access to the Internet to anyone, whatever age. They have said that they have no intention of providing filtering because they believe it's censorship."

Librarians frame the issue in those terms themselves, though with a more favorable spin. "Librarians have taken the position that without limiting adult reading material, they cannot limit reading material for children," says Louise Robbins, director of the University of Wisconsin School of Library and Information Studies in Madison. "The librarian's responsibility is to make as much information available as possible—given the constraints of budget, space and expertise—and let citizens make decisions about what materials they need," she says.

Is it constitutional to require libraries to install filtering?

When Congress passed the CDA five years ago making it a crime to transmit sexually explicit materials to minors across the Internet, the ACLU and the ALA challenged it in federal court as unconstitutional. As one of their arguments, the two groups contended that there was a less restrictive way to control youngsters' access to pornography on the Web: filters.

The Supreme Court unanimously agreed that the law violated the First Amendment. But now that Congress has passed a law requiring software filters in public and school libraries, the ACLU and the ALA say that it, too, is unconstitutional.

Supporters of the new law—CIPA—say that given their previous position, the ACLU and ALA are being disingenuous today in attacking filtering. "They waited to come out against filtering until the CDA was declared unconstitutional," maintains Burt of N2H2. "Then, as soon as the CDA was declared unconstitutional, they turned around and said, 'Wait. Filters don't work. You can't use them in libraries.'"

Lawyers for the two groups insist, however, that there is no inconsistency between their positions in the two

Are Computers the Answer . . .

Imagine reading Mark Twain's account of a trip to France in a Western literary journal published in 1868 while sitting at your home computer rather than standing in the dark and dusty stacks of a distant research library.

Imagine clicking on your computer and seeing a representation of Michelangelo's famous statue of David so detailed that you could make out the sculptor's individual chisel marks.

Imagine using your computer to microscopically examine a fragile fossil or botanical specimen held in a laboratory halfway around the globe and too delicate to be moved.

No need to imagine. Internet-linked computers already allow professional researchers or amateur scholars to access such information resources. And more digital wonders are on the way.

Rare books and manuscripts can now be viewed on a digital book at the National Institutes of Health's National Library of Medicine in Rockville, Md.

AP Photo/Evan Vucci

Soon, you may be able to whistle into a computer a few bars of a vaguely recalled musical composition and get back not only the name of the piece and the composer but also a complete account of the work and its historical and cultural background.

These 21st-century advances are redefining libraries—or "media centers," as some have been renamed—and creating countless new opportunities for serving patrons both inside and outside of the brick-and-mortar buildings. But new technologies also create logistical and financial strains on libraries, just as many are grappling with maintaining and preserving their primary collections of printed books, journals, magazines and newspapers.

At first blush, digitization—or converting printed material to digital form—may appear to be a panacea for a host of preservation and access problems. In fact, it poses a new set of preservation problems: Computers and word-processing systems obsolesce, disks and drives deteriorate.

"Scholars are just now becoming aware that digital media are not preservable now," says Abby Smith, program director of the Council on Library and Information Resources, a nonprofit group that studies issues affecting libraries.

In a draft report, a 15-member task force of scholars established by the council is calling for a more comprehensive and coordinated approach to preserving information resources from all media—including sound recordings, films and photographs.[1] Among the major recommendations: more money.

"There is no library that receives a steady stream of funding to ensure coordination of preservation of collections," Smith explains. "Preservation is an unfunded mandate, totally unfunded."

Library preservation issues have received unaccustomed attention over the past two months thanks to the publication of a controversial book sharply critical of how many libraries handle old print collections, including the Library of Congress. In his book *Double Fold*, novelist Nicholson Baker contends that out of an exaggerated fear of disintegrating newsprint and paper, many libraries have dismantled their collections of books and old newspapers—microfilming them at considerable expense and then trashing the originals to save space and storage costs.[2]

Baker was sufficiently concerned to use foundation grants and $26,000 of his own money to buy a trove of old U.S. newspaper collections that the British Museum was about to auction off. For now, he is storing the newspapers in a former textile mill in New Hampshire renamed the American Newspaper Repository.

cases. "We don't have a problem with blocking programs being available in libraries as an option for patrons who want to use them," the ACLU's Beeson says. "And certainly the use of these programs in the home doesn't present any constitutional problem, which is very different from using them in a library."

"It's the same problem," Beeson says of the two cases. "The government can't act as a censor on the Internet, whether it's by imposing criminal penalties or by restricting access in libraries."

The constitutional debate over CIPA turns on the question of how far Congress can go to limit the access of minors to sexually explicit materials without violating youngsters' free-speech rights or abridging adults' access to materials that are not legally obscene. Ob-

... To Libraries' Preservation Problems?

Librarians are as critical of Baker as he is of them. "They feel he's impugned the profession, and to a large extent he does," Smith says. She calls Baker's argument "one-sided," adding, "He appears not to have a grasp of the understanding of the economics of the situation."

Baker warns that digitization may lead to "a new wave of book wastage and mutilation" and argues that digital preservation is more costly and less permanent than technophiles seem to suggest. "Digital storage, with its eternally morphing and data-orphaning formats, . . . is not now an accepted archival storage medium," he writes.

Stephen Griffin, director of the National Science Foundation's (NSF) digital libraries initiative, acknowledges the difficulty. "There are all sorts of problems with electronic media," he says. "Your disk drives disintegrate. The software used to decipher what you wrote with your first word processor may be hard to come by."

"I don't think that digital technologies alone are a cure-all for printed materials, at least not yet," Griffin concludes.

The NSF initiative is sponsoring an array of projects to make better use of computer technology in accessing and analyzing information resources. "We're trying to make the best possible use of the Internet as a scholarly resource for the social good," Griffin explains. "We feel we can do that by funding projects that place very high-quality content on the Internet and that develop new technologies for helping to locate and to make that content available to users for a whole variety of purposes."

One of the NSF-funded projects is aimed at improving search capabilities, Griffin says. Search engines based on recognition of words or phrases are "inherently limited," he explains. The solution is to permit searches for broader concepts by tagging texts—for example, marking all references to "political reform" or "poverty." In similar vein, another project is aimed at making computer-based video collections searchable.

Some initiatives are already bearing fruit. In a project funded by the Andrew W. Mellon Foundation, the University of Michigan has put online a collection of 19th-century Americana encompassing 8,500 books and 50,000 journal articles. Smith says the online collection is far more accessible than the printed volumes—which the university did preserve.

"They were in secondary storage for years, never requested," Smith says. "And now they have 9,000 hits per week."

The Digital Archaeological Archive of Chesapeake Slavery depicts artifacts and digital images from Monticello and 20 other slave-quarter sites in the Chesapeake Bay region.

AP Photo/The Daily Progress, Andrew Shurtleff

[1] Council on Library and Information Resources, "The Evidence in Hand: The Report of the Task Force on the Artifact in Library Collections," March 2001 (www.clir.org).

[2] Nicholson Baker, *Double Fold: Libraries and the Assault on Paper*, 2001. For reviews, see *New York Times Book Review*, April 15, 2001, p. 8; *New York Review of Books*, April 26, 2001, p. 16.

scenity and child pornography are illegal under federal and state laws, but the standard for proving obscenity is difficult for prosecutors to meet.

However, the Supreme Court has given lawmakers some discretion to control youngsters' access to sexual material that is not legally obscene. In 1968, it upheld a New York law prohibiting the sale of adult magazines to anyone under 17 if the material was "harmful to minors." [6] Since then, the high court has repeatedly said that protecting children from indecency is a compelling governmental interest that can justify restrictions that would violate the First Amendment if applied to adults.

On the other hand, the court has ruled that regulations to protect minors from indecency cannot be sus-

Many Libraries Treat Kids Like Adults

Most of the nation's public libraries have policies on acceptable computer use. About half have different policies for adults and children.

Internet Policies at Public Libraries

Have acceptable-use policy	95.5%
Differentiate between young and adult users	46.3%

Source: National Commission on Libraries and Information Science, "Public Libraries and the Internet 2000: Summary Findings and Data Tables," Sept. 7, 2000.

BACKGROUND

Library Rights

The library profession's advocacy for intellectual freedom evolved gradually through the 20th century after an earlier period when librarians consciously acted as moral censors and arbiters of good taste. [9] The critical turning point came in 1939 with the American Library Association's adoption of the "Library Bill of Rights." The three-paragraph charter called on public libraries to select books on the basis of their "value and interest" without regard to the race, nationality or political or religious views of the authors and to represent all opinions "fairly and adequately."

In their first half-century—after the founding of the nation's first public library in Boston in 1854—the mission of free libraries was making books more readily available to people of limited means. The librarian and author Evelyn Geller writes in her history of this period that public libraries "were established in opposition not to censorship but to privilege." [10] Along with this mission went a corollary effort to lift the reading tastes of the masses and to protect them from "bad" literature.

Toward that end, many libraries either excluded or restricted access to books dealing with sexual subjects—literary classics as well as popular entertainment. They also weeded out other popular reading, such as the Pinkerton crime novels or books with what they considered untoward moral messages—including Horatio Alger's popular novels of boys rising over adversity and Mark Twain's *Huckleberry Finn* and *Tom Sawyer*. "As the library's audience becomes larger," ALA President Arthur Bostwick declared in a

tained if they limit the availability of non-obscene materials for adults. In one such case, the court struck down part of a "dial-a-porn" law that prohibited commercial telephone messages with either obscene or indecent communications. [7]

Lawyers attacking CIPA say the law runs afoul of that principle. "It's pretty clearly unconstitutional in that it's requiring libraries to make a choice by giving up funding or using filtering mechanisms that plainly block adults from having access to materials that are plainly protected," says Chmara, the ALA's lawyer.

CIPA supporters say that it merely requires libraries to filter already-illegal material. "I can't imagine the Supreme Court telling libraries that they can't block obscenity and child porn from computers," Burt says. And even if filters block access to some non-obscene material, supporters say the law solves the problem by giving adults a right to ask librarians to unblock the sites.

Opponents of the law insist that the likelihood of legitimate Web sites being blocked is greater than supporters acknowledge. And they say

that forcing library patrons to ask a librarian for access to sites with sexual information is itself unconstitutional. "There's a long line of Supreme Court decisions that say you can't force adults to ask for permission to access protected speech," the ACLU's Beeson says.

So far, only one court has ruled directly on the use of filtering. In November 1998, a federal judge in Virginia struck down a filtering policy adopted by the Loudoun County public library. As one of her reasons, Judge Leonie Brinkema said there was insufficient evidence that viewing pornography on library terminals was a serious problem. [8]

Supporters and opponents of the law disagree sharply on that point. "Pornography is becoming a staple in one library after another," says Janet LaRue, a lawyer with the conservative Family Research Council.

But librarians say the instances of misuse are relatively few. "We feel patrons use the Internet responsibly," says Dempsey in Chicago. "We don't feel there's any problem with rampant misuse of the Internet for objectionable material."

Chronology

Before 1900

First public libraries established in United States; librarians view role as moral censors.

1876
American Library Association (ALA) founded; for several decades, ALA leaders exhort librarians to seek to elevate public literary tastes.

1901-1950
ALA gradually moves toward advocating "freedom to read."

1920s-1940s

Censorship battles are fought over "subversive" literature.

1939
ALA adopts "Library Bill of Rights" amid censorship battles over *The Grapes of Wrath*; establishes Committee on Intellectual Freedom one year later.

1948
Library Bill of Rights amended to call for active steps to oppose censorship and enlist support of other groups.

1950s-1960s

Censorship fights persist over "subversive" literature, racial issues.

1951
ALA challenges loyalty oaths for librarians; also amends Bill of Rights to cover films, other non-print media.

1961
ALA backs integration of public libraries; also files friend of the court brief defending bookseller in *Tropic of Cancer* case.

1967
ALA establishes permanent Office of Intellectual Freedom; amends Bill of Rights to guarantee access without regard to age.

1970s-1980s

Censorship battles continue.

1970
Freedom to Read Foundation established as ALA's litigation arm.

1982
Supreme Court says school libraries can exclude books for "educational unsuitability," but cannot remove books on political grounds.

1990s
Congress seeks to limit sexually explicit material on the Internet, but is rebuffed in court challenges.

1996
Communications Decency Act (CDA) makes it a crime to transmit "indecency" on the Internet to youngsters under 18.

1997
U.S. Supreme Court unanimously strikes down CDA.

1998
Child Online Protection Act (COPA) criminalizes commercial transmission of "harmful to minors" material; fed-eral courts later block law from going into effect.

1998
Federal judge in Virginia bars filtering in Loudoun County case; ruling is not appealed.

2000s
Congress mandates filtering at libraries; library groups, patrons challenge law as unconstitutional.

March 2000
Filtering advocates publish report documenting use of computers in public libraries to access pornography on the Internet; state appeals court in California rules taxpayers cannot force libraries to install filters.

October 2000
Congressional commission calls for education, self-regulation to guide Internet use in libraries; takes no position on mandatory filtering.

December 2000
President Bill Clinton signs Children's Internet Protection Act (CIPA), requiring federally subsidized public or school libraries to use filtering software to prevent children from accessing Internet pornography.

March 2001
ALA, ACLU challenge CIPA in federal court on behalf of libraries, library patrons and organizations with Web sites; hearing before three-judge court set for July 23.

May 2001
Supreme Court agrees to hear government's effort to reinstate COPA.

Urban Libraries Have the Most Workstations

The nation's public libraries have an average of eight Internet workstations per library; libraries in cities have 17 stations, on average.

No. of Internet Stations

Rural	5
Suburban	9
Urban	17

Source: National Commission on Libraries and Information Science, "Public Libraries and the Internet 2000: Summary Findings and Data Tables," Sept. 7, 2000.

1908 speech, "the duty of sifting its material becomes more imperative."

There were countercurrents to this censorial attitude, even in the 19th century. The trustees of the Boston Public Library resisted public pressure to purge the shelves of "all objectionable matter" in the 1880s—and gained partial backing from the city's newspapers. "Nobody is forced to read what he does not wish to read," the *Sunday Herald* declared in an editorial. A few years later, San Francisco experienced a similar fight.

By the early 1900s, Geller writes, librarians advocating censorship were "increasingly on the defensive." The 1926 ALA catalog included some authors previously blacklisted, such as Oscar Wilde. But it still excluded such sexually themed works as *Lady Chatterly's Lover* and some politically controversial books, both fiction and non-fiction.

Political disputes first drew the ALA into resisting censorship. In 1929, the association unsuccessfully opposed a ban on importation of "seditious" literature. Five years later, the ALA made its first protest against the banning of a specific publication: a pamphlet entitled *You and Machines*, which had been prepared for use in Civilian Conservation Corps camps. The camps' director refused to circulate the pamphlet, saying that it might induce a desire to destroy existing political and economic structures. In a letter to President Franklin D. Roosevelt, ALA leaders called the censorship "unthinkable."

With freedom of speech under attack because of widespread Depression-era political agitation, the librarians' development of an anti-censorship ethos first found full voice from a librarian in the country's heartland. Forrest Spaulding, head of the Des Moines Public Library, wrote a bill of rights for libraries that was adopted by the library's trustees in November 1938. In early 1939, the Library Bill of Rights was published in library journals and was adopted with minor modifications by the ALA's governing council in June. Its three provisions opposed censoring books because of the author's political or religious beliefs, pledged to represent all opinions "as far as available material permits" and called for library meeting rooms to be available to people "on equal terms . . . regardless of their beliefs or affiliations."

That same year, the association had the chance to join battle over efforts to ban John Steinbeck's controversial novel *The Grapes of Wrath*. The portrait of harsh working conditions faced by migrant agricultural workers in California provoked a rash of bannings. The ALA responded indirectly by asking Spaulding to study current censorship and recommend a policy. At its next annual meeting, the ALA in May 1940 adopted Spaulding's recommendation to create a permanent committee—verbosely named the Committee on Intellectual Freedom to Safeguard the Rights of Library Users to Freedom of Inquiry. Eight years later, the name was shortened: the Committee on Intellectual Freedom.

Freedom to Read

Librarians have strengthened their commitment to defense of intellectual freedom in the six decades since the ALA adopted the Library Bill of Rights. In 1967, the ALA fortified the effort by creating an Office of Intellectual Freedom and a litigation arm, the Freedom to Read Foundation, in 1970. For their part, rank-and-file librarians gradually came to share the organization's commitment to intellectual freedom as what the University of Wisconsin's Robbins calls "the credo of librarianship." [11]

In 1948, the ALA took another step strengthening its position, when it amended the Library Bill of Rights to include a proactive anti-censorship provision. It stated that libraries must challenge book censorship—whether advocated by "volunteer arbiters of morals or political opinion" or by "organizations that would establish a coercive concept of Americanism." It also called on libraries to enlist support from science, education and book publishing groups to help resist "all abridgement of free access to ideas."

In the early years of the Cold War, the ALA opposed requiring loyalty oaths for librarians and labeling materials deemed "subversive." In response to efforts to suppress left-leaning films, the association in 1951 also amended the Bill of Rights to cover "all materials and media of communications used or collected by libraries."

The profession's fortified position on access to controversial titles was seen in the differing responses to the publication of two sexually themed works more than a decade apart. When Alfred Kinsey's *Sexual Behavior in the Human Male* was published in 1948, many librarians allowed circulation only

School Libraries Facing Filter Mandate

Most school libraries use filters on computers to block access to some sexual material on the Internet. And, for now at least, there are no legal challenges to the new law mandating filters in schools receiving federally subsidized rates for Internet connections.

Lawsuits filed by the American Library Association (ALA) and the American Civil Liberties Union against the new law—the Children's Internet Protection Act (CIPA)—apply only to the provisions affecting federally assisted public libraries. In a disappointment to many school librarians, the ALA concluded that it had no standing to represent schools in challenging the law.

"School library centers do not receive federal funds," explains Harriet Selverstone, a high school librarian in Norwalk, Conn., and president of the American Association of School Libraries, a division of the ALA. "The funds are sent to school districts."

Some school groups—including the National School Boards Association and the National Education Association (NEA), the largest teachers union—opposed the mandatory filtering proposal as it moved through Congress. Even so, filtering is more widespread in schools than in public libraries.

A survey of *School Library Journal* subscribers last year found that 53 percent of respondents said filtering was used at their schools. [1]

More recently, a U.S. Department of Education survey indicated that 74 percent of schools were using filtering software. [2] Among public libraries, only 25 percent use filtering: 10 percent use it on all terminals and another 15 percent use it on some.

Many schools using filtering seem satisfied with their experience. "It does protect [students] from a lot of crummy stuff, and it doesn't prevent them from getting to what they need to do," says Deborah Arlington, manager of e-mail and Web services for a regional agency serving 110 school districts in western New York. She says about 70 of the state's school districts use filters, including the largest: Buffalo.

The New York City school system has been using filters since 1999. Last month, when the Board of Education held a hearing on Internet-use policies, none of the witnesses discussed filtering, a spokeswoman said.

But in Connecticut, Selverstone says her school does not use filters and she opposes them. "I work with students who are dealing with a myriad of topics, and they would not be able to access the information if we had filters," she says.

A legal ruling against the public library provisions of the law might cast doubt on the school-related provision. But schools may have a weaker case to challenge the law because they function in part as surrogate parents, and because they have broader discretion to control information for students than libraries have for patrons.

In any event, an NEA spokeswoman says she is not aware of any plans to challenge the law on behalf of schools. And even without the law, school boards and administrators may elect to keep filters or install them where they are not already in use.

But tech-savvy students may outwit whatever filters are installed. "Kids are so smart, they override filters," says Selverstone. "Students are very adept technologically."

---

[1] See *School Library Journal*, Jan. 1, 2001. The results reflected returns from 465 school library subscribers out of a sample of 2,000—a lower than normal return rate, the magazine noted.

[2] National Center for Education Statistics, May 2001. Results were based on 1,104 returned questionnaires from a sample of 1,218 schools, a 91 percent return rate.

---

to specified types of patrons. "What God-given faculty has the librarian to determine who are the 'wrong people' to read Kinsey?" an ALA leader complained.

By contrast, after *Tropic of Cancer* was published in the U.S. in 1961, the ALA filed a friend-of-the-court brief in defense of a California bookseller convicted under that state's obscenity law for selling the book. The conviction was overturned.

The civil rights era raised new intellectual freedom issues for libraries. In 1960, with segregated public libraries still existing in parts of the South, the ALA's board declared its support for non-discrimination but added that it would not "intrude on local jurisdiction." However, after study by a special committee, the ALA adopted a more forthright position in early 1961: It advocated integration of libraries. "The rights of an individual to the use of a library should not be denied or abridged because of his race, religion, national origins or political views," the new Bill of Rights provision read.

In another expansion of the Bill of Rights, the ALA in 1967 moved to protect young people's access to information by stipulating that the use of a library should not be limited because of age. The move followed a conference on "Intellectual Freedom and the Teenager," jointly sponsored by the ALA's young adult services division and the American Association of School Librarians. Speakers unanimously emphasized the need for young people to have unlimited opportunity to explore issues of concern. Geller, writing in *Library Journal*, noted that the conference failed to deal with the issue of parental control of children's reading.

Librarians' actual practices, however, appeared to lag behind the Bill of Rights' rhetoric. A study by a California researcher, Marjorie Fiske, in 1958 reported that even though most librarians expressed "unequivocal freedom-to-read convictions," nearly two-thirds of those involved in book selection reported instances in which the controversial nature of a book or author resulted in a decision not to buy.

But the intellectual-freedom machinery established by the ALA at the end of the '60s helped fortify librarians' resistance to censorship. "The support system has helped librarians who have had materials challenged," the University of Wisconsin's Robbins says.

The ALA's Krug says the court record in censorship disputes is beneficial for librarians, even though the ALA generally relies on others to carry on the litigation. In the most important ruling, the U.S. Supreme Court turned aside an effort by outside groups to bar a list of controversial titles at a school library in Island Trees, N.Y. In a 5-4 ruling, the court in 1982 said school libraries cannot remove books on political grounds, though they can select books based on "educational unsuitability." [12]

"A lot of these [disputes] don't wind up in court judgments," adds Robert Peck, a lawyer and former president of the Freedom to Read Foundation. "More often than not, we provide legal advice and assistance, and the situation gets resolved."

Cyberspace Battles

The Internet opened up vast, new information resources for libraries and library patrons. But the prospect of children's easy access to sexually explicit material alarmed many parents—and some librarians—and embroiled libraries in the legal battles over efforts to regulate the Net. The ALA joined other First Amendment advocates in successfully challenging Congress' first

> "The Boston Public Library uses software filters on all computers in children's sections, but not on other PCs. The policy also allows children under 16 to use unfiltered terminals, but only with parental permission. "The key for us is permitting the parent to have [a] choice, to make that judgement for children."
>
> — *Bernard Margolis,*
> *Library President*

attempt to limit the availability of sexual material to youngsters on the Internet while also resisting calls for use of filtering software to control access in libraries. [13]

The CDA, signed into law in February 1996 as part of a broader telecommunications reform act, made it a federal crime to transmit online any "indecent" material to a person known to be under 18 or to display "patently offensive" material "in a manner available" to a person under 18. The law was immediately challenged in companion cases—one filed by the ACLU

and the other by the ALA and the Freedom to Read Foundation, along with online companies, booksellers, publishers, and others.

A little over a year later, the U.S. Supreme Court unanimously ruled the law unconstitutional. [14] The court acknowledged the legitimacy of the goal of protecting children from harmful materials, but concluded that the CDA's broad reach "effectively suppresses a large amount" of constitutionally protected speech for adults. Writing for the court, Justice John Paul Stevens also said that Internet users "seldom" encounter sexual material accidentally. And he also noted that one less-restrictive regulation would be to "tag" sexually explicit material so parents could use filtering software to control their children's access on computers in their homes.

Congress responded by approving the narrower COPA law in 1998, which seeks to ban commercial online transmission of material "harmful to minors." Again, the ACLU led a coalition of free-speech advocates challenging the law's constitutionality. (The Freedom to Read Foundation joined a friend-of-the-court brief urging that the law be struck down.) A federal court judge in Philadelphia blocked implementation of the law in February 1999 on the ground that the defenses permitted for online publishers—credit card or age verification—were inadequate.

The Third U.S. Circuit Court of Appeals upheld that ruling in June 2000, but on a different basis. It ruled that the use of local community standards in applying the "harmful to minors" provision was too restrictive on the Internet because online publishers have no way to tailor their sites to particular locales. The Supreme Court agreed on May 21 to the government's request to review the ruling. [15]

Meanwhile, the filtering controversy was finding its way into the court system. The library trustees for Loudoun County, Va.—a fast-growing exurban jurisdiction near Washington—adopted a mandatory-filtering policy for all computers in 1997. Under the policy, all library computers were to be equipped with software to block any sites displaying material deemed harmful to minors.

The effectiveness of the software used by the library—known as X-Stop—was one of the issues in a federal suit challenging the policy. Publishers of three Web sites—Safer Sex Page, Books for Gay and Lesbian Teens/Youth and Renaissance Transgender Association—established that their sites were blocked at least for a time even though they included no prohibited material. The library board, defending the policy, maintained that the software worked well and that bugs were worked out later.

In a thoroughgoing ruling, however, Judge Brinkema in November 1998 rejected the defense of the policy, point by point. A former librarian herself, Brinkema found that the complaints offered as evidence—one incident in another Virginia library and three other reported incidents from around the country—were "insufficient" to show that the policy was "reasonably necessary."

In any event, Brinkema said, the library could use less restrictive means to limit children's access—including privacy screens, monitoring of Internet use or filtering software. Moreover, she said filtering was legally defective because the library did not know what standards the software manufacturer was using to block sites, and a Web site publisher had no procedural safeguards to contest a blocking decision. The policy, the judge concluded, "offends the guarantee of free speech in the First Amendment and is, therefore, unconstitutional." [16]

Despite the judicial setback, congressional supporters of filtering began pushing legislation at the start of a new Congress in 1999 to mandate use of the software in any schools or public libraries that receive federal funds or federally mandated discounts for Internet services. The House and the Senate both approved versions of the legislation last year as amendments to the mammoth appropriations bill for the Departments of Labor, Health and Human Services and Education.

"We need to ensure that pervasive obscene and violent material is screened out and that our children are protected," Sen. John McCain, R-Ariz., a cosponsor of the Senate version, declared.

The Clinton administration had opposed the provision, calling instead for a softer measure to require libraries to adopt Internet use policies. Rather than send the entire spending bill back to Congress, however, Clinton signed it into law with the library-filtering mandate. Lawyers for the ACLU promptly said they would challenge the law. "This is a mandated censorship system by the federal government," ACLU attorney Christopher Hansen said. [17]

A month later, the ALA's executive board also voted unanimously to challenge the law. "No filtering software successfully differentiates constitutionally protected speech from illegal speech," the ALA said in a news release. Filters "are not effective in blocking all content that some may find objectionable, but they do block much useful and constitutionally protected information." [18]

CURRENT SITUATION

Filtering Practices

The Boston Public Library—the nation's oldest—uses software filters on all computer terminals in children's sections, but not on other PCs. Adopted four years ago, the policy also allows children under 16 to use terminals with unfiltered access, but only with parental permission.

The policy gives a "healthy respect" both to parental responsibility and to the First Amendment, according to the library's president, Bernard Margolis. "The key for us is permitting the parent to have that choice, to make that judgment for children," he says.Margolis likens Boston's policy to that of the Multnomah County library in Oregon. But the policies actually are different, says library director Cooper in Portland.

Children's terminals in Multnomah County libraries are set with age-appropriate home pages and links, Cooper explains, but a youngster can gain access to any site by typing in the necessary address. "We've made the decision not to limit children's access," he says.

The differing views on the filtering issue within the library community also emerged in testimony before a congressional subcommittee earlier this year. Two librarians testifying on April 4 before the House Energy and Commerce Subcommittee on Telecommunications and the Internet disagreed about the need for filtering or the wisdom of the federal law mandating the practice.

"CIPA will have a devastating impact on the ability of all library users to access valuable constitutionally protected material," Carolyn Caywood, a branch librarian in Virginia Beach, Va., told the subcommittee. She said the Virginia Beach library uses filters on terminals set aside for children's use but also allows youngsters to use terminals with unfiltered access.

But Laura Morgan, a reference librarian from Chicago, sharply criticized her system's opposition to filtering. "The easy availability of pornography on the Internet at the Chicago Public Library and in libraries across the nation has great potential for negatively affecting the staff, patrons (especially children) and the overall environment," Morgan said.

She became concerned about the issue when colleagues from the children's section told her that youngsters were "occasionally" accessing pornographic and violent Web sites on library computers. She also contended that "porn surfers" were creating a sexually hostile environment for female patrons and staff members.

Librarians at the Minneapolis Public Library have filed a complaint with the federal Equal Employment Opportunity Commission (EEOC) contending that they are subjected to a sexually hostile work environment by exposure to Internet pornography. The agency issued a finding of probable cause on May 24 and invited the librarians and library system to join it in trying to reconcile the dispute. An earlier attempt at mediation failed. The librarians said that time limits and ID requirements adopted by the library systemwere inadequate. [19]

In Tacoma, librarian Biek says he thinks the atmosphere in the system's libraries would be "disruptive" without filtering. "A number of libraries here in western Washington have had incidents of looking at kiddie porn," Biek says. He says he is not aware of any complaints that Tacoma's policy is too restrictive.

Cooper acknowledges receiving a few complaints about the lack of filtering in the Multnomah County system. "There are people who are very concerned about what kids, especially, might inadvertently see," she says. But she suspects many of the complaints come from non-library users. "We get way more complaints that we only allow people one hour a day on the computer," she adds.

In Boston, Margolis says he has personally received no complaints about the policy of filtering for children. He recalled one mother who told him that the policy gave her "added assurance" about allowing her children to use the library.

At the same time, he recalls, a mother who had given her teenage son permission to use unfiltered access was "amazed" at the kind of sexual material her son could access on the Internet. "But she also said that she would not change that," Margolis says.

Despite its use of filtering, the Boston Public Library is not a party to the lawsuits challenging CIPA. However, Margolis hopes the law is struck down. "I don't think the federal government should be intruding on our ability to deliver appropriate service," Margolis says. "This is more red tape [and] bureaucracy. And the policy and practice that we've had for over four years is working just fine."

Legal Issues

The ALA and the ACLU are mounting a broad legal assault against the mandatory filtering law, contending that it violates a half-dozen established free-speech principles. [20] The government has yet to file its first pleading in the case, but supporters of CIPA continue to defend its constitutionality.

For the moment, the government says it will not try to enforce the penalty provisions of the law before July 1, 2002. Meanwhile, school and public libraries are expected to comply with other provisions of the law, requiring the adoption of Internet-use policies and considering filtering options. With the government's decision to defer enforcement of the law, the ALA and the ACLU decided not to seek a preliminary injunction to formally block its provisions.

The two groups have assembled an array of plaintiffs to challenge the law, including 11 state, regional and local library associations extending—as the ACLU noted in its initial press release— "from Portland, Maine, to Portland, Oregon." Both suits included library patrons, including several who do not have home computers who said filtering would hamper their Internet access.

Several organizations that joined the ACLU suit claimed filtering would hinder access to their Web sites. Two of the sites—Out in America and PlanetOut—serve gay, lesbian, bisexual and transgendered persons. Three others—AfraidtoAsk.com, Safersex.org and Planned Parenthood's site—provide information about sexual issues.

In addition, an individual plaintiff—Jeffrey Pollock, a one-time Republican candidate for Congress from Oregon—claimed that he changed from supporting to opposing filtering after he discovered his own Web site was blocked by a filter. The offending material apparently related to Pollock's stand on abortion.

In their complaints, both the ALA and the ACLU contend that the law violates the First Amendment by imposing content- and viewpoint-based restrictions on constitutionally protected expression. Free-speech principles generally prevent the government from prohibiting or restricting speech based on viewpoint, but they allow some limited discretion to regulate speech by subject matter. For example, the Supreme Court in 1986 ruled that municipalities can use zoning laws to restrict the location of adult movie theaters or bookstores. [21]

Both suits also claim that mandatory filtering amounts to an impermissible "prior restraint." According to the ACLU complaint, the law "provides for and induces suppression of speech without any judicial determination that the speech is unprotected by law." Both suits also say that the law's provision allowing patrons to seek permission for unfiltered use of computers violates the Constitution by giving

Should public libraries use filters to block obscenity and pornography on the Internet?

David Burt
MARKET RESEARCH MANAGER, N2H2

WRITTEN FOR THE CQ RESEARCHER, MAY 2001

*i*n communities across America, a controversy is raging over how to cope with the problem of library patrons using Internet terminals to access illegal obscenity and child pornography.

Like many libraries, the Broward County, Fla., Public Library relies on "education" and "a policy" to encourage appropriate use of the Internet. But a lawsuit against the library uncovered the problems with such an education/policy approach. The *New Times* of Broward reported that access to Internet pornography in the library had led to "14 incidents of masturbation documented by library and police reports, two incidents of men exposing themselves and one instance of a man fondling a female patron."

Freedom of Information requests have uncovered thousands of other library pornography incidents from all over the country. The Greenville [S.C.] Public Library suffered similar problems. An internal report discovered that "a large number, perhaps 50 percent, of the users on one afternoon were young men going to pornography sites."

Library administrators found that "female staff . . . are intimidated by this activity." One female staffer stated: "I felt dirty coming home at the end of the day."

To stop the illegal activity and restore staff morale, the library board chose to install N2H2 filtering software. Since then, abuse of the Internet has stopped. Further, no patrons have complained about being denied access to legitimate sites.

This experience has been repeated across the county. After watching the failure of the education/policy approach, nearly 4,000 public libraries have chosen to install filtering software. According to a 2000 study by the U.S. National Commission on Libraries and Information Science, 24.6 percent of public libraries now use filters, an increase of 121 percent in two years.

Other research shows the filters are widely popular with the librarians who use them. Library researcher Ken Haycock, who recently studied the use of filters in public libraries, found that 76 percent of public librarians said they were "very/somewhat satisfied" with the decision to install Internet filter software. An eye-popping 90 percent of public librarians using filters responded that the software serves its purpose either "very well" or "somewhat well."

Public libraries don't stock *Hustler* next to *House & Garden* in their magazine section, so why should they offer Hustler.com? They shouldn't. Not when there is a tested, effective solution widely available.

Nancy Kranich
PRESIDENT, AMERICAN LIBRARY ASSOCIATION

WRITTEN FOR THE CQ RESEARCHER, MAY 2001

*f*ilters are neither the best nor the only means to protect children using the Internet in libraries. They give parents a false sense of security that their children are protected. No filter protects children from all objectionable content. But all filters block access to critical constitutionally protected speech about many subjects people need to know.

Filters cannot take the place of responsible use, informed by local community-based Internet access policies, user-education programs, links to great sites and safety guidelines. That is why ALA and many other organizations—including the federal Commission on Online Child Protection (COPA) and several filtering companies—oppose federal legislation mandating that libraries and schools utilize Internet-blocking technology. Laws like the Children's Internet Protection Act (CIPA) force libraries in economically disadvantaged areas to use already scarce resources to install expensive and unreliable filtering technologies or lose the vital federal funds they need to end the demoralizing effects of "digital discrimination" in underserved communities.

Thanks to the e-rate and other programs, 95 percent of America's libraries are now online, and libraries are the No. 1 point of access for those without computers at home, work or school. Librarians have worked hard to ensure that libraries provide a wide spectrum of information to our diverse communities. We do this not only by providing access to both print and online resources but also by instructing people how to use these resources efficiently and safely. We identify great sites for children and adults and schedule computer classes. The vast majority of library patrons use the Internet responsibly, guided by library policies that address appropriate use and invoke disciplinary action for violators. Approximately 95 percent of public libraries already have Internet policies.

Librarians care deeply about children. We have dedicated our careers to ensuring that adults and children enjoy an enriching experience and access to quality materials in libraries. We understand the enormous learning potential of the Internet and appreciate the responsibility we have as a society for ensuring that libraries remain safe and intellectually creative environments for everyone.

This will not be accomplished by imposing Draconian governmental controls over our libraries, but rather by allowing the parents and librarians in our local communities to tailor workable and effective policies to protect children from inappropriate material on the Internet.

librarians—as the ALA complaint puts it—"standardless, unfettered and unreviewable discretion" to control access to information.

Finally, both suits say the law fails a standard, three-part test for reviewing laws regulating speech. The test requires that a law advance a substantial or compelling governmental interest, that it be "narrowly tailored" to further that interest, and that it be no more restrictive than necessary to accomplish its goal.

Supporters of the law say the legal attacks overstate the impact of the statute. Taylor, of the National Law Center for Children and Families, emphasizes that the law only requires filtering for obscenity or child pornography—both of which are illegal under federal and state law.

"Those categories of speech are not protected speech for either of the age groups (adults or children)," Taylor says. "And the law only asks publicly funded institutions to restrict access to the information without restricting the information itself from the Internet."

Two First Amendment experts on opposite ends of the ideological spectrum, however, say the legal challenge is a strong one. Rodney Smolla, a liberal professor at the University of Richmond Law School, predicts the law will be struck down. Smolla says the Supreme Court's decision on the CDA indicates the justices are "unwilling" to give the government much leeway in limiting adults' access to information on the Internet, even to protect children from exposure to sexual material.

For his part, Douglas Kmiec, a conservative professor at Pepperdine Law School in Malibu, Calif., says the government can defend CIPA by citing so-called government speech cases, which give it some control over use of publicly funded institutions or programs. "I

don't think it's an easy question either way," Kmiec says, "but the government has a couple of additional arrows in its quiver" compared with the earlier CDA case.

The government is scheduled to file a motion to dismiss the suits on June 8. A hearing on the motion is sched-

> **"Filters are not going to block much legitimate sexual information."**
>
> *— Bruce Taylor, president*

> **"We continue to find accidental blocking of objectionable sites."**
>
> *— Ann Beeson, attorney*
> *American Civil Liberties Union*

uled for July 23. If the motion is denied, ALA and ACLU attorneys say they hope the trial can be scheduled by December.

OUTLOOK

Access Issues

Emmalyn Rood, a Portland, Ore., teenager, began to suspect two years ago that she might be a lesbian. She wanted to find out more about sexual-orientation issues, but did not want to use her computer at home lest her mother discover the research.

So, twice a week or so, Rood took the bus to downtown Portland to the main Multnomah County library, to get the information she wanted. She used the library's Internet services to access a number of Web sites, including PlanetOut.

Rood, now one of the plaintiffs in the ACLU's lawsuit against mandatory library filtering, "was able to connect with a friendly, welcoming queer community online," according to the complaint. And, because of the "information and support she received," Rood has since come out as a lesbian to her family and community.

Critics of CIPA say Rood's experience demonstrates the importance of unfiltered access to the Web in libraries—and the potential cost of using filters that block access to legitimate information about sexual issues. They emphasize that many library patrons have no other access to the Web because they have no personal computers in their homes. "The digital-divide problem is quite acute," says ACLU attorney Beeson. [22]

CIPA's funding penalties will have disproportionate effect on poor communities, Beeson explains, because they have no choice but to accept the federal funds and comply with the filtering mandate. "They'll get a dumbed-down version of the Internet," Beeson says.

Supporters of filtering minimize the digital divide issue by saying that library patrons have other ways to obtain information. "The public may not be able to get everything from a library," says Taylor of the National Law Center for Children and Families, "but they can get it from everywhere else."

Supporters and opponents of filtering also disagree about the extent of the "overblocking" problem. "Filters are not going to block much of the legitimate sexual information," Taylor says. But the ACLU's Beeson disagrees. "We continue to find accidental blocking" of unobjectionable sites, she says.

The overblocking issue is likely to be a major focus of any trial in the legal challenge against CIPA if the ALA and ACLU complaints survive the government's motion to dismiss—as seems likely. And Smolla at the University of Richmond says the issue is likely to hurt the likelihood of upholding the law. "To the extent that the software dramatically overscreens, it starts to fail the First Amendment standard," he says.

Whether or not the law is struck down, schools and libraries, as well as government agencies, could adopt an array of recommendations from the congressional COPA commission to help minimize children's access to Web porn. For instance, in addition to public education campaigns, the commission called for aggressive law enforcement programs to prosecute obscenity violations. It also called for federal regulations to discourage deceptive practices that entice children to sex-related sites. (*See box, p. 185.*)

But one member of the commission says the recommendations will not be sufficient to deal with the problem without filtering. "If you're concerned with limiting access to pornography, that's a way to go," says Robert Flores, vice president and senior counsel at the National Law Center. "But it doesn't get you all the way."

Even without the law, many libraries and schools may continue to use filtering. Supporters point to a public opinion poll showing that 92 percent of those surveyed supported the use of filters in schools to block sexual material, and 79 percent favored using filters to block hate speech. [23] On the other hand, opponents of filtering note that relatively few families—6 percent, according to one study—use filters in their own homes. [24]

In Philadelphia, Carol Williams still believes the law is unnecessary. She says she has seen no problems with kids' accessing pornography in libraries. In any event, she believes the issue is one of parental responsibility and government censorship. "Is the library responsible for what your child does or does not read when she's in the library?" she asks rhetorically.

"It blocks free speech," Williams says of filtering. "It not only blocks out obscene material, it blocks out informational sites."

In California, however, Kathleen R. says unrestricted library access to the Web interferes with her role as parent. "If my child can't borrow a book without my permission," she asks, "why can't it be the same way with the Internet?"

"Nobody knew that libraries were offering this," she continues. "It was even in the little kids' section, the Dr. Seuss, Hop-on-Pop section. They can say what they want, but this is a problem."

Notes

[1] The case is *Kathleen R. v. City of Livermore*, decided March 6, 2001, by the California Court of Appeal, First Appellate District. For news coverage, see *Los Angeles Times*, March 8, 2001, p. A3.

[2] For background, see Charles S. Clark, "The Future of Libraries," *The CQ Researcher*, May 23, 1997, pp. 457-480.

[3] See "Digital Chaperones for Kids," *Consumer Reports*, March 2001 (www.consumerreports.org).

FOR MORE INFORMATION

American Civil Liberties Union, 125 Broadway, New York, N.Y. 10004; (212) 549-2500; www.aclu.org. The ACLU represents plaintiffs challenging the Children's Internet Protection Act.

American Library Association, 50 East Huron St., Chicago, Ill. 60611; 1-(800) 545-2400; 1301 Pennsylvania Ave., N.W., #403; Washington, D.C. 20004; (202) 628-8410; www.ala.org. The ALA describes its mission as seeking to "enhance learning and ensure access to information for all."

Council on Library and Information Resources, 1755 Massachusetts Ave., N.W., #500, Washington, D.C. 20036; (202) 939-4750; www.clir.org. The private, nonprofit organization studies issues affecting libraries and other cultural heritage institutions.

Institute of Museum and Library Services, 1100 Pennsylvania Ave., N.W., Suite 802, Washington, D.C. 20506; (202) 606-8536; www.imls.gov. The independent federal agency provides assistance and support to all types of libraries: public, academic, research and school.

National Commission on Libraries and Information Science, 1100 Vermont Ave., N.W., Suite 820, Washington, D.C. 20005-3552; (202) 606-9200; www.nclis. gov/index.cfm. The 14-member commission provides research and statistics on libraries.

National Law Center for Children and Families, 3819 Plaza Drive, Fairfax, Va. 22030-2512; (703) 691-4626; www.nationallawcenter.org. The organization seeks to protect children and families from the effects of pornography through education and law enforcement.

4 Commission on Child Online Protection, "Final Report," Oct. 20, 2000 (www.copa-commission.org). For news coverage, see *The Wall Street Journal*, Oct. 19, 2000, p. A8; *The Washington Post*, Oct. 21, 2000, E1.

5 "Demographic Characteristics of Internet Users at the Tacoma Public Library, With Special Reference to the Issue of Internet Pornography," White Paper for the National Research Council Committee on Tools and Strategies for Protecting Kids from Pornography and Their Application to Other Inappropriate Material, Feb. 28, 2001 (www.nationalacademies.org).

6 The case is *Ginsberg v. New York* (1968).

7 The case is *Sable Communications of California, Inc. v. Federal Communications Commission* (1989).

8 The case is *Mainstream Loudoun v. Board of Trustees of the Loudoun County Library*, decided Nov. 23, 1998, in U.S. District Court, Eastern District of Virginia.

9 Background drawn from Evelyn Geller, *Forbidden Books in American Public Libraries, 1876-1939: A Study in Cultural Change*, (1984); Louise S. Robbins, *Censorship and the American Library, The American Library Association's Response to Threats of Intellectual Freedom, 1939-1969* (1996).

10 Geller, *op. cit.*, p. 11.

11 Robbins, *op. cit.*, p. 156.

12 The case is *Island Trees Free Union School District No. 26 v. Pico.*

13 Some background drawn from Robert S. Peck, *Libraries, the First Amendment, and Cyberspace: What You Need to Know* (2000), pp. 125-146.

14 The case is *Reno v. ACLU*, June 26, 1997. See Kenneth Jost, *The Supreme Court Yearbook*, 1996-1997, pp. 35-40.

15 The Third Circuit's decision, *ACLU v. Reno*, was issued June 22, 2000; the government's petition before the Supreme Court was filed under the name *Aschroft v. ACLU.*

16 The full text of the ruling can be found at www.aclu.org.

17 For news coverage, see *The New York Times*, Dec. 19, 2000, p. C4.

18 The Jan. 18, 2001, news release can be found at www.ala.org.

19 See (Minneapolis) *Star-Tribune*, May 25, 2001.

20 The complaints are available on the organizations' respective Web sites: www.ala.org and www.aclu.org.

21 The case was *Renton v. Playtime Theatres, Inc.* (1986).

22 For background, see Kathy Koch, "The Digital Divide," *The CQ Researcher*, Jan. 28, 2000, pp. 41-64.

23 Rebecca S. Weines, "Survey Finds Support for School Filters," *The New York Times*, Oct. 18, 2000.

24 The poll of 1,900 individuals was commissioned by the Digital Media Forum, a consortium of six public interest and consumer groups interested in media policy. The study was conducted by Jupiter Research, which researches the consumer online industry, cited in *Consumer Reports, op. cit.*

Bibliography
Selected Sources Used

Books

Baker, Nicholson, *Double Fold: Libraries and the Assault on Paper*, Random House, 2001.

Baker, a novelist, criticizes libraries' policies of microfilming and, more recently, digitizing newspapers, magazines and books for "preservation" and then discarding the original printed materials. The book includes detailed source notes and an 18-page list of references.

Geller, Evelyn, *Forbidden Books in American Public Libraries, 1876-1939: A Study in Cultural Change*, Greenwood, 1984.

Geller, a contributor to a number of library publications, recounts the library profession's transformation from serving as moral censor to actively advocating "the freedom to read." The book includes detailed source notes and a three-page bibliographical essay.

Jones, Barbara M., *Libraries, Access, and Intellectual Freedom: Developing Policies for Public and Academic Libraries*, American Library Association, 1999.

Jones, special-collections librarian at the University of Illinois at Champaign-Urbana, provides a practical guide for librarians on intellectual-freedom issues. The book includes a list of groups on both sides of freedom-to-read issues. The ALA also publishes the more comprehensive *Intellectual Freedom Manual* (5th ed., 1996).

Peck, Robert S., *Libraries, the First Amendment, and Cyberspace: What You Need to Know*, American Library Association, 1999.

Peck, a former president of the Freedom to Read Foundation, provides a detailed primer on First Amendment issues affecting libraries. The book includes detailed chapter notes, with case names and citations; ALA interpretations of the Library Bill of Rights; and the ALA Intellectual Freedom Committee's suggested policy on Internet use.

Reichman, Henry, *Censorship and Selection: Issues and Answers for Schools (3d ed.)*, American Library Association, 2001.

The book provides a guide for school librarians and media specialists, teachers and administrators on school freedom-to-read issues. Reichman is a history professor at California State University in Hayward and associate editor of the ALA's newsletter on intellectual freedom. The book includes several appendixes, including a six-page bibliography.

Robbins, Louise S., *Censorship and the American Library: The American Library Association's Response to Threats

to Intellectual Freedom, 1939-1969*, Greenwood, 1997.

Robbins, director of the University of Wisconsin's School of Library and Information Studies, traces the gradually strengthened role of the American Library Association in defending the freedom to read. The book includes detailed source notes and a three-page bibliography.

Articles

Maxwell, Nancy Kalikow, "Alternatives to Filters," *Library Technology Report*, March 2001.

The article discusses filters and alternative policies, such as privacy screens, computer positioning, family contracts, parental consent forms, patron authentication and "smart card" systems, content managers, outgoing data blockers, time limits, and so-called tap-on-the-shoulder policies.

Reports and Studies

American Civil Liberties Union, "Censorship in a Box: Why Blocking Software Is Wrong for Public Libraries," 1999 (*www.aclu.org*).

The ACLU tract attacks mandatory filtering in libraries as government censorship and advocates alternative measures, including time limits and privacy screens.

Burt, David, *Dangerous Access, 2000 Edition: Uncovering Pornography in America's Libraries*, Family Research Council, March 2000 (*www.frc.org*).

The 60-page report documents what it counts as more than 2,000 incidents of library patrons—"many of them children"—accessing pornography in public libraries. Most of the libraries surveyed did not respond. Burt is a former public librarian who now works for the filtering software company N2H2 in Seattle, Wash.

Commission on Online Child Protection, *Final Report*, October 2000 (*www.copacommission.org*).

The 95-page report concludes with 12 recommendations on reducing the access of minors to harmful material on the Internet, including public education, technological improvements and strengthened law enforcement, but not mandatory filtering in libraries or schools.

Council on Library and Information Resources, "The Evidence in Hand: The Report of the Task Force on the Artifact in Library Collections," March 2001 (*www.clir.org*).

The report addresses "the gap between the quantity of research materials that demand preservation and the insufficient funding available to meet that need."

11 School Vouchers Showdown

KENNETH JOST

Christine Suma has lived in Cleveland all her life. But no one in her family has ever attended a Cleveland public school — neither she, her husband nor any of their 12 children.

"The public schools don't have the best record in Cleveland," Suma explains. "I don't want my children where they may get an education and they may not. I don't want them where they might be safe or not. I don't want to take a risk with my children. I want a sure bet."

Like their parents, the Suma children have all gone to parochial schools in Cleveland. Up until 1996, the Sumas had to pay the tuition out of their own pockets. Today, however, the family receives about $1,500 in taxpayer funds for each of the children under a controversial school voucher program that faced a constitutional showdown before the Supreme Court. On June 27, 2002, the court upheld the constitutionality of the Cleveland voucher program, although the debate continues between voucher supporters and opponents.

Suma, who intervened in the case to urge the high court to uphold the program, says the vouchers provide the kind of school choices for her children already enjoyed by higher-income families. "I want my education tax dollars put where I want them to go," Suma says. "This voucher system is giving us opportunities."

Doris Simmons-Harris — a single mother of three children who have gone to Cleveland's public schools — has her complaints about the system

From *The CQ Researcher*, February 15, 2002. (Revised July 2002).

Christine Suma receives $1,500 a year in taxpayer funds per child for her children's Catholic school tuition in Cleveland. The controversial school voucher program faced a constitutional showdown before the U.S. Supreme Court.

Courtesy Institute for Justice

too. But she believes vouchers can only exacerbate the Cleveland schools' major problem: lack of money.

"Our quality went down since I went to school," Simmons-Harris says. "They cut out art classes and after-school activities because of money. My child's in a class in which every child doesn't have a book."

Two of Simmons-Harris' children have graduated from Cleveland schools; her younger son — who has a behavioral disability — is in high school now. She lent her name to the legal challenge against the voucher program in part because she believes the plan would ignore special-needs students like her son.

"He could never go to a private school because of his handicap," Simmons-Harris says. "The public schools take children with a handicap, but a private school would not."

The school vouchers debate has raged for more than a decade over an array of educational policy issues.[1] Advocates of "school choice" — largely, but not exclusively, political conservatives — say families deserve the chance to use public funds at whatever school, public or private, best serves their children's needs. And a voucher system, they say, will create competition that will force stultified public school systems to take needed steps to improve.

Opponents — including teachers' unions and school administrators as well as civil liberties and civil rights groups — argue that vouchers will benefit at most only a few students while diverting resources from the public schools that will continue to educate the vast majority of American youngsters.* In addition, they say neither of the two major public voucher programs operating today — in Cleveland and Milwaukee — has actually produced significant academic gains for the students using the vouchers to attend private schools. A third program, in Florida, has only 44 voucher students. (*See chart, p. 204.*)

So far, the Cleveland and Milwaukee programs both are also attracting fewer students than the number of vouchers that could be awarded. The Wisconsin legislature capped Milwaukee's program at 15 percent of the system's current enrollment; that would

---

* An estimated 47.2 million youngsters attended public schools and 5.9 million were in private schools in fall 2001, according to the National Center on Education Statistics. Catholic schools enroll close to 50 percent of private school students, other religious schools about 35 percent and nonsectarian schools about 15 percent.

allow slightly more than 15,000 students, but only 10,882 are currently receiving vouchers. In Cleveland the number of voucher students is theoretically limited by the size of the state appropriation for the program. But over the past three years the program has not spent some 37 percent of the $33.8 million allocated.

The issue has split racial and ethnic minorities, who constitute the major populations served by the big-city systems most often depicted by critics as "failing schools." School choice advocates have gained allies among African-Americans and Latinos by touting vouchers as an immediate option for minority youngsters to escape low-performing schools.

"For right now, vouchers are the only means to provide parents with the opportunity to select a school environment from a menu of schools that's best for their children," says Kaleem Caire, president of the two-year-old Black Alliance for Educational Options (BAEO).

Traditional civil rights groups, however, insist that vouchers will end up hurting most minority youngsters. "Vouchers might be good for the few poor kids who can take advantage of them," says Theodore Shaw, associate director of the NAACP Legal Defense and Educational Fund. "But systemically, they are going to further undercut public education, where the vast majority of African-American, Latino and poor children are going to remain."

Despite the broad-ranging debate, the issue facing the Supreme Court when it heard arguments Feb. 20 on the constitutionality of the Cleveland voucher program was a narrow one. The justices were asked to decide whether the program — now in its sixth year — aids religious schools in violation of the Establishment Clause, the Bill of Rights provision that bars any law "respecting the establishment of religion." The court eventually ruled that the program is not an unconstitutional endorsement of religion.

Opponents — who filed a federal court challenge to the plan after the Ohio Supreme Court gave its blessing to the program — emphasize that virtually all of the 4,456 students currently receiving vouchers are attending religious schools.

"This is nothing but a direct subsidy of the educational mission of religious denominations," says Barry Lynn, executive director of Americans United for Separation of Church and State. "And in the same way that one should not expect taxpayers to support churches, they should not be expected to support church-related educational facilities either."

Supporters counter that both the Cleveland and Milwaukee systems leave it up to parents to decide where to use the tax-paid stipends.

"The scholarship program is neutral on its face," says Clint Bolick, litigation director of the Institute for Justice, the Washington-based libertarian law firm that has spearheaded the voucher movement. "Funds are directed to religious schools only through the true private choices of individual parents, therefore satisfying Establishment Clause requirements."

The case — formally called *Zelman v. Simmons-Harris*, after Ohio's superintendent of public instruction, Susan Tave Zelman — reached the Supreme Court after a series of recent decisions that somewhat loosened the restrictions on government programs that benefit religious schools. In the most recent of those decisions, the court in *Mitchell v. Helms* in 2000 approved a federally funded program for lending computers and other equipment to parochial schools. [2]

Supporters and opponents of vouchers vow to continue their fight in state legislatures around the country, despite the court's decision.

Voucher proponents say they have the momentum on the issue. "The movement is progressing extremely well," says Bolick, "and I think it will

continue to produce educational opportunities for children regardless of what happens in the Supreme Court."

But opponents point out that legislatures in only three states — Wisconsin, Ohio, and, most recently, Florida — have approved voucher plans, while voters have rejected voucher or tuition tax-credit ballot proposals in five states since 1990. (*See chart, p. 208.*)

"It's very hard to believe that they have momentum, since every single ballot initiative has been defeated," says Robert Chanin, general counsel of the National Education Association (NEA), the country's largest teachers' union. "Everybody keeps proposing [voucher statutes], and nobody passes them."

Pollsters get somewhat different results on school vouchers depending on the phrasing of the question, but the most recent polls indicate that a majority of Americans oppose the idea, and that support has declined since the late 1990s. In the most favorable result for voucher advocates, 44 percent of respondents said last year that they would favor a proposal that would allow parents to send their children to any school of their choice with the government paying all or part of private school tuition; 54 percent of the respondents said they would oppose such a proposal. [3]

As the voucher debate continues, here are some of the major questions that divide supporters and opponents:

Do school voucher plans improve students' educational performance?

Six years into the Cleveland voucher program, student test scores have risen enough to encourage supporters, but not enough to impress or win over opponents. The results in other programs are similarly murky, though researchers generally appear to agree that African-American students in privately funded voucher schemes are making distinctive gains.

Researchers at Indiana University's Indiana Center for Evaluation have officially evaluated Cleveland's program each year since its inception. [4] They found no significant differences in academic progress between voucher students and comparable public school students after the first year. In the next two evaluations, they measured distinctive gains in language and science, but not in reading, mathematics or social studies.

In the most recent of the Indiana evaluations — published in September 2001 — researchers found that students who entered the voucher program as kindergartners had higher test scores as first-graders than other students, but by the end of third grade the gap had narrowed.

"Vouchers make at least a small but statistically significant difference," says Kim Metcalf, the center's director and an associate professor in the department of curriculum and instruction at the university's School of Education.

In Milwaukee's voucher program, scant information exists about students' academic performance, partly because test scores have not been collected since the 1994–95 school year, when the program was limited to secular schools and had few participants. The legislature dropped testing and evaluation requirements when it expanded the program. The official evaluator — John Witte, director of the University of Wisconsin's La Follette School of Public Affairs in Madison — reported no significant academic gains for voucher students compared to others, though research teams from Harvard and Princeton did find some distinctive gains for voucher students in some areas. [5]

Voucher supporters acknowledge that the evidence of academic gains is spotty at best. "The findings range from mildly positive to strongly positive," Bolick says. But, he adds, "I am unaware of any study that does not find at least mildly positive results from school choice in terms of academic performance. I expect those findings will grow stronger when later studies are done in terms of graduation rates."

"The impacts are not detectable for any groups other than African-Americans," says Paul E. Peterson, a prominent voucher advocate and director of the Program on Education Policy and Governance at Harvard's Kennedy School of Government in Cambridge, Mass.

Voucher opponents say studies show the programs do not produce the academic gains supporters predict. "There is almost nothing in the research literature that suggests vouchers succeed as an academic intervention," says Alex Molnar, a confirmed voucher opponent who taught at the University of Wisconsin in Milwaukee before moving to Arizona State University at Tempe last August. "There is no clear benefit one way or another with respect to the academic performance of students."

"When you get behind the hired guns or the committed proponents and look at the more objective [studies] — those written by researchers retained by a specific state — at best it's a wash," says Chanin, the NEA lawyer.

The evidence of gains among African-American students comes from three privately funded scholarship programs in Dayton, Ohio; New York City and Washington, D.C. A study by Peterson's group at Harvard released in September 2000 found that African-American students scored 6 percentiles higher in overall test performance than control-group students. But no statistically significant effects, positive or negative, were found among other ethnic groups. [6]

Peterson calls the gains for black students "fairly sizable" — comparable, he says, to the gains found in a recent class-size reduction experiment in Tennessee. "If you got that kind of impact in subsequent years, you could talk about reducing the test-score gap between blacks and whites," he says.

Indiana University's Metcalf acknowledges the gains but questions whether they can be attributed to vouchers. "We don't know how that effect was produced," he says. "One pos-

sible reason is that [scholarship students] have been put in classrooms with higher-achieving classmates whose families are more supportive of education. It may be a peer effect, not related to the productivity of the school itself."

Overall, two disinterested research organizations — the U.S. General Accounting Office and the Rand Corporation, the respected private research organization — find that the evidence of academic gains among voucher students is inconclusive so far. "Long-term effects on academic skills and attainment are as yet unexamined," Rand researchers write in a book-length study published last summer. [7] The GAO says "little or no" evidence of academic gains has been found in official evaluations in Milwaukee and Cleveland. [8]

For his part, Metcalf agrees that the evidence is inconclusive, but he sees a trend in favor of vouchers. "It isn't clear yet whether it's a good thing or a bad thing, but the data have not been negative about vouchers," Metcalf concludes.

Do voucher plans hurt public schools?

With no recent test scores, Milwaukee's voucher program offers no good opportunity to examine its effect on students receiving the stipends. But one prominent researcher says the decade-long experiment does provide useful — and encouraging — information about the effects on the overall performance of the city's public schools.

To test the hypothesis that vouchers will encourage public schools to change because of increased competition, Harvard economics Professor Caroline Hoxby studied academic performance in Milwaukee public schools since the start of the experiment. She found above-average gains in many of the schools — and particularly high gains in schools in low-income neighborhoods that she said faced the greatest "competition" from vouchers.

The Nation's Three Public Voucher Programs

Milwaukee's Parental Choice Program is the oldest and largest of the nation's three publicly funded voucher programs. Florida's "A-Plus" program is the newest, and the only statewide program. The Supreme Court ruled June 27, 2002, whether the Cleveland program violates the U.S. Constitution.

Program (Date Established)	Number of students receiving vouchers	Amount of voucher	Eligibility Requirements	Percentage of voucher students attending religious schools
Milwaukee Parental Choice Program (1990)	10,882	$5,553 (max.) (based on tuition)	Parents' income 175% of poverty level ($30,000 for household of four); child attended public school (any grade) or private school (K-3), enrolled in Choice program prior year.	70% (est.)
Cleveland Pilot Scholarship and Tutoring Program (1995)	4,456	$2,250 (max.; varies with income) (Parent pays min. 10% of tuition)	Parents' income up to 200% of federal poverty level ($35,000) for maximum amount; others receive $1,875; schools limited to $2,500 tuition.	96-99% *
Florida "A-Plus" Accountability and School Choice Program (1999)	44	$3,700 (max.)	Child attended Florida public school graded "F" in 2 out of 4 previous years (two schools so far); no income eligibility.	90.9%

* Lower figure for 1999-2000 school year, from Ohio Dept. of Education; higher figure for 2001-2002 school year from the education newsletter Catalyst-Cleveland.

Sources: Wisconsin Dept. of Public Instruction; Ohio Dept. of Education; Florida Dept. of Education

"Overall, . . . public schools made a strong push to improve achievement in the face of competition from vouchers," Hoxby writes in an academic paper on her study. [9] In an interview, she is more direct: "They improved a lot for three years in a row at an absolutely unprecedented rate. As an educational researcher, I've never seen improvement like that."

Rand researcher Brian Gill finds Hoxby's study provocative. "I don't think that's a definitive result, but it's certainly very promising," he says. But two other experts familiar with the Milwaukee program — with opposite viewpoints on vouchers — dismiss the report.

"I don't think there's any evidence" for Hoxby's conclusion, says Witte, who supports vouchers targeted at low-income students and is the official eval-uator of the Wisconsin project. "Test scores did go up, but they've now flattened out. I think they went up because there was an enormous push to get them up" — not because of the voucher program.

Voucher opponent Molnar also finds Hoxby's study unpersuasive. He says the test scores she used are "incomplete" and "not comparable" between different schools. More broadly, he says, Hoxby's conclusion requires "a series of [unrealistic] assumptions" about the reasons for the changes in reported test scores. "It's silly," Molnar says. "Schools and schooling are complex. [Hoxby's conclusion] flies in the face of all the things that we know about human beings and human nature."

A similar debate is raging over the effects of Florida's "A-Plus Accountability and School Choice Program," which provides vouchers to students attending public schools that fail to improve performance one year after receiving an "F" grade in a state evaluation. Jay P. Greene, a research associate at Harvard's Program on Education Policy and Governance, found evidence that schools that received a failing grade in 1999 — and thus faced the threat of vouchers — achieved test-score gains more than twice those recorded at other schools in Florida. But Gregory Camilli, a professor of education at Rutgers Graduate School of Education, concludes that Greene "vastly overestimated" the test score gains and contends that other aspects of Florida's program besides the threat of vouchers may be responsible for any improvements. [10]

Critics of vouchers say that far from helping, the stipends will actually hurt public schools — first, by providing incentives for better students to leave the public education system, and, second, by diverting money and other resources from already struggling public schools.

The evidence on the so-called cream-skimming issue is sketchy and inconclusive. Official evaluators Witte in Milwaukee and Metcalf in Cleveland say students entering the two voucher programs had achievement levels and demographic characteristics similar to other low-income public school students. On the other hand, the parents of voucher students — predominantly, single mothers — had slightly higher education levels and appeared more strongly motivated than parents of other students.

As for the fiscal impact, critics say the methods of funding both the Cleveland and Milwaukee programs take money from the public school systems. Supporters counter that both school systems continue to receive more per capita state aid than the cost of the vouchers, and that in any event the schools save money by having fewer students to educate.

Most broadly, voucher opponents contend that vouchers divert energy and attention, as well as money, from more productive education reforms.

"You've got powerful long-term studies that demonstrate the impact of early childhood education on the later educational success of children who participate in those programs," Molnar says. "Would I choose vouchers over that? No.

"What about reducing classroom size? The evidence suggests that that is a powerful intervention. What about providing high-quality educational opportunities for poor children over the summer? Research suggests that poor kids 'fall behind' because of what happens over the summer. Would I choose vouchers over any of those? No."

But Bolick of the Institute for Justice insists that the Cleveland and Milwaukee programs — as well as the newer, more limited program in Florida —

have pressured the school systems to change because of the fear of losing voucher students to private schools.

"The Cleveland system was one of the absolute worst in the country," Bolick says. "Two years ago, it failed every one of 28 of the state's criteria. This year, it passed three. These were the first stirrings of signs of life in an extremely troubled system."

Competition, Bolick says, is the key: "The rules of economics are not suspended at the schoolhouse door."

Do school voucher plans unconstitutionally subsidize religious schools?

When Milwaukee began its voucher program in 1990, the rules effectively limited participation to a handful of secular private schools established to serve low-income, minority students. Five years later, after lobbying by the Roman Catholic archdiocese and the business community, the Republican-controlled legislature expanded the program to include parochial schools.

"Catholic schools were the moving force on the 1995 legislation," Witte says. "The archdiocese was heavily involved."

The change — signed into law by then-Gov. Tommy Thompson, now President Bush's secretary of Health and Human Services — was immediately challenged in court as an unconstitutional subsidy for religious schools. But the Wisconsin Supreme Court rejected the challenge in 1998 — allowing the program to more than triple its enrollment at the beginning of the 1998-1999 school year.

Parochial-school advocates have battled over public-funding issues since the mid-1800s. In a series of decisions since 1948, the U.S. Supreme Court has approved some programs that provided aid to parochial-school students but barred more direct subsidies. The court's most recent decisions have loosened, but not eliminated, restrictions on the use of public funds at church-affiliated schools.

Church-state separationists argue that the use of vouchers at parochial schools violates the Constitution's prohibition against government establishment of religion. "The one central message [in the First Amendment] is that government is not intended to directly support religion — not one particular religion or religion in general," says Lynn of Americans United for Separation of Church and State.

But parochial-school advocates argue that both the Cleveland and Milwaukee programs meet the Supreme Court's guidelines on aid to religious schools. Scholarships are constitutional, says Mark Chopko, general counsel of the U.S. Conference of Catholic Bishops, if they are awarded "based on neutral, non-religious criteria that do not create incentives for choosing to attend religious schools."

Chopko acknowledges the financial problems facing parochial schools. "They're running at the line or below the line constantly," he says. But he forcefully denies that either of the programs in Cleveland or Milwaukee is a "bailout" for the parochial systems. "Absolutely not," he says.

Instead, Chopko views the programs as supporting Catholic schools' updated mission of providing education for mostly non-Catholic, mostly minority students in inner cities. "The participation of religious schools in these programs has been to qualify as providers of the assistance," Chopko continues. "The beneficiaries are really the children in these school districts."

Lynn, however, says Catholic schools — as well as schools operated by Christians, Jews, Muslims or other faiths — serve primarily religious purposes.

"Religious schools exist to promote faith," says Lynn, a United Church of Christ minister. "It doesn't just happen in a religion class. Religion imbues the curriculum in a Catholic school or a Muslim school from the time the bell rings in the morning until the children are dismissed in the afternoon."

Vouchers in Cleveland

March 3, 1995 *Federal judge, ruling in school desegregation case, orders state takeover of Cleveland public school system.*

June 28, 1995 *Ohio General Assembly approves Pilot Scholarship Program aimed at providing vouchers for low-income families in Cleveland; signed by Gov. George Voinovich on June 30.*

January 1996 *Challenge to voucher program filed in state court.*

July 31, 1996 *State court judge rules program constitutional.*

September 1996 *Program takes effect for 1996-97 school year.*

May 27, 1999 *Ohio Supreme Court rules program unconstitutional but says program does not improperly aid religious schools.*

June 29, 1999 *Gov. Bob Taft signs bill re-enacting program.*

July 20, 1999 *New challenge filed in federal court.*

Aug. 24, 1999 *Federal Judge Solomon Oliver issues preliminary injunction against program.*

Nov. 5, 1999 *Supreme Court, by 5-4 vote, stays injunction, allowing program to continue, pending further proceedings.*

Dec. 20, 1999 *Judge Oliver rules program unconstitutional.*

Dec. 11, 2000 *Federal appeals court in Cincinnati affirms lower court decision, 2-1.*

Sept. 25, 2001 *Supreme Court agrees to hear appeal by state, private schools and pro-voucher parents.*

Feb. 20, 2002 *U.S. Supreme Court hears arguments.*

June 27, 2002 *U.S. Supreme Court upholds constitutionality of the Ohio school voucher program.*

Opponents of the Cleveland program are basing their legal challenge on the evidence that the vast majority of the schools participating in the program are church-affiliated and enroll all but a small number of the voucher students. Of the 50 schools currently participating, only four are secular; the others include 37 Catholic schools, seven affiliated with other Christian denominations and two Islamic academies.

The opponents contend that the program inevitably channels students to parochial schools because of the relatively low limit on tuition — $2,500 —

that participating schools can charge. Catholic schools — subsidized by church funds — typically have lower tuition than secular private schools.

"When the government sets up a program and says you can spend this money only in the limited universe of schools — the vast majority of which are religious — that's not a free and independent choice by the parents," says the NEA's Chanin. "It's a choice dictated by the government."

Bolick says he expects more non-religious schools to participate in the programs over time. In any event, he

says, the predominant role of parochial schools in the programs today is no grounds for throwing them out.

"The question is whether the fact that only a few non-religious schools elected to throw an educational life preserver should mean that the whole voucher program should be invalidated," Bolick says. "In my view, to ask the question is to answer it."

Legal advocates and experts have differing views about how the court is likely to rule on the constitutional issues. Apart from that, however, Rand researcher Gill sees "no good reason" to exclude Catholic schools from voucher programs.

"There is some research indicating that they may have unique benefits" for at-risk students, especially African-Americans, Gill says. Another reason "is the common-sense notion that to exclude the largest number of private schools seems counterproductive."

BACKGROUND

Common Schools

Public and private education have co-existed throughout American history. [11] Church-affiliated schools dominated in Colonial times, but so-called common schools — tax-supported, secular public schools with compulsory, universal attendance — began to take shape in the 1800s and gained nearly complete acceptance by the start of the 20th century. Private and religious schools remained an important feature of U.S. education, but received only limited government assistance.

Thomas Jefferson advocated free, universal public education as early as 1779, but the creation of the common school is normally attributed to an education reform movement of the 1830s and '40s. [12] The most prominent of the reformers was Horace Mann, who —

as secretary of the board of education in Massachusetts from 1837 to 1849 — supervised the establishment of the country's first statewide educational system. Mann strongly believed in the value of education in promoting character and citizenship but disapproved of teaching what he called "doctrinal religion" — favoring one particular sect or denomination over another. [13]

The church-affiliated schools of Colonial times were — like the colonists themselves — predominantly Protestant. By the 1830s, however, Catholic immigration to the United States was increasing rapidly — first from Ireland and later in the century from Southern and Eastern Europe. The influx of Catholics engendered nativist intolerance among many Protestant Americans. For their part, Catholics, accustomed to religious schools in their native lands and resentful of the dominant Protestantism of American public schools, wanted their own schools.

The issue of public funding for religious schools flared as early as the 1820s, fueled both by the incipient common school movement and by anti-Catholic sentiment. [14] The Free School Society of New York City — forerunner of the public school system — successfully moved in 1822 to block church-affiliated schools from receiving grants from the city's school fund. Two decades later, New York Gov. William Seward called for public funding for parochial schools in order to ensure the education of the newly arriving Catholic immigrants. The legislature approved instead a bill barring public funds for any school that taught "any religious sectarian doctrine or tenet." The law left funding issues to local districts; New York City continued to bar funds for most parochial schools.

Divisions between public and parochial school advocates intensified after the Civil War. President Ulysses Grant recommended legislation in 1875 to prohibit the use of public funds "for the benefit of . . . any religious sect or denomination." As later introduced by Sen. James Blaine, R-Maine, the proposal called for barring funds to schools teaching "sectarian" tenets. The Blaine amendment became a partisan issue between Republicans and Democrats, who cultivated the Catholic vote in the North and Midwest. Although the amendment failed, Congress later required newly admitted states to establish public schools "free from sectarian controls." [15]

By the early 1900s, the public school system had taken shape with tax-supported education and compulsory-attendance laws in all states. Some public school advocates even tried to prohibit private and religious education. Oregon enacted such a law — with evident anti-Catholic motivation. In a landmark decision, the U.S. Supreme Court ruled it unconstitutional. Parents have a constitutional right to choose how to educate their children, the court ruled unanimously. [16]

Despite the constitutional protection, Catholic schools have had a hard time in the 20th century. Enrollment declined from 19th-century levels because of the increased availability of public schooling and — especially after World War II — because of growing assimilationist tendencies among Catholic families. Parochial schools received some government assistance, but over time financial aid was limited. The Supreme Court approved textbook loans and transportation for parochial-school students but eventually banned direct government funding in order to enforce separation of church and state. By the 1970s, many Catholic educators were openly asking whether Catholic schools could survive.

School Choice

The current school voucher movement originated not among parochial-school advocates but with a seminal academic article written in the mid-1950s by the libertarian economist Milton Friedman. [17] Support for the idea was originally limited to conservatives, but popular discontent with public education fed its growth, along with the conservative resurgence during Ronald Reagan's presidency in the 1980s. Then in the 1990s school choice supporters broadened their constituencies by successfully persuading many African-Americans that vouchers offered a way for black youngsters to escape inadequate, inner-city schools.

Friedman's 23-page article — simply entitled "The Role of Government in Education" — accepted the goal of compulsory universal education. [18] But he contended that government could accomplish that goal more effectively by giving families fixed amounts of money — vouchers — for them to use to enroll their children at schools, publicly or privately operated, that met certain standards of curriculum and instruction. The "denationalization of education," he said, would "widen the range of choice available to parents" by bringing about "a healthy increase in the variety of educational institutions available and in competition among them."

The article drew sufficient attention to prompt Virgil Blum, a Jesuit priest and political scientist at Marquette University, to found in 1957 a still-extant advocacy group, Citizens for Educational Freedom, to lobby for vouchers. A decade later, the liberal Harvard University sociologist Christopher Jencks endorsed a more regulated voucher system, with individual amounts adjusted to give greater benefits to low-income families. [19] Jencks' article in the journal *Public Interest* — "Are Public Schools Obsolete?" — prompted the Office of Economic Opportunity to offer grants to test the voucher concept in a few cities. One test — from 1972 to 1976 in a suburb of San Jose, Calif. — produced limited results and drew lukewarm reactions.

Interest in vouchers remained low through the 1970s, but President Rea-

Voters in Eight States Reject Vouchers

Voters overwhelmingly rejected providing parents with vouchers and tuition tax credits in the eight states that have voted on proposals. Since 1972, the votes against vouchers have been 60 percent or more.

Voucher Referenda, 1970-2000

State	Year	Election Result	
		Vote Against	**Vote For**
Michigan, Proposal C *	1970	43.2%	56.8%
Maryland, Question #18, General Election	1972	55.0	45.0
Michigan, Proposal H	1978	74.0	26.0
Colorado, Amendment 7	1992	66.8	33.2
California, Proposition 174	1993	70.0	30.0
Washington state, Initiative 173	1996	64.5	35.5
Michigan, Proposal 1	2000	69.0	31.0
California, Proposition 38	2000	70.7	29.3

Tuition Tax-Credit Referenda 1981-1998

State	Year	Vote Against	Vote For
Washington, D.C., Initiative 7	1981	89.0	11.0
Utah, Initiative C	1988	70.0	30.0
Oregon, Measure 11	1990	67.0	33.0
Colorado, Amendment 17	1998	60.3	39.7

* Proposal C amended the Michigan Constitution to prohibit any direct and indirect public funding to aid non-public elementary or secondary schools — thus the vote for the proposal was a vote against vouchers.

Source: People for the American Way Foundation, February 2002

gan gave the movement a major boost in the 1980s by endorsing a different school choice mechanism: tuition tax credits for private schools. The Reagan administration also boosted the voucher movement by the 1983 publication of the famous — some would say infamous — critique of the American education system, *A Nation at Risk.* Public school critics acclaimed the report — depicting U.S. students as falling behind students from other countries in such areas as science and math — as a needed wake-up call, but public school advocates denounced it as alarmist and thinly documented.

The new attention produced no concrete results, however. Congress spurned Reagan's tuition tax-credit proposal; and the vast majority of school officials, education advocacy groups and education policy experts continued to oppose vouchers through the 1980s.

Then at the end of the decade, two academics — Brookings Institution senior fellow John Chubb and Stanford University political scientist Terry Moe — breathed new life into the movement with their book, *Politics, Markets and America's Schools.* [20] They called for creation of a voucher-driven, competitive marketplace for ed-

ucation among public and private schools, including religious schools. Public-school bureaucracies would be replaced with "choice offices" and "parent information centers." Schools themselves would be minimally regulated and would be free to set their own admission policies subject only to non-discrimination requirements.

Chubb and Moe called the concerns about failing schools especially "grave" in inner cities and proposed higher stipends for students with "very special educational needs — arising from economic deprivation, physical handicaps, language difficulties, emotional problems and other disadvantages." [21] Apart from that proviso, however, Chubb and Moe presented their proposal as a universal reform, not one targeted at disadvantaged youngsters. But in the 1990s, school choice advocates discovered that targeting voucher proposals at low-income students was an effective strategy for moving the idea out of academic discussion and into the real world.

Voucher Experiments

V oucher proponents finally got a chance to test their theories in the 1990s in the two closely watched, sharply contested programs in Milwaukee and Cleveland. Both programs drew support from conservatives broadly critical of public education and African-Americans specifically disenchanted with inner-city public schools. Teachers' unions, civil rights groups and church-state separationists opposed both programs before they were established and — in court — afterward. Both sides looked to the Supreme Court for some word on the constitutional issues while girding for continuing fights regardless of how the court rules.

The prime mover for the Milwaukee voucher program was Polly Williams, a black Democratic state senator who

Chronology

Before 1950

"Common schools" become dominant pattern in U.S. education; private schools given constitutional protection but religiously affiliated systems struggle financially.

1884

U.S. Conference of Catholic Bishops calls for parochial schools in every parish, triggering unsuccessful congressional effort to bar government funds for religious schools.

1925

Supreme Court upholds parents' right to send children to private schools.

1950s–1970s

First stirrings of school voucher proposals, with limited effect; Catholic schools seek government funds as enrollment falls, but Supreme Court limits assistance by barring direct subsidies.

1955

Economist Milton Friedman publishes article calling for universal system of vouchers for parents to use to pay for children's education in public or private schools of their choice, but it has little immediate impact.

1973

Supreme Court bars direct government subsidies of parochial schools or tuition reimbursement or tax credits for parents of parochial-school students.

1980s *School choice movement gains strength.*

1983

U.S. Department of Education report, *A Nation at Risk*, damns public schools for "mediocre" education; public school advocates call report alarmist, undocumented.

1990s *Voucher programs established in Milwaukee, Cleveland; challenged in court with mixed results. Voters reject vouchers in several states.*

1990

Wisconsin legislature approves program to provide vouchers to low-income students in Milwaukee for use at non-religious schools; scholars John E. Chubb and Terry M. Moe detail proposal for universal voucher system in their book, *Politics, Markets and America's Schools.*

1995

Wisconsin legislature expands Milwaukee voucher program to allow parochial schools to participate; move brings court challenge based on separation of church and state.

1997

Supreme Court rules, 5-4, that school systems can provide federally funded remedial and enrichment services on the grounds of parochial schools.

1998

Wisconsin Supreme Court upholds constitutionality of Milwaukee voucher program in June; U.S. Supreme Court declines in November to review decision.

1999

Florida approves first statewide voucher program, providing stipends for students at schools that receive "failing" grade and do not improve performance after one year; Illinois approves tax credits for families for private-school tuition; Maine and Vermont supreme courts uphold exclusion of religious schools from public "tuitioning" programs; Cleveland federal judge rules voucher program unconstitutional, but Supreme Court allows program to continue, pending appeal.

2000s *Legal challenges to voucher programs continue; voters reject voucher proposals.*

June 28, 2000

U.S. Supreme Court upholds, 6-3, federally funded program to lend computers and other equipment to parochial schools; school choice advocates say opinions support constitutionality of vouchers.

Nov. 7, 2000

Voters in California, Michigan reject voucher proposals by 2-1 margins.

Dec. 11, 2000

Cleveland voucher program ruled unconstitutional by federal appeals court in Cincinnati by 2–1 vote.

Sept. 25, 2001

U.S. Supreme Court agrees to hear Cleveland voucher case; arguments heard Feb. 20, 2002.

June 27, 2002

U.S. Supreme Court upholds constitutionality of Ohio school voucher program.

Parochial Schools on the Move

New Catholic schools are going up in fast-growing suburbs and exurbs around the country, where they are attracting growing numbers of non-Catholic students. But total enrollment in Catholic schools has risen only slightly over the past decade, and Roman Catholic archdioceses are shuttering schools in many big cities that form their traditional base.

The modest growth over the past decade reverses a 40-year-long decline that saw Catholic school enrollment fall by half. The total number of schools has continued to decrease, however, and many of the remaining schools are struggling financially — often raising tuitions to come closer to covering their real costs. [1]

Despite the financial problems, Catholic educators present an upbeat picture of their system — which last year enrolled about 2.6 million students. Enrollment is increasing, they say, because Catholic schools offer a safe, quality education for inner-city families and a values-rich education for urban and suburban families alike.

"The state of many inner-city schools leads parents to want something a little more secure for their children," says Sister Glenn Anne McPhee, secretary for education of the U.S. Conference of Catholic Bishops in Washington.

Catholic schools are growing in the suburbs even though public school systems there are often regarded as providing a good education. "In suburban areas, parents are looking for more in the spiritual dimension of their children's education," says Sister Dale McDonald, director of public policy and research at the National Catholic Educational Association.

The parochial school system of today traces back to the decision by the bishops' conference in 1884 to call on every Catholic parish to establish a school. "Popular education has always been a chief object of the Church's care," the bishops declared in a pastoral letter. [2] In contrast to other Western countries, however, the United States has generally not provided direct funding for Catholic schools.

Despite the limited governmental support, Catholic school enrollment grew to more than 5 million by 1950. But a combination of factors caused enrollment to shrink drastically over the next 40 years. Catholics formed part of the population shift from city to suburb. Church attendance declined. And the number of nuns — who traditionally held most of the teaching positions — declined as fewer women entered religious orders.

By 1990, enrollment stood at around 2.5 million students. The number has increased about 2.7 percent since then, to 2,647,301 — including 2,004,037 elementary or middle-school students and 643,264 high school students. The figure includes about 358,000 non-Catholics, or nearly 14 percent of the total.

Hispanics comprise 11 percent of the total, and African-Americans about 8 percent; total minority enrollment is 26 percent.

With the nation's population shifts, new Catholic schools are going up in the suburbs and in the South and West: Some 54 new facilities were built last year. Out of 8,146 Catholic schools, nearly half — 44 percent — have waiting lists for admissions. But schools in inner cities are being closed or consolidated — 61 last year — usually because they are under capacity.

Catholic educators tout the academic benefits of parochial schools. John Witte, director of the University of Wisconsin's La Follette School of Public Affairs and formerly the official evaluator for Milwaukee's school voucher program, says research studies do document favorable results for Catholic schools.

For example, Catholic school students are less likely to drop out and more likely to go on to college and stay in college, Witte says. He also says that "the majority of studies" indicate some "achievement effects" in terms of higher test scores. But he adds that experts disagree whether those studies "have adequately controlled for selection into and expulsion from Catholic schools." [3]

Whatever the academic benefits, Catholic educators stress that religion is an integral part of the curriculum. "Our schools are still thoroughly Catholic," McPhee says. "Catholic values permeate all curriculum areas." McDonald, however, adds that the increased number of non-Catholics has made the schools "more inclusive."

Voucher proposals like those enacted in Milwaukee and Cleveland offer one source of financial support for Catholic schools, Catholic educators and officials acknowledge. But they insist that the church is committed to providing education in the inner city with or without vouchers.

"If there were no voucher program, we would continue to try to educate children in the same way," says Mark Chopko, general counsel of the bishops' conference. McPhee agrees: "The Catholic Church has made a commitment to remain in the inner city as a beacon of hope for many inner-city parents who want something that's not only safe but also very community-minded."

---

[1] See *United States Catholic Elementary and Secondary School Statistics, 2000-2001* (2001), www.ncea.org.

[2] Cited in Mark E. Chopko, "American and Catholic: Reflections on the Last Century in Catholic Church-State Relations." The paper will appear as a chapter in a forthcoming book on church-state relations being prepared by the DePaul University Center for Church/State Studies to be published by Carolina Academic Press in 2002.

[3] For background, see Anthony S. Bryk, Valerie E. Lee, and Peter B. Holland, *Catholic Schools and the Common Good* (1993).

---

began pushing the idea in the late 1980s to give black youngsters alternatives to the city's public schools. As approved by the Wisconsin legislature in 1990, the program provided vouchers up to $2,500 to a maximum of 950 low-income families to be used only at non-religious schools. Since then, the legislature has increased both the amount of the voucher and the number of participants, and opened the program in 1995 to participation by parochial schools. Today, voucher advocate Moe says the Milwaukee program was the first to show that vouchers could be "politically potent" when targeted solely at kids who need help the most." [22]

In Cleveland, the impetus for the voucher program came from a federal judge's March 1995 ruling in a school-desegregation suit, in which he ordered that the state take over the troubled city school system. The Ohio General Assembly responded in June by establishing a pilot voucher program in any school district subject to such a takeover order — effectively, only for Cleveland. The program provided up to 2,000 elementary-age students with vouchers worth up to $2,250 annually to attend any participating school. The schools had to limit their tuition for those students to $2,500. Low-income families had priority. Higher-income families were eligible for any unused vouchers, limited to $1,875, but with no cap on the participating schools' tuition.

Both programs drew swift legal challenges. In Milwaukee's case, a state trial court judge ruled in January 1997 that the expansion of the program to include parochial schools was unconstitutional. But the Wisconsin Supreme Court reversed that decision in June 1998, holding that the program did not violate church-state restrictions in either the state or U.S. constitutions. [23] Advocates on both sides of the issue looked to the U.S. Supreme Court to hear the opponents' appeal, but the justices in November 1998 declined to review the decision.

Opponents of the Cleveland program also filed their initial challenge in state court. A lower court judge found the program unconstitutional in July 1996. The Ohio Supreme Court gave opponents a temporary victory in May 1999 by ruling that the legislature had violated the state constitution's "single-subject" rule by including the program in an unrelated bill. [24] The legislature quickly fixed the problem, however. The Ohio justices also said that the program did not violate either the state or federal constitutions on religious grounds.

By the late 1990s, school choice advocates from coast to coast were pushing proposals for vouchers, tuition tax credits and privately run public schools known as charter schools. [25] Florida in 1999 became the first state to approve a statewide voucher program, but it was limited to students from schools that failed to meet state performance standards and then failed to improve a year afterward. It also provided vouchers for students with disabilities to attend a school of their choice.

In the same year, Illinois became the first state to give parents a direct tax credit for private-school tuition expenses. Two other states have tax-credit provisions for donations to groups providing scholarships to private schools: an individual tax credit in Arizona and a corporate credit in Pennsylvania.

On the other hand, school choice advocates failed in their efforts to get so-called tuitioning programs in Maine and Vermont opened up to participation by religious schools. Those programs give students in towns without a public high school vouchers to use at public or private schools elsewhere. The supreme courts in both states ruled in 1999 that religious schools could be excluded without improperly limiting parents' right to choose how to educate their children. [26] In addition, voters in six states defeated ballot initiatives to establish voucher programs — most notably in California, where voters in November 2000 defeated a proposal for universal $4,000 school vouchers by more than a 2-to-1 margin.

With the Supreme Court's refusal to consider the Milwaukee case, opposing camps looked to the Cleveland case as the most likely vehicle for settling the constitutionality question. Opponents moved into federal court following the Ohio Supreme Court's decision. In August 1999 — on the eve of a new school year — U.S. District Court Judge Solomon Oliver tentatively sustained the opponents' legal

challenge and issued a preliminary injunction against the program. School officials scurried to get a modification to allow students already receiving vouchers to continue at participating schools. Then in November the Supreme Court — dividing 5-4 along conservative-liberal lines — stayed the injunction, thus allowing the program to continue pending further legal proceedings.

A month later, Judge Oliver issued his final ruling, again holding that the program provided unconstitutional aid to religious schools. The federal appeals court agreed, in a 2-1 decision in December 2000. [27] While acknowledging that the program was neutral on its face, the appeals court majority said that in operation it promoted religion, primarily because the low tuitions that were permitted limited participation to Catholic schools.

In dissent, Judge James Ryan said the program passed constitutional muster. "Whether public funds find their way to a religious school is of no constitutional consequence," Ryan wrote, "if they get there as a result of genuinely private choice."

CURRENT SITUATION

Monitoring Programs

Ohio legislators established the Cleveland voucher program to give low-income students an alternative to what was seen as the city's failing public school system. But recent studies indicate that most of the 4,456 students currently using the vouchers have never attended Cleveland public schools.

In addition, the studies — by both a liberal-leaning research institute and

Supreme Court Takes Zig-Zag Course

Supreme Court decisions since 1930 have upheld some government programs providing aid to students attending religiously affiliated schools, but until recently the justices barred programs giving parochial schools direct subsidies. School choice advocates say the court's most recent decisions appear to support private-school vouchers, but opponents disagree.

Case	How the Court Voted
Cochran v. Louisiana Board of Education, 281 U.S. 370 (1930) Upholds providing textbooks to students at parochial and other schools.	9-0
Everson v. Board of Education of Ewing, 330 U.S. 1 (1947) Upholds New Jersey law providing reimbursement to parents for the cost of public transportation for students attending parochial and other non-public schools.	5-4
Board of Education of Central School District No. 1 v. Allen, 392 U.S. 236 (1968) Upholds New York state textbook-loan program for parochial and other non-public schools.	6-3
Lemon v. Kurtzman, 403 U.S. 602 (1971) Invalidates two "direct aid" statutes: Rhode Island law supplementing teacher salaries at non-public schools and Pennsylvania law reimbursing non-public schools for teacher salaries, textbooks and instructional materials. "Lemon test" bars aid to religious institutions unless it has a secular purpose, does not advance or inhibit religion and does not result in excessive governmental entanglement with religion.	9-0
Tilton v. Richardson, 403 U.S. 672 (1971) Upholds federal construction grants to church-affiliated colleges.	5-4
Levitt v. Committee for Public Education and Religious Liberty, 413 U.S. 472 (1973) Nullifies New York law providing per-capita payments to non-public schools for state-mandated testing and record keeping.	8-1
Hunt v. McNair, 413 U.S. 734 (1973) Upholds South Carolina law authorizing bonds for construction of secular facilities at church-affiliated or nonsectarian colleges and universities.	6-3
Committee for Public Education and Religious Liberty v. Nyquist, 413 U.S. 756 (1973) Invalidates New York "parochaid" statute providing maintenance and repair grants to non-public schools (9-0) and tuition reimbursement or tax credits for parents of students at non-public schools (7-2).	9-0, 7-2
Meek v. Pittinger, 421 U.S. 349 (1975) Upholds, 6-3, Pennsylvania law authorizing textbook loans for non-public schools, but strikes, by different 6-3 vote, loans of instructional materials and equipment.	6-3, 6-3

a reform-minded education newsletter — show that African-Americans are underrepresented among the participants, compared with their enrollment in the city's school system, and that a whopping 99.4 percent of the voucher students are attending religious schools. Only 25 Cleveland voucher recipients attend secular schools.

Critics say the newest information shows that the program has failed to meet the goals established by supporters to sell the idea to Ohio legislators. "If the goal of the program was to get students to leave the failing Cleveland public schools, the program has not achieved any of its aims," says Michael Charney, professional-issues director of the Cleveland Teachers Union. "And if the goal was to create competition and to give par-

Case	How the Court Voted
Roemer v. Maryland Board of Public Works, 426 U.S. 736 (1976) *Upholds program of general annual grants to private colleges, including church-related schools.*	**5-4**
Wolman v. Walter, 433 U.S. 229 (1977) *Upholds, 6-3, Ohio law providing non-public schools with textbooks and standardized testing and scoring, but strikes, 5-4, aid for instructional material, equipment and field trips.*	**6-3, 5-4**
Committee for Public Education and Religious Liberty v. Regan, 444 U.S. 646 (1980) *Upholds New York law reimbursing non-public schools for cost of administering, grading and reporting results of standardized tests.*	**5-4**
Mueller v. Allen, 463 U.S. 388 (1983) *Upholds Minnesota tax deduction for parents of children in public or private schools for tuition, textbooks or transportation.*	**5-4**
School District of Grand Rapids v. Ball, 473 U.S. 373 (1985) *Bars Grand Rapids, Mich., program reimbursing parochial schools for remedial and enrichment classes during school day (7-2) or after hours (5-4).*	**7-2, 5-4**
Aguilar v. Felton, 473 U.S. 402 (1985) *Bars New York City system from providing remedial and counseling services to disadvantaged students in non-public schools.*	**5-4**
Witters v. Washington Dept. of Services for the Blind, 474 U.S. 481 (1986) *Allows use of federal funds to aid blind seminary student.*	**9-0**
Zobrest v. Catalina Foothills School District, 509 U.S. 1 (1993) *Allows government to pay for sign-language interpreter to accompany deaf student to parochial school.*	**5-4**
Agostini v. Felton, 521 U.S. 203 (1997) *Allows New York City to use federal funds to provide remedial services to disadvantaged children on site at non-public schools; overrules Aguilar v. Felton.*	**5-4**
Mitchell v. Helms, 530 U.S. 793 (2000) *Upholds federally funded program lending computers and other instructional equipment to religious and other private schools. Four justices vote to uphold any neutral, secular aid program; Justices O'Connor and Breyer concur on narrower ground.*	**6-3**
Zelman v. Simmons-Harris, - U.S. - (2002) *Upholds constitutionality of Ohio law providing tuition vouchers for parents of students in Cleveland school system to use at participating schools.*	**5-4**

Sources: Joan Biskupic and Elder Witt, Guide to the U.S. Supreme Court (3d. ed.), 1997, pp. 490-498; Kenneth Jost, Supreme Court Yearbook 1996-1997, 1997, pp. 54-57; Supreme Court Yearbook, 1999-2000, 2000, pp. 63-66.

ents real choice, then the program has failed, because it doesn't include any of the elite private schools, [even as] it transfers $6 million to $8 million per year [away from] disadvantaged students in the Cleveland public school system."

However, Charney notes wryly, "If the goal of the program was to subsidize an economically failing parochial-school system, then it's succeeding."

Supporters, however, see it differently. "I think it's working wonderfully," says Rosa-Linda Demore-Brown, ex-

ecutive director of Cleveland Parents for School Choice. "The proof is in the testing, the parent level of satisfaction and the children. The children are very happy, doing very well."

Demore-Brown — mother of two grown children who attended both public and private schools — interprets test scores to show that voucher students are progressing academically and matching comparable public-school students. She blames the high proportion of students attending religious schools on the failure of elite private schools or suburban public schools to participate. "It's not that parents are looking to send their children to a religious school," she says.

A bare majority of Cleveland's voucher students — 53 percent — are African-American, according to a recent analysis by the education newsletter *Catalyst*. By comparison, African-Americans comprised 71 percent of the Cleveland public-school system's students. [28] But Demore-Brown, who is African-American, discounted the significance of the gap. "There are still more African-American children [than whites] receiving vouchers," she says.

Information about the percentage of voucher students who previously attended public schools comes from a report published in September by the liberal-leaning research institute Policy Matters Ohio. It shows that 21 percent of current voucher students previously attended Cleveland public schools while 33 percent had gone to private schools in the city. Most of the remaining 46 percent were entering kindergarten, but 6 percent of those had been attending preschool programs at private schools. [29]

Zach Schiller, the senior researcher who wrote the report, says it shows the voucher program "hasn't done what its proponents claimed." The program "has served students already going to private schools more than those who were attending public schools," he says. The organization also published the study in January showing the continuing rise in the percentage of voucher students attending religious schools. [30]

A separate analysis by *Catalyst* shows that the 10 Cleveland public schools that lost 17 or more students to vouchers over the last five years have test

scores somewhat higher than the district's overall average. In addition, 24 percent of the students at the 10 schools passed the Ohio Proficiency Test, compared with 16 percent for the district overall. [31]

Information about the Milwaukee program is less definitive because of the Wisconsin legislature's decision in 1995 to drop reporting and testing requirements for participating schools. The Roman Catholic archdiocese favored lifting the requirements, ostensibly to avoid government entanglement. But the University of Wisconsin's Witte believes voucher supporters wanted to reduce accountability. "I think the pro-voucher people didn't want anything that looked negative," he says.

In its latest report on the program, the legislature's auditing arm — the Wisconsin Legislative Audit Bureau — estimated that 70 percent of the voucher students were attending religious schools. About 62 percent of the voucher students were African-Americans, compared with 61 percent of the overall Milwaukee public school enrollment. [32]

The audit bureau's report notes that the so-called choice schools are not required to administer standardized tests. Nine of the 86 schools participating in the 1998–99 school year lacked accreditation and administered no standardized tests, the bureau found. It also noted that the state's Department of Public Instruction was investigating a complaint that 17 schools had violated program requirements, including rules requiring random admissions, prohibiting fees and requiring schools to allow pupils to opt out of religious activities. The complaint — filed by People for the American Way and the NAACP — is now in mediation.

"No one knows how [the Milwaukee program] is working because for the last six years there has been no data collected on the students participating in the voucher program," says Barbara Miner, managing editor of an education reform newsletter, *Rethink-*

ing Schools. "It's incredibly significant that we have no clue about how these kids in the voucher programs are performing academically." [33]

Aiding Religion?

Regardless of students' test scores, Cleveland's voucher program was decided in the Supreme Court over a different question: whether it impermissibly supported religious education. Opponents found the program so "heavily skewed toward religion" that it violated the Establishment Clause, while Ohio state officials and pro-voucher allies insisted the program was "religiously neutral."

Opponents said the relatively small size of the voucher — a maximum $2,250 — inevitably steered students to religious education because only low-tuition parochial schools were willing to participate. "The great majority of voucher program parents must send their children to sectarian private schools providing a religious education in order to obtain the benefits that the program offers," NEA lawyer Chanin wrote in his brief to the Supreme Court.

To the contrary, the Ohio attorney general's office argued, "[N]o social coercion or financial incentives influence parents toward selection of religious, as opposed to secular, schooling." Indeed, the state lawyers noted, voucher parents must pay at least 10 percent of the cost of any private education — creating a disincentive to leave the public schools. In his brief, the Institute for Justice's Bolick — representing Suma and other families receiving vouchers — argued that more secular schools will participate eventually, once legal challenges are resolved.

The law allows Cleveland students to use the vouchers at public schools outside the city, but none of the adjoining, suburban districts has ever agreed to participate. The size of the

At Issue

Will school vouchers help students from low-income families?

BOYCE W. SLAYMAN
VICE PRESIDENT
BLACK ALLIANCE FOR EDUCATIONAL OPTIONS

WRITTEN FOR THE CQ RESEARCHER, FEBRUARY 2002

*t*hinking people cannot ignore the mounting evidence that our knowledge-based economy is at long-term risk because of chronic shortages of high-skilled workers. Enlightened thinkers should also appreciate that our society cannot remain vibrantly democratic without effective education of the general population.

How will we ensure that our children receive the quality K-12 education that is critically necessary to reach a middle-class standard of living and otherwise thrive in the 21st century?

Given the continued failure of many urban public school systems to deliver quality education, parents want alternatives. Those with means can find them by moving or putting their children in private school. Those without means are trapped unless they can access resources to do the same.

Educational "choice" is about equalizing the playing field for low-income families. And the choices should include vouchers.

The Black Alliance for Educational Options actively supports parental choice to empower families and increase educational options for black children. We support choice because we see far too many low-income black children failing to realize their or their parents' aspirations for them within the current system. We believe that keeping the promise of educational opportunity for all requires turning away from 18th-century educational models and toward solutions that will work in a global, knowledge-based economy.

The debate about the desirability of school vouchers is over. Study after study — including both liberal and conservative research — shows that the majority of Americans support school vouchers and that African-American support is stronger than that of all other demographics. This is no accident of demography; it is a reality of geography. These are the parents of students trapped in largely urban and failing public school systems. They want better educational outcomes. They need choices.

No other domestic issue provokes such strong emotional responses, or is as important to the future of the republic, or creates such weird politics as educational choice. Yet, school choice, vouchers included, should not be viewed as a "left vs. right" issue. At its core, educational choice is a social- and economic-justice issue that is caught up in a very unproductive political maelstrom.

Without a strong education, our children will not have a real chance to engage in the practice of freedom and the process of transforming their world.

THEODORE M. SHAW
ASSOCIATE DIRECTOR-COUNSEL
NAACP LEGAL DEFENSE AND EDUCATIONAL FUND

WRITTEN FOR THE CQ RESEARCHER, FEBRUARY 2002

*f*rustrated with the failure of public school systems nationwide to provide quality education, some African-Americans have joined the voucher movement in seeking public subsidies for private-school tuition. The voucher movement is traditionally the terrain of white conservatives, including those who have abandoned public schools to escape racial desegregation and those who advocate public support for religiously sectarian education.

The U.S. Supreme Court currently is considering a Cleveland case in which two lower courts invalidated Ohio's voucher program. In that case, *Zelman v. Simmons-Harris*, the Institute for Justice, a conservative legal organization that cut its teeth opposing school desegregation and affirmative action, represents a group of black parents who support vouchers. Their brief asserts that voucher programs are necessary to fulfill *Brown v. Board of Education's* promise of "equal educational opportunity for all."

Putting aside the cynical manipulation of black parents' frustration with the failures of public schools, the voucher issue taps deep sensitivities. *Brown* held out the promise of equal educational opportunity. However, it was primarily about school desegregation and addressed quality education only to the extent that it was denied as a consequence of segregation. Almost 50 years after *Brown*, vast numbers of African-American children are still trapped in racially isolated and educationally failing schools.

The appeal of vouchers is understandable. All responsible parents do what they can to provide their children the best possible education. On a systemic level, however, vouchers are a disaster. Voucher programs signal the further abandonment of public schools; more practically, they skim badly needed financial resources and the most motivated and able students. Vouchers will further exacerbate the differences between private and public schools, which will continue to enroll the overwhelming majority of African-American students.

As the Cleveland case demonstrates, voucher programs usually serve white students — many of whom are already enrolled in private schools — in greater proportion than black students. Most voucher programs do not provide enough money to pay private-school tuition. Thus, their promise as a solution for the problems of black children is illusory.

Nothing short of a massive commitment to public schools by legislatures and policy-makers, reflected in money and reform, will produce equal educational opportunity for all.

voucher is cited as one deterrent to the suburban districts, but Bolick sees another motive. "Suburban schools do not want inner-city kids coming out to their schools," he says. "I don't think that's a noble explanation, but it's the world where we operate, sadly."

In their briefs, the opposing lawyers tried to fit the facts of the Cleveland case into differing Supreme Court precedents. Opponents relied principally on a 1973 decision, *Committee for Public Education and Religious Liberty v. Nyquist*, which struck down a New York "parochaid" law providing direct grants to religious schools. They said the voucher funds received by parochial schools in Cleveland amount to "direct unrestricted government payments" akin to those ruled unconstitutional in *Nyquist*.

Voucher supporters cited more recent Supreme Court decisions that uphold general government programs that provide assistance to students in religious or secular private schools. In 1993, for example, the court upheld the use of taxpayer funds to pay for an interpreter for a deaf student attending a religious high school. Most recently, the court in 1997 and 2000 upheld federally funded programs that provide remedial or enrichment services for disadvantaged students attending secular or religious private schools or allow local school districts to lend private schools computers and other equipment. As in those programs, voucher supporters argued, religious and secular schools are eligible for the Cleveland program because the funds go to religious schools only after "true, independent choice" by parents, not the government.

The case attracted an unusually large number of friend-of-the-court briefs on both sides. Lawyers representing the plaintiffs included attorneys from the NEA, the American Civil Liberties Union, People for the American Way and Americans United for Separation of Church and State. The

dozen or so friend-of-the-court briefs on their side came from education groups, such as the National School Boards Association, the NAACP Legal Defense Fund and the American Jewish Committee.

Voucher supporters drew more than 30 briefs from organizations or individuals, including conservative advocacy groups such as the American Center for Law and Justice, religious organizations such as the U.S. Conference of Catholic Bishops, and the Black Alliance for Educational Options. A group of 30, mostly conservative, constitutional law professors also urged the court to uphold the program.

The Bush administration weighed in, arguing to uphold the voucher program. In a brief filed by Solicitor General Theodore Olson, the government said the program "fits comfortably within [the] framework" of Supreme Court decisions allowing aid that benefits religious schools if it results from "genuinely independent and private choices of aid recipients."

O'Connor Seen as Key Vote

In recent cases, the court has been divided roughly along conservative-liberal lines on church-state separation issues. Chief Justice William Rehnquist and three fellow conservatives — Justices Antonin Scalia, Anthony Kennedy and Clarence Thomas — argued in the most recent case, *Mitchell v. Helms*, that any general government aid program operated on religiously neutral principles could pass constitutional muster under the Establishment Clause. Three liberal justices — John Paul Stevens, David Souter and Ruth Bader Ginsburg — said they would have ruled the computer loan program in question unconstitutional.

In the pivotal opinion, the centrist conservative Justice Sandra Day O'Connor voted to uphold the computer loan program but declined to join Thomas' broader opinion. O'Connor said the program did not have "the impermissible

effect of advancing" or endorsing religion, but she said "neutrality" was not a sufficient criterion for upholding the program. In rejecting any impermissible endorsement of religion, O'Connor said there was "significant" difference between a per-capita student aid program and "a true private-choice program." Justice Stephen Breyer, who usually votes with the liberals on church-state issues, joined O'Connor's opinion.

Lawyers on both sides agreed that O'Connor held the key to the Cleveland case. "There is no question that on Establishment Clause issues O'Connor has been the key vote," Bolick says. In their briefs, supporters of the Cleveland vouchers argued that it fits O'Connor's definition of a "true private-choice program."

Voucher opponents insisted, however, that the Cleveland program was more like the direct-aid programs prohibited under older Supreme Court decisions. "If the court rules consistently with the past, it will be unconstitutional," said Ralph Neas, president of People for the American Way, before the ruling. "But this is a very closely divided court right now."

OUTLOOK

Waiting for the Court

Five decades after his ground-breaking proposal for school vouchers, economist Friedman takes only scant satisfaction from the limited voucher programs enacted so far. "I have been much more optimistic than has been justified," Friedman told *Education Week* late last year. [34]

Friedman, now 89, contrasts his call for a universal system of vouchers to the programs enacted so far, which are targeted to low-income families. "A program for the poor will be a poor program," he said. "All parents should have the same choice."

Voucher proponents say the limited scope of the existing programs is a calculated strategy that bows to political realities. "It is very, very difficult for us to defeat the parade of hypotheticals that are raised against school choice programs," the Institute for Justice's Bolick says, referring to the string of unsuccessful school choice ballot measures. "It's better to get small programs started either through the legislatures or through private philanthropy and grow them through there."

However, opponents say voucher programs are small and few in number because the public does not really support them. "The public has spoken forcefully against vouchers in general," says Sandra Feldman, president of the American Federation of Teachers. Polls "make clear their preference for investing in public schools" rather than instituting vouchers, she says.

Voucher opponents think the Supreme Court decision to strike down the Cleveland program will be a decisive setback for supporters of the idea. "There will be no large-scale programs because you can't have a large program without sectarian schools," NEA lawyer Chanin says. However, since the court upheld the program, opponents will continue to fight them politically. "It won't change how the public feels," he says.

For their part, voucher supporters were confident of victory. "We designed a program to survive Supreme Court scrutiny," Bolick says. A ruling to uphold the program would "create tremendous momentum" for similar programs, he says. "School choice is one of the issues in which constitutional objections are often raised in the legislative process. A positive decision would remove a major obstacle."

Bolick says more voucher programs would promote the goal of equalizing educational opportunities regardless of income or race. "It would help vindi-cate the promise of *Brown v. Board of Education*," he says, referring to the Supreme Court's landmark 1954 decision outlawing racial segregation.

Arizona State University's Molnar disagrees. Expanded voucher programs, he says, will result in "a further exacerbation of the inequities that already exist in state-run educational systems."

Voucher opponents also say the programs will hamper other, more productive efforts to improve U.S. schools. "We do that by investing in schools, not by abandoning them," Feldman says.

But Hoxby, the Harvard economist, says voucher programs will stimulate needed changes. "If you really want public schools to be good, you want to have some forces that put some pressure on them to be good," she says.

In Cleveland, opponents concede that they cannot defeat the program except in court. "It's not a major issue in Cleveland," Charney of the local teachers' union says.

But Simmons-Harris, the parent plaintiff, still insists the program is bad for the schools. "Vouchers will take away from public schools," she says. "You're taking away from the masses for just the few."

School choice advocate Demore-Brown counters that voucher programs can be good for all students. "This is a win-win for everyone if they would just look at the total big picture," she says. "The bottom line is that these children we are educating today will run the country tomorrow. Everyone should be saying, 'Let's get these children educated and get this done right.'"

Notes

[1] For background, see Kathy Koch, "School Vouchers," *The CQ Researcher*, April 9, 1999, pp. 281-304; David Masci, "School Choice Debate," *The CQ Researcher*, July 18, 1997, pp. 625-648.

[2] See Kenneth Jost, *Supreme Court Yearbook, 1999-2000* (2000), pp. 61-66. For background, see Patrick Marshall, "Religion in Schools," *The CQ Researcher*, Jan. 12, 2001, pp. 1-24.

[3] "The 33rd Annual Phi Delta Kappa/Gallup Poll of the Public's Attitudes Toward the Public Schools," Phi Delta Kappan (September 2001), pp. 44-45, http://www.pdkintl.org/kappan/kimages/kpoll83.pdf. The telephone sample of 1,108 adults was conducted May 23-June 6, 2001.

[4] The annual evaluations are at www.indiana.edu/~iuice.

[5] See John F. Witte, *The Market Approach to Education: An Analysis of America's First Voucher Program* (2000), pp. 119-143; Jay P. Greene, Paul E. Peterson, and Jiangtao Du, "Effectiveness of School Choice: The Milwaukee Experiment," Program in Education Policy and Governance, John F. Kennedy School of Government, Harvard University (March 1997), www.ksg.harvard.edu/pepg; Cecilia Elena Rouse, "Schools and Student Achievement: More Evidence from the Milwaukee Parental Choice Program," Industrial Relations Section, Princeton University (January 1998); "Private School Vouchers and Student Achievement: An Evaluation of the Milwaukee Parental Choice Program," Princeton University (December 1996), www.irs.princeton.edu/pubs.

[6] William G. Howell, Patrick J. Wolf, Paul E. Peterson and David E. Campbell, "Test-Score Effects of School Vouchers in Dayton, Ohio, New York City, and Washington, D.C.: Evidence from Randomized Field Trials," Program on Education Policy and Governance, John F. Kennedy School of Government, Harvard University (August 2000), http://data.fas.harvard.edu/pepg.

[7] Brian P. Gill *et al.*, *Rhetoric Versus Reality: What We Know and What We Need to Know About Vouchers and Charter Schools* (2001), p. xvi.

[8] General Accounting Office, "School Vouchers: Publicly Funded Programs in Cleveland and Milwaukee" (August 2001), pp. 27-31.

[9] Caroline M. Hoxby, "How School Choice Affects the Achievement of Public School Students," paper presented at Hoover Institution, Stanford, Calif., Sept. 20-21, 2001 (http://post.economics.harvard.edu/faculty/hoxby/papers.html).

[10] See Jay P. Greene, "An Evaluation of the Florida A-Plus Accountability and School Choice Program," Manhattan Institute (2001), www.manhattan-institute.org; Gregory Camilli and Katrina Bulkley, "Critique of 'An Evaluation of the Florida A-Plus Accountability and School Choice Program,'" Education Policy Analysis Archives (March 4, 2001), www.epaa.asu.edu.

[11] Some background drawn from "Public Education in the United States" and "Private Education in the United States," *Encarta* (http://Encarta.msn.com) (visited January 2002).

[12] For background, see Lawrence A. Cremin, *The American Common School: An Historic Conception* (1951).

[13] *Ibid.*, pp. 191-203.

[14] Richard J. Gabel, *Public Funds for Church and Private Schools* (1937), pp. 351-361.

[15] *Ibid.*, pp. 523-525.

[16] The case is *Pierce v. Society of Sisters*, 268 U.S. 510 (1925).

[17] Some background drawn from Charles S. Clark, "Friends and Foes of Vouchers Envision Salvation for Poor and Tax Breaks for Rich," *The CQ Researcher*, July 26, 1996, pp. 662-663.

[18] Milton Friedman, "The Role of Government in Education," in Robert A. Solo (ed.), *Economics and the Public Interest* (1955), pp. 123-145.

[19] Christopher Jencks, "Is the Public School Obsolete?" *The Public Interest* (winter 1966), pp. 18-27.

[20] John E. Chubb and Terry M. Moe, *Politics, Markets, and America's Schools* (1990). See Richard L. Worsnop, "Brookings Book Sparks Debate Over Choice Plans," *The CQ Researcher*, May 10, 1991, p. 265.

[21] Chubb & Moe, *op. cit.*, p. 220.

[22] Terry M. Moe, *Schools, Vouchers, and the American Public* (2001), pp. 371-372.

[23] *Jackson v. Benson*, 578 N.W.2d 602 (Wis. 1998).

[24] For detailed state-by-state information from a pro-school choice organization, see Robert E. Moffit *et al.*, "School Choice 2001: What's Happening in the States," Heritage Foundation, 2001 (www.heritage.org/school).

[25] *Simmons-Harris v. Goff*, 711 N.E.2d 203 (Ohio 1999).

[26] The cases are *Bagley v. Raymond School Department*, Maine Supreme Court, April 23, 1999; *Chittenden Town School District v. Vermont Department of Education*, Vermont Supreme Court, June 11, 1999.

[27] *Simmons-Harris v. Zelman*, 234 F.3d 945 (CA6 2000)

FOR MORE INFORMATION

American Federation of Teachers, 555 New Jersey Ave., N.W., Washington, D.C. 2001; (202) 879-4400; www.aft.org. The country's second-largest teachers' union and its local affiliate, the Cleveland Teachers' Union, have both strongly opposed the Cleveland voucher plan.

Americans United for Separation of Church and State, 518 C St., N.E., Washington, D.C. 20002; (202) 466-3234; www.au.org. The church-state separationist group is part of the coalition legally challenging the Cleveland voucher program.

Black Alliance for Educational Options, 1710 Rhode Island Ave., N.W., Suite 200, Washington, D.C. 20036; (202) 544-9870; www.baeo.org/home/index.php. The two-year-old organization supports school vouchers.

Institute for Justice, 1717 Pennsylvania Ave., N.W., Suite 200, Washington, D.C. 20006; (202) 955-1300; www.ij.org. The libertarian public interest law firm has taken the lead role in the school choice movement, including lobbying and litigation on behalf of vouchers.

NAACP Legal Defense and Educational Fund, Inc., 99 Hudson St., 16th Floor, New York, N.Y. 10013; (212) 965-2200; and 1444 I St., N.W., Washington, D.C. 20005; (202) 682-1300; www.naacpldf.org. The longtime civil rights organization opposes vouchers.

National Education Association, 1201 16th St., N.W., Washington, D.C. 20036; (202) 833-4000; www.nea.org. The country's largest teachers' union has strongly opposed school vouchers and is part of the coalition that brought the challenge to the Cleveland program.

U.S. Conference of Catholic Bishops, 3211 4th St., N.E., Washington, D.C. 20017; (202) 541-3300; www.nccbuscc.org. The conference supports school vouchers; it also superintends the Catholic school system in the United States.

[28] Piet van Lier and Caitlin Scott, "Fewer choices, longer commutes for black voucher students," *Catalyst* (December 2001/January 2002) www.catalyst-cleveland.org. The newsletter, published six times a year, was founded in 1999; funders include the Cleveland Foundation, the George Gund Foundation and the Joyce Foundation.

[29] Zach Schiller, "Cleveland School Vouchers: Where the Students Come From," Policy Matters Ohio (September 2001), www.policymattersohio.org.

[30] Amy Hanauer, "Cleveland School Vouchers: Where the Students Go," *Policy Matters Ohio* (January 2002), *Ibid.* The study was

based on an earlier figure for the total number of voucher students: 4,202.

[31] Caitlin Scott, "Better district schools lose students to vouchers," *Catalyst* (December 2001/January 2002), www.catalyst-cleveland.org.

[32] "Milwaukee Parental Choice Program," Wisconsin Legislative Audit Bureau (February 2000), www.legis.state.wi.us.

[33] See www.rethinkingschool.org. The newsletter, now published on line, was founded by Milwaukee-area teachers in 1986.

[34] Mark Walsh, "Friedman Disappointed That Voucher Plans Aren't Bolder," *Education Week*, Dec. 12, 2001 (www.edweek.org).

Bibliography

Selected Sources

Books

Byrk, Anthony S., Valerie E. Lee and Peter B. Holland, *Catholic Schools and the Common Good*, Harvard University Press, 1993.

The authors trace the history of Catholic schools in the United States and detail largely positive research findings about their impact on student academic achievement and other outcomes. The book includes detailed source notes and a 14-page list of references. Byrk is a professor at the University of Chicago, Lee at the University of Michigan in Ann Arbor; Holland is superintendent of schools, Lexington, Mass.

Fuller, Bruce, and Richard F. Elmore, with Gary Orfield (eds.), *Who Chooses? Who Loses? Culture, Institutions, and the Unequal Effects of School Choice*, Teachers College Press, 1996.

The nine essays in this collection are by educational-policy experts representing a range of views on school choice. In their conclusion, co-editors Fuller and Elmore say school choice "may produce useful innovations in previously unresponsive systems" but also "seems to increase the social disparities between those who choose and those who do not." Fuller is a professor at the University of California-Berkeley School of Education and a coauthor of a more recent, critical paper, "School Choice: Abundant Hopes, Scarce Evidence of Results" (Policy Analysis for California Education, 1999); Elmore is a professor at Harvard's School of Education.

Moe, Terry M., *Schools, Vouchers, and the American Public*, Brookings, 2001.

The book, based in part on a national opinion survey, views vouchers as a growing — and increasingly popular — challenge to the traditional U.S. system of education. Includes extensive statistics, reference notes. Moe, a professor at Stanford University and fellow at the Hoover Institution, was coauthor with John E. Chubb of Politics, Markets and America's Schools (Brookings, 1990).

Peterson, Paul E., and Bryan C. Hassel (eds.), *Learning From School Choice*, Brookings, 1998.

Sixteen papers by pro-school choice authors cover voucher, charter school and public school choice programs. Includes tabular material, chapter notes. Peterson is director of Harvard's Program on Education Policy and Governance; Hassel is an education and policy consultant in Charlotte, N.C.

Viteritti, Joseph P., *Choosing Equality: School Choice, the Constitution, and Civil Society*, Brookings, 1999.

A professor at New York University argues that school choice can be a tool for promoting equal educational opportunity. Includes extensive chapter notes.

Witte, John F., *The Market Approach to Education: An Analysis of America's First Voucher Program*, Princeton University Press, 2000.

Witte examines Milwaukee's voucher program during its first five years — before the program was expanded to allow religious schools to participate. Witte, director of the La Follette School of Public Affairs at the University of Wisconsin-Madison, was the official evaluator of the voucher program during the period. Includes extensive tabular material and an eight-page list of references.

Reports and Studies

Gill, Brian P., P. Michael Timpane, Karen E. Ross and Dominic J. Brewer, *Rhetoric vs. Reality: What We Know and What We Need to Know About Vouchers and Charter Schools*, Rand 2001 (www.rand.org/publications).

The book-length study reviews the theoretical foundations for school vouchers and charter schools and the empirical evidence for their effectiveness. Includes source notes, 32-page list of references. Gill is a researcher in the Rand Corporation's Pittsburgh office.

Moffit, Robert E., Jennifer J. Garrett and Janice A. Smith, *School Choice 2001: What's Happening in the States*, Heritage Foundation, 2001 (www.heritage.org/schools).

The pro-choice think tank provides detailed information on public and private school choice programs in each of the 50 states, the District of Columbia and Puerto Rico. Includes appendix with list of national pro-choice organizations.

"The 33rd Annual Phi Delta Kappa/Gallup Poll of the Public's Attitudes Toward the Public Schools," *Phi Delta Kappan* (September 2001), pp. 41-58, http://www.pdkintl.org/kappan/kimages/kpoll83.pdf.

The telephone sample of 1,108 adults was conducted May 23-June 6, 2001. The 18-page report by the international education fraternity and the well-known polling organization covers public opinion on a range of education issues, including school vouchers and charter schools

U.S. General Accounting Office, "School Vouchers: Publicly Funded Programs in Cleveland and Milwaukee," August 2001 (GAO 01-914; www.gao.gov).

The 50-page report provides an objective overview of the operation of the Cleveland and Milwaukee voucher programs and the various studies of the programs' effectiveness. Includes three-page listing of studies.

12 Faith-Based Initiatives

SARAH GLAZER

J ohn Reese says he has finally kicked his 12-year cocaine habit. For that he thanks Teen Challenge, a Christian rehab program, the only one of the five treatment programs he tried that worked for him. The others, including Alcoholics Anonymous, failed to make an impact, according to Reese, 38, because they "aimed at the head but not the heart."

He credits the program with saving his marriage and ending the cycle of crimes he committed to feed his habit. Drug-free since last December, he works as a maintenance assistant at the Teen Challenge program in Brooklyn, N.Y., and is studying for the ministry.

"Until I came to terms with sin in my life, I would continually relapse," Reese says. Although he was not particularly religious before entering Teen Challenge, Reese, like other successful graduates, attributes the program's success to "the Jesus factor."

President Bush has praised Teen Challenge as an example of the religious groups he wants to make eligible for federal funding as part of his new faith-based initiative. Arguing that religious groups may be more successful than government bureaucracies in tackling intractable social problems, Bush has initiated a multipronged effort to allow churches and other faith-based groups to apply for federal grants to deliver a wide range of social services. [1]

But many questions have been raised about Teen Challenge, and many go to the heart of Bush's initiative:

From *The CQ Researcher,* May 4, 2001.

The Salvation Army mixes a Christian message with its wide array of community services. It has received federal funds since its founding in the late 19th century as a missionary group.

Should programs like Teen Challenge, which rely entirely on religious instructors rather than trained addiction counselors, receive taxpayers' dollars? And will the funding of Christian programs deprive social-service recipients of nonreligious alternatives? (*See story, p. 224.*)

Then there's the ultimate constitutional conundrum: If the "Jesus factor" is what works, how can the government support the program without violating the constitutional prohibition against promoting an individual group's religion?

Civil libertarians argue that any program that insists on acceptance of Christianity as part of its treatment, like Teen Challenge, should be barred from government support. The First Amendment is supposed to prevent the government from favoring one religion over another, says Rep. Robert C. Scott, D-Va., a leading opponent of Bush's initiative. "Which religious groups

should get federal money to convert people to their religion?" he asks.

Scott envisions a new form of religious pork barrel as different faiths jockey for federal funds and for local politicians' favor. "Who gets to feed at the public trough?" he asks. "You're talking about billions of dollars."

Until 1996, religious groups couldn't receive federal money unless they either set up a secular arm to deliver government-funded services or delivered secular services separately from their religious mission. But the little-noticed "charitable choice" provision of the 1996 Welfare Reform Act and three other laws signed by President Bill Clinton lowered the traditional wall between church and state. [2] Authored by then-Sen. John Ashcroft, R-Mo., now U.S. attorney general, charitable choice permits religious groups to apply directly for federal funds for welfare-to-work and drug treatment programs. However, such groups may not use federal funds for worship, conversion or religious instruction.

Concerned about the constitutional questions, the Clinton administration did little to promote the participation of religious groups. [3] By contrast, the budget proposed by the Bush White House would expand the types of social-service programs covered to include mentoring prisoners' children, helping fathers leave welfare and providing shelter for teen mothers.

The Bush administration is also supporting a House Republican bill to open nine additional programs — including juvenile delinquency prevention programs, senior citizens programs and housing grants — to direct bidding from religious groups. Because of its wide scope, the legislation will have to win the approval of numerous committees before reaching the floor, and the timetable for floor action is uncertain.

The new chief of the White House Office of Faith-Based and Community Initiatives, John J. DiIulio Jr., argues that the government's traditional reliance on secular, nonprofit organizations to carry out its social service agenda has failed.

"We have myriad programs for after-school literacy, and yet we have millions of children going through those programs and little evidence anyone ends up reading at or near grade level," he says. "We have spent scores of billions on housing rehab programs, and a third of the housing stock remains falling down. We have welfare-to-work programs that often succeed in getting none of their clients into long-term, living-wage jobs."

African-American and Latino churches are often the only local institutions in inner-city neighborhoods providing essential services like day care or job training, argues DiIulio, who became a champion of several inner-city ministers while studying their work as a social scientist at the University of Pennsylvania. He contrasts their holistic work with government programs that deal with disadvantaged youths one problem at a time — truancy, criminal violations, learning problems.

"The kid is a soul, a spirit, a body, an emotional self and a lived self," DiIulio says. "And the difference [in a faith-based organization] is the kid is a whole person, and the people providing the services are there so they can hook up with probation and the school and follow the kid through."

A recent poll illustrates the tension between supporting religious groups and crossing the line to government-supported religion. While the survey found broad public support for allowing religiously affiliated charitable organizations to apply for government funding, support drops off sharply if the groups encourage re-ligious conversion. And a majority of respondents worried the initiative would interfere with the separation between church and state. [4]

That tension reflects a unique American paradox, says Alan Wolfe, director of the Boisi Center for Religion and American Public Life at Boston College and author of *Moral Freedom*, a new book that deals with the issue. Americans are deeply religious, Wolfe says, but they have doubts about sects — as indicated by negative attitudes the poll found toward public funding of Scientologists and other sects — and they have reservations about "in-your-face" evangelism.

As Wolfe sees the problem, religious groups typically embrace a specific religious viewpoint. Teen Challenge, for example, espouses the view that Jesus Christ replaces the emptiness in the soul formerly filled by drugs. To support that approach, the government would have to support a specific religious viewpoint — which is what the Constitution appears to ban, Wolfe observes. "Exactly what makes the program work is what makes it unconstitutional," he says.

In addition, by law, religious institutions are allowed to discriminate on religious grounds in hiring so they can hire someone of their own faith. Bush's initiative would extend the exemption to religious groups even when they receive federal funds. Supporters of the provision argue the discrimination exemption is essential if religious groups are to preserve their identity.

Opponents say charitable choice gives carte blanche to groups to discriminate against employees on the basis of religious beliefs, which could then extend to race (some evangelical Christians, for example, oppose interracial dating) or sexual orientation (some religions view homosexuality as a sin).

Civil liberties groups are primed to challenge the hiring exemption in court. "The first call we get from anyone discriminated against on those grounds we would be happy to help them out," says Barry Lynn, executive director of Americans United for Separation of Church and State.

To Rep. Scott, an African-American, charitable choice provides nothing more than "the right to discriminate and the right to advance your religion."

Responding to DiIulio's concerns about inner-city blacks, Scott asks, "Why should we have to sell off our civil rights in order for you to spend money in the inner city?" He suggests that small black churches would be better served if the government offered to help them write grants under existing federal contracting rules. Under charitable choice, Scott predicts, "Those little churches are no more likely to get the money than they were before."

Several observers worry that the federal government could end up supporting fringe cults or religious groups that promote hate. Televangelist Pat Robertson has warned the initiative could open a "Pandora's box" by making funds available to Scientologists, the Nation of Islam or religious cults that employ "brainwashing techniques." [5]

The proposal has created strange bedfellows: Some evangelical Christians have sided with some African-American churches in supporting the proposal, while Baptist denominations that oppose the government's infringement on religion find themselves in the same camp with the American Civil Liberties Union (ACLU), which opposes any breach in the wall between church and state. Recently, labor groups came out against the proposal because it permits hiring discrimination. [6]

If there is a middle ground where liberals can meet conservatives from the faith community, it may be the idea that people need personal mentoring and some kind of inner transformation (an old conservative idea) as well as material help (the 1960s anti-poverty premise) to get out of poverty. Two dozen leading liberals, conservatives and religious leaders sent a consensus statement to the White House on April 27 supporting government assistance to faith-based groups. * The signers include John Castellani, president of Teen Challenge, and Harris Wofford, President John F. Kennedy's special assistant on civil rights and former head of the Corps for National Service under President Clinton.

"People who are inspired by their faith can add the sense of urgency that so many of these problems require," Wofford says, noting that 5,000 Americorps volunteers a year were assigned to faith-based programs, which were selected because they were often considered the best programs helping people in a community.

Although a majority of both houses approved charitable choice provisions in the last Congress, last week was the first time hearings have been held on the provisions. The additional scrutiny will shine a spotlight on the constitutional objections, which got little attention in the larger welfare reform debate in 1996. It may also bring new attention to the reality that millions of dollars in federal funds already go to religious groups like the Salvation Army, which mixes Christianity with its services for the homeless. [7]

As lawmakers and social-service providers debate constitutional and other questions about the initiative, these are some of the questions they are asking:

* The Consensus Group was organized by Search for Common Ground, USA.

Can religious groups provide social services more effectively than government agencies and secular groups?

Marvin Olasky's 1992 book, *The Tragedy of American Compassion*, is often cited as an influential source for President Bush's brand of "compassionate conservatism." Olasky, editor of the weekly Christian news magazine *World*, argues that the Great Society programs of the 1960s encouraged the poor to develop a sense of entitlement toward their welfare benefits rather than a sense of personal responsibility. He con-

John J. DiIulio Jr., head of the new White House Office of Faith-Based and Community Initiatives, argues that the government's traditional reliance on secular organizations to deliver social services has failed.

trasts the 1960s, when welfare rolls exploded, with the 1890s, when religious charities often required work in return for a handout.

Olasky argues that religious groups today are more successful at helping people out of poverty than government programs because they, like the 19th-century charities, challenge individuals to change from within.

"Isn't it time that we start managing by results, even if that means returning social services to those private and religious institutions that emphasize challenging compassion?" Olasky asked. [8]

Olasky's journalistic accounts claimed high success rates for religious groups among those they help, but there's virtually no social science evidence that they do better than non-religious groups. Similarly, writing of Teen Challenge and the Salvation Army last fall, DiIulio noted, "[W]e do not really know whether these faith-based programs or others like them outperform their secular counterparts, how they compare to one another or whether in any case it is the 'faith' in 'faith-based' that mainly determines any observed differences in outcomes." [9]

So far, the closest social scientists have come to an answer has been in the study of church attendance and juvenile delinquency. Recent University of Pennsylvania studies found that black youths from crime-ridden neighborhoods who attend church regularly are less likely to commit violent crime or use drugs than their peers. [10] But it's not clear if that's because the kinds of teens who attend churches already come from more law-abiding and less troubled families.

"Kids in church are choosing to be there. It's very likely to be a different kind of kid," says Mark Chaves, a sociologist at the University of Arizona. "Claims that we know these [faith-based organizations] are better are not justified."

In what may be the first systematic comparison to date, David Reingold, an assistant professor at Indiana University's School of Environmental and Public Affairs, compared how faith-based and secular groups in Indiana rated their effectiveness in providing social services. Faith-based groups rate themselves less effective than secular

Kicking Addiction at Teen Challenge

Seated in a semicircle, Bibles on their desks, a dozen men in a Brooklyn basement are preparing to visit local churches, where they will describe how their newly found faith in Jesus Christ is helping them to kick lives of addiction.

The men are all residents of Teen Challenge, a non-denominational Christian program that treats about 3,000 addicts each year at 150 drug rehabilitation centers nationwide. [1] Because the program does not use state-licensed addiction counselors, the Brooklyn branch is ineligible for state funding and relies entirely on private donations to provide free, yearlong residential treatment to each of its 45 men and women. However, that could all change under President George W. Bush's proposal to allow religious groups to apply for federal drug treatment funds under his proposed Faith-Based Initiative plan.

Many question whether taxpayers' dollars should fund such programs, in which the religious message is inextricable from the drug counseling — as it clearly is in this class. Prepping the students for their presentations, the teacher instructs, "You want to elevate Christ."

Work in the kitchen as well as daily prayer are important parts of the therapy for these two former drug abusers at the Teen Challenge program in Brooklyn.

His students respond in the same vernacular. "When people read of the pain and suffering Jesus Christ went through, [they'll realize that] most of us have been there: When you've got lots of years of bondage, hating that drink but knowing you need it," says a neatly dressed red-haired man in a madras shirt. "I've carried my own [cross], man."

His words are greeted by a chorus of "Amens" from the mixed group of African-American, Hispanic and white men, ranging from their 20s to middle-aged. The central message of the program is that addiction is a sin and that accepting Jesus Christ is the solution.

But several express doubts about how they will fare once they leave the program. "My greatest challenge will

be when I'm out in the street," says a young man recalling the worldly pull he felt in a recent conversation with an old friend from the streets.

"The temptation will still be there," the instructor answers. "We definitely are weak men, and that's why we need Christ."

When another student laments that drugs have impaired his mental faculties and his ability to memorize Bible verses, the teacher again is encouraging, a quality of the program successful graduates often praise. "It's going to take time. Don't rush it," the teacher says.

Women Confront Abuse

Most of the women at the Brooklyn Teen Challenge women's residence were sexually abused before they began using drugs, says Dave Batty, executive director of the center. Much of the women's counseling focuses on those old and painful issues, he says, adding, "Abuse issues are far more difficult to deal with than heroin addiction."

Although Batty says acceptance of Jesus Christ is the key to the program, when it comes to sexual abuse, he sounds like a mainstream psychologist. Intensive counseling is often necessary before the women can break the habit of turning to illegal drugs, he says.

Phyllis Jones, 48, a 1995 graduate of the program, says sexual abuse by a family member — starting when she was 4 — precipitated her drug use, which began with marijuana at 9 and heroin sniffing at 16. She ran away from another drug rehabilitation program, Odyssey House, in 1992, when she was pregnant with her first child. She recalled one particularly humiliating incident at Odyssey when the staff tied her by the wrist to another addict as they were squired to a medical clinic for prenatal treatment.

"There was a lot of condemnation" for being an addict, she says. "Your self-esteem was always torn down. Here [at Teen Challenge] they told me it was going to be OK." Jones was HIV positive and convinced she was about to

groups when it comes to an elaborate program like helping individuals find and keep a job, he found. But they think they're as effective in more traditional congregational activities like gathering food for the needy. [11]

"It shouldn't be that much of a surprise that faith-based organiza-tions are organized around meeting immediate needs — food pantries as opposed to job training," Reingold says.

die when her sister, a practicing Christian, got her into the Brooklyn Teen Challenge program in 1993.

The religious focus "was real strange at first," Jones says. But the combination of discipline and love from the female staff allowed her to come to terms with her past abuse and the void she had filled with men and drugs, she says. "I always say this is where I was reborn again," she says. At Teen Challenge, "I felt like I was somebody."

Today Jones is a counseler and teacher at Teen Challenge. She recently married and is studying to be a non-denominational minister and to get her license as a state-certified addiction counselor.

Some successful graduates of Teen Challenge say the program resonated with them because they had a religious upbringing. Maria Rodriquez, who was raised Catholic, said other programs failed to help her deal with her alcoholism, which she also says was rooted in a history of sexual abuse. She thinks the other programs failed because they lacked a religious component.

"I was looking for somebody real so I could be free of bondage inside," Rodriquez says. "Now I call God first." Rodriquez has been a house manager and teacher at Teen Challenge for the past six years.

Success Rates Questioned

A 1975 study of Teen Challenge's effectiveness by the National Institute on Drug Abuse (NIDA) found that while some people, like Jones and Rodriquez, thrived on the program's religious component, others were put off by it. "Too much religion" was a main reason cited by the 82 percent who drop out of the program before graduation. Teen Challenge's Web site highlights the study's finding that 67 percent of graduates remain drug-free seven years later. But, the NIDA study found that only 18 percent graduate, which casts doubt on the 67 percent success rate, say addiction experts. [2]

The program's Web site also claims an 86 percent success rate based on a 1995 study completed for a doctoral dissertation at Northwestern University. But that study also fails to count dropouts. According to the Northwestern study, Teen Challenge graduates reported returning to drug use less often than graduates of a hospital drug rehabilitation program, but not less than hospital program graduates who continued attending Alcoholics Anonymous support groups. [3] Critics also note that many drug treatment programs often are sent unwilling addicts by court order, while Teen Challenge selects its clients, choosing those who express an affinity for its religious approach.

Lack of Licensing Questioned

Addiction specialists also are concerned about the lack of licensed counselors at Teen Challenge, particularly in such potentially dangerous situations as detoxification.

"It is anti-intellectual, anti-professional and potentially dangerous to [addicted] patients to presume that all they need is spiritual advice," says Michael Miller, chairman of the public policy committee of the American Society for Addiction Medicine.

But John Castellani, president of Teen Challenge International USA, based in Springfield, Mo., responds that the program routinely sends addicts to detox at local hospitals before they enter Teen Challenge.

Teen Challenge's unlicensed status brought it to the attention of food stamp authorities in Texas. According to Castellani, the state threatened to cancel the food stamps that clients received at a Texas Teen Challenge center, on the grounds the program was unlicensed. However, then-Gov. Bush signed legislation permitting such unlicensed faith-based groups to remain eligible for government assistance.

Nevertheless, some Teen Challenge officials are ambivalent about the possibility of receiving federal funds other than food stamps, since federal law prohibits religious groups from spending federal funds on religious conversion, worship or instruction.

On the one hand, Batty says he would welcome government money for such non-spiritual items as a new sidewalk and new bathrooms for the facility. And, some program aspects that are not religiously oriented might be eligible for federal funding, such as job training, drug prevention programs and preparing students to take the GED (high school equivalency exams).

But, "the spiritual component is the key to our success," says Batty. "We're not willing to give that up just to get government money."

---

[1] Teen Challenge was created in 1961 by David Wilkerson, a Pennsylvania minister working with gang youth in Brooklyn. Today, Teen Challenge accepts addicts and alcoholics who are at least 17 years old; the Brooklyn program mainly treats adults.

[2] Catherine B. Hess, "Research Summation," Teen Challenge Training Center, and "An Evaluation of the Teen Challenge Treatment Program," National Institute on Drug Abuse, 1977.

[3] See Laurie Goodstein, "Church-Based Projects Lack Data on Results," *The New York Times*, April 14, 2001, p. A12 and "Teen Challenge is Proven Answer to the Drug Problem" at www.teenchallenge.com.

Similarly, in a national survey, Chaves found that religious congregations mainly get involved in emergency help — collecting food and clothing or giving temporary shelter to the homeless. [12]

"You sometimes get the impression that people think congregations are more likely to be holistic, more personal, more focused on transformational things, but that doesn't seem to be true," Chaves says. Only about

3 percent of congregations get federal funding, and fewer than 10 percent do personal transformational work, such as mentoring or drug rehabilitation, his study found. [13]

"It's not at all clear congregations would be good at this," Chaves maintains. The Mississippi Faith and Families Program, a state effort often held up as an exemplar to get churches to help women make the transition from welfare to work, "was a total failure," he says. "It was canceled six months after it started because congregations didn't know what to do."

Although DiIulio concedes that the belief that religious programs will outperform comparable programs is a hypothesis, not a "settled fact," he says he's willing to "make the same bet" as believers like Olasky that they will work better. [14]

What drives the confidence behind that bet? DiIulio's answer is the famous Woody Allen observation that "90 percent of life is showing up." In essence, DiIulio argues, black and Latino ministers and their congregational members succeed because they show up — because they live in the pockets of poverty where the neediest live.

"In most cases, these are volunteers who have first-hand knowledge and a personal stake," DiIulio maintains.

In addition, small church programs take a more flexible approach that responds more to an individual's needs than to an impersonal government mandate, DiIulio says. And, echoing Olasky, DiIulio says faith-based programs are more likely to require reciprocity from the people they serve in terms of work or behavior. DiIulio cites the Victory Fellowship, a Christian drug rehabilitation program founded by addict-turned-pastor Freddie Garcia in San Antonio in 1972, which works inside prisons and on the streets with gang members. The program, which puts a heavy emphasis on personal responsibility, makes former prisoners and addicts scrub down pews or wash pots if they violate the program's rules. "Generally in the faith community, a person may have had life troubles, but [the philosophy is] 'Now you're getting help, and you have to give respect in return,' " DiIulio says. "And that works."

African-American ministers may also play a crucial role as intermediaries between black youth and traditionally estranged institutions like the police, according to Christopher Winship, chairman of Harvard University's sociology department. Winship has studied the work of Eugene Rivers, pastor of the Azusa Christian Community, a Pentecostal church in Boston's impoverished Dorchester section. Rivers was a leading member of a group of ministers who founded the Ten Point Coalition in 1992 to tackle Boston's epidemic of gang-related deaths. DiIulio has often cited Rivers' work with youth as a prime example of what the federal government should fund.

Winship has argued that the Ten Point Coalition played a critical role in Boston's 72 percent drop in homicides between 1992 and 1997 by creating an "umbrella of legitimacy" for the police. Ministers like Rivers, who had previously been vocal critics of police stop-and-frisk tactics in black neighborhoods, began to visit gang members, promising swift retribution from the law if they continued the violence but help with school, jobs and pressure from gangs if they went straight. [15]

Although Winship has not studied the effectiveness of these programs specifically, when it comes to "messy moral issues" like youth violence and teen pregnancy, he suggests, ministers may be able to play a unique role. "Because we have a workable model, we've been able to convince a lot of kids to get out of gang-banging," Winship says.

Winship says he has also been impressed by the role these churches have played in partnership with community health centers, where they address inherently delicate issues like family relationships and sex. Ministers have a "unique moral standing" in their community, he has observed. "Maybe they're in a position to talk to people about the way they live their lives that standard nonprofits do not."

President Bush has been an enthusiastic supporter of ex-Watergate felon Charles W. Colson's Prison Fellowship Ministries. Boosters of the program claim recidivism rates four times lower than for those of prison-

> "A lot of what the faith-based initiative is about is trying to clarify the rules. Because the rules have been exceedingly unclear, faith-based groups have been scared to participate in public programs."
>
> — *Michael W. McConnell, constitutional law expert, University of Utah College of Law*

ers released without its help. [16] But Lynn of Americans United for Separation of Church and State notes it is often the only program a prison offers to help prisoners being released. Its success, Lynn suggests, could be the result of the extra family time obtained for fellowship participants, the fact that they are handpicked for the program or the help they receive in job placement rather than the Christian message.

Similar skepticism has been voiced about the high success rates with addicts claimed by Teen Challenge, which boasts a 67 percent cure rate.

Relatively little is known about the power of spirituality in drug-treatment programs like Alcoholics Anonymous, but community support may be as important as the religious factor, according to Richard K. Fuller, director of clinical and prevention research at the National Institute on Alcohol Abuse and Alcoholism (NIAA). Project Match, the largest such study conducted by NIAA, compared a spiritually oriented addiction-treatment program, Alcoholics Anonymous, to two other standard secular approaches, behavior and motivational enhancement therapy. The percentages rehabilitated were similar for all three treatment methods.

At the same time, addiction experts have expressed concern that counselors at programs like Teen Challenge lack the medical qualifications necessary to deal with detoxification, which can be fatal under some circumstances.

"We're very concerned that any lack of seriousness about this disease — alcohol dependence — as a real medical condition will potentially harm patients," says Geoff Laredo, director of NIAA's Office of Policy, Legislation and Public Liaison. "Would you go in for brain surgery without a qualified neurosurgeon?"

Counters DiIulio: "It's not always the case that certification equals qualification. After two decades of federal, state and local investments, we've seen relatively little evidence of success from even the most highly credentialed therapeutic programs. Many of the people who do that [work] at the grass roots may not have a Ph.D. in psychiatric social work but have themselves been drug addicts — and have no less concrete evidence of success than the professional, get-all-the-degree folks."

DiIulio has stressed repeatedly in public appearances that measurable results will be the new administration's most important criteria in deciding which groups get funded — for example, the number of drug addicts who remain abstinent, the number of children reading at grade level.

But James Q. Wilson, professor emeritus of management and public policy at the University of California at Los Angeles, notes that empirical tests are hard to arrange for small, understaffed activities. [17] Moreover, personal transformation, which is at the core of religion, is hard to measure with traditional statistics. "This is not an activity of which research foundations or schools of public policy know much," Wilson writes, even though, it's "a powerful force" that has shaped nations and cultures. [18]

Does government funding for religious groups violate the separation between church and state required by the Constitution?

The fundamental constitutional question raised by charitable choice is whether its provisions violate the separation between church and state set out by the First Amendment's so-called Establishment Clause: "Congress shall make no law respecting an establishment of religion or prohibiting the free exercise thereof."

At the root of the debate is a disagreement over what the Framers intended. Olasky, an early proponent of funding faith-based organizations, ar-gues that the Framers were trying to prevent the establishment of a state religion, not forbid all state aid to religion. Olasky is part of a wave of evangelical Christians who argue that the nation has gone too far in distancing itself from religion. Similarly, Wilson argues the Framers intended merely to prevent the government from imposing religious practices. [19]

But civil libertarians read the Establishment Clause as prohibiting any government support of religion. Eliot Mincberg, legal director of People for the American Way, is quick to recall James Madison's contention that not three pence of tax money should support any religion. [20]

Supreme Court decisions since the late 1940s have reflected both points of view. In the court's first decisive case, *Everson v. Board of Education of Ewing Township*, the court allowed New Jersey to reimburse parents for bus fare to parochial schools. But the 1947 ruling held, in a phrase borrowed from Thomas Jefferson, that the Establishment Clause erected a "wall of separation" between church and state. High court decisions during the 1970s supported this view (*see p. 232*).

Recent Supreme Court cases appear to be moving away from the principle laid down in earlier cases starting with *Everson* that there should "no direct aid" for religion. In the most recent case, *Mitchell v. Helms*, decided last year, the court declared that it was constitutional for the government to provide computers and other educational equipment to religious as well as public schools. In the closely watched case, four justices embraced the "neutrality" theory, arguing that aid to religious schools was constitutional as long as the aid is distributed even-handedly to religious and non-religious institutions alike according to secular criteria.

However the "neutrality" principle does not represent a majority position on the court. (Two justices said the government can't give aid that is used for religious instruction, and three said the government can't give aid likely to be used for religious instruction.)

"The honest answer is the law is uncertain as to what kind of aid to religious groups is impermissible," says Erwin Chemerinsky, a constitutional expert and professor of law at the University of Southern California (USC).

Chemerinsky thinks charitable choice violates the wall that separates church and state. "I think it will inevitably lead to coercion and to people participating in religions they don't believe in," he says. "I also think charitable choice will be a threat to religion. With government comes government monitoring and government conditions."

Charitable choice provisions in existing law forbid religious groups from using public funds for proselytizing, religious instruction or worship. But civil-liberties groups doubt that restriction could be enforced in practice.

"I've heard John DiIulio say the government can provide the chairs and someone else will provide the Bibles in a welfare-to-work program," Mincberg says. "That kind of mixing, where government is paying part of the cost, is a constitutional problem because it is government helping to promote the religious mission."

Some religious groups have expressed concern that the government would discriminate against minority religions seeking funding and against individual adherents of minority faiths.

Marc Stern, legal director of the American Jewish Congress, says "there's a sense of disquiet" among Jews and concern that the initiative would exclude them from social services, especially where they are few in number.

"In the panhandle of Oklahoma, nobody's going to fund a Jewish program instead of a Baptist program," he says. "This is designed for everybody but small religious groups." The Interfaith Alliance, representing 50 faiths from Christians and Jews to Bahai, opposes the initiative on similar grounds.

Several religious groups oppose charitable choice because they say it would interfere with religion. "We believe religion fares best when left unencumbered by the government," says K. Hollyn Hollman, general counsel for the Baptist Joint Committee on Public Affairs. "Charitable choice says you don't need to separate religious activity from government activity, and we think that causes a threat to the separation of church and state."

Hollman notes that religious organizations already have a constitutional mechanism for receiving state aid for social services — setting up a non-religious nonprofit designated in the Tax Code as a 501c(3). "If the thinking is to allow religious people to be involved, it's unneeded," she says.

But a constitutional expert who supports charitable choice, Michael W. McConnell of the University of Utah College of Law, says the government has sent conflicting signals as to how much religion is allowed in government-funded programs. The Salvation Army, a longtime recipient of federal funds, has not set up a separate secular branch, McConnell notes. Some of its missions have a strongly Christian flavor, while others have been told to tone down the religious element.

"A lot of what the faith-based initiative is about is trying to clarify what the rules are, because the rules have been exceedingly unclear in the past 20-30 years," McConnell says. "As a result, faith-based groups have been at the mercy of changing and conflicting regulations, which has made them scared to participate in public programs."

As a constitutional matter, McConnell sees nothing wrong with government funding of faith-based groups as long as the beneficiaries are not coerced into religious activities and have a non-religious alternative to choose from. "I say it's the separationists who are trying to restrict the range of beneficiaries' choices," he contends. "The First Amendment ought to be interpreted to

allow beneficiaries, if they choose, to select religiously oriented programs."

However critics note that while charitable choice provisions require a secular alternative be available, there is no requirement that a drug addict or other government beneficiary be informed that he has such a right.

Less public discussion has been focused on a provision of charitable choice that permits the use of vouchers to obtain social services from a religious group. DiIulio told the Manhattan Institute last month that vouchers might be a solution for a group like Teen Challenge, where religious counseling is inseparable from the drug-addiction treatment. Using vouchers might avoid the constitutional battle awaiting direct grants to religious groups. That's because the Supreme Court has given greater constitutional leeway to public aid received only indirectly by religious institutions (such as through vouchers) than it has to direct aid. [21] The court's decisions suggest that a method like vouchers would be constitutional as long as the voucher recipient is given a genuine choice between religious and non-religious groups.

Members of the evangelical community, including Olasky, prefer vouchers or tax credits to grants, which they see placing unworkable restrictions on a religious group's exercise of its faith. James Q. Wilson recently editorialized in favor of vouchers as permitting a church to help a homeless drug addict "without at the same time denying its own deep beliefs." [22] But vouchers would likely be more helpful for larger, better-known congregations than little urban ones, which might find themselves overlooked by people searching for social services.

Should faith-based groups be allowed to practice religious discrimination in hiring?

Charitable choice provisions exempt religious institutions from the 1964 Civil Rights Act prohibition

Will Churches Do More?

Will churches and other religious organizations expand their role in social services under President George W. Bush's faith-based initiative?

Nationwide, only a handful of large congregations currently deliver most of the faith-based social services, according to a national survey by University of Arizona sociologist Mark Chaves. In fact, the largest 10 percent of churches and synagogues account for more than half of congregational spending on social services, he says. Most of them have already set up separate, secular, nonprofit branches, which traditionally has been required in order for a church to receive federal support, Chaves says.

In light of his findings, Chaves doubts that many new churches will take advantage of new "charitable choice" laws designed to help churches apply for federal grants to deliver social services. Under the new laws churches are not required to set up separate social service entities in order to receive public aid.

But University of Pennsylvania associate professor of social work Ram Cnaan thinks many churches — especially in urban centers — will take advantage of the new rules. He surveyed 113 urban congregations in six cities and discovered an untapped well of social services, particularly in inner-city ministries. In Philadelphia, for instance, Cnaan found that black congregations were more likely than white congregations to offer the kinds of services Bush has targeted in his faith-based initiative: mentoring at-risk youth, providing child care and health education, tutoring adults and training young people to use computers. [1]

The aggregate annual value of social services contributed by Philadelphia congregations is estimated at $230 million, Cnaan found, with most of the help going to "unchurched" neighborhood youth. Cnaan found that four times as many non-members as congregation members receive services, ranging from feeding programs to teen recreation programs. [2]

Cnaan's findings also suggest that more churches would seek government grants if they knew about charitable choice. Cnaan found in a recent survey that most clergy had never heard of charitable choice, but 60 percent said they were interested in receiving federal funds for their social service programs.

In fact, on March 31, some 450 predominantly African-American Philadelphia clergy attended a meeting Cnaan helped organize to offer help in writing federal grant applications. "This clearly shows they're willing to do more if given a chance," Cnaan says.

Another sign of untapped potential cited by Cnaan is the recent outpouring of interest in congregations partnering with secular nonprofits. For instance, about 550 volunteers recently answered the call of Philadelphia congregations seeking mentors for prisoners' children, he says. Big Brothers/Big Sisters trained and then matched the volunteers to inmates' children, considered one of the most at-risk populations in the United States.

"We went and knocked on doors and got about 50 congregations to give us people," says Cnaan, who called it an enormous outpouring for one city.

The Rev. Eugene Rivers, a strong supporter of the Bush initiative, says his non-denominational church — founded by Harvard undergraduates — already gets government funds. Rivers contends that the faith-based initiative is needed for smaller churches that lack such expertise. Small churches ranging from 20 to 300 members account for 95 percent of black church attendance, he says, and "They're closest to the poor."

But skeptics argue that under charitable choice such small churches won't have the resources to deal with the many rules and regulations requiring auditing and accounting that will be imposed in order to ensure that faith-based organizations do not spend federal funds on prohibited activities, like conversion and worship.

---

[1] Ram A. Cnaan and Stephanie C. Boddie, *Black Church Outreach* (2001), University of Pennsylvania, Center for Research on Religion and Urban Society, pp. 1-2.

[2] Ram Cnaan and Gaynor I. Yance, "Our Hidden Safety Net," in E.J. Dionne Jr. and John J.DiIulio Jr., *What's God Got to Do With the American Experiment?* (2000), pp. 154-156.

---

against employers discriminating on the basis of religion. Religious organizations already have an exemption under Title VII of the act permitting them to hire people of their own faith. But the question is whether they should be allowed to discriminate once they take federal funds.

Proponents of the exemption argue that Roman Catholic organizations should be allowed to limit their employees to Catholics, much like Planned Parenthood can decide not to hire someone who is anti-abortion.

"I think it's quite arguable the exemption is constitutionally required," says McConnell of the University of Utah School of Law. "If we allow secular groups to confine their hiring to people who share their beliefs, it's highly questionable to say a group whose beliefs are religious in flavor has any less freedom than they do. If a battered-women's shelter has the right to hire feminists, why shouldn't Teen Challenge have the right to hire Christians?"

Chemerinsky of USC disagrees. "In our history, discrimination against religion, race and gender is something to be fought. The defense the other side gives [that groups should be allowed to hire someone who shares their worldview] concedes there will be more discrimination based on religion. And to me that's a bad thing."

Opponents say extending this exemption to federally funded groups creates a loophole where any federal contractor could discriminate in hiring by calling itself a religious organization. In practice, faith-based groups could use religious discrimination as a pretext for discriminating on other grounds like race, gender and sexual orientation, opponents argue. "If you discriminate on other bases and declare it's religious, then no [legal] case can be made," says Rep. Scott of Virginia.

Opponents have raised the specter of a religious group refusing to hire someone of another race because their religion forbids interracial dating or refusing to hire women if their faith disapproves of men and women mingling. A number of court cases have involved the legality of Christian schools firing unmarried female teachers after they became pregnant. At least two courts have said that the Title VII exemption would allow the schools to dismiss a female teacher for adultery but that a dismissal simply for pregnancy would raise the possibility of illegal sex discrimination. [23]

In the most relevant case that came up before the passage of charitable choice, and which may have been the impetus behind the exemption, a court in 1989 refused to allow the Salvation Army to fire an employee who was a Wiccan (a believer in witchcraft) because her salary was paid substantially with tax money. [24]

A pending suit against a state-funded religious organization in Kentucky could set a precedent for a constitutional challenge to charitable choice, according to the lawyers involved, even though it involves state, not federal funding. Alicia Pedreira was fired from her job as a therapist at the Kentucky Baptist Homes for Children, which contracts with the state to help at-risk youth, after her employees discovered she was a lesbian. A letter firing Pedreira ex-

plained that her "homosexual lifestyle is contrary to [the Home's] core values." In April, Pedreira and the ACLU filed a federal lawsuit in U.S. District Court in Louisville accusing the home of religious discrimination. [25]

But constitutional scholar McConnell says he sees no legal basis for the case. "To say a religious grantee can't [discriminate] where a secular grantee can is absurd," he says.

More than three-quarters of Americans surveyed oppose allowing federally funded religious groups to hire only people of the same faith, according to the recent Pew poll. [26] That may reflect Americans' deep suspicion of dogma and a general opposition to a "faith test," suggests Wolfe of Boston College. Yet if the belief by a program's employees in the salvation of souls is what makes the program work, there can't be effective programs without commitments to a specific faith, Wolfe adds. "Just about anything that would work would be unconstitutional," he concludes.

BACKGROUND

Fighting Poverty

The fundamental argument of Olasky's *The Tragedy of American Compassion* is that religiously based care historically has been the most effective way of tackling poverty.

"Typically, 100 years ago, if an able-bodied guy came to a homeless shelter, they would hand the guy an ax and say, 'Why don't you chop wood for an hour? 'It allowed people to see if he was willing to work," Olasky says approvingly. "For those who didn't have the right values, there was pressure to develop them. Today you have to challenge people that don't have

the values of work to develop them rather than enable them to stay at a low level of material help."

But several historians disagree with Olasky's argument that this early model of harsh compassion dating from the Puritans, which "stressed man's sinfulness," was more effective in eliminating poverty than the government programs of the 1960s.

Olasky argues that the poor were better off in 1890, when charity was in private hands, but the consensus view among historians is that the proportion of poor Americans was as high in the 19th century as it has ever been since, according to a critique of Olasky in *The American Prospect*. Journalist Eyal Press writes that Olasky's negative account of the 1960s "is curiously silent about Medicare, Medicaid and the expansion of Social Security, which many scholars credit with all but eliminating poverty among the elderly." [27]

The historical argument illuminates a central ideological divide between liberals, who tend to blame poverty on the structure of the economy, and conservatives, who traditionally blame poverty on the individual's lack of values. It also explains the suspicion of liberal groups that the faith-based initiative is just a pretext, as Jacob S. Hacker wrote in *The New Republic*, to "off-load ever-greater portions of the welfare burden onto faith-based groups," thereby jeopardizing the well-being of people who rely on the welfare state. [28]

Some scholars argue that the division between public and private charity has never been as clear-cut as the liberal-conservative debate would suggest. In his book *When Sacred and Secular Mix*, Stephen V. Monsma reports that the majority of religiously based nonprofits that could be considered "pervasively sectarian" by the Supreme Court's standards — and therefore constitutionally ineligible for taxpayers' funds — do, in fact, receive government funds. [29]

Chronology

1880s-1900s
Salvation Army pioneers religiously based social work, which it dubs "practical religion."

1879-1880
Salvation Army begins missionary work in the United States.

1902
Salvation Army receives its first public money for work with "fallen women."

1940s
Supreme Court declares that the First Amendment erected "a wall of separation" between church and state.

1947
In *Everson v. Board of Education of Ewing Township*, the court allows New Jersey to reimburse parents for bus fare to parochial schools.

1960s
Anti-poverty programs are enacted, but welfare rolls swell. Number of nonprofits grows to 250,000, partly in response to Great Society programs.

1964
President Lyndon B. Johnson declares his intention to create a Great Society "without the wretchedness of poverty."

1964-1965
Congress enacts the Economic Opportunity Act, Medicare, Medicaid and food stamp legislation.

1970s
Landmark Supreme Court decisions reiterate church-state separation.

1971
Lemon v. Kurtzman decision holds that aid to parochial schools must be secular in purpose and effect and must not entangle the government.

1980s
Supreme Court weakens its opposition to public aid to parochial schools.

1985
Supreme Court strikes down two programs providing remedial services to parochial students in *Grand Rapids School District v. Ball* and *Aguilar v. Felton*.

1987
A woman whose salary is paid partially by a federal grant successfully sues the Salvation Army for firing her for practicing the Wiccan religion. The case inspires then-Sen. John Ashcroft, R-Mo., to craft "charitable choice" provisions.

1988
Supreme Court approves federal grants to religiously affiliated charities in *Bowen v. Kendrick*.

1990s
Supreme Court opens door further to public aid to religion. Religious groups push for the right to receive federal funds without giving up their religious identity.

1995
Texas agency threatens to close a branch of Teen Challenge, a Christian drug rehab program, for not using licensed counselors. Gov. George W. Bush exempts faith-based groups in Texas from licensing. Ashcroft introduces "charitable choice" amendment.

1996
President Clinton signs welfare reform bill containing "charitable choice" provisions.

1997
In *Agostini v. Felton* the court upholds aid to parochial schools under the same program it had restricted 12 years earlier.

1998
Clinton signs the Community Services Block Grant bill containing "charitable choice" provisions.

2000s
Newly elected President Bush proposes his faith-based initiative.

June 28, 2000
In *Mitchell v. Helms*, the Supreme Court allows a government-funded computer loan program for parochial schools.

Oct. 17, 2000
Congress reauthorizes law permitting faith-based groups to seek federal aid for drug rehabilitation.

Jan. 29, 2001
President Bush creates Office of Faith-Based Initiatives.

March 28, 2001
Bill introduced to expand charitable choice to nine federal programs.

According to DiIulio, more than a third of the child care in the United States is faith-based, and mothers on welfare have been permitted to use vouchers for child care since 1990. The largest faith-based nonprofit, Lutheran Services in America, receives 39 percent of its $7 billion from government sources. The Salvation Army, which has received government funds since the 1890s, receives 18 percent of its $2.1 billion from government sources. [30]

With the expansion of federal domestic programs, nonprofit groups in general have taken an increasingly important role in social services. In the domestic sector, the federal government funds six private employees for every government employee, according to DiIulio, creating in essence a "government by proxy."

The Salvation Army, according to Lt. Col. Paul Bollwahn, the Army's national social services secretary, has insisted on retaining its Christian identity in its wide array of services for the poor, balking at past demands from a Department of Housing and Urban Development administrator that the Army remove a cross from the wall. While Bollwahn says the Army would not use government-funded programs to evangelize a homeless person, he says, "I wouldn't consider prayers a violation."

Church and State

The country's first political compromise between religious and non-religious factions was embodied in the Constitution's First Amendment, barring the government from establishing a religion. It was a compromise between Enlightenment thinkers like James Madison and Thomas Jefferson, who were suspicious of religion, and Baptists, akin to today's conservative evangelicals, who feared the government establishment of a liberal religion like the Anglican Church.

Today the heirs of Madison and Jefferson can be found in America's civil-liberties groups arguing that the Constitution was intended to prevent all aid to religion, while the Baptists' heirs argue that the First Amendment was intended to prevent the establishment of a state religion. "It meant both things," Boston College's Wolfe says.

Until the 1940s, there was little controversy about the unofficial recognition of religion in America, as evidenced by the widespread practice of prayers in public school. Anti-Catholic feeling, as much as civil-liberty concerns, characterized the predominantly Protestant nation's hostility to the alliance of church and state, according to some accounts. [31] When Catholic immigrants from Ireland began flooding America in the 1840s, Protestants strongly opposed government assistance to Catholic schools.

Supreme Court Rulings

In the late 1940s, a strong trend toward separation emerged, reflected in several historic court decisions. The 1947 *Everson v. Board of Education* ruling set forth the principle that there should be "no aid to religion" even though the case actually permitted parents to be reimbursed for their children's bus transportation to religious schools.

In 1971, in the landmark *Lemon v. Kurtzman* case, the court for the first time struck down a public program that provided money to a religious organization. [32] The court set out a three-part test for permitting assistance to parochial schools: aid had to be secular in purpose, secular in effect and must not entangle the government in its administration.

During the 1970s, the court continued to hand down rulings that further strengthened the wall between church and state. In 1985, the court struck down two other programs that provided remedial services to students in parochial schools in *Grand Rapids School District v. Ball* and *Aguilar v. Felton.*

But the court gradually weakened its restrictions against public aid to church-affiliated schools over the next decade or so, criticizing the *Lemon* test as too rigid in two cases in 1986 and in 1993. In each, the court stressed that the aid went to the individual not the school.

While most court cases have involved funding for religious elementary and secondary schools, the courts have drawn implications for other faith-based institutions providing social services. Only one modern case has focused specifically on social-services groups. In 1988, the Supreme Court approved health and welfare grants to religiously affiliated charities in *Bowen v. Kendrick.* [33] In 1997, in *Agostini v. Felton*, the court moved even further from its earlier separationist stance by upholding aid to parochial schools under the same government program it had restricted 12 years earlier in *Aguilar v. Felton.* Most recently, in *Mitchell v. Helms*, decided on June 28, 2000, the court voted, 6 to 3, to permit a government-funded computer-lending program to parochial schools to continue.

Charitable Choice

From the point of view of Ronald J. Sider, president of Evangelicals for Social Action, the application of the Supreme Court's no-aid policy by the courts has been "confusing," and rulings attempting to separate the secular aspects from religiously based programs have often seemed arbitrary.

"As a result of this legal confusion," Sider wrote last year, "some

Ex-Cop Reels Kids In

While on patrol during his 20-year career as a Washington, D.C., police officer, Tom Lewis often was approached by hungry, neglected children. More than one asked, "Will you be my daddy?" Lewis recalls. He often gave them food, but he was determined to find a better way to help.

"I promised God if I lived long enough to retire, I would do something about it," Lewis recalls. True to his vow, Lewis in 1990 opened the Fishing School in a rowhouse in a run-down neighborhood in northeast Washington.

Lewis had fixed up the building with help from his family and volunteers, and eventually expanded it into the abandoned house next door. Since then he has opened a second school in a nearby neighborhood. The two faith-based, after-school family and child-support centers are staffed by 14 paid employees and volunteers.

The centers' year-round programs serve up to 80 kids a day. Each afternoon staff members pick up the children at their local schools. The children, most of whom are in grades 1-8, typically stay at the Fishing School until 7:30 p.m., participating in activities designed to increase their educational and spiritual capacities.

Children take part in arts and crafts, singing, scripture reading and praying. They also receive computer instruction and learn Spanish. Tutors help with homework and regularly check with their teachers to see if the kids are on target to meet D.C. educational standards.

Parents are vital to the entire process, Lewis says. Sessions are held with parents to discuss the children's progress and offer support. Workshops help parents maintain a healthy family environment. Lewis says he does not want the Fishing School to take the children away from their families, but bring them back. "When programs work, children go back to their parents," he says.

When Lewis found out that many kids who attend the Fishing School don't go home to a cooked meal, he hired a cook, so every child would have a hot meal each evening.

Lewis says the many letters he's received from parents and teachers citing improvement at home and in school convince him that he's on the right track, as do improved report cards and reading and math test scores. Although there are no official statistics, Lewis estimates that about 80 percent of the Fishing School children graduate from high school. And several former Fishing School students have won college scholarships, he says.

The school receives no federal funds but solicits private donations and grants. Whenever he can, Lewis attends what he calls "hope meetings"— events where he tells his story and hopes someone will help. Lewis also hopes that passage of faith-based legislation will help alleviate his 14-hour days by allowing him to hire more trained staff.

There are no restrictions on who can attend the school, but programs do contain Christian-based themes and daily prayer. "If God made you, we'll take you," is his motto.

Lewis says faith-based groups like his are more effective than government services because there's "a sense of loving" at the Fishing School not found in public programs. "There is something that keeps the children here and coming back," he says.

— Scott Kuzner

Former policeman Tom Lewis, back row, center, started the Fishing School to help the neglected children he encountered on his beat. Now he serves 80 kids daily.

Courtesy Tom Lewis

agencies receiving public funds pray openly with their clients, while other agencies have been banned even from displaying religious symbols." [34]

The issue caught the attention of then-Texas Gov. George W. Bush in 1995, when the Texas Commission on Alcohol and Drug Abuse threatened to shut down a San Antonio branch of Teen Challenge for failing to employ licensed drug counselors. Bush backed the group, granting it an exemption from state regulation and signing a law exempting faith-based groups in Texas from state licensing requirements. [35]

In 1995, then-Sen. Ashcroft introduced the first charitable choice provision — which eventually became part of the 1996 welfare reform bill. In committee, Ashcroft made note of a 1987 court case assessing the Salvation Army $1.3 million in damages for firing an employee from a domestic-violence shelter for her association with the Wiccan religion. Ashcroft feared the case would "send a chill" through religious communities and argued for an amendment guaranteeing religious groups "the ability, frankly to be discriminating" in federal contracts. [36]

The provision was initially adopted as part of the conference agreement with very little notice. No hearings were held on the provision. The bill was signed into law on Aug. 22, 1996.

A charitable choice provision was also approved by Congress in 1998 as part of the Community Services Block Grant Program. In the 106th Congress, Congress enacted two overlapping charitable choice provisions that permitted religious groups to apply for grants to administer substance-abuse prevention and treatment programs. [37] In the Senate floor debate, Ashcroft said the purpose of the amendment was to put churches and other faith-based providers on "an equal footing" with other private organizations in providing federally funded services. He argued that when "people of faith" get involved "the results can be stunningly successful." [38]

The Salvation Army, which was actively involved in drafting the Ashcroft amendment, supported it in order to aid smaller religious groups that often participate in regional efforts like food pantries, according to Bollwahn. In addition, pressure from government contracts to be less religious had produced "antiseptic" programming at the Salvation Army, and a sense that the federal government was both ignoring and disparaging its historic Christian identity, he said.

But opponents observe that the Salvation Army may have had another motivation for supporting the provision exempting faith-based groups from the bar on religious discrimination in hiring — the wish to avoid future expensive settlements like the one they paid to resolve the suit by the fired Wiccan employee.

The impetus for today's fight over charitable choice stems from a "new fear" that a combination of Supreme Court decisions and cultural trends has "marginalized religion more than is necessary for religious freedom or desirable for the country," writes E.J. Dionne, a senior fellow at the Brookings Institution and *Washington Post* columnist, in introducing essays from both sides. [39] He cites the argument of Yale Law School Professor Stephen Carter that the country seems to have replaced old prejudices based on race and religion with a new prejudice against belief itself.

"The problem is, if you say the state should be neutral between religion and non-religion, you're choosing non-religion," says Boston College's Wolfe. "It looks fair to a non-believer, but it looks like the establishment of atheism to a believer."

CURRENT SITUATION

Legal Challenges?

F ew states have implemented the existing charitable choice provisions, and even fewer have given grants to faith-based organizations. According to the Center for Public Justice, a pro-religion think tank in Annapolis, Md., that supports charitable choice, fewer than 15 states have implemented charitable choice by issuing regulations or otherwise advertising the eligibility of faith-based groups.

Since passage of the 1996 provisions, only 84 religious groups in nine states have received government funds under the new provisions, according to the center. [40] The center primarily blames foot-dragging by state administrators but concedes some faith-based groups have been wary. In Philadelphia only one church — the African-American Cookman United Methodist — has received a grant under charitable choice — for job training.

"There are longstanding suspicions on both sides," says Stephen Lazarus, senior policy associate at the Center for Public Justice.

A legal challenge to the charitable choice laws has yet to be filed. "The reason there hasn't been a challenge to federal law yet is they haven't been implemented in the way the 'far right' wants them to," and thus there are few existing programs with much of a track record to challenge says Mincberg of People for the American Way. Court challenges aren't likely soon since lawyers for the opposition say any challenge would have to be posed against a specific program that has an established pattern of practice of using federal funds to promote religion. The Clinton Justice Department's stated concerns about the provisions' constitutionality and the Clinton administration's reluctance to implement the program have so far put a damper on the willingness of states to carry out the charitable choice provisions, Mincberg and other experts say.

However, lawyers are eyeing four cases challenging state funding for faith-based programs. These include the discrimination suit against Kentucky Baptist Homes; a suit in Texas challenging the constitutionality of funding a welfare-to-work program where the course text was the Bible; and a Wisconsin suit challenging the constitutionality of a faith-based, residential drug-treatment program that involved Bible study, chapel services and admission interviews that probe religious attitudes. [41]

At Issue

Should the federal government fund faith-based groups as proposed by President Bush?

STEPHEN LAZARUS
Senior Research Associate, Center for Public Justice

FROM "THE DISCRIMINATION OLYMPICS," APRIL 9, 2001, WWW.CPJUSTICE.ORG

*i*f advocating discrimination against religious groups were an Olympic sport, some opponents of "charitable choice" would be serious medal contenders. Consider, for example, the arguments made by some Washington lobby groups to deny faith-based organizations the right to provide social services as part of publicly funded welfare programs.

Bronze Medal—American Civil Liberties Union: "Government cannot fund the work of faith-based organizations because, under the Constitution, it can't fund religion." Nice try, but when government buys job training or transportation services from religious organizations, it is not buying "religion." It is buying a specific public service, just as it does from "secular" groups. In fact, charitable choice guidelines explicitly state that no public funds can be used for activities such as worship services or discipleship classes.

Silver Medal — People for the American Way: "Government cannot fund the work of faith-based organizations because they might use religion in hiring staff." It is essential to both the integrity and effectiveness of religious organizations that they hire staff committed to their programs. The Civil Rights Act of 1964 guarantees this right to faith-based groups. Charitable choice says they do not have to give it up when they use public funds.

Gold Medal — Baptist Joint Committee: "Government shouldn't fund the work of faith-based organizations, because whatever government funds, it controls." To keep faith-based groups "free" from government, [this argument] denies the right of faith communities to work with government, even if their faith leads them to do so. This is like the overprotective parent who forbids a child from ever going out to play because [his] child might meet the school bully — except that under this scenario, the playground is off limits for all children.

The argument also misses the mark because charitable choice rules now keep government on a pretty tight leash. These new guidelines require government to respect the rights of faith-based organizations to maintain their religious character. The law explicitly states that . . . they no longer have to turn their programs into "religion-free zones" as a condition of receiving public funds.

Instead of giving their blessing to unfair treatment of religious organizations in the public square, these medal winners should adopt a new game plan: Let government welcome all groups as potential teammates in serving the poor, regardless of their religious commitments, and let each group choose for itself whether or not it wants to participate.

AMERICANS UNITED FOR SEPARATION OF CHURCH AND STATE

FROM "THE BUSH FAITH-BASED INITIATIVE: WHY IT'S WRONG," APRIL 2001, WWW.AU.ORG

*u*nder the First Amendment, American citizens are free to decide on their own whether or not to support religious ministries, and the government must stay out of it. Bush's plan turns that time-tested constitutional principle of church-state separation on its ear.

At its core, Bush's plan throws the massive weight of the federal government behind religious groups and religious conversions to solve social problems. While houses of worship have played an important role in this country since its founding, these institutions have thrived on voluntary contributions.

The president's proposal will allow churches to legally discriminate on the basis of religion when hiring, despite receiving public dollars. A Bob Jones-style religious group, for example, could receive tax aid to pay for a social service job, but still be free to hang up a sign that says "Jews And Catholics Need Not Apply."

Under Bush's approach, religious institutions would receive taxpayer support to finance social services and would still be free to proselytize people seeking assistance, seriously threatening the religious freedom of beneficiaries.

Government always regulates what it finances, because public officials are obliged to make certain that taxpayer funds are properly spent. Once churches, temples, mosques and synagogues are financed by the public, some of their freedom will be placed in jeopardy by the almost certain regulation to follow.

Many supporters of Bush's proposal have insisted that faith-based institutions are better, and far more successful, than secular service providers. However, little empirical research supports these claims, and it is unwise to launch a major federal initiative with so little research in the area.

For years, public funds have provided services at religiously affiliated organizations. Catholic Charities and Lutheran Social Services, for example, often have received government grants and contracts. However, strict safeguards have been in place to protect the interests of taxpayers and the religious liberties of those receiving assistance. Independent religious agencies, not churches themselves, handled the public funds. Tax dollars supported only secular programs, and no religious discrimination with public funds was permitted.

Courts found this approach to be consistent with the First Amendment. Bush's plan radically alters that setup by allowing churches and other houses of worship to preach, proselytize and discriminate while providing public services.

Helping Welfare Families in Brooklyn

On Monday mornings, the staff at a storefront Pentecostal Baptist church in Brooklyn hauls the altar to a back room, pushes the chairs against the wall and sets up three offices to help welfare mothers find work.

Judah International Christian Center, an African-American church with about 50 members, is one of 16 religious groups that New York City has hired to help families whose welfare benefits are about to end. The program is the city's first attempt to carry out the so-called charitable choice provisions of the 1996 Welfare Reform Act, which permits religious institutions to receive federal funds for providing social services.

Under the nine-month, $3 million pilot program, which began last September, churches receive several hundred dollars for every person that they help find a job or that they help reconnect with the city's welfare system.

The faith-based groups are successfully reaching clients that didn't respond to letters and phone calls from government agencies and traditional contractors, says Joseph Capobianco, assistant director of the welfare-to-work division at the New York State Department of Labor. "These people are skeptical of government," he says. "The question is: Can organizations with a different relationship, based in the local community and who may know the individuals, do something to help them?"

So far, the churches' intensive door-knocking and phone calling has reached at least 800 individuals, Capobianco says.

In addition, Judah's intimate, one-on-one setting is a far cry from the city's crowded welfare offices, run by the Human Resources Administration (HRA), where mothers with children in tow can wait hours to see a caseworker. Further, many women perceive the jobs the city finds them, such as road clean-up, "degrading," says Keyon Sheppard, Judah's welfare project coordinator.

Judah takes a "holistic" approach to clients, not just finding a job but tackling individual issues, like self-esteem, drug addiction, domestic violence and the need for child care. "Our concern is the total person," Sheppard says. "We ask 'Who is this person?' and [figure out] how to go from where they are to where the HRA would like them to be.

"There's an entire mentality that goes with being a working person as opposed to being at home," he adds. "It's a change of mindset."

Sheppard says the church identifies itself as a faith-based organization when it contacts each welfare recipient, but the program does not discriminate against those of other faiths. "I am a person of faith and that's what makes it faith-based," says Judah's pastor, the Rev. Cheryl G. Anthony. "If a Muslim woman comes in and needs services, we are going to provide services and never question her about her beliefs."

Advocates for the poor question whether the faith-based initiative is an attempt to reduce the federal government's role in helping the poor by shifting the burden to churches.

The Rev. Anthony doesn't think so. "There is a partnership that can happen," Anthony says, "and we need to look at ways to have it happen."

"The fight is about [programs like] Teen Challenge and the program in Wisconsin, where religion is the methodology," says Stern of the American Jewish Congress, which is involved in several of the state challenges.

The Bush Initiative

Most congressional observers expect little controversy over the tax portion of Bush's initiative, which would encourage charitable giving to faith-based organizations by, among other things, permitting taxpayers who do not itemize to deduct their contributions. Sens. Rick Santorum, R-Pa., and Joseph I. Lieberman, D-Conn., introduced such a bill on March 21 to encourage charitable giving through tax incentives.

Most of the controversy is expected to focus on proposals to expand charitable choice to additional federal grant programs. In the House, a bill introduced on March 28 by Reps. J.C. Watts Jr., R-Okla., and Tony P. Hall, D-Ohio, with Bush administration support, incorporates direct aid to faith-based groups as well as the tax incentives. The bill would allow federal funds to flow directly to faith-based groups for nine new programs focusing on juvenile delinquency, crime prevention, housing grants, job training, senior citizens, child care, community development, domestic violence and hunger relief. [42]

Because the faith-based initiative involves so many programs, it is expected to move through multiple committees in many different bills, rather than as one legislative package.

Congressional attention is expected to focus first on Bush's proposal to open competitive bidding to faith-based groups to provide federally funded after-school programs for low-income children.

Bush's proposed budget includes $67 million for both faith-based and secular counseling of prisoners' children, $64 million for programs to promote marriage and help low-income fathers leave welfare, $33 million for group homes to provide shelter for teen mothers and $89 million in a "Compassion Capital Fund" to help start new charities. The Department of Justice budget under Bush's proposal would reallocate $5 million in Federal Bureau of Prisons funds to support faith-based counseling of prisoners about to be released. [43]

Opponents of the Bush initiative have focused much of their discussion on welfare families who will be pushed off the welfare rolls when the five-year federal clock runs out this year. They criticize Bush for opening welfare-to-work and other programs to an increasing number of competing providers without increasing the overall funding available for the disadvantaged.

"Bush is not proposing a bigger pie, he's proposing to divide that pie into a lot more slices. We're very concerned that the net effect will be worse," says Mincberg of People for the American Way. His organization is particularly troubled by Bush's proposal that states provide tax credits for donations to charities and finance it out of the state's share of federal welfare-to-work funds. [44] That's "literally robbing Peter to pay St. Paul."

Bush also has ordered an audit, expected to be completed this summer, to identify barriers to the participation of faith-based groups in federal grant programs administered by five Cabinet agencies. Most expect the investigation will lead to more aggressive implementation of existing laws to include faith-based groups in federal grant programs.

OUTLOOK

Falling Wall?

T his year will mark the first time Congress has held hearings on charitable choice and debated it in the full light of day.

Even if new legislation is passed, the debate will continue, since constitutional challenges in the courts are likely. The challenges are not expected, however, until programs have had time to work at the state and local level. While no Supreme Court ruling is likely anytime soon on charitable choice, constitutional scholars are watching a case challenging Cleveland school vouchers for clues on where the Supreme Court is heading on church vs. state issues.

Any change in the makeup of the Supreme Court during the Bush administration, some conservatives predict, would give a majority to the "neutrality" view shared by four justices that government aid to religion is constitutional as long as it is evenhanded. Currently there is no clear majority opinion on that question. But public-interest groups are already gearing up for the possibility that one of the three justices over age 70 will retire soon, enabling Bush to appoint another conservative.

The shifting and sometimes surprising alignments over the role of faith in America may make some fear that the wall between church and state is tumbling down, columnist Dionne has observed. But he suggests something more complex may be happening as the nation struggles over the appeal and the threat of religiously motivated help to the disadvantaged.

"The turn of the millennium in America may well be remembered as the time when the country renegotiated the relationship between r eligion and public life, faith and culture." [45]

Notes

[1] See David Nather, "Bush Social Policy Comes Into Focus with Cutbacks, Shift to Local Programs, *CQ Weekly*, April 14, 2001 p. 826.

[2] Under existing law, charitable choice applies to the four following domestic programs: Temporary Assistance to Needy Families (1996), Welfare-to-Work (1997); Community Services Block Grants (1998) and drug treatment under the Substance Abuse and Mental Health Services Administration (2000). For background, see Christopher Conte, "Welfare, Work and the States," *The CQ Researcher*, Dec. 6, 1996, pp. 1057-1080.

[3] David M. Ackerman *et al.*, "CRS Report for Congress: Charitable Choice: Constitutional Issues through the 106th Congress," Dec. 27, 2000, Congressional Research Service.

[4] The Pew Forum on Religion & Public Life and The Pew Research Center for the People & the Press, "Faith-Based Funding Backed, But Church-State Doubts Abound," April 10, 2001, p. 13. (59 percent of Americans oppose allowing groups that encourage religious conversion as part of their social services to compete for federal funds.)

[5] See Pat Robertson, "Mr. Bush's Faith-Based Initiative is Flawed," *The Wall Street Journal*, March 12, 2001.

[6] Labor unions, including the American Federation of State, County and Municipal Employees, joined with progressive religious groups, including the Union of American Hebrew Congregations, in a letter sent to Congress on April 11 urging rejection of Bush's faith-based plan. See Kevin Eckstrom, "Faith-Based Opponents, Supporters Gear up for Capitol Hill Battle," Religion News Service, April 12, 2001.

[7] For background, see Richard L. Worsnop, "Helping the Homeless," *The CQ Researcher*, Jan. 26, 1996, pp. 73-96.

[8] Marvin Olasky, *The Tragedy of American Compassion* (1992), p. 224.

[9] John J. DiIulio, Jr., "Godly People in the Public Square," *The Public Interest*, fall 2000, pp. 113-114.

[10] Byron R. Johnson, *The Role of African-American Churches in Reducing Crime among Black Youth*, University of Pennsylvania, Center for Research on Religion and Urban Civil Society (2001), and Johnson, *A Better Kind of High* (2000).

[11] David Reingold, "Empirical Evidence on Welfare Reform and Faith-Based Organizations," presented at 22nd Annual Research Conference of Association for Public Policy Analysis and Management, Seattle, Wash., November 2000.

[12] See Mark Silk, "Old Alliance, New Ground Rules," *The Washington Post*, Feb. 18, 2001, p. B3.

[13] Mark Chaves, "Congregations' Social Service Activities," Policy Brief No. 6, The Urban Institute, December 1999. at www.urban.org.

[14] DiIulio, *op. cit.*, p. 114.

[15] Christopher Winship and Jenny Berrien, "Boston Cops and Black Churches," *The Public Interest*, summer 1999, pp. 52-68.

[16] Robertson, *op. cit.* Also see Gustav Niebuhr, "Promise and Pitfalls Seen in Taking Religion to Prison," *The New York Times*, April 12, 2001, p. A26. For background, see "Prison-Building Boom," *The CQ Researcher*, Sept. 17, 1999, pp. 815-838.

[17] Wilson authored *The Moral Sense* (1993), an examination of the "moral sense" that Wilson argues governs human conduct throughout different periods.

[18] James Q. Wilson, "Religion and Public Life," in E.J. Dionne Jr. and John J. DiIulio Jr., eds., *What's God Got to Do With the American Experiment?* (2000), pp. 169-170.

[19] *Ibid.*, p. 167.

[20] From James Madison, "Memorial and Remonstrance" (1785) see www.au.org.

[21] Ackerman, *op. cit.*, p. 33.

[22] James Q. Wilson, "Why Not Try Vouchers?" *The New York Times*, April 27, 2001, p. A25.

[23] The two cases are *Vigars v. Valley Christian Center of Dublin, California* (1992) and *Ganzy v. Allen Christian School* (1998).

[24] The case *Dodge v. Salvation Army* is cited in Dionne, *op. cit.*, p. 141.

[25] Eyal Press, "Faith-Based Furor," *The New York Times Magazine*, April 1, 2001, p. 62.

[26] Pew, *op. cit.*

[27] Eyal Press, "Lead Us Not into Temptation," *The American Prospect*, April 9, 2001.

[28] Jacob S. Hacker, "Faith Healers," *The New Republic Online*, June 10, 1999. Hacker is a fellow at the New America Foundation.

[29] Stephen V. Monsma, *When Sacred and Secular Mix* (2000), p. 121. A "pervasively sectarian" organization is a term the Supreme Court has used to refer to "an institution in which religion is so pervasive that a substantial portion of its functions are subsumed in a religious mission." The court has generally barred the flow of tax funds to pervasively religious organizations.

FOR MORE INFORMATION

Americans United for Separation of Church and State, 518 C St., N.E., Washington, D.C. 20002; (202) 466-3234; www.au.org. This 60,000-member national organization advocates for church-state separation and opposes the faith-based initiative.

Manhattan Institute for Policy Research, 52 Vanderbilt Ave., 2nd Floor, New York, N.Y. 10017; (212) 599-7000; www.manhattan-institute.org. This research organization's Jeremiah Project, which was originally headed by John J. DiIulio Jr., studies and promotes the work of inner-city ministers in reducing youth violence.

Center for Public Justice, P.O. Box 48368, Washington, D.C. 20002-0368; (410) 571-6300. www.cpjustice.org. This policy research organization, whose stated purpose includes "to serve God," supports government funding for faith-based groups. It posts numerous studies and editorials on its Web site.

Pew Forum on Religion and Public Life, 1150 18th St., N.W., Suite 775, Washington, D.C. 20036-3823; (202) 955-5075; www.pewforum.org. The forum sponsors research and panel discussions on faith-based groups and related polls by the Pew Research Center for the People and the Press.

[30] Mark Silk, "Old Alliance, New Ground Rules," *The Washington Post*, Feb. 18, 2001, p. B3.

[31] Dionne and DiIulio, *op cit.*, p. 117.

[32] *Lemon v. Kurtzman*.

[33] *Bowen v. Kendrick*.

[34] Ronald J. Sider and Heidi Rolland Unruh, "No Aid to Religion?" in Dionne and DiIulio, *op. cit.*, p. 129.

[35] Press, *op. cit.*

[36] See Press, "Faith-Based Furor," *op. cit.*, p. 65.

[37] The two laws, both enacted in 2000, are the Children's Health Act and the Community Renewal Tax Relief Act. See Ackerman, *op cit.*

[38] *Ibid.*, p. 13.

[39] E.J. Dionne, "The Third Stage," in Dionne and DiIulio, *op. cit.*, p. 119.

[40] Amy Sherman, *The Growing Impact of Charitable choice: A Catalogue of New Collaborations Between Government and Faith-Based Organizations in Nine States*, Center for Public Justice (March 2000). See "Charitable Choice: Growing Impact," at www.cpjustice.org.

[41] The Texas suit, *American Jewish Congress and Texas Civil Rights Project v. Bost*, was originally filed in the state courts of Texas and was remanded by the District Court to the state court. The Wisconsin case, *Freedom from Religion Foundation v. Thompson*, was filed in the federal district court. *American Jewish Congress v. Bernik*, filed in Superior Court in San Francisco challenges California's state set-aside of $5 million for faith-based programs aimed at helping people re-enter the work force. See Memo from Marc D. Stern, American Jewish Congress "Re: Charitable Choice Litigation," Feb. 23, 2001.

[42] See "Highlights of Faith-Based Initiative Proposals," *CQ Weekly*, March 24, 2001, p. 661, and David Nather, "House GOP Bets on Passing Aid to 'Faith-Based' Groups; Senate Keys on Tax Incentives." *CQ Weekly*, March 24, 2001, p. 661.

[43] See David Nather, 'Bush Social Policy Comes Into Focus with Cutbacks, Shift to Local Programs,' *CQ Weekly*, April 14, 2001, p. 826.

[44] See David Nather, "Welfare Overhaul's Next Wave," *CQ Weekly*, March 17, 2001, p. 585.

[45] Dionne and DiIulio, *op cit.*, p. 115.

Bibliography
Selected Sources Used

Books

Dionne Jr., E. J., and John J. DiIulio Jr., eds., *What's God Got to Do with the American Experiment?* Brookings Institution Press, 2000.

This book of essays, edited by DiIulio, head of the Office of Faith-based and Community Initiatives, and *Washington Post* columnist Dionne, includes arguments for and against government funding of religious groups.

Glenn, Charles L., *The Ambiguous Embrace: Government and Faith-based Schools and Social Agencies*, Princeton University Press, 2000.

A Boston University professor advocates more government support for religious groups, but points out that groups like the Salvation Army have been forced to "secularize" their services to their detriment.

Monsma, Stephen V., *When Sacred and Secular Mix: Religious Nonprofit Organizations and Public Money*, Rowman & Littlefield.

A Pepperdine University professor argues that religious nonprofit organizations play a much larger role in providing social services with public money than one would think.

Olasky, Marvin, *The Tragedy of American Compassion*, Regnery, 1992.

Widely viewed as influential in spurring the Bush administration to fund faith-based groups, the editor of a weekly Christian news magazine argues that religious charities that require work with a handout have historically been more effective than government anti-poverty programs.

Articles

Cole, David, "Faith Succeeds where Prison Fails," *The New York Times*, Jan. 31, 1001.

A self-described "card-carrying liberal" favors public funding for faith-based groups on the grounds that they emphasize treatment rather than incarceration.

Foer, Franklin, and Ryan Lizza, "Holy War: The Faith-Based Slugfest," *The New Republic*, April 2, 2001, pp. 14-17.

The political implications of evangelical Christians' criticism of the faith-based initiative are discussed.

Press, Eyal, "Faith-Based Furor," *The New York Times Magazine*, April 1, 2001, pp. 62-65.

The firing of a lesbian from the Kentucky Baptist Homes for Children has been widely cited by civil libertarians as an illustration of the dangers of permitting faith-based groups to discriminate in hiring.

Press, Eyal, "Lead Us Not Into Temptation," *The American Prospect Online*, April 9, 2001.

The author casts a critical eye on the historical and political arguments for the faith-based initiative and the studies cited supporting the effectiveness of religious groups.

Silk, Mark, "Old Alliance, New Ground Rules," *The Washington Post*, Feb. 18, 2001, p. B3.

Silk, a professor at Trinity College, examines the potential of religious congregations to perform social services and suggests that if they get federal funding they could form a new interest group for the poor.

Szalavitz, Maia, "Why Jesus is not a Regulator," *The American Prospect*, April 9, 2001.

The author warns that efforts by the Bush administration to exempt religious groups from state licensing could lead to scandal.

Winship, Christopher, and Jenny Berrien, "Boston Cops and Black Churches," *The Public Interest*, summer 1999, pp. 52-68.

Harvard sociologist Winship praises Boston's black ministers' work with gangs, which has been widely cited by supporters of the faith-based initiative.

Reports

Cnaan, Ram A., "Keeping Faith in the City: How 401 Urban Religious Congregations Serve their Neediest Neighbors," Center for Research on Religion and Urban Civil Society, University of Pennsylvania.

This report has been widely cited as evidence that urban churches are actively providing social services outside their congregations.

Johnson, Byron, "The Role of African-American Churches in Reducing Crime Among Black Youth, 2001," Center for Research on Religion and Urban Civil Society, University of Pennsylvania.

The center established by John J. DiIulio Jr. finds that churchgoing reduces the likelihood that poor, black youth will be involved in violent crime.

Pew Forum on Religion and Public Life and The Pew Research Center for the People and the Press, "Faith-Based Funding Backed, but Church-State Doubts Abound," April 10, 2001.

Americans think religious groups can do a good job of providing social services but have doubts about how government funding of such groups would work in practice.

"Establish Justice"
— preamble to the Constitution of the United States

Race has been the dominant issue of equal justice in America from colonial times to the present day. Slavery divided the framers of the Constitution, and race continued to divide the nation even after the abolition of slavery following the Civil War. Since the Supreme Court's historic decision in *Brown v. Board of Education* in 1954, the Constitution has been read to prohibit official discrimination on the basis of race or color. But the dismantling of racial segregation has been slower and less complete than many people anticipated, and the use of "affirmative action" to remedy past discrimination against African Americans and other minorities has generated new controversies over the meaning of equality under the Constitution. Meanwhile, new issues were being raised under the constitutional guarantee of equal protection — including questions of sex discrimination and gay rights.

"School Desegregation" chronicles the legal strategy by civil rights groups that culminated in the Supreme Court's decision to outlaw racial segregation in public schools and the continuing legal and political battles over race and schools today at the fiftieth anniversary of the ruling. Most African American youngsters still attend prevalently black schools; similarly, most Latinos are enrolled in schools where Hispanics are the majority. Traditional civil rights groups call for stronger steps to break down the racial separation in schools. But some conservative interest groups and experts — including some African Americans and Hispanics — argue that integration is less important than other steps, such as curricular standards and public school accountability, to address the persistent racial gap in educational performance.

"Affirmative Action" traces the controversy over racial and ethnic preferences for minority applicants in the nation's colleges and universities. Traditional civil rights groups began advocating affirmative action in the 1960s to increase minority enrollment in higher education. Some unsuccessful white applicants viewed the policies as reverse discrimination and challenged them in courts as unconstitutional. The Supreme Court in 1978 ruled in favor of minority preferences but against fixed quotas. Twenty-five years later, the issue dramatically returned in a pair of cases from the University of Michigan. In two closely divided companion decisions, the court reaffirmed its previous position of permitting racial or ethnic preferences but barring quotas or any fixed bonus for minority applicants (*Grutter v. Bollinger, Gratz v. Bollinger,* June 23, 2003). Justice Sandra Day O'Connor, who cast pivotal votes in both cases, also called for affirmative action to end within another twenty-five years.

"Race in America" examines a wide range of legal and political issues affecting African Americans decades after the end of legal segregation and discrimination. Black Americans are better off today — socially, economically, and politically — but they continue to lag behind whites in wealth, income, life expectancy, school success and reduction in crime rates. Civil rights groups see these gaps as evidence of continuing institutionalized discrimination. Some conservatives, however, blame the disparities on social and cultural rather than anything legal or political.

"Single-Sex Education" analyzes the legal and policy debate over whether all-boy and all-girl schools enhance or hamper learning. Since the 1970s, Supreme Court rulings and federal and state laws have prohibited many forms of sex discrimination, but they have left room for some policies that treat men and women differently. Some court rulings have questioned the legality of single-sex public schools. In recent years, however, a diverse array of advocacy groups and experts have argued that boys and girls can learn better in single-sex environments, especially in the younger years. Since our report, the Bush administration proposed new rules on March 3, 2004, to make it easier for public school districts to establish single-sex schools or programs — rules strongly criticized by some women's rights organizations.

"Gay Marriage" covers the volatile debate over whether to extend legal recognition to same-sex unions. Many states and localities have laws prohibiting discrimination on the basis of sexual orientation, but gay rights groups have made limited progress at the national level. In 2003, however, the Supreme Court declared laws that ban gay sex to be unconstitutional. The ruling encouraged gay rights groups to intensify efforts to allow gay men and lesbians to marry — or to obtain marriage-like benefits under so-called civil unions. Social conservatives are strongly opposed and say that to recognize same-sex unions would hurt traditional marriage. Since our report, the Massachusetts Supreme Judicial Court ordered the state to allow gay couples to marry (*Goodridge v. Department of Public Health,* Nov. 18, 2003). President Bush responded on Feb. 24, 2004, by endorsing a constitutional amendment to limit marriage to heterosexual couples.

13 School Desegregation

KENNETH JOST

C ivil rights advocates consider Louisville-Jefferson County, Ky., a model of desegregation — but don't tell that to David McFarland.

McFarland says the county's claimed success in racial mixing comes at the expense of his children's education. In his view, Stephen and Daniel were denied admission to the school of their choice simply because they are white. "Diversity should not be used as an excuse for discrimination," he says.

The county's 19 traditional schools — with their reputation for good discipline, structured teaching and parental involvement — are so popular that they cannot accommodate all the students who want to attend. So students are assigned to schools by lottery.

To keep enrollments at each school within racial guidelines, a separate list of African-American applicants is maintained. The county's voluntary "managed-choice" program — which replaced a court-ordered desegregation plan in 2000 — is designed to prevent any school from having fewer than 15 percent or more than 50 percent African-American students.

The program works. In a county-wide system where African-Americans comprise about one-third of the 96,000 students, only one school has a majority-black enrollment.

Jefferson County was one of the first school systems in the country to begin integrating after the U.S. Supreme Court handed down its historic *Brown v. Board of Education* decision declaring racial segregation in schools unconstitutional. [1]

From *The CQ Researcher,*
April 23, 2004.

Fifty years after the Supreme Court handed down its historic Brown v. Board of Education *decision declaring racial segregation in public schools unconstitutional, most black and Latino students attend predominantly minority schools. At Birdwell Elementary in Tyler, Texas, 60 percent of the students are Hispanic.*

Getty Images/Mario Villafuerte

Today, as the 50th anniversary of the May 17, 1954, ruling approaches, Jefferson County stands in stark contrast to the ethnic and racial patterns in most other school districts. Across the country today, most black students attend majority-black schools, and an even larger percentage of Latino students attend majority-Latino schools — evidence of what civil rights advocates call resegregation.

In Louisville, McFarland and three other families sued in federal court to bar the school system from using race in any student assignments. [2] "It can't be fair to discriminate against a white male because he's a white male," says Ted Gordon, the plaintiffs' attorney. "That can't be fair in anybody's book."

School administrators, however, say a ruling for McFarland would effectively bring back racial segregation in Louisville. "We would be back to majority-white suburban schools and majority-black inner-city schools," says Byron Leet, lead attorney for the school system. "That would not be in the best interest of young people in the community, who have benefited greatly from attending desegregated schools."

The case is being closely watched at a time when school desegregation litigation nationwide is dormant, but parents in some areas are asking courts to block administrators from continuing to use race to promote integration.

"If the court decides that the sensitive way that Louisville has gone about trying to achieve integration is not acceptable, then I worry that there may be little or no way to reap the benefits of integration for our primary and secondary schools," says Chinh Quang Le, assistant counsel for the NAACP Legal Defense and Educational Fund, which filed a friend of the court brief on the side of the Louisville school system. The fund directed the court challenges against racial segregation that produced the *Brown* decision and remains the principal litigation center in school desegregation cases.

Today's pattern of school desegregation litigation underscores the changes in the nation's schools — and in the nation's attitudes toward race — since the *Brown* decision. [3] While the ruling is universally hailed, its promise is widely recognized as unfulfilled and its implications for educational policies today vigorously debated.

"*Brown v. Board of Education* is one of the signal legal events of our time," says Education Secretary Rod Paige, who himself attended racially segregated schools through college in his native Mississippi. But the ruling did not eliminate all the vestiges of segre-

Minority School Districts Receive Less Funding

School districts with high enrollments of minority or low-income students typically receive fewer funds compared to districts with more white or wealthier students. In 11 states, the funding gap between white and minority school districts is more than $1,000 per pupil.

Per-Pupil Funding Gaps Between Districts with High and Low Minority Enrollments

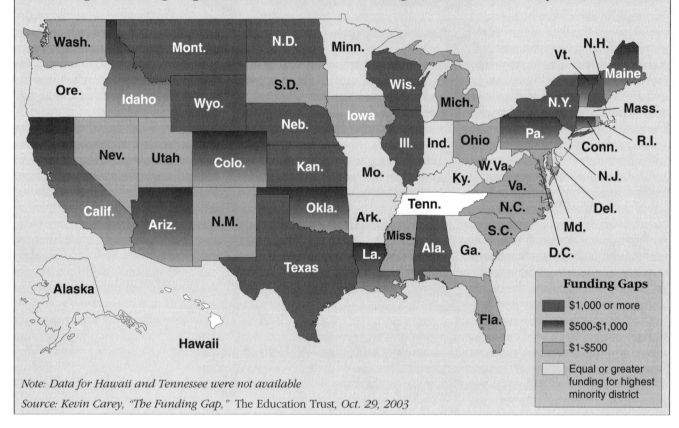

Funding Gaps

- $1,000 or more
- $500-$1,000
- $1-$500
- Equal or greater funding for highest minority district

Note: Data for Hawaii and Tennessee were not available

Source: Kevin Carey, "The Funding Gap," The Education Trust, Oct. 29, 2003

gation, Paige quickly adds. "If the goal was equality in education — to level the educational playing field for all children, especially children of color — we've yet to achieve that," he says.

"We have an unfulfilled promise of *Brown*," says Julie Underwood, general counsel for the National School Boards Association, which once resisted and now strongly supports desegregation. "If the civil rights people were actually seeking fully integrated public schools, we have not reached that point."

Civil rights advocates acknowledge that *Brown* fundamentally transformed American schools — and America itself. "Both whites and blacks have

been in far more integrated settings than anyone would have imagined before *Brown*," says Gary Orfield, a professor at Harvard's Graduate School of Education and director of the Harvard Civil Rights Project.

But Orfield and other desegregation advocates also maintain that the hard-won progress of the post-*Brown* era has not merely stalled but is now being reversed. "We've been going backward almost every place in the country since the 1990s," Orfield says.

A coterie of educational conservatives from academia and various advocacy groups challenge both this

view of present-day conditions and policies for the future. While praising the *Brown* decision, they argue that today's racial separation is not the result of law or policy and that race-conscious assignments violate *Brown*'s central meaning.

Brown "stands for the principles of integration and color-blindness," says Curt Levey, director of legal and public affairs for the Washington-based Center for Individual Rights.

"It's unfortunate that in the past few decades we have abandoned those principles in favor of racial preferences," Levey says. "It's just another form of discrimination." The center has represented plaintiffs challenging affirmative action in higher education and, in one case from Minneapolis, racial guidelines in public schools.

"Most of our schools became substantially racially balanced," says David J. Armor, a professor at George Mason University School of Public Policy in Fairfax, Va., and the leading academic critic of mandatory integration. Armor acknowledges that there's been "some resegregation of schools" but attributes the trend to changes in ethnic and racial residential patterns and the higher percentages of blacks and Latinos in public schools.

The debate over desegregation is waged against the disheartening persistence of large gaps in learning and achievement between whites, blacks and Latinos. "The magnitude of the gap is simply appalling," says Abigail Thernstrom, a senior scholar at the Manhattan Institute and co-author with her husband Stephan Thernstrom of a book on the subject. [4]

"A typical black student is graduating from high school with junior high school skills," Thernstrom says, citing figures from the National Assessment of Educational Progress (NAEP) — informally known as "the nation's report card." Hispanics, she says, "are doing only a tad better."

Traditional civil rights advocates acknowledge the gap, but they say that closing the gap requires more thoroughgoing desegregation and better funding for schools with large numbers of minority or low-income students. But educational conservatives discount those solutions, calling instead for changing "school culture" by improving discipline, teaching and student behavior.

One path to those changes, conservatives say, is "school choice" — vouchers that help students pay for private school tuition and charter schools that operate with freedom from traditional regulations. Traditional civil rights groups generally oppose vouchers and voice some doubts about char-

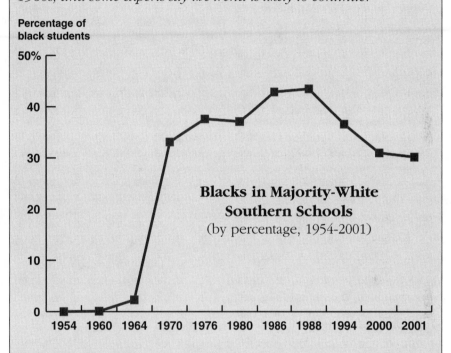

School-Integration Trend Reversing

The Supreme Court's landmark 1954 Brown v. Board of Education *ruling declared racial segregation in public schools unconstitutional. But after more than three decades, the desegration trend in U.S. schools reversed after 1988 — particularly in the South. Then a series of Supreme Court decisions between 1991 and 1995 eased the pressure on school districts to continue desegregation efforts. Today U.S. classrooms are almost as segregated as they were in the late 1960s, and some experts say the trend is likely to continue.*

Percentage of black students

Blacks in Majority-White Southern Schools
(by percentage, 1954-2001)

*Source: Gary Orfield and Chungmei Lee, "*Brown *at 50: King's Dream or* Plessy's *Nightmare?" The Harvard Civil Rights Project, January 2004*

ter schools, saying they drain support from public schools and risk further resegregation of minority students.

The policy debates underscore the shared view that *Brown* — despite its iconic status — has not proved a complete success. "You have to say it was a partial failure," says James Patterson, a professor emeritus of history at Brown University and author of a new account of the ruling and its impact.

Theodore Shaw, director of the Legal Defense Fund, agrees: "*Brown* changed everything and yet did not change everything."

As the nation prepares to unite in celebrating *Brown*, here are some of the issues that divide Americans 50 years later:

Is racial imbalance in schools increasing due to court actions?

North Carolina's Charlotte-Mecklenburg County school system in 1971 became the first in the country to operate under a court-ordered desegregation plan using wide-scale busing to achieve racial balance in school populations. Under the plan, African-Americans comprised between 30 percent and

Latinos' Unheralded Struggles for Equal Education

When school board officials in Lemon Grove, Calif., became concerned in 1930 that Mexican-American students were slowing down the Anglo pupils, they hit upon a simple solution: build a new school solely for the Mexican-Americans.

To the board's surprise, however, Mexican-Americans in the small border community protested, deriding the new facility as a "barn." And — more than two decades before the Supreme Court declared racial segregation in public schools unconstitutional — they won a lower-court order forcing the school board to dismantle the plans for a dual system of education. [1]

The Lemon Grove incident is one of many efforts by Latinos to fight for educational equity well before the Supreme Court's landmark 1954 decision in *Brown v. Board of Education.* The history of those efforts, however, has gone largely untold. "These cases are not taught, even in law school," says Margaret Montoya, a professor at the University of New Mexico School of Law.

Today, Latinos continue to receive far less attention in school desegregation debates than African-Americans even though Latinos now comprise the nation's largest ethnic minority, and Latino students are somewhat more likely than blacks to be in ethnically identifiable schools.

"We don't see an equal commitment on the part of educational equity for Latinos," says James Ferg-Cadima, legislative staff attorney for the Mexican American Legal Defense and Educational Fund (MALDEF) in Washington.

The Lemon Grove ruling was never appealed and had no further impact in California. Chicano families won a similar ruling from a lower court in Texas around the same time. It, too, did nothing to undo the advancing segregation of Mexican-American students in that state. [2]

In 1946, however, a federal appeals court in California ruled in favor of Mexican-American parents contesting school segregation in four districts in Orange County, south of Los Angeles. Ferg-Cadima says the case "could have been a precursor to *Brown v. Board of Education,*" but the school districts decided not to appeal. The ruling did lead to a law in 1947, however, that barred school segregation in the state. The act was signed by then-Gov. Earl Warren, who later became chief justice and author of the *Brown* decision. [3]

Perversely, Mexican-American families prevailed in some of their early legal efforts on the grounds that they were white and could not be segregated as black students were. "We have not been treated as a white subgroup, and we don't think of ourselves as a white subgroup," Montoya says. "But when the litigation was being developed, that seemed to be a reasonable way of trying to get kids educational rights." One consequence, Montoya adds, has been "to drive a wedge between Latinos and African-Americans."

The Supreme Court recognized Latinos as a separate group for desegregation purposes only in 1973 in a case from Denver. [4] By that time, however, the justices were about to pull back on school-desegregation remedies. "About the time we could have profited from *Brown* and used it ourselves, the protection starts crumbling," Ferg-Cadima says. Latinos have been the principal beneficiaries, however, of the Supreme Court's unanimous 1974 decision that school districts must make sure that non-English-speaking students are given language skills needed to profit from school attendance. [5]

Language is among the educational barriers distinctive to Latino students. Another, Ferg-Cadima says, is the migratory status of many Latino families, especially in agricultural areas in California, Texas and the Southwest.

Today, most Latino students attend majority-Latino schools in every region of the country, according to The Harvard Civil Rights Project. [6] As with African-American students, ethnic isolation for Latinos increased through the 1990s. The most intense segregation is found in the Northeast, where 45 percent of Hispanic students attend schools that are 90 to 100 percent Hispanic.

As for educational achievement, Latinos lag far behind white students and only slightly ahead of African-Americans. The average Latino student scored around the 25th percentile in both reading and mathematics in the 1999 National Assessment of Educational Performance — the so-called nation's report card. [7]

"The one lesson from *Brown* for all minority communities is that educational equity must be battled for on all fronts — it's something that has to be sought out," Ferg-Cadima says. "The schoolhouse gate isn't always open for our kids, so we have to fight for schools to be open and conducive to learning for all students."

---

[1] Robert R. Alvarez Jr., "The Lemon Grove Incident: The Nation's First Successful Desegregation Court Case," *The Journal of San Diego History,* Vol. 32, No. 2 (spring 1986). Alvarez is the son of the lead plaintiff in the case, *Alvarez v. Board of Trustees of the Lemon Grove School District.*

[2] See "Project Report: De Jure Segregation of Chicanos in Texas Schools," *Harvard Civil Rights-Civil Liberties Law Review,* Vol. 7, No. 2 (March 1972), pp. 307-391. The authors are Jorge C. Rangel and Carlos M. Alcala.

[3] See Vicki L. Ruiz, "'We Always Tell Our Children They Are Americans': *Méndez v. Westminster* and the California Road to *Brown v. Board of Education,*" *The College Board Review,* No. 200 (fall 2003), pp. 20-27. See also Charles Wollenberg, *All Deliberate Speed: Segregation and Exclusion in California Schools, 1855-1975* (1976), pp. 108-135.

[4] The case is *Keyes v. Denver School District No. 1,* 413 U.S. 921 (1973).

[5] The case, brought by non-English-speaking Chinese students in San Francisco, is *Lau v. Nichols,* 414 U.S. 563 (1974).

[6] Gary Orfield and Chungmei Lee, "Brown at 50: King's Dream or Plessy's Nightmare?," Harvard Civil Rights Project, January 2004, p. 21.

[7] Cited in Abigail Thernstrom and Stephan Thernstrom, *No Excuses: Closing the Racial Gap in Learning* (2001), pp. 19-20.

---

40 percent of the students at most of the schools through the 1970s and '80s. [5]

With public support for desegregation weakening, however, the school system shifted in the 1990s to volun-

tary measures to maintain racial balance — chiefly by attracting white students to majority-black schools by turning them into magnet schools. Then, at the end of the decade, white families successfully sued the school system, forcing it to dismantle the busing plan altogether. [6]

The result, combined with increasing percentages of African-American and Hispanic students in the system, has been a growing concentration of minorities in many schools. Today, more than one-third of the county's 148 schools have at least 80 percent non-white enrollment.

Civil rights advocates say Charlotte is one of many school systems where political and legal developments have contributed to a trend toward resegregation. "The federal court required Charlotte to resegregate," says Harvard's Orfield, "and they are resegregating — fast."

Critics of mandatory integration, however, say today's concentration of non-white students, particularly in urban school systems, largely reflects residential demographics. Nationwide, whites comprise only about 60 percent of students in public schools, compared to 80 percent in the late 1960s. In Charlotte today, 43 percent of the system's 114,000 students are black, and only 42 percent white.

"It's wrong to say that schools are segregated or becoming resegregated," says Abigail Thernstrom, a former member of the Massachusetts Board of Education. "Cities are becoming more heavily minority. There's nothing we can do about that. You can't helicopter kids in to get more white kids in the schools."

Orfield acknowledges that the increase in non-white enrollment poses "an obstacle" to racial mixing. But he and other desegregation advocates blame resegregation primarily on the courts, including the Supreme Court.

The percentage of black students attending majority-black schools was declining nationwide through the 1980s, Harvard Civil Rights Project reports show, but it increased during the 1990s — just as the Supreme Court

Three high school students in Clinton, Tenn., peacefully register their feelings about their school becoming the first in Tennessee to integrate, on Aug. 27, 1956. Many other protests were violent.

was signaling to federal courts that they could ease desegregation orders. "The only basic thing that's changed since [the 1980s] is the Supreme Court of the United States," Orfield maintains. [7]

"This is a demographic process," responds Armor, "and has little to do with what the courts are doing in the desegregation area."

Education Secretary Paige also argues that court rulings are not responsible for the increasing racial isolation of blacks or Latinos. "It's not our impression that these patterns are the result of current

legal practices," he says. "Ethnic communities cluster together because of a lot of different factors. Some of these factors include preferences; some are economic."

The Harvard civil rights report found that during the 1990s the trend toward integration was reversed, and the percentage of black students attending majority-black schools increased throughout the country. The percentage of Latino students attending majority-minority schools also increased in every region. Latinos are more likely than African-Americans to be in a racially or ethnically identifiable school, the report shows.

Educational conservatives, however, claim that Orfield presents a misleading picture by focusing exclusively on minority pupils' exposure to white students and not on white students' exposure to blacks and Latinos. "There are fewer white children who have no non-white classmates," says Stephan Thernstrom. "More and more white children have minority classmates."

More broadly, conservatives insist that talk of resegregation ignores the changes wrought by *Brown*. "There is no public school today that is segregated in the way that schools were routinely segregated before *Brown v. Board of Education*," says Roger Clegg, vice president and general counsel of the Center for Equal Opportunity, which opposes racial preferences. "Racial balance in a school that reflects the neighborhood is not segregation in the sense that we had segregation before *Brown*."

Shaw, of the Legal Defense Fund, counters that segregation never was

Minority Students Are Now More Isolated

The 1954 Brown *ruling led to widespread school integration, but today, due to resegregation, an overwhelming percentage of African-American and Latino students attend schools with predominantly non-white student bodies. Segregation has increased nationwide since 1991, when the Supreme Court began to relax pressure on school districts to integrate.*

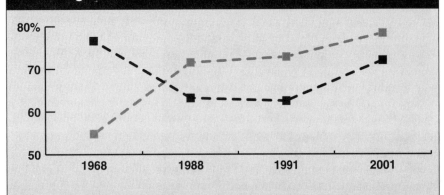

Percentage of Blacks and Latinos in 50-100% Minority Schools

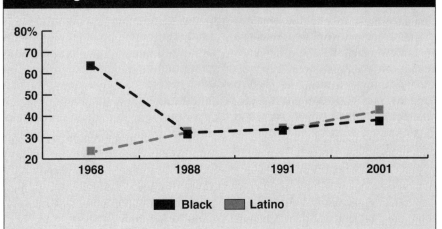

Percentage of Blacks and Latinos in 90-100% Minority Schools

■ **Black** ■ **Latino**

Source: "Brown at 50: King's Dream or Plessy's *Nightmare?" The Civil Rights Project, Harvard University, January 2004.*

Shaw and Orfield both say school boards should be allowed to consider race and ethnicity in pupil-assignment plans in order to promote integration. But educational conservatives oppose policies to deliberately increase racial mixing.

"I like racially mixed schools better than racially homogeneous schools," Abigail Thernstrom says. "But I do not want computer printouts that say you have no choice as to where to send your kids."

Do minorities suffer educationally because of racial isolation?

Black and Latino youngsters lag significantly behind whites (and Asian-Americans) on every significant measure of academic achievement. The "racial gap" in learning deeply troubles advocates and experts on both sides of the desegregation debate.

Traditional civil rights advocates largely blame racial isolation for the lagging performance of blacks and Latinos. There is "a very systematic relation" between segregation and the learning gap, Orfield says. "No one has ever made separate schools equal in American history on any scale."

Some critics of mandatory integration, however, see no solid evidence that racially mixed classrooms significantly benefit learning. "There is absolutely no reason to assume that because schools are heavily Hispanic or black that these children can't learn, that they have to sit next to whites or Asians in order to learn," Abigail Thernstrom says.

The social-science evidence on the issue is voluminous but less than clearcut. In his review of the literature, George Mason University's Armor concludes that racial composition "by itself" has "no significant effect on black achievement." When combined with other educational improvements, he says, desegregation has improved black achievement "to a limited but significant degree." [8]

eliminated completely and is increasing today. "The legal fiction is that we've severed the link between present-day segregation and our past segregated and discriminatory actions," Shaw says. "The truth is that the effects of decades and decades of segregation and discrimination were to segregate housing and to segregate other aspects of life.

"The busing remedies didn't eliminate the effects of that discrimination; they neutralized them," Shaw continues. "Once you get rid of the desegregation plans, those effects become operative once again."

Desegregation advocates strongly disagree with this minimalist view. Orfield says the effect of desegregation on achievement is "significant, but not transformative." But he adds that desegregation has a "huge" effect on "life chances," such as graduating from high school, going to college and "being able to live in an interracial world as an adult." [9]

In an examination of data from Charlotte-Mecklenburg schools, Roslyn Mickelson, a professor of sociology at the University of North Carolina in Charlotte, found that black and white students both had higher average scores on standardized tests if they had been in racially integrated schools. "There is a small but significant effect on test scores that cumulates over time," she says. [10]

Orfield and other desegregation advocates say the achievement gap for minority students results in part from underfunding of schools with high percentages of black or Latino students. "The resources aren't equivalent because those are often schools that have a badge of poverty," says Underwood of the school boards association. "So they have fewer resources." U.S. schools traditionally have received most of their funding from property taxes, so schools in wealthier neighborhoods usually had more resources than schools in districts with lower property values. [11]

Armor and the Thernstroms instead blame the racial gap primarily on social and cultural factors. "There are very strong correlations between single-parent households, low birth-weight and performance in school," says Abigail Thernstrom. Armor lists single-parent households as one of 10 "risk factors" for low academic achievement. Some of the others include poverty, limited education of parents, the size of the family and the age of the mother at pregnancy. [12]

The most incendiary aspect of the issue, perhaps, concerns the claim that some black students disdain academic achievement for fear of being ac-

cused by their peers of "acting white." The thesis is most often associated with the work of the late John Ogbu, an African-American professor of anthropology at the University of California, Berkeley, who died in 2003. Ogbu first aired the theory in a co-authored article about Washington, D.C., high school students in 1986 and repeated similar views in a book about students in the affluent Cleveland suburb of Shaker Heights. [13]

Education Secretary Paige subscribes to the theory based not only on Ogbu's research but also on his own experience as school superintendent in Houston. "I had a chance to see examples where some kids were not putting their best efforts into this in an effort to keep status among some of their peers," Paige says. "It exists."

Armor, however, discounts the theory, noting that the educational gap for African-Americans can be found at the earliest grades. Abigail Thernstrom also says the evidence is "not very good." She places greater blame on schools' failure to instill educational ambitions in minority youngsters. "Schools are delivering a wrong message — that this is a racist society, and there's a limit to how far you can go," she says.

But the Legal Defense Fund's Shaw says there is evidence of an "acting white" syndrome and says the issue needs more discussion among African-Americans. But he adds that some of the debate over the educational gap for black students has "the lurking sense of racial inferiority."

"If people come to this issue in good faith and they want to focus on the causes, the first thing they have to recognize is that there's still massive inequality," Shaw says. "By the time you get to high school, African-American students have had a completely different experience from white students. Let's not blame the victim. Let's fix the problem."

Would "school choice" policies help reduce the racial gap in educational

achievement for African-Americans and Latinos?

President Bush touts school vouchers, not integration, as the best way to help disadvantaged students get a better education. "When we find children trapped in schools that will not change, parents must be given another viable option," Bush told students and teachers at Archbishop Carroll High School in Washington on Feb. 13, 2004. The president used the appearance to plug a new law he had just signed to award vouchers to some 1,700 District of Columbia students per year to help pay tuition at private schools. [14]

Educational conservatives say "school choice" programs such as vouchers or charter schools will help improve schools by promoting innovation and overcoming resistance to change from public school administrators and teachers. Education Secretary Paige claims particular support for school choice among African-American families.

"My reading of the polls shows that African-American parents support choice, vouchers, strongly," Paige says. "The parents are supporters because the parents want the best education for the child."

The public school establishment strongly opposes vouchers, saying they would drain needed money from public schools. Underwood, the school boards association lawyer, says vouchers also "threaten any kind of diversity agenda that a school district may have." Private schools, she says, "can choose to discriminate. They can choose not to serve students with special needs or students who are poor or of a particular culture or ethnicity."

Local voucher programs are already operating in Milwaukee and Cleveland; Florida has a statewide program pushed by Gov. Jeb Bush, the president's brother. The programs are targeted to middle- and low-income families, but are small-scale because of limited funding. "Vouchers are going to be a sideshow for American education," Orfield says.

Charter schools — which operate under public auspices but free from some generally applicable regulations — are more widespread. [15] Some 2,700 charter schools were operating as of the 2002-2003 academic year. Many of them were established by black families and educators to serve the educational needs of African-American students. But Orfield and other desegregation advocates are skeptical that they will be better for black pupils than public schools.

"There is no evidence that charter schools are better than average," Orfield says, "and our studies show that they're more segregated than public schools."

Abigail Thernstrom counters that vouchers and charter schools "have the potential" to improve education for minority youngsters. "They have the potential for one very simple reason," she says. "They are out from under the constraints that make for such mediocre education in so many public schools."

Armor, however, sees no necessary benefit for minority youngsters from school choice programs. "I don't see personally why vouchers or charters would have any automatic impact on school quality," Armor says. "It might or might not. There's nothing intrinsic about charters that says those teachers are going to have a better subject mastery" than teachers at regular schools. As for vouchers, Armor says they "can also be used to go to a school that doesn't have better programs" than regular public schools.

Public-education groups cite underfunding as a major barrier to improving education for minority youngsters. Nationwide, schools with the highest minority or low-income enrollments receive $1,000 less per student than schools with the lowest minority or poverty enrollments, according to a report by the Education Trust, a Washington advocacy group. (*See map, p. 244.*)

"There is definitely a relationship between the amount of funding a district gets and academic performance," says Kevin Carey, a senior policy analyst with the group. "There are im-

portant issues besides money: organization, expectations for students, curricula, the way teachers are compensated. But money matters, too."

"We need to pay attention to sending resources where resources are needed," Underwood says, "so students with high educational needs get the resources they need to learn, so you really aren't leaving any child behind."

But Paige and other educational conservatives discount the importance of funding. "I don't accept that the achievement gap is a function of funding issues," Paige says. "It is a factor, but it is not *the* factor. The more important factors are those factors embedded in the No Child Left Behind Act: accountability, flexibility and parental choice — and teaching methods that work."

Orfield, however, says the No Child Left Behind Act has produced "confusion and frustration" for local school districts with scant evidence of help for minority pupils. [16] And the Legal Defense Fund's Shaw insists that school choice proposals could help only some minority students while leaving most of them behind.

"Most African-American students, like most students, are going to remain in public schools," Shaw says. "The promise of *Brown* isn't going to be realized by focusing on those few students who can escape from public schools. If we don't talk about fixing public education, then I think we betray not only *Brown* but also the fundamental notion of what public education is all about."

BACKGROUND

Long, Hard Road

The Supreme Court's celebrated decision in *Brown v. Board of Education* marks neither the beginning

nor the end of the campaign for equal education for black Americans. It was only a turning point in a struggle with roots in the 19th century that now extends into the 21st. [17]

Black youngsters received no education in the antebellum South and little schooling in the decades immediately after the abolition of slavery. Where blacks did go to school, they were segregated from whites in most (though not all) parts of the country, by law or custom. Some legal challenges to the practice in the 19th century succeeded, but the Supreme Court thwarted any broad attack on segregation with its 1896 decision in *Plessy v. Ferguson* upholding "separate but equal" in public transportation.

The NAACP — founded in 1909 — won its first victory against racial segregation in education in 1935, with a state court ruling to admit a black student to the University of Maryland's law school. Four years later, one of the winning lawyers, Thurgood Marshall, was named to head a separate organization: the NAACP Legal Defense and Educational Fund, Inc. The Inc. Fund — as it was then known — won important victories from the Supreme Court with two unanimous decisions in 1950 striking down segregationist practices in graduate education at state universities in Oklahoma and Texas. [18]

Meanwhile, Marshall had been helping organize local campaigns against segregation in elementary and secondary education in four Southern and Border States. The four cases, which were consolidated in the *Brown* decision, differed in their facts and in their legal histories: Black schools in Clarendon County, S.C., were mostly ramshackle shanties; those in Topeka, Kansas, were more nearly comparable to schools for whites. The federal judge in the Prince Edward County, Va., case found "no hurt or harm to either race" in dual school

Chronology

Before 1950

Racial segregation takes root in public schools — by law in the South, by custom elsewhere; NAACP begins challenging "separate but equal" doctrine in the 1930s.

———•———

1950s-1960s

Supreme Court outlaws racial segregation; ruling provokes massive resistance in South.

1950
Supreme Court bars racial segregation in public graduate education.

1954
Supreme Court rules racial segregation in public elementary and secondary schools unconstitutional on May 17, 1954 (*Brown I*).

1955
Court says schools must be desegregated "with all deliberate speed" (*Brown II*).

1957
President Dwight D. Eisenhower calls out Arkansas National Guard to maintain order when Little Rock's Central High School is integrated.

1964
Civil Rights Act authorizes federal government to bring school-desegregation suits and to withhold funds from schools that fail to desegregate.

1968
Impatient with limited desegregation, Supreme Court says school districts must dismantle dual school systems "now."

1970s-1980s

Desegregation advances, but busing triggers battles in many cities.

1971
Supreme Court upholds use of busing as desegregation tool.

1973
Supreme Court orders Denver to desegregate, making it the first non-Southern city ordered to integrate.

1974
Supreme Court bars federal courts from ordering cross-district busing to achieve desegregation . . . Start of busing in Boston provokes fierce opposition.

1975
Coleman report blames white-flight from urban public schools on court-ordered busing; desegregation advocates disagree.

Late 1980s
Integration peaks, with most African-American students still attending predominantly black schools in each of five regions across country.

———•———

1990s *Many school systems freed from court supervision; race-conscious assignments challenged as "reverse discrimination."*

1998, 1999
Federal courts strike racial preferences used for Boston Latin School, "magnet" schools in two Washington, D.C., suburban districts.

1991
Supreme Court allows judges to lift court orders if segregation has been eliminated to all "practicable" extent.

1995
Supreme Court says judges in desegregation cases should try to end supervision of school systems.

———•———

2000-Present

Brown's promise hailed, impact debated.

2001
President Bush wins passage of No Child Left Behind Act, providing penalties for school districts that fail to improve students' overall scores on standardized tests. . . . Federal court in September lifts desegregation decree for Charlotte-Mecklenburg schools in North Carolina.

2003
Supreme Court upholds affirmative action for colleges and universities. . . . Federal judge in December hears challenge to racial guidelines for Louisville-Jefferson County Schools; federal appeals court in same month considers suit to bar use of race as "tiebreaker" in pupil assignments in Seattle.

2004
Brown decision widely celebrated as 50th anniversary approaches; civil rights advocates decry "resegregation," while others say emphasis on racial balance is divisive and unproductive. . . . Federal appeals court to hear challenge in June to racial-balance transfer policy for Lynn, Mass., schools.

Success Asian-American Style

"U ncivilized, unclean and filthy beyond all conception . . . they know not the virtues of honesty, integrity or good faith," fulminated Horace Greeley, the 19th-century abolitionist and social reformer, describing Chinese immigrants. [1]

But the numbers today tell a different story. By any measure, Asian-Americans have been phenomenally successful academically. As a result, the concentration of Asian students in top American schools is wildly disproportionate to their ratio in the U.S. population.

For example, Asians make up approximately 70 percent of San Francisco's most prestigious public school, Lowell High, with Chinese-Americans alone constituting over 50 percent, although Chinese make up only 31.3 percent of the school district.

The excellent scholastic record of Asian students dates back at least to the 1930s, when California teachers wrote of "ideal" Japanese students who could serve as an example to other students. Their delinquency rate was one-third that of whites.

Today, although Asians make up only 3.8 percent of the U.S. population, Asian-Americans accounted for 27 percent of the freshman class at the Massachusetts Institute of Technology in the 2000-2001 school year, 25 percent at Stanford, 24 percent at the California Institute of Technology and 17 percent at Harvard; Asians were a phenomenal 40 percent of the freshmen at the University of California, Berkeley, in 1999. One in five American medical students is Asian. [2] Similarly, between 10 and 20 percent of the students at the nation's premier law schools are Asian.

The achievement gap between whites and Asians is greater than the gap between blacks and whites, by some measures. In 2001, 54 percent of Asian-Americans between ages 25 and 29 had at least a bachelor's degree, compared with 34 percent of whites and 18 percent of blacks.

Academics have long disputed the reasons for Asians' stellar performance. The controversial 1994 book, *The Bell Curve*, held that Asians did better because they were inherently more intelligent than others. But numerous academics attacked Richard J. Herrnstein and Charles Murray's methodology and racial conclusions. Some studies show that Asians, particularly Chinese, consistently score higher on IQ tests than other groups. [3] But there is increasing evidence that racial differences are minimal. [4]

Another explanation attributes the relative success of Asians in America to the socioeconomic and educational status of the Asian immigrants who were allowed to enter the United States. In 1965, immigration reforms allotted immigrant visas preferentially to people with needed skills. Many came from India or China with advanced degrees in medicine or technology.

The parents' educational and occupational attainments "far exceed the average for native-born Americans," according to Stephen L. Klineberg, a Rice University sociology professor studying Houston-area demographics. [5] With such parents, the children seem primed for success, but critics of socioeconomic explanations point out that even though many early Asian immigrants were mainly laborers and peasants, they still performed exceptionally well in school.

Most of those early Asian-Americans, mainly Chinese, lived in California, where school segregation developed quickly. By 1863, "Negroes, Mongolians and Indians" were prohibited from attending schools with white children. [6] Statewide restrictions were soon amended so non-white children could attend public schools with whites where no separate schools existed; in areas with fewer Chinese immigrants, they often attended schools with whites. San Francisco responded by building a separate school for Chinese children in 1885.

In 1906, Japanese and Koreans also were ordered to attend the so-called Oriental School in San Francisco, although the Japanese resisted, and by 1929 the vast majority of Japanese children attended integrated schools. [7] The courts and legislature ended legal segregation in California schools in 1947.

However, Chinese immigrants in California have staunchly opposed integration proposals that required their children to be bused out of local neighborhoods. "One time, in the 1960s and '70s, when integration of schools was the big issue, I almost got lynched in Chinatown by Chinese-Americans for supporting integration," said Ling-chi Wang, a professor of ethnic studies at Berkeley and veteran civil rights advocate. [8] More recently, Chinese-American parents successfully challenged a San Francisco school-integration plan, arguing that their children were losing out due to racial quotas at magnet schools. [9]

Today, regardless of their parents' income level or education, Asian students perform better academically than other groups, though

---

systems; the state judge in the Delaware case declared that state-imposed segregation "adversely affected" education for blacks. The federal judge in Topeka also had agreed that separate schools were harmful for blacks but abided by Supreme Court precedent in rejecting any relief for the plaintiffs.

The four cases were argued before the Supreme Court twice — first in December 1952 and then again in December 1953. The justices were divided after the first argument. Five or six justices appeared inclined to declare segregation unconstitutional, according to later reconstructions of the deliberations. [19] But Chief Justice Fred

M. Vinson hesitated to press for a final decision and accepted the suggestion of Justice Felix Frankfurter to ask for a reargument.

Vinson's death in September 1953 paved the way for the appointment of Chief Justice Earl Warren, who as governor of California had signed a law abolishing racial segregation in that

their performance does improve as parental education and income increase. The persistent performance gap, even accounting for socioeconomic factors, leads to a third explanation for Asians' success: the great emphasis put on education by Asian parents, higher academic expectations and the attitude that successful achievement is simply a question of hard work.

For instance, a study by Temple University's Laurence Steinberg of 20,000 Wisconsin and California students found that Asian-American students felt any grade below A- would anger their parents; for whites the anger threshold was B-, for blacks and Latinos a C-. And research shows that more than 50 percent of Asian-American high school seniors spend an hour or more per night on homework, compared to 30 percent of Latinos and less than 25 percent of whites. [10]

Education experts often blame the gap between how white children and new immigrants perform educationally on the language barriers faced by the immigrants. But evidence suggests that newly arrived Asians learn English faster than Latinos, thus breaking down those barriers faster. For instance, 1990 Census data showed that 90 to 95 percent of third-generation Asian-American children spoke only English at home, compared to only 64 percent of Mexican-Americans. [11]

But Asian immigrants are not a monolithic "model minority." Asians who arrive already speaking English, such as Filipinos or Indians, fare better educationally and economically. The poverty rate among Filipino immigrants — who come from a country with a 95 percent literacy rate — is only 6.3 percent, compared with 37.8 percent among the Hmong — a mostly uneducated ethnic group from Southeast Asia.

In Sacramento, where Hmong comprise about 8 percent of

Asians were segregated from whites in California schools at the end of the 19th century. In 1885, San Francisco built a separate school for Chinese children.

public school students, they are the lowest-performing group, according to Suanna Gilman-Ponce, director of the school district's multilingual education department. [12] For example, only 3 percent of the Hmong had a bachelor's degree, according to the 1990 census, compared with 24 percent of the nation as a whole.

But there is progress: Among the 25-to-34 age group, the first Hmong generation to grow up in the United States, 13.5 percent had degrees. And of the Vietnamese, many of whom also arrived as refugees, 26.9 percent had a college degree; the national average is 27.5 percent.

— *Kenneth Lukas*

[1] Quoted in Andrew Gyory, *Closing the Gate* (1998), p. 17.

[2] Abigail Thernstrom and Stephan Thernstrom, *No Excuses: Closing the Racial Gap in Learning* (2003), p. 85.

[3] Jeff Wise, "Are Asians Smarter?" *Time International*, Sept. 11, 1995, p. 60.

[4] Natalie Angier, "Do Races Differ? Not Really, Genes Show," *The New York Times*, Aug. 22, 2000, p. F1 and Steve Olson, "The Genetic Archaeology of Race," *The Atlantic Monthly*, April 2, 2001, p. 69.

[5] Quoted in Mike Snyder, "Survey: Area Asians Have Head Start," *The Houston Chronicle*, Oct. 1, 2002, p. A1.

[6] For background on Asians in California, see Charles Wollenberg, *All Deliberate Speed: Segregation and Exclusion in California Schools, 1855-1975* (1976).

[7] Bill Hosokawa, *Nisei: The Quiet Americans* (2002), pp. 85-89.

[8] Quoted in Sam McManis, "Activist Fights for Asian Americans at U.S. Labs," *San Francisco Chronicle*, March 27, 2002, p. A1.

[9] David J. Hoff, "San Francisco Assignment Rules Anger Parents," *Education Week*, June 4, 2003, p. 9. See also "All Things Considered," National Public Radio, Aug. 10, 2002, and April 5, 2004.

[10] Thernstrom, *op. cit.*, p. 94.

[11] *Ibid.*, pp. 111-113.

[12] Quoted in Erika Chavez, "Hmong Cry for Help Has Been Heard," *Sacramento Bee*, May 28, 2002, p. B1.

state's public schools. [20] Warren used his considerable political skills to forge the unanimous decision on May 17, 1954, which buried the "separate but equal" doctrine, at least in public education. "Separate educational facilities," Warren wrote near the end of the 13-page opinion, "are inherently unequal."

A year later, the justices rejected both Marshall's plea to order immediate desegregation and a federal recommendation that a specific timetable for desegregation be established. Instead, the court in *Brown II* ruled that the four school districts be required to admit pupils on a racially non-discriminatory basis "with all deliberate speed." [21]

Public opinion polls indicated a narrow majority of Americans favored the ruling, but the court's gradualist approach allowed the formation of what became massive resistance. More than 100 members of Congress signed the "Southern Manifesto" in 1956 vowing to use "all lawful means" to reverse the ruling. Most school districts

What Americans Think About School Desegregation

While 60 percent of Americans think classroom racial diversity is "very important," 66 percent think school officials should not try to increase the diversity of local schools.

In elementary school, were your classmates of many different races, or mostly the same race?

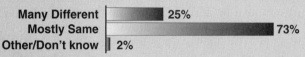

Many Different	25%
Mostly Same	73%
Other/Don't know	2%

Do the public elementary schools in your community today have kids mostly of the same race, or many different races?

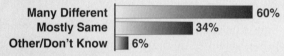

Many Different	60%
Mostly Same	34%
Other/Don't Know	6%

Did the Supreme Court make the right decision to end racial segregation in schools?

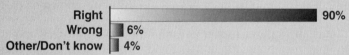

Right	90%
Wrong	6%
Other/Don't know	4%

How did ending racial segregation affect the quality of America's schools?

Better	45%
Worse	12%
No Change	34%
Other/Don't know	9%

How important is it that students of different races are in class together?

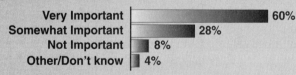

Very Important	60%
Somewhat Important	28%
Not Important	8%
Other/Don't know	4%

Should school officials try to increase the racial diversity of schools in your community?

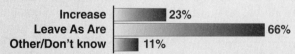

Increase	23%
Leave As Are	66%
Other/Don't know	11%

Source: Scripps Survey Research Center, Ohio University, www.newspolls.org. The national telephone survey of 1,013 people was taken Feb. 15-24, 2004.

dragged their feet, while even token integration efforts brought forth scattered bombings and violence and more widespread intimidation and harassment. In the most dramatic instance, President Dwight D. Eisenhower had to call out National Guardsmen in September 1957 to maintain order at Central High School in Little Rock, Ark., after nine black students were enrolled. As of 1964, only 2 percent of black students in the South were attending majority-white schools.

Facing resistance both active and passive, the Supreme Court left local federal courts largely on their own for nearly a decade. In 1964, however, Congress included provisions in the landmark Civil Rights Act that authorized the federal government to file school desegregation suits and to withhold funds from school districts that failed to desegregate. Four years later, the court — with Marshall now serving as the first African-American justice — announced that its patience was at an end. The justices rejected a "freedom of choice" plan offered by a rural Virginia school board and declared that school districts had to develop plans to dismantle dual systems "root and branch" — and to do it "now."

Given patterns of residential segregation, many plans devised by federal judges inevitably involved busing — typically, transporting black students to schools in predominantly white areas. Many white parents objected, but the court — under a new chief justice, Warren Burger — unanimously ruled in the *Charlotte-Mecklenburg* case in 1971 that courts had discretion to order busing as part of a desegregation plan.

Bumps in the Road

In the 1970s and '80s, desegregation advanced generally in the South and in most of the rest of the country. But the use of busing as a principal tool for racial mixing provoked fierce protests in some cities and widespread opposition from officials and the public at large. Meanwhile, Latino enrollment in public schools began to increase dramatically — and so, too, did the percentage of Latino students attending predominantly Latino schools.

The busing issue dominated the headlines and the policy debates in the 1970s, obscuring the less dramatic evidence of changes in public schools, especially in the South. From 1968 to 1988, the percentage of black students attending predominantly minority schools fell sharply in the South — from more than 80 percent to around 55 percent — and declined significantly in every other region except the Northeast.[22] As historian Patterson notes, most of the heavily black schools in the South were more nearly comparable to white schools by the end of the 1980s, salaries for black teachers were more nearly equal to those for whites and teaching staffs were integrated.

Public education in the South, he concludes, "had been revolutionized" — thanks to pressure from the then-Department of Health, Education and Welfare and rulings from federal courts.[23]

For many Americans, however, desegregation came to be understood only as court-ordered transportation of stu-

dents out of their neighborhoods to distant schools of uncertain character and quality. The polarizing issue erupted most dramatically in ostensibly liberal Boston, where a federal judge ordered racial mixing between heavily white South Boston and predominantly black Roxbury. Patterson notes that

Pioneering civil rights attorney Thurgood Marshall, shown here in 1957, successfully argued the landmark Brown v. Board of Education *case before the U.S. Supreme Court. President Lyndon B. Johnson appointed Marshall to the high court in 1967.*

Library of Congress

on the first day of the plan in September 1974, only 10 of the 525 white students assigned to Roxbury High School showed up, while buses carrying 56 black pupils bound for South Boston High School were stoned.[24]

Busing had few vocal supporters. President Gerald Ford, a Republican,

complained that busing "brought fear to black students and white students." President Jimmy Carter, a Democrat, was lukewarm toward the practice. Sociologist James Coleman — who authored an influential report in 1968 documenting the educational achievement gap for African-American students — added respectability to the anti-busing critique with a report in 1975 blaming "white flight" from central-city schools on court-ordered busing and calling instead for voluntary desegregation.[25]

Civil rights supporters countered that opponents were exaggerating the costs and disruption of court-ordered busing when their real objection was to racial mixing altogether. They also sharply disputed Coleman's "white flight" theory, insisting that the movement of whites to the suburbs — and the resulting concentration of African-Americans in inner cities — stemmed from social and economic trends dating from the 1950s unrelated to school desegregation.

The Supreme Court itself acknowledged the logistical problems of busing in some of its decisions, but the justices couched their emerging disagreements on desegregation in legalistic terms. In 1973, the court established a critical distinction between "de jure" segregation — ordered by law — and "de facto" segregation resulting only from residential segregation. The ruling allowed a lower court to enforce a desegregation plan, but only on the grounds that the school district had intentionally drawn zones to separate black and white pupils. (The ruling also recognized Hispanic students as an identifiable class for desegregation purposes.) In a partial dissent, Justice Lewis F. Powell Jr. criticized the distinction between "de facto" and "de jure" segregation, saying any racial separation of students was constitutionally suspect.

A year later, the court dealt integration advocates a more serious setback in a 5-4 ruling that barred transportation of students across school-district lines to achieve desegregation. The ruling struck down a desegregation plan for the heavily black Detroit school district and the predominantly white schools in surrounding Wayne County suburbs. For the majority, Chief Justice Burger said school district lines "could not be casually ignored." In dissent, Marshall called the ruling "a large step backwards."

Three years later, the court dealt another blow to desegregation advocates by ruling — in a case from Pasadena, Calif. — that a school district was not responsible for resegregation of students once it had adopted a racially neutral attendance plan.

The rulings combined with political opposition and socioeconomic trends to stall further increases in racial mixing of students by the end of the 1980s. The percentage of black students attending predominantly minority schools increased after 1988 in the South and West and after 1991 in the Northeast, Midwest and Border States. The Supreme Court, under the leadership of conservative Chief Justice William H. Rehnquist, then eased the pressure on school districts to continue desegregation efforts with three more decisions between 1991 and 1995.

The rulings — in cases from Oklahoma City; suburban DeKalb County, Ga.; and Kansas City — effectively told federal judges to ease judicial supervision once legally enforced segregation had been eliminated to the extent practicable. For the majority, Rehnquist wrote in the Kansas City case that federal judges should remember that their purpose was not only to remedy past violations but also to return schools to the control of local and state authorities.

Reversing Directions?

By the mid-1990s, traditional civil rights advocates were strongly criticizing what they termed the resegregation of African-American and Latino students. Critics of mandatory integration replied that legal segregation and its effects had been largely eliminated and that apparent racial and ethnic separation reflected residential neighborhoods and the growing proportion of African-American and Latino students in public schools.

As federal courts backed away from desegregation suits, white students brought — and in a few cases won — so-called reverse-discrimination suits contesting use of race in school-assignment plans. Meanwhile, some civil rights supporters shifted direction by bringing school-funding cases in state courts.

School-desegregation litigation all but petered out during the 1990s. Nearly 700 cases remain technically alive nationwide, but a law professor's examination of the period 1992-2002 found only 53 suits in active litigation. [26] Professor Wendy Parker of the University of Cincinnati College of Law also showed that school districts had succeeded in every instance but one when they asked for so-called unitary status — in order to get out from under further judicial supervision of desegregation decrees — even if enrollments continued to reflect racial imbalance.

In addition, Parker said judges were somewhat lax in requiring racial balance of teaching staffs and that any racial imbalance in teaching assignments invariably mirrored a school's racial composition: Schools with a disproportionate number of black teachers were predominantly black, those with disproportionate numbers of white teachers were predominantly white.

Meanwhile, a few federal courts were curbing school districts' discretion to consider race in assigning students to elite or so-called magnet

Police escort school buses carrying African-American students into South Boston in 1974, implementing a court-ordered busing plan to integrate schools.

schools. In 1998, the 1st U.S. Circuit Court of Appeals had ruled against the use of "flexible race/ethnicity guidelines" for filling about half of the places each year at the elite Boston Latin School. The court said the Boston School Committee had failed to show that the policy either promoted diversity or helped remedy vestiges of past discrimination. [27]

The next year, another federal appeals court ruled in favor of white students' claims that school boards in two suburban Washington, D.C., school districts — Montgomery County, Md., and Arlington, Va. — violated the Constitution's Equal Protection Clause by considering race in magnet-school placements. In both rulings, the 4th U.S. Circuit Court of Appeals said the use of race was not narrowly tailored to achieve the goal of diversity. The Supreme Court refused to hear the school districts' appeals. [28]

With federal courts seemingly uninterested in desegregation initiatives, civil rights groups put more resources into school-funding challenges before state legislatures or courts. [29] The various efforts, pushed in some 40 states, generally aimed at narrowing or eliminating financial disparities between well-to-do and less-well-off school districts. Funding-equity advocates succeeded in part in several states — sometimes through court order, sometimes by legislative changes spurred by actual or threatened litigation.

The initiatives helped cause a shift in education-funding sources away from the historic primary reliance on local property taxes. Today, just over half of local education funding comes from state rather than local revenues, according to Carey, of the Education Trust. Nonetheless, school districts with high minority or low-income enrollments still receive fewer funds compared to districts with more white or wealthier students.

The limited progress on funding issues gave civil rights advocates only slight consolation for the evidence of increasing racial imbalance in public schools. By 2001, at least two-thirds of black students and at least half of Latino students nationwide were enrolled in predominantly minority schools. Significantly, the Northeast is more segregated: More than half of black students (51 percent) and nearly half of Latino students (44 percent) attended intensely segregated schools with 90 to 100 percent minority enrollment. "We've been going backward almost every place in the country since the 1990s," Harvard's Orfield says.

Critics of mandatory integration, however, viewed the figures differently. They emphasized that white students' exposure to African-American and Latino students has continued to increase. In any event, they say, residential patterns, city-suburban boundary lines and the increasing percentages of African-American and Latino students in overall enrollment make it impractical to achieve greater racial mixing in many school districts.

"The proportion of minorities in large districts is growing," says George Mason's Armor. "When it crosses 50 percent, whatever your racial-assignment plan, you're going to have minority schools."

For his part, President Bush has pushed education reform aimed in part at helping low-income students but without adopting traditional civil rights goals or rhetoric. "American children must not be left in persistently dangerous or failing schools," Bush declared as he unveiled — on Jan. 23, 2001, his second full day in office — what eventually became the No Child Left Behind Act. Approved by Congress in May 2001, the law prescribes student testing to measure academic progress among public school students and provides

financial penalties for school districts that fail to improve student performance.

Education Secretary Paige says the law seeks to continue the effort to improve educational opportunities for all students started by *Brown v. Board of Education*. The law passed with broad bipartisan support. By 2004, however, many Democrats were accusing the administration of failing to provide funding to support needed changes, while many school administrators were criticizing implementation of the law as excessively rigid and cumbersome.

CURRENT SITUATION

Race-Counting

S chools in Lynn, Mass., were facing a multifaceted crisis in the 1980s, with crumbling buildings, tattered textbooks, widespread racial strife and rapid white flight. To regain public confidence, the school board in 1989 adopted a plan combining neighborhood-school assignments with a transfer policy that included only one major restriction: No child could transfer from one school to another if the move would increase racial imbalance at either of the schools involved.

The Lynn school board credits the plan with stabilizing enrollment, easing race relations and helping lift academic performance throughout the 15,000-student system. But lawyers for parents whose children were denied transfers under the plan are asking a federal appeals court to rule that the policy amounts to illegal racial discrimination.

'We've Yet to Achieve' Equality of Education

Secretary of Education Rod Paige was interviewed on March 24, 2004, in his Washington office by Associate Editor Kenneth Jost. Here are verbatim excerpts from that interview.

On his experience attending racially segregated schools:

"The fact that [white students] had a gym was a big deal. They played basketball on the inside. They had a big gym with lights and stuff on the inside. We played basketball on the outside with a clay court. We played up until the time that you couldn't see the hoop any more. . . . I wanted to take band, but there was no music. I wanted to play football, but there was no football team [until senior year]. . . . The concept of separate but equal is not at all academic for me. It is very personal. And even today . . . I don't know what I missed."

On the impact of the Brown v. Board of Education decision:

"Was the goal to take 'separate but equal' away . . . ? The answer would be [yes], in a very strong and striking way. If the goal was equality education, to level the educational playing field for all children, especially children of color, the answer is we've yet to achieve that."

On the resegregation of black and Latino students:

"Ethnic communities cluster together because of a lot of different factors. Some of these factors include preferences; some are economic. So our goal should be now to provide a quality education for a child no matter where they are in this system."

On efforts to promote racial balance in schools:

"If anybody is in a segregated school based on unfairness, then, yes, they should work against that. But . . . we don't want to get integration confused with educational excellence. We want to provide educational excellence to kids no matter what their location is [or] the ethnic makeup of their community."

Secretary of Education Rod Paige

U.S. Dept. of Education

On the use of race in pupil assignments:

"A person should not be disadvantaged because of the color of their skin. Nor should that person be advantaged because of the color of their skin. . . . That's the principle I would apply to any set of circumstances."

On "equal" opportunities for African-American and Latino students:

"I've got to come down on the side that there's a large amount of lower expectations for minority kids. . . . If there are lower expectations for a child, then the answer to your question has to be that there is not a fair opportunity."

On causes of the "racial gap" in learning:

"There are three drivers. One is the quality of instructional circumstances. . . . The second is the quantity of it . . . And the third one is student engagement. Learning is an active activity between the teacher and the student. So the student does have some responsibility here in terms of student engagement."

On underfunding of minority and low-income schools:

"I don't accept that the achievement gap is a function of funding issues. I think it is a factor, but it is not *the* factor. . . . The more important factors are those embedded in the No Child Left Behind Act: accountability, flexibility and parental choice — and teaching methods that work."

On school choice proposals — vouchers and charter schools:

"My reading of the polls show[s] that African-American parents support choice, vouchers, strongly. . . . The parents are supporters because [they] want the best education for the child. . . . Enforcing monopolistic tendencies on schools is a detriment to schools. The people who force these monopolistic tendencies on schools deny schools the opportunity to innovate, create and reach their potential."

"They're denying school assignments based on the color of the kid who's asking for the assignment," says Michael Williams, a lawyer with the Boston-based Citizens for the Preservation of Constitutional Rights.

The case — expected to be argued in September 2004 before the 1st U.S. Circuit Court of Appeals in Boston — is one of several nationwide where school boards with voluntary integration plans are facing legal actions

At Issue

Should the federal government do more to promote racial and ethnic diversity in public schools?

GARY ORFIELD
DIRECTOR, THE HARVARD CIVIL RIGHTS PROJECT
CO-AUTHOR, "BROWN AT 50: KING'S DREAM OR
PLESSY'S NIGHTMARE?"

WRITTEN FOR *THE CQ RESEARCHER*, APRIL 2004

*t*he federal government has taken no significant, positive initiatives toward desegregation or even toward serious research on multiracial schools since the Carter administration. In fact, Presidents Richard M. Nixon, Gerald Ford, Ronald Reagan and both George Bushes were generally opposed to urban desegregation and named like-minded appointees to run the major federal civil rights and education agencies. Attorney General John Ashcroft, for example, fought desegregation orders in St. Louis and Kansas City, and Reagan Supreme Court appointee Chief Justice William H. Rehnquist has consistently opposed urban desegregation.

Between 1965 and 1970, federal leadership played a decisive role in ending educational apartheid in the South and transforming it into the nation's most desegregated region. Southern schools were the most integrated for more than three decades, during which time black achievement, graduation and college attendance increased, and educational gaps began to close. But those schools now are seriously resegregating.

President Nixon largely ended enforcement of the 1964 Civil Rights Act in schools and intentionally stirred up national division over busing as part of his "Southern strategy." Then, in two separate 5-4 decisions in 1973 and 1974, four Nixon justices helped block school-finance equalization and desegregation across city-suburban lines. The federal government never enforced the Supreme Court's 1973 decision recognizing Latinos' right to desegregation. And in the 1990s the Rehnquist court thrice ended desegregation orders, effectively producing resegregation. Nearly 90 percent of the heavily segregated minority schools produced by this process have high rates of poverty and educational inequality.

Federal policy could help reverse the resegregation trend. First, leaders must make the compelling case that desegregation, properly implemented, is valuable for all students, preparing them to live and work in a multiracial society. Second, judicial vacancies and civil rights enforcement agencies should be staffed with progressives. Third, the desegregation-aid program could be revived to help suburbs experiencing racial change without preparation or resources.

In addition, serious research needs to be done on resegregation. Educational choice programs should forbid transfers that increase segregation and reward those that diminish it. And magnet school programs should be expanded. Finally, fair-housing enforcement should be greatly increased and policies adopted to help stabilize desegregated neighborhoods.

DAVID J. ARMOR
PROFESSOR OF PUBLIC POLICY, SCHOOL OF PUBLIC
POLICY, GEORGE MASON UNIVERSITY

WRITTEN FOR *THE CQ RESEARCHER*, APRIL 2004

*t*o answer this question, we must ask three related questions. First, do legal constraints prevent the promotion of diversity in public schools? The answer is yes. The Supreme Court has provided a legal framework for using race in public policy, and the justices recently clarified that framework in two cases involving college admissions in Michigan. Racial diversity can be a compelling government purpose, but policies must be narrowly tailored to reflect the use of race or ethnicity as only one factor, not the predominant factor, in the policy.

Applying this framework to public schools, race could not be used as the primary basis for assigning students to schools (as in old-fashioned busing plans), unless a school district was remedying illegal segregation. The use of race might be justified for controlling enrollment in a voluntary magnet school on the grounds that students should be allowed to choose racially diverse programs, but even this limited use of race is being challenged in the courts. The Supreme Court has yet to rule on diversity for K-12 public schools.

Second, does diversity bring clear social and educational benefits to public school children? Diversity unquestionably has social value, since it allows children from different backgrounds to learn about other cultures and how to work together. However, it is hard to find social outcomes that have consistently benefited from desegregation. For example, race relations have sometimes worsened after desegregation programs, particularly if they involved mandatory busing. Moreover, the formal educational value of diversity has not been proven, since large-scale school-desegregation programs have not reduced the racial gap in academic achievement.

The third question we must ask is what kind of promotion, if any, might be appropriate for the federal government? Federal agencies have an important but limited role in policies for K-12 public schools. They conduct research, sponsor special programs, conduct assessment and recently adopted policies to raise academic standards and accountability under the No Child Left Behind Act. Given the legal constraints on diversity programs and the uncertain educational benefits of diversity in K-12 schools, I do not think promoting diversity should be a high priority at this time.

However, since there is still a debate over the educational benefits of racial diversity programs, it would be appropriate for the federal government to sponsor research to help resolve this important issue.

aimed at eliminating any use of race in student assignments. Attorneys for the school boards are vigorously defending race-conscious policies.

"You cannot ignore race and expect that the issue will not be present in your school system," says Richard Cole, senior counsel for civil rights in the Massachusetts attorney general's office, who is defending the Lynn plan. "The only way is to take steps to bring kids of different racial groups together."

Meanwhile, the federal appeals court for Washington state is considering a challenge to the Seattle School District's use of race as one of several factors — a so-called "tiebreaker" — in determining assignments to oversubscribed schools. The 9th Circuit appeals court heard arguments on Dec. 14, 2003, in a three-year-old suit by the predominantly white Parents Involved in Community Schools claiming that the policy violates equal-protection guarantees. [30]

Opposing experts and advocates in the desegregation debate are also closely watching the Louisville case, where U.S. District Judge John Heyburn II is expected to rule by the end of the school year on Jefferson County's racial guidelines for pupil assignments. And in another case, a conservative public-interest law firm is in California state court claiming that a statewide initiative barring racial preferences prevents the Berkeley school system from asking for racial information from students and families or using the information for assignment purposes. [31]

Schools in Lynn, a gritty former mill town 10 miles north of Boston, were in "dire straits" in the 1980s before adoption of the integration plan, according to Cole. Attendance was down; violence and racial conflict were up. White students — who comprised more than 80 percent of the enrollment as of 1977 — were fleeing the schools at the rate of 5 percent a year. There was also evidence that white students were being allowed to transfer out of predominantly black schools in

Stanton Elementary School, in Stanton, Ky., reflects the current status of school integration in most of the nation. Most public schools are as segregated today as they were in 1969. During the 2000-2001 school year, for instance, only 30 non-white students were enrolled in the 2,500-student Stanton school district.

violation of the district's stated rules.

The school board adopted a multipronged strategy to try to stem white flight and improve schools for white and minority youngsters alike, Cole says. A neighborhood-school assignment plan was combined with the construction of new schools, including magnet schools, using funds under a state law to aid racial-balance programs. Cole says attendance rates and achievement levels are up, discipline problems down and enroll-

ment stabilized. The district's students are 58 percent minority, 42 percent white.

The citizens' group, which had earlier filed a suit that forced Boston to drop its use of busing for desegregation, sued Lynn schools in August 1999. Williams acknowledges the school system's past problems and more recent progress. But he says all of the improvements resulted from "race-neutral stuff that could have happened if the plan had not included a racial element."

U.S. District Judge Nancy Gertner rejected the group's suit in a 156-page ruling in December 2003. "The Lynn plan does not entail coercive assignments or forced busing; nor does it prefer one race over another," said Gertner, who was appointed by President Bill Clinton. "The message it conveys to the students is that our society is heterogeneous, that racial harmony matters — a message that cannot be conveyed meaningfully in segregated schools." [32]

Legal Defense Fund Director Shaw calls the legal challenges to voluntary desegregation plans "Orwellian." "Our adversaries have this perverted sense of the law and the Constitution that holds mere race consciousness — even if it's in support of desegregation — as discriminatory," he says.

But Clegg of the Center for Equal Opportunity says schools should not assign students on the basis of race or ethnicity. "The social benefits to achieving a predetermined racial or ethnic mix are very small compared to the social costs of institutionalized racial and ethnic discrimination," he says.

Race-Mixing?

Some two-dozen Washington, D.C., high school students gathered on a school day in late February for a "dialogue" with the president of the American Bar Association and the city's mayor about *Brown v. Board of Education*. Dennis Archer, a former mayor of Detroit, is black — as is Washington's mayor, Anthony Williams. And so, too, are all but three of Woodson High School's 700 students.

The students — chosen from an advanced-placement U.S. history course — listen respectfully as Archer and Williams relate the story of the *Brown* case and the implementation of the ruling over the ensuing 50 years. The students' questions, however, make clear that they feel little impact from the ruling in their daily lives.

"Why is there such a small percentage of white students in D.C. schools?" Danyelle Johnson asks. Wesley Young echoes the comment: "I feel that to make it better we should be like Wilson [High School] and have different races in schools," he says, referring to a well-regarded integrated school in a predominantly white neighborhood.

"It's really hard for me to make [*Brown*] relevant to them," assistant principal Phyllis Anderson remarks afterward, "because they've been in an all-black environment all their lives, and their parents before them."

With 84 percent of its 65,000 public school students black, another 10 percent Hispanic and only 5 percent white, Washington provides an extreme, but not unrepresentative, example of the situation in central-city school districts throughout the country. Nationwide, central-city black students typically attend schools with 87 percent minority enrollment, according to the Harvard Civil Rights Project. For Latinos, the figure is 86 percent. This "severe segregation" results from residential segregation and the "fragmentation" of large metropolitan regions into separate school districts, the project's most recent survey explains. [33]

The Supreme Court's 1974 ruling barring court-ordered interdistrict desegregation plans virtually eliminated the possibility of racial mixing between inner cities and suburbs except in countywide systems like those in Louisville-Jefferson County and Charlotte-Mecklenburg County. The court's ruling in the Kansas City desegregation case in 1995 also limited federal judges' power to order costly improvements for central-city schools in an effort to attract white students from the suburbs.

Over the past decade or so, middle-class blacks and Latinos have themselves migrated to the suburbs, but because of residential segregation the movement has not fundamentally changed the pattern of racial isolation in the schools, according to the Harvard report. Even in the suburbs of large metropolitan areas, the typical black student attends a school that is 65 percent minority, the typical Latino a school that is 69 percent minority. [34]

Federal courts, meanwhile, have been freeing dozens of school districts from judicial supervision by declaring the segregated systems dismantled and granting the districts "unitary status." In an examination of 35 such districts, the Harvard study found that black students' exposure to whites had fallen in all but four — typically, by at least 10 percent. "Desegregation is declining rapidly in places the federal courts no longer hold accountable," the report concludes. [35]

The Legal Defense Fund's Shaw says the trends result from judicial solicitude for school districts that once practiced segregation. "If a snapshot reveals a desegregated district," he says, "the court can grant judicial absolution, and the district can return to a segregated status."

The Manhattan Institute's Abigail Thernstrom counters that the focus on racial mixing is beside the point. "Teach the kids instead of worrying about the racial composition of the school," she says. "Otherwise, we're chasing demographic rainbows. Cities aren't going to get whiter. And they're not going to get more middle-class."

OUTLOOK

Mixed Records

Fifty years after the Supreme Court declared the end of racial segregation, the four communities involved in the historic cases present mixed records on the degree of progress in bringing black and white children together in public schools. [36]

Topeka — home of Oliver Brown and his daughter Linda, then in elementary school — achieved "substantial levels of integration" while under a court-ordered desegregation plan, according to the Harvard Civil Rights Project. But integration has receded slightly since the system was declared unitary and judicial supervision was ended in 1999.

As of 2001, black students in Topeka were in schools with 51 percent white enrollment — down from 59 percent in 1991. Just outside the city limits, however, better-off suburban school districts have predominantly white enrollments. "The city was then, as it is now, physically and emotionally segregated," Ronald Griffin, a black professor at Washburn University Law School in Topeka, remarked at a symposium in 2002. "That has not changed." [37]

The Delaware case "led to the merger and full desegregation of all students" in Wilmington and adjoining suburban districts, the Harvard report says. The federal court lifted judicial supervision in 1996, but Wilmington and the entire state remain as some of the most integrated school systems in the country, according to the report.

The two Southern communities involved in the four cases present a sharp contrast. Prince Edward County, Va., resisted integration to the point of closing all public schools from 1959 until the Supreme Court ordered them reopened in 1964. Today, however, the school system has an integration level "far above the national average" and student achievement in line with other Virginia districts, despite a predominantly black enrollment, according to the Harvard report.

In Clarendon County, S.C., however, School District Number One in tiny Summertown has only 60 white students among a total enrollment of 1,100. Other white students attend a private academy set up at the start of desegregation in 1969. When an *Education Week* reporter recently asked Jonathan Henry — a great-great-grandson of one of the plaintiffs — about his interactions with white students, Henry seemed "bewildered. . . . He really doesn't know any." [38]

The legacy of the *Brown* cases is "mixed," according to historian Patterson. "It seems in the early 2000s to be somewhat more complicated, somewhat more mixed than anybody in the 1970s could have imagined."

"We are miles ahead because of *Brown*," Education Secretary Paige says. "But we have yet to achieve" the goal of equal educational opportunities for all students.

Whatever has or has not been accomplished in the past, the nation's changing demographics appear to be combining with law and educational policy to push ethnic and racial mixing to the side in favor of an increased emphasis on academic performance. Schools "are going to be more racial-

ly identifiable," the Legal Defense Fund's Shaw says. "I don't see any public policy right now that's going to turn that around."

Critics of mandatory integration applaud the change. "At the end of the day, what you want to ask is, 'Are the kids getting an education?'," Abigail Thernstrom says. "The right question is what are kids learning, not whom are they sitting next to."

The emphasis on academic performance makes the challenges for schools and education policy-makers all the more difficult, however, not less. "The black kid who arrives at school as a 5- or 6-year old is already way, way behind, and it just gets worse as they go on," historian Patterson says. "There's only so much the schools can do."

Latino youngsters enter school with many of the same socioeconomic deficits, often combined with limited English proficiency. In any event, the debates about educational policy have yet to catch up with the fact that Latinos are now the nation's largest minority group. [39] "We don't see an equal commitment on the part of educational equity for Latinos," says James Ferg-Cadima, an attorney for the Mexican American Legal Defense and Educational Fund.

"It's a major challenge for all of us to work together collegially to make sure that our children get the education they deserve," ABA President Archer says. "We're going to have to do a lot more to make sure all of our children in public schools — or wherever they are — graduate with a good education and can be competitive in a global economy."

Notes

[1] The decision is *Brown v. Board of Education of Topeka*, 347 U.S. 483 (1954). The ruling came in four consolidated cases from

Topeka; Clarendon County, S.C.; Prince Edward County, Va.; and Wilmington-Kent County, Del. In a companion case, the court also ruled racial segregation in the District of Columbia unconstitutional: *Bolling v. Sharpe*, 347 U.S. 497 (1954).

[2] The case is *McFarland v. Jefferson County Public Schools*, 3:02CV-620-H. For coverage, see Chris Kenning, "School Desegregation Plan on Trial," *The* (Louisville) *Courier-Journal*, Dec. 8, 2003, p. 1A, and subsequent daily stories by Kenning, Dec. 9-13. McFarland's quote is from his in-court testimony.

[3] For background, see Kenneth Jost, "Rethinking School Integration," *The CQ Researcher*, Oct. 18, 1996, pp. 913-936.

[4] Abigail Thernstrom and Stephan Thernstrom, *No More Excuses: Closing the Racial Gap in Learning* (2003). For a statistical overview, see pp. 11-23.

[5] Some background drawn from Roslyn Arlin Mickelson, "The Academic Consequences of Desegregation and Segregation: Evidence From the Charlotte-Mecklenburg Schools," *North Carolina Law Review*, Vol. 81, No. 4 (May 2003), pp. 1513-1562.

[6] The decision is *Belk v. Charlotte-Mecklenburg Board of Education*, 269 F.3d 305 (4th Cir. 2001). For coverage, see Celeste Smith and Jennifer Wing Rothacker, "Court Rules That Schools Unitary," *The Charlotte Observer*, Sept. 22, 2001, p. 1A.

[7] See Gary Orfield and Chungmei Lee, "*Brown* at 50: King's Dream or *Plessy's* Nightmare," The Civil Rights Project, Harvard University, January 2004.

[8] David J. Armor, "Desegregation and Academic Achievement," in Christine H. Rossell *et al.*, *School Desegregation in the 21st Century* (2001), pp. 183-184.

[9] See Orfield and Lee, *op. cit.*, pp. 22-26.

[10] Mickelson, *op. cit.*, pp. 1543ff.

[11] For background, see Kathy Koch, "Reforming School Funding," *The CQ Researcher*, Dec. 10, 1999, pp. 1041-1064.

[12] See David J. Armor, *Maximizing Intelligence* (2003).

[13] See John Ogbu, *Black Students in an Affluent Suburb: A Study of Academic Disengagement* (2003).

[14] Quoted in Justin Blum, "Bush Praises D.C. Voucher Plan," *The Washington Post*, Feb. 14, 2004, p. B2. For background, see Kenneth Jost, "School Vouchers Showdown," *The CQ Researcher*, Feb. 15, 2002, pp. 121-144.

[15] For background, see Charles S. Clark, "Char-

ter Schools," *The CQ Researcher*, Dec. 20, 2002, pp. 1033-1056.

[16] See Gary Orfield *et al.*, "No Child Left Behind: A Federal-, State- and District-Level Look at the First Year," The Civil Rights Project, Harvard University, Feb. 6, 2004.

[17] For a recent, compact history, see James T. Patterson, Brown v. Board of Education: A *Civil Rights Milestone and Its Troubled Legacy*, 2001. The definitive history — Richard Kluger, *Simple Justice: The History of* Brown v. Board of Education *and Black America's Struggle for Equality* — was republished in April 2004, with a new preface and final chapter by the author.

[18] The decisions are *Sweatt v. Painter*, 339 U.S. 629, and *McLaurin v. Oklahoma State Regents for Higher Education*, 339 U.S. 637. Sweatt required Texas to admit a black student to its main law school even though a "black" law school was available; McLaurin ruled that the University of Oklahoma could not deny a black student use of all its facilities, including the library, lunchroom and classrooms.

[19] For a recent reconstruction of the deliberations, see National Public Radio, "All Things Considered," Dec. 9, 2003.

[20] See Charles Wollenberg, *All Deliberate Speed: Segregation and Exclusion in California Schools, 1855-1975* (1976), p. 108.

[21] The case is *Brown v. Board of Education of Topeka*, 349 U.S. 294 (1955).

[22] "Brown at 50," Harvard Civil Rights Project, *op. cit.*, Appendix: Figure 5.

[23] Patterson, *op. cit.*, p. 186.

[24] *Ibid.*, p. 173.

[25] James S. Coleman, Sara D. Kelly and John A. Moore, *Trends in School Segregation, 1968-1973*, The Urban Institute, 1975. The earlier report is James S. Coleman, *et al.*, *Equality of Educational Opportunity*, U.S. Department of Health, Education and Welfare, 1966.

[26] Wendy Parker, "The Decline of Judicial Decisionmaking: School Desegregation and District Court Judges," *North Carolina Law Review*, Vol. 81, No. 4 (May 2003), pp. 1623-1658.

FOR MORE INFORMATION

Center for Equal Opportunity, 14 Pidgeon Hill Dr., Suite 500, Sterling, VA 20165; (703) 421-5443; www.ceousa.org. Opposes the expansion of racial preferences in education, employment and voting.

Center for Individual Rights, 1233 20th St., N.W., Suite 500, Washington, DC 20036; (202) 833-8400; www.cir-usa.org. A nonprofit, public-interest law firm that opposes racial preferences.

Harvard Civil Rights Project, 125 Mt. Auburn St., 3rd floor, Cambridge, MA 02138; (617) 496-6367; www.civilrightsproject.harvard.edu. A leading civil rights advocacy and research organization.

Mexican American Legal Defense and Educational Fund, 1717 K St., N.W. Suite 311, Washington, DC 20036; (202) 293-2828; www.maldef.org. Founded in 1968 in San Antonio, MALDEF is the leading nonprofit Latino litigation, advocacy and educational outreach organization.

NAACP Legal Defense and Educational Fund, Inc., 99 Hudson St., 16th floor, New York, NY 10013; (212) 965-2200; www.naacpldf.org. The fund's nearly two-dozen attorneys litigate on education, economic access, affirmative action and criminal justice issues on behalf of African-Americans and others.

National School Boards Association, 1680 Duke St., Alexandria, VA 22314; (703) 838-6722; www.nsba.org. The association strongly supports school desegregation.

[27] The case is *Wessmann v. Gittens*, 160 F.3d 790 (1st Cir. 1998).

[28] The decisions are *Tuttle v. Arlington County School Board*, 195 F.3d 698 (4th Cir. 1999) and *Eisenberg v. Montgomery County Public Schools*, 197 F.3d 123 (4th Cir. 1999).

[29] See Koch, *op. cit.*

[30] The case is *Parents Involved in Community Schools v. Seattle School District No. 1*. For coverage, see Sarah Linn, "Appeals Judges Told of Schools' Racial Tiebreaker," The Associated Press, Dec. 16, 2003.

[31] The case is *Avila v. Berkeley Unified School District*, filed in Alameda County Superior Court. For coverage, see Angela Hill, "Suit Accuses District of Racial Bias," *The Oakland Tribune*, Aug. 9, 2003.

[32] The decision is *Comfort v. Lynn Schools Committee*, 283 F Supp, 2d 328 (D.Mass. 2003). For coverage, see Thanassis Cambanis, "Judge OK's Use of Race in School Assigning," *The Boston Globe*, June 7, 2003, p. A1.

[33] Orfield and Lee, *op. cit.*, p. 34.

[34] *Ibid.*

[35] *Ibid.*, pp. 35-39.

[36] *Ibid.*, pp. 11-13, 39 (Table 21).

[37] Quoted in Vincent Brydon, "Panel: Segregation Still Exists in U.S. Schools," *The Topeka Capital-Journal*, Oct. 26, 2002. The Topeka district has a Web site section devoted to the *Brown* case (www.topeka.k12.ks.us).

[38] Alan Richard, "Stuck in Time," *Education Week*, Jan. 21, 2004.

[39] For background, see David Masci, "Latinos' Future," *The CQ Researcher*, Oct. 17, 2003, pp. 869-892.

Bibliography

Selected Sources

Books

Armor, David J., *Forced Justice: School Desegregation and the Law*, Oxford University Press, 1995.

A professor of public policy at George Mason University offers a strong critique of mandatory desegregation. Includes table of cases and seven-page bibliography.

Cushman, Clare, and Melvin I. Urofsky (eds.), *Black, White and Brown: The School Desegregation Case in Retrospect*, Supreme Court Historical Society/CQ Press, 2004.

This collection of essays by various contributors — including the lawyer who represented Kansas in defending racial segregation in *Brown* — provides an historical overview of the famous case, from a variety of perspectives.

Klarman, Michael J., *From Jim Crow to Civil Rights: The Supreme Court and the Struggle for Racial Equality*, Oxford University Press, 2004.

A law professor at the University of Virginia offers a broad reinterpretation of racial issues, from the establishment of segregation through the *Brown* decision and passage of the Civil Rights Act of 1964. Includes extensive notes and a 46-page bibliography.

Kluger, Richard, *Simple Justice: The History of* Brown v. Board of Education *and Black America's Struggle for Equality*, Vintage, 2004.

A former journalist and book publisher has written a definitive history of the four school-desegregation suits decided in *Brown v. Board of Education*. Originally published by Knopf in 1976, the book has been reissued with a new chapter by the author.

Ogletree, Charles J., Jr., *All Deliberate Speed: Reflections on the First Half Century of* Brown v. Board of Education, Norton, 2004.

A well-known African-American professor at Harvard Law School offers a critical examination of the unfulfilled promise of the *Brown* decision. Includes notes, case list.

Patterson, James T., Brown v. Board of Education: *A Civil Rights Milestone and Its Troubled Legacy*, Oxford University Press, 2001.

A professor emeritus of history at Brown University provides a new compact history of *Brown* and its impact.

Rossell, Christine H., David J. Armor and Herbert J. Walberg (eds.), *School Desegregation in the 21st Century*, Praeger, 2001.

Various academics examine the history and current issues involving desegregation. Rossell is a professor of political science at Boston University, Armor a professor of public policy at George Mason University and Walberg a professor emeritus of education and psychology at the University of Illinois, Chicago. Includes chapter notes, references.

Thernstrom, Abigail, and Stephan Thernstrom, *No Excuses: Closing the Racial Gap in Learning*, Simon & Schuster, 2003.

An academic-scholar couple provides a strongly argued case for adopting educational reforms, including school choice, instead of racial mixing to reduce the learning gap for African-American and Latino pupils. Abigail Thernstrom is a senior scholar at the Manhattan Institute; Stephan Thernstrom is a professor of history at Harvard. Includes detailed notes.

Articles

Cohen, Adam, "The Supreme Struggle," *Education Life Supplement, The New York Times*, Jan. 18, 2004, p. 22.

A *Times* editorial writer offers an overview of the 1954 *Brown* decision and its impact.

Henderson, Cheryl Brown, "*Brown v. Board of Education* at Fifty: A Personal Perspective," *The College Board Review*, No. 200 (fall 2003), pp. 7-11.

The daughter of Oliver Brown, first-named of the 13 plaintiffs in *Brown v. Board of Education of Topeka*, provides a personal reflection on the landmark case. Henderson is executive director of the Brown Foundation for Educational Equity, Excellence and Research in Topeka (www.brown-vboard.org).

Hendrie, Caroline, "In U.S. Schools, Race Still Counts," *Education Week*, Jan. 21, 2004.

This broad survey of racial issues in public schools was the first of a five-part series marking the 50th anniversary of *Brown*. Other articles appeared on Feb. 18 (Charlotte-Mecklenburg County, N.C.), March 10 (Chicago; Latinos), April 14 (Arlington, Va., challenges of integration), with a final story scheduled for May 19 (parental choice).

Reports and Studies

Orfield, Gary, and Chungmei Lee, "*Brown* at 50: King's Dream or *Plessy's* Nightmare?" The Civil Rights Project, Harvard University, January 2004.

The project's most recent analysis of school-enrollment figures finds that racial separation is increasing among African-American and Latino students.

14   Affirmative Action

Jennifer Gratz wanted to go to the University of Michigan's flagship Ann Arbor campus as soon as she began thinking about college. "It's the best school in Michigan to go to," she explains.

The white suburban teenager's dream turned to disappointment in April 1995, however, when the university told her that even though she was "well qualified," she had been rejected for one of the nearly 4,000 slots in the incoming freshman class.

Gratz was convinced something was wrong. "I knew that the University of Michigan was giving preference to minorities," she recalls. "If you give extra points for being of a particular race, then you're not giving applicants an equal opportunity."

Gratz went on to earn a degree from Michigan's less prestigious Dearborn campus and a job in San Diego. But she also became the lead plaintiff in a showdown legal battle in the long-simmering conflict over racial preferences in college admissions.

On the opposite side of Gratz's federal court lawsuit was Lee Bollinger, a staunch advocate of race-conscious admissions policies who served as president of the University of Michigan for five-and-a-half years before leaving in June 2002 to assume the presidency of Columbia University.

"Racial and ethnic diversity is one part of the core liberal educational goal," Bollinger says. "People have different educational experiences when they grow up as an African-American, Hispanic or white."

From *The CQ Researcher*,
September 21, 2001.
(Revised April 29, 2004).

First-year engineering students at the University of Michigan–Ann Arbor gather during welcome week. A federal judge ruled in December 2000 that the school's race-based admissions system in 1995 was illegal but that a revised system adopted later was constitutional. The case is widely expected to reach the Supreme Court.

Gratz won a partial victory in December 2000, when a federal judge agreed that the university's admissions system in 1995 was illegal. The ruling came too late to help her, however, and Judge Patrick Duggan went on to rule that the revised system the university adopted in 1998 passed constitutional muster.

Some three months later, however, another federal judge ruled in a separate case that the admissions system used at the university's law school was illegal. Judge Bernard Friedman said the law school's admissions policies were "practically indistinguishable from a quota system."

The decision came in a suit filed by Barbara Grutter, who unsuccessfully sought admission to the law school in December 1996 while in her 40s after having raised a family and worked as a health care consultant. Grutter, who is white, blamed her rejection on minority preferences used by the law school.

The two cases — *Gratz v. Bollinger* and *Grutter v. Bollinger* — went on

to be argued together before the federal appeals court in Cincinnati and then again before the U.S. Supreme Court. Then, in a dramatic day at the high court, the justices issued companion rulings on June 23, 2003, that upheld the law school's policies, but struck down the college's system.

The law school system satisfied constitutional standards, Justice Sandra Day O'Connor wrote in the 5-4 decision, because it was narrowly tailored to achieve the goal of attaining a diverse student body. Writing for a different 6-3 majority, however, Chief Justice William H. Rehnquist said the college's admissions system was unconstitutional because it awarded minority candidates a fixed numerical bonus without individualized consideration of the applicants' backgrounds and records.[1]

The rulings were aimed at resolving legal uncertainty stemming from the long time span — 23 years — since the Supreme Court's only previous full-scale ruling on race-based admissions policies: the famous *Bakke* decision. In that fractured ruling, *University of California Regents v. Bakke*, the high court in 1978 ruled that fixed racial quotas were illegal but allowed the use of race as one factor in college admissions.[2]

After Bakke, race-based admissions policies became widespread in U.S. higher education — "well accepted and entrenched," according to Sheldon Steinbach, general counsel of the pro-affirmative action American Council on Education.

Roger Clegg, general counsel of the Center for Equal Opportunity, which opposes racial preferences, agrees with Steinbach but from a different

Despite Progress, Minorities Still Trail Whites

A larger percentage of young adult African-Americans and Hispanics have completed college today than 20 years ago. But college completion rates for African-Americans and Hispanics continue to be significantly lower than the rate for whites. Today, the national college completion rate — 30 percent — is more than triple the rate in 1950.

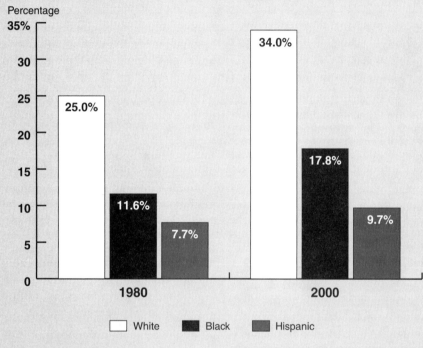

Percentages of College Graduates, Ages 25–29

Source: U.S. Department of Education, "Digest of Education Statistics," 2001 edition.

The race-based admissions policies now in use around the country have evolved gradually after the passage of federal civil rights legislation in the mid-1960s. By 1970, the phrase "affirmative action" had become common usage to describe efforts to increase the number of African-Americans (and, later, Hispanics) in U.S. workplaces and on college campuses.[4] Since then, the proportions of African-Americans and Hispanics on college campuses have increased, though they are still underrepresented in terms of their respective proportions in the U.S. population. (*See chart, p. 267.*)

Michigan's efforts ranged from uncontroversial minority-outreach programs to an admissions system that explicitly took an applicant's race or ethnicity into account in deciding whether to accept or reject the applicant. The system formerly used by the undergraduate College of Literature, Science and the Arts had separate grids for white and minority applicants. It was replaced by a system that used a numerical rating with a 20-point bonus (out of a total possible score of 150) for "underrepresented minorities" — African-Americans, Hispanics and Native Americans (but not Asian-Americans). The law school's system — devised in 1992 — was aimed at producing a minority enrollment of about 10 percent to 12 percent of the entering class.

Critics of racial preferences say they are not opposed to affirmative action. "Certainly there are some positive aspects to affirmative action," says Michael Rosman, attorney for the Center for Individual Rights in Washington, which represented the plaintiffs in the Michigan cases. Rossman says he approves of increased recruitment of minorities and reassessment by colleges of criteria for evaluating applicants. But, he adds, "To the extent that suggests that they have carte blanche to discriminate between people on the basis of race, it's not a good thing."

perspective. "Evidence is overwhelming that racial and ethnic discrimination occurs frequently in public college and university admissions," Clegg says.[3]

Higher-education organizations and traditional civil rights groups say racial admissions policies are essential to ensure racial and ethnic diversity at the nation's elite universities — including the most selective state schools, such as Michigan's Ann Arbor campus. "The overwhelming majority of students who apply to highly selective institutions are still white," says Theodore Shaw, di-

rector of the NAACP Legal Defense and Educational Fund, which represented minority students who intervened in the two Michigan cases. "If we are not conscious of selecting minority students, they're not going to be there."

Opponents, however, say racial preferences are wrong in terms of law and social policy. "It's immoral. It's illegal. It stigmatizes the beneficiary. It encourages hypocrisy. It lowers standards. It encourages the use of stereotypes," Clegg says. "There are all kinds of social costs, and we don't think the benefits outweigh those costs."

Higher-education officials respond that they should have discretion to explicitly consider race — along with a host of other factors — to ensure a fully representative student body and provide the best learning environment for an increasingly multicultural nation and world. "Having a diverse student body contributes to the educational process and is necessary in the 21st-century global economy," Steinbach says.

As colleges and universities examine the impact of the Supreme Court's rulings in the University of Michigan cases, here are some of the major questions being debated:

Should colleges use race-based admissions policies to remedy discrimination against minorities?

The University of Michigan relies heavily on high school students' scores on standardized tests in evaluating applications — tests that have been widely criticized as biased against African-Americans and other minorities. It gives preferences to children of Michigan alumni — who are disproportionately white — as well as to applicants from "underrepresented" parts of the state, such as Michigan's predominantly white Upper Peninsula.

Even apart from the university's past record of racial segregation, those factors could be cited as evidence that Michigan's admissions policies were racially discriminatory because they had a "disparate impact" on minorities. And the Supreme Court, in *Bakke*, said that racial classifications were constitutional if they were used as a remedy for proven discrimination.

But Michigan did not defend its racial admissions policies on that basis. "Every public university has its share of decisions that we're now embarrassed by," Bollinger conceded. But the university defended its use of race — along with an array of other factors — only as a method of produc-

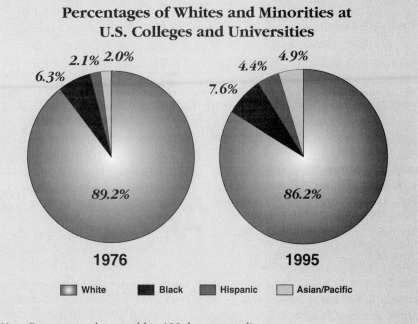

Minority Enrollments Increased

African-Americans and Hispanics make up a larger percentage of the U.S. college population today than they did in 1976, but they are still underrepresented in comparison to their proportion of the total U.S. population. Hispanics comprise 12.5 percent of the population, African-Americans 12.3 percent.

Percentages of Whites and Minorities at U.S. Colleges and Universities

1976: 6.3% · 2.1% · 2.0% · 89.2%

1995: 7.6% · 4.4% · 4.9% · 86.2%

White · Black · Hispanic · Asian/Pacific

Note: Percentages do not add to 100 due to rounding.

Source: U.S. Dept. of Education, "Digest of Education Statistics," 2001 edition.

ing racial diversity, not as a way to remedy current or past discrimination.

Some civil rights advocates, however, insist that colleges and universities are still guilty of racially biased policies that warrant — even require — explicit racial preferences as corrective measures.

"Universities should use race-conscious admissions as a way of countering both past and ongoing ways in which the admission process continues to engage in practices that perpetuate racism or are unconsciously racist," says Charles Lawrence, a professor at Georgetown University Law Center in Washington.

Opponents of racial preferences, however, say colleges should be very wary about justifying such policies on the basis of past or current discrimination against minorities. "The Supreme Court has been pretty clear that you can't use the justification of past societal discrimination as a ground for a race-based admissions policy at an institution that did not itself discriminate," says Stephen Balch, president of the National Association of Scholars, a Princeton, N.J.-based group of academics opposed to racial preferences.

Balch defends alumni preferences, the most frequently mentioned example of an admissions policy that disadvantages minority applicants. "It's not at all unreasonable for colleges and universities to cultivate their alumni base," Balch says. In any event, he adds, "As student bodies change, the effect of that policy will change."

For his part, Rosman of the Center for Individual Rights says racial preferences are not justified even if colleges are wrong to grant alumni preferences or to rely so heavily on standardized test scores. "If you have criteria that discriminate and are not

sororities until the 1960s, allowed white students to refuse to room with black students and did not hire its first black professor until 1967. The evidence also showed that black students reported continuing discrimination and racial hostility through the 1980s and into

Judge Friedman rejected similar arguments in the final portion of his March 27, 2001, ruling in the law school case. "This is a social and political matter, which calls for social and political solutions," Friedman wrote. "The solution is not for the law school, or any other state institution, to prefer some applicants over others because of race."

Gratz v. Bollinger: Race and College Admissions

Jennifer Gratz, a white woman, sued the University of Michigan contending she was improperly denied admission because of race. The lawsuit is shaping up as a key battle in the long-simmering conflict over racial preferences in college admissions.

"I see benefits from different opinions, different thoughts on any number of subjects. But I don't think that's necessarily race coming through. I don't think like every other white person. ... Your race doesn't mean that you're going to think this way or that way."

Jennifer Gratz, B.S., University of Michigan, Dearborn

"You get a better education and a better society in an environment where you are mixing with lots of different people — people from different parts of the country, people from different parts of the socioeconomic system, people from abroad, and people from different races and ethnicities."

Lee Bollinger, former president, University of Michigan

Should colleges use race-based admissions policies to promote diversity in their student populations?

Michigan's high schools graduated some 100,000 students in 1999. Out of that number, only 327 African-American students had a B-plus average and an SAT score above 1,000 — the kind of record needed to make them strong contenders for admission to the University of Michigan's Ann Arbor campus based on those factors alone.

University officials cited that stark statistic to underline the difficulty in admitting a racially diverse student body — and to justify their policy of giving minority applicants special consideration in the admissions process. Without the bonus for minority applicants, the number of African-American and Hispanic students "would drop dramatically" from the current level of about 13 percent of undergraduates to "somewhere around 5 percent," according to Elizabeth Barry, the university's associate vice president and deputy general counsel.

Opponents of racial preferences dismiss the warnings. "It's certainly not inevitable that the number of students from racial and ethnic minorities will decline" under a color-blind system, Rosman says. In any event, he says that diversity is "not a sufficiently powerful goal to discriminate and treat people differently on the basis of race."

The dispute between supporters and opponents of racial admissions policies turns in part on two somewhat

educationally justified, then the appropriate response is to get rid of those criteria, not to use 'two wrongs make a right,'" Rosman says.

Minority students intervened in both the undergraduate and law school suits to present evidence of discrimination by the university and to use that evidence to justify the racial admissions policies. In the undergraduate case, evidence showed that the university refused to desegregate fraternities and

the '90s.

In his Dec. 13, 2000, ruling, Judge Duggan acknowledged the evidence but rejected it as a justification for the admissions policies. The racial segregation occurred too long ago to be a reason for current policies, Duggan said. He also rejected the minority students' argument that the racial impact of alumni preferences, standardized test scores and other admissions criteria justified preferences for minority applicants.

rarefied issues. Supporters claim to have social-science evidence to show that racial and ethnic diversity produces quantifiable educational benefits for all students — evidence that opponents deride as dubious at best. *(See story, p. 276.)* The opposing camps also differ on the question of whether the *Bakke* decision allows colleges to use diversity as the kind of "compelling government interest" needed to satisfy the so-called strict-scrutiny standard of constitutional review. *(See story, p. 270.)*

Apart from those specialized disputes, opponents of racial preferences argue simply that they constitute a form of stereotyping and discrimination. "We don't believe that there is a black outlook or an Asian outlook or a white experience or a Hispanic experience," Clegg says. "Students are individuals, and they should be treated as individuals, not as fungible members of racial and ethnic groups."

Some critics — including a few African-Americans — also say racial preferences "stigmatize" the intended beneficiaries by creating the impression that they could not be successful without being given some advantage over whites. "There is no way that a young black at an Ivy League university is going to get credit for [doing well]," says Shelby Steele, a prominent black critic of racial preferences and a research fellow at the Hoover Institution at Stanford University. "There's no way that he's going to feel his achievements are his own."

Supporters of racial admission policies, however, say that race plays an independent and important role in American society that colleges are entitled to take into account. "It is reasonable for educational institutions to believe that race is not a proxy for something else," Bollinger says. "It is a defining experience in American life — and therefore an important one for this goal" of educational diversity.

White supporters of affirmative action generally deny or minimize any supposed stigmatization from race-conscious policies. Some blacks acknowledge some stigmatizing effects, but blame white racism rather than affirmative action. "The stigmatizing beliefs about people of color," Professor Lawrence writes, "have their origin not in affirmative action programs but in the cultural belief system of white supremacy."[5]

The two judges in the Michigan cases reached different conclusions on the diversity issue. In his ruling in the undergraduate case, Duggan agreed with the university's argument that a "racially and ethnically diverse student body produces significant education benefits, such that diversity, in the context of higher education, constitutes a compelling governmental interest under strict scrutiny."

Ruling in the law school case, Judge Friedman acknowledged that racial diversity may provide "educational and societal benefits," though he also called for drawing "a distinction . . . between viewpoint diversity and racial diversity." Based on his interpretation of *Bakke*, however, Friedman said these "important and laudable" benefits did not amount to a compelling interest sufficient to justify the law school's use of race in admissions decisions.

Should colleges adopt other policies to try to increase minority enrollment?

Texas and Florida have a different approach to ensuring a racial mix in their state university systems. Texas' "10 percent plan" — adopted in 1997 under then-Gov. George W. Bush — promises a spot in the state university to anyone who graduates in the top 10 percent of any high schools in the state. Florida's plan — adopted in 1999 under Gov. Jeb Bush, the president's brother — makes the same commitment to anyone in the top 20 percent.

The plans are drawing much attention and some favorable comment as an ostensibly race-neutral alternative to racial preferences. But major participants on both sides of the debate over racial admissions policies view the idea with skepticism.

"It's silly to suggest that all high schools are equal in terms of the quality of their student body," Clegg says. "And therefore it makes no sense to have an across-the-board rule that the top 10 percent of every high school is going to be admitted."

Both Clegg and Rosman also say that a 10 percent-type plan is dubious if it is adopted to circumvent a ban on explicit racial preferences. "Any neutral policy that is just a pretext for discrimination would have to survive strict scrutiny," Rosman says.

Supporters of race-based admissions are also unenthusiastic. "The only reason they work is because we have segregated high schools, segregated communities," Shaw says. "From a philosophical standpoint, I'd rather deal with race in a more honest and upfront way and make a more principled approach to these issues."

In the Michigan lawsuits, the university cited testimony from a prominent supporter of racial admissions policies in opposition to 10 percent-type plans. "Treating all applicants alike if they finished above a given high school class rank provides a spurious form of equality that is likely to damage the academic profile of the overall class of students admitted to selective institutions," said former Princeton University President William G. Bowen, later president of the Andrew W. Mellon Foundation in New York City.

Rosman looks more favorably on another alternative: giving preferences to applicants who come from disadvantaged socioeconomic backgrounds. "It's not a bad idea to take into account a person's ability to overcome obstacles," he says. "That's useful in assessing a person's qualifications."

In his testimony, however, Bowen also criticized that approach. Young-

What Does *Bakke* Mean? Two Judges Disagree

The Supreme Court's 1978 decision to prohibit fixed racial quotas in colleges and universities but to allow the use of race as one factor in admissions was hailed by some people at the time as a Solomon-like compromise.

But the meaning of the high court's famous *Bakke* decision was sharply disputed. And the disagreement lay at the heart of conflicting rulings by two federal judges in Michigan on the legality of racial preferences used at the University of Michigan's flagship Ann Arbor campus.

In upholding the flexible race-based admissions system used by the undergraduate College of Literature, Science and the Arts in December 2000, Judge Patrick Duggan said *Bakke* means that colleges can evaluate white and minority applicants differently in order to enroll a racially and ethnically diverse student body.

But Judge Bernard Friedman rejected that widely held interpretation in his March 2001 decision striking down the law school's use of race in admissions. Friedman — like Duggan an appointee of President Ronald Reagan — said that racial and ethnic diversity did not qualify as a "compelling governmental interest" needed under the so-called strict scrutiny constitutional standard to justify a race-based government policy.

The differing interpretations stem from the Supreme Court's unusual 4-1-4 vote in the case, *University of California Regents v. Bakke*. Four of the justices found the quota system used by the UC-Davis Medical School — reserving 16 out of 100 seats for minorities — to be a violation of the federal civil rights law prohibiting racial discrimination in federally funded institutions. Four others — led by the liberal Justice William J. Brennan Jr. — voted to reject Alan Bakke's challenge to the system.

In the pivotal opinion, Justice Lewis F. Powell Jr. found the UC-Davis admissions system to be a violation of the constitutional requirement of equal protection but said race could be used as a "plus" factor in admissions decisions. The "attainment of a diverse student body," Powell wrote, "clearly is a constitutionally permissible goal for an institution of higher education."

Under Supreme Court case law, it takes a majority of the justices — five — to produce a "holding" that can serve as a precedent for future cases. In a fractured ruling, the court's holding is said to be the "narrowest" rationale endorsed by five justices. But Brennan's group did not explicitly address the question of diversity. Instead, they said that race-based admissions decisions were justified to remedy past discrimination — a proposition that Powell also endorsed.

Critics of racial preferences in recent years have argued that the Brennan group's silence on diversity means that they did not join Powell's reasoning. On that basis, these critics say, Powell's opinion cannot be viewed as a controlling precedent. They won an important victory when the federal appeals court in New Orleans adopted that reasoning in the so-called *Hopwood* case in 1996 striking down the University of Texas Law School's racial preferences.

In his ruling in the Michigan law school case, Friedman also agreed with this revisionist view of *Bakke*. "The diversity rationale articulated by Justice Powell is neither narrower nor broader than the remedial rationale articulated by the Brennan group," Friedman wrote. "They are completely different rationales, neither one of which is subsumed within the other."

But in the undergraduate case, Duggan followed the previous interpretation of *Bakke*. Brennan's "silence regarding the diversity interest in *Bakke* was not an implicit rejection of such an interest, but rather, an implicit approval of such an interest," Duggan wrote.

The two judges also differed on how to interpret later Supreme Court decisions. Duggan cited Brennan's 1990 majority opinion in a case upholding racial preferences in broadcasting — *Metro Broadcasting, Inc. v. Federal Communications Commission* — as supporting the use of diversity to justify racial policies. But Friedman said other recent rulings showed that the Supreme Court had become much more skeptical of racial policies than it had been in 1978. Among the decisions he cited was the 1995 ruling, *Adamant Constructors v. Pena* that overruled the *Metro Broadcasting* holding.

Reporters follow Alan Bakke on his first day at the University of California-Davis Medical School on Sept. 25, 1978. The Supreme Court ordered him admitted after ruling that the school violated his rights by maintaining a fixed quota for minority applicants.

AP Photo/Walt Zeboski

sters from poor black and Hispanic families are "much less likely" to excel in school than those from poor white families, Bowen said. On that basis, he predicted that a "class-based" rather than race-based admissions policy "would substantially reduce the minority enrollments at selective institutions."

For its part, the University of Michigan stressed that its system gave up to 20 points to an applicant based on socioeconomic disadvantage — the same number given to minority applicants. "We consider a number of factors in order to enroll a diverse student body," Barry said while the system was in use, "because race is not the only element that's important to diversity in education."

In their rulings, Duggan and Friedman both favorably noted a number of alternatives to race-based admissions policies. Friedman suggested the law school could have increased recruiting efforts or decreased the emphasis on undergraduate grades and scores on the Law School Aptitude Test. He also said the school could have used a lottery for all qualified applicants or admitted some fixed number or percentage of top graduates from various colleges and universities. Friedman said the law school's "apparent failure to investigate alternative means for increasing minority enrollment" was one factor in rejecting the school's admissions policies.

For his part, Duggan noted the possibility of using race-neutral policies to increase minority enrollment when he rejected the minority students' critique of such policies as alumni preferences. "If the current selection criteria have a discriminatory impact on minority applicants," Duggan wrote, "it seems to this court that the narrowly tailored remedy would be to remove or redistribute such criteria to accommodate for socially and economically disadvantaged applicants of all races

and ethnicities, not to add another suspect criteria [sic] to the list."

BACKGROUND

Unequal Opportunity

African-Americans and other racial and ethnic minority groups have been underrepresented on college campuses throughout U.S. history. The civil rights revolution has effectively dismantled most legal barriers to higher education for minorities. But the social and economic inequalities that persist between white Americans and racial and ethnic minority groups continue to make the goal of equal opportunity less than reality for many African-Americans and Hispanics.

The legal battles that ended mandatory racial segregation in the United States began with higher education nearly two decades before the Supreme Court's historic ruling in *Brown v. Board of Education*.[6] In the first of the rulings that ended the doctrine of "separate but equal," the court in 1938 ruled that Missouri violated a black law school applicant's equal protection rights by offering to pay his tuition to an out-of-state school rather than admit him to the state's all-white law school.

The court followed with a pair of rulings in 1950 that similarly found states guilty of violating black students' rights to equal higher education. Texas was ordered to admit a black student to the state's all-white law school rather than force him to attend an inferior all-black school. And Oklahoma was found to have discriminated against a black student by admitting him to a previously all-white state university but denying him the opportunity to use all its facilities.

At the time of these decisions, whites had substantially greater educational opportunities than African-Americans. As of 1950, a majority of white Americans ages 25-29 — 56 percent — had completed high school, compared with only 24 percent of African-Americans. Eight percent of whites in that age group had completed college compared with fewer than 3 percent of blacks. Most of the African-American college graduates had attended all-black institutions: either private colleges established for blacks or racially segregated state universities.

The Supreme Court's 1954 decision in *Brown* to begin dismantling racial segregation in elementary and secondary education started to reduce the inequality in educational opportunities for whites and blacks, but changes were slow. It was not until 1970 that a majority of African-Americans ages 25-29 had attained high school degrees.

Changes at the nation's elite colleges and universities were even slower. In their book *The Shape of the River*, two former Ivy League presidents — Bowen and Derek Bok — say that as of 1960 "no selective college or university was making determined efforts to seek out and admit substantial numbers of African-American students." As of 1965, they report, African-Americans comprised only 4.8 percent of students on the nation's college campuses and fewer than 1 percent of students at select New England colleges.[7]

As part of the Civil Rights Act of 1964, Congress included provisions in Title IV to authorize the Justice Department to initiate racial-desegregation lawsuits against public schools and colleges and to require the U.S. Office of Education (now the Department of Education) to give technical assistance to school systems undergoing desegregation. A year later, President Lyndon B. Johnson delivered his famous commencement speech at historically black Howard University that laid the foundation for a more proactive approach to equalizing opportunities for African-Americans. "You do not take a person," Johnson said, "who, for years, has been hobbled by chains and liberate him, bring him up to the starting line of a race and then say, 'You are free to compete with all the others,' and still justly believe that you have been completely fair."[8]

Affirmative Action

Colleges began in the mid-1960s to make deliberate efforts to increase the number of minority students. Many universities instituted "affirmative action" programs that included targeted recruitment of minority applicants as well as explicit use of race as a factor in admissions policies. White students challenged the use of racial preferences, but the Supreme Court — in the *Bakke* decision in 1978 — gave colleges and universities a flashing green light to consider race as one factor in admissions policies aimed at ensuring a racially diverse student body.

The federal government encouraged universities to look to enrollment figures as the criterion for judging the success of their affirmative action policies. By requiring universities to report minority enrollment figures, the Nixon administration appeared to sug-

President Lyndon B. Johnson signs the Civil Rights Act on July 2, 1964. Race-based admissions policies now in use around the country evolved gradually from the landmark law.

AP Photo

gest that race-conscious admissions were "not only permissible but mandatory," according to Bowen and Bok. But universities were also motivated, they say, to remedy past racial discrimination, to educate minority leaders and to create diversity on campuses.

As early as 1966, Bowen and Bok report, Harvard Law School moved to increase the number of minority students by "admitting black applicants with test scores far below those of white classmates." As other law schools adopted the strategy, enrollment of African-Americans increased — from 1 percent of all law students in 1965 to 4.5 percent in 1975. Similar efforts produced a significant increase in black students in Ivy League colleges. The proportion of African-American students at Ivy League schools

increased from 2.3 percent in 1967 to 6.7 percent in 1976, Bowen and Bok report.[9]

Critics, predominantly but not exclusively political conservatives, charged that the racial preferences amounted to "reverse discrimination" against white students and applicants. Some white students challenged the policies in court. The Supreme Court sought to resolve the issue in 1978 in a case brought by a California man, Alan Bakke, who had been denied admission to the University of California Medical School at Davis under a system that explicitly reserved 16 of 100 seats for minority applicants. The 4-1-4 decision fell short of a definitive resolution, though.

Justice Lewis F. Powell Jr. cast the decisive vote in the case. He joined four justices to reject Davis' fixed-quota approach and four others to allow use of race as one factor in admissions decisions. In summarizing his opinion from the bench, Powell explained that it meant Bakke would be admitted to the medical school but that Davis was free to adopt a more "flexible program designed to achieve diversity" just like those "proved to be successful at many of our great universities."[10]

Civil rights advocates initially reacted with "consternation," according to Steinbach of the American Council on Education. Quickly, though, college officials and higher-education groups took up the invitation to devise programs that used race — in Powell's terms — as a "plus factor" without

Chronology

Before 1960

Limited opportunities for minorities in private and public colleges and universities.

1938
Supreme Court says Missouri violated Constitution by operating all-white law school but no school for blacks.

1950
Supreme Court says Texas violated Constitution by operating "inferior" law school for blacks.

1954
Supreme Court rules racial segregation in public elementary and secondary schools unconstitutional; ruling is extended to dismantle racially segregated colleges.

1960s–1980s

Civil rights era: higher education desegregated; affirmative action widely adopted, approved by Supreme Court if racial quotas not used.

1964
Civil Rights Act bars discrimination by federally funded colleges.

1978
Supreme Court rules in *Bakke* that colleges and universities can consider race as one factor in admissions policies.

1980s
Supreme Court leaves *Bakke* unchanged.

1990s
Opposition to race-based admissions policies grows.

1995
President Clinton defends affirmative action; University of California ends use of race and sex in admissions.

1996
University of Texas law school's use of racial preferences in admissions ruled unconstitutional in *Hopwood* case; California voters approve Proposition 209 banning state-sponsored affirmative action in employment, contracting and admissions.

1997
Texas Gov. George W. Bush signs law guaranteeing admission to University of Texas to top 10 percent of graduates in state high schools.

1998
Washington state voters approve initiative barring racial preferences in state colleges and universities.

1999
Gov. Jeb Bush of Florida issues executive order banning racial preferences but granting admission to state colleges to top 20 percent of graduates in all state high schools.

2000s
Legal challenges to affirmative action continue.

Dec. 4, 2000
University of Washington Law School's former admissions system — discontinued after Proposition 200 — is upheld by federal court.

Dec. 13, 2000
University of Michigan undergraduate admissions policies upheld by federal judge, though former system ruled illegal.

March 26, 2001
Supreme Court agrees to hear new appeal in *Adarand* case.

March 27, 2001
University of Michigan Law School admissions policies ruled unconstitutional by federal judge.

June 2001
Supreme Court declines to review conflicting rulings in *University of Washington, University of Texas* cases.

Aug. 27, 2001
Federal appeals court in Atlanta rules University of Georgia admissions system giving bonuses to all non-white applicants is unconstitutional.

May 2002
University of Michigan Law School admissions system upheld by federal appeals court in Cincinnati by 5-4 vote; court issues no ruling in challenge to admissions policies at Michigan's undergraduate college.

December 2002
Supreme Court agrees to take up challenges to admissions policies for undergraduates and law students at University of Michigan.

June 23, 2003
Supreme Court upholds, 5-4, use of race in admissions at University of Michigan Law School, but rules racial preferences in undergraduate admissions unconstitutional by 6-3 vote; in pivotal opinion, Justice Sandra Day O'Connor calls for racial preferences to end in 25 years..

Minority Preferences: Will They Disappear in 25 Years?

We take the Law School at its word that it would "like nothing better than to find a race-neutral admissions formula" and will terminate its race-conscious admissions program as soon as practicable. ... It has been 25 years since Justice Powell first approved the use of race to further an interest in student body diversity in the context of public higher education. Since that time, the number of minority applicants with high grades and test scores has indeed increased. ... We expect that 25 years from now, the use of racial preferences will no longer be necessary to further the interest approved today."

Justice Sandra Day O'Connor, majority opinion, *Grutter v. Bollinger*

"I agree with the Court's holding that racial discrimination in higher education admissions will be illegal in 25 years... For the immediate future, however, the majority has placed its *imprimatur* on a practice that can only weaken the principle of equality embodied in the Declaration of Independence and the Equal Protection Clause. ... It has been nearly 140 years since ... the Nation adopted the Fourteenth Amendment. Now we must wait another 25 years to see this principle of equality vindicated.

Justice Clarence Thomas, separate opinion, *Grutter v. Bollinger*

"However strong the public's desire for improved education systems may be, ... it remains the current reality that many minority students encounter markedly inadequate and unequal educational opportunities. Despite these inequalities, some minority students are able to meet the high threshold requirements set for admission to the country's finest undergraduate and graduate educational institutions. As lower school education in minority communities improves, an increase in the number of such students may be anticipated. From today's vantage point, one may hope, but not firmly forecast, that over the next generation's span, progress toward nondiscrimination and genuinely equal opportunity will make it safe to sunset affirmative action."

Justice Ruth Bader Ginsburg, separate opinion, *Grutter v. Bollinger*

setting aside any seats specifically for minority applicants. The ruling, Steinbach says, "enabled institutions in a creative manner to legally provide for a diverse student body."

The Supreme Court avoided re-examining *Bakke* after 1978, but narrowed the scope of affirmative action in other areas. The court in 1986 ruled that government employers could not lay off senior white workers to make room for new minority hires, though it upheld affirmative action in hiring and promotions in two other decisions that year and another ruling in a sex-discrimination case a year later. As for government contracting, the court ruled in 1989 that state and local governments could not use racial preferences except to remedy past discrimination and extended that limitation to federal programs in 1995.[11]

All of the court's decisions were closely divided, but the conservative majority made clear their discomfort with race-specific policies. Indeed, as legal-affairs writer Lincoln Caplan notes, none of the five current conservatives — Chief Justice William H. Rehnquist and Associate Justices Sandra Day O'Connor, Antonin Scalia, Anthony M. Kennedy and Clarence Thomas — had ever voted to approve a race-based affirmative action program prior to the Michigan cases.[12]

Negative Reaction

A political and legal backlash against affirmative action emerged with full force in the 1990s — highlighted by moves in California to scrap race-conscious policies in the state's university system and a federal appeals court decision barring racial preferences in admissions in Texas and two neighboring states. But President Bill Clinton rebuffed calls to scrap federal affirmative action programs. And colleges continued to follow race-conscious admissions policies in the absence of a new Supreme Court pronouncement on the issue.

In the first of the moves against race-conscious admissions, the 5th U.S. Circuit Court of Appeals in New Orleans in March 1996 struck down the University of Texas Law School's system that used separate procedures for white and minority applicants with the goal of admitting a class with 5 percent African-American and 10 percent Mexican-American students.[13] The ruling in the *Hopwood* case unanimously rejected the university's attempt to justify the racial preferences on grounds of past discrimination. Two judges also rejected the university's diversity defense and directly contradicted the prevailing interpretation of Bakke that diversity amounted to a "compelling governmental interest" justifying race-based policies.[14]

The ruling specifically applied only to the three states in the 5th Circuit — Louisiana, Mississippi and Texas — but observers saw the decision as significant. "This is incredibly big," said John C. Jeffries Jr., a University of Virginia law professor and Justice Powell's biographer. "This could affect every public institution in America because all of them take racial diversity into account in admissions."[15]

Four months later, the University of California Board of Regents — policy-making body for the prestigious, 162,000-student state university system — narrowly voted to abolish racial and sexual preferences in admissions by fall 1997. The 14-10 vote approved a resolution submitted by a black businessman, Ward Connerly, and supported by the state's Republican governor, Pete Wilson. Connerly was also the driving force behind a voter initiative — Proposition 209 — to abolish racial preferences in state government employment and contracting as well as college and university admissions. Voters approved the measure, 54 percent to 46 percent, in November 1996.

In the face of opposition from UC President Richard Atkinson, the move to scrap racial preferences was delayed to admissions for the 1998-1999 academic year. In May 1998, the university released figures showing a modest overall decline in acceptances by non-Asian minorities to 15.2 percent for the coming year from 17.6 percent for the 1997-1998 school year. But the figures also showed a steep drop in the number of black and Hispanic students in the entering classes at the two most prestigious campuses — Berkeley and UCLA. At Berkeley, African-American and Hispanic acceptances fell to 10.5 percent from 21.9 percent for the previous year; at UCLA, the drop was to 14.1 percent from 21.8 percent.

The Supreme Court did nothing to counteract the legal shift away from racial preferences in education. It declined in 1995 to review a decision by the federal appeals court in Richmond, Va., that struck down a University of Maryland scholarship program reserved for African-American students. A year later, the justices refused to hear Texas' appeal of the *Hopwood* decision; and a year after that they also turned aside a challenge by labor and civil rights groups to Proposition 209. Instead, the high

court concentrated on a series of rulings beginning in June 1993 that limited the use of race in congressional and legislative redistricting.[16] And in June 1995 the court issued a decision, *Adarand Constructors, Inc. v. Peña*, that limited the federal government's discretion to give minority-owned firms preferences in government contracting.[17]

With affirmative action under sharp attack, Bowen and Bok came out in 1998 with their book-length study of graduates of selective colleges that they said refuted many of the criticisms of race-based admissions. Using a database of some 80,000 students who entered 28 elite colleges and universities in 1951, 1976 and 1989, the two former Ivy League presidents confirmed the increase in minority enrollment at the schools and the impact of racial preferences: More than half the black students admitted in 1976 and 1989 would not have been admitted under race-neutral policies, they said. But they said dropout rates among black students were low, satisfaction with their college experiences high and post-graduation accomplishments comparable with — or better than — white graduates.[18]

The Bowen-Bok book buttressed college and university officials in resisting calls to scrap racial preferences. While voters in Washington state moved to eliminate race-based admissions with an anti-affirmative action initiative in 1998, no other state university system followed the UC lead in voluntarily abolishing the use of race in weighing applications.

In Texas, then-Gov. George W. Bush sought to bolster minority enrollment in the UT system after *Hopwood* by proposing the 10 percent plan — guaranteeing admission to any graduating senior in the top 10 percent of his class. (Florida Gov. Jeb Bush followed suit with his 20 percent plan two years later.) Many schools — both public and private — re-examined their ad-

missions policies after *Hopwood*. But, according to Steinbach, most of them "found that what they had was satisfactory."

Legal Battles

Critics of race-based admissions kept up their pressure on the issue by waging expensive, protracted legal battles in four states: Georgia, Michigan, Texas and Washington. The cases produced conflicting decisions. The conflict was starkest in the two University of Michigan cases, where two judges, both appointed in the 1980s by President Ronald Reagan, reached different results in evaluating the use of race at the undergraduate college and at the law school.

The controversy in Michigan began in a sense with the discontent of a longtime Ann Arbor faculty member, Carl Cohen.[19] A professor of philosophy and a "proud" member of the American Civil Liberties Union (ACLU), Cohen had been troubled by racial preferences since the 1970s. In 1995 he read a journal article that described admissions rates for black college applicants as higher nationally than those for white applicants. The article prompted Cohen to begin poking around to learn about Michigan's system.[20]

As Cohen tells the story, administrators stonewalled him until he used the state's freedom of information law to obtain the pertinent documents. He found that the admissions offices used a grid system that charted applicants based on high school grade point average on a horizontal axis and standardized test scores on a vertical axis — and that there were separate grids or different "action codes" (reject or admit) for white applicants and for minority applicants. "The racially discriminatory policies of the university are blatant," Cohen says today. "They are written in black and white by the

Evidence of Diversity Benefits Disputed

The University of Michigan defended its race-based admissions policies not only with law but also with evidence of the educational benefits of having a racially mixed student body. But opponents of racial preferences dismissed the evidence as distorted and biased.

The largest of the studies introduced as evidence in the two federal court lawsuits over the university's undergraduate and law school admissions policies runs 850 pages. Written by Patricia Gurin, chairman of the Psychology Department, it contains detailed statistics derived from a national student database and surveys of Michigan students. Gurin contends that students "learn more and think in deeper, more complex ways in a diverse educational environment."[1]

In addition, Gurin says students "are more motivated and better able to participate in an increasingly heterogeneous and complex democracy." And students who had "diversity experiences" during college — such as taking courses in Afro-American studies — also had "the most cross-racial interactions" five years after leaving college.

University of Michigan student Agnes Aleobua speaks out against a court ruling in March 2001 that the law school's race-based admission policy is illegal.

The National Association of Scholars, which opposes racial preferences, released two lengthy critiques of Gurin's study after the trials of the two suits. The studies were included in a friend-of-the-court brief filed in the appeals of the rulings.[2]

In the major critique, Thomas E. Wood and Malcolm J. Sherman contend that the national student database actually shows "no relationship" between the proportion of minorities on campus and educational benefits. They also say that "diversity activities" had only a "trivial impact" on educational outcomes.

The university also included "expert reports" from William G. Bowen and Derek Bok, the two former Ivy League university presidents who co-authored the pro-affirmative action book *The Shape of the River*. Bowen and Bok repeat their conclusions from the 1998 book that black students admitted to the "highly selective" colleges and universities studied did "exceedingly well" after college in terms of graduate degrees, income and civic life.[3] About half of the blacks admitted to the schools would not have been admitted under race-neutral policies, Bowen and Bok say.

In their reports for the Michigan suits, Bowen and Bok briefly acknowledge that black students at the schools had lower grades and lower graduation rates than whites. In an early critique of the book, two well-known critics of racial preferences — Abigail and Stephan Thernstrom — call Bowen and Bok to task for glossing over the evidence of poor performance by black students. They note that the dropout rate for black students — about 20 percent — was three times higher than for whites and that black students' grades overall were at the 23rd percentile — that is, in the bottom quarter.[4]

The studies are the tip of a large iceberg of academic literature that has sought to examine the effects of diversity in colleges and universities. In one of the most recent of the studies to be published, a team of authors from Pennsylvania State University concluded that the evidence is "almost uniformly consistent" that students in a racially or ethnically diverse community or engaged in "diversity-related" activities "reap a wide array of positive educational benefits."[5] In their own study of students at seven engineering schools, the scholars found what they called "a small, if statistically significant, link between the level of racial/ethnic diversity in a classroom and students' reports of increases in their problem-solving and group skills."

---

[1] Gurin's report can be found on the university's Web site:www.umich.edu.

[2] Thomas E. Wood and Malcolm J. Sherman, "Is Campus Racial Diversity Correlated With Educational Benefits?", National Association of Scholars, April 4, 2001 (www.nas.org). Wood is executive director of the California Association of Scholars; Sherman is an associate professor of mathematics and statistics at the State University of New York in Albany.

[3] William G. Bowen and Derek Bok, *The Shape of the River: Long-Term Consequences of Considering Race in College and University Admissions,* 1998. Bowen is a former president of Princeton University, Bok a former president of Harvard University.

[4] Stephan Thernstrom and Abigail Thernstrom, "Reflections on The Shape of the River," *UCLA Law Review,* Vol. 45, No. 5 (June 1999), pp. 1583-1631. Stephan Thernstrom is a history professor at Harvard; his wife is a senior fellow at the Manhattan Institute and a member of the Massachusetts Board of Education.

[5] Patrick T. Terenzini et al., "Racial and Ethnic Diversity in the Classroom: Does It Promote Student Learning?", Journal of Higher Education (September/October 2001), pp. 509–531. Terenzini is a professor and senior scientist with the Center for the Study of Higher Education at Pennsylvania State University.

university. It's just incredible."

Cohen wrote up his findings in a report that he presented later in the year at a meeting of the state chapter of the American Association of University Professors. The report also found its way to a Republican state legislator, Rep. Deborah Whyman, who conducted a hearing on the issue and later held a news conference to solicit unsuccessful applicants to challenge the university's admission system. They forwarded about 100 of the replies to the Center for Individual Rights, a conservative public-interest law firm already active in challenging racial preferences.

Gratz and a second unsuccessful white applicant — Patrick Hamacher — were chosen to be the named plaintiffs in a class-action suit filed in federal court in Detroit in October 1997. The center filed a second suit on behalf of Grutter against the law school's admission system in December 1997. Grutter thought she deserved admission based on her 3.8 undergraduate grade-point average 18 years earlier and a respectable score on the law school admission test (161, or 86th percentile nationally). After the rejection, she did not enroll elsewhere.

The cases proved to be long and expensive. By fall 2000, the university said it had spent $4.3 million defending the two suits, not counting personnel costs; the center had spent $400,000, including salaries, and also received the equivalent of $1 million in pro bono legal services from a Minneapolis firm helping to litigate the suits. Among the key pieces of evidence was a long report by an Ann Arbor faculty member — psychology professor Patricia Gurin — concluding that diversity in enrollment has "far-reaching and significant benefits for all students, non-minorities and minorities alike." The center countered with a lengthy study issued under the auspices of the National Association of Scholars that analyzed the same data and found "no connection . . . be-

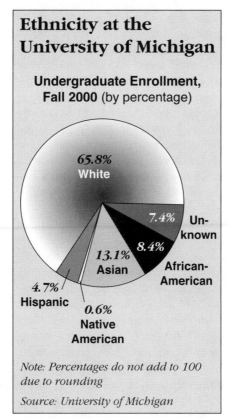

Ethnicity at the University of Michigan

Undergraduate Enrollment, Fall 2000 (by percentage)

65.8% White

7.4% Unknown

8.4% African-American

13.1% Asian

4.7% Hispanic

0.6% Native American

Note: Percentages do not add to 100 due to rounding

Source: University of Michigan

tween campus racial diversity and the supposed educational benefits."

In the meantime, the university revised its undergraduate admissions system, beginning with the entering class of 1999. The race-based grids and codes were replaced by a numerical system that assigned points to each applicant based on any of a number of characteristics. An applicant from an "underrepresented minority group" — African-Americans, Hispanics and Native Americans — was given 20 points. (One hundred points was typically required for admission, according to Cohen.) The same number was given to an applicant from a disadvantaged socioeconomic status, to a white student from a predominantly minority high school or to a scholarship athlete, according to university counsel Barry. The most important single factor, she added, was an applicant's high school grades.

Judge Duggan's Dec. 13, 2000, ruling in the undergraduate case sustained the plaintiffs' complaint against the

system used when Gratz and Hamacher had been rejected. Duggan said that the "racially different grids and codes based solely upon an applicant's race" amounted to an "impermissible use of race." But Duggan said the revised system was on the right side of what he called "the thin line that divides the permissible and the impermissible."

Three months later, however, Judge Friedman on March 27, 2001, struck down the law school's admission system. Evidence showed that the school had used a "special admissions" program since 1992 aimed at a minority enrollment of 10 percent to 12 percent.

Friedman relied on a statistical analysis that showed an African-American applicant's relative odds of acceptance were up to 400 times as great as a white applicant's. Friedman rejected the use of diversity to justify the racial preferences, but in any event said the law school's system was not "narrowly tailored" because there was no time limit and there had been no consideration of alternative means of increasing minority enrollment.

The two Michigan cases took on added significance in June 2001 when the Supreme Court declined for a second time to hear Texas' appeal in the *Hopwood* case or to hear the plaintiffs' appeal of a ruling by the 9th U.S. Circuit Court of Appeals upholding a discontinued system of racial preferences at the University of Washington Law School. Then on Aug. 27, 2001, the 11th U.S. Circuit Court of Appeals issued a ruling striking down the University of Georgia's admissions system.[21]

The Sixth U.S. Circuit Court of Appeals decided to hear the two Michigan cases together in October 2001 before the full court instead of three-judge panels. Seven months later, the appeals court on May 14, 2002, issued a sharply divided, 5-4 decision upholding the law school admissions system. The majority said the school considered race along with other factors in an effort to admit enough minority students so that all students could enjoy "the educational benefits of an academically diverse student body." The dissenting judges maintained that the procedures were indistinguishable from a numerical quota.

The appeals court did not rule on the undergraduate case at the same time and issued no explanation for the omission. The Center for Individual Rights asked the Supreme Court to review the law school ruling and later — with the college case still undecided — asked the justices to bypass the appeals court and take jurisdiction of Gratz's case too. The university opposed reviewing the law school case, but agreed that if review was granted the two cases should be heard together.

The Court granted certiorari in both cases on December 2, 2002. By the time the cases came to be argued, they had attracted a record number of friend-of-the-court briefs: eighty-one in all, more than two-thirds of them supporting the university. Court watchers noted in particular briefs filed by a group of retired military officers stressing the importance of affirmative action in producing a racially diverse officer corps and a separate brief by the Michigan-based General Motors Corp. defending affirmative action as a means of a diverse workforce at supervisory and managerial levels. On the opposite side, the Bush administration urged the Court to hold procedures at both schools unconstitutional but did not call for prohibiting any consideration of race in admissions.

CURRENT SITUATION

Split Decisions?

The Supreme Court's rulings in the Michigan cases — issued togeth-

er on June 23, 2003 — appeared at quick glance to be a compromise of sorts: upholding the law school policies while ruling the college's admissions system unconstitutional. On closer examination, though, affirmative action supporters stressed that the law school decision squarely held — and the undergraduate case acknowledged — that universities could use individualized race-conscious admissions procedures to promote the compelling government interest in diversity.

Writing for the majority in *Grutter*, Justice O'Connor said the law school's admissions policies satisfied the constitutional requirement that any government use of race be "narrowly tailored" to achieve a compelling interest — in this case, attaining a diverse student body. The law school, she wrote, "engages in a highly individualized, holistic review of each applicant's file, giving serious consideration to all the ways an applicant might contribute to a diverse educational environment."

In contrast to the undergraduate admissions procedures, O'Connor said, the law school "awards no mechanical, predetermined diversity 'bonuses' based on race or ethnicity." Under the law school program, an applicant's race or ethnicity was not "the defining feature" of his or her application, she wrote. And even though the law school explicitly sought a "critical mass" of minority admittees, O'Connor said that the admissions program "does not operate as a quota."

O'Connor ended her opinion, though, by suggesting that race-conscious admissions policies should not be permanent. Colleges and universities, she said, should include "sunset provisions" and "periodic reviews" to determine whether racial preferences are still needed to achieve student body diversity. Citing the twenty-five year period since *Bakke*, O'Connor concluded, "We expect that 25 years from now, the use of racial preferences will no longer be necessary to further the interest approved today." O'Connor's

opinion — was joined by the court's four liberal-leaning justices: John Paul Stevens, David H. Souter, Ruth Bader Ginsburg and Stephen G. Breyer. The four dissenting justices — William H. Rehnquist, Antonin Scalia, Anthony M. Kennedy and Clarence Thomas — each wrote opinions explaining why they disagreed with the decision to uphold the law school's admissions program.

Writing for all four, Rehnquist said the procedures appeared to be "a carefully managed program designed to ensure proportionate representation of applicants from selected minority groups." Rehnquist also faulted the majority for what he called "unprecedented" deference to the law school's defense of its program. In a lone opinion, Kennedy also criticized the majority for what he called a "perfunctory" review of the program. But Kennedy explicitly agreed that racial diversity was a constitutionally legitimate goal in higher education.

In the longest of the dissents, Thomas strongly criticized affirmative action on both legal and practical grounds. Referring to diversity as "classroom aesthetics," Thomas said the majority made "no serious effort" to explain its educational benefits. In practice, he said, racial preferences provoked resentment among unsuccessful applicants while most blacks admitted under the policies were "tarred as undeserving." Thomas also warned the decision would produce further "controversy and litigation." Scalia joined Thomas's opinion and wrote a shorter dissent of his own.

Both Thomas and Scalia did note their agreement with the Court's suggestion that race-conscious admissions policies should be terminated in twenty-five years. From the other side, Ginsburg wrote a concurring opinion somewhat discounting the deadline. " . . . [O]ne may hope, but not firmly forecast, that over the next generation's span, progress toward nondiscrimination and genuinely equal opportunity will make it safe to sunset

At Issue

Should colleges eliminate the use of race in admissions?

THOMAS E. WOOD
EXECUTIVE DIRECTOR, CALIFORNIA ASSOCIATION OF SCHOLARS, CO-AUTHOR OF CALIFORNIA PROP. 209

WRITTEN FOR THE CQ RESEARCHER, SEPTEMBER 2001

Colleges should eliminate the use of race in admissions. One cannot prefer on the basis of race without discriminating against others on the basis of race. Treating people differently on the basis of their race violates the Constitution's guarantee of equal protection under the laws.

There is only one national database for higher education that is in a position to adequately address this question whether, or to what extent, campus racial diversity is a necessary component of educational excellence. So far, the American Council on Education/Higher Education Research Institute database has failed to find any connection between campus racial diversity and any of the 82 cognitive and non-cognitive outcome variables incorporated in the study.

Proponents claim that the abandonment of racial classifications will result in the resegregation of higher education. Since preferences have been used to increase the number of minorities in the past, their abandonment will lead in the near term to lower numbers for minorities (though only in the most elite institutions of higher education).

But the claim that abandoning the use of race in college admissions will lead to resegregation implies that all or virtually all minorities who are presently enrolled in the most elite institutions are there only because they have been given preferences, which is both untrue and demeaning. The claim also ignores the fact that the country was making significant progress toward diversity *before* the advent of racial preferences in university admissions in the mid-to-late 1970s.

This analysis is confirmed by the experience of Texas, California and Washington, which already have bans on racial classifications in university admissions. The experience in these states has been that while there is an initial decline when racial classifications are abandoned (though only in the most elite institutions), the underlying trend toward greater diversity resumes after the initial correction.

For some, of course, any regression from the numbers that are obtainable through the use of preferences is unacceptable. At its heart, this is the view that racial diversity is a value that trumps all others. But that is a view that has clearly been rejected by the courts, and for good reason. Diversity is an important public policy goal, but there is a right way and a wrong way to pursue it. Racial classifications are the wrong way.

ANGELO ANCHETA
DIRECTOR, LEGAL AND ADVOCACY PROGRAMS, CIVIL RIGHTS PROJECT, HARVARD LAW SCHOOL

WRITTEN FOR THE CQ RESEARCHER, SEPTEMBER 2001

Affirmative action policies advance the tenet that colleges, like the workplace and our public institutions, should reflect the full character of American society. Race-conscious admissions policies not only promote the integration ideal first realized in *Brown v. Board of Education* but also help create educational environments that improve basic learning and better equip students for an increasingly diverse society.

The U.S. Supreme Court upheld race-conscious admissions over 20 years ago in *Regents of the University of California v. Bakke*. Yet, affirmative action opponents, armed with the rhetoric of quotas and tokenism for the unqualified, persist in trying to undermine *Bakke*. Educators know that quotas are illegal under *Bakke* and that granting admission to the unqualified serves no one's interest. Colleges have been highly circumspect, employing carefully crafted policies that consider all applicants competitively and that use race as only one of many factors in admissions decisions.

Nevertheless, recent litigation challenging affirmative action in Texas, Washington, Georgia and Michigan portends that the Supreme Court will soon revisit *Bakke*. But the case that promoting educational diversity is, in the language of the law, "a compelling governmental interest" and that race-conscious admissions policies can best serve that interest has only strengthened in recent years.

The latest findings show that student-body diversity significantly improves the quality of higher education. Studies at the University of Michigan have found that diverse learning environments can enhance students' critical-thinking skills, augment their understanding and tolerance of different opinions and groups, increase their motivation and participation in civic activities and better prepare them for living in a diverse society. Several studies support these findings and further show that interaction across races has positive effects on retention rates, satisfaction with college, self-confidence and leadership ability.

Without race-conscious admissions, the student-body diversity necessary to advance these educational outcomes would be lost. The declining enrollment of minority students at public universities that have abandoned affirmative action strongly suggests that the "color-blind" path is not the path to equal opportunity; nor is it the path to the highest-quality education.

Affirmative action policies reflect the reality that race has always shaped our educational institutions. Justice Blackmun's admonition in *Bakke* thus remains as vital as ever: "In order to get beyond racism, we must first take account of race. There is no other way."

affirmative action," she wrote. Breyer joined her opinion.

Writing for the majority in *Gratz*, Rehnquist said the program violated the Equal Protection Clause because its use of race was "not narrowly tailored to achieve the interest in educational diversity that [university officials] claim justifies their program." The automatic distribution of 20 points, he said, had the effect of making race the decisive factor "for virtually every minimally qualified underrepresented minority applicant."

Rehnquist rejected the college's argument that the volume of applications made it "impractical" to adopt the kind of individualized review of applications approved by the Court in the law school case. "The fact that the implementation of a program capable of providing individualized consideration might present administrative challenges does not render constitutional an otherwise problematic system," he wrote.

Rehnquist was joined by the other three dissenters from the law school case and O'Connor. In a concurring opinion, O'Connor said the undergraduate admissions system was "a nonindividualized, mechanical one" that did not provide for "a meaningful individualized review of applicants." Breyer concurred in the judgment; he said he concurred in O'Connor's opinion "except insofar as it joins that of the Court."

The dissenters objected on procedural and substantive grounds. Procedurally, Stevens and Souter said that Gratz and Hamacher had no standing to seek to enjoin the further use of the admissions policies because they had both graduated from different schools and were no longer seeking admission. On the merits, Souter and Ginsburg both said they would uphold the admissions program. In her opinion, Ginsburg said racial policies aimed at "inclusion" should be treated more favorably than policies aimed at "exclusion." Breyer said he joined that part of Ginsburg's opinion.

OUTLOOK

Reform or Status Quo?

The Supreme Court's decisions in the Michigan cases heartened supporters of affirmative action and disappointed opponents. For their part, university officials across the country generally said the rulings would allow them to continue using racial preferences in admissions with only minor modifications if any.

Affirmative action supporters were beaming after announcement of the decisions. "This is a wonderful day," University of Michigan president Mary Sue Coleman told reporters on the Supreme Court plaza. The decisions, she said, provided "a green light to pursue diversity" and "a road map to get us there."

Liberal interest groups also praised the decisions. "The Court has reiterated America's commitment to affirmative action, and the nation is better off for it," said Vincent Warren, a staff attorney with the American Civil Liberties Union who worked on the cases. "They're not willing to turn the clock back," said Theodore Shaw of the NAACP Legal Defense and Educational Fund. "That's the message for the nation.

Conservative groups, which had generally expected a clear-cut victory in the cases, tried to conceal their disappointment by depicting the rulings as a partial win. Terrence Pell, president of the Center for Individual Rights, said the rulings would make it "more difficult" for universities to use race-based admissions procedures. Clint Bolick, vice president of the libertarian Institute for Justice, said the decisions "will leave the nation racially polarized."

Both Pell and Bolick also contended that the rulings did nothing to address racial gaps in elementary and secondary education. "Racial preferences in postsecondary education make us think that we are solving that problem when in fact it is growing," Bolick said. "For that reason, this decision is a tragedy for all Americans."

President Bush cautiously praised the decisions for recognizing "the value of diversity" while requiring universities to "engage in a serious, good faith consideration of workable race-neutral alternatives."

Coleman told reporters that the university would quickly revise its undergraduate admissions policies in line with the Court's ruling in time for the class entering the college in 2004. Officials representing other colleges and universities said the rulings cleared up legal confusion over the issues and predicted the decisions would lead to few changes.

The ruling "has the effect of defining current practices as constitutional," said Barmak Nassirian, associate executive director of the American Association of Collegiate Registrars and Admissions Officers. "There are very few institutions that would be negatively affected by the undergraduate decision."

But Pell warned universities not to use the rulings as a "fig leaf" to preserve the status quo. "Some schools are determined to continue to take race into account, and it's business as usual for them," Pell said. He said the center would monitor responses to the decisions and challenge any schools that used a "mechanistic" formula to favor minority candidates.

Notes

[1] For extensive information on both cases, including the texts of the two rulings and other legal documents, see the University of Michigan's Web site (www.umich.edu) or the Web site of the public-interest law firm representing the plaintiffs, the Center for Individual Rights (www.cir-usa.org).

[2] The legal citation is 438 U.S. 265; Supreme Court decisions can be found on a number of

Web sites, including the court's official site: www.supremecourtus.gov. For background, see Kenneth Jost, "Rethinking Affirmative Action," *The CQ Researcher*, April 28, 1995, pp. 369-392.

[3] See Robert Lerner and Althea K. Nagai, "Pervasive Preferences: Racial and Ethnic Discrimination in Undergraduate Admissions Across the Nation," Center for Equal Opportunity, Feb. 22, 2001 (www.ceo-usa.org).

[4] For background, see David Masci, "Hispanic Americans' New Clout," *The CQ Researcher*, Sept. 18, 1998, pp. 809-832; David Masci, "The Black Middle Class," *The CQ Researcher*, Jan. 23, 1998, pp. 49-72; and Kenneth Jost, "Diversity in the Workplace," *The CQ Researcher*, Oct. 10, 1997, pp. 889-912.

[5] Charles R. Lawrence III and Mari J. Matsuda, *We Won't Go Back: Making the Case for Affirmative Action* (1997), p. 127. Matsuda, Lawrence's wife, is also a professor at Georgetown law school.

[6] For background, see Joan Biskupic and Elder Witt, *Guide to the U.S. Supreme Court* (3d ed.), 1997, pp. 362-363. The cases discussed are *Missouri ex rel. Gaines v. Canada*, 305 U.S. 337 (1938); *Sweatt v. Painter*, 339 U.S. 629 (1950); and *McLaurin v. Oklahoma State Regents for Higher Education*, 339 U.S. 637 (1950).

[7] William G. Bowen and Derek Bok, *The Shape of the River: Long-Term Consequences of Considering Race in College and University Admissions* (1998), pp. 4-5. Bowen, a former president of Princeton University, is now president of the Andrew W. Mellon Foundation in New York City; Bok is a former president of Harvard University and now University Professor at the John. F. Kennedy School of Government at Harvard.

[8] Reprinted in Gabriel J. Chin (ed.), *Affirmative Action and the Constitution: Affirmative Action Before Constitutional Law, 1964-1977*, Vol. 1 (1998), pp. 21-26.

[9] Bowen and Bok, *op. cit.*, pp. 6-7.

[10] Description of the announcement of the decision taken from Bernard Schwartz, *Behind Bakke: Affirmative Action and the Supreme Court* (1988), pp. 142-150.

[11] The cases are *Wygant v. Jackson Bd. of Education*, 476 U.S. 267 (1986); *Johnson v. Trans-*

portation Agency of Santa Clara County 480 U.S. 646 (1987); *City of Richmond v. J.A. Croson Co.* 488 U.S. 469 (1989); and *Adarand Constructors, Inc. v. Peña* 575 U.S. 200 (1995).

[12] Lincoln Caplan, *Up Against the Law: Affirmative Action and the Supreme Court* (1997), p. 16.

[13] The case is *Hopwood v. Texas*. Some background on this and other cases in this section drawn from Girardeau A. Spann, *The Law of Affirmative Action: Twenty-Five Years of Supreme Court Decisions on Race and Remedies* (2000).

[14] The legal citation is *Hopwood v. Texas*, 78 F.2d 932 (5th Cir. 1996). In a subsequent decision, the appeals court on Dec. 21, 2000, reaffirmed its legal holding, but upheld the lower court judge's finding that none of the four plaintiffs would have been admitted to the law school under a race-blind system. See *Hopwood v. Texas*, 236 F.2d 256 (5th Cir. 2000).

[15] Quoted in Facts on File, March 28, 1996.

[16] For background, see Jennifer Gavin, "Redis-

tricting," *The CQ Researcher*, Feb. 16, 2001, pp. 113-128; Nadine Cahodas, "Electing Minorities," *The CQ Researcher*, Aug. 12, 1994, pp. 697-720.

[17] The legal citation is 515 U.S. 200.

[18] For a critique, see Stephan and Abigail Thernstrom, "Reflections on the Shape of the River," *UCLA Law Review*, Vol. 46, No. 5 (June 1999), pp. 1583-1631.[19] For a good overview, see Nicholas Lemann, "The Empathy Defense," *The New Yorker*, Dec. 18, 2000, pp. 46-51. See also Carl Cohen, "Race Preference and the Universities — A Final Reckoning," *Commentary*, September 2001, pp. 31-39.

[20] "Vital Signs: The Statistics that Describe the Present and Suggest the Future of African Americans in Higher Education," *The Journal of Blacks in Higher Education*, No. 9 (autumn 1995), pp. 43-49.

[21] The Washington case is *Smith v. University of Washington Law School*, 9th Circuit, Dec. 4, 2000; the Georgia case is *Johnson v. Board of Regents of the University of Georgia*, 11th Circuit, Aug. 27.

Bibliography

Selected Sources Used

Books

Bowen, William G. , and Derek Bok, *The Shape of the River: Long-Term Consequences of Considering Race in College and University Admissions*, Princeton University Press, 1998.

The book analyzes data on 80,000 students admitted to 28 selective private or public colleges and universities in 1951, 1976 and 1989 to examine the impact of race-based admissions on enrollment and to compare the educational and post-graduation experiences of white and minority students. Includes statistical tables as well as a nine-page list of references. Bowen, a former president of Princeton University, heads the Andrew W. Mellon Foundation; Bok is a former president of Harvard University and now a professor at Harvard's John F. Kennedy School of Government.

Caplan, Lincoln, *Up Against the Law: Affirmative Action and the Supreme Court*, Twentieth Century Fund Press, 1997.

The 60-page monograph provides an overview of the Supreme Court's affirmative action rulings with analysis written from a pro race-conscious policies perspective. Caplan, a longtime legal-affairs writer, is a senior writer in residence at Yale Law School.

Chin, Gabriel J. (ed.), *Affirmative Action and the Constitution: Affirmative Action Before Constitutional Law, 1964-1977* (Vol. 1); *The Supreme Court "Solves" the Affirmative Action Issue, 1978-1988* (Vol. 2); *Judicial Reaction to Affirmative Action, 1988-1997* (Vol. 3), Garland Publishing, 1998.

The three-volume compendium includes a variety of materials on affirmative action from President Lyndon B. Johnson's famous speech at Howard University in 1965 to President Bill Clinton's defense of affirmative action in 1995 as well as the full text of the federal appeals court decision in the 1995 Hopwood decision barring racial preferences at the University of Texas Law School. Chin, who wrote an introduction for each volume, is a professor at the University of Cincinnati College of Law.

Edley, Christopher Jr., *Not All Black and White: Affirmative Action, Race, and American Values*, Hill & Wang, 1996.

Edley, a Harvard Law School professor, recounts his role in overseeing the Clinton administration's review of affirmative action in 1995 as part of a broad look at the issue that ends with measured support for affirmative action "until the justification for it no longer exists."

Schwartz, Bernard, *Behind Bakke: Affirmative Action and the Supreme Court*, New York University Press.

Schwartz, a leading Supreme Court scholar until his death in 1997, was granted unusual access to the private papers of the justices for this detailed, behind-the-scenes account of the Bakke case from its origins through the justices' deliberations and final decision.

Spann, Girardeau A., *The Law of Affirmative Action: Twenty-Five Years of Supreme Court Decisions on Races and Remedies*, New York University Press, 2000.

The book includes summaries — concise and precise — of major Supreme Court decisions from Bakke in 1978 to Adarand in 1995 Spann is a professor at Georgetown University Law Center.

Steele, Shelby, *A Dream Deferred: The Second Betrayal of Black Freedom in America*, HarperCollins, 1998.

Steele, a prominent black critic of affirmative action and a research fellow at the Hoover Institution at Stanford University, argues in four essays that affirmative action represents an "extravagant" liberalism that "often betrayed America's best principles" in order to atone for white guilt over racial injustice.

Articles

Lawrence, Charles R. III, "Two Views of the River: A Critique of the Liberal Defense of Affirmative Action," *Columbia Law Review*, Vol. 101, No. 4 (May 2001), pp. 928-975.

Lawrence argues that liberals' "diversity" defense of affirmative action overlooks "more radical substantive" arguments based on "the need to remedy past discrimination, address present discriminatory practices, and reexamine traditional notions of merit and the role of universities in the reproduction of elites." Lawrence is a professor at Georgetown University Law Center.

PBS NewsHour, "Admitting for Diversity," Aug. 21, 2001 (www.pbs.org/newshour).

The report by correspondent Elizabeth Brackett features interviews with, among others, Barbara Grutter, the plaintiff in the lawsuit challenging the University of Michigan Law School's race-based admissions policies, and the law school's dean, Jeffrey Lehman.

Thernstrom, Stephan, and Abigail Thernstrom, "Reflections on The Shape of the River," *UCLA Law Review*, Vol. 46, No. 5 (June 1999), pp. 1583-1.

The Thernstroms contend that racial preferences constitute a "pernicious palliative" that deflect attention from real educational problems and conflict with the country's unrealized egalitarian dream. Stephan Thernstrom is a professor of history at Harvard University; his wife Abigail is a senior fellow at the Manhattan Institute and a member of the Massachusetts State Board of Education. An earlier version appeared in Commentary (February 1999).

15 Race in America

ALAN GREENBLATT

When Joe Moore got out of jail in June, the 60-year-old hog farmer told reporters, "I just want to go home, look at TV and stay out of trouble." After her release, Kizzie White, 26, hugged her two children and said, "I'm going to be the best mother I can to them." [1]

Moore and White were among the more than three-dozen, mostly black residents of the West Texas town of Tulia convicted of drug crimes four years ago solely on the now-discredited testimony of an undercover police officer widely labeled as a racist.

Many white Americans believe that race no longer matters in America, now that public schools have been integrated, blacks can vote and race-based job and housing discrimination are illegal. Yet racial incidents like Tulia continue to erupt, periodically shattering Americans' complacency about race and signaling to many observers that racist sentiments still linger in some psyches.

Often the eruptions spill into the streets — usually in response to allegedly racist police actions — such as the riots that broke out in Cincinnati in April 2001 or in Benton Harbor, Mich., this past June.

Lately, some of the incidents — particularly in the South — appear to represent a longing by some for the pre-1960s era of segregation. In Georgia this spring, white high-school students held a prom at which African-American students pointedly were excluded — a year after the school's first integrated prom. That followed the downfall last fall of Sen. Trent Lott of Mississippi, who was forced to resign as majority leader after

From *The CQ Researcher,*
July 11, 2003.

Benny Robinson hugs his daughter Jada after he and other African-Americans in Tulia, Texas, were released from prison in June. Some three-dozen residents — mainly blacks — were convicted of drug charges based on the now-discredited testimony of a racist policeman. Although African-Americans have made economic, political and social progress over the last four decades, such incidents periodically erupt, shattering Americans' complacency about race.

saying America would have been better off if then-Gov. Strom Thurmond of South Carolina had won the presidency in 1948, when he was an ardent segregationist.

And some of the racially tinged incidents have been particularly conscience-searing: the murder of James Byrd Jr., chained behind a truck in Jasper, Texas, and dragged to death; the broomstick sodomizing of Haitian immigrant Abner Louima and the shooting of unarmed African immigrant Amadou Diallo by New York policemen; the beating in Los Angeles of Rodney King.

Such cases bring into dramatic focus the often diametrically opposing ways in which whites and blacks view race relations in America, especially when the criminal-justice system is involved. Many whites saw the acquittal of O.J. Simpson in the murder of his ex-wife Nicole Simpson and her friend Ron Gold-

man as a miscarriage of justice, while blacks generally viewed it as a triumph over racist police tactics. Similarly, blacks in Tulia celebrated the release of their fellow citizens as righting a racial injustice while whites continued to question the prisoners' innocence.

And even the Supreme Court's landmark approval recently of the University of Michigan's use of affirmative action in law-school admissions was viewed differently by some blacks and whites (*see pp.* 291, 300).

But many Americans — whites as well as blacks — say the nation's racial problems go beyond racial preferences and the criminal-justice system. They say discrimination still exists despite civil-rights laws, undercutting blacks educationally and economically. Although African-Americans have made economic, political and social progress over the last four decades, by several objective measures they are trailing whites:

- Median income among black men is only 73 percent as high as that of white men, and only 84 percent for black women compared with white women. [2]
- Blacks are 60 percent less likely than whites to receive access to sophisticated medical treatments such as coronary angioplasty and bypass surgery. [3]
- Minorities are far more likely to pay higher, "predatory" mortgage rates than whites. [4]
- A majority of black students score below the basic level in five out of seven subject areas on the National Assessment of Educational Progress (NAEP) tests, compared to only about 20 percent of white students. [5]

White Students Are the Most Isolated

The average white student in the United States attends a school made up of 80 percent whites. Similarly, most black students attend schools in which the majority of their fellow students are the same race as themselves. Asians are the most integrated in American schools.

Racial Composition of Schools Attended by the Average . . .

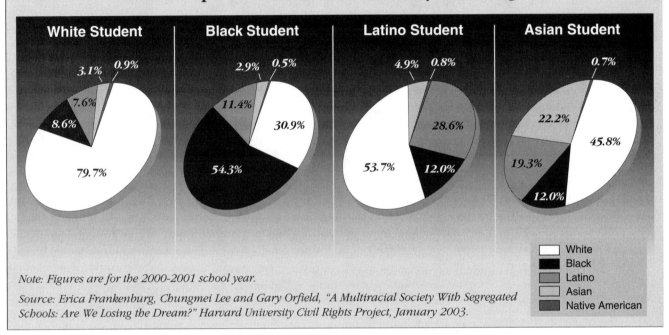

White Student
- 79.7%
- 8.6%
- 7.6%
- 3.1%
- 0.9%

Black Student
- 54.3%
- 30.9%
- 11.4%
- 2.9%
- 0.5%

Latino Student
- 53.7%
- 28.6%
- 12.0%
- 4.9%
- 0.8%

Asian Student
- 45.8%
- 22.2%
- 19.3%
- 12.0%
- 0.7%

Legend:
- White
- Black
- Latino
- Asian
- Native American

Note: Figures are for the 2000-2001 school year.

Source: Erica Frankenburg, Chungmei Lee and Gary Orfield, "A Multiracial Society With Segregated Schools: Are We Losing the Dream?" Harvard University Civil Rights Project, January 2003.

- One in five black men spends part of his life in prison — seven times the rate for whites. [6] Blacks are 13 percent of the U.S. population, but make up more than 40 percent of the prisoners on Death Row. [7]

Meanwhile, some social critics warn that Latinos and Arabs increasingly experience discrimination in the United States. Latinos, expected to become the nation's largest minority group in the next few years, struggle with levels of poverty and education similar to those of blacks. And Arabs and civil-liberties advocates say the nation's war on terrorism subjects Middle Easterners to widespread harassment. (*See sidebar, p. 300.*)

Some social scientists say that civil-rights laws are working and that blacks' lack of achievement is often due to lack of hard work and criminal behavior, not racism. Moreover, they point to progress in a number of areas, including the recent decision by New Jersey to stop racial profiling by its state troopers.

Gary Orfield, co-director of the Harvard Civil Rights Project, says the racial divide still appears to be widest in public education. Despite decades of court-ordered school integration, more than one in six black children attends a school comprised of 99-100 percent minority students; by comparison, less than 1 percent of white public-school students attend such schools.

Many observers have expected the Republican Party to adopt a more conciliatory stance toward blacks, who overwhelmingly favor Democrats in elections for all levels of office. Indeed, a day after 12 of the Tulia defendants were released from prison, the Bush administration barred federal officers from using race or ethnicity as a factor in conducting investigations (except in cases involving terrorism or national security). [8]

But some African-American leaders question the Bush administration's commitment to fighting racism. "Bush represents anathema to our struggle for social justice," says civil-rights activist Jesse Jackson. "He would not permit [Secretary of State Colin] Powell to go to the U.N. conference on racism in South Africa; he has sought to stock the courts with anti-civil rights judges; he is anti-affirmative action. . . . We are simply on different teams." [9]

Less than a month after Lott stepped down, President Bush spoke out against the University of Michigan's use of racial preferences.

Bush's supporters, however, say he has appointed as many women and minorities to top government jobs as Bill Clinton, whose administration was the most racially diverse in history. "The president is very committed to diversity of thought, of professional background, of geography, ethnicity and gender," said Clay Johnson, who coordinated appointments for Bush. By March 2001, he noted, 27 percent of Bush's selections were women, and 20 to 25 percent were minorities. [10]

Like many conservatives, Bush believes that the interests of blacks, as well as whites, are best served by race-neutral policies. "As we work to address the wrong of racial prejudice, we must not use means that create another wrong, and thus perpetuate our divisions," he said.

Indeed, Heather Mac Donald, a senior fellow at the Manhattan Institute, says "the white establishment is doing everything it can to hire as many black employees as it can. If you are a black high-school student who graduates with modest SATs today, you're going to have colleges beating down your door to try and persuade you to come."

But David Wellman, a white professor of community studies at the University of California, Santa Cruz, sees an opposite reality. "Race not only matters, but whites have an advantage because blacks have a disadvantage," says Wellman, co-author of the forthcoming book *Whitewashing Race*. "That's the dirty little secret that nobody wants to talk about anymore.

"Everyone wants to believe that racism has been essentially solved through legislation," he insists. "Unfortunately, when you look at the evidence in terms of education, crime and welfare, it's just shocking how important race continues to be."

Some scholars argue that, absent overt discrimination, blacks must share much of the blame if their circumstances are not equal to whites. "The grip of the Cult of Victimology encourages the black American from birth to fixate upon remnants of racism and resolutely down-

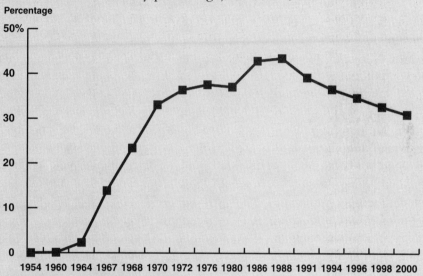

Re-Segregation Increasing in Southern Schools

By 1988 — after decades of court-ordered desegregation — the South had become the country's most integrated region, with 43.5 percent of black students attending majority-white schools. But by 2000 the percentage had dropped to 31 percent, following the abandonment of busing and other school-desegregation efforts in the 1990s.

Black Students in Majority-White Southern Schools
(by percentage, 1954-2000)

Source: Southern Education Reporting Service

play all signs of its demise," writes John McWhorter, a professor at the University of California, Berkeley. [11]

Faith Mitchell, deputy director of the National Research Council's Division on Behavioral and Social Sciences, acknowledges that her fellow African-Americans have made much progress — but only to a point. "Yes, you have a growing black middle class," she says, "but it's still disproportionately small relative to the rest of the black population. The lower class is growing faster." [12]

As blacks and whites examine race relations in the United States, here are some of the questions they are asking:

Is discrimination still a problem in the United States?

In 1988, when a residential treatment center opened in Indianapolis

for convicted child molesters, neighbors accepted it with little comment. But three years later, when it was converted into a facility for homeless veterans — half of them black — neighborhood whites vandalized a car and burned a cross.

"An all-white cadre of child molesters was evidently acceptable," wrote Randall Kennedy, a black Harvard law-school professor, "but the presence of blacks made a racially integrated group of homeless veterans intolerable!" [13]

The Indianapolis case was unusually overt, says Leonard Steinhorn, an American University professor and co-author of the book *By the Color of Our Skin: The Illusion of Integration and the Reality of Race.* Most opposition to racial integration is much more subtle,

Are Blacks Losing Political Clout?

Even at age 100, Sen. Strom Thurmond, R-S.C., was a lightning rod for debates about racism. In Washington, powerful Mississippi Sen. Trent Lott lost his job as majority leader last year for waxing nostalgic for segregation at a 100th birthday party for Thurmond, who died recently. Lott told the celebration he wished the centenarian had won the presidency back in 1948, when he ran as a segregationist.

And in South Carolina this spring, GOP state legislators angered some of their Democratic colleagues by including several pictures of a young Thurmond in the state legislative manual. "Nobody could dispute the fact that Strom Thurmond was probably the No. 1 racist Dixiecrat of the day," says state Sen. Robert Ford.

Ford, an African-American and veteran of the civil-rights movement, believes Thurmond sincerely tempered his views on race later in his career. Still, Ford took to the Senate floor to express his dismay over the pictures of a younger, unreconstructed Thurmond in the manual.

Several Republican legislators said Ford was making a big deal out of nothing, or, worse, that he was unnecessarily criticizing a man revered as an icon throughout South Carolina. "They don't want to hear anything negative about Strom Thurmond," Ford says. "They are living in another world."

In fact, whites in the state literally do live in a different world. Because of redistricting maneuvers, South Carolina blacks live in predominantly black political districts. Conversely, most districts are so dominated by whites that politicians representing those districts have no practical incentives to consider the needs or historical sensitivities of African-Americans. This political segregation encourages both black and white politicians to pick fights over racially charged matters — such as disputes about pictures of Thurmond or whether to allow the Confederate flag to fly over state buildings — because they get high-profile coverage back home.

"On both sides of the aisle, they log onto largely symbolic issues," says Dick Harpootlian, who recently stepped down as chairman of the South Carolina Democratic Party.

"If you want to get re-elected and you're black, you don't want to talk to white voters," Harpootlian says. "If you're white and running for re-election, you don't want to talk to blacks.

We've institutionalized this idea that race predominates over any other interest."

The Voting Rights Act of 1982 encouraged some blacks to join with Republicans to create majority-black districts after the 1980 and 1990 censuses — mostly in the South. The deal allowed African-Americans to create districts that would likely elect blacks. For Republicans, concentrating black voters into a relatively few districts weakened Democratic candidates' chances in neighboring districts.

Partly as a result, there are about 600 black state legislators in the United States today — twice as many as there were in 1970. But now that Democrats are losing power in the South, black legislators in the South are in the dubious position of becoming more important in a national party that has become less powerful.

Former Sen. Carol Moseley Braun, D-Ill., one of only two blacks ever elected to the U.S. Senate in modern times, is seeking the Democratic presidential nomination.

Getty Images/Linda Spillers

"African-Americans now have a seat at the table but no plate, no forks and nothing to eat," Harpootlian says. "African-Americans have no influence in our legislature now — zero, nada, none."

Although today there are more black elected officials at all levels of government than in earlier years, the trend appears to have peaked, at least for now. Over the last 40 years, only one African-American has been elected governor — L. Douglas Wilder of Virginia — and only two blacks have been elected to the U.S. Senate — Edward W. Brooke, R-Mass., and Carol Moseley Braun, D-Ill.

Blacks have enjoyed the most real political power at the city level — but even that power is receding. New York, Los Angeles, Chicago, Denver, Oakland, Cleveland, St. Louis, Baltimore, Seattle, Minneapolis, Dallas and numerous other cities had black mayors during the 1980s and '90s but have white mayors today.

University of Maryland political scientist Ronald Walters says that as increasing numbers of blacks moved out of the center cities, whites have gained the upper hand because they vote in greater numbers. "It's sort of a cycle of expectations that didn't pan out," Walters says. "There was a lot of euphoria around the first generation of black mayors and what they could accomplish."

But just as blacks were taking the reins of power, Walters points out, urban populations began declining, and aid to cities began drying up. "The irony was that they couldn't accomplish a whole hell of a lot. The whole conservative movement at the state and national level robbed them of the ability to do much."

he says. "Today, a black person moves in and most white people accept it, or even like it," Steinhorn says. "But one or two families get nervous and move out. More blacks may move in, because they see that the first blacks have been accepted. Then a couple more whites say we better move.

"It's a slow and gradual phenomenon, not the spontaneous, overnight reaction we saw in the past," Steinhorn explains. Even if the African-Americans share the same socioeconomic footing as the whites, most whites will not stay in a neighborhood once it becomes more than 10 to 15 percent black, he says.

But some observers argue that segregation today is more a matter of choice than of bigotry. "White flight is just as widespread as ever," says Jared Taylor, editor of *Amer ican Renaissance* magazine, who has been described as a white nationalist. "Even if few people acknowledge it, people prefer the company of people like themselves, and race is an important ingredient. Given the chance, they spend their time in homogeneous groups. It is part of human nature."

Taylor's sentiments are echoed by Carol Swain, a black professor of law and political science at Vanderbilt University. "Clearly, discrimination exists, and in very subtle ways," she says, but it is "human nature for people to favor their own group." Indeed, many "black separatists" argue that African-Americans can achieve more by running their own businesses in their own communities, rather than seeking opportunities among whites.

"I would prefer to see more integration," says Bob Zelnick, chairman of the Boston University journalism department and a member of the conservative Citizens' Initiative on Race and Ethnicity. "But I don't think it's a mark of failure if people prefer to live among their own kind. There's some lingering discrimination [in the United

Most Inmates Are Black, Hispanic

Minorities represented nearly two-thirds of the 1.8 million American men over age 18 in local jails and state or federal prisons in 2002.

Men in U.S. Jails and Prisons
(as of June 30, 2002)

		Percentage of Inmate Total	Percentage of Race in U.S. Population
White	630,700	34.0%	75.0%
Black	818,900	44.0	13.0
Hispanic	342,500	18.5	12.0
Total	**1,848,700**		

Note: American Indians, Alaska Natives, Asians, Native Hawaiians and other Pacific Islanders are included in the total.

Source: U.S. Department of Justice, Bureau of Justice Statistics, "Prison and Jail Inmates at Midyear 2002," April 2003

States], but I think the determined middle-class or upper-middle-class minority family that seeks to live in a white neighborhood can do so."

Zelnick is "not overly concerned" about segregated patterns of residential living, but only "so long as you have real opportunity for African-Americans to get access to educational opportunity and institutions of higher learning, and as long as you have access to employment opportunities after college or high school."

But others are quick to point out that educational opportunities are not, in fact, allocated evenly to all races. They cite a recent decision in which the New York Court of Appeals found that the city's longstanding system of providing less money to inner-city schools than to wealthier suburban schools violates the state Constitution because it deprives students of an equal education. The court gave the state 13 months to change the funding formulas that provide less money for urban students — a common practice in American school districts. [14]

Meanwhile, Harvard history Pro-

fessor Stephan Thernstrom says studies show residential segregation has been declining since the 1960s. "[Segregation] is now at the lowest level since 1920," he says. Real estate agents and home sellers are more interested in closing the deal than engaging in discrimination. If residential segregation exists, he says, it's largely a matter of choice.

But some racial separation may not be by mutual choice. A recent Urban Institute analysis of home-loan applications in Chicago and Los Angeles found that information was withheld from blacks and Hispanics in "statistically significant patterns of unequal treatment" that "systematically favor whites." [15] In another study, African-American women had access to about half as many rental properties as white males because of disparities in the information the women received. [16]

Meanwhile, Southern public schools are "re-segregating." According to researchers at the Harvard Civil Rights Project, the proportion of black students in majority-white Southern schools has

Predatory Lending on the Rise

The number of subprime home-mortgage loans — or loans with high interest rates, exorbitant fees and harmful terms — has skyrocketed in recent years. The increase in these so-called predatory loans has been most dramatic in minority communities, particularily among Latinos. At the same time, the number of prime, or lower-rate, loans decreased for blacks but increased for whites and Latinos. Subprime loans are intended for people who are unable to obtain a conventional prime loan at the standard bank rate. The loans have higher interest rates to compensate for the potentially greater risk that these borrowers represent, but Fannie Mae (Federal National Mortgage Association) estimates that as many as half of all subprime borrowers could have qualified for a lower-cost mortgage. Elderly homeowners, communities of color, and low-income neighborhoods are the most severely affected by such practices. Subprime loans represented 9 percent of all conventional home-purchase loans in the U.S. in 2001.

Increases in Subprime and Prime Lending, 1995-2001

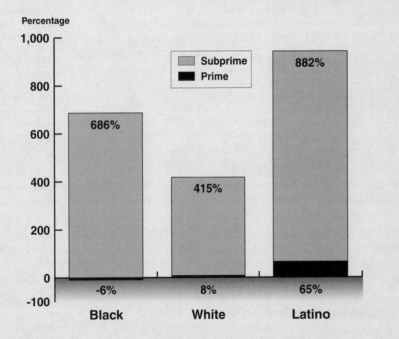

Source: ACORN (Association of Community Organizations for Reform Now), "Separate and Unequal: Predatory Lending in America," November 2002

reached its lowest level since 1968. [17] (*See graph, p. 285.*)

Moreover, American University's Steinhorn says, many forms of de facto discrimination still are practiced today, such as requiring black job applicants — but not whites — to take writing tests; department store security guards following blacks more closely than whites; and drug stores failing to carry African-American hair-care products to discourage their patronage.

"It doesn't have to be legalized, high-profile segregation to be meaningful," Steinhorn says. "This is the stuff of life. If it's death by a thousand cuts, that's as powerful as being told you have to sit at the back of the bus."

Are blacks still economically disadvantaged due to racism?

Nearly everyone agrees that blacks, generally, are far better off financially than they were 40 years ago. But blacks still hold a fraction of whites' accumulated assets. For instance, the proportion of blacks that own their own homes has doubled since 1940, but it is still about a third below the rate for whites. [18]

Are these financial disparities between the races due to racism or to socioeconomic factors and differences in education levels? Steinhorn and others say the persistent separation of the races has negative financial consequences for blacks. Segregation, for instance, can prevent blacks from having access to the social networks that can lead to good jobs. Some economists also argue that urban blacks suffer from "spatial mismatch" — unequal access to suburban jobs located near white residential areas. High crime rates also hamper black wealth creation.

"Crime depresses the property values in cities and neighborhoods that blacks tend to live in," says George R. La Noue, a political scientist at the University of Maryland, Baltimore County.

Much of the racial disparity in wealth is the result of the historical legacy of segregation, according to Steinhorn and others. Black families simply have not had time to accrue wealth to match the generations of inherited property and other assets enjoyed by whites. Blacks also have a harder time investing in major assets, such as real estate.

"There is no question that minorities are less likely than whites to obtain mortgage financing and that, if successful, they receive less generous loan amounts and terms," concluded a 1999 Urban Institute study. [19]

Education is perhaps the biggest factor affecting black incomes. Blacks consistently trail behind whites on standardized tests, and people who achieve higher test scores usually can command higher salaries.

But the University of California's McWhorter says the disparity in education levels can't be attributed solely to racism. "A cultural trait is the driving factor in depressing black scholarly performance," he writes. "A wariness of books and learning for learning's sake as [being] 'white' has become ingrained in black American culture." [20]

Harvard's Thernstrom, co-author of a forthcoming book on racial disparities in education, *No Excuses: Closing the Racial Gap in Learning*, says the education gap largely explains the income gap. Too many studies unfairly compare income levels for blacks and whites who have completed the same level of education, he argues. But blacks score more poorly on standardized tests than whites at the same grade level, indicating that they are not receiving the same level of instruction.

"When you measure educational achievement — not by the time you've spent under a school roof, but by what you know — the disparity in racial income mostly disappears," he says. "People of different races with equal levels of cognitive skills have earned about the same amount of money in our society for the past 25 years. Even if employers aren't discriminating at all on the basis of race, they are paying higher-skilled workers more."

Thernstrom believes that blacks' poor test scores are not so much due to racism but to flaws in K-12 public education in general. He says concentrating efforts on improving schools would aid education in general while also aiding blacks and other minorities.

"In a society committed to equal opportunity, we still have a racially identifiable group of educational have-nots — young African-Americans and Latinos," write Thernstrom and his

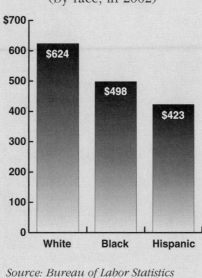

Whites Earn the Most

The average white worker made $126 a week more than the average black worker in 2002, and $201 a week more than the average Hispanic.

Median Weekly Income
(by race, in 2002)

White: $624
Black: $498
Hispanic: $423

Source: Bureau of Labor Statistics

wife and co-author, Abigail Thernstrom, a senior fellow at the Manhattan Institute and a member of the U.S. Civil Rights Commission. "They place some blame on members of these groups for failing to place an emphasis on education and for a cultural work ethic that sometimes equates achievement with "acting white or selling out."

But the Thernstroms place heavier blame on schools for failing to adapt to group cultural differences and for not demanding high standards from their students. "Plenty of white and Asian kids are also being shortchanged," they write, "but it is the black and Hispanic [statistics] that suggest appalling indifference." [21]

Many people on the other side, however, citing the recent New York appeals court decision, point out that American school-funding policies —

which unlike any other industrialized country are based on property values — are clearly lopsided against poorer school districts, which often are made up primarily of blacks, Latinos and other minorities.

However, William E. Spriggs, executive director of the National Urban League's Institute for Opportunity and Equality, says even highly educated blacks suffer higher unemployment rates than whites. "Year after year, the unemployment rate for [black] college graduates has continued to climb," Spriggs says, "whereas for whites, it's been fairly stable."

But the disparities don't end there, adds Spriggs, a former president of the black National Economics Association. Blacks with the same skills as whites earn 10 to 20 percent less, he says. "Every hour at work, to make 80 cents on somebody else's dollar is a huge disadvantage," he says. "You can't start the race 20 percent behind."

William Rodgers, an economics professor at the College of William and Mary in Williamsburg, Va., and former chief economist at the Department of Labor in the Clinton administration, agrees that economic disparities cannot be explained entirely by differences in education. "Even if they come in with skills and education like their white counterparts, minorities are still experiencing labor-market discrimination," he says, with blacks receiving fewer callbacks and job offers.

The University of Maryland's La Noue admits that racism and discrimination persist, but he says other factors — such as limited educational opportunities — also can affect members of all races. Thus he opposes trying to alleviate income disparities through racial quotas or special race-based programs, because he says they are unfair to whites with limited opportunities.

For the same reason, La Noue opposes government programs that set aside a certain percentage of contracts for minority-owned companies. "Too often in this area, we created race-based solutions that are not really congruent with the problems we're trying to solve, and based on gross generalizations that all people of one race are privileged and all people of another race are disadvantaged," he says.

Is the criminal-justice system racially biased?

Black comedian Richard Pryor used to joke about going to court seeking justice in America. "And that's exactly what I saw," he said. "Just us."

Indeed, blacks comprise 13 percent of the country's population but more than 40 percent of the U.S. prison population, according to the Washington-based Sentencing Project. A black male born in 1991 stands a 29 percent chance of spending time in prison, compared with 4 percent for white males. In 1995, one in three black men between the ages of 20 and 29 was either in prison, on probation or on parole. [22]

Many African-Americans argue that more blacks are in jail because police and prosecutors target blacks. Many blacks say they have been pulled over for the "crime" of "driving while black." "Nothing has poisoned race relations more," writes Harvard's Kennedy, "than racially discriminatory policing, pursuant to which blacks are watched, questioned and detained more than others." [23]

Lawsuits challenging the constitutionality of racial profiling have led to settlements in California, Maryland and other states, many of which have revised their policies for stopping motorists. [24] In

Demonstrators reflect both sides of the affirmative-action debate following the Supreme Court's June 23 ruling supporting the University of Michigan's use of race as a factor in admissions.

Getty Images/Alex Wong

March, New Jersey became the first state to ban profiling. [25] And in June, President Bush banned racial profiling at the federal level — except in cases involving terrorism and national security.

But the Manhattan Institute's Mac Donald, author of *Are Cops Racist?* says police don't target blacks because of race. "It's not racism that sends police departments into black neighborhoods," she says. "It's crime."

Merely comparing numbers of stops and arrests with raw census data is an exercise in false logic, she argues. "The way the anti-police activists are spinning numbers is very clever," Mac Donald says. Comparing arrest records for blacks and whites is just as spurious as

complaining that too few senior citizens are arrested, despite the fact that they don't commit as many violent crimes as younger people, she says.

Complaints about profiling, Mac Donald warns, can make police officers wary of going after black offenders, for fear of exceeding their allowable quota of African-American arrests. In Cincinnati, where police changed their tactics after blacks rioted in 2001, arrests dropped by 30 percent in 2002, but homicides reached a 15-year high, she notes. [26]

In a widely cited study, Michael Tonry, director of the University of Cambridge's Institute of Criminology, maintains that more blacks are locked up because they commit more "imprisonable crimes." [27]

Perhaps more poignantly, Jesse Jackson once said, "There is nothing more painful for me at this stage in my life than to walk down the street and hear footsteps and start to think about robbery and see it's somebody white and feel relieved." [28]

Still, some critics say when blacks do commit crimes, they can't get a fair shake from the criminal-justice system. Although even critics of the system admit that data is scarce comparing how blacks and whites are sentenced for committing the same crimes, the University of California's Wellman cites studies in Georgia and New York that show racial differences in the prison terms imposed for similar offenses.

Members of the Congressional Black Caucus — including Rep. John Conyers, D-Mich., the ranking Democrat on the Judiciary Committee —

Few Changes Seen in Racial Admissions Plans

College and university officials expect few changes in admissions practices following the Supreme Court's qualified approval of affirmative action. But opponents of affirmative action vow to continue their fight in court and elsewhere.

Most undergraduate and graduate schools with race-conscious admissions policies use an individualized application process akin to the University of Michigan Law School's system approved by the high court on June 23, education officials and experts say. They add that only a few schools award all minority applicants a fixed, quantitative bonus similar to the point system used at Michigan's undergraduate college, which the court found unconstitutional.

The court's ruling "has the effect of defining current practices as constitutional," says Barmak Nassirian, associate executive director of the American Association of Collegiate Registrars and Admissions Officers. "There are very few institutions that would be negatively affected by the undergraduate decision."

The head of the conservative public-interest law firm that represented unsuccessful white applicants to Michigan, however, says the court's action will make it more difficult for universities to use racial preferences by precluding the mechanistic formulae that he believes are common. Terence Pell, president of the Washington-based Center for Individual Rights, warns universities not to use the rulings as a "fig leaf" to preserve the status quo.

"Some schools are determined to continue to take race into account, and it's business as usual for them," Pell said after the court's decisions. The center plans to monitor responses to the decisions, Pell said, and challenge any schools claiming to review applicants individually but still using a "mechanistic" formula to favor minority candidates. [1]

Immediately after the rulings, Michigan President Mary Sue Coleman greeted reporters at the Supreme Court with a broad smile. "This is a wonderful day," she said, adding that the undergraduate college would be able to change its system to comply with the court's decision by the fall. [2]

The court's 6-3 ruling in the undergraduate case — *Gratz v. Bollinger* — faulted the College of Literature, Science and the Arts for awarding minority applicants a fixed bonus of 20 points out of a maximum score of 150, with 100 points needed to qualify for admission. By contrast, the 5-4 majority in the law-school case — *Grutter v. Bollinger* — found that the admissions process used by the law school was constitutional because officers considered race or ethnicity as only one factor in trying to achieve a "critical mass" of minority candidates needed for a diverse student body.

Nassirian says the rulings will speed a movement already under way among colleges and universities toward what admissions officers call "full-folder review" of applicants. "Most applicants want to be treated fairly," he says, "and they don't want to be eliminated on the basis of two or three data elements."

But Bradford Wilson, executive director of the National Association of Scholars, in Princeton, N.J., notes that the undergraduate college defended its fixed-bonus system on the grounds that individualized review was impossible given its large volume of applications. "I just don't see how it's possible to do what the Supreme Court called meaningful, individualized review without having a virtual army of [undergraduate] admissions officers reviewing applicants," says Wilson, whose group opposed both Michigan admissions procedures.

The court's rulings came after a period of retrenchment on affirmative action in some states, including three with big public-university systems: Texas, California and Florida. Texas had to suspend racial preferences in admissions after a March 1996 federal appeals-court decision in a suit against the University of Texas Law School. [3] California voters approved an initiative in November 1996, Proposition 209, which barred consideration of race or national origin in admissions. And in February 2000, Gov. Jeb Bush, R-Fla., adopted a so-called "One Florida" program that similarly ended the use of race in admissions at state universities.

In Texas, Larry Faulkner, president of the university's Austin campus, said the school would resume some form of racial admissions policies for the class entering in fall 2004. [4] University of California President Richard Atkinson, however, said the school would continue to comply with the state's initiative barring race-based admissions. In Florida, Bush also reaffirmed the policy against considering race in university admissions.

All three states also adopted so-called percentage plans for state universities to admit any high-school graduate with a class rank above a fixed cutoff point — the top 10 percent, for example, in Texas. In a brief opposing the Michigan admissions policies, the Bush administration endorsed the ostensibly race-neutral alternative to racial preferences. Percentage plans are designed to create diversity by ensuring representation from all schools, including those that are predominantly black or Hispanic.

But in her majority opinion in the Michigan law-school case, Justice Sandra Day O'Connor said such approaches "may preclude" individualized assessment of applicants and prevent universities from achieving diversity in other respects besides race.

— ***Kenneth Jost***

[1] Quoted in Diana J. Schemo, "Group Vows to Monitor Academia's Responses," *The New York Times*, June 24, 2003, p. A22. For other statements and materials, see the center's Web site: www.cir.org.

[2] For the text of a letter on the ruling that Coleman sent to the university community and other materials, see the university's Web site: http://www.umich.edu/~urel/admissions/.

[3] The case is *Hopwood v. University of Texas Law School*, 78 F.3d 392.(5th Cir. 1996). The ruling, which the U.S. Supreme Court declined to review, also covered the states of Louisiana and Mississippi.

[4] Reaction from the three states is compiled in Jeffrey Selingo, "Decisions May Prompt Return of Race-Conscious Admissions at Some Colleges," *The Chronicle of Higher Education*, July 4, 2003, p. S5.

often complain that sentencing guidelines are much harsher for crack cocaine, predominantly used and sold by blacks, than for powder cocaine, used primarily by whites. But critics of that argument note the Black Caucus pushed hard for tough laws against crack precisely because it is a scourge in predominantly black communities. [29]

But the biggest disparities result because of where police concentrate their enforcement efforts, says Marc Mauer, assistant director of the Sentencing Project. "Drug use and abuse cuts across race and class lines, but drug-law enforcement is primarily located in the inner cities," Mauer says. Moreover, he points out, white suburban teenagers caught with drugs might be sent to treatment programs instead of being prosecuted, but similar treatment isn't offered to blacks: "In a low-income community, those resources aren't provided to the same extent, so [drug possession] is much more likely to be defined as a criminal-justice problem."

Critics of the criminal-justice system also argue that street crimes are prosecuted more harshly than white-collar crimes, which primarily are committed by whites. But that's because tax fraud and securities abuse are less of a societal concern than armed robbery, says Harvard sociologist Christopher Jencks. "Given a choice, almost everyone would rather be robbed by a computer than at gunpoint," he writes. [30]

Racial disparities also exist in the use of the death penalty, according to a recent Maryland study. It found that blacks who murdered whites were far more likely to face the death penalty than either white killers or blacks who killed other blacks. [31] A court-appointed committee in Pennsylvania announced in March that the state should halt executions pending a study of racial bias. [32] Several other states have commissioned studies to determine whether the death penalty is applied more often or unfairly to blacks.

"Generally, discrimination based on the race of the defendant has tremendously declined," says David Baldus, a University of Iowa law professor who has studied racial bias in the death penalty. "But discrimination based on the race of victim has continued."

BACKGROUND

Road to Emancipation

By 1619, the first African slaves had been brought to Virginia, and by the 1640s slavery was well-established, mostly in the Southern colonies. Between 1680 and 1750, the colonies' blacks — who were virtually all slaves — grew from just under 5 percent of the population to more than 20 percent. [33] As slavery grew, so did the repressiveness of racial laws governing non-slaves. In the early 18th century, free blacks endured higher taxes and more severe criminal punishments than white colonials, with several Southern states denying them suffrage.

However, whites turned to blacks for support in their war against the British during the American Revolution. In part, this was a natural outgrowth of the egalitarian ideals that had become the rallying call for the Americans — even though the Continental Congress had struck anti-slavery language from Thomas Jefferson's draft of the Declaration of Independence.

"How is it that we hear the loudest yelps for liberty among the drivers of Negroes?" mocked British author Samuel Johnson. [34]

But British commanders had promised freedom to any slave who fought on their side, so the Americans matched the offer. By 1775, George Washington, who had originally opposed recruiting black soldiers, wrote:

"Success will depend on which side can arm the Negroes the faster." [35]

By war's end, most colonies and the Continental Congress were enlisting blacks, with the understanding that freedom would be their reward for fighting. Thousands served as soldiers and laborers, while thousands more took advantage of the confusion of war to flee from white masters in the South.

But the promises of freedom turned out, in many cases, to be empty ones. After the war, most of the New England states banned slavery, but the Southern states, of course, continued the practice.

Many of the economic gains made by blacks during the war were short-lived, and their political and legal status soon slipped as well. The Fugitive Slave Law of 1793 pledged the aid of federal courts in returning escaped slaves to their masters. With fear of slave revolts growing, abolitionism never took root in the South, and by the early 19th century several Northern states had disenfranchised free blacks.

A number of frontier states barred not just slaves but all blacks, purely out of racial hatred, as contemporary debates made clear. Then a new Fugitive Slave Act in 1850 expanded the role of the federal government in the search for escaped slaves.

Life for freed blacks was tenuous, indeed, a situation made abundantly clear by the Supreme Court's 1857 *Dred Scott* decision. The infamous ruling determined that runaway slaves like Scott remained the property of their masters, even after they had escaped to free states. The court also said persons of African descent could never become citizens with the right to sue, and overturned bans on slavery in the frontier territories.

In early 1861, Congress approved a constitutional amendment protecting the institution of slavery, but it was never ratified by the requisite three-quarters of the states. The measure apparently was designed to allay Southerners' fears that the 1860 election of President Lincoln

Chronology

1940s-1950s
World War II and its aftermath presage big changes for African-Americans as the migration north intensifies and the civil-rights movement takes off.

1941
World War II causes an immediate shortage of industrial labor at home, increasing the migration of Southern African-Americans to Northern urban areas.

1947
Jackie Robinson joins the Brooklyn Dodgers, becoming the first black to play Major League Baseball.

July 26, 1948
President Harry S Truman ends racial segregation in the armed forces.

1954
The Supreme Court's landmark *Brown v. Board of Education* ruling overturns the previous "separate but equal" policy in public education.

1955
Rosa Parks refuses to give up her seat on a city bus to a white man, sparking the Montgomery, Ala., bus boycott. The Rev. Dr. Martin Luther King Jr. emerges as a civil-rights leader.

1960s *The civil-rights movement prompts Congress to enact legislation aimed at ending discrimination.*

1961
President John F. Kennedy uses the term "affirmative action" for the first time, ordering federal contractors to give preferential treatment to minorities in hiring.

1963
Dr. King gives his stirring "I Have a Dream" speech at the Lincoln Memorial in Washington.

1964
The Civil Rights Act prohibits job discrimination based on race, sex or national origin.

1965
President Lyndon B. Johnson signs the Voting Rights Act. In September he orders federal contractors to actively recruit minorities.

1968
Dr. King is assassinated, touching off race riots in many U.S. cities.

1970s-1980s
New policies like affirmative action are adopted, prompting a backlash among whites.

1970
President Richard M. Nixon requires contractors to set goals for minority employment.

1978
In *University of California Regents v. Bakke*, the Supreme Court rules that universities can use race as a factor in admissions, but may not impose quotas.

1980
Affirmative-action foe Ronald Reagan is elected to the presidency. The Justice Department begins attacking racial quotas.

1990s-2000s
As affirmative action is challenged in the courts, racist-tinged incidents continue to shock the nation.

1991
Black motorist Rodney King is kicked and beaten by white Los Angeles police officers; their acquittal in 1992 touches off major rioting. Eventually they are convicted of civil-rights violations.

1993
Supreme Court rules in *Shaw v. Reno* that race cannot be used as the "predominant" factor in drawing political districts.

1996
Voters in California approve Proposition 209 outlawing the use of race or gender preferences at all state government institutions.

1998
Three white men in Jasper, Texas, drag black James Byrd Jr. to death behind their pickup truck. Two are sentenced to death; a third is sentenced to life in prison.

2002
Sen. Trent Lott says the country would have been better off if then-segregationist Gov. Strom Thurmond had been elected president in 1948; after outcry, Lott steps down as Senate majority leader.

Jan. 15, 2003
President Bush announces that his administration sides with affirmative-action opponents against University of Michigan admissions policies.

June 2003
Supreme Court upholds the University of Michigan's qualified use of race as a factor in admissions. . . . Blacks riot in Benton Harbor, Mich., to protest allegedly racist police tactics.

The N-Word and Other Racist Symbols

"If you want to rile up black folk," says jazz singer Rene Marie of Atlanta, Ga., "wave the Confederate flag, sing 'Dixie' or say 'nigger.' "

Marie notes that the words to "Dixie" are not objectionable in and of themselves. But they hold negative connotations for her fellow African-Americans because it was the South's Civil War anthem and was sometimes sung by white Southerners in reaction to the civil-rights movement. Marie wants to reclaim "Dixie" to protest her feelings of being excluded from mainstream Southern culture even though she was born in the region. "That song talks about longing for the South. Well, a majority of black people are from the South — they should be able to express those feelings, too."

Marie's emotionally vulnerable version, though, speaks to different memories of the Old South. On stage, she segues from "Dixie" into "Strange Fruit," the graphic song about lynching made famous by jazz singer Billie Holiday. But with its pounding rhythm and wrenching cries, Marie's rendition is more aggressive than Holiday's.

Marie remembers being nervous about how audiences would respond to the medley, particularly black listeners. Now, when she starts "Dixie," her fans applaud. Still, the combined effect of the two songs is harrowing, an angry reminder of the uglier legacies of the South.

Some black performers and other African-Americans have sought to reconfigure the meaning of "nigger," which Los Angeles prosecutor Christopher Darden famously called the "filthiest, dirtiest, nastiest word in the English language" during the O.J. Simpson murder trial. It has been "a familiar and influen-

tial insult" at least since the 1830s, writes Harvard University Professor Randall Kennedy in his recent book about the hateful word. [1]

Today, many blacks use the term to mean "friend" or simply to signify a black person. [2] "When we call each other 'nigger,' it means no harm," says the rap star and actor Ice Cube. "But if a white person uses it, it's something different, it's a racist word." [3]

Black comedian Chris Rock jokes about the differences between black people and "niggers," yet follows that up with a story in which he punches a white fan for repeating the same material. For blacks, whites using the word are offering an insulting reminder that they are perceived as inferior, a caste at a level to which whites can never sink. (Sen. Robert C. Byrd, D-W. Va., who as a young man belonged to the Ku Klux Klan, had to apologize for twice referring to "white niggers" during a Fox TV appearance in 2001.)

Over the past year, local governments from Baltimore to San Jose have passed resolutions denouncing the use of the word. [4] Indeed, it remains such a potent insult that some white people claim not to be racist just because they refrain from saying it. A mobster who referred to blacks as "spades," "shines" and "coons" insisted to author Studs Terkel that he was nonetheless not a racist. "Did you ever hear me say 'nigger'? Never!" [5]

Whites and blacks also remain in conflict over the Confederate flag. For African-Americans, the "stars and bars" are a reminder not only of the South's fight to preserve slavery but also its resistance to desegregation. Some states returned to waving Confederate flags, or added aspects of it to their official state

— who had advocated banning slavery in the territories — threatened slavery in the South. Unconvinced, 11 Southern states seceded from the Union, beginning in 1861. The country was soon at war.

Rise of 'Jim Crow'

On Jan. 1, 1863, Lincoln issued his Emancipation Proclamation, freeing all slaves in the territories and Border States. Although Lincoln had not wanted to make slavery the central issue of the conflict between the North and the South, the Confederacy still focused on it. Even before issuing the proclamation, Lincoln — like

Washington — recognized that putting blacks to use as soldiers had become "a military necessity."

After the North's victory, Congress passed the 13th, 14th and 15th amendments to the Constitution, which vacated the *Dred Scott* decision and gave blacks citizenship and the vote. Southern states wishing to rejoin the Union had to ratify the amendments.

After an anti-abolitionist assassinated Lincoln in 1865, his successors were reluctant to advocate further civil rights for blacks, and the Supreme Court did little to encourage enforcement of the civil-rights laws that existed.

In fact, emboldened by court interpretations that elevated states' rights

above those of blacks, Southern states passed a series of so-called Jim Crow laws stripping blacks of stature and legal protections. Named after a minstrel character, the legislation was carefully written in race-neutral language to pass constitutional muster. Most infamously, the Supreme Court in 1896 upheld segregation laws, ruling in *Plessy v. Ferguson* that "separate but equal" accommodations did not intrinsically benefit one race over another.

Oklahoma soon required "separate but equal" telephone booths. New Orleans kept black and white prostitutes segregated. Florida and North Carolina made it illegal for whites to read textbooks that had been used by blacks. [36] Meanwhile, throughout

flags, during the 1950s and '60s to symbolize their defiance of civil-rights pressures.

Since 1999, the National Association for the Advancement of Colored People (NAACP) has organized economic boycotts of states that fly the Confederate flag. South Carolina has since taken the flag down from its Capitol, while Mississippi voters opted to keep it flying. In Georgia, Republican Gov. Sonny Perdue was elected last fall largely on his pledge to let voters decide whether to restore the Confederate cross to the state flag. [6]

Many Southern whites argue that the Confederate flag, which some Southerners call the "battle flag," is not meant to be racist, but represents their heritage and is an expression of pride.

"Actually, in the South the battle flag is so ubiquitous it doesn't have a single meaning," says William Rolen, Southern-heritage defense coordinator for the Council of Conservative Citizens in Tennessee. Not only is the emblem found on countless bumper stickers, but Confed-

Georgia voters will decide in March whether to restore the traditional Confederate battle symbol (shown above in the 1956 flag) to the state flag.

Liaison/Erik S. Lesser

erate flag T-shirts marketed to children are million-sellers. But dozens of Southern school districts have banned them. [7]

"It's just totally inconceivable that any other group that stood for something so vile and was defeated would be given this place of honor," says William Spriggs, executive director of the National Urban League's Institute for Opportunity and Equality, referring to Southern capitals that fly the flag. "One could not imagine that the mayor of Paris would fly a Nazi flag because the Germans ruled France for part of World War II."

[1] Randall Kennedy, *Nigger: The Strange Career of a Troublesome Word* (2002), p. 4.

[2] Clarence Page, "A Word That Wounds — If We Let It," *Chicago Tribune*, Oct. 12, 1997, p. 25.

[3] Quoted in Kennedy, *op. cit.*, p. 41.

[4] Sarah Lubman, "Black Activists in S.J. Mount Campaign to Eliminate Slur," *San Jose Mercury News*, Jan. 28, 2003, p. A1.

[5] Studs Terkel, *Race: How Blacks and Whites Think and Feel About the American Obsession* (1992), p. 5.

[6] See "Phew," *The Economist*, May 3, 2003, p. 33.

[7] "Dixie Chic," *People*, March 10, 2003, p. 100.

the first half of the 20th century, Southern schools for blacks received only a fraction of what was spent to educate whites. As Mississippi Gov. James K. Vardaman put it in 1909, "Money spent today for the maintenance of public school for Negroes is robbery of the white man, and a waste upon the Negro." [37]

In many places, blacks were systematically deprived of the right to vote, and between the post-Civil War Reconstruction period and the turn of the century their turnout dropped 90 percent or more in some Southern states. The Supreme Court, increasingly influenced by Justice (and ex-klansman) Edward White, was deaf to the loudest complaints about voting-rights abuses.

Some Southern leaders even bragged about the region's concerted efforts to marginalize — and even eliminate — blacks. "We have done our level best," said Ben Tillman of the South Carolina Constitutional Convention. "We have scratched our heads to find out how we could eliminate the last one of them. We stuffed ballot boxes. We shot them. We are not ashamed." [38]

By the turn of the century, lynchings were more common in some years than legal executions. In a recent history of lynching, author Philip Dray notes that more than 3,400 blacks were lynched between 1882 and 1944. "Is it possible for white America to really understand blacks' distrust of the legal system, their fears of racial profiling and the police, without understanding how cheap a

black life was for so long a time in our nation's history?" Dray asks. [39]

Blacks began to move north searching for better jobs and more political opportunity. Racial tensions during the economic upheaval that followed World War I led to riots in 1919 in about two-dozen Northern cities. But whites were unable to drive the blacks out, despite dozens of fire-bombings of black homes.

Instead, beginning in the 1920s, whites left the cities in droves, a phenomenon called "white flight." Jobs often followed the whites to the suburbs. By 1940, 80 percent of the country's urban blacks lived in segregated neighborhoods, compared to less than a third in 1860. [40] Meanwhile, none of the five Deep South states — home to 40 percent of the nation's black population — had even a single black policeman. [41]

Civil-Rights Era

As in the Revolutionary and Civil wars, the pressures of World War II helped move desegregation forward. In 1941, as thousands of African-Americans were planning to march on Washington to protest hiring discrimination in the defense industries, President Franklin D. Roosevelt signed an executive order barring such discrimination and creating a Fair Employment Practices Committee (FEPC) to investigate such complaints. (Although the planned march was canceled, the idea was to re-emerge in 1963, providing the occasion for civil-rights leader Martin Luther King Jr.'s celebrated "I Have a Dream" speech.)

Meanwhile, Southern blacks continued migrating by the millions to Northern cities in search of factory jobs; more than 3 million African-Americans moved north between 1940 and 1960. [42]

In 1948, President Harry S Truman — bowing to pressure from blacks, whom he needed for political support, and his personal revulsion at how some black veterans were physically attacked when they returned home from the war — signed an executive order desegregating the armed services. His action, coupled with a strong civil-rights plank in the Democratic Party's presidential platform that year, prompted many Southerners to walk out of the Democratic convention to protest the party's new commitment to civil-rights. South Carolina Gov. Strom Thurmond then ran for president as the nominee of the States' Rights Party, better known as the Dixiecrats, as an opponent of integration. Thurmond carried four Southern states.

On May 17, 1954, in the landmark *Brown v. Board of Education* decision, the U.S. Supreme Court unanimously declared that separate educational facilities are "inherently unequal" and thus violate the Constitution's 14th Amendment, which guarantees all citizens "equal protection under the law."

The Rev. Dr. Martin Luther King Jr. delivered his stirring "I Have a Dream" address during the March on Washington in August 1963. The assassination of the civil-rights leader five years later touched off race riots in many cities.

AFP Photo

The court ordered schools to be desegregated "with all deliberate speed." But the South was recalcitrant. Several years after the decision, less than 2 percent of Southern black students attended integrated schools. [43]

But if Southern whites were defiant, so, increasingly, were Southern blacks. In 1955 in Montgomery, Ala., Rosa Parks refused to give up her bus seat to a white man. Her arrest sparked a bus boycott led by King, which eventually prompted a Supreme Court decision banning segregation on buses.

Other blacks pressed their demands for equal rights through lunch-counter sit-ins, marches and "freedom rides." They were met with violence, as were orders to desegregate schools. In 1957 President Dwight D. Eisenhower federalized the Arkansas National Guard to force the entry of nine black students into Little Rock's Central High School. Five years later, President John F. Kennedy made the same decision in response to white violence when James Meredith became the first black to enroll in the University of Mississippi.

On June 11, 1963, after a confrontation over Gov. George Wallace's refusal to allow black students to register at the University of Alabama, Kennedy announced in a televised address that he would push Congress to pass a civil-rights bill that had been languishing for years. As was often the case during the 1960s, Kennedy couched the importance of the bill in terms of improving America's image abroad — an important strategic consideration during the Cold War.

Five months later Kennedy was assassinated, and President Lyndon B. Johnson vowed that passing the civil-rights bill would be a fitting memorial. Johnson eventually outlasted the filibuster — the obstructionist tactic typically employed by Southern senators — against such bills. [44] The Senate voted to close debate and passed the most important piece of civil-rights legislation in the nation's history — the Civil Rights Act of 1964 — outlawing discrimination in employment and public accommodations. [45]

However, King and others continued a series of non-violent protests in the South, including a 1965 march from Selma to Montgomery, Ala., to protest state and local discrimination against blacks seeking the right to vote. They were met by state troopers wielding cattle prods, nightsticks and rubber hoses wrapped in barbed wire.

In response, Johnson proposed a law to "strike down restrictions to voting in all elections — federal, state and local — which have been used to deny Negroes the right to vote." The Voting Rights Act, cleared by Congress in 1965, outlawed literacy tests and similar qualification devices used to keep blacks off the rolls. Johnson signed the bill in full knowledge that it might weaken his party in the South.

That same year, Johnson ordered federal contractors to take "affirmative action to ensure that [black] applicants are employed." He had declared earlier, "You do not take a person who, for years, has been hobbled by chains and liberate him, bring him up to the starting line in a race and then say, 'you are free to compete with all the others.' " [46]

After King was assassinated in 1968, blacks rioted in 125 cities, mostly in the North. Within days, Congress passed an open-housing law — the Fair Housing Act — which had previously languished, but included no enforcement provisions. [47]

A Dream Deferred?

The Johnson administration proved to be the high-water mark for civil-rights legislation, although new versions of the Civil and Voting Rights acts have since been passed.

By the 1970s, de jure (legal) segregation was finished, voting rights for blacks were secure for the first time in U.S. history and economic improvements for many blacks had become irreversible. By 1970, 22 percent of black men and 36 percent of black women were holding white-collar jobs — four to six times the percentages, respectively, in 1940.

But some of the laws had little or no enforcement power. The rigor with which anti-discrimination laws were enforced would vary from one administration to the next. Meanwhile, the focus of anti-discrimination efforts broadened to include women, Hispanics, Native Americans and the young. (The voting age was lowered from 21 to 18 in 1970 as part of a Voting Rights Act extension.)

One of the major controversies between the races during the 1970s concerned the attempt to force integration by busing children out of their home neighborhoods in order to balance schools' racial demographics. Some of the stiffest resistance occurred in the North, notably in Boston, where a photograph of a white crowd holding a black man and attempting to impale him with an American flag won a Pulitzer Prize. The focus of numerous court challenges, busing has since been discontinued.

Since the 1970s, Johnson's prediction about Southern whites bolting the Democratic Party has largely come true. President Richard M. Nixon, a Republican, initially opposed the 1970 Voting Rights extension, responding to pressure from Southerners objecting to aspects of the law that applied only to their region. In the face of a growing political backlash against race-based preferential treatment in education or employment, the once solidly Democratic South has turned to a modern Republican Party that favors color-blind policies of equal opportunity for all. Beginning in 1968, working-class whites began to abandon the Democrats in presidential politics, and the party would go on to lose four out of the next five presidential contests.

Republicans aggressively encouraged the exodus of disaffected white voters from the Democratic Party. In 1980, GOP presidential nominee Ronald Reagan was accusing "strapping young bucks" and Cadillac-driving "welfare queens" of abusing the welfare system. "If you happen to belong to an ethnic group not recognized by the federal government as entitled to special treatment, you are the victim of reverse discrimination," he said. [48]

Reagan slashed funding for federal equal-protection agencies, but his administration was unable to limit affirmative-action programs. Meanwhile, in 1996, a federal court ruled that the University of Texas law school could not use affirmative action to create a diverse student body. That same year, California voters barred the state from using race as a factor in employment, contracts or university admissions. Black freshman enrollment dropped throughout the University of California system, but has since recovered except at the flagship Berkeley campus. [49]

Even many African-Americans worry that affirmative-action programs have primarily helped the most affluent blacks instead of the neediest. And the policy has not lowered poverty rates among African-Americans: Since 1970, the overall poverty rate for blacks has not budged, dragged down by ever-burgeoning numbers of households headed by single women. [50]

Persistent Poverty

Both liberal and conservative writers blame persistent poverty on high rates of unwed pregnancy, particularly among teenagers. But while liberals generally blamed the pregnancies on poverty, conservatives blamed what they felt were wrong-headed welfare policies that rewarded out-of-wedlock births, perpetuating cycles of poverty from generation to generation. In 1996, Congress changed the welfare law to limit the lifespan of benefits and require recipients, including mothers, to work. Republicans claim that the new law has done more to lift black families out of poverty than any of the Johnson-era Great Society programs. [51]

Fostering Integration on Campus and Beyond

I rini Bekhit was born in Egypt, but she feels right at home at the New Jersey Institute of Technology (NJIT) in Newark. When her fellow students socialize, some separate along racial or ethnic lines, but Bekhit says most students are working so hard they don't have time for the racial rivalries that mark many other campuses. Even many of the fraternities are racially mixed. "Everyone here is so different, it becomes a non-issue," Bekhit says. "You get used to it just from walking around."

U.S. News & World Report magazine ranked NJIT the eighth-most-diverse doctorate-granting campus in the nation. [1] The school is 20 percent Asian, 9 percent black, 9 percent Hispanic and 18 percent foreign-born. Dean of Students Jack Gentul says the school has fewer racial problems than New York University — which has the country's largest proportion of international students — where he ran diversity programs for 15 years.

"The degree of integration here is much greater, and I don't know why," he admits. "I would certainly get another Ph.D. if I could explain it well. I wish I could bottle it."

Most successfully integrated institutions work hard to create and maintain an inclusive atmosphere. The armed services, desegregated by President Harry S Truman in 1948, are often touted as an exceptionally strong example of integration — and one of the rare places in American life where whites routinely take orders from blacks.

"There are aspects of military culture that were conducive to change despite massive resistance," says Sherie Merson, co-author of a study of military integration. Those aspects include the military's culture of meritocracy; its sense of shared purpose, to which individuals subordinate their individual identities; and its command-and-control structure, which can impose programs over the objections of those individuals.

Moreover, the Department of Defense diligently runs racial-awareness programs to keep biases from coloring decisions. "What really makes the difference is the training we give. It helps officers realize they have to treat each person fairly and with respect, and they don't allow any embedded biases to cause them to treat one person better than another," says Capt. Robert Watts, commander of the Defense Equal Opportunity Management Institute.

Weldon Latham, who runs the corporate-diversity practice at

The U.S. armed services, desegregated by President Harry S Truman in 1948, are generally considered a strong example of successful integration.

Holland & Knight, one of the nation's biggest and most diverse law firms, says that although blacks are still underrepresented in corporate America, many big companies have taken major strides toward integrating their work forces. "The enlightened CEOs get it — and get it for the right reason, the same reason they get everything else — the bottom line," Latham says.

America's shifting demographics and the ever-increasing pursuit of markets overseas have made it advantageous for companies to have staffs that match, to some extent, the profile of their customers, he points out.

Yet even organizations that strive to recruit blacks find that racial disparities can slip back into their midst. Blacks have never been as well represented in the military officer corps as among enlisted personnel, and even their share of the enlisted ranks has been slipping in recent years as the job market has improved.

Affluent Shaker Heights, Ohio, is often touted for having bucked the trend toward residential segregation that is pronounced in the Cleveland area. The city has long devoted about a half-million dollars annually to providing low-interest loans to people willing to buy houses in neighborhoods where their race is underrepresented. "Shaker Heights has been as aggressive as any place in trying to address the issue," says Ronald Ferguson, who teaches at Harvard University's Kennedy School of Government and is senior research associate at Harvard's Weiner Center for Social Policy. "It's trying to maintain racial and, to a lesser degree, socioeconomic diversity."

Yet city officials say their vaunted loan program has found fewer takers of late, largely because interest rates are so low generally. As a result, locals worry about the re-segregation of many blocks. They are especially concerned that white parents have begun pulling their children from the public schools.

NJIT's Gentul finds it heartening to know that in little pockets effort at racial integration and understanding can work. But Harry Holzer, a labor economist at Georgetown University, finds himself discouraged by the fact that such situations are difficult to replicate, or sustain. "You can end your career with a broken heart," he says, "because there are great model programs here or there, and you try to re-create them or bring them up to scale, and they fail."

---

[1] "Step 2: Choose the Right School," *U.S. News & World Report*, Sept. 13, 2002, p. 45.

Despite persistent poverty, a black middle class has arisen, primarily the result of public and nonprofit-sector employment, with middle-class blacks disproportionately entering jobs in government, the postal service, teaching and social work. In 2000, African-Americans made up 35 percent of the nation's postal clerks and 25 percent of the social workers, but only 5 percent of the lawyers and engineers and 4 percent of the dentists. [52] Yet, even critics of affirmative action agree that it helped accelerate, albeit slowly, the entry of African-Americans into the professional class.

In 1990, concerned that a series of Supreme Court rulings had weakened employment-discrimination law, Congress passed a tough, new Civil Rights Act to counteract the decisions. After lengthy negotiations and a major fight over the appointment of African-American Clarence Thomas to the Supreme Court, an initially reluctant President George Bush signed the new law in 1991. [53] The law expanded the anti-discrimination law to cover women and the disabled, as well as racial groups, and boosted the power of the Equal Employment Opportunity Commission (EEOC).

The Supreme Court was heavily involved in racial politics during the 1990s as well. The Justice Department had interpreted the 1982 Voting Rights Act to mean that, whenever possible, legislative districts with a high likelihood of electing blacks or other minorities should be drawn. After the redistricting cycle of the early 1990s, this led to large increases in the numbers of African-Americans elected to Congress and state legislatures.

However, the Supreme Court took exception to the Justice Department's earlier interpretation. In cases involving majority-minority congressional districts, the court ruled in the 1990s that such districts violated the 14th Amendment rights of white voters and said race could not be used as a "predominant" factor in drawing legislative districts. [54] In another voting-rights controversy, the

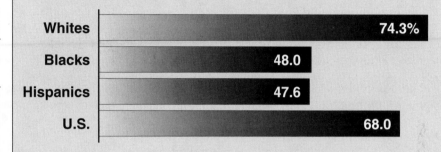

Minority Homeownership Lags

Despite increases in minority homeownership during the 1990s, large gaps remain between whites, blacks and Hispanics. Nearly three-quarters of whites owned homes in 2002, compared with less than half the blacks and Hispanics.

U.S. Homeownership Rates
(percentage of each race that owns a home)

Whites	74.3%
Blacks	48.0
Hispanics	47.6
U.S.	68.0

Sources: The White House (www.whitehouse.gov); U.S. Census Bureau

U.S. Civil Rights Commission investigated hundreds of complaints stemming from the 2000 presidential election alleging racial discrimination in Florida and elsewhere.

Meanwhile, the age-old debate continues about the harmful effects the legacy of slavery might be having on today's African-Americans. Since 1989, Rep. Conyers repeatedly has introduced legislation calling for reparations — payments to the descendants of slaves — sparking controversy in the states and on college campuses. [55]

With racial discrimination outlawed by the federal government, the political goals of blacks seeking to improve their standing in society became less clear. An age-old split widened between African-Americans who favored confrontation or reparations and those who favored individual improvement. As a result, many observers argue that black conservatives have "sold out"; others say civil-rights activists continue to be pessimistic about race relations to serve their own cause.

In essence, the "double-consciousness" for black Americans that the celebrated civil-rights leader and author W.E.B. Du Bois wrote about a century ago — "to be both a Negro and an American, without being cursed and spit upon by his fellows, without having the doors of opportunity closed roughly in his face" — continues today. [56]

CURRENT SITUATION

Affirmative-Action Ruling

The Supreme Court's June 23 decisions involving two University of Michigan admissions policies turned on the question of whether racial preferences are discriminatory toward other groups, such as whites.

Anti-Arab Sentiment on the Rise

For Yashar Zendehdel, an Iranian student at the University of Colorado, confusion over the number of academic credits he listed on his immigration paperwork led to a harrowing 26 hours in a federal jail. He was eventually cleared of any wrongdoing, but remains furious that he was treated like a criminal. [1]

"I couldn't believe it," Zendehdel said. "It was awful. I have never been to jail before. Government officials are wasting American people's tax money, my time, their time." [2]

"Discrimination against Arab-Americans and those perceived to be Arab-American has been a much bigger problem" since the Sept. 11, 2001, terrorist attacks by 19 Arab Muslims, says Laila Al-Qatami, of the American-Arab Anti-Discrimination Committee. "We've seen a lot more discrimination and hate-crime cases and a greater variety of cases."

In 2001, the FBI recorded 481 attacks against Middle Easterners, Muslims and Sikhs, compared with 28 attacks reported the previous year. [3] Job-discrimination complaints from Muslims roughly doubled after Sept. 11, from 542 in 2001 to 1,157 in 2002, according to the U.S. Equal Employment Opportunity Commission. [4]

And despite President Bush's declaration that Islam is a "religion of peace," some prominent politicians and religious leaders have made inflammatory remarks about Islam and Muslims. The Rev. Franklin Graham, son of the Rev. Billy Graham, called Islam "a very evil and wicked religion." Jerry Vines, former president of the Southern Baptist Convention, denounced the Islamic prophet Muhammad as a "demon-possessed pedophile." [5]

And Rep. John Cooksey, R-La., recommended that airline personnel selectively question Arab passengers. "If I see someone who comes in that's got a diaper on his head and a fan belt wrapped around the diaper on his head, that guy needs to be pulled over," Cooksey told a Louisiana radio interviewer. [6]

Moreover, some of the government's post-9/11 anti-terrorism programs have exacerbated Arabs' feelings of persecution and discrimination. The FBI began monitoring American mosques and encouraging thousands of Arab-Americans to undergo voluntary interviews. Many were arrested when they showed up. Recently, the FBI interviewed 5,000 Iraqis in the U.S. in an attempt to pre-empt terrorism related to the war in Iraq. [7]

The new National Security Entry-Exit Registration System (NSEERS) — created by Attorney General John Ashcroft under a congressional mandate — required tens of thousands of mostly Arab and Muslim men living in the United States to be fingerprinted by the government during so-called special-registration sweeps. [8]

The program also has begun registering foreigners at U.S. borders who meet government criteria as potential threats or persons of interest. So far, the programs have documented visitors from 155 countries, says Jorge Martinez, a Justice Department spokesman.

In some instances, large Arab turnouts at registration locations have overloaded officials and forced them to detain hundreds of people until they could be fully documented, complains James Zogby, president of the Washington-based Arab American Institute.

"If you take all these pieces and you put them together, it

By a 5-4 vote in *Grutter v. Bollinger*, the court granted continuing legal favor to the law school's practice of affirmative action. The case centered on a challenge to the law school's policy of using race as a "plus factor" in accepting students. The court found that using race as one factor among many in determining individual admissions was acceptable.

But in *Gratz v. Bollinger*, by a 6-3 vote, the justices found unconstitutional the undergraduate school's practice of granting 20 points, on a 150-point scale, to blacks and Latinos just because of their race. Quantifying race as a universal value, the court said, was unacceptable.

"In order to cultivate a set of leaders with legitimacy in the eyes of the citizenry," wrote Justice Sandra Day

O'Connor in the majority opinion in *Grutter*, "it is necessary that the path to leadership be visibly open to talented and qualified individuals of every race and ethnicity." The law school engages in a "highly individualized, holistic review of each applicant's file," she wrote, in which race counts as a factor but is not used in a "mechanical way." For that reason, O'Connor explained, the policy was in keeping with a 1978 court ruling on affirmative action that permits using race as a "plus factor."

The court's ruling that decisions can be made based on race as long as they are not done in a purely quantitative manner struck some observers as hazy. But the biggest complaints were lodged by those who thought the court had given credence to the

notion that members of some races should be granted advantages that are not enjoyed by all.

"Racial classifications in the United States have a long and ugly history," wrote U.S. Civil Rights Commissioner Thernstrom. "Racial subordination was all about double standards, with different entitlements depending on your racial identity. Nevertheless, the highest court in the land has now embraced them. It is a bleak day in American constitutional law." [57]

Affirmative-action supporters, however, echoed O'Connor's assertion that creating a diverse leadership class through more racially balanced admissions to top universities was a societal good worth preserving. For them, the court's decision was a cheering answer to a long series of attacks on

produces a lot of fear in the Arab-American community," adds Al-Qatami.

Others say the registration programs are tantamount to racial profiling, a practice recently banned by the Bush administration. "The NSEERS program and special registration was a disaster," Zogby says, "and it clearly targeted Muslims and Arabs."

But the Justice Department insists registration programs only targeted people from countries that sponsor terrorism or harbor Al-Qaeda members. "The registration programs have absolutely nothing to do with race or religion," Martinez says. "People from certain countries were registered because they presented a higher national-security threat, and it's just coincidence that those countries happen to be a majority Arab and Muslim."

Others doubt the efficacy of registration programs. "So far, registration programs haven't netted much," Al-Qatami says. "If we just focus on certain ethnic or racial characteristics, we're going to miss other people who also commit crimes and terrorism," such as Richard Reid — the British Al-Qaeda sympathizer convicted of trying to destroy an airliner with a shoe bomb.

Government officials counter that national security trumps concerns over racial profiling. "When it relates to a national-security investigation, efforts to identify terrorists may include factors like race and ethnicity," Martinez says.

On a more positive note, law enforcement has won praise for prosecuting backlash crimes against Arab-Americans. Martinez notes the Justice Department has investigated more than 500 alleged backlash crimes, and 13 have been prosecuted successfully.

"Clearly, after Sept. 11 there was a directive that the government would take backlash crimes against Arab-Americans and Muslims seriously in an effort to stem hate crimes," Zogby says.

To strengthen ties with the Arab community, the FBI recently established an Arab-American Advisory Committee in Washington similar to committees in several other cities. [9] "Both law enforcement and the Arab-American community believe that a community-policing situation was the ideal way to break down the barriers of mistrust," says Zogby, a member of the D.C. advisory committee. "We've been able do some good stuff together."

Others are more cautious. "Some positive things have come out of the experience," Al-Qatami says, "but we still have a long way to go."

— *Benton Ives-Halperin*

[1] Eric Hoover, "Closing the Gates: A Student Under Suspicion," *The Chronicle of Higher Education*, April 11, 2003, p. 12.

[2] Maria Bondes, "Foreign Students to Leave U. Colorado?" *Colorado Daily*, Jan. 7, 2003.

[3] Darryl Fears, "Hate Crimes Against Arabs Surge, FBI Finds," *The Washington Post*, Nov. 26, 2002, p. A2.

[4] Equal Employment Opportunity Commission fact sheet, June 11, 2003.

[5] Laurie Goodstein, "Seeing Islam as 'Evil' Faith, Evangelicals Seek Converts," *The New York Times*, May 27, 2003, p. A1.

[6] "National Briefing South: Louisiana: Apology From Congressman," *The New York Times*, Sept. 21, 2001, p. A16.

[7] "Under Suspicion," *The Economist*, March 29, 2003.

[8] Patrick J. McDonell, "Nearly 24,000 Foreign Men Register in U.S," *Los Angeles Times*, Jan. 19, 2003, p. A22.

[9] Alan Lengel and Caryle Murphy, "FBI, Arab Community Join Forces With Panel," *The Washington Post*, March 29, 2003, p. B1.

affirmative action, including state-ballot initiatives banning the practice in California and elsewhere.

"A diverse and racially integrated campus benefits all students and ultimately, all of America," says Marc Morial, president of the National Urban League. "The court clearly upheld the argument that the government has a compelling interest in promoting diversity in education and the workplace."

Thus, the notion of helping members of minority groups, such as blacks and Latinos, through some formal process rather than relying on "colorblind" admissions and hiring policies, is, legally, here to stay. However, O'Connor also expressed the hope that race-based admissions policies would no longer be necessary in 25 years.

Advocates of such policies point to public universities in California, Florida and Texas that have devised new formulas for continued minority enrollment after dumping affirmative action. Admission is either guaranteed to the top students from each high school, including those where students are predominantly minorities, or they seek out low-income students, who are disproportionately black or Latino. The university systems have maintained or even increased their minority enrollments, except at their flagship campuses. [58]

The cases in many ways demonstrate the shifting political dynamics when race is at issue. When the court considered affirmative-action policies in *University of California Regents v. Bakke* in 1978, hardly any corpora-

tions engaged in the issue. In the Michigan case this time, however, a group of five-dozen *Fortune* 500 companies filed an *amicus* brief with the court, arguing that diverse campuses better prepare future workers for a global economy, especially in a country whose demographic trends suggest that whites no longer will account for a majority of the population by 2050.

Three days after the Michigan ruling, the Supreme Court used a Georgia case, *Georgia v. Ashcroft*, to signal a new direction in the ways blacks and other minorities can be represented politically. For the past 20 years, Justice Department officials have interpreted the Voting Rights Act to mean that whenever a legislative district could be created with a majority of minority voters,

At Issue

Should colleges be allowed to use race as a factor in admissions?

DAVID W. DEBRUIN
ATTORNEY, JENNER & BLOCK

EXCERPTED FROM A BRIEF FILED IN THE U.S. SUPREME COURT,
GRUTTER V. BOLLINGER, **FEB. 18, 2003.**

*d*iversity in higher education is a compelling government interest not only because of its positive effects on the educational environment itself, but also because of the crucial role diversity in higher education plays in preparing students to be the leaders this country needs in business, law and all other pursuits that affect the public interest. . . .

[B]y enriching students' education with a variety of perspectives, experiences and ideas, a university with a diverse student body equips all of its students with the skills and understanding necessary to succeed in any profession. Those skills include the ability to understand, learn from, and work and build consensus with individuals from different backgrounds and cultures. . . .

There are several reasons for the importance of maintaining diversity in higher education. First, a diverse group of individuals educated in a cross-cultural environment has the ability to facilitate unique and creative approaches to problem-solving arising from the integration of different perspectives.

Second, such individuals are better able to develop products and services that appeal to a variety of consumers and to market offerings in ways that appeal to those consumers. Third, a racially diverse group of managers with cross-cultural experience is better able to work with business partners, employees and clientele in the United States and around the world. Fourth, individuals who have been educated in a diverse setting are likely to contribute to a positive work environment, by decreasing incidents of discrimination and stereotyping.

Overall, an educational environment that ensures participation by diverse people, viewpoints and ideas will help produce the most talented workforce. The thrust of the government's position is that it is permissible to take affirmative steps to ensure educational diversity — a goal that itself includes consideration of race. The United States defends particular admissions programs it prefers in Texas, Florida and California explicitly on the ground that those programs allegedly continue to produce, at least in raw numbers, the same racial and ethnic diversity in enrollment.

Institutions of higher learning must be allowed to prepare students to thrive in an increasingly diverse environment. The best way to do this is to ensure that students learn in an environment of diversity, including racial and cultural diversity. Accordingly, institutions of higher learning should be able to use "competitive consideration of race and ethnic origin" in pursuit of a diverse student body.

GEORGE W. BUSH
PRESIDENT OF THE UNITED STATES

EXCERPTED FROM REMARKS MADE ON JAN. 15, 2003

*o*ur Constitution makes it clear that people of all races must be treated equally under the law. Yet we know that our society has not fully achieved that ideal. Racial prejudice is a reality in America. It hurts many of our citizens. As a nation, as a government, as individuals, we must be vigilant in responding to prejudice wherever we find it. Yet, as we work to address the wrong of racial prejudice, we must not use means that create another wrong, and thus perpetuate our divisions.

America is a diverse country, racially, economically and ethnically. And our institutions of higher education should reflect our diversity. A college education should teach respect and understanding and goodwill. And these values are strengthened when students live and learn with people from many backgrounds. Yet quota systems that use race to include or exclude people from higher education and the opportunities it offers are divisive, unfair and impossible to square with the Constitution. . . .

The University of Michigan has established an admissions process based on race. At the undergraduate level, African-American students and some Hispanic students and Native American students receive 20 points out of a maximum of 150, not because of any academic achievement or life experience, but solely because they are African-American, Hispanic or Native American. To put this in perspective, a perfect SAT score is worth only 12 points in the Michigan system. Students who accumulate 100 points are generally admitted, so those 20 points awarded solely based on race are often the decisive factor.

At the law school, some minority students are admitted to meet percentage targets while other applicants with higher grades and better scores are passed over. This means that students are being selected or rejected based primarily on the color of their skin. The motivation for such an admissions policy may be very good, but its result is discrimination, and that discrimination is wrong.

Some states are using innovative ways to diversify their student bodies. Recent history has proven that diversity can be achieved without using quotas. Systems in California and Florida and Texas have proven that by guaranteeing admissions to the top students from high schools throughout the state, including low-income neighborhoods, colleges can attain broad racial diversity. In these states, race-neutral admissions policies have resulted in levels of minority attendance for incoming students that are close to, and in some instances slightly surpass, those under the old race-based approach.

At Issue

Is the Confederate flag a racist symbol?

SANFORD CLOUD, JR.
PRESIDENT AND CEO, NATIONAL CONFERENCE FOR COMMUNITY AND JUSTICE

EXCERPTED FROM THE NCCJ WEB SITE, DATED 2002

*h*istorically, the Confederate flag was a symbol during the Civil War of the Confederate States of America, which defended the rights of individual states that maintained their economy through slave labor. Although the Civil War ended 138 years ago, the battle over the legacy of slavery, segregation and civil rights continues.

Through the years, the Confederate flag has taken on additional negative connotations because it was used as a symbol of resistance during the civil-rights movement and is currently a prominent symbol of active white-supremacist groups. This is not to say that all individuals who bear the Confederate flag are racist. However, the symbolic meaning of the flag is that of white domination and Southern pride.

Some people assert that the Confederate flag is a symbol of their heritage; however, for many people of color and religious minorities across the United States and other communities around the world, it represents hatred, bigotry, racism, and anti-Semitism. This symbol is a very powerful nonverbal communication tool that, according to the Anti-Defamation League (ADL), generates deep meaning, intent and significance in a compact, immediately recognizable form. Members of racist organizations often use the symbol along with more specific images associated with their groups. Independent racists can avoid association with a specific group, and perhaps prosecution of that group by law enforcement, by opting for more universal racist symbols.

The National Conference for Community and Justice (NCCJ) maintains that the Confederate flag is a visible, confrontational racist symbol that represents racial oppression, segregation and slavery. As noted by Kweisi Mfume, president and CEO of the National Association for the Advancement of Colored People, "The [Confederate] flag is representative of an era that epitomized everything that was wrong and inhumane in this country and should be stripped of any sovereignty context and placed into a historical context." NCCJ concurs with this sentiment and calls for the removal of the Confederate flag from all public properties with allowances for its usage in appropriate historical and educational contexts.

All people of goodwill need to recognize that the Confederate flag . . . is an attack on the freedoms of our nation. Similarly, racism has no boundaries, and this issue cannot be confined to the Southern states. NCCJ therefore calls on all residents of the United States to actively oppose the usage of the Confederate flag and denounce it as a visible public statement that is offensive in nature.

WILLIAM ROLEN
DIRECTOR AND SOUTHERN HERITAGE DEFENSE COORDINATOR, COUNCIL OF CONSERVATIVE CITIZENS

WRITTEN FOR THE CQ RESEARCHER, MAY 2003

*f*or thirty years, the 1956 Georgia flag flew peacefully over every public building in the state. Not many people seemed disturbed by the large Confederate portion of the flag, which was put there in 1956 to honor the Southern soldiers who had fought and died defending Georgia against the atrocities of Gen. Sherman.

Then in 1991, the NAACP national convention passed a resolution condemning the Confederate flag as racist. From that year on, the Confederate flag and other Confederate icons have been subjected to relentless vitriolic wrath. One by one, Confederate flags have been removed, banned or desecrated simply because threats from the NAACP terrify the political status quo in virtually every Southern state.

The problem with the Confederate flag does not involve illicit connections with the klan or any other "guilt by association" flummery. The NAACP took aim at the Confederate flag because the emblem is revered by most Southerners. Confederate flag decals stick on every type of vehicle from trucks to tricycles. Confederate-flag clothing, from Dixie Outfitter T-shirts to G.R.I.T.S. (Girls Raised In The South) swimsuits are ordinary sights. The images of celebrities like Elvis and Hank Williams are superimposed on Confederate flags sold at truck stops and souvenir shops. Only a very jaundiced eye sees racism lurking behind every Southern-cross belt buckle and bandana worn on race day at Talledega.

Certainly, the Confederate flag honors the Southern soldier and the memory of generals Lee, Jackson, and Beauregard. More significantly, the Confederate flag represents the continuum of Southern experience. Does the flag have a racial dimension? Yes, but the racial connotations are no more negative than the FUBU (For Us, By Us) clothing that is designed, marketed and intended only for blacks.

The Confederate flag is not an aggressive symbol. No one is trying to hoist the Confederate colors over the Capitol of Vermont, nor are Confederate flag ski jackets a fashion statement on the slopes of Aspen. The Confederate flag is largely a regional phenomenon, and one of multiple interpretations. The NAACP, however, allows for only one, narrow viewpoint.

The time has come to honor and respect the Confederate flag for all the sacrifices Southerners have made over the last 20 years to display the symbol with honor, dignity and pride. And a word of caution to the NAACP: The harder you try to pull it down, the higher it will fly.

Getty Images/Scott Olson

Getty Images/Mike Simons

Police Tactics Spark Riots

The racially tinged incidents that periodically break out across the country are often provoked by outrage in the black community over police tactics that are seen by many African-Americans as heavy-handed and racist. At least five homes were torched and up to 15 people injured during a riot in Benton Harbor, Mich., in mid-June following the death of a black motorcyclist during a police chase (top). Police arrest a demonstrator during a protest march outside Cincinnati in June 2001. (bottom). The march followed riots sparked by the fatal shooting of an unarmed black man by a white policeman.

such districts should be created. Majority-minority districts have led to more black and Latino representation in both Congress and state legislatures over the past dozen years.

But some blacks and Democrats argued that majority-minority districts actually weaken political representa-

tion for blacks: By "packing" most black voters within racially separate districts, politicians from neighboring "bleached" (all-white) districts have no natural incentive to represent black interests. The state of Georgia created a map of state Senate districts that broke up some majority-black districts, in favor of creating more districts in which blacks could compete politically.

It's now widely believed that black politicians can win office in districts where blacks make up less than a majority of the electorate. Giving blacks a real opportunity, rather than an assured win, is good enough to protect their interests in the current racial climate, according to Swain of Vanderbilt Law School and other black scholars.

The Justice Department opposed Georgia's map, but the high court upheld the plan, 6-3. Writing for the majority, Justice O'Connor wrote that "various studies have suggested that the most effective way to maximize minority voting strength may be to create" districts "where minority voters may not be able to elect a candidate of choice but [can] play a substantial, if not decisive role, in the electoral process."

Bush Administration

M any people predicted that after Lott lost his Senate leadership post for pro-segregationist remarks, the Republicans might show an increased interest in '60s-style civil-rights legislation. That has not been the case. With the momentum for race-specific programs slowing, the Congressional Black Caucus and African-American advocates have begun focusing on seeking equal treatment under laws and programs that apply to all Americans, advocating increased funding for domestic priorities like education and health. Meanwhile, Republicans continue to argue that race-neutral, market-based proposals will work better than further government intrusions into private-sector practices.

President Bush opposes race-specific government-aid programs. Afterschool programs that get federal aid are often in minority neighborhoods, because they are targeted at poor districts. In his fiscal 2004 budget, Bush proposed cutting federal grants to afterschool programs by 40 percent, to $600 million. It appears that Congress will fund the grants at last year's level of $1 billion, but that is still well below the $1.75 billion authorized by Bush's No Child Left Behind education-reform law.

In response to the Supreme Court's affirmative-action decisions and O'Connor's comments about the need for affirmative action fading after 25 years, Bush said he was glad that the court shared his vision of a color-blind America.

On June 17, Bush announced a new policy designed to severely curtail racial profiling by federal law-enforcement officers. Agents running auto-theft or drug investigations, for instance, cannot stop black or Latino motorists based on the "generalized assumption" that members of those racial or ethnic groups are more likely to commit such crimes.

If a specific description identifies a suspect as black, however, the agents can target blacks as part of their search. The new policy also exempts national-security cases in "narrow" circumstances. Immigration officers, for example, can continue to require registration by visitors from Middle Eastern countries thought to foster terrorism.

Skeptics, though, wonder whether cash-strapped states and the federal government will pick up a larger tab for funding anti-poverty programs and other measures that apply not only to blacks but also to a much-expanded pool of disadvantaged citizens of all races.

At a recent forum, Stephen Goldsmith, a special adviser to the president, said, "There is now a broad consensus that a work-based benefit system is where we want to be." But he acknowledged

that even if there is consensus about work being the best way to help low-income Americans, there isn't agreement about how much money to provide for such a system. [59]

As Congress prepares to consider its latest reauthorization of the welfare-reform law, black and Latino activists are concerned that states are not properly monitoring civil rights in the law's assistance programs. They want Congress to beef up enforcement, claiming that African-American and Hispanic women have not been given support services equal to members of other races.

Similarly, as Congress prepares to reauthorize the Workforce Investment Act of 1998, which consolidated dozens of job-training programs into block grants to the states, members of the Congressional Black Caucus are concerned that the law's data-collection requirements make it harder to determine whether African-Americans are being discriminated against.

Some black advocates claim that blacks, Asians and Hispanics are being steered toward less-useful training — into areas such as résumé writing — rather than more potentially lucrative occupational job training.

Action in the States

California, Maryland and New Jersey have recently revised their racial-profiling policies in an effort to discourage bias among their troopers. Mac Donald, at the Manhattan Institute, argues that the increasing number of states and cities requiring police to record interactions with civilians on the basis of race will have a "chilling effect . . . on legitimate police work," as police officers avoid "all but the most mandatory and cursory interactions with potential minority suspects." [60] Nevertheless, about 20 other states are either setting up commissions to study racial profiling or considering legislation to curb the practice.

Meanwhile, as part of the ongoing debate about whether the descendants of slaves should receive reparations, several states also are considering establishing commissions to determine the effects of slavery on contemporary African-Americans.

In some states, the most pressing racial issues are largely symbolic. In his successful campaign for governor of Georgia last year, Republican Sonny Perdue promised voters a referendum on restoring a Confederate emblem to the state flag that had been removed in 2001.

California voters next year will vote on the "Racial Privacy Initiative," which would prohibit state and local agencies, such as schools and the Department of Motor Vehicles, from asking people about their racial identities or including voluntary racial check-off boxes on their forms. The goal is to end policies of racial classification that serve to separate people into different categories.

Critics worry that blocking racial-data collection will make it harder to track civil-rights abuses and may also hamper medical research. The initiative's main sponsor is conservative activist Ward Connerly, who also sponsored California's 1996 initiative ending state affirmative-action programs.

OUTLOOK

Lingering Problems?

The nation's historic blend of European colonialists, displaced Native Americans, African slaves and immigrants from around the world has made for an often-volatile racial mix. Given current predictions that by 2050 no racial group will comprise a majority of the population, racial relations are expected to evolve in complex ways.

Optimists believe that the demographic changes, along with the changes in social norms that make open discrimination against blacks taboo, will eventually lead to a society that is less divided and concerned about race. "It may be no accident," says Harvard's Thernstrom, "that the first state to bar racial preferences by constitutional amendment, California, is also the state with the most complex racial mix."

But even some optimists say racism will remain potent for a long time. "Hopefully, we've set in motion enough positive activities where we do ultimately get to a color-blind society," says Weldon Latham, corporate-diversity director at the giant Holland & Knight law firm. "But it's many decades from now."

Similarly, while University of California, Berkeley psychologist Jack Glaser sees racism declining, "Sadly, I can't imagine that it will ever go away," he says. "People are pretty hard-wired to see things in categories. You can put people into very arbitrary groups, and they know it's arbitrary, but they will still show favor to members of their group."

During his recent tenure as president of the American Bar Association (ABA), Oklahoma City attorney William G. Paul made diversity his top priority because, he said, his profession is 92.5 percent white. He has been heartened by the scholarship fund the ABA established and by data showing that blacks and other minorities are better represented in law schools than they are, as yet, in the legal profession itself.

"I didn't find anyone voicing any opposition," recalls Paul, who is white. Yet he admits that habits and the status quo are so ingrained that achieving equality even in his high-profile profession is "going to require a multi-decade effort."

Indeed, the most pessimistic observers of race relations predict that there could yet be a new backlash against blacks and minorities, mirroring the historic setbacks blacks faced following the Revolutionary and Civil wars. "I don't really think the white population is going to lose its powers or prestige because its numbers are going down," says *Two Nations* author Andrew Hacker.

Even without ill will or conscious discrimination, recent history suggests that institutions long dominated by whites will continue to be dominated by whites, with few exceptions. "If you assume attitudes and expectations are institutionalized," says Mitchell, of the National Research Council, "time won't make a difference."

Notes

1 Lee Hockstader, "For Tulia 12, 'It Feels So Good,'" *The Washington Post*, June 17, 2003, p. A1.

2 Andrew Hacker, *Two Nations: Black & White, Separate, Hostile, Unequal* (3rd ed. 2003, originally published 1992), p. 111.

3 Sheryl Gay Stolberg, "Cultural Issues Pose Obstacles in Cancer Fight," *The New York Times*, March 14, 1998, p. A1.

4 Margery Austin Turner and Felicity Skidmore, ed., "Mortgage Lending Discrimination: A Review of Existing Evidence," The Urban Institute, June 1999, p. 1.

5 Stephan Thernstrom and Abigail Thernstrom, *America in Black and White: One Nation, Indivisible* (1997), p. 222. See "The Nation's Report Card," National Assessment of Educational Progress, National Center for Education Statistics. http://nces.ed.gov/nationsreportcard/.

6 Hacker, *op. cit.*, p. 222.

7 Thernstrom and Thernstrom, *op. cit.*, p. 274.

8 Eric Lichtblau, "Bush Issues Racial Profiling Ban But Exempts Security Inquiries," *The New York Times*, June 18, 2003, p. A1.

9 Quoted in Bettijane Levine, "Harry Belafonte won't retreat from slavery remarks," *Chicago Tribune*, Oct. 23, 2002, p. 1.

10 See Ellen Nakashima and Al Kamen, "Bush Official Hails Diversity," *The Washington Post*, March 31, 2001, p. A10.

11 John McWhorter, *Losing the Race: Self-Sabotage in Black America* (2000).

12 For background, see David Masci, "The Black Middle Class," *The CQ Researcher*, Jan. 23, 1998, pp. 49-72.

13 Randall Kennedy, *Nigger: The Strange Career of a Troublesome Word* (2002), p. 27.

14 See Greg Winter, "State Underfinancing Damages City Schools, New York Court Finds," *The New York Times*, June 27, 2003, p. A1. For background on school funding issues, see Kathy Koch, "Reforming School Funding," *The CQ Researcher*, Dec. 10, 1999, pp. 1041-1064.

15 Office of Policy Research and Development, "All Other Things Being Equal: A Paired Testing Study of Mortgage Lending Institutions," U.S. Department of Housing and Urban Development, April 2002, p. 10, http://www.huduser.org/Publications/PDF/aotbe.pdf.

16 Douglas S. Massey and Garvey Lundy, "Use of Black English and Racial Discrimination in Urban Housing Markets: New Methods and Findings," *Urban Affairs Review 36* (2001): 470-96.

17 Erica Frankenburg, Chungmei Lee and Gary Orfield, "A Multiracial Society With Segregated Schools: Are We Losing the Dream?" Harvard University Civil Rights Project, January 2003, p. 28, http://www.civilrightsproject.harvard.edu/research/reseg03/AreWeLosingtheDream.pdf.

18 Thernstrom and Thernstrom, *op. cit.*, p. 199.

19 Turner and Skidmore, *op. cit.*

20 McWhorter, *op. cit.*

21 Thernstrom and Thernstrom, *op. cit.*

22 Mark Mauer, "The Crisis of the Young African-American Male and the Criminal Justice System," testimony submitted to the U.S. Commission on Civil Rights, April 15-16, 1999.

23 Randall Kennedy, *Race, Crime, and the Law* (1997), p. x.

24 For background, see Kenneth Jost, "Policing the Police," *The CQ Researcher*, March 17, 2000, pp. 209-240.

25 David Kocieniewski, "New Jersey Adopts Ban on Racial Profiling," *The New York Times*, March 14, 2003, p. B5.

26 The Associated Press, "Cincinnati Police Want Community Pact Ended," *The Washington Post*, April 30, 2003, p. A8.

27 Michael Tonry, *Malign Neglect: Race, Crime, and Punishment in America* (1995), p. 79.

28 Quoted in Kennedy 1997, p. 15. See Clarence Page, "Message to Jackson: The Word Is Crime, Not Black Criminals," *Chicago Tribune*, Jan. 5, 1994, p. 15.

29 See Kennedy 1997, pp. 370 ff.

30 Quoted in Kennedy 1997, p. 14.

31 Adam Liptak, "Death Penalty Found More Likely If Victim Is White," *The New York Times*, Jan. 8, 2003, p. A12.

32 Henry Weinstein, "Panel Urges Halt to Executions in Pa.," *Los Angeles Times*, March 5, 2003, p. 15.

33 Philip A. Klinkner with Rogers M. Smith, *The Unsteady March: The Rise and Decline of Racial Equality in America* (1999), p. 12.

[34] Quoted in Philip S. Foner, *From Africa to the Emergence of the Cotton Kingdom* (1975), p. 303.

[35] Quoted in Klinkner and Smith, *op. cit.*, p. 18.

[36] Lerone Bennett, Jr., *Before the Mayflower: A History of Black America* (5th ed., 1984; originally published 1962), p. 257.

[37] Quoted in Thernstrom and Thernstrom, *op. cit.*

[38] Quoted in Bennett, *op. cit.*

[39] Philip Dray, *At the Hands of Persons Unknown: The Lynching of Black America* (2002), p. iii.

[40] Klinkner and Smith, *op. cit.*

[41] Thernstrom and Thernstrom, *op. cit.*

[42] *Ibid.*, p. 79.

[43] Gerald N. Rosenberg, *The Hollow Hope: Can Courts Bring About Social Change?* (1991), p. 50.

[44] Thurmond had led a record-breaking filibuster of 24 hours and 18 minutes against the Civil Rights Bill of 1957.

[45] *Congress and the Nation*, Vol. 1, p. 1635.

[46] *Congress and the Nation*, Vol. 2, p. 356.

[47] Niel J. Smelser, William Julius Wilson and Faith Mitchell, eds., *America Becoming: Racial Trends and Their Consequences, Vol. 1* (2001), p. 321.

[48] Quoted in Klinkner and Smith, *op. cit.*

[49] Carol Pogash, "Berkeley Makes Its Pitch to Top Minority Students," *Los Angeles Times*, April 20, 2003, Part 2, p. A6.

[50] Thernstrom and Thernstrom, *op. cit.*

[51] For background, see Sarah Glazer, "Welfare Reform," *The CQ Researcher*, Aug. 3, 2001, pp. 601-632.

[52] Hacker, *op. cit.*, p. 130.

[53] *Congress and the Nation*, Vol. VIII, p. 757.

[54] For background see Jennifer Gavin, "Redistricting," *The CQ Researcher*, Feb. 16, 2001, pp. 113-128.

[55] For background, see David Masci, "Reparations Movement," *The CQ Researcher*, June 22, 2001, pp. 529-552.

[56] W.E.B. Du Bois, *The Souls of Black Folk* (1933).

[57] Abigail Thernstrom, "Court Rulings Add Insult to Injury," *Los Angeles Times*, June 29, 2003, p. M1.

[58] Mitchell Landsberg, Peter Y. Hong and Rebecca Trounson, " 'Race-Neutral' University Admissions in Spotlight," *Los Angeles Times*, Jan. 17, 2003, p. 1.

[59] Quoted in David Callahan and Tamara Draut, "Broken Bargain: Why Bush May Be Destroying A Hard-Won Consensus on Helping the Poor," *The Boston Globe*, May 11, 2003, p. H1.

[60] Heather Mac Donald, "A 'Profiling' Pall on the Terror War," *The Washington Post*, May 5, 2003, p. A21.

FOR MORE INFORMATION

American Civil Rights Institute, P.O. Box 188350, Sacramento, CA 95818; (916) 444-2278; www.acri.org. A group dedicated to educating the public about programs that promote race and gender preferences.

Center for Equal Opportunity, 14 Pidgeon Hill Dr., Suite 500, Sterling, VA 20165; (703) 421-5443; www.ceousa.org. A think tank promoting color-blind policies.

Center for Individual Rights, 1233 20th St., N.W., Suite 300, Washington, DC 20036; (202) 833-8400; www.cir-usa.org. A public-interest law firm that has challenged affirmative-action policies.

Centre for New Black Leadership, 202 G St., N.E., Washington, DC 20002; (202) 546-9505; www.cnbl.org. An advocacy organization supporting policies that "enhance the ability of individuals and communities to develop market-oriented, community-based" solutions to economic and social problems.

The Civil Rights Project, 125 Mt. Auburn St., 3rd Floor, Cambridge, MA 02138; (617) 496-6367; www.civilrightsproject.harvard.edu. A Harvard-affiliated think tank.

Joint Center for Political and Economic Studies, 1090 Vermont Ave., N.W., Suite 1100 Washington, DC 20005-4928; (202) 789-3500; www.jointcenter.org. Founded to train black elected officials, it studies issues of importance to black Americans.

Leadership Conference on Civil Rights, 1629 K St., N.W., 10th Floor, Washington, DC 20006; (202) 466-3311; www.civilrights.org. A coalition of 180 national organizations promoting civil-rights legislation and policy.

The Manhattan Institute, 52 Vanderbilt Ave., 2nd Floor, New York, NY 10017; (212) 599-7000; www.manhattan-institute.org. A think tank that fosters "greater economic choice and individual responsibility."

National Association for the Advancement of Colored People, 4805 Mt. Hope Dr., Baltimore, MD 21215; (877) NAACP-98; www.naacp.org. Century-old organization committed to improving the civil rights of African-Americans and other minorities.

National Conference for Community and Justice, 475 Park Ave. South, 19th Floor, New York, NY 10016; (212) 545-1300; www.nccj.org. Formerly the National Conference of Christians and Jews, it fights bias and racism in America.

National Urban League, 120 Wall St., 8th Floor, New York, NY, 10005; (212) 558-5300; www.nul.org. Consortium of community-based organizations that promotes access to education, economic activity and civil rights among African-Americans.

Southern Poverty Law Center, 400 Washington Ave., Montgomery, AL 36104; (334) 956-8200; www.splcenter.org/splc.html. A group that fights discrimination through educational programs, litigation and its maintenance of the Civil Rights Memorial.

U.S. Commission on Civil Rights, 624 Ninth St., N.W., Washington, DC 20425; (202) 376-7700; www.usccr.gov. Government agency that investigates complaints about discrimination.

Bibliography

Selected Sources

Books

Correspondents of *The New York Times*, *How Race Is Lived in America*, **Times Books, 2001.**

A collection of the *Times'* Pulitzer Prize-winning series of reporting about how issues of race still affect American society.

Hacker, Andrew, *Two Nations: Black & White, Separate, Hostile, Unequal*, **3rd ed. 2003 (originally published 1992).**

A political scientist finds race to be an "obdurate" problem, portraying an America in which blacks and whites are still separate and unequal, with illustrations drawn largely from census figures.

Kennedy, Randall, *Nigger: The Strange Career of a Troublesome Word*, **Pantheon, 2002.**

A Harvard Law School professor examines the history and usage of "the paradigmatic slur" and what it expresses about racial enmities.

Kennedy, Randall, *Race, Crime, and the Law*, **Pantheon, 1997.**

The Harvard law professor analyzes issues at the intersection of race and the criminal-justice system, including anti-drug laws, the death penalty and jury selection.

Klinkner, Philip A., with Rogers M. Smith, *The Unsteady March: The Rise and Decline of Racial Equality in America*, **University of Chicago Press, 1999.**

The authors survey African-American rights from Colonial times to the late 1990s and conclude that each period of advancement for blacks has been followed by a lengthy backlash. Klinkner teaches government at Hamilton College; Smith teaches race and politics at Yale University.

McWhorter, John, *Losing the Race: Self-Sabotage in Black America*, **Free Press, 2000.**

A linguistics professor at the University of California, Berkeley argues that African-Americans cling to a "Cult of Victimology" that keeps them fixated on racism at the expense of making improvements in their own lives.

Patterson, Orlando, *The Ordeal of Integration: Progress and Resentment in America's "Racial" Crisis*, **Civitas/Counterpoint, 1997.**

A Harvard sociologist examines the state of progress among Afro-Americans and the impact various ideologies have on public policy.

Smelser, Neil J., William Julius Wilson and Faith Mitchell, eds., *America Becoming: Racial Trends and Their Consequences, Vols. I and II*, **National Academy Press, 2001.**

Essays from a National Research Council conference on race cover trends in housing, labor, income, justice and other issues.

Steinhorn, Leonard, and Barbara Diggs-Brown, *By the Color of Our Skin: The Illusion of Integration and the Reality of Race*, **Dutton, 1999.**

Two American University professors — one white, one black — conclude that America has not successfully integrated.

Thernstrom, Stephan, and Abigail Thernstrom, *America in Black and White: One Nation Indivisible*, **Simon & Schuster, 1997.**

The authors trace the history of U.S. race relations and political, social and economic trends since the civil-rights movement. They argue that race-neutral policies are a better cure for society's ills than race-conscious ones. Stephan Thernstrom teaches history at Harvard; Abigail Thernstrom is a senior fellow at the Manhattan Institute.

Reports and Studies

Frankenburg, Erika, Chungmei Lee and Gary Orfield, "A Multiracial Society With Segregated Schools: Are We Losing the Dream?" *Civil Rights Project*, **January 2003; http://www.civilrightsproject.harvard.edu/research/reseg03/AreWeLosingtheDream.pdf.**

Harvard researchers find that schools are re-segregating, with most whites attending predominantly white schools and many blacks and Hispanics attending "apartheid schools" with almost entirely minority student bodies.

Office of Policy Research and Development, *All Other Things Being Equal: A Paired Testing Study of Mortgage Lending Institutions, U.S. Department of Housing and Urban Development*, **http://www.huduser.org/Publications/PDF/aotbe.pdf, April 2002.**

The report concludes that blacks and Hispanics often receive less favorable treatment than whites when applying for mortgages.

Rawlston, Valerie A., and William E. Spriggs, "Pay Equity 2000: Are We There Yet?" National Urban League Institute for Opportunity and Equality, April 2001; http://www.nul.org/departments/inst_opp_equality/word/reports_statistics/pay_equity_report.doc.

A study of federal contractors finds that women and minorities make about 73 cents for every dollar earned by non-Hispanic white men, in large part due to differences in the types of work they do. White men are still paid more, however, for doing the same jobs.

16 Single-Sex Education

KENNETH JOST

Parents, friends and guests strain for a clear view as the graduates file in, resplendent in white academic gowns. Some of the members of this New York City high school class of 2002 are smiling broadly. Others are more solemn as the familiar strains of "Pomp and Circumstance" waft through the packed auditorium.

With the audience seated and the welcome delivered, the 34 graduates are introduced one by one in a slide show, along with the names of the colleges that all but one of the seniors will be attending in the fall.

The college acceptance record is unique for a New York City public school in one of the city's marginal neighborhoods. Even more unusual, all of the graduates are girls — self-described "pioneers" in a six-year-old experiment aimed at improving learning and boosting self-confidence by giving the girls a school of their own, away from the competition and distraction of adolescent boys.

"What a wonderful gift," exclaims Principal Kathleen Ponze, "when the girls come here and we say, 'This is all for you.' "

Welcome to The Young Women's Leadership School of East Harlem: TYWLS, pronounced "Twills" by students and faculty. [1] Founded in 1996, it is one of the success stories being cited by a growing number of advocates of single-sex education as examples for public school systems around the country seeking to improve education for girls and boys alike.

"Single-sex education works better,"

From *The CQ Researcher,*
July 12, 2002.

The Jefferson Leadership Academies provide single-gender education to boys and girls from low-income families in Long Beach, Calif. The Bush administration wants federal regulations to make it easier for school districts to experiment with single-sex education, now offered in only 13 schools nationwide.

Jefferson Leadership Academies

says Leonard Sax, a family physician and psychologist in Poolesville, Md., near Washington, D.C. and founder of the fledgling National Association for the Advancement of Single-Sex Public Education. "Kids who attend single-sex schools not only do better academically but also have a better attitude toward school and a better outlook on life."

After sitting in on three classes at TYWLS in May, Secretary of Education Rod Paige enthused, "Visiting this school fortifies my already strong belief that these kinds of schools should be available for parents." [2]

Paige is giving the idea more than lip service. He has ordered a rewrite of federal regulations to make it easier for

school districts to experiment with single-sex schools and classes. The Education Department will also be in charge of doling out money that Congress added to President Bush's education-reform package for school districts to pay for those experiments.

Support for single-sex education is far from unanimous, however. Coeducational schools have predominated in U.S. public education for more than a century — and appear to be popular among the vast majority of students from kindergarten through college. Experts are divided on the claimed academic benefits of single-sex education. And many women's and civil rights groups fear that the movement diverts attention and resources from improving public schools for the vast majority of students or risks undercutting the federal law — known as Title IX — that prohibits sex discrimination in schools or colleges receiving federal funds.

"I understand that the Harlem girls' school is doing very well, and it should be," says Nancy Zirkin, director of public policy and government affairs at the American Association of University Women (AAUW). "But what is the collateral damage done by pulling kids out and focusing on one school and leaving the other ones behind? I would think it would not improve public schools."

The movement for single-sex education follows a decades-long debate about how well girls are doing in public schools, and a more recent debate over boys' performance as well. [3] A 1992 AAUW report charged that schools were "shortchanging" girls by "depriving [them] of classroom attention, ignor-

Same-Sex Schools Target Minority Students

Only 13 public schools in the United States currently operate all or some of their classes on a single-sex basis, according to education experts. Virtually all serve minority communities.

Charter School of San Diego San Diego, Calif. Founded: 2000 Enrollment: 40 girls and 40 boys	The 1,300-student school for grades 7-12 offers single-sex classes in grades 7 and 8. Boys and girls are more comfortable asking questions and interacting in single-sex classrooms, says Director Mary Bixby.
Jefferson Leadership Academies Long Beach, Calif. Founded: 1999 Enrollment: 1,120 boys and girls, grades 6-8	Parents in this low-income community felt that coeducational classes provided too many distractions for students, prompting the conversion to single-sex classes.
Lewis Fox Middle School Hartford, Conn. Founded: 1995 Enrollment: 80 boys and girls in 7th and 8th grades	Students in the single-sex program (total school enrollment is 900) perform 15-20 percent better on standardized tests than citywide averages.
Maria Mitchell Elementary School Denver, Colo. Founded: 1998 Enrollment: 60 4th- and 5th-grade students; 540 total enrollment	Principal Reginald Robinson says the program works because 4th- and 5th-graders are "too inquisitive" about the opposite sex to concentrate on classwork.
Moten Elementary School Washington, D.C. Founded: Fall of 2001 Enrollment: 362 boys and girls, grades 4-6	When this inner-city school switched to single-sex classes and revamped its curriculum, students' standardized test scores rose by an average of 40 percentage points.
Paducah Middle School Paducah, Ky. Founded: 2001 Enrollment: 30 boys and 18 girls in 6th grade	Although performance has not been measured for the pilot program, all 6th- and 7th-graders will attend single-sex classes in the future.

ing the value of cooperative learning and presenting texts and lessons in which female role models are conspicuously absent." [4]

More recently, some experts and advocates have complained that schools shortchange boys by starting them at school at an age when they are developmentally behind girls and then constraining their natural instincts toward physical activity and healthy competition. "As competitiveness and individual initiative are discouraged, classroom discipline loosened and out-

lets for natural rambunctiousness eliminated, schoolboys tend to tune out," writes Christina Hoff Sommers in her book *The War Against Boys.* [5]

The answer to both problems, single-sex education advocates say, is simple: Let boys be boys and girls be girls. "The solution is to let boys and girls attend separate classes, so that you can take advantage of the sex differences" in learning styles, Sax says.

Others say that the supposed differences between boys and girls are being exaggerated. "There are much

greater differences among girls and among boys than there are between girls and boys," say education experts Patricia Campbell and Ellen Wahl. [6]

For the present, the United States offers relatively few places to test the opposing arguments, especially in the public school setting. Only a dozen or so public schools are known to be offering single-sex enrollment or classes. Parochial and private schools were once predominantly single-sex, but are far less so today. In higher education, the number of women's schools has

Philadelphia High School for Girls Philadelphia, Pa. Founded: 1848 Enrollment: 1,400 girls, grades 9-12	The magnet school is open to exceptional applicants citywide and sends 95 percent of its graduates to college. Half of the students are from homes with family incomes below the poverty line.
Robert Coleman Elementary School Baltimore, Md. Founded: 1993 Enrollment: Pre-K - 5th grade	After Principal Hattie Johnson separated classes by gender at the predominantly minority school, test scores rose to among the highest in Baltimore and discipline problems all but vanished.
San Francisco 49ers Academy Palo Alto, Calif. Founded: 1997 Enrollment: 90 boys and 90 girls	Boys and girls' schools operate separately at this middle school. Although classes are single-sex, recess and extracurricular activities are coeducational.
The Young Women's Leadership School New York, N.Y. Founded: 1996 Enrollment: 365 students, grades 7-12	The Harlem school sends almost 100 percent of its students to four-year colleges; 59 percent are Latina, 40 percent African-American.
Thurgood Marshall Elementary School Seattle, Wash. Founded: 2000 Enrollment: 356 boys and girls, grades K-5	After Principal Ben Wright instituted single-sex classes, test scores rose and discipline problems declined. The students are 97 percent minority, and 80 percent receive subsidized lunches.
Western High School Baltimore, Md. Founded: 1844 Enrollment: 1,050 girls	More than 80 percent African-American, Western boasts the third-highest SAT scores in Baltimore and a college acceptance rate of 99 percent in 2001.
Young Women's Leadership School Chicago, Ill. Founded: 2000 Enrollment: 300 girls, grades 7-12	With a curriculum focused on leadership, science and technology, the school serves a student body that is over 80 percent minority, and 65 percent of the students come from poor families.

declined sharply over the past four decades, and men's colleges have all but disappeared: Only three remain. (*See story, p. 320.*)

Perhaps surprisingly, academic experts on both sides of the debate say that increasing the number of single-sex schools or classes would be beneficial, at least in terms of research. "We see some of these studies with large samples indicating some positive effect from single-sex schooling," says Rosemary Salomone, a professor at St. John's University School of Law in Ja-

maica, N.Y. "We won't know unless we permit the programs to survive."

"Anyone who says the research is definitive either way is not accurate," says David Sadker, a professor of education at American University in Washington and a skeptic of single-sex education. "There's still a lot to learn."

Meanwhile, TYWLS founder Ann Rubenstein Tisch is convinced the school provides an invaluable option. "I know that some of our students, our stars, would have done well in any school," says Tisch, a former tele-

vision reporter turned education activist. "But I also know that there are many others who would never, never have made it were it not for the environment that we offer them. There's got to be something to it."

As the debate over single-sex education continues, here are some of the questions being considered:

Does single-sex education enhance learning?

Australian researcher Kenneth Rowe examined the academic records of some 270,000 high school seniors in an effort to identify what factors really make a difference in students' learning. One of his key findings, according to a press release, was that both girls and boys attending single-sex schools scored 15-22 percentile points higher than their counterparts in coeducational schools.

Advocates of single-sex education in the United States point to the big differential as the strongest proof yet that separating boys and girls improves learning for both genders. "That's enormous," Sax says.

But Rowe, principal research fellow with the Australian Council on Education Research, himself insists that Sax and others are distorting his findings. In his formal paper, Rowe explained that the differences between single-sex and coeducational schools "pale into insignificance" compared to differences attributable to teacher training and ability. Today, Rowe says bluntly that the single-sex school debate amounts to "little more than epistemological claptrap." [7]

The advocates of single-sex education claim its benefits derive in part from biological realities. Boys' and girls' brains develop differently, they say — differences especially significant for learning in early years. Then, as they get older, boys and girls distract each other from academics because of normal social and sexual development.

"If you put a 15-year-old boy next to a 15-year-old girl, his mind is not going to be on geometry, or Spanish or English," Sax says. "It's going to be on that girl sexually. He's got the hormones of a grown man, but the brain of a 10-year-old."

In earlier years, Sax and others say, girls typically begin to read at a younger age and are also less distractible in the classroom. Advocates of single-sex education say these differences set up a dynamic unhelpful for boys' learning.

"To the extent that boys experience school in a competitive way and some boys aren't learning to read as readily,

their response is to say that reading is girls' stuff, not boys' stuff," says Christopher Wadsworth, executive director of the International Boys' School Coalition. "That can lead to an attitude that is not conducive to development."

In addition, girls'-school advocates say, single-sex education helps girls overcome the male sexism that still exists in public schools. "Girls are at center stage with only girls in the audience," says Meg Milne Moulton, co-executive director of the National Coalition of Girls' Schools. "They get 100 percent of the attention."

"No girl in a single-sex school is able to say, 'I can't do it because no girl can do it' — because there is some girl who is doing it," adds Cornelius Riordan, a professor of sociology at Providence College.

Critics of single-sex education say these claims are largely unsubstantiated. "People think it helps girls' self-esteem or makes boys calmer," the AAUW's Zirkin says. "This is anecdotal. This is pulling things out of the air. There is not the scientifically based research for anybody to make an informed decision."

Academics on both sides of the issue want more and better studies. "There is not definitive research," says Sadker, of American University.

Riordan, however, insists that although the subject is "overpoliticized and underresearched," the research favors single-sex schooling. "All of the studies consistently show small positive effects for boys and girls," he says. "The effects are stronger for girls than for boys, and the positive effects are always larger for disadvantaged students."

Riordan cites a study he published more than a decade ago comparing boys and girls from the 1972 and 1982 graduating classes at American single-sex or coeducational Catholic high schools. After adjusting for ability and background, Riordan found that minority girls and minority boys in single-sex schools did better — about the equiv-

alent of one grade year — than minority girls or boys respectively in coeducational schools. Girls from more representative cross-sections also did better in single-sex schools, but boys' scores were slightly higher in coeducational schools. [8]

Today, Riordan has refined his argument. In a paper presented in various forums over the past several years, he says, "only females of low socioeconomic status are likely to show significant gains (along with boys) in single-sex schools."

Riordan posits a dozen "theoretical rationales" for why single-sex schools have positive effects — including such hypothetical advantages as reduced sex bias in teacher-student interactions, reduced sex differences in curricula and more successful role models for girls. But, he points out, the fact that attendance at a single-gender school today requires an affirmative decision by students and parents — which he calls "a pro-academic" choice — is perhaps the single most important factor contributing to the positive effects.

"That student realizes, 'I'm going to go to a school where it's not business as usual,' " Riordan explains. " 'I'm going to have to work.' "

Critics of single-sex education say all the more explicitly that any benefits are most likely attributable to other factors. "A lot of the effects are [due to the fact that] they're good schools, not because they're single-sex," Sadker says.

"The elements that make for good schools would work whether it's single-sex or coed," Zirkin says. "The elements are attention to core academics, qualified teachers, smaller classrooms, discipline and a sense of community and parental involvement. These are the elements that will enable any child in any situation to learn. To say that it's a single-sex school that's achieved such good results really begs the question."

Rowe says his research does indicate advantages from single-sex education, but "gender-class grouping" is not the critical factor, he insists. "Whether schools are single-sex or coed or have single-sex classes within coed settings matters far less than the quality of the teaching and learning provided," he says.

Do single-sex schools reinforce gender stereotypes?

A two-year pilot project in six California public school districts from 1998-2000 affords the best opportunity to date to study the effects of single-sex schools in U.S. public systems. But researchers who studied the effects on gender-related issues report mixed results.

Professors Amanda Datnow of the University of Toronto, Lea Hubbard of the University of California at San Diego and Elisabeth Woody of the University of California at Berkeley found that — as proponents predicted — boys and girls in single-gender settings engaged in more candid conversations about such issues as gender roles than boys and girls in coeducational schools. [9] They also found that eliminating distractions from the opposite sex helped academic learning, especially for girls.

On the other hand, the researchers also found that single-gender classes actually exacerbated teasing and disruptive behavior among boys and cattiness among girls. In addition, teachers perpetuated stereotypes about gender roles — depicting men, for example, as primary wage earners for families. Teachers also based disciplinary and instructional practices on gender stereotypes: Boys received more discipline and were taught in individualistic settings, while girls were treated in a more nurturing manner and afforded opportunities for collaborative work.

"There is a tendency to teach to a particular notion of boys and a particular notion of girls," Datnow says. "There's really much more variation among boys or among girls as there is between boys and girls."

But advocates of single-sex education believe it helps reduce gender stereotyping. "You break down gender stereotypes by letting the sexes be separate," Sax says. "When you put boys and girls together, you intensify the gender roles. The boys do things that are thought of as typical for boys, and girls do things that are thought of as typical for girls."

"Girls are judged in their own right, not in relation to each other or in relation to the other gender," says Moulton, of the National Coalition of Girls' Schools. "It's a lot easier for a girl to be a girl in a single-gender setting."

Boys, too, find it easier to be themselves in a single-sex setting, Wadsworth says. "Freed from the need to impress girls, boys are more open," he says. "They allow themselves to be more vulnerable to making mistakes."

In her visits to same-sex schools, Salomone of St. John's University says she was struck by boys' willingness to engage in what would be considered "feminine activities," like choir or drama club. "At one school, I saw a whole classroom of boys playing the violin," she recalls.

Riordan says single-sex schools also reduce the incidence of sexual harassment. "A great deal of sexual harassment occurs on school grounds, even in classes," he says. "That does not occur in single-sex schools."

But Datnow and Hubbard reported what they called an unexpected type of harassment of students attending single-sex schools. Students from coeducational schools would tease them with homophobic comments, reflecting an assumption that enrollment in a single-sex school either meant someone was or might become gay or lesbian.

Opponents contend that single-sex schools are more likely to strengthen rather than weaken gender stereotyping. "The concern is the perpetuation of stereotypes in the name of protecting [boys and girls] by taking steps that

indeed don't protect either sex but in fact perpetuate the stereotypes that hamstring their development in life," says Donna Lieberman, executive director of the New York Civil Liberties Union. "The school system should not be about reinforcing those."

For his part, Sadker of American University believes single-sex schools "can promote gender stereotypes or hinder them. Being single-sex of itself will do neither."

From her study of the California experiment, Datnow concludes that teachers will be the determining factor on whether single-sex schools increase or decrease gender stereotyping. "Teachers need relevant training and support to address student needs in a single-sex setting so they don't presume that all girls learn in a particular way or that boys are naturally rowdy and need kinetic activities," she says.

Datnow says the schools in the California experiment did not provide that kind of support. "Most of the schools did not have a strong ideological commitment to single-sex education," she says. "The administrators were particularly attracted by the generous grant offered by the state."

Do single-sex schools help or hurt the goal of gender equity?

Desperate to keep the city's black teenagers out of prison or the morgue, Detroit's school board decided to open three all-male academies in 1991. The new schools — initially designed to serve about 250 students from preschool through fifth grade — were to offer an Afrocentric curriculum and a mentoring program aimed at improving students' academic performance, character and self-esteem.

Shortly before the academies were to open, however, two women with young daughters sued the school district in federal court, claiming that barring girls from the new schools would amount to sex discrimination in vio-

Helping Young Women in Harlem

Lori-Anne Ramsay did not speak up much at the coeducational public high school she attended in New York City. "When I was in physics class, I expected all the boys to be smarter than me," Ramsay recalls.

In two years at The Young Women's Leadership School (TYWLS) in East Harlem, however, Ramsay has blossomed. She graduated in June with honors and in September will be off to Bates College in Maine to study economics.

Ramsay credits much of her success to TYWLS' all-girl environment. "It allows you to focus more," Ramsay says. "Having the opposite sex in the room is a distraction."

But Ramsay concedes there are downsides to a single-sex school. "The social aspects are not all that good," she says. "If you're not a person who goes out and makes friends, you definitely suffer."

Ramsay's classmates and her teachers generally echo her positive feelings toward the six-year-old experiment in public, single-sex education. A few, however, note some disadvantages or credit the school's success primarily to other factors. "It's the school itself — the teachers, the staff," says Oberlin-bound graduate Jasmine Cruz-Oquendo.

"Our school is unique not only because it is single-sex but also because we have small classes, very dedicated teachers and kids have to apply to be here," says Spanish teacher Roseanne Demammos. "Certainly, some of the students could have experienced the same success" at a coeducational school.

Principal Kathleen Ponze also acknowledges the school's small size — 370 students in grades 7-12 — necessarily limits its offerings: There are only two advanced-placement courses, for example. "It's extremely difficult to meet the needs of every kid," Ponze says. She also laments the limited social opportunities the school can provide.

Still, TYWLS tries to fill the gaps. The school partners with New York University for a drama club and with an all-boys Catholic school for socials. And juniors and seniors can take courses at nearby Hunter College. "We don't have any of the frills here," Ponze says. "We try to make the frills."

More worrisome has been the high staff turnover. Ponze is the school's third principal, and more than a dozen teachers left last year. "The school is very demanding of its faculty as well as its students," says Demammos. "It's not necessarily the right situation for everyone."

This year, however, staffing has stabilized. "We appear to have stopped the bleeding," Ponze says.

A visitor to the school — housed on five floors of a nondescript office building in southernmost East Harlem — sees little to suggest shortcomings, however. The school is clean, the walls decorated with student projects, the girls neatly uniformed in plaid skirts or navy trousers with white blouses under vests or blazers. Classrooms use tables instead of rows of desks, to encourage girls to study together, rather than competitively.

As with most of the nation's two-dozen or so single-sex public schools, the students are overwhelmingly from minorities — in TYWLS's case, primarily Latina and African-American. Of 34 seniors, 23 live at or below the poverty level. Twenty-two graduates will be the first in their families to attend college. But Columbia-bound valedictorian Maryam Zohny follows three older siblings to college.

TYWLS founder Ann Rubenstein Tisch got the idea for the school while covering education stories as an NBC correspondent. "I didn't think we were doing enough for inner-city kids," she says. "If it's OK for affluent boys and girls, and Catholic boys and girls, wouldn't it follow that it would work in another community?"

lation of Title IX and the equal-protection provisions of both the Michigan and U.S. constitutions. Judge George Woods agreed. The "important" purpose of helping the city's black youth, Woods said, "is insufficient to override the rights of females to equal opportunities." [10]

Opponents of single-sex education say separate schools for boys and girls necessarily violate students' rights to equal educational opportunities. "Single-sex public schools are contrary to the spirit of Title IX and — as a practical matter — impossible to police under the Equal Protection Clause," says Martha Davis, senior counsel of

the National Organization for Women (NOW) Legal Defense and Education Fund. "The notion that you can have separate but equal is as false for women as it is for minorities."

"Focusing special attention on one sex over the other is a violation of the public trust," Davis adds. "We need to be addressing the ills that kids in an urban setting face regardless of their gender."

"In every legal challenge about the establishment of a boys school or a girls school, [it] has always been found that the boys school has been superior," says Leslie Annexstein, senior counsel with the National Women's

Law Center in Washington. She notes that Pennsylvania courts ordered Philadelphia's all-boys Central High School to adopt an open admissions policy in 1984 after finding that the school's facilities were superior to those at a counterpart all-girls school. [11]

Advocates of single-sex schools believe the opponents are fighting battles from the past. "We're beyond that," Providence College's Riordan says. "That was a generation ago. Today, we're talking about schools that would be equal in resources, equal in prestige: We have laws in place to assure that. I don't think that in today's world there's a remote possibility that the

Tisch, who married into the family that controls the Loews Corp., set up a foundation to help support the school — to the tune of about $200,000 last year. New York's Board of Education pays for the building, teachers and books and supplies. Classes have about 20-22 students — a low teacher-student ratio that depends on several budgeting arrangements with the Board of Education.

TYWLS graduates gather around 2002 commencement speaker Alma Powell, wife of Secretary of State Colin Powell. All but one of the girls will attend college this fall.

For the coming year, the school has 550 applicants for 60 seventh-grade slots and 1,200 applicants for three openings in the ninth grade.

In contrast to the student body, two-thirds of the 26-member teaching staff is white. Ponze acknowledges the disparity but notes that she recently hired five persons of color, including an assistant principal.

Teachers cite a range of experiences indicating that single-sex education can benefit girls in and out of the classroom. "By not having [boys], they were able to compete with themselves," says science teacher Melissa Melchior. "There wasn't that level where guys would dominate."

Tisch's foundation helps buy curricular materials, gives some summer scholarships and pays for a full-time college counselor. That last investment pays off. For the second year in a row, all of the school's seniors gained admittance to four-year colleges, although one graduate is joining the Navy instead — for financial reasons.

The school is listed in *New York* magazine as one of the city's top public high schools, but the admissions policy is targeted to applicants performing at or below grade level. Applicants must tour the school with a family member. Once a student is admitted, she and her parents or guardians sign a contract promising to support the school's mission of rigorous academics, attendance and "thoughtful habits of mind" and to keep the lines of communication open between parents and the school.

"Socially, girls become less competitive with each other when there aren't any boys around," says math teacher Deb Carlson-Doom. "There's less sparring in general because there aren't boys."

The graduating students echo their teachers' observations. "We could be ourselves," says Karla Carballo. "We didn't have to pretend to be anyone else."

Many stress the close bonds of sisterhood with their classmates. "It was a lot of support," says Leslie Cortez. "It was very much a family."

"The girls are so united, so focused on [each other's] education," says Denise Fernandez. "It's not for everyone, but it was good for me."

school for boys or the school for girls would take on greater prestige or would have greater resources."

"There are pretty strong lobbies and awareness on both sides," says Moulton, of the National Coalition of Girls Schools. "By serving one population, I don't see you disserving another."

In its most recent decision on the issue, the U.S. Supreme Court ordered the state of Virginia to admit female students to the previously all-male Virginia Military Institute (VMI). In a 7-1 decision, the court held that the state's plan to provide a military program for women at another public university was insufficient. [12]

"VMI should serve as an object lesson of what not to do," Salomone says. But, she adds, "you can see the factual distinctions between VMI and the kind of second-generation [single-sex] programs that we see growing up around the country."

The Education Department, in its announcement that it was considering changes in Title IX, said it wants to provide "more flexibility" to permit single-sex classes and schools "while at the same time ensuring appropriate safeguards against discrimination." The final proposal, the department promises, "will ensure that educational opportunities are not limited to students based on

sex, and that single-sex classes are not based on sex-role stereotypes."

Critics of single-sex schools are still concerned. "Is this the first step toward undoing Title IX?" Sadker asks. "Can you undo a civil rights protection like this without endangering that protection?"

"There's a perception that the gender problem has been solved," Datnow says. "If we're going to experiment, there needs to be some very specific language around gender equity and some monitoring. We can't simply devolve money to the local level and let them take it away. There needs to be some accountability."

Young Women's Leadership School

BACKGROUND

'Tide of Coeducation'

Coeducation gradually emerged during the 19th century as the dominant practice in the United States, first in primary and secondary education and later at the college level. Historians David Tyack and Elisabeth Hansot say economics was a major impetus for what they call a "tide of coeducation." [13] Particularly with the advent of the one-room schoolhouse, it became cheaper and more efficient to educate boys and girls together than to operate separate schools for both sexes. Feminists of the day also viewed coeducation as a necessary step in women's emancipation, and some education policymakers believed it would benefit boys and girls alike.

The earliest schools and colleges in Colonial America were for boys only. Girls were educated in informal settings — at home or in so-called "dame schools," which evolved from mere child tending into a forerunner of the American primary school. Coeducation began making inroads early, however. The 19th-century education reformer Horace Mann observed that one of the first educational improvements in Colonial New England was to begin "smuggling" girls into schools for limited periods after the boys had left. By the American Revolution, some reformers were arguing that, just like boys, girls had a right to — and a need for — a good education.

Coeducation became "embedded" in public schools in the first half of the 19th century, Tyack and Hansot write. Small towns and rural communities could not afford to go beyond single, one-room schoolhouses; larger cities also found separate schools impractical. Women's-rights advocates thought coeducation the most likely way to make girls' education more nearly equal to that of the boys.

A broader rationale emerged by the second half of the 19th century. In an important paper, William Harris, superintendent of St. Louis schools and later U.S. commissioner of education, argued in 1870 that mixing the sexes in the classroom improved instruction and discipline for boys and girls by merging their different abilities and allowing pupils of each gender to serve as a "counter-check" on the other. [14]

Despite the advance of coeducation, upper-class families continued to send their sons and daughters to single-sex schools through the 19th century — and, less uniformly, through the 20th century.

Meanwhile, in the late 19th century some prominent academics began attacking coeducation. In his book *Sex in Education*, Edward Clarke, a professor at the Harvard Medical School, argued in 1873 that academic competition with boys overloaded girls' brains and interfered with the development of their reproductive organs. With Darwinian theories much in vogue, Clarke's views attracted interest and support, but they had little effect on schools' practices.

Coeducation came under more sustained challenge in the 20th century — first, in the early 1900s, from male educators complaining of boys' lagging educational performance compared to girls, and, in recent decades, from feminist critics who accuse schools of shortchanging girls.

The so-called "boy problem" consisted simply of boys' doing less well than girls. For example, more boys repeated grades or dropped out of school than girls. Some educators blamed the "feminization" of schooling that supposedly resulted from the preponderance of female teachers. To solve the problem, some educators called simply for "differentiation" in instruction by gender, but others went further and called for segregating classes by sex. Some experiments were tried — to mixed reviews — but eventually fizzled out.

Since the early days, educators and advocates seeking to improve schooling for girls contended with a tension between women's roles in the home and family and their roles in the workplace and society. In the 1800s, schooling had been aimed at making girls "better wives and mothers," Tyack and Hansot write. But in the early-20th century, reformers established "scientific" home economics courses for girls to counter a perceived deterioration in family life.

With the emergence of a strengthened women's movement in the latter-20th century, the tension became more manifest. Feminists discovered what Tyack and Hansot call "the hidden injuries" of coeducation: perpetuation of male dominance and an "implicit hidden curriculum of sex stereotyping in coeducational public schools."

Gender Equity

The feminist critique of public education contributed to the passage of a federal law — Title IX of the Education Amendments of 1972 — aimed at guaranteeing gender equity in federally financed schools, colleges and universities. The effects of the law have been felt mainly in higher education — most visibly, perhaps, in athletics. [15] Women's groups marking the 30th anniversary of the law this year say it has prompted significant progress, but has fallen short of equalizing opportunities for boys and girls in K-12 education or for men and women in colleges and universities.

The National Organization for Women (NOW) included a demand for "equal and unsegregated educa-

Chronology

1800s-1960
Coeducation becomes dominant practice in U.S. public schools by turn of century; many Catholic, private schools continue as single-sex.

1960s-1970s
Civil-rights era produces new concerns about "gender equity" in education; many men's and women's colleges become coeducational.

1967
National Organization for Women calls for "equal and unsegregated" education as part of the group's women's bill of rights.

1972
Congress passes Title IX, barring sex-based discrimination in any federally financed school, college or university; law permits single-sex admissions policies at elementary and secondary schools and private colleges and universities.

1975
Department of Health, Education and Welfare issues Title IX regulations, which generally bar single-sex classes or programs in K-12 except for contact sports, sex education, choir; women's-rights groups later complain of weak enforcement.

1977
Supreme Court, divided 4-4, upholds appeals court ruling allowing all-male policy at Philadelphia's Central High School.

1979
Women outnumber men in U.S. colleges and universities for first time except during wartime.

1980s
Title IX brings changes in K-12, higher education; court rulings tilt against single-sex schools.

1982
Supreme Court strikes down all-female admissions policy at Mississippi University for Women's School of Nursing.

1984
Supreme Court limits enforcement of Title IX by ruling that penalty for violation does not require funds cut-off for entire college — only for affected program or department; Pennsylvania state court requires open admissions at all-male Central High School because of unequal funding of counterpart school for girls.

1990s
Interest in single-sex education increases.

1991
Detroit drops plan for academies for African-American boys after federal court ruling; Milwaukee also opens to girls its planned school for minority boys after opposition is voiced.

1992
American Association of University Women issues report charging that public schools are "shortchanging" girls.

1995
American Association of University Women (AAUW) gives guarded endorsement to single-sex policies on short-term basis.

1996
Young Women's Leadership School opens in East Harlem; civil-rights groups file complaint with Department of Education, but no action is taken.

1997
AAUW adopts more critical stance toward single-sex policies.

1998
California provides grants to school districts for single-sex programs; six districts participate, with mixed results; most drop experiment when state ends grants in 2000.

2000s
Single-sex education gains support from Congress, Bush administration.

2000
Australian researcher finds girls and boys do better in single-sex schools than in coeducational settings but says quality of teaching is more important; conservative author Barbara Hoff Sommers argues in *The War Against Boys* that public schools are shortchanging boys, not girls.

2001
Senate includes incentive grants for single-sex schools and classes in President Bush's education-reform package.

2002
Bush signs No Child Left Behind Act on Jan. 8, with funds for single-sex demonstration projects; Department of Education on May 8 starts process of revising Title IX regulations to make it easier for schools to adopt single-sex policies; at least four single-sex schools to open at start of new school year.

How Title IX Prevents Discrimination

Title IX of the Education Amendments of 1972 seeks to guarantee gender equity in federally financed schools, colleges and universities. The Bush administration would rewrite the regulations to make it easier for school districts to experiment with single-sex schools. [1]

"No person in the United States shall, on the basis of sex, be excluded from participation in, be denied the benefits of, or be subjected to discrimination under any education program or activity receiving Federal financial assistance."

Current Title IX Regulations:

Area Regulated	Impact of Law	What Title IX Regulations Say
Admissions	Discrimination prohibited, with exceptions	"No person, shall on the basis of sex, be denied admission, or be subjected to discrimination in admission, by any recipient." Single-sex institutions of higher education were grandfathered; non-vocational elementary and secondary schools were exempted.
Housing	Separation permitted	"Separate housing on the basis of sex," if "proportionate in quantity to the number of students of that sex applying for housing" and "comparable in quality and cost to the student."
Comparable facilities	Separation permitted	"Separate toilet, locker room and shower facilities on the basis of sex"if "comparable to such facilities provided for students of the other sex."
Access to course offerings	Separation permitted, in certain cases	"Grouping of students in physical education classes and activities by ability as assessed by objective standards of individual performance developed and applied without regard to sex." "Grouping of students by sex within physical education classes or activities during participation in wrestling, boxing, rugby, ice hockey, football, basketball and other sports, the purpose or major activity of which includes bodily contact." "Separate sessions for boys and girls" in "[p]ortions of classes in elementary and secondary schools which deal exclusively with human sexuality . . ." "Requirements based on vocal range or quality which may result in a chorus or choruses of one or predominantly one sex."
Athletics	Separation permitted	"Separate teams for members of each sex where selection for such teams is based upon competitive skill or the activity involved is a contact sport," provided that for non-contact sports students of both sexes must be allowed to try out for a team unless the school sponsors teams for both sexes. "Unequal aggregate expenditures for male and female teams allowed, but may be considered "in assessing equality of opportunity for members of each sex."

[1] 34 Code of Federal Regulations sections 106.21, 106.32-34, 106-41.

tion" in the women's bill of rights approved by the group at its second national conference in 1967. Five years later, though, Congress was preoccupied with racial busing issues when it worked on reauthorizing federal aid to education programs and gave little attention to what emerged as Title IX.

As enacted, the law forbade discrimination on the basis of sex in any "education program or activity" receiving federal financial assistance. (*See box, p. 318.*) However, the law specifically exempted admissions policies at public elementary and secondary schools and private undergraduate institutions. [16]

Writing the regulations to implement Title IX took three years. As issued in July 1975 by what was then the Department of Health, Education and Welfare, the regulations included several provisions sought by feminists to make public elementary and secondary coeducation more nearly identical for both sexes. School districts were generally barred from offering single-sex activities or programs, except for contact sports or sex education. Any other single-sex admissions policy, courses or services were legal only if the school district offered "comparable" courses, services or facilities to persons of the opposite sex. [17]

Two years later, the NOW Legal Defense Fund called enforcement of the regulations "indifferent, inept, ignorant of the law itself or bogged down in red tape." [18] The record improved under President Jimmy Carter — partly because of a court order to enforce the law — but enforcement again lagged in the 1980s under President Ronald Reagan. Women's-rights groups, however, began winning enactment of gender-equity laws at the state level. And school administrators, fearful of litigation, generally moved to comply with the law. In one highly visible area, girls' participation in high school sports increased fivefold

in the 1970s — while still lagging far behind boys' programs in number and funding. [19]

The Supreme Court missed an opportunity to deal with the issue at the K-12 level in 1977 when the justices — divided 4-4 with one justice not participating — left standing a lower court's decision upholding Philadelphia's Central High School all-male admissions policy. [20] The justices also limited the impact of Title IX by ruling in 1984 that the penalty for violating the law would be to cut off federal funds only for the specific programs or departments guilty of discrimination, not the entire institution. [21]

In two other decisions, however, the high court made clear that single-sex admissions policies at public colleges and universities would be difficult to sustain. In 1982, the court struck down the exclusion of men from the Mississippi University for Women's School of Nursing. Then in a heavily publicized case in 1996, the court similarly struck down VMI's all-male policy. In her opinion for the court in the VMI case, Justice Ruth Bader Ginsburg said any form of sex discrimination in higher education could be upheld under the 14th Amendment's Equal Protection Clause only if a state presented an "exceedingly persuasive justification" for the policy. [22]

Through the mid-1990s, the Department of Education's Office of Civil Rights (OCR) — the unit charged with enforcing Title IX — reported that the relatively few complaints involving single-gender issues at the K-12 level had all been "resolved." [23] The office took no action against the Philadelphia High School for Girls and Baltimore's all-girl Western High School after receiving assurances that both schools were — nominally — open to boys as well.

In a similar vein, the office told school systems contemplating single-gender classes that unless the class-

es were open to students of both sexes they would be violating Title IX. And OCR officials told the Prince George's County, Md., school board to open all its mentoring programs to boys and girls after finding that the multimillion-dollar boys program was significantly bigger than the program for girls.

Single-Sex Revival

Single-sex education drew renewed interest through the 1990s from researchers, advocacy groups and policymakers. Some local initiatives were thwarted by legal challenges, but others survived opposition. By decade's end, at least 10 single-sex public schools were operating in the United States. Academic proponents of single-sex education accumulated evidence seeking to show its benefits, but some researchers and advocacy groups remained unconvinced. Meanwhile, congressional efforts to encourage single-sex experiments finally culminated in the provision in the president's education-reform bill to authorize incentive grants for school districts wishing to experiment with separate schools or classrooms for boys or girls. [24]

Detroit's effort to establish Afrocentric academies for young black males in 1991 ran up against concerted opposition from the national ACLU, the NAACP Legal Defense Fund and the NOW Legal Defense and Education Fund, and then a federal court suit. In his ruling blocking the plan, Judge Woods noted that the Detroit school board had acknowledged "an equally urgent" crisis facing female students. He also said the school board had failed to show that "the coeducational factor" was to blame for the school system's failures. The academies opened with a stated policy of accepting boys or girls. Opposition to a similar plan in Milwaukee forced officials there also

Women's Colleges Refuse to Fade Away

When feminist educator Mary Lyon founded Mount Holyoke Female Seminary in western Massachusetts in 1837, American women had very few opportunities for higher education. There were a few other female "seminaries" in New England and the South, but only one college — Oberlin in Ohio — admitted women to study alongside men. [1]

By the late-20th century, however, U.S. higher education had become overwhelmingly coeducational — not only at public colleges and universities, most of which had been coeducational from their founding, but also at formerly all-male universities such as Harvard and Yale.

Women's place in higher education changed so much that Mount Holyoke's administrators, faculty, students and alumnae twice within the last three decades seriously considered following the trend toward coeducation. And both times — most recently in the mid-1990s — Mount Holyoke College, as it is now called, decided to remain exclusively for women.

"In the world, women still do not have equal opportunity," says Patricia Vandenberg, director of communications for the 2,000-student college. "There is a real sense that a women's college like Mount Holyoke that challenges women and expects them to achieve gets results that the world needs."

Mount Holyoke is one of a dwindling number of women's colleges in the United States, however. From a high of nearly 300 all-female institutions in the 1960s, the number of women's colleges today has dropped to around 70, according to the Washington-based Women's College Coalition. The sharp drop began in the late 1960s, according to coalition President Jadwiga Sebrechts. More than half ceased operating as women's institutions within a five-year span at the turn of the decade.

About half of those former women's colleges — including such prominent schools as Vassar and Bennington — became coeducational. About half of the others merged with brother institutions, including many Catholic colleges. The remainder simply closed their doors.

The movement toward coeducation continued apace over the next two decades. Meanwhile, men's colleges became all but extinct. Today, only three remain: historically black Morehouse College in Atlanta with about 3,000 students; Hampden-Sydney College in Hampden-Sydney, Va. (1,000 students); and Wabash College in Crawfordsville, Ind. (860 students).

In public education, two Supreme Court decisions sharply limit the states' freedom to establish or maintain single-sex institutions. The two rulings — requiring admission of men to the Mississippi University for Women in 1982 and of women to all-male Virginia Military Institute in 1996 — both require states to show an "exceedingly persuasive justification" for treating men and women differently in public higher education. [2]

Today, only three public women's colleges remain. One of those — Douglass College of Rutgers University in New Jersey — is part of a coeducational university. The other two — Mississippi University for Women and Texas Woman's University — both admit men, but state in promotional materials that their mission is to further women's education.

Despite the declining number of women's colleges, enrollment is increasing. Over the past decade, the number of students has nearly doubled — from about 50,000 in 1990 to 98,000 today. Mount Holyoke has maintained its enrollment at around 2,000, but applications have increased by about 44 percent since the mid-'90s, according to Vandenberg.

---

to allow boys and girls to apply for the new school.

Tisch drew similar opposition from civil rights and women's organizations when she started The Young Women's Leadership School. A coalition that included NOW New York City, the New York Civil Liberties Union and the New York Civil Rights Coalition filed a complaint with OCR, charging that the planned school violated Title IX and state and local anti-discrimination laws. Anne Conners, president of New York City NOW, called the school "a Band-Aid approach to gender equity for girls." Six years later, OCR has not acted on the complaint. "It didn't stop us from doing what we

wanted to and needed to do," Tisch says.

California tried a more ambitious experiment in single-gender schooling in the late 1990s, but the pilot program shrank for lack of political support. Legislation pushed by Republican Gov. Pete Wilson provided $500,000 apiece to school districts to operate equivalent single-gender academies at the middle and high school levels for boys and girls. Six school districts participated in the program from 1998-2000: Four operated as schools-within-a-school, while two operated self-contained single-gender schools.

In their report on the program, Datnow and Hubbard found that the school

districts were careful to provide equal resources for boys and girls, and that single-gender classes reduced distractions. But they also said the participating school districts appeared to be primarily interested in getting more money to address needs of at-risk students rather than using single-gender classes to improve learning or reduce gender stereotyping. In any event, the program proved to be "not sustainable," Datnow and Hubbard conclude. Wilson's Democratic successor, Gray Davis, ended state support for the project; only two of the single-sex programs are still operating.

As the 1990s ended, single-sex education was being vigorously debated both among experts and advocacy

Women's Colleges Decline, Enrollments Rise

Although the number of U.S. women's colleges has been declining for 40 years, enrollments nearly doubled over the past decade.

Women's college advocates make parallel arguments to those being advanced for all-girl schools at the elementary and secondary levels: the need to give women a better opportunity to develop self-esteem and confidence and to present more women as role models in the curriculum and at the institution itself.

"It's much, much easier for men to be validated as learners in most educational settings," Sebrechts says. "For women, when they are in a women-centered setting, it is often the first time that they've been feeling that kind of validation."

"The environment is different," Vandenberg says. "We have almost 50 percent women faculty. Students' peers are other smart women."

For its part, the American Association of University Women — the major organization opposing expanded single-sex education at the K-12 level — does not oppose private women's colleges. "Women's colleges came up at a time when there was no other way," says Nancy Zirkin, the association's director of

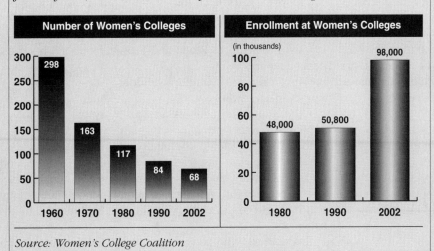

Source: Women's College Coalition

public policy. "It's a completely different set of circumstances."

Despite a high retention rate of around 80 percent, Vandenberg concedes that some women leave Mount Holyoke to go to coeducational schools. The women who stay can find plenty of men at the other members of a five-college consortium — Amherst, Hampshire, Smith and the University of Massachusetts-Amherst — located within a nine-mile radius.

Overall, students and alumnae continue to favor maintaining Holyoke as a women's college, Vandenberg says. "I don't see it changing in the near future," she concludes.

---

[1] For background, see Irene Harwarth, Mindi Maline and Elizabeth DeBra, "Women's Colleges in the United States: History, Issues, and Challenges," U.S. Dept. of Education, Office of Educational Research and Improvement (www.ed.gov/offices/OERI/PLLI/webreprt.html), June 1997; and Barbara M. Solomon, *In the Company of Educated Women: A History of Women and Higher Education in America* (1985).

[2] The cases are *Mississippi University for Women v. Hogan*, 458 U.S. 718 (1982), and *United States v. Virginia*, 518 U.S. 515 (1996).

---

groups and on Capitol Hill. In 1995, the AAUW voiced "guarded enthusiasm" for single-sex classes on a short-term basis to compensate for past discrimination against girls. [25]

A 1997 AAUW symposium on single-sex education included speakers on both sides. Riordan of Providence College presented his research concluding that single-sex schools "work for boys and girls," in particular for girls and minority boys or girls. But in her review of research in the field, Valerie Lee, a professor of education at the University of Michigan, concluded that separating students by gender was "misguided." In publishing the proceedings, the AAUW adopted a largely critical

tone, concluding that there was "no evidence that single-sex education in general 'works' or 'is better' than co-education." [26]

Meanwhile in Washington, lawmakers were pushing proposals in Congress to encourage local school systems to experiment with single-sex programs. The Senate approved money for demonstration grants in 1994 as part of an omnibus education bill, but the provision was dropped from the final version. Sen. Kay Bailey Hutchison, R-Texas, introduced a bill in 1995 to give school districts a waiver from Title IX for single-gender programs for disadvantaged pupils, but it died in committee. Through the rest of the

decade, other proposals similarly failed to advance.

With a new Congress and a new administration, single-sex advocates picked up a visible and influential ally: former first lady Hillary Rodham Clinton, New York's newly elected junior senator. Clinton — a graduate of Wellesley College, one of the nation's most prestigious women's schools — teamed with Hutchison last year to insert funding for single-sex schools and classes into President Bush's education-reform bill as it moved through the Senate. "There should not be any obstacle to providing single-sex choice within the public school system," Clinton, a Democrat, said during Senate debate on June 7.

The amendment passed by voice vote and stayed in the final bill. As enacted, the law authorized up to $450 million for a variety of demonstration projects, including single-gender schools or classes, but Congress ended up appropriating only $385 million. The law — which Bush signed on Jan. 8 — directed the secretary of Education to issue guidelines and criteria for grants within 120 days of enactment.

CURRENT SITUATION

Starting New Schools

Lynn Spampinato helped introduce single-sex classes five years ago at Maria Mitchell Elementary School in inner-city Denver. She credits the decision with an academic turnaround that slashed by 50 percent the number of students at the school scoring in the lowest quarter on a nationwide achievement test.

Now, back in her native Pennsylvania, Spampinato hopes to introduce what she calls "gender-separate" education to help turn around a high-poverty, all-black middle school in Philadelphia. As regional director for a private company named to manage three failing schools in the troubled Philadelphia system, Spampinato plans literally to cut FitzSimons Middle School in half and divide the 660 students into separate "leadership academies" — one for boys and one for girls.

"We hope to take the social pressure off the kids and really raise the standards," she says. "We believe that in a gender-separate environment, we can do a lot in building self-esteem, developing character and creating a very safe, homey place for children to excel."

FitzSimons is one of at least four public schools across the country likely to open with single-sex classrooms for the first time when the new academic year starts later this summer. Others include Brighter Choice Charter School in Albany, N.Y.; William A. Lawson International Peace and Prosperity Preparatory Academy for Boys in Houston; and Southern Middle School in Louisville, Ky.

Other education activists are busily putting together plans for single-sex schools to open later. A conference of boys' schools late last month heard organizers making pitches for two new all-boy schools for minority neighborhoods in Brooklyn and Lower Manhattan.

Spampinato, who served as an administrator in the Philadelphia school system for two years before assuming her current position with Victory Schools, Inc., took her idea to the city's newly created School Reform Commission. The commission supplanted the former Board of Education after the state took over the city's public schools in December 2001. "They were very supportive if we had community support," Spampinato says.

So far, Spampinato says she has found "more support than dissent" from parents. "One of the things that parents are most concerned about is safety," she says. "They seem to like it [from] that perspective."

The *Philadelphia Inquirer*, however, found divided reaction among teachers and students. [27] Reporter Susan Snyder described teachers as "on the fence," with some questioning whether the plan would make any difference in academic performance. Students' opinions were said to be divided along gender lines: "Girls liked the idea, but boys didn't."

Spampinato acknowledges that the changed attitude in Washington has helped her push the idea. "The secretary of Education is offering support," she says. "There will be

new funding." A graduate herself of a Catholic girls' high school in Pittsburgh, Spampinato believes single-sex education should be available for low-income youngsters in the same way that it has been available in private or parochial schools for families who could afford it.

Organizers of the other new single-sex schools voice similar sentiments. "This is an option that is widely available for private schools, says Tom Carroll, chairman of Brighter Choice, scheduled to open with 90 kindergartners and first-graders divided by gender. "Wherever these schools are set up, people are fighting to get into them." [28]

In Louisville, Southern Middle School will separate the students for most classes, though boys and girls will be together for some activities — such as band and choir — and at lunch. Principal Anita Jones says the plan will reduce distractions for students. "They'll focus on education instead of on the opposite sex," she says. "This isn't a panacea . . . but we had to do something." [29]

Houston's new boys' academy — already being designated as WALIPP Prep — is expected to open in a predominantly black neighborhood. The school is aimed at giving black students strong male role models and mentors. "What I want to do is develop strong men, and I think that can be done by bringing strong men around these boys," says Audrey Lawson, whose husband is pastor of a local Baptist church. [30]

Revising Federal Rules?

Advocates of single-sex education are urging the Department of Education to impose few requirements for public school systems wanting to institute single-sex schools or classes. Opponents are urging the department

At Issue

Should federal regulations make it easier for school districts to establish single-sex schools or classes?

CORNELIUS RIORDAN
PROFESSOR OF SOCIOLOGY
PROVIDENCE COLLEGE

WRITTEN FOR THE CQ RESEARCHER, JULY 2002

yes

Since evaluation is a concurrent part of funding for all school reform efforts, a wealth of data exists on most reform programs. Scientific investigation of education programs has become the benchmark, as it should, for judging the promise of any reform. In fact, the reauthorization of the Elementary and Secondary School Act of 2001 has raised the level of research to a higher level, calling for more studies using rigorous, scientifically-based, objective procedures to obtain valid knowledge.

Yet, research on single-sex schooling has never been conducted in a scientific manner in the public sector. Until now, the politicalization of the issue by opposition groups has closed down the scientific process on single-sex schools.

Despite the posturing by opponents and proponents, no one knows the full extent to which single-sex schools are more effective than coeducational schools, and for what types of students, and at what grade levels and for how long. There is simply not enough research on the issue to make such a determination, especially in the public sector. The relaxing of Title IX guidelines by the Department of Education will provide the necessary first step towards increasing the number of single-sex schools and classes so the research can be conducted.

What do we know from the high-quality empirical studies that have been done, primarily in the private sector? Single-sex schools help to improve student achievement. They work for girls and boys, whites and non-whites, but this effect is limited to students of low socioeconomic status and/or students who are disadvantaged historically.

The major factor that conditions the strength of single-sex effects is social class, and since class and race are inextricably linked, the effects are also conditioned by race, and sometimes by gender. Impoverished, desperate and powerless children in lower-tiered schools stand to gain the most from single-sex schools. There is no evidence in the United States showing that they would do better in coeducational schools.

Single-sex schools are no longer limited to providing an alternative educational avenue for some girls; today some boys also need this type of school organization in order to learn effectively.

Moreover, single-sex schools can help to bring about greater race and social-class equity that have now become the final frontiers in establishing true equality of educational opportunity for everyone.

DAVID SADKER
PROFESSOR OF EDUCATION,
AMERICAN UNIVERSITY

WRITTEN FOR THE CQ RESEARCHER, JULY 2002

no

The proposed loosening of the rules on creating single-sex public schools is problematic for several reasons, but I will focus on three: the need for research, the potential misuse of such schools and the nation's history of gender-biased funding.

First, the effectiveness of single-sex schools is a big educational question mark. Some studies show that they are more effective for girls than boys, others that only lower-class students benefit and still others that such schools intensify gender stereotypes and homophobia. Critics point out that many of the academic successes of these schools may be due to smaller classes, engaged parents and well-trained teachers, not to the fact that they are single sex. No wonder there is confusion!

We need to craft a thoughtful, controlled and studied implementation of single-sex schooling to untangle this conflicting body of research. The administration's proposed loosening of the regulations sidesteps the many unanswered research questions, creating schools rather than examining them. I predict that some will fail and some will succeed, and we will miss many opportunities to learn why.

My second concern is some of these schools could do harm. While the girls' schools in Harlem and Chicago seem to be successes, the college-prep model is not the only one out there. Many supporters of single-sex schools describe the very different schools that they would create, ranging from schools built on each sex's unique "brain structure" to schools teaching that female submission is part of a "natural law." Their idea of a good girls' school is one focusing on child rearing and de-emphasizing careers in science, while boys would learn how to read by using war poetry. In the failed California experiment, single-sex schools were seen as a means to discipline boys. Without clear protections from unfair treatment, sex-role stereotypes may be intensified, and individual needs ignored.

My final point is a history lesson, reminding us why Title IX restricted single-sex schools in the first place. Three decades ago, Philadelphia, Boston and most major cities were proud of their single-sex schools. While the cities argued that the girls' and boys' schools were "comparable," the courts found the girls' schools underfunded and clearly inferior.

Without safeguards requiring "equitable" schools, we may once again create two sets of schools, separate and unequal. This gender gap in educational spending is a trend we should reverse, not promote, and Title IX is a law we should strengthen, not weaken.

to leave Title IX regulations completely unchanged. Alternatively, they say school systems should be required to justify any single-sex schools or classes and to be subject to prior approval and continuing oversight from federal officials.

The opposing positions emerge in comments filed before a July 8 deadline in response to a "notice of intent to regulate" issued by the department's Office of Civil Rights (OCR) on May 8. The notice asked for comments on a series of questions to be considered in drafting rules designed "to provide more flexibility for educators to establish single-sex classes and schools at the elementary and secondary level."

The major participants in the debate appear to agree on only one of the major questions presented: participation in single-sex schools or classes should be voluntary, not mandatory, for students and families. But they disagree sharply on other questions.

Supporters says schools should not be required to "explain the benefits" of single-sex classes before instituting the practice. While saying that the benefits are well established, Sax, of the National Association for the Advancement of Single-Sex Public Education, warns that a future administration opposed to single-sex education could use such a requirement to block proposed programs.

Opponents, however, insist that existing law dictates that school districts justify any use of single-sex classes. "Both Title IX and the Constitution properly place the burden of justifying single-sex programs on the school

district choosing to establish such programs," the National Women's Law Center says. The center says that school districts should be required to seek approval from OCR before implementation of any single-sex classes and that OCR "must monitor the implementation . . . to ensure continued compliance with the law."

Opponents are also calling for several other conditions for establishing single-sex schools or classes that supporters warn could effectively prevent school districts from adopting such programs. Most significantly, they say single-sex schools or classes must be provided for both sexes rather than relying

Mount Holyoke College in western Massachusetts is among a dwindling number of U.S. women's colleges. Twice in recent years it considered following the trend toward coeducation — but decided to remain exclusively for women.

on a coeducational school or class to serve students who do not have a single-sex program available to them. And the opponents say that schools or classes for both sexes must be "equal," not just "comparable" — as the department's notice suggested.

"Equality, not comparability, must be the standard," the NOW Legal Defense Fund says, "and only a single-sex option could meet that standard."

Supporters, however, say school districts should be allowed to establish

programs for students of one gender but not the other. "The needs of each sex are often different," Providence College's Riordan writes. "Thus, the emphasis of a school for boys should not be required to be comparable to the emphasis of a school for girls."

"Where a school district offers a single-sex school for girls, it should suffice to prove that it offers equal opportunities to boys in a coed school," says Salomone of the St. John's University School of Law. Pointing to the Supreme Court's decision in the VMI cases, she says the ruling does not require programs to be "exactly identical" for both sexes. A stricter standard, she says, "could hobble" single-sex initiatives.

The opposing sides have a measure of agreement on one minor question in the notice: "Are there any classes which should not be permitted to be single-sex?" Citing past and continuing gender discrimination in vocational training, the NOW Legal Defense Fund says there should be no "general green light" for single-sex vocational or technical classes.

Sax says he is "sympathetic" to the concern that single-sex classes in some subjects could "reinforce gender stereotypes." For that reason, he says, the rules might prohibit girls-only cosmetology classes or boys-only computer classes.

Groups opposing any change in the rules include two powerful education lobbies — the National Education Association and the National Congress of PTAs — as well as the American Civil Liberties Union. "Public schools have the obligation to ensure that both females and males can obtain an education in a coeducational setting free from sex discrimination," the ACLU says.

Supporters counter that single-sex programs will promote rather than retard the goal of equal educational opportunity. "Impoverished, desperate and powerless children in lower-tiered schools stand to gain the most from single-sex schools," Riordan writes.

Another comment period will be required once OCR officials draft a proposed rule — making it unlikely that a final rule will be adopted before fall, at the earliest.

OUTLOOK

A New Era?

Single-sex education seemed on the verge of virtual extinction in the United States a decade ago. Separate schools for boys and girls were widely thought to be illegal in public education and were becoming less and less popular among private or parochial schools as well as colleges and universities.

The cumulative effect of guardedly favorable research studies and reconsideration of boys' and girls' respective learning styles and behavior, however, has put single-sex education back on the map. With the Bush administration's support for revising the legal rules on single-sex education, advocates are predicting a sharp increase in the number of single-sex schools or classes at the elementary and secondary levels, while critics and skeptics are softening their previous opposition.

"I really think that we are on the brink of a new era," says Sax, of the National Association for the Advancement of Single-Sex Public Education. "In the next few years, we're going

to see a tremendous increase in the number of single-sex schools."

Sax notes not only the new schools expected to open this year or next but also the recent disclosure that Moten Elementary School in southeast Washington, D.C., had quietly instituted single-sex classes without notifying the school system's central office. The move came to light only when officials noticed a sharp increase in students' test scores and asked for an explanation. [31] "I suspect that there are other schools out there that we don't know about," Sax says.

The AAUW's Zirkin emphasizes that even with the four new schools slated to open later this summer, the number of single-sex public schools remains tiny. "I don't call four a trend," she says. Along with other opponents or critics, however, Zirkin now calls for carefully constructed pilot projects to study the effectiveness of single-sex schools or classes — without any changes in the Title IX regulations covering sex discrimination at federally financed schools and colleges.

"The parameters have to be designed in such a way as to not disadvantage girls or boys, so that there isn't sex stereotyping of girls going on and so that there isn't any bias from the get-go," Zirkin says. "Then evaluate the pilot project and see where you are."

Academic skeptics are also muting their criticisms. "As a choice for some students, this is worth trying," the University of Toronto's Datnow says. American University's Sadker agrees on the need for more research but cautions against exaggerating the potential benefits of single-sex education or ignoring the potential costs to other public schools.

"It's fine to have limited single-sex schools that we can evaluate and judge in an objective way, not a politicized way, because we could learn from that," Sadker says. "I am against

saying this is a solution to the problem: Let's pull off the most active girls and parents from the public school system and put them in a single-sex schools."

Long-time proponent Riordan of Providence College cautions advocates that even with support from the administration and Congress, advances in single-sex education will be slow in coming. "It takes an awful lot of effort to open a school even when there's no one against you," Riordan says. He says a realistic expectation is for the number of single-sex schools to double over the next three to five years.

"What we may see is an increase in coeducational schools of single-sex classes," says Wadsworth of the International Boys' School Coalition. "That could be done with changes that are less complex as long as it's viewed as legally viable."

Meanwhile, at Harlem's Young Women's Leadership School, Principal Ponze says she is baffled by the debate. "I don't understand why this should be a bone of contention," she says. "Why can't there be this choice for girls?"

Creating single-sex schools, Ponze concludes, "should be as easy as the demand in the community creates. If that's what the community wants, then the community should have the right to open single-sex schools or classrooms."

Notes

[1] The school's Web site is at www.tywls.org; information about the loosely affiliated Young Women's Leadership Charter School of Chicago can be found at www.ywcls.org.

[2] Quoted in Katherine Roth, "Ahead of New Federal Guidelines, Education Secretary Visits Single-Sex Public School," The Associated Press, May 30, 2002.

[3] For background, see Sarah Glazer, "Boys' Emotional Needs," The CQ Researcher, June

18, 1999, pp. 521-544; and Charles S. Clark, "Education and Gender," *The CQ Researcher*, June 3, 1994, pp. 481-504.

[4] American Association of University Women Educational Foundation, *How Schools Shortchange Girls* (1992).

[5] Christina Hoff Sommers, *The War Against Boys: How Misguided Feminism Is Harming Our Young Men* (2000).

[6] See Patricia B. Campbell and Ellen Wahl, "What's Sex Got to Do With It? Simplistic Questions, Complex Answers," in *Separated by Sex: A Critical Look at Single-Sex Education for Girls* (1998), American Association of University Women Educational Foundation, p. 64.

[7] Kenneth J. Rowe, "Gender Differences in Students' Experiences and Outcomes of Schooling? Exploring 'Real' Effects from Recent and Emerging Evidence-Based Research in Teacher and School Effectiveness," Oct. 31, 2000 (www.acer.edu.au). The April 17, 2000, press release, "Boys and Girls Perform Better at School in Single-Sex Environments," can also be found on the Web site.

[8] Cornelius Riordan, *Girls and Boys in School: Together or Separate?* (1990), pp. 110-113.

[9] Amanda Datnow, Lea Hubbard and Elisabeth Woody, "Is Single Gender Schooling Viable in the Public Sector? Lessons From California's Pilot Program," May 2001, http://www.oise.utoronto.ca/depts/tps/adatnow/research.html#single. For a shortened version, see Amanda Datnow and Lea Hubbard, "Are Single-Sex Schools Sustainable in the Public Sector?" in Datnow and Hubbard (eds.), *Gender in Policy and Practice: Perspectives on Single-Sex and Coeducational Schooling* (forthcoming, July/August 2002).

[10] *Garrett v. Board of Education of School District of Detroit*, 775 F.Supp 1004 (E.D. Mich. 1991). For coverage, see Mark Walsh, "Detroit Admits Female Students," *Education Week*, Sept. 4, 1991.

[11] The case is *Newberg v. School District of Philadelphia*, 478 A.2d 1352 (Pa. Super. Ct. 1984).

[12] The case is *United States v. Virginia*, 518 U.S. 515 (1996). See Kenneth Jost, *The Supreme Court Yearbook, 1995-1996* (1996), pp. 38-42.

[13] David Tyack and Elisabeth Hansot, *Learning Together: A History of Coeducation in American Schools* (1990), p. 11. Further back-

ground drawn from their account.

[14] William T. Harris, "St. Louis School Report for 1870," summarized in Tyack and Hansot, *op. cit.*, pp. 101-103.

[15] For background, see Jane Tanner, "Women in Sports," *The CQ Researcher*, May 11, 2001, pp. 401-424.

[16] See U.S. Dept. of Education, "Guidelines on Current Title IX Requirements Related to Single-Sex Classes and Schools," *Federal Register*, May 3, 2002, www.ed.gov/offices/OCR/t9-guidelines-ss.html.

[17] *Ibid.*

[18] Project on Equal Education Rights, NOW Legal Defense and Education Fund, "Stalled at the Start: Government Action on Sex Bias in the Schools" (1977), pp. 33-39, cited in Tyack and Hansot, *op. cit.*, p. 256.

[19] *Ibid.*, p. 264.

[20] The case is *Vorcheimer v. School District of Philadelphia*, 532 F.2d 880 (3d. Cir. 1976), affirmed by an equally divided court, 430 U.S. 703 (1977).

[21] The case is *Grove City College v. Bell*, 465 U.S. 555 (1984).

[22] The cases are *Mississippi University for Women v. Hogan*, 458 U.S. 718 (1982) and *United States v. Virginia*, 518 U.S. 515 (1996).

[23] See U.S. General Accounting Office, *Public Education: Issues Involving Single-Gender*

Schools and Programs, May 1996, pp. 7-11.

[24] Some background drawn from *ibid*.

[25] American Association of University Women Educational Foundation, "Growing Smart: What's Working for Girls in Schools," 1995, pp. 2, 10-11.

[26] American Association of University Women Educational Foundation, "Separated by Sex: A Critical Look at Single-Sex Education for Girls," 1998, pp. 2-3. Riordan's paper appears at pp. 53-62, Lee's at pp. 41-52.

[27] See Susan Snyder, "A School Trial Will Separate the Sexes," *The Philadelphia Inquirer*, June 17, 2002, p. A1.

[28] Quoted in Rick Karlin, "School Champions Single-Sex Classes," (Albany) *Times Union*, May 9, 2002, p. A1.

[29] Quoted in Chris Kenning, "Southern Middle Will Separate Boys, Girls," *The* (Louisville) *Courier-Journal*, June 18, 2002.

[30] Quoted in Melanie Markley, "Helping Boys Make the Grade," *Houston Chronicle*, May 2, 2002, p. A1.

[31] See Justin Blum, "Scores Soar at D.C. School With Same-Sex Classes," *The Washington Post*, June 27, 2002, p. A1.

Bibliography

Selected Sources

Books

Datnow, Amanda, and Lea Hubbard, eds., *Gender in Policy and Practice: Perspectives on Single-Sex and Coeducational Schooling*, **Routledge, forthcoming (July/August 2002).**

An anthology of 16 articles by experts representing a range of views on single-sex and coeducational schools. Datnow is an assistant professor of education at the University of Toronto; Hubbard is an assistant research scientist in sociology at the University of California-San Diego.

Faragher, John Mack, and Florence Howe, *Women and Higher Education in American History*, **W.W. Norton, 1988.**

Includes 10 essays on the history of women and higher education in America.

Riordan, Cornelius, *Girls and Boys in School: Together or Separate?* **Teachers College, 1990.**

Reviews the then-existing research on academic results of single-sex and coeducational schools. Includes 16-page list of references. Riordan is a professor of sociology at Providence College and an advocate of expanded single-sex education. His more recent review of the issue is included in the Datnow and Hubbard anthology.

Sadker, Myra, and David Sadker, *Failing at Fairness: How America's School Cheat Girls*, **Charles Scribners' Sons, 1994.**

Non-technical survey of issues that authors say keep females from achieving as well as males in school. David Sadker is a professor of education at American University; his wife was also a professor at American until her death in 1995.

Solomon, Barbara M., *In the Company of Educated Women: A History of Women and Higher Education in America*, **Yale University Press, 1985.**

Details the history of higher education for women from the evolution of "seminaries" for women into women's colleges in the 19th century through the expansion of coeducation and the decline in the number and student population of women's colleges in the late 20th century. Includes detailed notes, 28-page bibliography.

Sommers, Christina Hoff, *The War Against Boys: How Misguided Feminism Is Harming Our Young Men*, **Simon & Schuster, 2000.**

Sommers, a fellow at the American Enterprise Institute, criticizes claims that schools shortchange girls, arguing instead that boys are being shortchanged by school systems that "fail to address the problem of male underachievement."

Stabiner, Karen, *All Girls: Single-Sex Education and Why It Matters*, **Riverhead, forthcoming (August 2002).**

Journalistic account of a pivotal year in the lives of two young women — one white and the other African-American — attending all-girls' schools, located on opposite coasts: an elite Los Angeles prep school and The Young Women's Leadership School in East Harlem, N.Y.

Tyack, David, and Elisabeth Hansot, *Learning Together: A History of Coeducation in American Schools*, **Yale University Press, 1990.**

Traces the history of coeducation in America from its gradual evolution through the 19th century through the critiques from gender-equity advocates in the 1970s and '80s. Includes detailed notes. Tyack is professor emeritus and Hansot professor emerita at Stanford University's School of Education.

Articles

Ransome, Whitney, and Meg Milne Moulton, "Why Girls Schools? The Difference in Girl-Centered Education," *Fordham Law Journal*, **Vol. 29, No. 2 (December 2001), pp. 589-599.**

Arguments for single-sex education for girls by the executive directors of the National Coalition of Girls' Schools.

Webb, Stephen H., "Defending All-Male Education: A New Cultural Moment for a Renewed Debate," *Fordham Law Journal*, **Vol. 29, No. 2 (December 2001), pp. 601-610.**

Defense of single-sex education for boys by an associate professor of religion and philosophy at Wabash College, in Crawfordsville, Ind.

Reports and Studies

American Association of University Women, *How Schools Shortchange Girls: The AAUW Report*, **1992.**

Critical report compiled by Wellesley College Center for Research on Women claimed girls are shortchanged by less attention in classrooms and fewer role models than boys. Includes detailed notes, appendixes.

American Association of University Women Educational Foundation, "Separated by Sex: A Critical Look at Single-Sex Education for Girls," 1998.

The 93-page report includes a somewhat critical summary and an overview of research followed by four papers by experts representing a range of views presented at an AAUW-sponsored symposium. Each paper includes detailed notes. For an earlier, less critical report, see American Association of University Women Educational Foundation, "Growing Smart: What's Working for Girls in Schools," 1995.

17 Gay Marriage

KENNETH JOST

As a lawyer with Gay and Lesbian Advocates and Defenders (GLAD), Mary Bonauto sympathized with the couples who came to her for help. Many of their problems — health benefits that could not be shared, child-custody limits, tax penalties — grew out of the inability of same-sex couples to be legally married.

But throughout most of the 1990s, Bonauto fended off the gay-marriage issue as premature: Not yet, she would say, the time is not right. In 1998, however, she and other GLAD lawyers decided the time for action had come, and under a unique provision of Vermont's constitution they sued the state.

In a stunning decision in December 1999, the Vermont Supreme Court ordered the legislature to grant gay and lesbian couples the same legal benefits enjoyed by married heterosexuals. Over protests from social conservatives, the legislature created a new, marriage-like legal status for same-sex couples: "civil unions." [1]

Now Bonauto is hoping to go even further in Massachusetts. Hillary and Julie Goodridge and six other gay and lesbian couples represented by GLAD are anxiously awaiting a decision from the state's highest court in a suit — *Goodridge v. Massachusetts Department of Public Health* — that could make Massachusetts the first state to recognize gay marriage.

The Goodridges see nothing extraordinary about their legal plea. Instead, they find it more surprising that the law gives them no opportunity to

From *The CQ Researcher,*
September 5, 2003.

Massachusetts could become the first state to recognize gay marriage if the state's highest court rules in favor of Hillary and Julie Goodridge, here with their daughter Annie, and other gay couples. Gay-rights advocates say homosexuals need and deserve the same symbolic and practical benefits for their relationships enjoyed by heterosexuals. But religious groups and social conservatives say legal recognition for same-sex couples runs counter to historical tradition, moral order and the best interests of children and society at large.

Mainframe Photographics, Inc.

formalize their relationship even though they have been together for 16 years and have been raising a daughter together for the last eight.

"We have a child. We own real estate together. We have wills. We have health-care proxies. But we have no legal relationship to each other," Julie explains. "That's what we're trying to change with the marriage case."

Gay-rights advocates emphasize the distinction between legalizing civil marriage between same-sex couples and gaining religious recognition for gay marriages. "Every religion can decide for itself whether to perform or

honor any marriage," says Evan Wolfson, a longtime gay-rights litigator, who is now executive director of the New York-based advocacy group Freedom to Marry. "But no religion should be able to dictate who gets a civil marriage license."

Even so, an array of religious and conservative advocacy groups strongly opposes legal recognition for same-sex couples, saying it runs counter to historical tradition, moral order and the best interests of children and society at large.

"We favor the tradition of a one-man, one-woman marriage," says Connie Mackey, vice president of the Family Research Council, a Washington-based Christian organization. "We reject the attempts of the gay community to foist its agenda on the general public."

"Marriage means the union of one man and one woman," says Ron Crews, president of the Massachusetts Family Institute, which filed a friend-of-the-court brief in the Massachusetts case. "It's a risky business for courts or legislatures to get into the business of changing the definition of a word."

"Only the relationship between a man and a woman has a natural association with the generation of new children," says Daniel Avila, an attorney with the Massachusetts Catholic Conference. "No other relationship has that potential."

Advocates of same-sex marriage counter that allowing gay men and lesbians to marry would strengthen their relationships and also provide concrete legal protections and economic benefits.

Support for Gay Relationships Drops

Americans' support for legal homosexual relations and gay civil unions rose steadily from the 1960s through the 1980s but declined measurably after the Supreme Court struck down a Texas anti-sodomy law on June 26. The ruling had been hailed as clearing the way for new gay civil rights, but recent polls appear to indicate a backlash against recognizing same-sex relationships.

Should homosexual relations between consenting adults be legal?

43%	43%	60%	35%	48%	46%
1977		**May 5-7, 2003**		**July 25-26, 2003**	

Should homosexual couples be allowed to form legal civil unions?

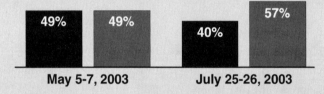

49%	49%	40%	57%
May 5-7, 2003		**July 25-26, 2003**	

In general, should homosexuals have equal rights in terms of job opportunities?

88%

9%

Should homosexual couples have the legal right to adopt a child?

49%

48%

Do you favor a constitutional amendment that would define marriage as between a man and a woman, thus barring marriages between gay or lesbian couples?

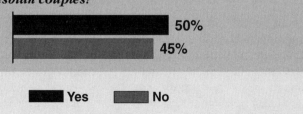

50%

45%

■ Yes   ■ No

Source: Gallop Poll, 1977; USA Today/CNN/Gallup Poll, May 5-7, July 25-26, 2003

"Only marriage conveys the love and commitment that others automatically understand and respect," Bonauto says. "Only marriage provides a legal safety net protecting the couple's emotional bonds and their economic security."

"Civil marriage is a powerful and important affirmation of love, a source of social recognition and support, and the legal gateway to a vast array of protections, responsibilities and benefits, most of which cannot be replicated in any other way," Wolfson says.

Supporters also say legalizing same-sex marriage will help, not hurt, the increasing number of children being raised by gay or lesbian parents. "It means a great deal to the kids that their parents have all the support and acknowledgment that a family deserves," Wolfson says. (*See story, p. 338.*)

The seven couples who filed suit in Massachusetts have been together for periods ranging from three to more than 30 years. Four of the couples have children. (*See box, p. 334.*) In a news conference when the suit was filed in April 2001, several of the plaintiffs noted practical problems that they had encountered because they were not married. But the Goodridges also say they were prompted to join the suit by a surprising exchange with their then 5-year-old daughter Annie.

One night, after listening to the Beatles' song "All You Need Is Love," Hillary asked Annie if she knew any people who loved each other. Annie listed several of her mothers' married friends.

"What about Mommy and Ma?" Hillary asked, using the names she and Julie had taken for themselves before Annie's birth.

"If you loved each other," Annie replied, "you'd get married."

The Supreme Judicial Court of Massachusetts heard arguments in the case on March 4. The state attorney general's office urged the seven justices to reject the suit, saying the legislature had a rational basis — encouraging procreation and child rearing — for limiting marriage to heterosexual couples. Moreover, argued Assistant State Attorney General Judith Yogman, any change was up to the legislature, not the courts.

The court's unofficial deadline for a decision passed in mid-July, but Bonauto says she is not surprised that the justices are taking their time with the case. "This is an opinion that is being watched very carefully," she says. "The pressure here is tremendous."

The gay-marriage issue has simmered for decades but did not become a priority for gay-rights advocates till the 1990s. Before the Vermont case, state courts in Hawaii and Alaska issued preliminary rulings in favor of gay marriage, but the court moves were thwarted by state constitutional amendments.

In the meantime, however, the Netherlands and Belgium became the first and second countries to recognize same-sex marriage, both by parliamentary action. Then in June the Canadian government announced that it would bow to a ruling by Ontario's highest provincial court and prepare legislation to legalize marriage for same-sex couples throughout the country.

The issue moved to the top of the U.S. political agenda following a landmark decision by the Supreme Court that invalidated state laws against gay sex. The June 26 ruling in *Lawrence v. Texas* said homosexuals have the right to engage in physically intimate conduct without government intervention.

The opinion did not deal directly with same-sex marriage. But Bonauto says the ruling supports the gay-marriage suit. "*Lawrence* confirmed what we had already been arguing —

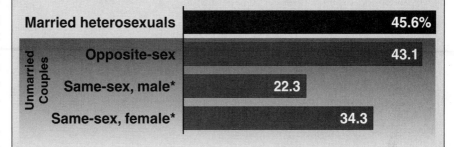

Many Gay Couples Have Children

Nearly a quarter of the gay couples living together and a third of the lesbians are raising children. Among heterosexuals, 46 percent of married couples and 43 percent of unmarried couples have children.

Average percentage of U.S. households with children under 18

Married heterosexuals	**45.6%**
Unmarried Couples — **Opposite-sex**	43.1
Unmarried Couples — **Same-sex, male***	22.3
Unmarried Couples — **Same-sex, female***	34.3

* The children either belong to one of the partners or are biologically unrelated, such as foster children or adoptees.

Source: "Married-Couple and Unmarried-Partner Households: 2000," Census 2000, U.S. Census Bureau

that if a right is fundamental for some, it's fundamental for all," she says. "There's not a gay exception in the Constitution."

A leading academic opponent of same-sex marriage says the *Lawrence* decision has mobilized partisans on both sides of the issue. "It has certainly energized the gay-rights movement," says Lynn Wardle, a professor at Brigham Young University Law School in Provo, Utah. "It's also going to energize the conservative, pro-family movement. So there are going to be political clashes."

Gay-marriage supporters hope — and opponents fear — that a ruling to recognize same-sex relationships in one state will have a cascading effect in other states. Opponents hope that so-called defense-of-marriage (DOMA) laws enacted by Congress and 37 states will allow individual states to refuse to recognize same-sex marriages granted elsewhere.

President Bush entered the debate

on July 30 by saying his administration is looking at ways to "codify" the definition of marriage as one man, one woman. Some opponents of gay marriage say a constitutional amendment is needed, but acknowledge that it will be difficult to win the two-thirds majority in Congress and approval by three-fourths of the states to ratify an amendment.

For their part, all but two of the Democratic presidential candidates favor granting legal benefits to same-sex couples, but only three contenders — all of whom are low in the polls — favor gay marriage. [2]

Meanwhile, opinion polls indicate an apparent backlash on the issue in the weeks since the *Lawrence* decision. Support for civil unions had been increasing, but it dropped by 10 percentage points or more in polls conducted in May and July. (*See box, p. 330.*)

As the issue proceeds in the courts and elsewhere, here are some of the major questions being debated:

Blessing Gay Marriage Widely Opposed in U.S.

Former Boston priest Jon Schum does not think of himself as a renegade, but he goes against the Roman Catholic Church's official teachings: He lives in a committed relationship with another man and performs commitment ceremonies for gay and lesbian couples.

Schum never sought out opportunities to officiate at same-sex ceremonies. But people who heard about him through Dignity, a gay Catholic organization, asked him to help them celebrate their unions "in the context of their Catholic traditions."

The half-dozen ceremonies Schum has performed over the past two years have had most of the trappings of a Catholic wedding, including scripture readings and exchanged vows and rings. He believes they are fully Catholic in substance as well. "The love between gay and lesbian persons is just as real, just as authentic, just as holy, just as sacramental, as the love between any married persons," Schum says.

The church hierarchy, however, strongly opposes any recognition for same-sex unions, either within the church or in law. "There are absolutely no grounds for considering homosexual unions to be in any way similar or even remotely analogous to God's plan for marriage and family," the Vatican said in a doctrinal statement on July 31. The statement said Catholic lawmakers have "a moral duty" to oppose any moves to recognize gay marriage. [1]

The U.S. Conference of Catholic Bishops had earlier issued a similar statement opposing "attempts to grant the legal status of marriage" to same-sex relationships. "No same-sex union can realize the full and unique potential which the marital relationship expresses," the conference's secretariat for family, laity, women and youth said in a June 3 policy statement.

The blessing of same-sex unions also is opposed by most other U.S. denominations, including Eastern Orthodoxy, the Southern Baptist Convention and other evangelical Protestant denominations, the Church of Jesus Christ of Latter-day Saints, the Orthodox and Conservative branches of Judaism, and Islam. [2]

The Episcopal Church U.S.A. officially recognized the blessing of same-sex unions at its August convention in Minneapolis but declined to establish a liturgy for those ceremonies. The compromise culminated a tumultuous convention dominated by a sharp debate over the eventual election of an openly gay priest, V. Gene Robinson, as bishop of New Hampshire. [3]

Among other mainline Protestant denominations, the United Methodist Church bans same-sex ceremonies while the Presbyterian Church U.S.A. allows clergy to officiate at same-sex rituals but specifies that such events differ from marriages. The Evangelical Lutheran Church plans a report on the issue in 2005.

Meanwhile, ministers in the predominantly gay Universal Fellowship of Metropolitan Community Churches have performed same-sex commitment ceremonies since 1968. The Unitarian Universalist Association and the United Church of Christ advocate tolerance for same-sex unions. Judaism's liberal Reform branch gives rabbis the option of presiding at gay commitment ceremonies.

Would recognizing same-sex unions benefit gay men and lesbians?

Bill Flanigan and Robert Daniel, a gay couple in San Francisco, did all that they could to formalize their relationship. They registered as domestic partners, as permitted under a San Francisco ordinance, and Daniel executed a health-care proxy allowing Flanigan to make medical decisions relating to Daniel's treatment for AIDS.

The preparations were not enough, however, when a critically ill Daniel was admitted to the University of Maryland's Shock Trauma Center in Baltimore on Oct. 16, 2000. Hospital personnel barred Flanigan from Daniel's room for four hours until Daniel's mother and sister arrived to give permission. By then, Daniel was uncon-

scious, his eyes taped shut. He died with no chance for the two men to say goodbye.

Lawyers for Lambda Legal Defense and Education Fund, an advocacy group for gays, say the hospital's refusal shows that gay men and lesbians can gain the practical benefits that heterosexual couples take for granted only if they are allowed to legally marry. "We are a nation divided by discrimination in marriage," says attorney David Buckel. "Bill and Robert paid a terrible price for that discrimination."

Some opponents of same-sex marriage object to any legal steps to permit gay couples to enjoy marriage-like benefits. "What makes them different from other kinds of people who might want to get the same benefits of marriage?" asks Mackey of the Family Re-

search Council. "Why special rights for this group of people?"

Other opponents, however, say they have no objections to gay couples enjoying some of the benefits of marriage as long as marriage itself is reserved for heterosexuals. "Much that they are asking to be done can be done without the radical redefinition of the word 'marriage,' " says Crews, of the Massachusetts Family Institute. "There are things that are already available for those who want to be in a relationship that doesn't qualify for marriage."

In fact, many gay and lesbian couples already structure their affairs jointly. They buy houses together, name each other in their wills and — in a few states — jointly adopt children. Domestic-partnership provisions rec-

Clergy members who perform same-sex ceremonies see their roles as part of their pastoral duties. "I consider myself a priest who is trying to live out his ministry in the best way possible," Schum says. "This is the work that I'm called to do."

Schum says he was "angry," but not surprised, by the Vatican statement on same-sex marriage. "The tone of the letter is cruel," he says. "It's uninformed. It's unjust. It just reflects the unwillingness of the hierarchy to have any kind of dialogue with gay and lesbian Catholics and to have any kind of dialogue about the new knowledge about homosexuality."

Marianne Duddy, former executive director of Dignity, has similar reactions to the Vatican statement today, five years after she was "married" to her partner by a Catholic priest. "I felt incredibly sad and incredibly attacked," says Duddy, a clinical social worker in Boston. "The Vatican is totally depersonalizing us."

The Vatican statement also opposed adoption by gay or lesbian persons, saying it "would actually mean doing violence to these children" because it would put them in unhealthy home environments. Duddy, who is in the process of adopting a foster daughter who has lived with her and her partner since early 2002, says that part of the statement was "especially hurtful."

U.S. Catholics appear divided on the issue. A survey by the Pew Forum on Religion in Public Life last spring found support for gay marriage among U.S. Catholics had increased to 38 percent from 27 percent in 1996.[4] The survey was conducted before the U.S. Supreme Court's decision striking down state anti-sodomy laws in late June. Other polls since that time have indicated a decline in public support for gay marriage.

Specifically, a *Washington Post* poll conducted in August just after the Episcopal Church's action found that a large majority of Americans — 60 percent — oppose church sanctions of homosexual relationships. In fact, nearly half of all churchgoing Americans said they would leave their churches if their minister blessed gay couples. Slightly fewer — 58 percent — opposed civil unions, which would grant gay partners some of the legal rights of married couples without the involvement of a religious institution.[5]

---

[1] "Considerations Regarding Proposals to Give Legal Recognition to Unions Between Homosexual Persons," July 31, 2003, www.vatican.va. For coverage, see Frank Bruni, "Vatican Exhorts Legislators to Reject Same-Sex Unions," *The New York Times*, Aug. 1, 2003, p. A1; Alan Cooperman and David von Drehle, "Vatican Instructs Legislators on Gays," *The Washington Post*, Aug. 1, 2003, p. A1.

[2] "Few U.S. Religions Bless Same-Sex Unions," The Associated Press, Aug. 7, 2003.

[3] For coverage, see Alan Cooperman, "Episcopal Church Ratifies Compromise on Gay Unions," *The Washington Post*, Aug. 8, 2003, p. A2; Monica Davey, "Episcopal Church Leaders Reject Proposal for Same-Sex Union Liturgy," *The New York Times*, Aug. 8, 2003, p. A20.

[4] Pew Forum on Religion and Public Life, "Religion and Politics: Contention and Consensus," July 24, 2003 (http://www.pewforum.org).

[5] Richard Morin and Alan Cooperman, "Majority Against Blessing Gay Unions," *The Washington Post*, Aug. 14, 2003, p. A1.

---

ognized by some city and state governments and a growing number of private employers allow an employee to designate a gay or lesbian partner for health benefits.

Gay-marriage advocates, however, complain that homosexual couples cannot achieve these benefits without making special efforts. "It's time-consuming and complicated," says Mark Strasser, a professor at Capital University Law School in Columbus, Ohio. In addition, some of the rights and benefits of marriage simply cannot be achieved without changes in the law, such as spousal support in the event of a breakup or the confidentiality of marital communications.

"Access to health care, medical decision-making, inheritance, taxation, immigration — the list literally goes on and on," says Wolfson, of Freedom to Marry. "Gay people have the same needs for structure, support and responsibility that straight people do."

Gay couples also want the symbolic recognition of their relationships that only marriage can convey. "Marriage is an important vocabulary" in defining a relationship, Wolfson says.

Strasser says marriage constitutes "a public statement" as well as "an internal recognition" about a couple's commitment to each other.

Lawyers in the Massachusetts case stress both the practical and symbolic benefits of marriage for gay and lesbian couples. "Only 'marriage' conveys the love and commitment that others automatically understand and respect," GLAD attorney Bonauto says. "Only 'marriage' provides a legal safety net protecting the couple's emotional bonds and their economic security."

In its brief, the state acknowledges the policy arguments for affording same-sex couples some of the benefits accorded to married couples, but it says the issue is not for the courts to decide. The legislature is "best suited to decide whether, when and how to make such a basic and far-reaching change in Massachusetts law," the state's attorneys contend.

In the past, some gay-rights advocates have been opposed to or unenthusiastic about pushing for marriage rights, viewing the issue either as a low priority or as an undesirable assimilation to "straight" social norms. Today, the gay community appears to be largely unified on the issue and committed to making it a priority.

Meet the Massachusetts Plaintiffs

The seven gay couples who filed suit in Massachusetts seeking the right to marry have had long-term relationships ranging from three to 32 years. The suit — Goodridge v. Massachusetts Department of Public Health *— could make Massachusetts the first state in the country to recognize gay marriage.*

Julie and Hillary Goodridge
Julie, 45, investment adviser; Hillary, 46, grant administrator. Together, 16 years; commitment ceremony, 1995; one daughter, Annie, 8.

David Wilson and Robert Compton
David, 58, business executive; Rob, 53, dentist. Together, three years; commitment ceremony, October 2000

Gloria Bailey and Linda Davies
Gloria, 62; Linda, 57; joint psychotherapy practice. Together, 32 years

Richard Linnell and Gary Chalmers
Rich, 39, nurse; Gary, 37, school teacher. Together, 14 years; one son, Paige, 10.

Maureen Brodoff and Ellen Wade
Maureen, 50, lawyer; Ellen, 54, lawyer, private practice. Together, 20-plus years; one daughter, Kate, 14.

Gina Smith and Heidi Norton
Gina, 38, researcher; Heidi, 38, law program director, both with Center for Contemplative Mind in Society. Together, 12 years; commitment ceremony, 1993; two sons: Avery, 6; Quinn, 3.

Ed Balmelli and Michael Horgan
Ed, 42, computer engineer; Michael, 43, computer systems administrator. Together, seven years; civil union, Vermont, October 2000.

Source: Gay and Lesbian Advocates and Defenders (www.glad.org.).

For his part, Brigham Young University's Wardle acknowledges that homosexual couples could benefit from legal recognition. But, "the benefits would be enjoyed by a very few, a very small group," he points out. "The costs would be borne by society as a whole."

Would recognizing same-sex unions hurt heterosexual marriage?

The United States has the highest divorce rate of any industrialized country, with somewhere between one-third and one-half of all marriages ending in a break-up. The number of oppo-site-sex couples living together without being married is also high: nearly 5.5 million households — 9.1 percent of all households in the United States. [3]

Opponents of same-sex marriage cite those figures as evidence that traditional marriage is in trouble. Legal recognition of gay and lesbian couples, they say, can only add to the pressures on an institution they consider vital to American society.

"Marriage is the most preferred institution in the law, and for good reason," Wardle says. "It contributes to a society in which rights, values and cultures are passed on, and liberties are protected. It is critical to our way of life."

Recognizing gay marriage "breaks down thousands of years of culture," adds the Family Research Council's Mackey. "It would have a very strange effect."

But proponents say recognizing same-sex unions would have no effect on heterosexual couples, while strengthening homosexual relationships.

"Same-sex couples are interested in the exact same thing that different-sex couples are interested in," Buckel says. "Any time you have people committing to being legally responsible for each other, that's good for communities."

"It's nonsense to say that gay couples taking on a commitment and building a life together takes anything away from anyone else," Wolfson says. "There is enough marriage to share. It's not as though gay couples are going to use up all the marriage licenses."

Opponents are most specific in warning about the potential effects on children from legalizing gay marriage. When pressed to list other possible consequences, Mackey says there might be pressure to bestow marriage-like benefits on other living arrangements. "If an aunt and a niece are living together, why would they not be privileged to the same tax laws?" Mackey asks.

Mackey also suggests that legalizing gay marriage might increase the divorce rate and the incidence of opposite-sex couples living together. "There would be no reason to marry at all," she says. Asked if recognizing gay marriage would promote homosexuality, Mackey replies, "Absolutely, yes."

In its brief in the *Goodridge* case, the Massachusetts attorney general's office acknowledges that public attitudes toward "non-traditional marriages" have changed since enactment of the state's marriage laws. The brief significantly avoids any specific criticisms of gay or lesbian relationships and makes no claim that recognizing same-sex

Here are the seven gay couples that filed suit in Massachusetts seeking the right to marry; Julie and Hillary Goodridge are at far right. A ruling in the suit— Goodridge v. Massachusetts Department of Public Health — *is expected at any time.*

unions would affect the behavior of heterosexual couples.

A coalition of conservative religious groups, however, argues in a friend-of-the-court brief that recognizing homosexual marriage "would institutionalize a radically different vision of sexual relationships." The groups, including the Massachusetts Catholic Conference and the National Association of Evangelicals, suggest that recognizing homosexual marriage would "teach that fundamentally the sexes do not need each other and can — perhaps ought to — live separately."

The plaintiffs' brief does not specifically address the potential effect on heterosexual couples, but an amicus brief filed by a group of 26 social and legal historians points out that court-mandated changes in marriage law — such as striking down anti-miscegenation (racial intermarriage) laws — are now widely accepted. Al-

lowing same-sex couples to marry, the historians argue, "represents the logical next step in . . . reforming marriage to fit the evolving nature of committed intimate relationships and the rights of the individuals in those relationships."

Bonauto says flatly there would be no effect on heterosexual marriage if same-sex marriage is recognized. "Right now, gay and lesbian people are working side by side with non-gay people in the workplace," she says. "Gay and lesbian people are making commitments to each other, gay and lesbian parents are sending children to school. None of that will change with marriage."

"Gay and lesbian families are already part of the community," Bonauto continues. "We're talking about providing them with more legal protections. It's not going to be an issue in changing anyone else's life."

Wardle, however, maintains that the effect on society would be substantial — and detrimental. "You have to look at the children who would be raised in their homes. What message would be sent to society as a whole as to the equality of men and women? What message are we sending to children who are growing up in this society? What kind of message does society send about the value of this institution, about the value of the commitment to this institution?" he asks.

"Marriage is suffering already," Wardle adds. "Marriage and marriage-based families are already carrying a heavy load."

Are children helped or hurt by being raised in homosexual households?

Lawyers for the state of Vermont urged the state Supreme Court four years ago to uphold the ban on same-sex marriage primarily on the grounds that preserving traditional marriage was essential to "legitimize" children and provide for their security. The court rejected the argument.

Many gay couples already adopt children or give birth through assisted reproductive techniques, the justices said. Excluding same-sex couples from the legal protections of marriage, the Vermont court concluded, "exposes their children to the precise risks that the State argues the marriage laws are designed to secure against."

Advocates and opponents of same-sex marriage sharply disagree about the effects of raising children in homosexual households. Opponents insist that a traditional marriage is the best setting for raising children. "Every reputable social study done to date is that the optimal setting for child rearing is a married mom and dad in a home, not just two adults," says Crews, of the Massachusetts Family Institute.

In fact, some opponents of same-sex marriage even contend that being raised in a gay household harms children. "The homosexual lifestyle is inconsistent with the proper raising of children," writes Timothy Dailey, a former research associate with the Family Research Council. "Homosexual relationships are characteristically unstable and are fundamentally incapable of providing children the security they need." [4]

Supporters of same-sex marriage maintain that social-science studies, in fact, show that children raised in homosexual households do as well as children from heterosexual homes. (*See sidebar, p. 338*) "Gay people make fit and loving parents, and the children raised show happy, healthy lives," says Wolfson, of Freedom to Marry.

Legal recognition for gay couples, law Professor Strasser adds, would strengthen their ability to raise children. "This is a way of helping them cement those couples, so children can be raised well and can thrive," Strass-

er says. "This is a reason to recognize, not a reason not to recognize."

The debate turns in part on social-science evidence that is sharply disputed. Supporters of same-sex marriage say studies consistently show no significant differences between children raised in gay households and those raised by straight couples. Opponents of same-sex marriage say the studies are methodologically flawed and ideologically biased.

Two gay-friendly researchers have added to the debate recently by reinterpreting previous studies as showing that children raised in gay households are more tolerant of homosexual behavior than children from straight households. Researchers Judith Stacey of New York University and Timothy Biblarz of the University of Southern California in Los Angeles view that result favorably, but opponents of same-sex marriage claim the study substantiates their argument that gay parenting is bad for children. [5]

The Massachusetts attorney general's office cites the Stacey-Biblarz study — along with other research — to contend that evidence of the effect of homosexual parenting is "inconclusive." Despite changing sex roles, the state's lawyers argue, the legislature "could still rationally believe that a favorable setting for raising children is a two-parent family with one parent of each sex."

On the opposite side, a coalition of mental-health and social-welfare organizations told the state high court in a friend-of-the-court brief that it is "beyond scientific dispute" that children of gay and lesbian parents are "as well adjusted and psychologically healthy" as those of heterosexual parents.

Same-sex marriage advocates note that virtually all states permit — and many encourage — adoption of children by gay or lesbian parents because it helps relieve the burdens on overcrowded and underfunded state

foster-care systems.

"This is a major difficulty for the state — how to deal with children who've been taken out of the home," Strasser says. "The notion that somehow the children would be better off in the system than having two loving, same-sex adults caring for them — it's an amazing argument to make."

Some opponents of same-sex marriage acknowledge the benefits of gay adoption but say it does not require broader legal recognition for gay couples. "If we redefine marriage, then it becomes very difficult for the state to distinguish on a legal basis a married couple and someone else wanting to adopt," says Avila, of the Massachusetts Catholic Conference. "There may be very good reasons for maintaining the presumption in favor of a married couple."

Other opponents of same-sex marriage, however, are simply opposed to gay adoption. "We've got too many children in our foster-care and social-service systems," Crews says. "But you don't have to radically redefine marriage to tackle a problem of the needs of children."

BACKGROUND

'More Than Brothers'

Men have paired up with men and women with women throughout history and around the globe seeking companionship, support and — often — physical love. These same-sex relationships have enjoyed some measure of social acceptance. But in the West, religious and secular authorities have been virtually unanimous in condemning homosexual relationships at least since the Middle Ages.

Chronology

1950s-1970s
U.S. gay-liberation movement emerges; gay marriage debated.

1951
Publication of *The Homosexual in America*.

1969
Gay-liberation movement energized after two days of rioting, triggered by police raid on Stonewall Inn, a popular New York City gay bar; many early leaders are skeptical of or opposed to gay marriage.

1971
In first American appellate decision on same-sex marriage, Minnesota Supreme Court upholds refusal to issue marriage license for gay couple.

1979
First National Gay and Lesbian Civil Rights March draws estimated 100,000 people to Washington, D.C.

1980s
Gay rights advances, but social conservatives strengthen their opposition; AIDS becomes an epidemic.

1984
Berkeley, Calif., becomes first city to provide domestic-partner benefits for gays and lesbians.

1986
U.S. Supreme Court upholds state laws prohibiting consensual homosexual sodomy.

1987
Sweden provides most legal benefits of marriage to cohabiting couples, including same-sex couples; similar laws enacted in Denmark (1989) and Norway (1993).

1990s
First U.S. court rulings to hint at recognition of same-sex unions provoke strong resistance from social conservatives.

1993
Hawaii Supreme Court says state must justify its prohibition of same-sex marriages. . . . second gay-rights march on Washington draws crowd officially estimated at 300,000.

1994
Historian John Boswell publishes book claiming medieval Catholic Church routinely sanctified same-sex unions; thesis is widely publicized and criticized.

1996
U.S. Supreme Court on May 20 invalidates Colorado initiative barring anti-gay discrimination measures. . . . President Bill Clinton on Sept. 21 signs Defense of Marriage Act, denying federal recognition to same-sex marriages and buttressing similar refusals by states; 37 states enact similar laws by 2003. . . . Hawaii trial court on Dec. 2 rules ban on same-sex marriage is unconstitutional.

1998
Alaska trial judge on Feb. 27 issues preliminary ruling requiring state to justify same-sex marriage ban. . . . Alaska voters approve constitutional amendment on Nov. 3 prohibiting homosexual marriage; Hawaii voters approve amendment same day authorizing legislature to bar same-sex marriage.

1999
Vermont Supreme Court on Dec. 20 orders state to allow same-sex couples to enjoy legal benefits accorded to heterosexuals.

2000-Present
Gay-rights advocates and social conservatives continue to battle over same-sex unions.

2000
California voters on March 7 approve Proposition 22 barring recognition of same-sex marriages. . . . Vermont Gov. Howard Dean on April 26 signs legislation creating "civil union" status for same-sex couples, effective July 1. . . . The Netherlands on Sept. 12 enacts first nationwide law officially recognizing same-sex marriage.

2001
Seven gay and lesbian couples file same-sex marriage suit in state court in Boston on April 11. Trial judge upholds ban on same-sex marriage on May 8, 2002.

2002
New York Times in September becomes most prominent newspaper to publish announcements of same-sex commitment ceremonies.

2003
Belgium recognizes same-sex marriage on Jan. 30. . . . Supreme Judicial Court of Massachusetts hears arguments March 4 in gay-marriage suit. . . . Ontario's high court on June 10 orders the province to immediately allow same-sex couples to marry. . . . U.S. Supreme Court on June 26 rules state laws banning gay sex unconstitutional. . . . Three Democratic candidates for president endorse gay marriage in July 15 forum before gay-rights group; six others favor granting legal benefits to same-sex couples. . . . President Bush says on July 30 he wants to "codify" definition of marriage as between one man, one woman.

Disputed Studies Give Gay Parents Good Marks

Mark Brown always wanted to have children, but his partner Bob Cesario liked the quiet privacy of a kid-free home. After more than 20 years together, however, the one-time college sweethearts finally decided a few years ago they were ready — as Mark puts it — "to get pregnant."

Now, with a 4-year-old daughter and infant son in their Los Angeles home, Mark goes to the office every day, while Bob's acting career is on hold as he devotes most of his time to parenting.

"He's the stay-at-home dad, the soccer mom," Mark says. "He's the primary caregiver while I'm out making a living."

Their children, Ella and Sander Brown, are among the estimated 1 million to 9 million youngsters being raised in the United States today by gay or lesbian parents — by either same-sex couples or single parents. [1] The number is almost certainly on the rise, as gay men and lesbians increasingly turn to adoption, co-parenting, surrogacy or assisted reproduction to bring children into their lives and homes.

Gay-advocacy groups are proud of the trend. "There are all sorts of kids being raised out there in wonderful homes headed by gay parents," says David Buckel, a staff attorney with Lambda Legal Defense and Education Fund in New York City.

Religious and social conservatives, however, view the development as a dangerous social experiment. "The traditional structure of one-man-one-woman marriage is clearly the best structure for raising children," says Connie Mackey, vice president for government affairs at the Washington-based Family Research Council.

But a range of child welfare, medical, and other professional groups agree with gay organizations that children who grow up in same-sex households fare as well overall as children raised by heterosexual parents. In the most comprehensive position paper on the issue, a task force of the American Academy of Pediatrics concludes, "No data have pointed to any risk to children of growing up in a family with one or more gay parents." [2]

The report, published in February 2002, catalogued some 20 published research papers studying gay and lesbian parents and their children. It concluded that there was "no systematic difference" between gay and non-gay parents in emotional health, parenting skills or attitudes toward parenting.

Most studies also indicate no substantial differences in emotional and social development or in gender identity and sexual orientation between children of gay parents and those of heterosexual parents. If anything, some studies suggest advantages for children raised by homosexual parents — such as greater tolerance of diversity or less aggressiveness than children raised by heterosexuals.

Critics generally claim the studies are flawed — because of poor design, small sample size or researchers' bias. The studies "are all gravely deficient," Robert Lerner and Althea Nagai, partners in a social-science research consulting firm, write in a paper posted on an anti-gay marriage Web site. [3]

However, one British study often cited by critics found that children raised by lesbians were slightly more likely to consider having a same-sex partner than children of single mothers. The study examined 27 households in each group and conducted follow-up interviews with 46 children from the two groups 14 years later. [4]

Lynn Wardle, a law professor at Brigham Young University in Provo, Utah, says the study proves children of homosexual parents are "more likely to experiment with homosexual behavior." He goes on to say that homosexuality among adolescents "is associated with" alcohol and drug abuse and multiple sexual partners. "Before we endorse [gay parenting], we ought to think very seriously about what life would be like for those children," Wardle says.

Ellen Perrin, the head of the pediatrics group's task force and a professor at New England Medical Center in Boston, says critics like Wardle ignore a second finding of the study: that the number of children who eventually identified themselves as homosexual was roughly equal in the two groups. She says it was "no surprise" that more children of lesbian parents were open to same-sex behavior because they had grown up with someone who had a same-sex partner.

One gay-friendly researcher, however, says she suspects that further studies may show that a "slightly higher minority" of children of homosexual parents turn out to be "not exclusively heterosexual" than children of straight parents. But Judith Stacey, a professor of sociology at New York University, adds, "The majority of gay people have straight parents, and the majority of gay parents have straight kids."

For his part, Brown scoffs at the notion that a parent's sexual orientation affects his or her child's. "Every gay person I know was raised by extremely heterosexual parents," Brown says. "I don't think it has any bearing whatsoever."

Stacey, along with a colleague at her former school, the University of Southern California, shifted the debate on gay parenting somewhat when they co-wrote a 2001 article claiming evidence of "beneficial effects" on children raised in homosexual households. She and Timothy Biblarz — who are both heterosexual — concluded in the paper that there was "suggestive evidence" of "modest and interesting" differences between children raised by gay parents and those raised by straight parents. [5]

Stacey says that many of those differences are likely to be

Present-day advocates of gay marriage — notably, Yale law Professor William Eskridge in his book *The Case for Same-Sex Marriage* — find historical analogues dating back to the Biblical accounts of David and Jonathan and Ruth and Naomi. [6] Eskridge notes that same-sex relationships between men were common in ancient Greece — witness Plato's discourse on love in the dialogue *Symposium* — and that the Roman Emperor Nero had a for-

advantages, not disadvantages, for the kids in gay households. She suspects the unconventional path to parenthood taken by gay men and lesbians is responsible for the differences. "Gay parenting is one of the most planned forms of parenting," Stacey says. "You don't have accidental kids, you don't have unplanned kids." Heterosexuals, Stacey adds, are much more likely to "wander backwards into parenting."

Brown and Cesario, both 48, took a somewhat conventional path to parenthood: adoption. They adopted Ella through an agency and 4-month-old Sander through a private placement. Both children are biracial: mixed black and white. Under an executive order signed by California Gov. Gray Davis in 1999, the two men adopted both children jointly. Gay or lesbian couples in most other states have to follow a two-step procedure, with adoption first by one of the partners and then a "second-parent adoption" by the other.

Adoption by gay or lesbian couples is prohibited by law in three states and generally not allowed by judges in several others. A constitutional challenge to Florida's statute, which prohibits adoption by gay or lesbian individuals or couples, is currently pending before the federal appeals court in Atlanta. [6] Mississippi's law prohibits adoption by gay or lesbian couples, but not individuals; Utah's prohibits adoption by any cohabiting couple.

Other homosexuals take more difficult paths to parenthood, parallel to routes chosen by infertile heterosexual parents. Some gay men "co-parent" with single lesbians or lesbian couples — often, with sperm provided by the man used to artificially inseminate the birth mother. Some women use sperm from anonymous donors for an otherwise natural birth. Some gay men provide sperm to a woman who serves as surrogate mother — so-called traditional surrogacy. And some men or women use so-called "gestational surrogacy" — where a woman's embryo is fertilized with a man's sperm and then implanted in a woman who carries the child to term.

Experts and advocates on both sides agree that further studies are needed about the effects of gay parenting on children. "There is an awful lot that we don't know about children of parents who

Courtesy Mark Brown

After more than 20 years together, Mark Brown, left, and his partner Bob Cesario are raising a 4-year-old daughter and an infant son. Bob, an actor, is the "stay at home dad," says Mark, who works full time.

are gay or lesbian," Perrin says. "But there is also an awful lot that we don't know about the children of parents who are heterosexual."

Wardle agrees. "There are a few things we know that raise startling issues," he says. "There are also a lot of things we don't know because these [parenting arrangements] are so new."

Brown, a television writer and producer who is co-president of the Los Angeles gay fathers group the Pop Luck Club, believes most gay parents are "extremely conscientious, conscious and very loving." He adds, "Children thrive in a loving environment, whether that child has a single parent, a gay parent or a straight parent."

As for marriage, Brown and Cesario have not given it much thought. "We joke sometimes that it would jinx us," Brown says. "Our relationship has worked so well that if we formalized it, we might get divorced."

Brown has had second thoughts, however, since the family returned from a niece's wedding in Boston in June. Ella enjoyed the wedding a lot, Brown says, and asked afterward whether he and Cesario were married. "Daddy and Poppa are married in our hearts and minds," Brown told her.

"I would love to get married," Brown says now. "It would be particularly joyous for us to get married in front of our children. If it were legal, I'd go out and get married tomorrow."

---

[1] Edward O. Laumann, "National Health and Social Life Survey, 1995," cited in American Academy of Pediatrics, "Technical Report: Coparent or Second-Parent Adoption by Same-Sex Parents," Vol. 109, No. 2 (February 2002), pp. 341-344.

[2] *Ibid.*, p. 344.

[3] Robert Lerner and Althea K. Nagai, "No Basis: What the Studies *Don't* Tell Us About Same-Sex Parenting," January 2001 (www.marriagewatch.org).

[4] S. Golombok, F. Tasker, C. Murray, "Children Raised in Fatherless Families From Infancy: Family Relationships and the Socioemotional Development of Children of Lesbian and Single Heterosexual Mothers," in *Journal of Child Psychology and Psychiatry*, Vol. 38 (1997), pp. 783-791.

[5] Judith Stacey and Timothy J. Biblarz, "(How) Does the Sexual Orientation of Parents Matter?" *American Sociological Review*, Vol. 66 (April 2001), pp. 159-183. Biblarz is an associate professor of sociology at USC.

[6] The case is *Lofton v. Kearney*, 01-16723-DD. The Florida law was upheld by a U.S. District Court Aug. 30, 2001; the case was argued before the 11th U.S. Circuit Court of Appeals in March.

---

mal wedding ceremony with his male lover Sporus.

"Same-sex marriages are a commonplace in human history," Eskridge writes, and have been "tolerated in most societies" except in the West.

Opponents of same-sex marriage view the history differently. They emphasize that the Bible condemns homosexuality: "Thou shalt not lie with mankind, as with womankind: it is abomination" (*Leviticus*, 18:22). Despite the acceptance of same-sex relationships in ancient Greece and Rome, they emphasize — as Eskridge acknowledges — that attitudes changed by the time of the late Roman Empire. Accounts of male-male couplings assumed a satirical tone, and an imperial decree in 342 A.D. prescribed execution for men who married other men.

The divergent views of history emerged dramatically with the publication of a controversial 1994 book, *Same-Sex Unions in Premodern Europe*, by Yale historian John Boswell. [7] The first openly gay tenured professor at an Ivy League college, Boswell found evidence in some 60 liturgical manuscripts from the eighth through the 16th centuries to support his thesis that the medieval Catholic Church routinely sanctified same-sex unions.

Prayers for uniting "brothers" appeared in manuscripts alongside prayers for betrothals and marriages, Boswell reported. The ceremonies included rituals associated with marriage: the burning of candles, the placing of the two parties' hands on the Gospel, the joining of their right hands, crowning, a kiss and sometimes circling around the altar, according to Boswell. These rites "most likely signified a marriage in the eyes of most ordinary Christians," he concluded. [8]

Critics argued that Boswell — who died six months after the book's publication — exaggerated, misconstrued or misrepresented the ceremonies described in the liturgies. They contend-

Demonstrators in Chicago march in celebration of the U.S. Supreme Court's landmark June 26 ruling striking down a Texas law against gay sex. The ruling did not deal directly with same-sex marriage, but gay-rights advocates say it supports the gay-marriage suit pending in Massachusetts.

Getty Images/Scott Olson

ed that the ceremonies blessed fraternal adoptions or friendships, not physical relationships. "To try to make scripture condoning the homosexual lifestyle or somehow blessing it, it's just not there," says Crews, a Presbyterian minister.

In a sympathetic assessment on a gay-history Web site, Fordham University Professor Paul Halsall today calls Boswell's thesis "groundbreaking" but acknowledges criticisms from various experts, including some openly gay professors.

But James Brundage, a professor of law and history at the University of Kansas who specializes in the medieval period, says Boswell's thesis has

few supporters today. "The academic historians no longer take that book all that seriously," he says.

Whatever acceptance same-sex relationships had enjoyed earlier, European religious and secular authorities adopted unambiguous opposition, according to Eskridge. Beginning in the 13th century, governments enacted the first laws prohibiting "crimes against nature," he writes, and prior ecclesiastical laws "came to be more stringently enforced." [9]

Despite the opposition, same-sex relationships survived in the modern West, both in Europe and in the United States. Homosexual subcultures have existed in many European cities since the 18th century and by the beginning of the 20th century in such U.S. cities as New York, Chicago, San Francisco and Washington.

Typically, same-sex couples were discreet, but by the mid-20th century interest in openly partnering was increasing. By the 1960s, the early forerunners of today's gay-rights groups were debating marriage, and some couples were engaging in mock wedding ceremonies. As Eskridge concludes, however, "these 'marriages' enjoyed neither legal recognition nor the prospect of legal recognition." [10]

Coming Out

In the 1970s, gay and lesbian couples began trying to legally marry, but courts uniformly rebuffed their efforts through the 1980s. However, the issue was not a high priority within the growing gay-rights movement. Opinions were divided about the importance — or even the value — of marriage. Besides, gay-rights advocates had more pressing issues to pursue, such as job discrimination, anti-sodomy laws and AIDS. [11]

The debate within the gay and lesbian community dated to 1951, when the first major homosexual manifesto in the United States was published: *The Homosexual in America*, written by the pseudonymous Donald Webster Cory. In a chapter on relationships, Cory concluded that homosexuals should be allowed to marry. But he reached that view only after what Eskridge calls an "agonized" discussion citing self-hatred and promiscuity as impediments to stable relationships among gay men.

The nascent gay-liberation movement emerged energized and radicalized after a police raid on the Stonewall Inn, a popular Greenwich Village bar, touched off two days of rioting by homosexual activists in New York City in 1969. Marriage, however, was not a widely shared goal. Leaders of the Gay Liberation Front denounced it as "one of the most insidious and basic sustainers of the system" and family as "the microcosm of oppression." Marriage, in this view, stifled sexual freedom, oppressed women and propped up the capitalist system.

Demand for formalized relationships was nonetheless emerging among gay and lesbian couples by the late 1960s. The gay-welcoming Universal Fellowship of Metropolitan Community Churches began conducting ceremonies for same-sex couples in 1968. Gay and lesbian synagogues followed suit in the early '70s. In Minnesota, a gay couple — Richard John Baker and James Michael McConnell — were married in a religious ceremony in 1970 and then unsuccessfully applied for a state marriage license. They sued in state court, contending that the denial of the license was unconstitutional. In the first appellate decision in the United States on same-sex marriage, the

Minnesota Supreme Court rejected their plea in 1971. [12]

Public officials and courts in other jurisdictions responded in kind, with only isolated exceptions. In 1975, the Boulder County (Colo.) clerk issued marriage licenses to at least six same-sex couples after receiving approval from the county district attorney. After public protests, the state attorney general ordered the practice stopped. In Washington, D.C., a city councilman introduced a proposal to legalize gay marriage but withdrew it after strong opposition from religious groups. Gay couples who took the issue to court ran into a stone wall. As Yale law Professor Eskridge notes, between 1971 and 1993 every judge to consider the issue ruled that same-sex couples had no statutory or constitutional right to marry. [13]

With divided opinion within the community and stout resistance without, gay-rights advocates put marriage on a back burner through the 1980s and concentrated on other issues — with some success. In 1981, Wisconsin became the first state to prohibit discrimination on the basis of sexual orientation in housing, employment or public accommodations. Many states repealed anti-sodomy laws used to prosecute homosexual behavior, though advocates of gay rights were disappointed by the U.S. Supreme Court's 1986 decision upholding the constitutionality of such measures. [14] Nonetheless, gay-rights advocates won a measure of recognition for same-sex couples by persuading some city and state governments — starting with Berkeley, Calif., in 1984 — to provide domestic-partner benefits to gays.

The debate over marriage within the gay community became more visible in 1989 after an extraordinary debate between two top officials of the Lambda Legal Defense and Education Fund published in a gay journal. Executive Director Thomas Stoddard argued that marriage was "the issue most likely to lead ultimately to a world free from

discrimination against lesbians and gay men." Legal Director Paula Ettelbrick countered that marriage would force homosexuals "into the mainstream" and divert the movement's efforts at broader social reforms. [15]

Despite the ongoing debate, most gay men and lesbians responding to a mail-in survey in 1994 in *The Advocate*, a gay newsmagazine, wanted the option of getting married. Among gay men, 59 percent said they would want to marry another man if they could, and another 26 percent said they might. In a similar survey of lesbians in 1995, seven of 10 respondents said they would marry if legally permitted. [16]

Defending Marriage

Efforts to win legal recognition for same-sex unions intensified during the 1990s — spurred by favorable court rulings in Hawaii and Alaska and by an apparent increase in monogamy among gay and lesbian couples. Despite growing social acceptance of homosexuality, however, the new trend in the courts provoked a forceful backlash. The Hawaii and Alaska rulings were effectively nullified by state constitutional amendments, while Congress and two-thirds of the states passed laws aimed at barring recognition of same-sex marriage. However, at decade's end, Vermont had became the first state to grant same-sex couples marriage-like benefits in a newly created status: civil unions.

The Hawaii case began with a suit filed in 1991 in state court by three homosexual couples seeking to invalidate the statutory exclusion of same-sex marriage on either state or federal constitutional grounds. [17] A trial judge rejected the suit, but the Hawaii Supreme Court gave the plaintiffs a precedent-setting interim victory in May 1993. The court ruled that the same-sex marriage ban amounted to discrimination on the

Lifting the Lid on Gay Domestic Violence

Like many of Stephen's rages, it comes on unexpectedly. One minute, he is preparing dinner, "chatting and bopping around." The next, he is livid, furious that his lover, Patrick, has cut the carrots wrong.

"Look at these!" he shouts. "These are no good! With one swipe of his hand, the carrots are off the cutting board and onto the floor.

Seconds later, he is pummeling Patrick in the head, the face, the chest. Terrified, Patrick runs to the bedroom.

So begins *Men Who Beat the Men Who Love Them*, Patrick Letellier and David Island's account of same-sex domestic abuse. [1]

The 1991 book was the first to address the taboo topic of same-sex partner abuse, a problem that had been largely overlooked by the domestic-violence movement. Lettelier and Island raised the then-radical notion that domestic abuse is as prevalent in gay couples as it is among straight couples, affecting an estimated 500,000 gay men nationwide.

"Domestic violence [is] the third-largest health problem facing gay men today," they wrote. [2]

While research into domestic violence among homosexuals is still in its infancy and often anecdotal, at least one large-scale scientific study corroborates the authors' claim. [3] It surveyed 2,881 gay men from four cities and found that two in five respondents had experienced domestic violence. Other smaller studies suggest that domestic violence may occur in an even greater number of lesbian relationships. [4] By comparison, domestic violence occurs in 25 to 33 percent of straight relationships. [5]

Despite these findings, many straight people doubt there is much same-sex domestic violence. Most people are socialized to see men as dominant and women as passive and cannot picture men as victims and women as batterers, researchers say.

Claire Renzetti, a sociology professor at Saint Joseph's College in Philadelphia, says that when she speaks about the topic in public, people "act really surprised, or almost find it humorous, like it's one more oddity."

Gays and lesbians themselves often are reluctant to discuss homosexual abuse. Lesbian women may be unwilling to shatter a "utopic vision of a peaceful, women-centered world," and gay men may want to maintain the illusion that they are somehow more evolved than the paternalistic, dominant society they live in, explains Sandra E. Lundy, a Boston lawyer and author of a 1993 *New England Law Review* article about homosexual abuse. [6]

Others feel so threatened by societal homophobia that they don't want to acknowledge internal problems. "When you're always focused on the violence from without, seeing it from within can be very scary," says Melissa Bates, a victim advocate with the Violence Recovery Program at Fenway Community Health in Boston.

The gay community may also be suppressing the problem out of fear that statistics on same-sex domestic violence will be exploited to derail gay marriage, says Rachel Baum, associate director of the New York City-based National Coalition of Anti-Violence Programs, which compiles statistics on abuse. "People don't want to give ammunition to antis who would say our relationships are sick and wrong," she says.

Victim advocates say the silence surrounding same-sex abuse, coupled with a lack of role models for healthy same-sex relationships, empowers batterers and makes it harder for victims to recognize that they are in abusive relationships.

"Batterers will try to define reality for their partners," says

basis of sex and could be upheld under Hawaii's constitution only if the state could show a "compelling" government interest to justify it. [18]

When the case was back in the trial court, the state defended the same-sex marriage ban on the ground that gay and lesbian couples would not be sufficiently good parents. Rejecting the argument, the judge ruled the same-sex marriage ban unconstitutional in December 1996 but stayed the decision pending appeal. While the appeal was pending, opponents of same-sex marriage won voter ratification of a constitutional amendment in November 1998 authorizing the legislature to limit marriage to heterosexual couples. In 1999,

the state Supreme Court interpreted the amendment to retroactively validate the same-sex marriage ban — eliminating any need for legislative action. [19]

A similar suit filed by a gay couple in Alaska started along a comparable course but was cut short by a constitutional amendment at an earlier stage. The judge in the case gave the plaintiffs a preliminary victory in February 1998 by ruling that the state had to justify denying them their "fundamental" right to choose a partner. [20] The state appealed to Alaska's Supreme Court, but within the year the legislature approved and voters ratified a constitutional amendment defining marriage as a union between one man and one woman.

The Hawaii case raised fears among opponents that a final ruling for the plaintiffs could force the other 49 states to recognize gay marriages sanctioned there. As the suit moved toward trial, Congress moved quickly — in an election year — to enact federal legislation aimed at thwarting any state court rulings in favor of gay marriage. The Defense of Marriage Act (DOMA) — passed overwhelmingly by both houses and signed into law by President Bill Clinton on Sept. 21, 1996 — declared that states were not obligated to recognize any same-sex marriages that might be legally sanctioned in other states. It also defined marriage and spouse in heterosexual terms for federal law, thus

Beth Leventhal, executive director and founder of The Network/La Red, a Boston organization serving battered lesbians. "If it is the victim's first relationship after coming out, they will tell them, 'This is how we do things.' "

Even for those who decide to come forward, help is scant or non-existent. While a handful of hotlines and counseling programs have cropped up in major cities over the last 20 years, huge swaths of rural America remain without any services. "Victims can be a long way from resources in terms of mountain ranges, snow, you name it," says Denise de Percin, executive director of the Colorado Anti-Violence Program, which serves the entire state.

Battered-women's shelters are geared toward heterosexuals and may either refuse to serve lesbians or fail to screen applicants, enabling batterers to infiltrate the system.

Gay men and transgender individuals have even fewer shelter options, mostly limited to short-term emergency housing at hotels.

Only a handful of cities have treatment programs for batterers, forcing many to seek help at 12-step programs, anger-management classes and couples counseling. Meanwhile, treatment of same-sex violence by police forces varies dramatically. While some police forces are trained to handle same-sex domestic-violence calls, others have a hard time distinguishing victim from aggressor. [7]

Some officers "make judgments based on who the bigger partner is, or who the more butch or masculine partner is," Bates says. "Sometimes, even the victim is arrested." In cases where the victim fights back, law enforcement may label the violence "mutual abuse," assuming that it is a fight between equals.

Victims encounter even more inconsistencies in the courts. In some states, domestic-violence law applies only to heterosexual couples; in others, judges may issue mutual restraining orders.

Laws that prevent same-sex couples from adopting also work against victims. When the biological parent is the batterer, he or she can threaten that if the victim leaves he or she will never see the child again. [8]

Facing the prospect of institutional "re-victimization" by the police and courts, many victims choose not to come forward.

Shawna Virago, director of the domestic-violence survivor program at Community United Against Violence in San Francisco, says education about domestic abuse in general is the solution.

"It's a national epidemic of violence, and it's not being addressed," Virago says.

— *Kelly Field*

[1] David Island and Patrick Letellier, *Men Who Beat the Men Who Love Them* (1991), p. 1.

[2] *Ibid.*

[3] Gregory L. Greenwood, *et al.*, "Battering Victimization Among a Probability-Based Sample of Men Who Have Sex With Men," *American Journal of Public Health*, December 2002, pp. 1964-1969.

[4] Gwat-Yong Lie and S. Gentlewarrier, "Intimate Violence in Lesbian Relationships: Discussion of Survey Findings and Practice Implications," *Journal of Social Service Research*, 1991, p. 146.

[5] National Coalition Against Domestic Violence.

[6] Sandra E. Lundy, "Abuse That Dare Not Speak Its Name: Assisting Victims of Lesbian and Gay Domestic Violence in Boston," *New England Law Review*, winter 1993.

[7] National Coalition of Anti-Violence Programs, "Lesbian, Gay, Bisexual and Transgender Domestic Violence in 2002," July 2003, p. 17.

[8] Beth Leventhal and Sandra E. Lundy, eds., *Same Sex Domestic Violence* (1999), p. 21.

precluding homosexual couples from filing joint tax returns or obtaining any spousal benefits under Social Security or other federal programs. [21]

Some state legislatures had already approved comparable laws before Congress acted; more followed suit over the next few years. By the end of 2000, more than 30 states had so-called "mini-DOMAs" on the books. The list included three measures approved by voters in 2000: a ballot initiative adopted in March in California and constitutional amendments ratified in November in Nebraska and Nevada. All of the laws specifically defined marriage as the union of one man and one woman. Some appeared simply

to bar same-sex marriage by the state's own residents; most went further and barred recognition of same-sex marriages sanctioned in other states, too.

Meanwhile, however, three homosexual couples in Vermont had won a landmark victory from the state's Supreme Court. In a nearly unanimous decision in December 1999, the court said that the state had to grant same-sex couples "the common benefits and protections that flow from marriage under Vermont law." The court left it up to the state legislature whether to legalize marriage — as the lone dissenting justice argued — or to create some form of "parallel 'domestic-partnership' system." [22] With no room to

maneuver, the legislature in April 2000 approved a bill creating a "civil union" status for homosexuals; then-Democratic Gov. Howard Dean signed it into law, to take effect on July 1.

'Marriage Equality'

Vermont's civil-union law was less than a year old when seven gay and lesbian couples filed a new suit seeking to legalize gay marriage in neighboring Massachusetts. *Goodridge v. Massachusetts Department of Public Health* became a major showdown on the issue, with a total of 26 friend-of-the-court briefs filed on both sides before the state's highest court heard arguments in March 2003.

Meanwhile, same-sex marriage was advancing in other countries — first in the Netherlands in September 2000 and then in Belgium and Canada in 2003. In addition, gay-marriage advocates say the U.S. Supreme Court's June 26 decision striking down state anti-sodomy laws laid the groundwork for broader legal equality for homosexuals in the United States.

The seven Massachusetts plaintiff couples stressed the practical problems resulting from being unable to marry. [23] Hillary Goodridge recalled that even with a legal document known as a health-care proxy she had difficulty visiting her partner Julie in the hospital when Julie had a difficult childbirth. Teacher Richard Linnell noted that his health insurance covered the child he jointly adopted with his partner, Gary Chalmers, but he had to pay extra for Chalmers. Gloria Bailey and Linda Davies said that as they considered retirement, they realized that they would face taxes that married couples would not have to pay in selling their home or their joint psychotherapy practice.

"Unequal treatment is inconsistent with the Constitution," Jennifer Levi, a GLAD attorney, said at an April 2001 news conference announcing the suit. "All these couples seek is equality."

Acting Gov. Jane Swift responded by restating her opposition to same-sex marriage. "I think that marriage and the recognition of marriage is an important institution in our commonwealth and in our country and should be for heterosexual couples," said Swift, a Republican.

In his 26-page opinion rejecting the suit a year later, Judge Thomas Connolly relied on what he called the "centuries-old" definition of marriage and the "central" role of procreation in marriage. "Recognizing that procreation is marriage's central purpose, it

is rational for the legislature to limit marriage to opposite-sex couples who, theoretically, are capable of procreation," Connolly wrote. The judge said the plaintiffs should direct the plea to the legislature, not the courts. [24]

European countries, in fact, were dealing with the issue legislatively rather than judicially. Three Scandinavian countries had passed laws several years earlier granting legal benefits to same-sex couples: Sweden in 1987, Norway in 1989 and Denmark in 1993. The Netherlands went further in September 2000, legalizing marriage between persons of the same sex. The measure passed the Dutch parliament 109-33 after drawing opposition only from a few small Christian parties. Belgium, predominantly Catholic, followed suit in January 2003, but only after a more protracted parliamentary debate.

Justices on Massachusetts' high court actively questioned lawyers for both sides when the *Goodridge* case was before them on March 4. [25] "Why do you think that this is an issue that we should decide?" Justice Roderick Ireland asked Bonauto, representing the couples. Justice Martha Sosman asked whether a ruling for the couples would lead to recognizing polygamy.

But one justice noted the seeming paradox in allowing same-sex couples to adopt children, but not to marry each other. "Are those ideas somewhat at odds?" Justice John Greaney asked Judith Yogman, the assistant state attorney general handling the case. Some observers saw the questioning as encouraging for the plaintiffs, but others cautioned against making predictions.

While the Massachusetts justices deliberated the case, the Canadian government took steps to become the third Western country to officially recognize same-sex marriage. Prime Minister Jean Chretien announced on June 17 that his government would prepare legislation to recognize gay marriage — a week after Ontario's highest court

ordered immediate recognition of same-sex marriage in Canada's most populous provinces. [26] Provincial courts in British Columbia and Quebec had also backed gay marriage in earlier rulings.

The U.S. Supreme Court's 6-3 decision striking down anti-sodomy laws gave gay-marriage advocates further encouragement. Justice Anthony M. Kennedy's opinion for the majority noted that the case did not involve "whether the government must give formal recognition to any relationship that homosexual persons seek to enter."

In dissent, however, Justice Antonin Scalia said the June 26 ruling left laws limiting marriage to opposite-sex couples on "pretty shaky grounds." *Newsweek's* cover story on the decision framed the issue dramatically: "Is Gay Marriage Next?" [27]

CURRENT SITUATION

Making Commitments

Deb Price and Joyce Murdoch have been a committed couple since 1985, but the two Washington, D.C., journalists feel like newlyweds since they were married in Toronto on June 27.

"Tears welled up in my eyes as I realized that after 18 years together, Joyce and I were being legally wed," Price, a reporter for *The Detroit News*, writes in her syndicated gay-lifestyle column. She says she and Murdoch "have been dizzy" adjusting to their new status as "spouses." [28]

"Both of us were really shocked at how moving it felt, how we had this feeling of being brought back into this institution that goes back thousands of years," says Murdoch, managing editor for politics at the weekly magazine

At Issue

Should gay marriage be legally recognized?

MARY BONAUTO
CIVIL RIGHTS PROJECT DIRECTOR, GAY AND LESBIAN ADVOCATES AND DEFENDERS (GLAD)

EXCERPTED FROM THE GLAD WEB SITE, AUG. 15, 2003

marriage is a major building block for strong families and communities. Weddings are an opportunity for friends, family and neighbors to come together to recognize a couple's lifelong commitment to one another. This occasion strengthens a couple's bond and marks their inclusion as a family into the communities of which they are a part.

But marriage is much more than that. First, it is a unique relationship — synonymous with "family" — so that if you are "married," no one would dare challenge a person's right to be by his or her spouse's side. The word itself is one of the protections. Second, it is a gateway to hundreds of legal protections established by the state and over 1,000 by the federal government. Married couples can take for granted rights of hospital visitation, security for their children and rights of inheritance.

While gay and lesbian families can protect themselves in limited ways by creating wills, health-care proxies and co-parent adoptions, this does not come close to emulating the automatic protections and peace of mind that marriage confers. People cannot contract their way into changing pension laws, survivorship rights, worker's-compensation dependency protection or the tax system, to name just a few.

Marriage is also a social institution of the highest importance, the ultimate expression of love and commitment. While it remains exclusive to opposite-sex couples, gay men and lesbians will continue to fall short of the status of full citizenship, marking them and their children with a stamp of inferiority. Denying the security that marriage can bring only serves to weaken gay and lesbian families and the communities of which they are a part.

Far from undermining marriage, the struggle for full equality for gay and lesbian couples is an acknowledgement of the importance marriage has in society and the power it has over all our lives. Increasing access to marriage for adults in committed relationships will strengthen the institution, not weaken it. Marriage will not be destroyed by allowing same-sex couples to marry, just as it was not destroyed by women's equality within marriage or the repeal of interracial marriage bans.

In seeking the freedom to marry, gay and lesbian couples simply ask that their relationships be given the same respect under law accorded to others, so that they may obtain the security and protection their families need.

RON CREWS
PRESIDENT, MASSACHUSETTS FAMILY INSTITUTE

WRITTEN FOR THE CQ RESEARCHER, AUGUST 2003

the push for legalizing homosexual "marriage" is based on at least three myths: that same-sex sexual behavior is genetic and unchangeable, that homosexual relationships are just like marriage between a man and a woman and that children raised by same-sex couples do just as well as those with a married mother and father. None of these myths is true.

The definition of marriage is based on the fact that all human beings from conception have, in every cell of their bodies, either XX chromosomes if they are female or XY chromosomes if they are male. Even a sex-change operation and hormone treatments cannot change those chromosomes.

These permanent distinctions make for a permanent definition of what it means to be married. This has been the legal, social, historical and theological definition of marriage throughout the ages.

On the other hand, sexual orientation, or same-sex attraction, can and does change. Jeffrey Satinover, psychiatrist and author of *Homosexuality and the Politics of Truth*, states that a major study, conducted for U.S. agencies tracking the AIDS epidemic found that 75 percent of boys who at age 16 think they are homosexual become permanently heterosexual by age 25 without any intervention. Furthermore, the average lifespan of those who practice homosexual sex is reduced by approximately 20 years, often leaving children orphaned.

Same-sex couples may look in some respects like a married couple, but they are missing the essential element. They may have children; but an orphanage has children. That does not make it a marriage. They may have long-term committed relationships. Parents and children, brothers and sisters and friends have long-term committed relationships. That does not make a marriage. Only the union of a woman and a man, with immutable XX and XY chromosomes in every cell of their bodies, representing the two halves of the human race, can make a marriage and produce the next generation.

That next generation needs a mother and a father. Every reputable social science study done to date has affirmed that children do best, by whatever measure is used, when they have a married mom and dad. Deliberately depriving a child of a mother or father is cruel and unfair.

Do people with same-sex attraction deserve to be treated with dignity? Absolutely! Do we need to change the definition of marriage to please them? Absolutely not!

National Journal. "It was this wonderful new page."

Price and Murdoch are among the hundreds of U.S. couples who have crossed into Canada to be married since Ontario's provincial court ruled in favor of same-sex marriage on June 10. Canada beckons not only because it is geographically close but also because it imposes no citizenship or residency requirement — unlike the other countries to recognize same-sex marriage, the Netherlands and Belgium.

The sudden surge of cross-border gay marriages is only one sign of the increasing visibility of same-sex couples throughout the United States. More than 200 U.S. newspapers — most prominently, *The New York Times* — now publish same-sex couples' announcements of commitment ceremonies. [29] *Bride's* magazine, the leading mass-circulation bridal magazine, has a one-page news story about same-sex unions in its current issue. [30]

Recognition of same-sex couples by the mainstream media has been dramatically mirrored on network TV. This year's Tony Awards featured two winning male gay-partner song writers sharing a celebratory kiss. And this summer's new reality show "Boy Meets Boy" follows high-profile gay-oriented shows like the over-the-top "Will and Grace" and the new make-over show "Queer Eye for the Straight Guy," in which five gay men transform clueless straight men into cool guys.

Karen Ahlers and Michelle Blair walk down the aisle after exchanging symbolic marriage vows at First Parish Church of Framingham, Mass., on Aug. 2. Gay-rights advocates say religious groups can decide for themselves whether to perform marriages but shouldn't have a say in whether civil marriages are legalized. Episcopal Church leaders in early August gave U.S. dioceses the option of blessing same-sex unions.

Getty Images/Douglas McFadd

For its part, the U.S. Census Bureau reported in March that it found 594,000 same-sex couples living together in its 2000 population count — a threefold increase over the number recorded in 1990. [31] The number — almost equally divided between gay and lesbian couples — represents about 1 percent of households nationwide.

Demographers and other experts on gay issues say that the actual number is almost certainly higher. The reported increase since 1990 is attributed in large part to an increased willingness of same-sex couples to disclose their status.

"Many gay and lesbian couples felt more comfortable acknowledging their relationship to the government [in 2000] than they did in 1990," says Gary Gates, a research associate at the Urban Institute, a liberal-leaning research organization in Washington. "That results from the increasing acceptance of same-sex couples in our society."

About one-third of the lesbian couples (34.3 percent) and one-fourth of the gay couples (22.3 percent) have children in their households, according to Census data. The comparable figure is 45.6 percent for married-couple households and 43.1 percent for unmarried opposite-sex couples.

The Census data also showed an increase in the number of unmarried opposite-sex couples — from 3.2 million in 1990 to 5.5 million in 2000. Social conservatives found the statistics distressing.

"It's a continuing trend that has been growing," Allan Carlson, a fellow at the Family Research Council, told *The New York Times.* "It's not a healthy thing. The commitments that go with cohabitation are not as firm or strong as marriage." [32]

Gates says other Census data indicate that same-sex couples are in between unmarried opposite-sex couples and married couples on other measures of social stability. Two-thirds of same-sex couples own their homes — compared to 43 percent of unmarried opposite-sex couples and 81 percent of married couples. Slightly over one-third (38 percent) of same-sex couples live in the same households as five years ago — compared to 18 percent for unmarried opposite-sex couples and 58 percent of married couples.

"I find it fascinating that even in the absence of marriage, gay and lesbian couples exhibit traits that have fairly high measures of stability," Gates says. "At the same time, there are many rights and privileges associated with marriage that same-sex couples don't have. Over the lifetime, it's much more difficult to be a same-sex couple than a married couple."

After 12 years together, Martin Grochala and Fred Reuland have been through those problems: the difficulties of being open about their relationship, the fear of rejection by friends or family and the extra steps that a gay couple has to take to maintain a household and protect their lives and property. When the Chicago couple observed a commitment ceremony in July, however, the friend they selected to preside urged them to view those difficulties as a cause for celebration rather than regret.

"Yes, there are challenges," Grochala says today. "But rather than saying woe are us, he told us those challenges are wonderful opportunities to be the best persons we can be."

Debating Marriage

Gay-rights advocates are broadening and intensifying their push for same-sex marriage while waiting for what many expect to be a favorable ruling from the Massachusetts high court. Opponents, in turn, are stepping up their efforts to thwart any state court rulings to sanction same-sex relationships through federal legislation or a constitutional amendment, if necessary.

Opinion polls indicate a decline in support for same-sex relationships since the Supreme Court's June decision in the Texas anti-sodomy case. Anti-gay

Ten States Have Laws on Adoption by Gays

Although laws in only 10 states specifically allow gay and lesbian couples to adopt kids, 96 percent of all U.S. counties have at least one same-sex couple raising children under 18.

States Allowing Adoption by Gay Couples

California	Pennsylvania
Connecticut	Massachusetts
Illinois	Vermont
New Jersey	Washington
New York	Wisconsin

Source: Urban Institute, May 30, 2003

groups say the shift amounts to a backlash against gay marriage and other parts of what they call the gay agenda. Gay-rights advocates depict the shift as a short-term dip and cite the majority support for same-sex marriage among young people as an indication of the long-term trend of public opinion on the issue.

Gay-rights groups are working to mobilize support for same-sex marriage from like-minded organizations and individuals outside the gay and lesbian community. Lambda Legal, for example, is gathering endorsements from a wide variety of religious and civil-liberties organizations, political figures and celebrities from entertainment, business and other professions. "As with any civil-rights movement, there is a need to reach out to allies, particularly non-gay allies," Freedom to Marry's Wolfson explains.

In the largest effort for mass support, Human Rights Campaign, the gay political-action organization, is using a Web site (www.millionformarriage.org) to seek 1 million signatures on a pe-

tition supporting gay marriage. As of early September, the site claimed more than 155,000 signatures.

On the opposite side, socially conservative groups are stepping up their media and outreach efforts on the issue. "The gay community has forced the agenda," says Mackey of the Family Research Council, "so people are now having to respond."

As one example, the Traditional Values Coalition, a conservative Christian group, says it is sending out 1.5 million mailings a month to conservative voters to enlist support for a constitutional amendment to bar same-sex marriage. "I call this the defining moment for American Christianity," the Rev. Lou Sheldon, founder of the group, told *The Washington Post*. "What is at stake is no less than the doctrine of creation." [33]

Opponents are focusing in part on a possible amendment to the U.S. Constitution to block any state from recognizing same-sex marriage or from being required to recognize a same-sex marriage granted in any other state. Three days after the Supreme Court decision in the gay-sex case, Senate Majority Leader Bill Frist, R-Tenn., told a television interviewer that he "absolutely" supported a constitutional amendment to bar gay marriage. In August, however, Frist said the issue was not on the Senate's agenda for the rest of the year. [34]

For his part, President Bush told a news conference on July 30 that he favors legally limiting marriage to heterosexual couples. "I believe marriage is between a man and a woman, and I believe we ought to codify that one way or the other, and we have lawyers looking at the best way to do that," Bush said.

A proposed amendment introduced by Rep. Marilyn Musgrave, R-Colo., would define marriage only as "a union of a man and a woman." It would then stipulate that the U.S. Constitution, state constitutions or state

Gay-Marriage Issue Poses Political Risks

The gay-marriage issue poses risks for both Republicans and Democrats in next year's presidential election. Some conservatives, like former presidential candidate Gary Bauer — now president of the conservative American Values group — say it will be a defining "values" issue for voters.

President Bush will no doubt by pressured to elaborate on his marriage-is-between-a-man-and-a-woman position. In doing so, he'll have to keep the Christian right wing of his party happy without alienating moderate GOP and independent voters favoring individual privacy over government intrusiveness.

"I can't imagine the White House being AWOL on that debate and just repeating, 'We believe marriage is between a man and a woman,' " Bauer says. "You've got to put a policy on the table to implement the values of your supporters. Otherwise, why would your supporters continue to be engaged in your coalition?" [1]

Meanwhile, Vice President Dick Cheney's wife Lynn — a conservative stalwart — calls the idea that government has any business in people's bedrooms "a stretch." [2] Cheney's daughter is gay, as is Democratic presidential candidate Richard Gephardt's. Both are actively campaigning for their fathers.

Still another branch of the GOP, the gay Log Cabin Republicans, may also push Bush to take a stand. "The Bush administration is going to have to decide to go on record" embracing gays "as part of the American family and the Republican Party," said Patrick Guerriero, the former Melrose, Mass., mayor who now heads the group.

Democratic candidates also have been reluctant to endorse gay marriage. At a July forum sponsored by Human Rights Campaign, all nine Democratic presidential candidates endorsed same-sex partnership benefits, but none of the major candidates has embraced gay marriage.

The gay-marriage issue could affect Democrats' performance in the Midwest, the southern Border States, rural areas and among over-50 Americans — all key demographic segments where support for gay rights is weaker than among urban, coastal and younger voters.

---

[1] Quoted in Susan Page, "Gay Rights Tough to Sharpen into Political 'Wedge Issue,' " *USA Today*, July 28 2003, p. A10.

[2] Frank Rich, "Gay Kiss: Business As Usual," *The New York Times*, June 22, 2003.

---

or federal laws cannot be construed to require that "marital status or the legal incidents thereof be conferred upon unmarried couples or groups."

Some opponents of gay marriage are not convinced a constitutional amendment is necessary. "We would favor defense-of-marriage acts in every state and if necessary a constitutional amendment," Mackey says. Others think Musgrave's amendment may not go far enough. "We want to see an amendment that would prevent civil unions and domestic partnership, one that would prevent the legal recognition of same-sex partnerships no matter what you call it," says Sandy Rios, president of Concerned Women of America.

Gay-marriage supporters, on the other hand, say the amendment goes too far by effectively prohibiting any marriage-like arrangements between same-sex partners. The amendment "limits all the indicia of marriage," including rights of inheritance, child support or health-care decision making, according to Vincent Samar, who teaches a course on

sexual orientation and the law at Chicago's Kent College of Law. Samar calls the amendment "dangerous." [35]

To be ratified, a constitutional amendment must be approved by two-thirds majorities in both houses of Congress and then by legislatures in three-fourths (38) of the states. Supporters acknowledge ratification faces an uphill battle. But a recent opinion poll indicates majority support for either a law or constitutional amendment to ban gay marriage.

The poll, conducted for The Associated Press by International Communications Research, reported that 52 percent of respondents favored and 41 percent opposed a law to ban gay marriage. A constitutional amendment to define marriage as one man and one woman was supported by 54 percent of respondents and opposed by 42 percent. The poll also found a majority — 53 percent — opposed to laws allowing gays or lesbians to form a civil union with marriage-like benefits.

OUTLOOK

Brave New World?

In his argument for recognizing same-sex marriage in the mid-1990s, Yale law Professor Eskridge predicted the move would bring about significant changes in the gay community and in society at large. Same-sex marriage, he wrote, "civilizes gays" — by fostering commitment, reducing promiscuity and promoting integration into the larger culture. It also "civilizes America," Eskridge said, by replacing homophobic "group hatred" with the kind of "group acceptance and cooperation" that is a source of American strength and pride.

Opponents of same-sex marriage envision significant change, too — but not for the better. Invoking the image of novelist Aldous Huxley's negative utopia, lawyers with the Marriage Watch

Project at Catholic University, say in their amicus brief in the *Goodridge* case that the "proposed 'brave new world' of marriage" would necessarily lead to legalizing incest and polygamy [and] leave "moral restraints . . . consigned to the ash heap."

Advocates of same-sex marriage today dispute the dire predictions from opponents but also minimize, to some extent, the likely changes for the gay community or society at large. "Gay married couples will pay their taxes, enroll their kids in school and fight over who takes out the garbage just like other married couples, and it will do nothing to undermine anyone else's marriage and family," says Wolfson of Freedom to Marry.

For the moment, however, acceptance of gay marriage seems to be receding, according to the three polls conducted for national news organizations since the Supreme Court's *Lawrence* decision in late June. The AP poll, the most recent of the three, indicates likely trouble for any political candidate who takes up the issue. Close to half of those surveyed said they would be less likely to support a presidential candidate who backs civil unions (44 percent) or gay marriage (49 percent), while only around 10 percent said they would be more likely.

A dose of political reality is also deflating the euphoria within the gay community about the moves toward same-sex marriage in Canada. The government's planned legislation to legalize same-sex marriage nationwide faces uncertain prospects for passage, according to news accounts. Some members of Canada's Parliament are suggesting the issue be put before the voters in a national referendum. Polls indicate Canadians are almost equally divided on the subject.

Gay-marriage advocates in the United States play down the recent poll numbers as a momentary dip. With suits advancing in Arizona and New Jersey and the Massachusetts case still awaiting decision, they profess confidence that a breakthrough is imminent. [36] "Within a year, we will see gay couples legally married in the United States," Wolfson says, "and Americans will accept that."

Opponents denounce the courts' role on the issue. "The only way the gay agenda is moved forward is from runaway courts," says Mackey of the Family Research Council. "We think that's a very serious problem when the courts take on something that they shouldn't."

For his part, gay-marriage opponent Wardle, of Brigham Young University, says he is resigned to unfavorable rulings from some state courts: "It will mean that gay relationships recognized in one state will not be recognized in some other states."

However, Wardle and gay-marriage advocate Strasser at Capital University Law School both believe the Supreme Court is unlikely to endorse same-sex marriage any time soon.

Individual state legislatures, however, could decide to provide marriage-like benefits to homosexual couples even without court action. The California legislature is on the verge of approving a bill to give registered domestic partners — including gay and lesbian couples — an array of benefits, including the ability to ask for child support and alimony and t he right to health coverage under a partner's plan. The bill, approved by the state Senate on Aug. 28 and awaiting final approval of amendments by the Assembly, would also give domestic partners the same privilege for marital confidentiality enjoyed by heterosexuals. Democratic Gov. Gray Davis supports the bill and has promised to sign it when it reaches his desk. [37]

With no definitive resolution on the issue on the horizon, both sides appear to be preparing for a long struggle. Opponents believe public opinion is on their side and will ultimately prevail. "In spite of what you're seeing in pop culture and in the media, in the absence of anything pushing back on the gay agenda, in spite of that silence except from groups like ours, Americans seem to be resonating with what we believe to be true," says Rios of Concerned Women of America.

"If the masses of the people decide they're going to have to take this on, marriage will be codified as one man, one woman."

Gay-marriage supporters, however, note that other civil-rights movements have struggled long and hard to win over public opinion. "Our civil-rights movement will be on the same type of slow-but-sure march toward equality in marriage," says Lambda Legal Defense attorney Buckel.

"The outcome is inevitable," he continues. "It's about family. Anybody who has a family knows how far they will go to get the protections that family needs."

Notes

[1] For general background, see the following *CQ Researcher* reports: Kenneth Jost, "Gay Rights Update," April 14, 2000, pp. 305-328; Richard L. Worsnop, "Gay Rights," March 5, 1993, pp. 193-216; Charles S. Clark, "Marriage and Divorce," May 10, 1996, pp. 409-432.

[2] Darryl Fears, "3 Support Same-Sex Marriage; Democrats Appear At Rights Forum," *The Washington Post*, July 16, 2003, p. A8.

[3] U.S. Census Bureau, "Married-Couple and Unmarried-Partner Households: 2000," *Census 2000 Special Reports*, February 2003, pp. 1-13.

[4] Timothy J. Dailey, "Homosexual Parenting: Placing Children at Risk," Family Research Council, Oct. 30, 2001.

[5] Judith Stacey and Timothy J. Biblarz, "(How) Does the Sexual Orientation of Parents Matter?" *American Sociological Review*, Vol. 66 (April 2001), pp. 159-183.

[6] Background drawn from William N. Eskridge Jr., *The Case for Same-Sex Marriage: From Sexual Liberty to Civilized Commitment* (1996), pp. 15-50. The chapter can also be found at "Peo-

ple with a History: An Online Guide to Lesbian, Gay, Bisexual, and Trans History," a Web site maintained by Fordham University Professor Paul Halsall (www.fordham.edu/halsall/pwh).

[7] John Boswell, *Same-Sex Unions in Premodern Europe* (1994). For representative reviews, see Marina Warner, "More Than Friendship," *The New York Times Book Review*, Aug. 28, 1994, p. 7; Wendy Doniger, "Making Brothers," *Los Angeles Times Book Review*, July 31, 1994, p. 1; and Camille Paglia, "Plighting Their Troth," *Book World* (*The Washington Post*), July 17, 1994, p. X1. For a compendium of sources, see "People with a History," *op. cit.*

[8] Boswell, *op. cit.*, p. 191.

[9] Eskridge, *op. cit.*, p. 35.

[10] *Ibid.*, p. 44.

[11] Background drawn from Eskridge, *op. cit.*, pp. 51-86.

[12] The case is *Baker v. Nelson*, 191 N.W.2d 185 (Minn. 1971).

[13] Eskridge, *op. cit.*, p. 56. The cases from eight states are listed in footnote 28, at pp. 232-233.

[14] The case is *Bowers v. Hardwick*, 478 U.S. 186 (1986).

[15] The debate, originally published in *OUT/LOOK, National Lesbian and Gay Quarterly* (fall 1989), is reprinted in Suzanne Sherman (ed.), *Lesbian and Gay Marriage: Private Commitments, Public Ceremonies* (1992), pp. 13-26. Stoddard died in 1997; Ettelbrick, currently family policy director of the National Gay and Lesbian Task Force, is now more supportive of efforts to win legal recognition of same-sex relationships.

[16] Janet Levin, "Sexual Relations: The 1994 Advocate Survey of Sexuality and Relationships: The Men," *The Advocate*, Aug. 23, 1994, pp. 32-33; Janet Levin, "Lesbian Sex Survey: The 1995 Advocate Survey of Sexuality and Relationships: The Women," *The Advocate*, Aug. 22, 1995, pp. 26-27.

[17] For background on the lead plaintiffs, Ninia Baehr and Genora Dancel, see Eskridge, *op. cit.*, pp. 1-4.

[18] The decision is *Baehr v. Lewin*, 852 P.2d 44 (Hawaii 1993).

[19] The decision is *Baehr v. Miike*. The Hawaii Supreme Court decision, not officially published, can be found at 1999 *LEXIS* 391.

[20] The decision is *Brause v. Bureau of Vital Statistics*, 1998 WL 88743 (Alaska Super.).

FOR MORE INFORMATION

Concerned Women for America, 1015 15th St., N.W., Suite 1100, Washington, DC 20005; (202) 488-7000; www.cwfa.org. Conservative advocacy group opposed to gay marriage and other parts of what it calls the "homosexual agenda."

Family Research Council, 801 G St., N.W., Washington, DC 20001; (202) 393-2100; www.frc.org. Nationwide pro-family group opposed to gay marriage.

Freedom to Marry, 116 West 23rd St, Suite 500, New York, NY 10011; (212) 851-8418; www.freedomtomarry.org. Gay-marriage advocacy group seeks to mobilize supporters outside gay-lesbian community.

Gay and Lesbian Advocates and Defenders, 30 Winter St., Suite 800, Boston, MA 02108; (617) 426-1350; www.glad.org. Regional gay-rights organization representing plaintiffs in Massachusetts gay-marriage case.

Lambda Legal Defense and Education Fund, Inc., 120 Wall St., Suite 1500, New York, NY 10005-3904; (212) 809-8585; www.lambdalegal.org. National gay-rights organization representing plaintiffs in New Jersey gay-marriage case.

Massachusetts Family Institute, 381 Elliot St., Newton, MA 02464; (617) 928-0800; www.mafamily.org. Pro-family organization, founded in 1991, opposed to gay marriage.

---

[21] See *1996 CQ Almanac*, pp. 5-26 — 5-29.

[22] The case is *Baker v. State*, 744 A.2d 864 (Vt. 1999).

[23] For coverage, see Trudy Tynan, "Gay couples sue over right to marry in Massachusetts," The Associated Press, April 11, 2001; Yvonne Abraham, "Gays Seek Right to Marry," *The Boston Globe*, April 12, 2001, p. A1; Linda Bock, "Gays Seek OK for Marriage," *The* (Worcester) *Telegram and Gazette*, April 12, 2001, p. A1.

[24] For coverage, see Kathleen Burge, "Judge Dismisses Same-Sex Marriage Suit," *The Boston Globe*, May 9, 2002, p. B6.

[25] For coverage, see Kathleen Burge, "SJC Peppers Lawyers on Same-Sex Marriage," *The Boston Globe*, March 5, 2003, p. A1.

[26] The case is *Halpern v. Canada* (A.G.), C39172 (Court of Appeal for Ontario, June 10, 2003). http://www.ontariocourts.on.ca/decisions/2003/june/halpernC39172.htm

[27] Evan Thomas, "The War Over Gay Marriage," *Newsweek*, July 7, 2003, pp. 38-45.

[28] Deb Price, "Gay Newlyweds Embrace Canadian Marriage," *The Detroit News*, July 7, 2003.

[29] Three states have no newspapers that publish same-sex couples' announcements: Mississippi, Oklahoma and South Dakota. For a complete list, see the Gay and Lesbian Alliance Against Defamation's Web Site: www.glaad.org.

[30] David Toussaint, "Outward Bound," *Bride's*, September-October 2003, p. 346.

[31] U.S. Census Bureau, *op. cit.*

[32] Quoted in Christopher Marquis, "Total of Unmarried Couples Surged in 2000 U.S. Census," *The New York Times*, March 13, 2003, p. A22.

[33] Quoted in Evelyn Nieves, "Family Values Groups Gear Up for Battle Over Gay Marriage," *The Washington Post*, Aug. 17, 2003, p. A6.

[34] See Bill Swindell and John Cochran, "Gay Marriage Debate Holds Land Mines for Both Parties," *CQ Today*, Aug. 1, 2003.

[35] Appearance on PBS "NewsHour with Jim Lehrer," July 31, 2003.

[36] The New Jersey case is *Lewis v. Harris*, L-00-4233-02 (Hudson County Superior Court), filed June 26, 2002. The Arizona case is *Standhardt vs. Superior Court*, 1 CA-SA-03-0150, argued before the Arizona Court of Appeal on Aug. 19, 2003.

[37] See Carl Ingram, "Domestic Partners Bill OKd," *Los Angeles Times*, Aug. 29, 2003, p. B1.

Bibliography

Selected Sources

Books

Boswell, John, *Same-Sex Unions in Premodern Europe*, Villard, 1994.

Presents highly controversial thesis by the late, openly gay Yale historian that the medieval Catholic Church routinely conducted ceremonies solemnizing "same-sex unions" between men. Heavily annotated; includes texts of manuscripts, translated. Draws on author's earlier work, *Christianity, Social Tolerance, and Homosexuality: Gay People in Western Europe from the Beginning of the Christian Era to the Fourteenth Century* (University of Chicago Press, 1980).

Eskridge, William N., *The Case for Same-Sex Marriage: From Sexual Liberty to Civilized Commitment*, Free Press, 1996.

A professor at Yale Law School strongly argues for legal recognition of same-sex marriage. Chapters cover history of same-sex marriage, debate within gay and lesbian community, mainstream objections to same-sex marriage, and constitutional arguments for recognition. Includes notes, list of court cases and 20-page list of references.

Lewin, Ellen, *Recognizing Ourselves: Ceremonies of Gay and Lesbian Commitment*, Columbia University Press, 1998.

A professor of anthropology and women's studies at the University of Iowa provides a comprehensive account of gay and lesbian commitment ceremonies in the United States, including the author's own. Includes notes and 10 pages of references. For an older collection of vignettes of gay and lesbian couples, see Suzanne Sherman (ed.), *Lesbian and Gay Marriage: Private Commitments, Public Ceremonies* (Temple University Press, 1992).

Strasser, Mark, *On Same-Sex Marriage, Civil Unions, and the Rule of Law: Constitutional Interpretation at the Crossroads*, Praeger, 2002.

A professor at Capital University Law School, Columbus, Ohio, argues for recognition of same-sex marriage with analysis of legal developments from Hawaii Supreme Court ruling through enactment of Vermont "civil union" legislation. Includes notes, list of court cases and bibliography. For earlier titles, see *The Challenge of Same-Sex Marriage: Federalist Principles and Constitutional Protections* (Praeger, 1999); and *Legally Wed: Same-Sex Marriage and the Constitution* (Cornell University Press, 1997).

Wardle, Lynn D., Mark Strasser, William C. Duncan and David Orgon Coolidge (eds.), *Marriage and Same-Sex Unions: A Debate*, Praeger, 2003.

Carefully balanced essays by some 20 contributors on historical, philosophical and constitutional views of same-sex marriage. Includes two-page table of cases. Wardle and Strasser are identified under their individual titles. Duncan is assistant director of the Marriage Law Project, Columbus School of Law, Catholic University of America; Coolidge was the project's director before his death in 2002.

Articles

Bumiller, Elisabeth, "Why America Has Gay Marriage Jitters," *The New York Times*, Aug. 10, 2003, Sec. 4, p. 1.

Analyzes public opinion on gay marriage after polls registered drop in popular support.

Thomas, Evan, "The War Over Gay Marriage," *Newsweek*, July 7, 2003, pp. 38-45.

Journalistic analysis of gay-marriage issue immediately following U.S. Supreme Court's decision striking down state anti-sodomy laws.

Wardle, Lynn D., "A Critical Analysis of Constitutional Claims for Same-Sex Marriage," *Brigham Young University Law Review*, Vol. 1996, No. 1, pp. 1-101.

Comprehensively criticizes arguments for recognizing same-sex marriage; also notes "imbalance" in legal literature on the issue. Wardle is a professor at Brigham Young University's J. Ruben Clark School of Law. For a more recent article, see "'Multiply and Replenish': Considering Same-Sex Marriage in Light of State Interests in Marital Procreation," *Harvard Journal of Law and Public Policy*, Vol. 24, No. 3 (summer 2001), pp. 771-814.

Reports and Studies

American Academy of Pediatrics, "Technical Report: Coparent or Second-Parent Adoption by Same-Sex Parents," Vol. 109, No. 2 (February 2002), pp. 341-344.

Task force of pediatricians' group examines some 20 studies to conclude that children raised by gay or lesbian parents fare as well as children raised in heterosexual households.

Cahill, Sean, Mitra Ellen and Sarah Tobias, "Family Policy: Issues Affecting Gay, Lesbian, Bisexual and Transgender Families," National Gay and Lesbian Task Force Policy Institute, 2002.

Comprehensively catalogs from an advocacy perspective laws and policies affecting gay and lesbian individuals and families.

Lerner, Robert, and Althea K. Nagai, "No Basis: What the Studies Don't Tell Us About Same-Sex Parenting," January 2001 (www.marriagewatch.org).

Critique by two social scientists of studies purporting to show that children raised by gay or lesbian parents fare as well as those raised in heterosexual households.

Constitution of the United States

We the People of the United States, in Order to form a more perfect Union, establish Justice, insure domestic Tranquility, provide for the common defence, promote the general Welfare, and secure the Blessings of Liberty to ourselves and our Posterity, do ordain and establish this Constitution for the United States of America.

Article I

Section 1. All legislative Powers herein granted shall be vested in a Congress of the United States, which shall consist of a Senate and House of Representatives.

Section 2. The House of Representatives shall be composed of Members chosen every second Year by the People of the several States, and the Electors in each State shall have the Qualifications requisite for Electors of the most numerous Branch of the State Legislature.

No Person shall be a Representative who shall not have attained to the age of twenty five Years, and been seven Years a Citizen of the United States, and who shall not, when elected, be an Inhabitant of that State in which he shall be chosen.

[Representatives and direct Taxes shall be apportioned among the several States which may be included within this Union, according to their respective Numbers, which shall be determined by adding to the whole Number of free Persons, including those bound to Service for a Term of Years, and excluding Indians not taxed, three fifths of all other Persons.][1] The actual Enumeration shall be made within three Years after the first Meeting of the Congress of the United States, and within every subsequent Term of ten Years, in such Manner as they shall by Law direct. The Number of Representatives shall not exceed one for every thirty Thousand, but each State shall have at Least one Representative; and until such enumeration shall be made, the State of New Hampshire shall be entitled to chuse three, Massachusetts eight, Rhode-Island and Providence Plantations one, Connecticut five, New-York six, New Jersey four, Pennsylvania eight, Delaware one, Maryland six, Virginia ten, North Carolina five, South Carolina five, and Georgia three.

When vacancies happen in the Representation from any State, the Executive Authority thereof shall issue Writs of Election to fill such Vacancies.

The House of Representatives shall chuse their Speaker and other Officers; and shall have the sole Power of Impeachment.

Section 3. The Senate of the United States shall be composed of two Senators from each State, [chosen by the Legislature thereof,][2] for six Years; and each Senator shall have one Vote.

Immediately after they shall be assembled in Consequence of the first Election, they shall be divided as equally as may be into three Classes. The Seats of the Senators of the first Class shall be vacated at the Expiration of the second Year, of the second Class at the Expiration of the fourth Year, and of the third Class at the Expiration of the sixth Year, so that one third may be chosen every second Year; [and if Vacancies happen by Resignation, or otherwise, during the Recess of the Legislature of any State, the Executive thereof may make temporary Appointments until the next Meeting of the Legislature, which shall then fill such Vacancies.][3]

No Person shall be a Senator who shall not have attained to the Age of thirty Years, and been nine Years a Citizen of the United States, and who shall not, when elected, be an Inhabitant of that State for which he shall be chosen.

The Vice President of the United States shall be President of the Senate, but shall have no Vote, unless they be equally divided.

The Senate shall chuse their other Officers, and also a President pro tempore, in the Absence of the Vice President, or when he shall exercise the Office of President of the United States.

The Senate shall have the sole Power to try all Impeachments. When sitting for that Purpose, they shall be on Oath or Affirmation. When the President of the United States is tried, the Chief Justice shall preside: And no Person shall be convicted without the Concurrence of two thirds of the Members present.

Judgment in Cases of Impeachment shall not extend further than to removal from Office, and disqualification to hold and enjoy any Office of honor, Trust or Profit under the United States: but the Party convicted shall nevertheless be liable and subject to Indictment, Trial, Judgment and Punishment, according to Law.

Section 4. The Times, Places and Manner of holding Elections for Senators and Representatives, shall be prescribed in each State by the Legislature thereof; but the Congress may at any time by Law make or alter such Regulations, except as to the Places of chusing Senators.

The Congress shall assemble at least once in every Year, and such Meeting shall [be on the first Monday in December],[4] unless they shall by Law appoint a different Day.

Section 5. Each House shall be the Judge of the Elections, Returns and Qualifications of its own Members, and a Majority of each shall constitute a Quorum to do Business; but a smaller Number may adjourn from day to day, and may be authorized to compel the Attendance of absent Members, in such Manner, and under such Penalties as each House may provide.

Each House may determine the Rules of its Proceedings, punish its Members for disorderly Behaviour, and, with the Concurrence of two thirds, expel a Member.

Each House shall keep a Journal of its Proceedings, and from time to time publish the same, excepting such Parts as may in their Judgment require Secrecy; and the Yeas and Nays of the Members of either House on any question shall, at the Desire of one fifth of those Present, be entered on the Journal.

Neither House, during the Session of Congress, shall, without the Consent of the other, adjourn for more than three days, nor to any other Place than that in which the two Houses shall be sitting.

Section 6. The Senators and Representatives shall receive a Compensation for their Services, to be ascertained by Law, and paid out of the Treasury of the United States. They shall in all Cases, except Treason, Felony and Breach of the Peace, be privileged from Arrest during their Attendance at the Session of their respective Houses, and in going to and returning from the same; and for any Speech or Debate in either House, they shall not be questioned in any other Place.

No Senator or Representative shall, during the Time for which he was elected, be appointed to any civil Office under the Authority of the United States, which shall have been created, or the Emoluments whereof shall have been encreased during such time; and no Person holding any Office under the United States, shall be a Member of either House during his Continuance in Office.

Section 7. All Bills for raising Revenue shall originate in the House of Representatives; but the Senate may propose or concur with Amendments as on other Bills.

Every Bill which shall have passed the House of Representatives and the Senate, shall, before it become a Law, be presented to the President of the United States; If he approve he shall sign it, but if not he shall return it, with his Objections to that House in which it shall have originated, who shall enter the Objections at large on their Journal, and proceed to reconsider it. If after such Reconsideration two thirds of that House shall agree to pass the Bill, it shall be sent, together with the Objections, to the other House, by which it shall likewise be reconsidered, and if approved by two thirds of that House, it shall become a Law. But in all such Cases the Votes of both Houses shall be determined by yeas and Nays, and the Names of the Persons voting for and against the Bill shall be entered on the Journal of each House respectively. If any Bill shall not be returned by the President within ten Days (Sundays excepted) after it shall have been presented to him, the Same shall be a Law, in like Manner as if he had signed it, unless the Congress by their Adjournment prevent its Return, in which Case it shall not be a Law.

Every Order, Resolution, or Vote to which the Concurrence of the Senate and House of Representatives may be necessary (except on a question of Adjournment) shall be presented to the President of the United States; and before the Same shall take Effect, shall be approved by him, or being disapproved by him, shall be repassed by two thirds of the Senate and House of Representatives, according to the Rules and Limitations prescribed in the Case of a Bill.

Section 8. The Congress shall have Power To lay and collect Taxes, Duties, Imposts and Excises, to pay the Debts and provide for the common Defence and general Welfare of the United States; but all Duties, Imposts and Excises shall be uniform throughout the United States;

To borrow Money on the credit of the United States;

To regulate Commerce with foreign Nations, and among the several States, and with the Indian Tribes;

To establish an uniform Rule of Naturalization, and uniform Laws on the subject of Bankruptcies throughout the United States;

To coin Money, regulate the Value thereof, and of foreign Coin, and fix the Standard of Weights and Measures;

To provide for the Punishment of counterfeiting the Securities and current Coin of the United States;

To establish Post Offices and post Roads;

To promote the Progress of Science and useful Arts, by securing for limited Times to Authors and Inventors the exclusive Right to their respective Writings and Discoveries;

To constitute Tribunals inferior to the supreme Court;

To define and punish Piracies and Felonies committed on the high Seas, and Offences against the Law of Nations;

To declare War, grant Letters of Marque and Reprisal, and make Rules concerning Captures on Land and Water;

To raise and support Armies, but no Appropriation of Money to that Use shall be for a longer Term than two Years;

To provide and maintain a Navy;

To make Rules for the Government and Regulation of the land and naval Forces;

To provide for calling forth the Militia to execute the Laws of the Union, suppress Insurrections and repel Invasions;

To provide for organizing, arming, and disciplining, the Militia, and for governing such Part of them as may be employed in the Service of the United States, reserving to the States respectively, the Appointment of the Officers, and the Authority of training the Militia according to the discipline prescribed by Congress;

To exercise exclusive Legislation in all Cases whatso-ever, over such District (not exceeding ten Miles square) as may, by Cession of particular States, and the Acceptance of Congress, become the Seat of the Government of the United States, and to exercise like Authority over all Places purchased by the Consent of the Legislature of the State in which the Same shall be, for the Erection of Forts, Magazines, Arsenals, dock-Yards, and other needful Buildings;—And

To make all Laws which shall be necessary and proper for carrying into Execution the foregoing Powers, and all other Powers vested by this Constitution in the Government of the United States, or in any Department or Officer thereof.

Section 9. The Migration or Importation of such Persons as any of the States now existing shall think proper to admit, shall not be prohibited by the Congress prior to the Year one thousand eight hundred and eight, but a Tax or duty may be imposed on such Importation, not exceeding ten dollars for each Person.

The Privilege of the Writ of Habeas Corpus shall not be suspended, unless when in Cases of Rebellion or Invasion the public Safety may require it.

No Bill of Attainder or ex post facto Law shall be passed.

No Capitation, or other direct, Tax shall be laid, unless in Proportion to the Census or Enumeration herein before directed to be taken.[5]

No Tax or Duty shall be laid on Articles exported from any State.

No Preference shall be given by any Regulation of Commerce or Revenue to the Ports of one State over those of another; nor shall Vessels bound to, or from, one State, be obliged to enter, clear, or pay Duties in another.

No Money shall be drawn from the Treasury, but in Consequence of Appropriations made by Law; and a regular Statement and Account of the Receipts and Expenditures of all public Money shall be published from time to time.

No Title of Nobility shall be granted by the United States: And no Person holding any Office of Profit or Trust under them, shall, without the Consent of the Congress, accept of any present, Emolument, Office, or Title, of any kind whatever, from any King, Prince, or foreign State.

Section 10. No State shall enter into any Treaty, Alliance, or Confederation; grant Letters of Marque and Reprisal; coin Money; emit Bills of Credit; make any Thing but gold and silver Coin a Tender in Payment of Debts; pass any Bill of Attainder, ex post facto Law, or Law impairing the Obligation of Contracts, or grant any Title of Nobility.

No State shall, without the Consent of the Congress, lay any Imposts or Duties on Imports or Exports, except what may be absolutely necessary for executing it's inspection Laws: and the net Produce of all Duties and Imposts, laid by any State on Imports or Exports, shall be for the Use of the Treasury of the United States; and all such Laws shall be subject to the Revision and Controul of the Congress.

No State shall, without the Consent of Congress, lay any Duty of Tonnage, keep Troops, or Ships of War in time of Peace, enter into any Agreement or Compact with another State, or with a foreign Power, or engage in War, unless actually invaded, or in such imminent Danger as will not admit of delay.

Article II

Section 1. The executive Power shall be vested in a President of the United States of America. He shall hold his Office during the Term of four Years, and, together with the Vice President, chosen for the same Term, be elected, as follows

Each State shall appoint, in such Manner as the Legislature thereof may direct, a Number of Electors, equal to the whole Number of Senators and Representatives to which the State may be entitled in the Congress: but no Senator or Representative, or Person holding an Office of Trust or Profit under the United States, shall be appointed an Elector.

[The Electors shall meet in their respective States, and vote by Ballot for two Persons, of whom one at least shall not be an Inhabitant of the same State with themselves. And they shall make a List of all the Persons voted for, and of the Number of Votes for each; which List they shall sign and certify, and trans-mit sealed to the Seat of the Government of the United States, directed to the President of the Senate. The President of the Senate shall, in the Presence of the Senate and House of Representatives, open all the Certificates, and the Votes shall then be counted. The Person having the greatest Number of Votes shall be the President, if such Number be a Majority of the whole Number of Electors appointed; and if there be more than one who have such Majority, and have an equal Number of Votes, then the House of Representatives shall immediately chuse by Ballot one of them for President; and if no Person have a Majority, then from the five highest on the list the said House shall in like Manner chuse the President. But in chusing the President, the Votes shall be taken by States, the Representation from each State having one Vote; A quorum for this Purpose shall consist of a Member or Members from two thirds of the States, and a Majority of all the States shall be necessary to a Choice. In every Case, after the Choice of the President, the Person having the greatest Number of Votes of the Electors shall be the Vice President. But if there should remain two or more who have equal Votes, the Senate shall chuse from them by Ballot the Vice President.][6]

The Congress may determine the Time of chusing the Electors, and the Day on which they shall give their Votes; which Day shall be the same throughout the United States.

No Person except a natural born Citizen, or a Citizen of the United States, at the time of the Adoption of this Constitution, shall be eligible to the Office of President; neither shall any Person be eligible to that Office who shall not have attained to the Age of thirty five Years, and been fourteen Years a Resident within the United States.

In Case of the Removal of the President from Office, or of his Death, Resignation, or Inability to discharge the Powers and Duties of the said Office,[7] the Same shall devolve on the Vice President, and the Congress may by Law provide for the Case of Removal, Death, Resignation or Inability, both of the President and Vice President, declaring what Officer shall then act as President, and such Officer shall act accordingly, until the Disability be removed, or a President shall be elected.

The President shall, at stated Times, receive for his Services, a Compensation, which shall neither be encreased nor diminished during the Period for which he shall have been elected, and he shall not receive within that Period any other Emolument from the United States, or any of them.

Before he enter on the Execution of his Office, he shall take the following Oath or Affirmation:—"I do solemnly swear (or affirm) that I will faithfully execute the Office of President of the United States, and will to the best of my Ability, preserve, protect and defend the Constitution of the United States."

Section 2. The President shall be Commander in Chief of the Army and Navy of the United States, and of the Militia of the several States, when called into the actual Service of the United States; he may require the Opinion, in writing, of the principal Officer in each of the executive Departments, upon any Subject relating to the Duties of their respective Offices, and he shall have Power to grant Reprieves and Pardons for Offences against the United States, except in Cases of Impeachment.

He shall have Power, by and with the Advice and Consent of the Senate, to make Treaties, provided two thirds of the Senators present concur; and he shall nominate, and by and with the Advice and Consent of the Senate, shall appoint Ambassadors, other public Ministers and Consuls, Judges of the supreme Court, and all other Officers of the United States, whose Appointments are not herein otherwise provided for, and which shall be established by Law: but the Congress may by Law vest the Appointment of such inferior Officers, as they think proper, in the President alone, in the Courts of Law, or in the Heads of Departments.

The President shall have Power to fill up all Vacancies that may happen during the Recess of the Senate, by granting Commissions which shall expire at the End of their next Session.

Section 3. He shall from time to time give to the Congress Information of the State of the Union, and recommend to their Consideration such Measures as he shall judge necessary and expedient; he may, on extraordinary Occasions, convene both Houses, or either of them, and in Case of Disagreement between them, with Respect to the Time of Adjournment, he may adjourn them to such Time as he shall think proper; he shall receive Ambassadors and other public Ministers; he shall take Care that the Laws be faithfully executed, and shall Commission all the Officers of the United States.

Section 4. The President, Vice President and all civil Officers of the United States, shall be removed from Office on Impeachment for, and Conviction of, Treason, Bribery, or other high Crimes and Misdemeanors.

Article III

Section 1. The judicial Power of the United States, shall be vested in one supreme Court, and in such inferior Courts as the Congress may from time to time ordain and establish. The Judges, both of the supreme and inferior Courts, shall hold their Offices during good Behaviour, and shall, at stated Times, receive for their Services, a Compensation, which shall not be diminished during their Continuance in Office.

Section 2. The judicial Power shall extend to all Cases, in Law and Equity, arising under this Constitution, the Laws of the United States, and Treaties made, or which shall be made, under their Authority; — to all Cases affecting Ambassadors, other public Ministers and Consuls; —to all Cases of admiralty and maritime Jurisdiction; —to Controversies to which the United States shall be a Party; —to Controversies between two or more States; —between a State and Citizens of another State;[8] —between Citizens of different States; —between Citizens of the same State claiming Lands under Grants of different States, and between a State, or the Citizens thereof, and foreign States, Citizens or Subjects.[8]

In all Cases affecting Ambassadors, other public Ministers and Consuls, and those in which a State shall be Party, the supreme Court shall have original Jurisdiction. In all the other Cases before mentioned, the supreme Court shall have appellate Jurisdiction, both as to Law and Fact, with such Exceptions, and under such Regulations as the Congress shall make.

The Trial of all Crimes, except in Cases of Impeachment, shall be by Jury; and such Trial shall be held in the State where the said Crimes shall have been committed; but when not committed within any State, the Trial shall be at such Place or Places as the Congress may by Law have directed.

Section 3. Treason against the United States, shall consist only in levying War against them, or in adhering to their Enemies, giving them Aid and Comfort. No Person shall be convicted of Treason unless on the Testimony of two Witnesses to the same overt Act, or on Confession in open Court.

The Congress shall have Power to declare the Punishment of Treason, but no Attainder of Treason shall work Corruption of Blood, or Forfeiture except during the Life of the Person attainted.

Article IV

Section 1. Full Faith and Credit shall be given in each State to the public Acts, Records, and judicial Proceedings of every other State. And the Congress may by general Laws prescribe the Manner in which such Acts, Records and Proceedings shall be proved, and the Effect thereof.

Section 2. The Citizens of each State shall be entitled to all Privileges and Immunities of Citizens in the several States.

A Person charged in any State with Treason, Felony, or other Crime, who shall flee from Justice, and be found in another State, shall on Demand of the executive Authority of the State from which he fled, be delivered up, to be removed to the State having Jurisdiction of the Crime.

[No Person held to Service or Labour in one State, under the Laws thereof, escaping into another, shall, in Consequence of any Law or Regulation therein, be discharged from such Service or Labour, but shall be delivered up on Claim of the Party to whom such Service or Labour may be due.][9]

Section 3. New States may be admitted by the Congress into this Union; but no new State shall be formed or erected within the Jurisdiction of any other State; nor any State be formed by the Junction of two or more States, or Parts of States, without the Consent of the Legislatures of the States concerned as well as of the Congress.

The Congress shall have Power to dispose of and make all needful Rules and Regulations respecting the Territory or other Property belonging to the United States; and nothing in this Constitution shall be so construed as to Prejudice any Claims of the United States, or of any particular State.

Section 4. The United States shall guarantee to every State in this Union a Republican Form of Government, and shall protect each of them against Invasion; and on Application of the Legislature, or of the Executive (when the Legislature cannot be convened) against domestic Violence.

Article V

The Congress, whenever two thirds of both Houses shall deem it necessary, shall propose Amendments to this Constitution, or, on the Application of the Legislatures of two thirds of the several States, shall call a Convention for proposing Amendments, which, in either Case, shall be valid to all Intents and Purposes, as Part of this Constitution, when ratified by the Legislatures of three fourths of the several States, or by Conventions in three fourths thereof, as the one or the other Mode of Ratification may be proposed by the Congress; Provided [that no Amendment which may be made prior to the Year One thousand eight hundred and eight shall in any Manner affect the first and fourth Clauses in the Ninth Section of the first Article; and][10] that no State, without its Consent, shall be deprived of its equal Suffrage in the Senate.

Article VI

All Debts contracted and Engagements entered into, before the Adoption of this Constitution, shall be as valid against the United States under this Constitution, as under the Confederation.

This Constitution, and the Laws of the United States which shall be made in Pursuance thereof; and all Treaties made, or which shall be made, under the Authority of the United States, shall be the supreme Law of the Land; and the Judges in every State shall be bound thereby, any Thing in the Constitution or Laws of any State to the Contrary notwithstanding.

The Senators and Representatives before mentioned, and the Members of the several State Legislatures, and all executive and judicial Officers, both of the United States and of the several States, shall be bound by Oath or Affirmation, to support this Constitution; but no religious Test shall ever be required as a Qualification to any Office or public Trust under the United States.

Article VII

The Ratification of the Conventions of nine States, shall be sufficient for the Establishment of this Constitution between the States so ratifying the Same.

Done in Convention by the Unanimous Consent of the States present the Seventeenth Day of September in the Year of our Lord one thousand seven hundred and Eighty seven and of the Independence of the United States of America the Twelfth. IN WITNESS whereof We have hereunto subscribed our Names,

George Washington,
President and deputy from Virginia

[The language of the original Constitution, not including the Amendments, was adopted by a convention of the states on September 17, 1787, and was subsequently ratified by the states on the following dates: Delaware, December 7, 1787; Pennsylvania, December 12, 1787; New Jersey, December 18, 1787; Georgia, January 2, 1788; Connecticut, January 9, 1788; Massachusetts, February 6, 1788; Maryland, April 28, 1788; South Carolina, May 23, 1788; New Hampshire, June 21, 1788.

Ratification was completed on June 21, 1788.

The Constitution subsequently was ratified by Virginia, June 25, 1788; New York, July 26, 1788; North Carolina, November 21, 1789; Rhode Island, May 29, 1790; and Vermont, January 10, 1791.]

Amendments

Amendment I

(First ten amendments ratified December 15, 1791.)

Congress shall make no law respecting an establishment of religion, or prohibiting the free exercise thereof; or abridging the freedom of speech, or of the press; or the right of the peo-ple peaceably to assemble, and to petition the Government for a redress of grievances.

Amendment II

A well regulated Militia, being necessary to the security of a free State, the right of the people to keep and bear Arms, shall not be infringed.

Amendment III

No Soldier shall, in time of peace be quartered in any house, without the consent of the Owner, nor in time of war, but in a manner to be prescribed by law.

Amendment IV

The right of the people to be secure in their persons, houses, papers, and effects, against unreasonable searches and seizures, shall not be violated, and no Warrants shall issue, but upon probable cause, supported by Oath or affirmation, and particularly describing the place to be searched, and the persons or things to be seized.

Amendment V

No person shall be held to answer for a capital, or otherwise infamous crime, unless on a presentment or indictment of a Grand Jury, except in cases arising in the land or naval forces, or in the Militia, when in actual service in time of War or public danger; nor shall any person be subject for the same offence to be twice put in jeopardy of life or limb; nor shall be compelled in any criminal case to be a witness against himself, nor be deprived of life, liberty, or property, without due process of law; nor shall private property be taken for public use, without just compensation.

Amendment VI

In all criminal prosecutions, the accused shall enjoy the right to a speedy and public trial, by an impartial jury of the State and district wherein the crime shall have been committed, which district shall have been previously ascertained by law, and to be informed of the nature and cause of the accusation; to be confronted with the witnesses against him; to have compulsory process for obtaining witnesses in his favor, and to have the Assistance of Counsel for his defence.

Amendment VII

In Suits at common law, where the value in controversy shall exceed twenty dollars, the right of trial by jury shall be preserved, and no fact tried by a jury, shall be otherwise re-examined in any Court of the United States, than according to the rules of the common law.

Amendment VIII

Excessive bail shall not be required, nor excessive fines imposed, nor cruel and unusual punishments inflicted.

Amendment IX

The enumeration in the Constitution, of certain rights, shall not be construed to deny or disparage others retained by the people.

Amendment X

The powers not delegated to the United States by the Constitution, nor prohibited by it to the States, are reserved to the States respectively, or to the people.

Amendment XI (Ratified February 7, 1795)

The Judicial power of the United States shall not be construed to extend to any suit in law or equity, commenced or prosecuted against one of the United States by Citizens of another State, or by Citizens or Subjects of any Foreign State.

Amendment XII (Ratified June 15, 1804)

The Electors shall meet in their respective states and vote by ballot for President and Vice-President, one of whom, at least, shall not be an inhabitant of the same state with themselves; they shall name in their ballots the person voted for as President, and in distinct ballots the person voted for as Vice-President, and they shall make distinct lists of all persons voted for as President, and of all persons voted for as Vice-President, and of the number of votes for each, which lists they shall sign and certify, and transmit sealed to the seat of the government of the United States, directed to the President of the Senate; — The President of the Senate shall, in the presence of the Senate and House of Representatives, open all the certificates and the votes shall then be counted; — The person having the greatest number of votes for President, shall be the President, if such number be a majority of the whole number of Electors appointed; and if no person have such majority, then from the persons having the highest numbers not exceeding three on the list of those voted for as President, the House of Representatives shall choose immediately, by ballot, the President. But in choosing the President, the votes shall be taken by states, the representation from each state having one vote; a quorum for this purpose shall consist of a member or members from two-thirds of the states, and a majority of all the states shall be necessary to a choice. [And if the House of Representatives shall not choose a President whenever the right of choice shall devolve upon them, before the fourth day of March next following, then the Vice-President shall act as President, as in the case of the death or other constitutional disability of the President. —][11] The person having the greatest number of votes as Vice-President, shall be the Vice-President, if such number be a majority of the whole number of Electors appointed, and if no person have a majority, then from the two highest numbers on the list, the Senate shall choose the Vice-President; a quorum for the purpose shall consist of two-thirds of the whole number of Senators, and a majority of the whole number shall be necessary to a choice. But no person constitutionally ineligible to the office of President shall be eligible to that of Vice-President of the United States.

Amendment XIII (Ratified December 6, 1865)

Section 1. Neither slavery nor involuntary servitude, except as a punishment for crime whereof the party shall have been duly convicted, shall exist within the United States, or any place subject to their jurisdiction.

Section 2. Congress shall have power to enforce this Article by appropriate legislation.

Amendment XIV (Ratified July 9, 1868)

Section 1. All persons born or naturalized in the United States, and subject to the jurisdiction thereof, are citizens of the United States and of the State wherein they reside. No State shall make or enforce any law which shall abridge the privileges or immunities of citizens of the United States; nor shall any State deprive any person of life, liberty, or property, without due process of law; nor deny to any person within its jurisdiction the equal protection of the laws.

Section 2. Representatives shall be apportioned among the several States according to their respective numbers, counting the whole number of persons in each State, excluding Indians not taxed. But when the right to vote at any election for the choice of electors for President and Vice President of the United States, Representatives in Congress, the Executive and Judicial officers of a State, or the members of the Legislature thereof, is denied to any of the male inhabitants of such State, being twenty-one years of age,[12] and citizens of the United States, or in any way abridged, except for participation in rebellion, or other crime, the basis of representation therein shall be reduced in the proportion which the number of such male citizens shall bear to the whole number of male citizens twenty-one years of age in such State.

Section 3. No person shall be a Senator or Representative in Congress, or elector of President and Vice President, or hold any office, civil or military, under the United States, or under any State, who, having previously taken an oath, as a member of Congress, or as an officer of the United States, or as a member of any State legislature, or as an executive or judicial officer of any State, to support the Constitution of the United States, shall have engaged in insurrection or rebellion against the same, or given aid or comfort to the enemies thereof. But Congress may by a vote of two-thirds of each House, remove such disability.

Section 4. The validity of the public debt of the United States, authorized by law, including debts incurred for payment of pensions and bounties for services in suppressing insurrection or rebellion, shall not be questioned. But neither the United States nor any State shall assume or pay any debt or obligation incurred in aid of insurrection or rebellion against the United States, or any claim for the loss or emancipation of any slave; but all such debts, obligations and claims shall be held illegal and void.

Section 5. The Congress shall have power to enforce, by appropriate legislation, the provisions of this Article.

Amendment XV (Ratified February 3, 1870)

Section 1. The right of citizens of the United States to vote shall not be denied or abridged by the United States or by any State on account of race, color, or previous condition of servitude.

Section 2. The Congress shall have power to enforce this Article by appropriate legislation.

Amendment XVI (Ratified February 3, 1913)

The Congress shall have power to lay and collect taxes on incomes, from whatever source derived, without apportionment among the several States, and without regard to any census or enumeration.

Amendment XVII (Ratified April 8, 1913)

The Senate of the United States shall be composed of two Senators from each State, elected by the people thereof, for six years; and each Senator shall have one vote. The electors in each State shall have the qualifications requisite for electors of the most numerous branch of the State legislatures.

When vacancies happen in the representation of any State in the Senate, the executive authority of such State shall issue writs of election to fill such vacancies: Provided, That the legislature of any State may empower the executive thereof to make temporary appointments until the people fill the vacancies by election as the legislature may direct.

This amendment shall not be so construed as to affect the election or term of any Senator chosen before it becomes valid as part of the Constitution.

Amendment XVIII (Ratified January 16, 1919)

Section 1. After one year from the ratification of this Article the manufacture, sale, or transportation of intoxicating liquors within, the importation thereof into, or the exportation thereof from the United States and all territory subject to the jurisdiction thereof for beverage purposes is hereby prohibited.

Section 2. The Congress and the several States shall have concurrent power to enforce this Article by appropriate legislation.

Section 3. This Article shall be inoperative unless it shall have been ratified as an amendment to the Constitution by the legislatures of the several States, as provided in the Constitution, within seven years from the date of the submission hereof to the States by the Congress.][13]

Amendment XIX (Ratified August 18, 1920)

The right of citizens of the United States to vote shall not be denied or abridged by the United States or by any State on account of sex.

Congress shall have power to enforce this Article by appropriate legislation.

Amendment XX (Ratified January 23, 1933)

Section 1. The terms of the President and Vice President shall end at noon on the 20th day of January, and the terms of Senators and Representatives at noon on the 3d day of January, of the years in which such terms would have ended if this Article had not been ratified; and the terms of their successors shall then begin.

Section 2. The Congress shall assemble at least once in every year, and such meeting shall begin at noon on the 3d day of January, unless they shall by law appoint a different day.

Section 3.[14] If, at the time fixed for the beginning of the term of the President, the President elect shall have died, the Vice President elect shall become President. If a President shall not have been chosen before the time fixed for the beginning of his term, or if the President elect shall have failed to qualify, then the Vice President elect shall act as President until a President shall have qualified; and the Congress may by law provide for the case

wherein neither a President elect nor a Vice President elect shall have qualified, declaring who shall then act as President, or the manner in which one who is to act shall be selected, and such person shall act accordingly until a President or Vice President shall have qualified.

Section 4. The Congress may by law provide for the case of the death of any of the persons from whom the House of Representatives may choose a President whenever the right of choice shall have devolved upon them, and for the case of the death of any of the persons from whom the Senate may choose a Vice President whenever the right of choice shall have devolved upon them.

Section 5. Sections 1 and 2 shall take effect on the 15th day of October following the ratification of this Article.

Section 6. This Article shall be inoperative unless it shall have been ratified as an amendment to the Constitution by the legislatures of three-fourths of the several States within seven years from the date of its submission.

Amendment XXI (Ratified December 5, 1933)

Section 1. The eighteenth Article of amendment to the Constitution of the United States is hereby repealed.

Section 2. The transportation or importation into any State, Territory, or possession of the United States for delivery or use therein of intoxicating liquors, in violation of the laws thereof, is hereby prohibited.

Section 3. This Article shall be inoperative unless it shall have been ratified as an amendment to the Constitution by conventions in the several States, as provided in the Constitution, within seven years from the date of the submission hereof to the States by the Congress.

Amendment XXII (Ratified February 27, 1951)

Section 1. No person shall be elected to the office of the President more than twice, and no person who has held the office of President, or acted as President, for more than two years of a term to which some other person was elected President shall be elected to the office of the President more than once. But this Article shall not apply to any person holding the office of President when this Article was proposed by the Congress, and shall not prevent any person who may be holding the office of President, or acting as President, during the term within which this Article becomes operative from holding the office of President or acting as President during the remainder of such term.

Section 2. This Article shall be inoperative unless it shall have been ratified as an amendment to the Constitution by the legislatures of three-fourths of the several States within seven years from the date of its submission to the States by the Congress.

Amendment XXIII (Ratified March 29, 1961)

Section 1. The District constituting the seat of Government of the United States shall appoint in such manner as the Congress may direct:

A number of electors of President and Vice President equal to the whole number of Senators and Representatives in Congress to which the District would be entitled if it were a State, but in no event more than the least populous State; they shall be in addition to those appointed by the States, but they shall be considered, for the purposes of the election of President and Vice President, to be electors appointed by a State; and they shall meet in the District and perform such duties as provided by the twelfth Article of amendment.

Section 2. The Congress shall have power to enforce this Article by appropriate legislation.

Amendment XXIV (Ratified January 23, 1964)

Section 1. The right of citizens of the United States to vote in any primary or other election for President or Vice President, for electors for President or Vice President, or for Senator or Representative in Congress, shall not be denied or abridged by the United States or any State by reason of failure to pay any poll tax or other tax.

Section 2. The Congress shall have power to enforce this Article by appropriate legislation.

Amendment XXV (Ratified February 10, 1967)

Section 1. In case of the removal of the President from office or of his death or resignation, the Vice President shall become President.

Section 2. Whenever there is a vacancy in the office of the Vice President, the President shall nominate a Vice President who shall take office upon confirmation by a majority vote of both Houses of Congress.

Section 3. Whenever the President transmits to the President pro tempore of the Senate and the Speaker of the House of Representatives his written declaration that he is unable to discharge the powers and duties of his office, and until he transmits to them a written declaration to the contrary, such powers and duties shall be discharged by the Vice President as Acting President.

Section 4. Whenever the Vice President and a majority of either the principal officers of the executive departments or of such other body as Congress may by law provide, transmit to the President pro tempore of the Senate and the Speaker of the House of Representatives their written declaration that the President is unable to discharge the powers and duties of his office, the Vice President shall immediately assume the powers and duties of the office as Acting President.

Thereafter, when the President transmits to the President pro tempore of the Senate and the Speaker of the House of Representatives his written declaration that no inability exists, he shall resume the powers and duties of his office unless the Vice President and a majority of either the principal officers of the executive departments or of such other body as Congress may by law provide, transmit within four days to the President pro tempore of the Senate and the Speaker of the House of Representatives

their written declaration that the President is unable to discharge the powers and duties of his office. Thereupon Congress shall decide the issue, assembling within forty-eight hours for that purpose if not in session. If the Congress, within twenty-one days after receipt of the latter written declaration, or, if Congress is not in session, within twenty-one days after Congress is required to assemble, determines by two-thirds vote of both Houses that the President is unable to discharge the powers and duties of his office, the Vice President shall continue to discharge the same as Acting President; otherwise, the President shall resume the powers and duties of his office.

Amendment XXVI (Ratified July 1, 1971)

Section 1. The right of citizens of the United States, who are eighteen years of age or older, to vote shall not be denied or abridged by the United States or by any State on account of age.

Section 2. The Congress shall have power to enforce this Article by appropriate legislation.

Amendment XXVII (Ratified May 7, 1992)

No law varying the compensation for the services of the Senators and Representatives shall take effect, until an election of Representatives shall have intervened.

Source: The Constitution of the United States of America, as Amended. House Document No. 106–214. Washington, D.C.: Government Printing Office, 2000.

Notes

1. The part in brackets was changed by section 2 of the Fourteenth Amendment.
2. The part in brackets was changed by the first paragraph of the Seventeenth Amendment.
3. The part in brackets was changed by the second paragraph of the Seventeenth Amendment.
4. The part in brackets was changed by section 2 of the Twentieth Amendment.
5. The Sixteenth Amendment gave Congress the power to tax incomes.
6. The material in brackets was superseded by the Twelfth Amendment.
7. This provision was affected by the Twenty-fifth Amendment.
8. These clauses were affected by the Eleventh Amendment.
9. This paragraph was superseded by the Thirteenth Amendment.
10. Obsolete.
11. The part in brackets was superseded by section 3 of the Twentieth Amendment.
12. See the Nineteenth and Twenty-sixth Amendments.
13. This amendment was repealed by section 1 of the Twenty-first Amendment.
14. See the Twenty-fifth Amendment.

Index

Page numbers in italics indicate photographs and illustrations

Index

Index

advise and consent, 50, 52–53
analysis of voting by judges, 58–59
background to, 50–55
bipartisan procedures for, 49–50
"blue slip" procedure and, 46
chronology of, 51
confirmation process, politicizing of, 47–48
current situation of, 55–59
Federalist Society and, 52–53
ideology and, 45, 46, 57
"midnight judges," 50
outlook, 59–60
political battles and, 43, 45
Republican appointees, 44
retirement and, 59–60
selection process, politicizing by President Bush, 45–47
special interest groups and, 50
vacancies on bench, 43
Federal Trade Commission (FTC), 165, 170
Federal Violent Crime Control and Law Enforcement Act of 1994, 133–134
Federation of American Scientists, 6, 18
Feingold, Russell D. (D-Wis.), *23*
campaign financing reform and, 23, 25
challenges to law and, 36
enacting reform legislation and, 33
on constitutionality of Bipartisan Campaign Act, 37
on releasing information on detainees, 7
Feinstein, Dianne (D-Calif.), 50
Feldman, Sandra, 217
Felker v. Turpin (1996), 118
FEMA (Federal Emergency Management Agency), 18
Fenway Community Health, 342
FEPC (Fair Employment Practices Committee), 296
Ferg-Cadima, James, 246, 262
Ferguson, Ronald, 298
Fernandez, Denise, 315
Fetal murder laws, 142, 148
Fields, Kenneth, 70
Figueroa, Juan, 56
Filtering software. *See* Libraries, *subheading:* Internet use in
Financial Information Privacy Protection Act of 2001, 174
Financial Institution Privacy Act, 174
Financial Services Roundtable, 164
Firearm Owner's Protection Act of 1986, 133
First Amendment, 96, 175, 182, 193. *See also* Bipartisan Campaign Reform Act; *Buckley v. Valeo* (1976)
anti-abortion groups and, 145
campaign financing and, 23, 24, 25, 26, 27–28, 30, 32, 34
CIPA and, 197
Establishment Clause, 202, 226
express advocacy test, 27, 32
faith-based initiatives and, 228, 235
gag rule, 90
independent expenditures and, 30
independent speech issue and, 27
libraries and Internet use and, 192

public funding for state judicial candidates and, 49
separation of church and state under, 232
Fisher, Louis, 9
Fishing School, 233
Fiske, Marjorie, 192
Fitzgerald, Peter, 49–50
FitzSimons Middle School, 322, 527
organizations and campaign financing, 26
Flanigan, Bill, 332
Flanigan, Timothy, 53
Fleischer, Ari, 34
Flores, Robert, 197
Florida school voucher program, 201, 204, 205. *See also* Schools, *subheading:* vouchers
Flynn, Stephen, 20
Food and Drug Administration (FDA), 153
Food stamps, 231
Ford, Gerald R., 29, 96, 255, 259
Ford, Robert, 268
Ford v. Wainwright (1986), 118
Foreign Assistance Act of 1974, 5
Foreign Intelligence Surveillance Act of 1978, 95
Foreign Intelligence Surveillance Court of Review, 7, 100
Foreign policy, 15, 19. *See also specific presidents*
Fortas, Abe, 57
Fourth Amendment, 7, 89–90, 96, 162
Fox, Rebecca, 141, 157
Frank, Barney (D-Mass.), 53
Frankel, Marvin, 133
Frankfurter, Felix, 74, 252
Frase, Richard, 131
Fraud in health-care, 91
Free Congress Foundation, 101
Free Congress Research and Education Foundation, 47, 50, 55
Freedom of Access to Clinic Entrances Act (FACE), 149, 151
Freedom of Choice Act, 151
Freedom of Information Act (FOIA) requests, 100, 101
Freedom to Marry, 329
Freedom to Read Foundation, 189, 192
Free School Society, 207
Free speech. *See* First Amendment
Friedman, Bernard, 265, 268, 269, 271, 277
Friedman, Milton, 207, 209, 216–217
Frist, Bill (R-Tenn.), 347
Frost, Martin, 63, *64,* 80
FTC (Federal Trade Commission), 165, 170
Fugitive Slave Law of 1793, 292
Fullbright, J. William (D-Ark.), 14
Fuller, Richard K., 227
Furman v. Georgia (1971), 117

Gag rule, 90
Garcia, Freddie, 226
Gas industry, 5
Gates, Gary, 346, 347
Gay and Lesbian Advocates and Defenders (GLAD), 329
Gay Liberation Front, 341
Gay marriage, 329–351

adoption and, 332, 339, 347
amendment, marriage, 348
background, 336–344
benefits of, 332–334
Canada and, 331, 344, 349
children and, 331, 332, 335–336, 338–339
chronology of, 337
current situation, 344–348
debating marriage, 347–348
defending marriage, 341–343
domestic violence, 342–343
effect of recognition on heterosexual marriage, 334–335
marriage equality, 343–344
Massachusetts case on, 334
outlook, 348–349
political risks of, 348
public opinion poll data on, 330, 333
religious organizations and, 332–333
Geller, Evelyn, 188, 190, 191
General Accounting Office, 103
General Motors, 278
Genetic discrimination, 165, 176
Geneva Convention, 93, 100
Gentul, Jack, 298
GeoCities, 171
Georgia v. Ashcroft (2003), 68, 301
Gephardt, Richard A., *3,* 9, 348
Gerhardt, Michael, 45, 48, 50, 59–60
Gerry, Elbridge, 69
Gerrymandering. *See* Redistricting
Gertner, Nancy, 260
Getgood, Susan, 182
Gill, Brian, 204, 206
Gilman-Ponce, Suanna, 253
Gilmore, Gary, 115, 117
Gingrich, Newt, 33
Ginsberg, Benjamin, 29
Ginsburg, Ruth Bader
abortion and, 151
affirmative action and, 274, 278, 280
appointment of, 51, 54
church-state separation issues and, 216
Federalist Society and, 53
on campaign finance laws, 29
on death penalty, 122
redistricting and, 78
single-sex education and, 319
GLAD. *See* Gay and Lesbian Advocates and Defenders
Glaser, Jack, 306
Global warming, 19
Gold, Laurence, 27
Goldberg, Jackie, 134
Goldman, Janlori, 166, 167–168, 177
Goldman, Ron, 283
Goldman, Sheldon, 43, 50, 54, 59
Goldsmith, Stephen, 305
Gonzales, Alberto, 45, 46, 54–55
Goodridge, Hillary, 329, *329,* 330, 334, *335,* 344
Goodridge, Julie, 329, *329,* 330, 334, *335,* 344
Goodridge v. Massachusetts Department of Public Health (2004), 330–331, 334–335, 337, 343–344, 349
Gora, Joel, 27, 29

proposal for easing warrant requirements, 92

sneak-and-peek, 89, 95, 97, 100

telegrams, 172

telephone calls, 172–173

Warren, Earl, 246, 252–253

Warren, Roger, 49

Warren, Vincent, 280

Warshaw, Shirley Anne, 10

Wartime and civil liberties, 93–94

Washington, George, 50, 57, 172, 292

Washington Area Clinic Task Force, 141

Washington Legal Foundation, 119

Washington state's three-strikes laws, 133, 134

Watergate scandal, 8

Watt, Melvin (D-N.C.), 67

Watts, J. C., Jr. (R-Okla.), 236

Watts, Robert, 298

Waxman, Seth, 50

Weapons of mass destruction, 3n, 10

Weich, Ronald, 167, 168

Welfare Reform Act of 1964, 236

Welfare Reform Act of 1996, 221

Wellesley College, 321

Wellman, David, 285, 290

Wellstone, Paul, 16

Wertheimer, Fred, 24, 26, 27, 28, 35, 39

Western High School, 319

Wetstone, Gregory, 18, 19

When Sacred and Secular Mix (Monsma), 230

Whitaker, Reg, 161

White, Byron R., 69

White, Edward, 295

White, Kizzie, 283

White, Penny, 48, 49

White, Ronnie, 47, 51

White flight, 295

White House Office of Faith-Based and Community Initiatives, 222

Whitewashing Race (Wellman), 285

Whyman, Deborah, 277

Wicharaya, Tamasak, 132

Wilde, Oscar, 190

Wilder, L. Douglas, 286

Wilkerson, David, 225n1

Will, George, 119

William A. Lawson International Peace and Prosperity Preparatory Academy for Boys, 322

Williams, Anthony, 261

Williams, Carol, 181, 197

Williams, Michael, 258, 260

Williams, Polly, 208, 210

Wilson, Bradford, 291

Wilson, David, 334

Wilson, James Q., 226, 228

Wilson, Pete, 275

Wilson, Woodrow, 11, 13, 14, *14*, 52

Winner-take-all system, targeting, 67

Winship, Christopher, 226

Winter, Ralph, 35

Wiretaps, 92, 96, 97, 172

Wisconsin Legislative Audit Bureau, 214

Wisconsin Right to Life, 49

Witnesses, right to confront, 102

Witte, John, 203, 204, 205, 210, 214

Witten, Roger, 25, 26, 29, 39

Witters v. Washington Dept. of Services for Blind (1986), 213

Wofford, Harris, 223

Wolfe, Alan, 222, 230, 232, 234

Wolfson, Evan, 329, 330, 333, 334, 336, 347, 349

Wolman v. Walter (1977), 213

Women

abortion. *See* Abortion

single-sex education. *See* Single-sex education

Women's College Coalition, 320

Wood, Thomas E., 276, 279

Woods, George, 314, 319

Woodson v. North Carolina (1976), 117

Woodward, George, 57

Woody, Elisabeth, 313

Wootton, James, 48, 49

Workforce Investment Act of 1998, 305

World Summit on Sustainable Development, 19

World Trade Center attacks, 95, 96

World War I and harassment of ethnic Germans, 89

World War II

internment of Japanese-Americans, 94

war-crimes trials after, 99

Wray, Christopher, 100

Wright, Ben, 311

Wright, Ron, 122

Wright, Wendy, 154

X-Stop, 193

Yogman, Judith, 331, 344

You and Machines (Civilian Conservation Corps), 190

Young, Wesley, 261

Youngstown Sheet and Tube Co. v. Sawyer (1952), 5, 11, 14

The Young Women's Leadership School of East Harlem (TYWLS), 309, 314–315, 320, 325

Yucca Mountain, 18–19

Yugoslavian air strikes by U.S., 9

Zelman, Susan Tave, 202

Zelman v. Simmons-Harris (2002), 202, 213, 215

Zelnick, Bob, 287

Zendehdel, Yashar, 300

Zirkin, Nancy, 309, 312, 321, 325

Zobrest v. Catalina Foothills School District (1993), 213

Zogby, James, 300, 301

Zohny, Maryam, 314

Zoning laws and adult movies and books stores, 194